COOK'S

ILLUSTRATED

~ 2005 ~

$29.95

Published by
America's Test Kitchen
17 Station Street
Brookline, MA 02445

ISBN: 0-936184-92-2
ISSN: 1068-2821

To get home delivery of *Cook's Illustrated,* call 800-526-8442 inside the U.S., or 515-247-7571 if calling from outside the U.S., or subscribe online at www.cooksillustrated.com.

In addition to Annual Hardbound Editions available from each year of publication (1993–2005), *Cook's Illustrated* offers the following cookbooks and DVD sets:

The America's Test Kitchen Family Cookbook

The Best Recipe Series
The Cook's Illustrated Guide to Grilling and *Barbecue*
Best American Side Dishes
Cover & Bake
The New Best Recipe
Steaks, Chops, Roasts, and Ribs
Baking Illustrated
Restaurant Favorites at Home
Perfect Vegetables
The Quick Recipe
Italian Classics
American Classics
Soups & Stews

**The America's Test Kitchen Series
(companion cookbooks and DVD sets
to our hit public television series)**
Cooking at Home with America's Test Kitchen
    (2006 season companion cookbook)
America's Test Kitchen Live!
    (2005 season companion cookbook)
Inside America's Test Kitchen
    (2004 season companion cookbook)
Here in America's Test Kitchen
    (2003 season companion cookbook)
The America's Test Kitchen Cookbook
    (2002 season companion cookbook)
The *America's Test Kitchen* 2005 Season 4-DVD
    Boxed Set
The *America's Test Kitchen* 2004 Season 4-DVD
    Boxed Set

The How to Cook Master Series
How to Make a Pie
How to Make an American Layer Cake
How to Make Salad
How to Grill
How to Make Simple Fruit Desserts
How to Cook Holiday Roasts and Birds
How to Make Stew
How to Cook Shrimp and Other Shellfish
How to Barbecue and Roast on the Grill
How to Cook Garden Vegetables
How to Make Pot Pies and Casseroles
How to Sauté
How to Make Sauces and Gravies
How to Make Muffins, Biscuits, and Scones
How to Cook Chicken Breasts

Additional books from the editors of
Cook's Illustrated **magazine**
The Cook's Bible
The Cook's Illustrated Complete Book of
    Pasta and Noodles
The Best Kitchen Quick Tips
The Kitchen Detective
1993–2005 Master Index
2005 Cook's Country Annual Edition

To order any of our cookbooks listed above, give us a call at 800-611-0759 inside the U.S., or at 515-246-6911 if calling from outside the U.S.

You can order subscriptions, gift subscriptions, and any of our books by
visiting our online store at www.cooksillustrated.com

BC=Back Cover

NUMBER SEVENTY-TWO

JANUARY & FEBRUARY 2005

COOK'S
ILLUSTRATED

Pasta with Chicken
and Broccoli

Italian Pork Chops

Beef Brisket
Fork Tender and Moist

Chicken Teriyaki
Quick Broiler Method

Better
Cornbread

German Chocolate
Cake
Big Flavor, Easier Method

Recipe Rescue
Fixing Kitchen Disasters

Cocoa Taste Test
Hearty Scrambled Eggs
Rating "Saucier" Pans
Black Bean Soup
Glazed Winter Vegetables

www.cooksillustrated.com

$5.95 U.S./$6.95 CANADA

0 2>

0 74470 62805 7

CONTENTS

January & February 2005

www.cooksillustrated.com

HOME OF AMERICA'S TEST KITCHEN

Founder and Editor	Christopher Kimball
Executive Editor	Jack Bishop
Senior Editors	Jolyon Helterman
	Dawn Yanagihara
Editorial Manager, Books	Elizabeth Carduff
Test Kitchen Director	Erin McMurrer
Senior Editors, Books	Julia Collin Davison
	Lori Galvin
Senior Writer	Bridget Lancaster
Managing Editor	Rebecca Hays
Associate Editor, Books	Keith Dresserr
Associate Editor	Sandra Wu
Science Editor	John Olson
Web Editor	Lindsay McSweeney
Copy Editor	India Koopman
Test Cooks	Stephanie Alleyne
	Erika Bruce
	Sean Lawler
	Jeremy Sauer
	Rachel Toomey
	Diane Unger-Mahoney
	Sarah Wilson
Assistant Test Cooks	Garth Clingingsmith
	Charles Kelsey
	Nina West
Editorial Assistant, Books	Elizabeth Wray
Assistant to the Publisher	Melissa Baldino
Kitchen Assistants	Barbara Akins
	Nadia Domeq
	Maria Elena Delgado
	Ena Gudiel
Editorial Intern	Elizabeth Bomze
Contributing Editors	Matthew Card
	Elizabeth Germain
Consulting Editors	Shirley Corriher
	Jasper White
	Robert L. Wolke
Proofreader	Jean Rogers
Design Director	Amy Klee
Designer	Heather Barrett
Staff Photographer	Daniel van Ackere
Vice President Marketing	David Mack
Sales Director	Leslie Ray
Retail Sales Director	Jason Geller
Corporate Sponsorship Specialist	Laura Phillipps
Sales Representative	Shekinah Cohn
Marketing Assistant	Connie Forbes
Circulation Director	Bill Tine
Circulation Manager	Larisa Greiner
Products Director	Steven Browall
Direct Mail Director	Adam Perry
Customer Service Manager	Jacqueline Valerio
Customer Service Representative	Julie Gardner
E-Commerce Marketing Manager	Hugh Buchan
Vice President Operations	James McCormack
Senior Production Manager	Jessica Lindheimer Quirk
Production Manager	Mary Connelly
Book Production Specialist	Ron Bilodeau
Production Assistants	Jeanette McCarthy
	Jennifer Power
	Christian Steinmetz
Systems Administrator	Richard Cassidy
WebMaster	Aaron Shuman
Chief Financial Officer	Sharyn Chabot
Controller	Mandy Shito
Staff Accountant	Maya Santoso
Office Manager	Saudiyah Abdul-Rahim
Receptionist	Henrietta Murray
Publicity	Deborah Broide

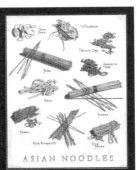

ASIAN NOODLES

ASIAN NOODLES Flat, transparent rice sticks, made from only rice flour and water, are commonly used to make pad thai and Vietnamese pho. Thinner rice vermicelli are often used in soups or chilled salads. Both rice sticks and vermicelli are "cooked" by means of soaking in hot water rather than boiling. Cellophane noodles (also called bean threads or glass noodles) are made from mung bean flour and are also soaked before being eaten. Chinese egg noodles, such as those used for lo mein, can be either thick or thin, fresh or dried. Broad, flat chow foon rice noodles have a mild flavor and slippery texture that work well as a base for stir-fries. Japanese yam noodles called *shirataki* add a bouncy, springy texture to brothy dishes. Soba noodles, made from buckwheat flour, have an earthy, nutty flavor and are served in both hot and cold preparations. Delicate Japanese somen noodles are made from wheat flour and resemble fine angel hair pasta. Fat, chewy udon noodles are also made from wheat flour and are typically used in hearty soups. Japanese ramen noodles can be purchased fresh, dried, frozen, or—in instant soup packets—fried. COVER (*Oranges*): Elizabeth Brandon, BACK COVER (*Asian Noodles*): John Burgoyne

For list rental information, contact: ClientLogic, 1200 Harbor Blvd., 9th Floor, Weehawken, NJ 07087; 201-865-5800; fax 201-867-2450.
Editorial Office: 17 Station St., Brookline, MA 02445; 617-232-1000; fax 617-232-1572. Subscription inquiries, call 800-526-8442.
Postmaster: Send all new orders, subscription inquiries, and change of address notices to Cook's Illustrated, P.O. Box 7446, Red Oak, IA 51591-0446.

PRINTED IN THE USA

THE LAST PICTURE SHOW

As a kid in Vermont, I wasn't familiar with the notion of choice. Cows had to be milked twice a day. Horses had to be watered down at the stream behind the barn. The pigs and Angus had to be grained. Fences had to be checked and fixed. True, corn could be planted early or late, and haying does involve decision making, since you don't want mown hay to be caught in a hard rain. Calvin Coolidge probably summed up a farmer's view of indecision pretty well when he said, "When you don't know what to do, do the work in front of you." I've spent most of my life following this simple dictum.

Just last summer I had to purchase a new pickup—the flatbed of my old Ford was rotted out, the brakes were gone, and it was leaking oil. So I took a trip down to the Ford dealership in Greenwich. Did I want a crew cab or a super cab? Did I want the deluxe Lariat or the King Ranch option? Did I need the towing package? How about roof lights and sideboard lights, and what type of sound system did I require? Was I interested in the 150, the 250, or the 350? I could even get a Harley-Davidson limited edition pickup, all in black, with a special monogrammed bed liner.

When it comes to eating out, I have grown quite fond of church suppers, not just because one gets to visit with neighbors but because there is no choice involved, except when it comes to dessert. The church in Pawlet has been raising money for its new spire, and we have been attending its monthly pork dinners. It's $9 for adults and $4.50 for kids under 12. The menu usually includes coleslaw, red Jell-O (as a side dish), mashed potatoes, rolls, applesauce, green peas, stuffing, pork, and gravy. You can drink coffee, lemonade, or iced tea, and for dessert you sometimes get a choice. Last weekend it was yellow cake with a whipped pineapple frosting or chocolate cake with a fudge frosting. (Our family voted in a block for the chocolate, although the pineapple cake seemed to be more popular with other folks because the frosting was thicker.) And you can always depend on the crowd. We'll see our town's last farmer, Charlie Bentley; Valerie and her son, Charles; our minister, Rev. Bort, and his wife, Joan, who plays the organ and sings; Jean and Jack, our neighbors across the valley; Roy and Jane Gatlin; and, of course, Gerald Ennis from Salem, who shows up at our farm from time to time just to see what's going on.

Christopher Kimball

I'm not suggesting that country living offered no choices. Old country stores had quite a lot to offer. You were likely to find None Such Mince Meat, I. D. Gilmor & Company Celebrated Biscuits, Fine Quality Pressed Hops, Slade's Assorted Marjoram, and Bird's Eye Diamond Matches. A good store also carried large displays of colored threads, penny candies, poultry remedies, a dozen brands of tobacco, tea, coffee, fabric, and almost anything you might want in the way of dry goods. And, if old-fashioned country stores were anything like ours is today, you could find just about any type of gossip you might want, from suspicions about who is jacking deer out of season to the darkest speculation about marital infidelities.

But, on the whole, there was plenty of work to do, not much cash money, and little time to spend it. In fact, when I was a kid on the farm, money didn't seem to have much currency. The things that were prayed for included good weather, deliverance from sickness, and a bit of luck in love. When a new pickup was purchased, it looked just like the old one—the same model and color—so it was no cause for celebration. In fact, life didn't offer many choices: One simply got out of bed and went to work.

Today, in our mountain town, things haven't changed much. If we want to see a movie, we head down to Hathaway's Drive-In. Unlike a multiplex, there is no choice—it's two movies for six bucks, and they don't start until twilight. Last July I took the kids down to see a double feature. We got there a few minutes early. Two young boys were throwing a football, a 5-year-old started playing on the metal supports for the screen as if they were a jungle gym, there were plenty of army and air force T-shirts, a young couple sat close together in a green Mustang, and the station wagons were parked backward so the families inside could sit and look out through the open hatchbacks.

The movie started, and my kids had moved out onto blankets, eating Milk Duds, fries, and popcorn. I was alone in the pickup, sitting in the same spot I had with my parents 40 years ago. Since that time, I have made a lot of choices, not all of them good ones, but I have had enough sense to know where home is. Pickup trucks, candy wrappers, the enormous night sky, french fries, ice cream cones, a bottle rocket hissing upward, and Hollywood two stories high—that's home to me. It's easy to fall for the promise of the big screen; maybe there *is* something better in the next town. But there is something to be said for knowing every inch of a place where the rain falls on farmhouses that hold no secrets and where there is nothing old-fashioned about hot fries and a $6 drive-in.

After a bit, mosquitoes drove the kids back into the pickup. I wondered if, in another generation, some of my kids would return to Hathaway's with their children. My season would have ended by then and it would be their turn. Or maybe they would make other choices and end up on the far side of the world. But perhaps Calvin Coolidge was right. If we are confused by a sea of choices, we ought simply to do the work in front of us. Then we just follow the path ahead, one step at a time, the path that leads to a summer night, the hopeful flicker of the big screen, and then the drive home to a high mountain valley and a farmhouse at the end of the road.

FOR INQUIRIES, ORDERS, OR MORE INFORMATION:

www.cooksillustrated.com

At www.cooksillustrated.com, you can order books and subscriptions, sign up for our free e-newsletter, or renew your magazine subscription. Subscribe to the Web site and you'll have access to 12 years of *Cook's* recipes, cookware tests, ingredient tastings, and more.

COOKBOOKS

We sell more than 40 cookbooks by the editors of *Cook's Illustrated*. To order, visit our bookstore at www.cooksillustrated.com or call 800-611-0759 (or 515-246-6911 from outside the U.S.).

COOK'S ILLUSTRATED Magazine

Cook's Illustrated magazine (ISSN 1068-2821), number 72, is published bimonthly by Boston Common Press Limited Partnership, 17 Station Street, Brookline, MA 02445. Copyright 2005 Boston Common Press Limited Partnership. Periodicals postage paid at Boston, Mass., and additional mailing offices, USPS #012487. POSTMASTER: Send address changes to Cook's Illustrated, P.O. Box 7446, Red Oak, IA 51591-0446. For subscription and gift subscription orders, subscription inquiries, or change-of-address notices, call 800-526-8442 in the U.S. or 515-247-7571 from outside the U.S., or write us at Cook's Illustrated, P.O. Box 7446, Red Oak, IA 51591-0446.

≥ COMPILED BY INDIA KOOPMAN ≤

Fresh Ground Pepper on the Go

What do you think of the built-in "grinder" in the new jar of McCormick peppercorns?

HEATHER CHAMBERLAIN
GLENDALE, CALIF.

➤ McCormick's new offering of black peppercorns in a jar with its own grinder at first struck us as superfluous: Most cooks own a pepper mill, so why buy a disposable one? Then we bought one and tried it and realized it's the sort of thing that comes in handy for stocking a vacation home, taking on a picnic, or stowing in a backpack on a camping trip. The $1.99 jar has a removable cap, under which is a simple grinding mechanism encircled in a band of hard black plastic. To use it, you simply remove the cap, turn the jar upside down, and twist the plastic band. What you get is a coarse grind, good for seasoning a salad, steak, or sandwich just before you eat it. The grind isn't adjustable, so you're out of luck if you want a fine grind that will melt into your food. The cap snaps back snugly after use, eliminating the opportunity for spills. (Yes, we tested it by dropping it and by carrying it around in a knapsack for a couple of days.)

McCormick's jar of whole peppercorns with a built-in grinder makes sense for vacation homes, camping trips, box lunches, and picnics.

The New Crisco

You recently tested several alternatives to Crisco that don't contain partially hydrogenated, or trans, fat (May/June 2004). It is my understanding that Crisco is now available without trans fat. Have you tried it?

HERMAN VENTURA
MILILANI, HAWAII

➤ The J. M. Smucker Company, manufacturer of Crisco, released its new product, Zero Grams Trans Fat Crisco, in spring 2004, promising that it would produce exactly the same results as the original Crisco when used in any recipe. To make the original product, Smucker puts soybean and cottonseed oils through a process of partial hydrogenation. The partially hydrogenated fat that's created in the process is, as you say, the source of the unhealthy trans fat in Crisco. The new product is made from nonhydrogenated

sunflower and soybean oils and from cottonseed oil that has been through a process of complete hydrogenation. When an oil is completely, or fully, hydrogenated, it becomes a saturated fat—considered better for you than trans fat but not as healthy as unsaturated fat, which is found in many unadulterated vegetable oils.

To see how this new product performs, we prepared our pie crust, biscuit, and fried chicken recipes with both the original and the new Crisco. The pie crusts and biscuits made with each type of Crisco browned equally well, as did both batches of fried chicken. In fact, we couldn't tell the difference between the chicken fried in the original and new

Can a new Crisco product measure up?

Crisco. The chicken tasted the same, and the skin was equally crisp.

In the case of the pie crust and biscuits, we could not discern a different taste, but there was a slight difference in texture. The pie crust made with the original product was a bit more tender, while the crust made with the new product was a bit more stiff and crackerlike. Likewise, the biscuits made with the original Crisco were slightly more tender and also a little more fluffy than their Zero Grams Trans Fat counterparts. Because the overall differences were so slight, we would not hesitate to try the new Crisco in any recipe that calls for vegetable shortening.

Really, Truly Browned Meat

I have two questions about browning meat. First, when a recipe says to brown the meat, does it just mean to cook it till it loses its pink color or to cook it until it gets a dark brown sear? Second, when browning cubes of beef to make a stew, the meat often gives off so much liquid that it is really boiling in liquid instead of frying. Is there a way to avoid this?

LAURA LYNN LEWIS
LUBBOCK, TEXAS

➤ When a recipe says to brown the meat, it is calling for a deep brown sear and a discernibly thick crust on all sides—something that's best obtained by quick cooking over high heat. If you're browning meat for stew, that means putting the meat in a hot pan and not turning it until the first side is well seared, about two or three minutes. Then continue cooking the other sides

of the meat until they, too, are well seared, about one or two minutes per side. When making stew, the goal is not to cook the meat through—that will happen when you stew it—but to achieve the browning that will develop flavor in the meat itself and that will create *fond*—browned bits left behind in the pan that when deglazed will add still more flavor to the stew.

When beef for a stew essentially steams in its own liquid—as you describe—it loses the opportunity for good flavor development and can develop a bland, liverlike flavor. Definitely not a good thing. There are several steps you can take to ensure that meat browns properly. First, make sure the meat is dry before it goes into the pan; pat it down thoroughly with paper towels. This is especially important with previously frozen meat, which often releases a great deal of water. Second, when you're ready to put the meat in the pan, make sure the pan is hot by preheating it over high heat until any oil or fat you've added to the pan is shimmering or close to smoking. Finally, make sure not to overcrowd the pan; there should be at least ¼ inch of space between the pieces of meat. If there isn't, the meat is likely to steam instead of brown. If need be, cook the meat in two or three batches to keep from crowding the pan.

Are Shallots Worth the Expense?

Is there a reason for using shallots instead of onions? My grocery store sells shallots for $2.99 a pound and onions for $1.29 a pound. Why pay twice as much for shallots?

MARGARET BARNES
WEST HARTFORD, CONN.

➤ Shallots have a unique flavor that is milder and more delicate than that of onions, and, of course, they are also much smaller than most onions. When shallots and onions are cooked, the differences between them show up even more. In a quick-cooking pan sauce for steak, for example, a shallot's mild flavor will meld much more smoothly with that of the other ingredients. A finely minced shallot will also melt into the sauce until it's all but indiscernible. No matter how finely you mince an onion, it's not going to disappear into an otherwise silky sauce. An onion also needs much more cooking time before its flavor will mellow.

In addition, a raw shallot will add gentle heat to a vinaigrette or salsa, with a minimum of crunch. Use a raw onion in the same recipe and the pungent onion crunch may seem out of place.

Label Watch:
Flour and Protein Content

You talk a lot about the protein content of flour and what is best for, say, bread versus pastry. But the flour in the supermarket doesn't show a protein percentage; the "Nutrition Facts" label on the bag gives only the number of grams of protein per serving. Is there a way to figure out the percentage of protein from the information on the bag?

JON SCHUSTER
SEATTLE, WASH.

The Nutrition Facts label on a bag of flour does not provide a very accurate indication of protein content. We looked at five popular all-purpose flours, and the labels on all five listed a serving size of 30 grams and a protein content per serving of 3 grams. If you do the math, you get a protein content of 10 percent. But the actual protein content of each of these flours is quite different: 10.5 percent for both Gold Medal and Pillsbury, 11 percent for Hodgson Mill, 11.7 percent for King Arthur, and an average of 11.7 percent for Heckers/Ceresota. What's going on? Rounding. When a label says "3 grams," the actual number can be anything from 2.6 grams to 3.4 grams. That translates to anything from 8.3 percent protein to 11.7 percent.

A much better guide to the protein content of flour is its general category, which is clearly stated on the bag. In the supermarket, you'll usually find three basic categories: bread flour, with a protein content in the range of 12 to 14 percent; all-purpose, 10 to 12 percent; and cake, usually 6 to 8 percent. The higher the protein content, the more structure and chew in the end product (as in a chewy rustic Italian loaf made with bread flour); the lower the protein content, the more tender the end product (a meltingly soft butter cake made with cake flour). All-purpose, true to its name, covers lots of the territory in between.

Recipe Timing: Boiling Water

For many years I have been trying to decipher the instructions for boiling times. Should I boil an item from the time it goes into the water or from the time the water returns to a boil? Does the same formula hold for both blanching vegetables and cooking lobster?

RICHARD M. BRICKMAN
VIRGINIA BEACH, VA.

Hmmm. We realized this was a good question when we turned to a number of our recipes for blanching and found that we don't specify whether the water must return to a boil before you start counting the seconds or minutes. We can't speak for other recipe writers, but in our recipes for blanching you start counting from the moment you plunge the fruit or vegetable into the boiling water. The goal in blanching is not to cook foods through but usually to aid in skinning

WHAT IS IT?

I picked up this item for $10 in a barn full of antiques in Ipswich, Mass., just because it looked interesting. Can you identify it?

LEE PARADIS
ARLINGTON, MASS.

Ipswich may be best known for its clams, but, like several other towns on Massachusetts' North Shore that date back to Colonial times, it's also enjoyed for its "collectibles," which include everything from baked bean pots to scrimshaw to oak beams salvaged from old barns. One of our editors came across the same item that you found in a store in neighboring Essex.

What is it? She learned from one of the proprietors that it's a juicer. Made from cast aluminum and measuring about 9 inches long by 4 inches high and 5 inches wide (at the juice-collecting end), the juicer works by means of a handle that when pressed pushes against the flat side of a ladle-like container that holds the juice (see the illustration). A slotted, removable hopper sits inside the ladle to hold back the pulp and seeds. The juice is then simply poured out through the spout in the container.

This tool is the perfect size for juicing an orange, but it will also neatly juice a lime or lemon or even a small grapefruit. Testers were impressed by its efficiency and ease of use—lots of juice squeezed with one press of the handle, making it easier to use than our favorite hand juicer and reamer, both of which, like all such devices, require pressure as well as twisting and turning. Testers also liked the fact that the slotted hopper could be removed for cleaning. All of that said, this hand-press juicer is rather bulky and would be awkward to store. What's more, to our knowledge, it's no longer being manufactured.

This unusual but efficient juicer squeezes every last drop out of oranges, lemons, limes, and even small grapefruit.

(peaches and tomatoes) or to soften till crisp/tender (vegetables for a crudité). If you don't start counting till the water returns to a boil, the food will be overcooked.

For foods meant to be cooked all the way through, from lobster to boiled potatoes, you generally start counting once the water returns to a boil. At least that's the way it works in our recipes. And if the recipe gives a range (say 20 to 30 minutes for good-size potatoes), it's always best to start checking for doneness early—once those potatoes are overcooked, there's no going back.

Eliminating Gas from Beans

Why do beans sometimes cause gas? Is there something I can do to reduce the discomfort?

MADELEINE HOWE
RUTLAND, VT.

For some, the greatest obstacle to preparing beans is not the lack of a good recipe but an aversion to the discomfort associated with digestion. The creation of unwanted intestinal gas begins with the arrival of small chains of carbohydrates (called oligosaccharides) into the large intestine. People cannot digest these molecules efficiently, but bacteria residing at the end of the gut do and produce gas as a byproduct. Some sources say that presoaking or precooking beans alleviates gas production by removing these carbohydrates.

Our science editor decided to put these theories to the test by measuring the amount of one of the most prevalent small carbohydrates in black beans, stachyose.

His results gave the theories some credence. Beans soaked overnight in water and then cooked and drained showed a 28 percent reduction in stachyose. The precooking, quick-soak, method, consisting of a one-minute boil followed by a soak for an hour, was more effective, removing 42.5 percent of the stachyose. Though these results were encouraging, we thought we could do better.

We tried several recommended ingredients that are purported to "neutralize" the offending compounds as beans cook: epazote, kombu (giant kelp), bay leaves, and baking soda. None of these seemed to do much in the pot, though it is possible that they act only during digestion.

Our conclusion: Though the quick-soak method is not our first choice because of its negative effect on the texture of the beans, if beans cause you significant discomfort, this approach was the most effective at reducing the amount of the offending compounds.

SEND US YOUR QUESTIONS We will provide a complimentary one-year subscription for each letter we print. Send your inquiry, name, address, and daytime telephone number to Notes from Readers, Cook's Illustrated, P.O. Box 470589, Brookline, MA 02447, or to notesfromreaders@bcpress.com.

Quick Tips

≥ COMPILED BY ERIKA BRUCE ≤

Storing Sharp Utensils

Fondue forks, paring knives, skewers, and all manner of small, sharp objects can present a danger when tossed haphazardly into a kitchen drawer: The next time you reach into the drawer, you're likely to get poked. Tired of this routine, Toni Bocci of Cordova, Alaska, came up with the idea of securing those pointy tips in leftover wine corks, which not only protects hands but also keeps sharp edges from getting dull.

Neater French Toast

No one likes to waste French toast batter by dripping it all over the stovetop while transferring soaked slices of bread from bowl to skillet. Mitch Kramer of Middlebury, Vt., discovered a clever way to soak up each and every drop. He simply places one piece of plain bread between the bowl and the skillet. Once he's used up all of the other slices, he uses the catchall slice for the last piece of French toast.

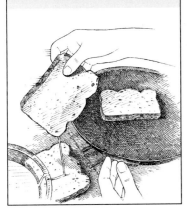

Rolling Pin Storage

Storing large, awkward rolling pins with handles and ball bearings is often difficult, especially with limited drawer and cupboard space. Elizabeth McCarthy of San Mateo, Calif., came up with a clever solution.

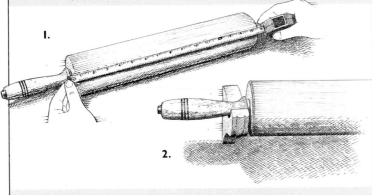

1. Measure the distance between the handles of the rolling pin.
2. Measure that same distance at a convenient spot on your kitchen wall and mount two inexpensive curtain rod holders from the hardware store, one at each end. Then simply suspend your rolling pin by its handles.

Neater Egg Sandwiches

Fried-egg sandwiches always seem to taste better when made with English muffins or bagels, but how do you fry a round egg of just the right size—one that won't flop messily over the sides of the sandwich? Lou Verret of Portland, Ore., does the job with large cookie cutters, making round fried eggs that are a perfect fit for English muffins.

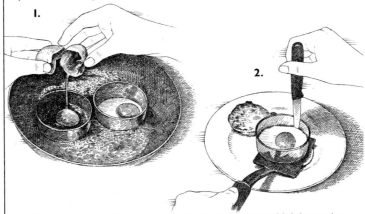

1. Butter one or more 2½- to 3-inch round cookie cutters. Melt butter in a nonstick skillet, then place the cutters in the skillet, being sure not to scrape the pan's surface. Pour one egg into each cutter and season with salt and pepper. Cover the pan and cook to the desired doneness.
2. Remove both the egg and the cutter with a spatula. If necessary, run a paring knife around the inside of the cutter to loosen the egg.

Convenient Oil Dispenser

Pour spouts are a great way to mete out just the right amount of cooking oil for a sauté or a salad, but some people—including Christopher Huang of Honolulu, Hawaii—don't have cupboards tall enough to fit both the bottle and the spout. He figured out a way to get just a splash of oil from the bottle without using a spout.

1. Remove the plastic cap from the oil and poke a small hole through the safety seal under the cap with a paring knife. Replace the cap and store as usual.
2. When you need a little oil, just remove the cap, invert the bottle, and give it a squeeze or a shake.

The Perfect Grind

Measuring fresh-ground pepper for a recipe can be tricky. A coffee grinder works, but, if you're like us, you end up grinding much more than you need. Matthew Bartram of Scarborough, Ontario, solved the problem by counting the number of grinds his pepper mill required to produce ¼ teaspoon of pepper and then marking the number on a piece of tape affixed to the mill.

Chopsticks to the Rescue

Most cooks like to keep a pump soap dispenser near the kitchen sink for hand washing. But it's wasteful to discard the last drops of soap that always collect in the bottom of the bottle. Cathie Brenner of Brookline, Mass., found a fast, neat way to get the soap from one bottle to another. Insert a long chopstick into the neck of the second bottle and invert the first bottle on top. The soap will cling to the chopstick and trickle down more readily.

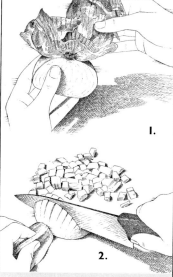

Getting a Grip While Slicing Onions

Piper Cole of Menlo Park, Calif., came up with this tip to make dicing or slicing onions even easier. After trimming the top of the onion and halving it pole to pole, she follows the steps below.

1.

2.

1. Carefully peel the outer layers from each half down to—but not all the way off—the root end.
2. When you have diced or sliced most of the onion, hold on to the outer layers to stabilize the root end as you finish cutting.

"Instant" Oatmeal

A quick bowl of hot oatmeal can start the day on a warm note. But reaching for those gluey instant packets just isn't worth it. Jaxson Eryck Brandt of Glendive, Mont., came up with a way to have the best of both worlds: instant homemade oatmeal.

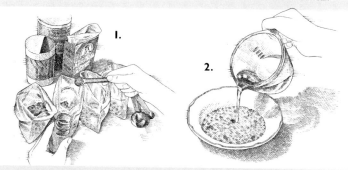

1.

2.

1. Measure the dry ingredients for one serving of oatmeal into a sandwich-size zipper-lock bag; we like ½ cup quick-cooking (or one-minute) oats, ¼ teaspoon cinnamon, 1 tablespoon brown sugar, a pinch of salt, and 1 tablespoon dried fruit. Repeat with as many bags as you like.
2. To cook, empty a bag into a bowl and add ⅔ cup boiling water. Stir, cover with plastic wrap, and let sit for 5 minutes. Uncover, stir again, and breakfast is ready.

Trash Bag Tips

A. Sheryl Siegel of Englewood, Colo., found a clever way to save both time and space while changing her trash bags. She stores the container of trash bags in the bottom of the trash can; when a full bag is removed, all she has to do is reach down and grab a fresh bag to replace it.

B. Betty Wibby of Traverse City, Mich., likes to recycle plastic shopping bags by using them to line small trash cans (about 12 inches tall), but she finds the bags have an annoying habit of sliding to the bottom of the can. To solve this problem, she attaches small adhesive coat hooks on either side of the can, about 4 inches from the top. To secure the bag, she simply slips the bag handles around the hooks.

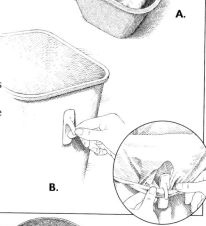

A.

B.

Peeling Egg Shells—Fast

When making recipes such as egg salad or deviled eggs, which call for several hard-cooked eggs, Greg Star of Needham, Mass., has a quick and easy way to loosen and remove the shells.

1. After draining the hot water from the pot used to cook the eggs, shake the pot back and forth to crack the shells.
2. Add enough ice water to cover the eggs and let cool. The water seeps under the broken shells, allowing them to be slipped off without a struggle.

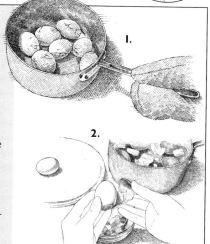

1.

2.

Perfect Fried Eggs

Nothing is worse than cooking a perfect fried egg only to tear it while transferring the egg from the skillet to a plate. Brenda Bilodeau of Leeds, Maine, avoids this mishap by applying cooking spray to the spatula, which allows her to gently slide the cooked eggs onto the plate.

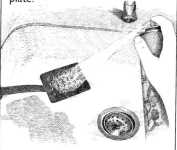

Freezing Leftover Wine

Often tempted to toss out that last bit of wine from an unfinished bottle, Jolie Teope-Tam of Chicago, Ill., tried freezing it instead. Now when she needs a little wine to finish a sauce, there is no need to open a fresh bottle. Measure 1 tablespoon of wine into each well of an ice cube tray and freeze. Use a paring knife to remove each wine cube, then store in a zipper-lock bag. Add frozen cubes to sauces as desired.

Preventing Boil-Overs

Most cooks with electric stoves who need to quickly cool down a hot pot move it to another burner. Instead of risking a burn while trying to move a large pot of angrily bubbling water, Ames Rich of Winston-Salem, N.C., tosses in one or two ice cubes. This brings down the temperature quickly and takes up the slack while the heating element slowly cools down.

Pork Chops with Vinegar and Peppers

This Italian dish of juicy pork chops cooked with sweet peppers and vinegar can lose a lot in translation. Could we reinterpret this classic for modern American cooks?

> BY BRIDGET LANCASTER

Pork chops with vinegar peppers are a welcome change from the pork chop doldrums. Braised to fall-off-the-bone tenderness in a sauce made of little more than sweet red vinegar peppers right out of the jar, the pork chops arrive at the table smothered, juicy, and full of big, tart vinegar flavor. Well, I like vinegar almost as much as I love pork chops, so I gathered a multitude of recipes to test in hopes of reproducing this dish.

In a land where pork is still full of fat, this must make a great supper. Sadly, all that the lean supermarket pork in this country had to contribute to the dish was chalky chops. And my first sauces were harsh and musty tasting—not at all what I had in mind. Modern takes on the recipe eschewed the braising technique altogether, sautéing the chops on their own and then building a vinegar pepper pan sauce. This approach, too, was a letdown. The chops were bland and dry, the sauce no more than an afterthought. I had a long way to go.

Chop Shop

Choosing the proper pork chop was my first challenge. With their big pork flavor, tender rib chops were tasters' favorite, followed by center-cut chops. Blade chops were tasty but lost out because they were also quite tough. Rib chops are available with or without their bone, but I found that the bone helped to retain both flavor and juiciness.

Armed with the proper chop, I approached the recipe from two different directions. For my first round of tests, I browned the chops in a skillet and then braised them slowly in a vinegar pepper sauce. To my surprise, no matter what the cooking time, the chops always turned out stewed and chalky. I suspected that the vinegar was the culprit, so I performed a test using a mix of vinegar and water to braise one batch of chops and water alone for another. I was right. The pork chops braised in vinegar were more tender, but at a cost. The texture was unpleasantly chalky.

My next thought was to brown the pork chops and then top them with the vinegar pepper sauce at the very end (as when using a pan sauce).

Homemade vinegar peppers (ready in just minutes) transform ordinary pork chops into a satisfying Italian supper.

These chops fared a little better. Although they were a bit dry and tough, they browned beautifully. The problem was that the pan sauce didn't taste like pork and there was no sign of bright vinegar flavor in the chops.

I quickly solved the dry pork chop problem by bathing the chops in a brine of salt, sugar, and water for half an hour before cooking them. (On a whim, I tried adding a little vinegar to the brine, but this again led to chalky chops.) The brined chops retained much more moisture, and the sugar in the brine produced a terrific browned crust. Juiciness aside, however, these pork chops were still tough and tasted nothing like vinegar or peppers. The next time I browned the chops quickly, added the vinegar peppers to the pan, and simmered the vinegar down for just a few minutes (much less time than required for a braise). This approach showed promise. The pork started to taste like the sauce and the sauce started to take on the flavor of the pork, but the

texture of the chops, from soggy crust to tough interior, was still all wrong.

My next attempt again started with browning the chops, but this time I pulled them out of the pan as soon as they formed a beautiful browned crust (which took just a few minutes). I placed the chops, still raw inside, on a plate while I made the sauce. When the sauce had reduced, I placed the chops back in the pan, being careful not to pile the peppers on top and cover the crisp, browned crust. Then I put the skillet in a hot oven to quickly bring the chops up to a safe internal temperature and (I hoped) to allow them to absorb some of the vinegar and pepper flavor. This stovetop/oven combo was a huge improvement: The crust was intact, the chops were still juicy, and they were saturated with the flavor of the tart sauce.

A Pack of Peppers

The pork chops were great: juicy, tender, full of flavor—and, except for one minor detail, I could have stopped there. But that minor detail was the vinegar peppers. The flavor that they were giving to the sauce and pork was dull, stewed, and a bit bitter. Because jarred peppers are readily available and because there are plenty of brands to choose from, I thought I could easily find a sweet red pepper packed in vinegar that would please the masses. Not so. Maybe fancy supermarkets carry exotic imported peppers from afar that would work, but the jarred peppers taken off my local supermarket shelves were a big disappointment—dull or bitter, with a vinegar flavor that walked the line between acrid and musty.

Well, if supermarkets couldn't provide, then I'd make my own vinegar peppers. Back to the market I went to pick up some fresh red bell peppers. I followed the lead of a few recipes and roasted the peppers in the oven until they were charred. After peeling the blackened skin away, I marinated the peppers in vinegar for a few hours. The end result was flabby peppers that took too much time to make.

My other option was to sauté strips of peppers in the skillet until soft before adding the vinegar. Unfortunately, these peppers cooked down to a mush by the time the vinegar had reduced. Next I tried sautéing the peppers briefly, just to take off the raw crunch, added a cup of vinegar (enough to cover the peppers) to the pan, and simmered the lot. This did the trick. The pepper strips were still plump enough to enjoy and had taken on flavor from the vinegar. But, oh, what flavor! Once I tempered the harshness of the vinegar with some water, I had achieved easy, homemade, perfect vinegar peppers.

The Vinegar Itself

The last component to test was the vinegar itself, and although recipes mostly called for white wine vinegar, I tested champagne, cider, red wine, balsamic, and plain old white vinegar as well. Champagne vinegar was too sweet, cider was too "down-home," and red wine vinegar was too harsh. Balsamic vinegar was interesting—bold and sweet—but a few tasters complained that it was "not authentic" (it made for a great variation, though). There's a reason that people pull the bottle of white wine vinegar (a smooth, high-quality brand, please) off the shelf for this recipe. It offers a clean, sweet taste that marries perfectly with the peppers and the pork.

My last step was to boost the flavor of the sauce. In went some onion for roundness and sweetness. Garlic and anchovy added complexity. Also welcome was a hint of rosemary, added simply by steeping a whole sprig in the sauce for a few minutes. To finish the sauce, I added parsley for color and butter for richness. Finally, a hit of vinegar added just before serving (anywhere between a teaspoon and a couple of tablespoons, depending on your personal pucker tolerance), and no one will complain about this dish being dull again.

PORK CHOPS WITH VINEGAR AND SWEET PEPPERS
SERVES 4

For this recipe, we prefer rib chops, but center-cut chops, which contain a portion of tenderloin, can be used instead. If you do not have time to brine the chops, "enhanced" pork (pork injected with a salt, water, and sodium phosphate solution, so stated on the package label) presents an acceptable solution; the enhanced meat will have more moisture than unbrined natural chops. To keep the chops from overcooking and becoming tough and dry, they are removed from the oven when they are just shy of fully cooked; as they sit in the hot skillet, they continue to cook with residual heat. The vinegar stirred into the sauce at the end adds a bright, fresh flavor. We advise, however, that you taste the sauce before you add the vinegar—you may prefer to omit it.

Two Keys to Better Browning

PAT — PRESS

Do not rinse the chops after removing them from the brine; simply pat them dry with paper towels (left). Because the sugar in the brine has not been rinsed off the surface, the chops will brown better than if they had been rinsed. To ensure that the entire surface of the chop comes into contact with the hot pan, press the top of the chop with a spoon or spatula to push the meat into the pan.

I	cup sugar
	Table salt
4	bone-in pork rib chops, each ¾ to I inch thick and 7 to 9 ounces (see note)
	Ground black pepper
2	tablespoons olive oil
I	large onion, chopped fine (about I ¼ cups)
I	large red bell pepper, stemmed, seeded, and cut into ¼-inch-wide strips (about I ½ cups)
I	large yellow bell pepper, stemmed, seeded, and cut into ¼-inch-wide strips (about I ½ cups)
2	anchovy fillets, minced (about 2 teaspoons)
I	sprig fresh rosemary, about 5 inches long
2	medium garlic cloves, minced or pressed through garlic press (about 2 teaspoons)
¾	cup water
½	cup white wine vinegar, plus optional 2 tablespoons to finish sauce
2	tablespoons cold unsalted butter
2	tablespoons chopped fresh parsley leaves

1. Dissolve sugar and ½ cup table salt in 2 quarts water in large container; add pork chops and refrigerate 30 minutes. Remove chops from brine; thoroughly pat dry with paper towels, season with ¾ teaspoon pepper, and set aside.

2. Adjust oven rack to middle position; heat oven to 400 degrees. Heat oil in heavy-bottomed ovensafe 12-inch nonreactive skillet over medium-high heat until oil begins to smoke; swirl skillet to coat with oil. Place chops in skillet; cook until well browned, 3 to 4 minutes, using spoon or spatula to press down on center of chops to aid in browning. Using tongs, flip chops and brown lightly on second side, about 1 minute. Transfer chops to large plate; set aside.

3. Set skillet over medium-high heat. Add onion and cook, stirring occasionally, until just beginning to soften, about 2 minutes. Add peppers, anchovies, and rosemary; cook, stirring frequently, until peppers just begin to soften, about 4 minutes. Add garlic; cook, stirring constantly, until fragrant, about 30 seconds. Add water and ½ cup vinegar and bring to boil, scraping up browned bits with wooden spoon. Reduce heat to medium; simmer until liquid is reduced to about ⅓ cup, 6 to 8 minutes. Off heat, discard rosemary.

4. Return pork chops, browned side up, to skillet; nestle chops in peppers, but do not cover chops with peppers. Add any accumulated juices to skillet; set skillet in oven and cook until center of chops registers 135 to 140 degrees on instant-read thermometer, 8 to 12 minutes (begin checking temperature after 6 minutes). Using potholders, carefully remove skillet from oven (handle will be very hot) and cover skillet with lid or foil; let stand until center of chops registers 145 to 150 degrees on instant-read thermometer, 5 to 7 minutes. Transfer chops to platter or individual plates. Swirl butter into sauce and peppers in skillet; stir in optional 2 tablespoons vinegar, if using, and parsley. Adjust seasonings with salt and pepper, then pour or spoon sauce and peppers over chops. Serve immediately.

PORK CHOPS WITH BALSAMIC VINEGAR AND SWEET PEPPERS

Balsamic vinegar adds rich flavor and color.

Follow recipe for Pork Chops with Vinegar and Sweet Peppers, substituting balsamic vinegar for white wine vinegar and adding 1 tablespoon chopped fresh thyme along with parsley in step 4.

STEP-BY-STEP | PICK APART A PEPPER

I. Using chef's knife, cut ½ inch from top and bottom of pepper.

2. Slice from top to bottom, then flatten pepper with skin side facing down.

3. Pull out seedbed, then trim white ribs from inside pepper.

4. Cut pepper lengthwise into ¼-inch strips.

Better Chicken Teriyaki

Tired of food-court chicken teriyaki wannabes, we were determined
to develop a simple but authentic recipe.

≥ BY SANDRA WU ≤

When the fish isn't so fresh and the soba's just so-so, you can usually count on chicken teriyaki as a reliable standby at most Japanese restaurants. But with so many lackluster Americanized adaptations out there—including everything from skewered chicken chunks shellacked in a corn-syrupy sauce to over-marinated, preformed chicken breast patties—what is the real deal? Traditionally, chicken teriyaki is pan-fried, grilled, or broiled, with the sauce added during the last stages of cooking. In fact, the Japanese term *teriyaki* can be translated as *teri*, meaning "shine" or "luster"—referring to the glossy sauce—and *yaki*, meaning "to broil."

The chicken is most often served off the bone and cut into thin strips. The sauce itself—unlike most bottled versions—consists of just three basic ingredients: soy sauce, sugar, and either mirin (a sweet Japanese rice wine) or sake.

The half-dozen test recipes I assembled were, for the most part, disappointing. The most promising recipes had one thing in common: The skin was left on. Despite minor complaints about the sauce being too watery, tasters seemed to like a marinated and broiled version best, followed by one in which the chicken was pan-fried and simmered in sauce during the final minutes of cooking. While the skin kept the meat tender and moist, it also had a major flaw: its chewing-gum-like texture. I had to come up with a way to keep the skin crisp, even with the addition of sauce. A skillet or broiler—or perhaps a tag-team effort employing both—would be integral to getting me there.

The Right Cut

Although chicken thighs were clearly preferred by tasters over chicken breasts, I couldn't give up on the ubiquitous boneless, skinless variety just yet. But in subsequent tests, whether the chicken breasts were seared and broiled, solely broiled, marinated, or left plain and sauced at the end, they always ended up unappealingly dry, bland, and even a little rubbery around the edges compared with the thigh meat. The deeper, meatier taste of the thighs stood up nicely to the salty profile of the teriyaki sauce, while the breast meat acted as not much more than a one-dimensional backdrop, contributing little flavor of its own.

With the thighs now an established standard, the questions of bone-in or bone-out, skin-on or skin-

To keep the skin on the chicken crisp, hold back the teriyaki sauce until serving time.

off, begged to be answered. The skin seemed to create a protective barrier against the heat source, keeping the meat moist, so it would have to be left on. Because most skin-on chicken thighs are sold with the bone attached, we would have to bone them ourselves if we wanted to serve the meat in easy-to-eat strips. Even with a sharp paring knife and a straightforward technique, it took kitchen novices a few tries before they felt completely comfortable with the procedure. But the effort was well worth it. Not only did boning the chicken thighs allow the meat to cook faster, it also made cutting the pieces of hot chicken into strips much easier (and less messy). If you want to skip the knife work, you can cook and serve the chicken with the bone in, but the presentation is not nearly as nice and everyone will have to work harder at the table.

Potato-Chip-Crisp Skin

Because most of the recipes I came across in my research called for marinating the meat to infuse it with as much flavor as possible, all of my initial efforts began with this step. But whether I pricked the skin with a fork or slashed it with a knife, mari-

nating the thighs in the teriyaki sauce caused the skin to become unattractively flabby. A combination of searing the thighs and then finishing them under the broiler yielded the most promising results, but once the meat received its final dredge in a reduced portion of the marinade (which I now referred to as a sauce) to get that glazy shine, the skin always slipped back into sogginess.

Exhausted at the thought of having to refine a long-winded process of boning, marinating, searing, reducing, and broiling that didn't seem to work, I solicited the advice of my colleagues in the test kitchen. One suggested browning unmarinated thighs skin side down in a 12-inch skillet, weighting them with a Dutch oven, followed by simmering them skin side up in the reducing sauce. Frustrated and covered in splotches of chicken grease, I turned to another colleague, who suggested something so simple, so obvious, that I wondered why I hadn't thought of it sooner. "Why not just broil the chicken without marinating it and spoon the sauce on at the end?" she asked. I had gotten so caught up with trying to infuse the meat with flavor that I had all but forgotten a main principle of traditional teriyaki: applying the sauce at the end.

After playing musical racks with the oven broiler to get the thighs up to the requisite 175-degree temperature without burning the skin or leaving it pale and fatty, I found that placing the rack in the middle (about 8 inches from the heat source) provided the most consistent level of browning and crispness for the lightly salt-and-peppered thighs. On the middle rack, the skin turned almost as crispy as a potato chip, but there were still some spots where the fat didn't render completely. To remedy this problem, I slashed the skin, which allowed the heat to penetrate more easily, and tucked the exposed edges of meat underneath the skin while smoothing out the tops, which reduced the occurrence of dips and bumps where small pockets of fat had gotten trapped.

All about the Sauce

With the chicken taken care of, it was time to concentrate on the sauce. Bottled teriyaki sauce (see the tasting on page 9) was uniformly rejected in favor of a homemade sauce, which took just five minutes to prepare. Working with various amounts of soy sauce, sugar, and mirin (which tasters preferred to sake), I found that the best balance of sweetness and saltiness was achieved with equal

STEP-BY-STEP | PREPARING CHICKEN THIGHS

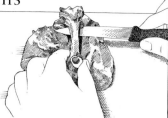

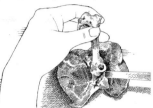

1. After trimming excess skin and fat (leave enough skin to cover meat), cut slit along white line of fat from one joint to other joint to expose bone.

2. Using tip of knife, cut/scrape meat from bone at both joints.

3. Slip knife under bone to separate meat completely from bone.

4. Discard bone. Trim any remaining cartilage from thigh.

5. Cut three diagonal slashes in skin. Do not cut into meat.

6. Tuck meat under skin and lightly flatten thigh to even thickness.

---

amounts of soy sauce and sugar (½ cup) and with a smaller amount of mirin (2 tablespoons), which added a slightly sweet, wine flavor. In terms of consistency, getting the sauce glazy (but neither as thick as molasses nor as thin as water) was difficult. No matter how carefully I watched the sauce simmer, it either was too thin or became tacky while the soy sauce burned, producing what one person called a "strangely bologna-like" flavor. A minimal amount of cornstarch (½ teaspoon) quickly solved this problem. Although the sauce was now clean and balanced, it needed more depth, which was achieved through the addition of some grated ginger and minced garlic. With at-once crisp and moist, sweet and salty glazed chicken now available at home, I would never have to eat food-court teriyaki again.

CHICKEN TERIYAKI
SERVES 4 TO 6

If you prefer to serve whole bone-in thighs and thereby skip the step of boning the chicken, trim the thighs of excess skin and fat, position the oven rack about 12 inches from the heat source, and increase the broiling time to 20 to 26 minutes, rotating the pan once halfway through the cooking time. This recipe was developed to work in an in-oven broiler, not the drawer-type broiler typical of older gas ovens. Mirin, a sweet Japanese rice wine, is a key component of teriyaki; it can be found in the international section of most major supermarkets and in most Asian markets. If you cannot find it, use 2 tablespoons white wine and an extra teaspoon of sugar. If desired, low-sodium soy sauce can be used in place of regular soy sauce. Serve with steamed rice, preferably short grain.

8   bone-in, skin-on chicken thighs (about 5 ounces each), trimmed, boned, and skin slashed (see illustrations 1 through 5 above)
     Table salt and ground black pepper
½   cup soy sauce
½   cup sugar
½   teaspoon grated fresh ginger
1   medium garlic clove, minced or pressed through garlic press (about 1 teaspoon)
2   tablespoons mirin
½   teaspoon cornstarch

1. Position oven rack about 8 inches from heat source; heat broiler. Season chicken thighs with salt and pepper; set thighs skin side up on broiler pan (or foil-lined rimmed baking sheet fitted with flat wire rack), tucking exposed meat under skin and lightly flattening thighs to be of relatively even thickness (see illustration 6). Broil until skin is crisp and golden brown and thickest parts of thighs register 175 degrees on instant-read thermometer, 8 to 14 minutes, rotating pan halfway through cooking time for even browning.

2. While chicken cooks, combine soy sauce, sugar, ginger, and garlic in small saucepan; stir together mirin and cornstarch in small bowl until no lumps remain, then stir mirin mixture into saucepan. Bring sauce to boil over medium-high heat, stirring occasionally; reduce heat to medium-low and simmer, stirring occasionally, until sauce is reduced to ¾ cup and forms syrupy glaze, about 4 minutes. Cover to keep warm.

3. Transfer chicken to cutting board; let rest 2 to 3 minutes. Cut meat crosswise into ½-inch-wide strips. Transfer chicken to serving platter; stir teriyaki sauce to recombine, then drizzle to taste over chicken. Serve immediately, passing remaining sauce separately.

TASTING: Bottled Teriyaki Sauces

Considering that a great teriyaki sauce can be had in a mere five minutes with six not terribly exotic ingredients, bottled sauces can hardly boast convenience. But how do they taste? We sampled seven leading brands to find out.

Our 19 tasters had difficulty identifying many of these sauces as teriyaki. Several brands resembled hoisin, oyster, or even barbecue sauce. Of the three that met tasters' standards for teriyaki, Annie Chun's All Natural received top marks. A second tasting pitted Annie Chun's against our homemade teriyaki sauce. Our judges deemed Annie Chun's harsh in comparison to the brighter-tasting and better-balanced sauce we had made ourselves. –Garth Clingingsmith

DECENT

ANNIE CHUN'S All Natural Teriyaki Sauce
"Smooth, rich texture" and indisputable teriyaki flavor, but cannot compare to homemade.

TOLERABLE

SOY VAY Veri Veri Teriyaki
No one objected to the "whoa, garlic" flavor, but offensive "little floaties" of sesame and onion turned many away.

SUN LUCK Honey Mirin Teriyaki Sauce
Overwhelming sweetness tended to overshadow the "fishy" and "chemical" flavors. Surprisingly, a few tasters asked, "Where's the salt?"

NOT RECOMMENDED

HOUSE OF TSANG Tokyo Teriyaki Hibachi Grill Sauce "Gluelike texture" and "molasses-like" sweetness reminded tasters of oyster sauce.

KIKKOMAN Lite Teriyaki Marinade & Sauce
This watery sauce was dominated by "loads of ginger" and "vinegary acidity."

KIKKOMAN Teriyaki Marinade & Sauce
"This is straight soy," summed up tasters' responses to this thin and salty sauce.

SAN-J Traditional Japanese Teriyaki Stir-Fry & Marinade "Peppery, scorched harshness" made this "Japanese A-1" tough to swallow.

Rethinking Cornbread

Brushing regional differences aside, we wanted both a tender, fluffy crumb and a thick, crunchy crust. But what we wanted most of all was sweet corn flavor.

> BY ERIKA BRUCE

Deeply rooted in American history, cornbread has been around long enough to take on a distinctly different character depending on where it is made. In the South, it has become a squat, savory skillet bread used for sopping up pot liquor, the tasty liquid left behind by cooked meat or vegetables or what have you. In cooler Northern regions, where it has become more cake than bread, it is light, tender, and generously sweetened. Despite these regional variations in texture and appearance, however, cornbread has remained unfortunately constant in one respect: It lacks convincing corn flavor.

Wanting to avoid a regional food fight, I figured that everyone—north or south of the Mason-Dixon line—could agree on one simple notion: Cornbread ought to be rich with the flavor of corn. A deeply browned crust also seemed far from controversial, and, when it came to texture, I attempted a reasonable regional compromise: moist and somewhat fluffy but neither cakey nor heavy. Could this humble dish finally unite North and South? I was prepared to work very hard toward this end.

Choosing the Right Cornmeal

I started out with a Northern-style recipe calling for equal amounts of flour and cornmeal. (It is customary for Southern-style recipes to minimize or eliminate the flour altogether.) My first tests involved the cornmeal. The different brands ran the gamut from fine and powdery to coarse and uneven, yielding wild variations in texture, from dry and cottony to downright crunchy, but not one produced very much corn flavor. I quickly came to the conclusion that my recipe, like it or not, would have to call for a national brand of cornmeal to avoid these huge textural swings. The obvious option was Quaker yellow cornmeal, which is available in every supermarket from New Orleans to Portland, Maine. Although my choice may rightfully be considered heretical by many cornbread mavens, it was the only way I could be sure my recipe would deliver consistent results.

Reliable though it is, Quaker cornmeal is degerminated—robbed of the germ (the heart of the kernel) during processing. It is thus also

Can this flavorful cornbread with a fluffy crumb and crisp crust please everyone?

robbed of flavor. (In whole-grain cornmeal, the germ is left intact.) By using degerminated cornmeal, I was now taking a step backward in my quest to build more corn flavor. Increasing the amount of cornmeal to compensate caused the cornbread to lose its lightness. And tasters didn't care for the abundance of hard, crunchy grains. My next move was to soak the cornmeal in boiling water before mix-

ing it with the other ingredients (a common recipe directive), reasoning that this would both soften the cornmeal and extract more of its flavor. But the added moisture made the cornbread even heavier and slightly rubbery, while contributing not a bit of extra corn flavor. Relenting, I reduced the cornmeal (I now had more flour than cornmeal), which produced the best texture thus far and alleviated any grittiness or heaviness.

Putting the Corn Back into Cornbread

To boost corn flavor, a few recipes added fresh corn to the batter. While appreciating the sweet corn taste, tasters objected to the tough, chewy kernels. Chopping the corn by hand was time-consuming. Pureeing the corn in the food processor was much quicker and broke down the kernels more efficiently. With pureed corn, my recipe was finally starting to taste good.

The dairy component up until now had been whole milk. To compensate for the extra liquid exuded by the pureed corn, I reduced the amount, but this just made the cornbread bland. I tried substituting a modest amount of buttermilk, which produced both a lighter texture and a tangier flavor. The sweetener also had an effect on texture; honey and maple syrup added nice flavor accents, but they also added moisture. Granulated and light brown sugars made for a better texture, but the light brown sugar did more to accentuate the corn flavor. Two eggs worked well in this bread, offering structure without cakiness. A modest amount of baking powder boosted by a bit of baking soda (to react with the acidic buttermilk) yielded the best rise.

The fat used in cornbread can vary from bacon drippings to melted butter or vegetable oil. Cooking bacon for this relatively quick recipe seemed an unnecessary step, and butter indisputably added more flavor and color than vegetable oil. Because I was already using the food processor for the corn, I decided to avoid dirtying another bowl and added all of the wet ingredients together. I even added

A Corny Solution

FRESH   **CANNED**   **FROZEN**

The secret to cornbread with real corn flavor is pretty simple: Use corn, not just cornmeal. We tried fresh cooked corn (cut right from the cob), rinsed canned corn, and thawed frozen corn. Fresh corn was best, but frozen was nearly as good—and a lot easier to use.

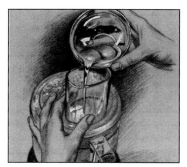

1. Puree corn—along with brown sugar, buttermilk, and eggs—to eliminate coarse texture of whole kernels.

2. Create well in center of dry ingredients, then pour in wet ingredients, except for butter.

3. After couple of initial folds, add warm melted butter.

4. Working quickly but gently, fold mixture together just until dry ingredients are moistened.

the light brown sugar to the wet mix to eliminate the pesky lumps it had been forming in the flour mixture. Then I noticed that some recipes added the melted butter last. This created subtle streaks of unmixed butter in the batter, but, as the bread baked, the butter rose to the surface and created a more deeply browned top crust and a stronger butter flavor. Now my recipe, too, would add the butter last. For the best flavor and texture, my recipe would also add a lot more butter than many others—a whole stick.

Although the increase in butter and the adjustment to the mixing method improved the browning, the bread was still missing a thick and crunchy crust. Southern cornbreads, which usually showcase such a crust, are baked in fat-coated, piping-hot cast-iron skillets. Because some cooks don't own a cast-iron (or any other ovenproof) skillet, I tried an 8-inch-square baking dish. Heating it in the oven or on the stovetop before adding the batter was not only awkward but dangerous (especially with Pyrex, which can shatter

RECIPE TESTING:
Where North & South Don't Meet

SOUTHERN CORNBREAD   NORTHERN CORNBREAD

A typical Southern cornbread contains more cornmeal than flour and no sweetener at all, and it is cooked in a skillet to make sure the exterior is well browned and crisp. The texture is crumbly, making this thin cornbread an ideal partner to saucy dishes. In contrast, a typical Northern cornbread is made with more flour than cornmeal and a fair amount of sweetener. Because it is cooked in a baking pan, the exterior is very pale. The texture is cakey, making this thick cornbread ideal for breakfast or a snack.

if handled this way). Most recipes that call for a baking dish use a moderate oven temperature of 350 degrees. A hotter oven—the kind used in many Southern recipes with a skillet—was better. Baked at 400 degrees, the crust was both crunchy and full of buttery, toasted corn flavor.

Do I really think that this one cornbread recipe will please the whole country? Regional loyalties being what they are, probably not. But if you are looking for big corn flavor, a good crust, a light (but not cakelike) texture, and an easy-to-make recipe, this is one cornbread that just might make the trip from North to South.

ALL-PURPOSE CORNBREAD
MAKES ONE 8-INCH SQUARE

Before preparing the baking dish or any of the other ingredients, measure out the frozen kernels and let them stand at room temperature until needed. When corn is in season, fresh cooked kernels can be substituted for the frozen corn. This recipe was developed with Quaker yellow cornmeal; a stone-ground whole-grain cornmeal will work but will yield a drier and less tender cornbread. We prefer a Pyrex glass baking dish because it yields a nice golden-brown crust, but a metal baking dish (nonstick or traditional) will also work. The cornbread is best served warm; leftovers can be wrapped in foil and reheated in a 350-degree oven for 10 to 15 minutes.

1½	cups (7½ ounces) unbleached all-purpose flour
1	cup (5½ ounces) yellow cornmeal (see note)
2	teaspoons baking powder
¼	teaspoon baking soda
¾	teaspoon table salt
¼	cup (1¾ ounces) packed light brown sugar
¾	cup (3½ ounces) frozen corn kernels, thawed
1	cup buttermilk
2	large eggs
8	tablespoons (1 stick) unsalted butter, melted and cooled slightly

1. Adjust oven rack to middle position; heat oven to 400 degrees. Spray 8-inch-square baking dish with nonstick cooking spray. Whisk flour, cornmeal, baking powder, baking soda, and salt in medium bowl until combined; set aside.

2. In food processor or blender, process brown sugar, thawed corn kernels, and buttermilk until combined, about 5 seconds. Add eggs and process until well combined (corn lumps will remain), about 5 seconds longer.

3. Using rubber spatula, make well in center of dry ingredients; pour wet ingredients into well. Begin folding dry ingredients into wet, giving mixture only a few turns to barely combine; add melted butter and continue folding until dry ingredients are just moistened. Pour batter into prepared baking dish; smooth surface with rubber spatula. Bake until deep golden brown and toothpick inserted in center comes out clean, 25 to 35 minutes. Cool on wire rack 10 minutes; invert cornbread onto wire rack, then turn right side up and continue to cool until warm, about 10 minutes longer. Cut into pieces and serve.

SPICY JALAPEÑO-CHEDDAR CORNBREAD

Shred 4 ounces sharp cheddar cheese (you should have about 1⅓ cups). Follow recipe for All-Purpose Cornbread, reducing salt to ½ teaspoon; add ⅜ teaspoon cayenne, 1 medium jalapeño chile, cored, seeded, and chopped fine, and half of shredded cheddar to flour mixture in step 1 and toss well to combine. Reduce sugar to 2 tablespoons and sprinkle remaining cheddar over batter in baking dish just before baking.

BLUEBERRY BREAKFAST CORNBREAD

Follow recipe for All-Purpose Cornbread, reducing salt to ½ teaspoon; add 1 cup fresh or frozen blueberries (do not thaw frozen blueberries) to flour mixture in step 1 and toss well to coat berries. Reduce buttermilk to ¾ cup and add ¼ cup maple syrup to food processor along with buttermilk. Sprinkle 2 tablespoons granulated sugar over batter in baking dish just before baking.

Pasta with Chicken and Broccoli

This restaurant-chain classic can be as off-putting as a bad horror movie: drab colors, tough meat, and a main character—the pasta—with no bite.

≥ BY JULIA COLLIN DAVISON ≤

Pseudo-Italian chain restaurants known for cheap wine and doughy breadsticks are often also notorious for serving dreadful plates of chicken and broccoli with ziti. Drowned in a fatty cream sauce whose only flavor is that of old chopped garlic, this dish needed serious help. I wanted to reclaim this wholly American dish with fresh, crisp broccoli, tender chicken, and a clean-flavored sauce.

Right off the bat, I decided that boneless, skinless chicken breasts were the best choice and tested various cooking methods, including microwaving, broiling, sautéing, and poaching (simmering in a liquid). Not surprisingly, microwaving produced bland chicken with a steamed taste, and the timing was tricky. Broiling and sautéing produced meat with the most flavor, but the nicely seared edges of the chicken turned tough and stringy after being tossed with the pasta and sauce. Poaching the chicken—in the pasta water or the simmering sauce—produced meat that was tender and juicy, but the flavor was badly washed out.

Wanting the flavor provided by a sauté and the tenderness that comes with poaching, I put my mind to combining these methods. Lightly cooking the chicken with a little butter in a skillet until it just began to turn golden, I removed it from the pan when it was still underdone. After building a sauce in the now-empty skillet, I returned the chicken to the pan and let it simmer in the sauce until fully cooked. That did the trick; I now had chicken that was tender and flavorful.

Turning my attention next to the broccoli, my first disastrous attempt at simmering it right in the sauce infused the whole dish with an off flavor and a dirty color. Steaming it on the stovetop or in the microwave was OK, but neither was as easy as blanching, given that there was already a pot of boiling water going for the pasta.

Up until now, I had been making a sauce by thickening heavy cream with flour and butter (that is, a roux) and had determined that garlic, red pepper flakes, fresh herbs, and white wine were all crucial for flavor. But tasters wanted more. I tried omitting the roux and letting the cream simmer and thicken on its own, but this produced a sauce that was much too fatty. I then tried replacing portions of the cream with chicken broth and was relieved to finally hear some compliments. The flavor of the wine, garlic, and herbs

began to show, and there was a significant boost in chicken flavor. Incrementally increasing the amount of broth and decreasing the amount of cream, I churned out sauce after sauce to better and better reviews until the cream had been completely eliminated. The broth-based sauce tasted clean and fresh, enhancing the flavors of the crisp broccoli and tender chicken rather than obfuscating them. Rounded out with a few tablespoons of butter, a handful of Asiago cheese, and some sun-dried tomatoes, the sauce finally carried some serious flavor. Now this was a dish worth staying home for.

PASTA WITH CHICKEN, BROCCOLI, AND SUN-DRIED TOMATOES
SERVES 4

Be sure to use low-sodium chicken broth in this recipe; regular chicken broth will make the dish extremely salty. The broccoli is blanched in the same water that is later used to cook the pasta. Remove the broccoli when it is tender at the edges but still crisp at the core—it will continue to cook with residual heat. If you can't find Asiago cheese, Parmesan is an acceptable alternative.

- 4 tablespoons unsalted butter
- 1 pound boneless, skinless chicken breasts, trimmed of fat and cut crosswise into ¼-inch slices
- 1 small onion, chopped fine (about ⅔ cup)
  Table salt
- 6 medium garlic cloves, minced or pressed through garlic press (about 2 tablespoons)
- ¼ teaspoon red pepper flakes
- 2 teaspoons roughly chopped fresh thyme leaves
- 2 teaspoons all-purpose flour
- 1 cup dry white wine
- 2 cups low-sodium chicken broth
- 1 bunch broccoli (about 1½ pounds), florets trimmed into 1-inch pieces (about 6 cups), stems discarded
- ½ pound penne, ziti, cavatappi, or campanelle
- 2 ounces finely grated Asiago cheese (1 cup), plus extra for serving
- 1 jar (7 to 8½ ounces) oil-packed, sun-dried tomatoes, rinsed, patted dry, and cut into ¼-inch strips (about 1 cup)
- 1 tablespoon minced fresh parsley leaves
  Ground black pepper

1. Bring 4 quarts water to rolling boil, covered, in stockpot.

2. Meanwhile, heat 1 tablespoon butter in 12-inch nonstick skillet over high heat until just beginning to brown, about 1 minute. Add chicken in single layer; cook for 1 minute without stirring, then stir chicken and continue to cook until most, but not all, of pink color has disappeared and chicken is lightly browned around the edges, about 2 minutes longer. Transfer chicken to clean bowl; set aside.

3. Return skillet to high heat and add 1 tablespoon butter; add onion and ¼ teaspoon salt and cook, stirring occasionally, until browned about edges, 2 to 3 minutes. Stir in garlic, red pepper flakes, thyme, and flour; cook, stirring constantly, until fragrant, about 30 seconds. Add wine and chicken broth; bring to simmer, then reduce heat to medium and continue to simmer, stirring occasionally, until sauce has thickened slightly and reduced to 1¼ cups, about 15 minutes.

4. While sauce simmers, add 1 tablespoon salt and broccoli to boiling water; cook until broccoli is tender but still crisp at center, about 2 minutes. Using slotted spoon, transfer broccoli to large paper towel–lined plate. Return water to boil; stir in pasta and cook until al dente. Drain, reserving ½ cup pasta cooking water; return pasta to pot.

5. Stir remaining 2 tablespoons butter, Asiago, sun-dried tomatoes, parsley, and chicken into sauce in skillet; cook until chicken is hot and cooked through, about 1 minute. Off heat, season to taste with pepper. Pour chicken/sauce mixture over pasta and add broccoli; toss gently to combine, adding pasta cooking water as needed to adjust sauce consistency. Serve immediately, passing additional Asiago separately.

Preparing Broccoli

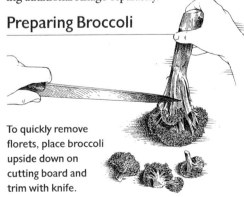

To quickly remove florets, place broccoli upside down on cutting board and trim with knife.

Moist and Tender Braised Brisket

When this notoriously tough cut finally turns tender, it's often dry as a bone.
Could we have our brisket both ways?

⇒ BY SEAN LAWLER ⇐

Texans smoke it, the Irish pickle it, and Germans smother it in sauerkraut and prunes. Cooks from around the world may never see eye to eye on what to do with a beef brisket, but they all agree it takes time. Brisket would therefore seem an ideal cut for braising, as it takes hours of slow cooking to soften this workhorse muscle, which runs down the chest of the steer and is otherwise as tough as leather. Sadly, this patience is usually rewarded with shreds of dry, chewy meat, as brisket tends to give up its last ounce of moisture just as it finally becomes fork tender.

My goal was a braised brisket that was both moist and tender, with a simple sauce that complemented this naturally flavorful cut. The down-home recipes I sampled used diversionary tactics to attack the problem of dry, chewy meat, either emptying the spice rack into the pot or slathering the brisket in sticky sweet sauces made from cola, chili sauce, or powdered soup mix. More traditional recipes took a minimalist approach, braising the meat with onions in a watery broth (if not actually water). Neither strategy could disguise or remedy the basic problem: meat that was either tough or bone-dry and impossible to cut without shredding it into stringy bits.

All braises struggle with this same Catch-22. For the normally tough meat to become tender, its connective tissues must be broken down, which requires hours of low-temperature, moist-heat cooking. As the meat cooks, the muscle fibers slowly contract, expelling moisture and often leaving the meat dry. The amount and distribution of the fat in the meat can make a big difference in the outcome of a braise. A chuck roast will taste succulent after a proper braise because of its relatively high and even distribution of fat. In a brisket, most of the fat is located in an exterior cap and in a few thick layers—it is not marbled throughout. As a result, fat renders into the sauce rather than basting the interior of

We discovered that for the best results, brisket should be cooked, cooled overnight, sliced, and then gently reheated.

the meat, which is rather lean. (This is especially true of flat cut brisket; see the "Shopping" box on page 14 for more information.)

For all these reasons, the *Cook's* standard braising technique, in which the meat is browned in a Dutch oven, then braised with wine, broth, and aromatics in a 300-degree oven until tender, delivered disappointing results. While tender, the brisket was quite dry and had an unappealing boiled flavor, and the sauce was thin and greasy. The sliced and sautéed onions I added to the pot lent a welcome sweetness, but after almost four hours they had all but disintegrated. Last, the meat appeared to cook unevenly; by the time the center of the brisket was tender, the outer layers

of meat were falling apart in shreds.

A Better Braise

Looking for a better way to braise, I tested an assortment of cooking vessels and techniques. To improve the flavor of the sauce, I ran a test with much less liquid than goes into a standard braise—just a half cup each of wine and broth. The resulting sauce was indeed flavorful, but, in such a shallow pool of liquid, the meat cooked unevenly. (The portions exposed to the air took longer to cook.) I then came across an unusual recipe that called for searing the brisket in a skillet before cooking it in a wrapper of aluminum foil along with the wine and broth used to deglaze the pan. The good news was that this brisket cooked evenly— the meat was always in contact with liquid—and the sauce was flavorful. But the meat was still dry.

Not as common with beef as with pork and chicken, brining was nonetheless one way to try to reduce the moisture loss. Unfortunately, tasters found that even a mild brine resulted in meat and sauce that were unpalatably salty. Overnight marinades in wine and herbs, suggested by some traditional Eastern European recipes, left the briskets mushy and sour tasting. Some brisket recipes recommended cooking the meat fat side up and poking holes through the fat and into the meat to help the rendered fat penetrate and baste the meat. While this step did make for some improvement in the moistness of the brisket, overall the meat was still too dry.

If I couldn't keep the moisture from leaving the meat in the first place, could I get the meat to reabsorb some of the liquid after cooking? Until this point, I had been removing the brisket from the sauce and letting it rest on a cutting board before attempting—and failing—to cut it into thin, neat slices. (Like a flank steak, brisket has long muscle fibers and must be sliced against the grain to avoid being chewy. These same long fibers, however, turn into shreds once the

Beef Brisket

A whole beef brisket weighs up to 12 pounds. It is usually sold in two pieces, the flat (or first) cut and the point cut. The flat cut is leaner and thinner, with a rectangular shape and an exterior fat cap. It is more commonly available at supermarkets than the point cut, which has an oblong, irregular shape and contains large interior pockets of fat.

We found the point cut to be marginally more flavorful but, more important, much less prone to drying out, thanks to all the extra fat. Unfortunately, more than a few tasters found the point cut too fatty to enjoy, and it was next to impossible to carve it into neat slices. All in all, it seemed a better cut for barbecuing than braising.

The flat cut is easier to sear and to slice, provided it has cooled. Butchers usually trim away some or all of the fat cap, but try to find one with at least ¼ inch of fat in place, as it will help to keep the meat moist during cooking. (It can be hard to tell how much fat is in place because supermarkets often wrap the brisket with the fat side hidden.) If the fat cap is very thick and untrimmed in places, cut it down to a thickness of about ¼ inch.

A flat cut brisket roast usually weighs between 4 and 5 pounds, though butchers occasionally cut them into smaller 2- to 3-pound roasts. You can substitute two of these smaller cuts if that is all that is available, although the cooking time may vary. –S.L.

FLAT CUT

POINT CUT

A 4- to 5-pound flat cut brisket with a decent cap of fat (top) is ideal for braising. We find its meat to be leaner and easier to slice than the highly marbled and knobby point cut brisket (bottom), but either will work in our recipe.

A debate sprang up in the test kitchen over the proper thickness of the finished sauce. "Gravy" enthusiasts wanted a thick sauce that would cling to the meat, while their opponents backed a thinner, more natural jus. But everyone agreed that too much flour, stirred into the skillet while building the sauce, resulted in a sauce than was overly pasty; just 2 tablespoons were enough to give the sauce the proper body. To further thicken the sauce, I put it back on the stove to simmer while slicing the finished brisket. Just before serving, I added a few teaspoons of cider vinegar to brighten the flavor, and tasters unanimously approved.

Now I had the best of both worlds—tender and moist—and the recipe could be made the day before serving, making it perfect for a midweek supper or even for entertaining.

ONION-BRAISED BEEF BRISKET
SERVES 6

This recipe requires a few hours of unattended cooking. It also requires advance preparation. After cooking, the brisket must stand overnight in the braising liquid that later becomes the sauce; this helps to keep the brisket moist and flavorful.

Defatting the sauce is essential. If the fat has congealed into a layer on top of the sauce, it can be easily removed while cold. Sometimes, however, fragments of solid fat are dispersed throughout the sauce; in this case, the sauce should be skimmed of fat after reheating. If you prefer a spicy sauce, increase the amount of cayenne to ¼ teaspoon. You will need 18-inch-wide heavy-duty foil for this recipe. If you own an electric knife, it will make easy work of slicing the cold brisket. Good accompaniments to braised brisket include mashed potatoes and egg noodles.

If you would like to make and serve the brisket on the same day, after removing the brisket from the oven in step 4, reseal the foil and let the brisket stand at room temperature for an hour. Then transfer the brisket to a cutting board and

connective tissue has been dissolved, making the meat difficult to slice.) Next I tested letting the meat rest, and even cool, in the sauce before slicing it, in hopes that it would reabsorb some of the flavorful liquid it had lost. Twenty minutes in the sauce had little effect on the meat, but after an hour-long rest the brisket was noticeably better.

Encouraged, I let the meat cool overnight in the sauce. The next day, I noticed two big improvements: The excess fat had congealed on top of the sauce and was easy to remove, and the cold brisket was now easy to slice without shredding. Once reheated in the sauce, the overnight brisket was dramatically improved on all counts— moist, flavorful, and meltingly tender. Weighing pieces of brisket that had rested overnight in the sauce showed that they had, in fact, gained several ounces. In effect, they had reabsorbed some of their juices from the sauce, which made the meat less dry.

A Better Sauce

Until now, my working recipe had called for equal parts red wine and beef broth as braising liquids. While my goal was a sauce with a lot of beef flavor, past tastings had shown that most canned beef broths taste salty and artificial. I tested a variety of liquids in different combinations and found that, indeed, tasters preferred chicken broth to beef for its cleaner flavor. To boost the flavor of the sauce, I doubled the quantities of both broth and wine, then allowed them to reduce before placing the braise in the oven. As for the other ingredients in the sauce, tasters loved the sweetness of onions—sliced thick to stand up to the long cooking time—but agreed that carrots and celery were unnecessary. Brown sugar complemented the onions, while paprika and a pinch of cayenne contributed a bit of spice and heat. Garlic, tomato paste, bay leaves, and a few sprigs of fresh thyme rounded out the flavors.

TECHNIQUE | A BETTER WAY TO COOK BRISKET

1. Use Dutch oven or cast-iron skillet to weight meat as it browns.

2. Carefully pour sauce and onions into foil-lined baking dish.

3. Place brisket on top of sauce, fat side up, nestling meat into liquid and onions.

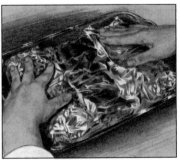

4. Fold flaps of foil to wrap brisket securely, but do not wrap too tightly.

continue with the recipe to strain, defat, and reheat the sauce and slice the meat; because the brisket will still be hot, there will be no need to put it back into the oven once the reheated sauce is poured over it.

1	beef brisket roast, 4 to 5 pounds, flat cut preferred (see shopping note on page 14)
	Table salt and ground black pepper
	Vegetable oil
3	large onions (about 2½ pounds), halved and sliced ½ inch thick
1	tablespoon light or dark brown sugar
3	medium garlic cloves, minced or pressed through garlic press (about 1 tablespoon)
1	tablespoon tomato paste
1	tablespoon paprika
⅛	teaspoon cayenne
2	tablespoons all-purpose flour
1	cup low-sodium chicken broth
1	cup dry red wine
3	dried bay leaves
3	sprigs fresh thyme
2	teaspoons cider vinegar (to season sauce before serving)

1. Adjust oven rack to lower-middle position; heat oven to 300 degrees. Line 13 by 9-inch baking dish with two 24-inch-long sheets of 18-inch-wide heavy-duty foil, positioning sheets perpendicular to each other and allowing excess foil to extend beyond edges of pan. Pat brisket dry with paper towels. Place brisket fat side up on cutting board; using dinner fork, poke holes in meat through fat layer about 1 inch apart. Season both sides of brisket liberally with salt and pepper.

2. Heat 1 teaspoon oil in 12-inch skillet over medium-high heat until oil just begins to smoke. Place brisket fat side up in skillet (brisket may climb up sides of skillet); weight brisket with heavy Dutch oven or cast-iron skillet and cook until well browned, about 7 minutes. Remove Dutch oven; using tongs, flip brisket and cook on second side without weight until well browned, about 7 minutes longer. Transfer brisket to platter.

Worth the Wait

SLICED RIGHT AWAY   **RESTED, THEN SLICED**

Sliced straight from the pot, brisket almost invariably shreds (left). Letting the cooked brisket rest overnight in the braising liquid allows the meat to absorb some of these juices, and the result is meat that slices neatly and tastes better (right).

3. Pour off all but 1 tablespoon fat from pan (or, if brisket was lean, add enough oil to fat in skillet to equal 1 tablespoon); stir in onions, sugar, and ¼ teaspoon salt and cook over medium-high heat, stirring occasionally, until onions are softened and golden, 10 to 12 minutes. Add garlic and cook, stirring frequently, until fragrant, about 1 minute; add tomato paste and cook, stirring to combine, until paste darkens, about 2 minutes. Add paprika and cayenne and cook, stirring constantly, until fragrant, about 1 minute. Sprinkle flour over onions and cook, stirring constantly, until well combined, about 2 minutes. Add broth, wine, bay, and thyme, stirring to scrape up browned bits from pan; bring to simmer and simmer about 5 minutes to fully thicken.

4. Pour sauce and onions into foil-lined baking dish. Nestle brisket, fat side up, in sauce and onions. Fold foil extensions over and seal (do not tightly crimp foil because foil must later be opened to test for doneness). Place in oven and cook until fork can be inserted into and removed from center of brisket with no resistance, 3½ to 4 hours (when testing for doneness, open foil with caution as contents will be steam-ing). Carefully open foil and let brisket cool at room temperature for 20 to 30 minutes.

5. Transfer brisket to large bowl; set mesh strainer over bowl and strain sauce over brisket. Discard bay and thyme from onions and transfer onions to small bowl. Cover both bowls with plastic wrap, cut vents in plastic with paring knife, and refrigerate overnight.

6. About 45 minutes before serving, adjust oven rack to lower-middle position; heat oven to 350 degrees. While oven heats, transfer cold brisket to cutting board. Scrape off and discard any congealed fat from sauce, then transfer sauce to medium saucepan and heat over medium heat until warm, skimming any fat on surface with wide shallow spoon (you should have about 2 cups sauce without onions; if necessary, simmer sauce over medium-high heat until reduced to 2 cups). While sauce heats, use chef's or carving knife to slice brisket against grain into ¼-inch-thick slices, trimming and discarding any excess fat, if desired; place slices in 13 by 9-inch baking dish. Stir reserved onions and vinegar into warmed sauce and adjust seasoning with salt and pepper. Pour sauce over brisket slices, cover baking dish with foil, and bake until heated through, 25 to 30 minutes. Serve immediately.

Recipe Rescue

Ever wish there was an emergency hotline you could call for advice when a recipe takes a turn for the worse? These tips and guidelines are the next-best thing to a 24-hour food emergency operator. BY SEAN LAWLER

TROUBLESHOOTING AT THE STOVETOP

When certain things burn there is no going back, and the successful cook learns to recognize the point of no return. Scorched oil and garlic, for example, will contribute a burnt, bitter flavor to the finished dish. In this case, it's best to wipe the pan clean and start over. And most such problems can be avoided by choosing the proper pan, cooking fat, and burner setting for the job. That said, here's what to do if . . .

The food won't simmer slowly.
If it's hard to get your stovetop burners to maintain a very low flame (necessary when trying to cook soups or stews at a bare simmer), improvise a flame tamer out of a thick ring of aluminum foil. Set the foil ring on the burner, then place the pot on top.

The pan gets too dark.
Searing meat in a pan produces a crusty, brown *fond*, which is the key to great flavor in many soups, stews, and sauces. But when those dark brown bits begin to turn black, you've got a good thing gone bad. When searing cutlets over high heat, for example, it's often the areas of the pan between the pieces of meat that are the first to blacken. To guard against this, shift the position of the food to cover the darker spots. The juices released from the meat will help to deglaze the pan. When searing a large quantity of meat in batches, it may be necessary to deglaze the empty pan with water, wine, or stock between batches.

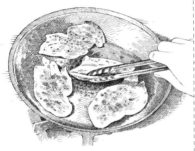

Melting butter starts to burn.
Blackened butter will impart a bitter flavor to a finished dish and should be thrown away. However, slightly browned butter is no problem—in fact, it has a pleasantly nutty flavor. To keep it from browning further, add a small amount of vegetable oil to the pan. With its higher smoke point, vegetable oil is more resistant to burning and will help keep the butter from burning.

Food sticks to the pan.
Food that initially sticks to the pan usually releases on its own after a crust begins to form. As long as the food is not burning, wait a minute or two and then try again. For stubbornly stuck pieces of meat or fish, dip a thin, flexible spatula into cold water and slide the inverted spatula blade underneath the food.

WHEN SEASONINGS GO AWRY

If you've added too much salt, sugar, or spice to a dish, the damage is usually done. In mild cases, however, the overpowering ingredient can sometimes be masked by the addition of another from the opposite end of the flavor spectrum. Consult this chart for ideas. (By the way, a potato is useless—see the box on page 17.) And remember to account for the reduction of liquids when seasoning a dish—a perfectly seasoned stew will likely taste too salty after several hours of simmering. Your best bet: Season with a light hand during the cooking process, then adjust the seasoning just before serving.

IF YOUR FOOD IS . . .	ADD . . .	SUCH AS . . .
Too salty	An acid or sweetener	Vinegar; lemon or lime juice; canned, unsalted tomatoes; sugar, honey, or maple syrup
Too sweet	An acid or seasonings	Vinegar or citrus juice; chopped fresh herb; dash of cayenne; or, for sweet dishes, a bit of liqueur or espresso powder
Too spicy or acidic	A fat or sweetener	Butter, cream, sour cream, cheese, or olive oil; sugar, honey, or maple syrup

Meat is undercooked.
The meat has rested and been sliced, and it's underdone in the center. Simply putting the slices in the oven to finish cooking is not a good idea—the slices will dry out and quickly turn gray. Boston chef Gordon Hamersley has the solution: Place the sliced meat on a wire rack set over a baking sheet, then cover the meat with lettuce leaves before putting it under the broiler. The meat will gently steam under the lettuce, without drying out.

ILLUSTRATION: JOHN BURGOYNE

FROM TOO THICK OR THIN TO JUST RIGHT

Soups, stews, and sauces often need some last-minute adjustments, even if the recipe was followed to the letter. Why? The moisture and fat content of foods can vary a great deal. If your sauce is . . .

Too thick Gradually add more water, broth, canned tomatoes, or whatever liquid is appropriate. Remember to correct the seasoning before serving.

Too thin Simmering the liquid until the desired consistency is reached is the simplest option but not necessarily the best one. Time will not always permit a lengthy simmer, which may also overcook any meat or vegetables in the dish. Here are some better options.

Butter: Whisking cold butter into a sauce just before serving adds richness and body.

Cornstarch: Soups and stews can be thickened with cornstarch, provided it is first dissolved in a small amount of cold water to prevent lumps.

Bread: Many vegetable and bean soups are thickened by pureeing some of the soup, then adding it back to the pot. When that's not an option, use bread to thicken a watery soup. Soak several pieces of crusty bread in some of the broth, then puree it in a blender or food processor until smooth, adding more broth if necessary. Add the mixture back to the soup and stir to combine.

POTATOES TO THE RESCUE?
Popular kitchen lore holds that a few chunks or slices of raw potato will absorb excess salt from an overseasoned soup or stew. Is this true? To find out, we oversalted several pots of chicken stock to varying degrees, removed samples, then added raw potatoes and simmered until they were tender. After discarding the potatoes, we held a blind taste test to see if we could discern any difference in the salt levels. We could not. To be sure, we tested the stocks with a sodium probe and found little difference. Common sense supports these results: A potato may soak up a small quantity of the salty liquid, but it is powerless to reduce the overall concentration of salt in the liquid.

SMART FIXES FOR BAKED GOODS

Here's how to fix common problems that arise when baking.

Cream won't whip.
Check to make sure that your bowl and whisk (not to mention the cream) are very cold. Place the bowl and whisk in the freezer or fill the bowl with ice water.

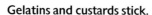

Gelatins and custards stick.
If your crème caramel (or another custard or a gelatin dessert) won't slip out of its ramekin, dip the mold in hot water for about 15 seconds. As a last-ditch measure, run a small paring knife around the inside of the mold to loosen the contents.

Baked goods burn.
Badly burnt baked goods are usually not worth salvaging, but a few burnt corners can be easily removed with a Microplane grater. If the scarring is noticeable, brush the grated areas with an egg wash and return to the oven until just browned, no more than five minutes.

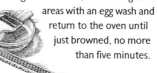
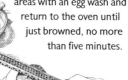

Bread dough rises too slowly.
Place the dough in a warm, draft-free, and preferably humid place. The inside of a turned-off oven is ideal. To maximize the effect, place a baking pan filled with boiling water on the oven rack beneath the dough.

Cake layers bake unevenly.
As long as the damage will be covered with icing, use a serrated bread knife to remove the domed portion of the cake layer.

Chocolate seizes.
If chocolate is melted over a burner that's too hot, it will "seize," taking on a greasy, curdled appearance. Provided the problem is not too severe, it can be corrected by adding boiling water to the chocolate, a tablespoon at a time, and stirring vigorously after each addition.

Muffins stick to the tin.
Pass the bottom of the muffin tin over a medium-low burner several times to heat the pan and try again to shake the muffins loose. Also try using a grapefruit knife to gently dig down under the muffin and set it free.

Better Black Bean Soup

With its thin, gray broth and weak flavor, has this restaurant standard passed its prime?

≥ BY REBECCA HAYS ≤

Black beans (or turtle beans) have always been a staple in Mexican, Cuban, and Caribbean kitchens, but they really came into vogue in the United States with the introduction of black bean soup in the 1960s. The Coach House restaurant in New York City popularized the soup, which was an all-day affair. It started with soaked beans that simmered for hours with, among other ingredients, parsnips, carrots, beef bones, and smoked ham hocks. The pureed soup was finished with a splash of Madeira, chopped hard-cooked eggs, and thinly sliced lemon. Refined? Yes. Realistic for the modern cook? No. The good news is that today's recipes, heavily influenced by Latin American cuisine, are easier to prepare. The bad news is that as restaurant recipes have been simplified, flavor has suffered.

Testing five soups shed light on specific problems. Asked to record their impressions, tasters chose the words "watery" and "thin" to describe the texture of most soups and either "bland" and "musty" or "over-spiced" and "bitter" to describe the taste. The soups were given low marks for appearance, too; all had unattractive purple/gray tones; none were truly black.

Bean Town

When beans are the star ingredient, it's preferable to use the dried variety, not canned—the former release valuable flavor into the broth as they cook, while the latter generally make vapid soup. (I simmered five brands of dried beans, including an organic variety and beans from the bulk bin of a natural foods store, and there were only minor variations in flavor. In short, brand doesn't seem to matter.) We've also learned that there's no reason to soak dried beans overnight—doing so only marginally reduces the cooking time and requires too much forethought. Similarly, the "quick-soak" method in which the beans are brought to a boil, then soaked off heat for an hour, is disappointing in that it causes many of the beans to explode during cooking.

As for seasoning, a teaspoon of salt added at the outset of cooking provided tastier beans than salt added at the end of cooking. We've found that salting early does not toughen the skins of beans, as some cooks claim. In addition to salt, I threw a couple of aromatic bay leaves into the pot.

Sour cream and avocado offset the spiciness of this soup, while minced red onion and cilantro add freshness and color.

I knew I didn't want to make from-scratch beef stock, so I focused on more time-efficient flavor builders, starting with a smoky ham hock. While tasters liked the meaty flavor offered by the ham hock, it also made them want more—not just more meat flavor (hocks are mostly bone) but real meat. I turned to untraditional (for black bean soup) cured pork products: salt pork, slab bacon, and ham steak. Ham steak contributed a good amount of smoky pork flavor and decidedly more meat than any of the other options, making it my first choice.

Aside from the ham flavor, the soup tasted rather hollow. I found improvement with a soffrito, a Spanish or Italian preparation in which aromatic vegetables and herbs (I used green pepper, onion, garlic, and oregano) are sautéed until softened and lightly browned. But my soffrito needed refinement.

Fragrant oregano was replaced with cumin, which had a warmer, more likable taste. I slowly incorporated the ground spice, working my way up to 1½ tablespoons. (Freshly ground and toasted whole cumin seed was not worth the bother. See our recommendations on ground cumin on page 19.) Sounds like a lot? It is, but I was after big flavor, and when the cumin toasted along with

the aromatics, its pungency was tempered. I also replaced the bitter green pepper with minced carrot and celery for a sweeter, fresher flavor.

My colleagues urged me not to be shy with minced garlic and hot red pepper flakes: I added six cloves and ½ teaspoon, respectively. The soup was now a hit, layered with sweet, spicy, smoky, and fresh vegetable flavors. While the Coach House recipe called for homemade beef stock, my aggressive seasonings meant that a mixture of water and canned broth was all that was needed.

Through Thick and Thin

My colleagues were united in their request for a partially pureed soup, refusing both ultra-smooth mixtures and chunky, brothy ones. Even after pureeing, though, a thickener seemed necessary. Simply using less liquid in the soup and mashing some of the beans ameliorated the texture somewhat, but the soup still lacked body. A potato cooked in the soup pureed into an unpleasant, starchy brew. Flour, cooked with the oil in the soffrito to form a roux, and cornstarch, stirred into the soup at the end of cooking, both worked. I decided to call for cornstarch, which lets the cook control the thickness (or thinness) of the finished soup by adding more or less of the slurry (cornstarch and water paste) to the pot.

I was finally satisfied, save for the soup's unappealing gray color. As often happens, the solution came to me in a roundabout way. While our food scientist was looking into remedies for the gas-causing effects of beans in digestion (see "Eliminating Gas from Beans" on page 3), we noticed that a side effect of cooking beans with baking soda is that the beans retain their dark color. The coating of the black beans contains anthocyanins (colored pigments) that change color with changes in pH: A more alkaline broth makes them darker, and a more acidic broth makes them lighter. I experimented by adding various amounts of baking soda to the beans both during and after cooking. The winning quantity was a mere ⅛ teaspoon, which produced a great-tasting soup (there was no soapy aftertaste, as was the case with larger quantities) with a darker, more appetizing color than unadulterated beans. Problem solved.

Classic additions to black bean soup include Madeira, rum, sherry, or scotch from the liquor cabinet and lemon, lime, or orange juice from the citrus bin. Given the other flavors in the soup, lime juice seemed the best fit. Because it is acidic, too much lime juice can push the color of the soup toward pink. Two tablespoons added flavor without marring the color.

Without an array of colorful garnishes, even the best black bean soup might be dull. Sour cream and diced avocado offset the soup's heat, while red onion and minced cilantro contribute freshness and color. Finally, wedges of lime accentuate the bright flavor of the juice that's already in the soup.

BLACK BEAN SOUP
MAKES ABOUT 9 CUPS, SERVING 6

Dried beans tend to cook unevenly, so be sure to taste several beans to determine their doneness in step 1. For efficiency, you can prepare the soup ingredients while the beans simmer and the garnishes while the soup simmers. Though you do not need to offer all of the garnishes listed below, do choose at least a couple; garnishes are essential for this soup as they add not only flavor but texture and color as well. Leftover soup can be refrigerated in an airtight container for 3 or 4 days; reheat it in a saucepan over medium heat until hot, stirring in additional chicken broth if it has thickened beyond your liking.

Beans

1	pound (2 cups) dried black beans, rinsed and picked over
4	ounces ham steak, trimmed of rind
2	dried bay leaves
5	cups water
1/8	teaspoon baking soda
1	teaspoon table salt

Soup

3	tablespoons olive oil
2	large onions, chopped fine (about 3 cups)
1	large carrot, chopped fine (about 1/2 cup)
3	medium celery ribs, chopped fine (about 1 cup)
1/2	teaspoon table salt
5–6	medium garlic cloves, minced or pressed through garlic press (about 1 1/2 tablespoons)
1/2	teaspoon red pepper flakes
1 1/2	tablespoons ground cumin
6	cups low-sodium chicken broth
2	tablespoons cornstarch
2	tablespoons water
2	tablespoons juice from 1 to 2 limes

Garnishes

Lime wedges
Minced fresh cilantro leaves
Finely diced red onion
Diced avocado
Sour cream

1. **FOR THE BEANS:** Place beans, ham, bay, water, and baking soda in large saucepan with tight-fitting lid. Bring to boil over medium-high heat; using large spoon, skim scum as it rises to surface. Stir in salt, reduce heat to low, cover, and

simmer briskly until beans are tender, 1 1/4 to 1 1/2 hours (if necessary, add another 1 cup water and continue to simmer until beans are tender); do not drain beans. Discard bay. Remove ham steak (ham steak darkens to color of beans), cut into 1/4-inch cubes, and set aside.

2. **FOR THE SOUP:** Heat oil in 8-quart Dutch oven over medium-high heat until shimmering but not smoking; add onions, carrot, celery, and salt and cook, stirring occasionally, until vegetables are soft and lightly browned, 12 to 15 minutes. Reduce heat to medium-low and add garlic, pepper flakes, and cumin; cook, stirring constantly, until fragrant, about 3 minutes. Stir in beans, bean cooking liquid, and chicken broth. Increase heat to medium-high and bring to boil, then reduce heat

to low and simmer, uncovered, stirring occasionally, to blend flavors, about 30 minutes.

3. **TO FINISH THE SOUP:** Ladle 1 1/2 cups beans and 2 cups liquid into food processor or blender, process until smooth, and return to pot. Stir together cornstarch and water in small bowl until combined, then gradually stir about half of cornstarch mixture into soup; bring to boil over medium-high heat, stirring occasionally, to fully thicken. If soup is still thinner than desired once boiling, stir remaining cornstarch mixture to recombine and gradually stir mixture into soup; return to boil to fully thicken. Off heat, stir in lime juice and reserved ham; ladle soup into bowls and serve immediately, passing garnishes separately.

BLACK BEAN SOUP
WITH CHIPOTLE CHILES

The addition of chipotle chiles in adobo—smoked jalapeños packed in a seasoned tomato-vinegar sauce—makes this a spicier, smokier variation on Black Bean Soup.

Follow recipe for Black Bean Soup, omitting red pepper flakes and adding 1 tablespoon minced chipotle chiles in adobo plus 2 teaspoons adobo sauce along with chicken broth in step 2.

TESTING EQUIPMENT: **Inexpensive Dutch Ovens**

Our test kitchen is stocked with our favorite Dutch ovens, made by All-Clad and Le Creuset, but we know that many cooks don't want to shell out $200 for these pots. Could we find a cheaper option that worked as well? To find out, we gathered four inexpensive Dutch ovens and ran them through a series of kitchen tests.

The good news: With one exception, these pans did not embarrass themselves when pitted against our favorite Dutch ovens. Although we aren't ready to trade in our All-Clad or Le Creuset for one of these cheaper options, if you're on a budget, it's nice to know you can still get the job done. Our favorite was the Tramontina Dutch Oven, which is larger and lighter than the other recommended options. –Garth Clingingsmith

FAVORITE

TRAMONTINA Sterling II 7-Quart Dutch Oven, $56.95
A heavy "tri-ply" base of aluminum sandwiched between stainless steel maintains very even heat over the large cooking area. The lightweight lid sputters over a pot of boiling water, however, and the pan takes a long time to heat up.

RECOMMENDED

INNOVA 7-Quart Oval Oven with Lid, $49.99
Awkward oval design causes cool spots in the oven's narrow "ends," resulting in slightly uneven browning. Aside from the annoying shape, this is an affordable option for cooks who like typically expensive enameled cast iron.

LODGE Pro-Logic 7-Quart Dutch Oven, $44.99
Great results, but lugging this 17-pound cast-iron behemoth around the kitchen is, literally, a pain. We would prefer a lighter pan that does not require periodic seasoning and performs nearly as well.

NOT RECOMMENDED

NORDIC WARE 6-Quart Covered Stock Pot, $17.99
This ultra-light aluminum pan was a poor performer in all tests. Even over low heat, the pan ran hot, and it was difficult to maintain a simmer. Its diameter is smaller than that of the other models, so we had to brown chicken in batches.

Hearty Scrambled Eggs

Why do additional ingredients quickly transform fluffy eggs into a watery mess?

⇒ BY NINA WEST AND ERIN MCMURRER ⇐

What's not to love about fluffy, bright yellow, featherweight scrambled eggs? Back in 1998, we discovered that adding milk to the eggs makes the curds soft and pliable, while cooking them over high heat in a constant folding motion coagulates the eggs quickly and efficiently. It was, therefore, a great disappointment when we discovered that our quick, simple recipe ran into trouble as soon as we attempted to add any other ingredients. Just a sprinkle of sautéed vegetables or browned sausage caused the eggs to become watery, discolored, and heavy. As it turned out, the difference between scrambled eggs and "hearty" scrambled eggs was much bigger than we expected.

The biggest problem was "weeping": Additional ingredients seemed to promote water loss in the eggs during cooking. Our first thought was that the temperature of the added ingredients might be a key factor. But from tests in which we tried adding both room-temperature and refrigerated ingredients, we learned that their temperature made little difference to the eggs. We thought perhaps adding a binder would inhibit water loss, so we tried cornstarch, cream cheese, mayonnaise, and bread crumbs—all to no avail. Then we suspected that milk, one of the ingredients in the original recipe, might be the source of the problem, considering that it is mostly water. We eliminated the milk but found that the recipe could not live without it; dairyfree scrambled eggs were tough.

Another thought was that the high heat of the recipe was causing the eggs to cook too quickly, seize, and squeeze out their moisture (evident in the gray, unappetizing puddle of liquid on our plate). Although even the slightest bit of overcooking will cause eggs to lose their moisture and high heat makes split-second timing essential, the heat itself was not the problem. To the contrary, the steam created by cooking over high heat was crucial to the light, fluffy texture that was the hallmark of our recipe. Nonetheless, to reduce the margin of error, we reduced the heat to medium. The texture of these eggs was slightly more substantial but certainly not inappropriate for a hearty egg dish. So far, so good—but the added ingredients were still causing our scrambled eggs to turn watery.

We figured out how to keep scrambled eggs light and fluffy while adding hearty ingredients like sausage, cheese, and vegetables.

We wondered if the method we were using to combine the ingredients in the pan was a factor. Our current approach was to sauté onions, add the beaten eggs, and then fold the ingredients together until the eggs cooked through. For the next test, we removed the sautéed onions from the pan and wiped it clean before cooking the eggs, folded in the sautéed onions when the eggs were nearly done, then let the eggs finish cooking off the heat. Finally, some good news. The weeping was reduced, and the eggs had managed to hold on to their pristine yellow hue.

Because the onions were adding moisture to the eggs, we wondered if we should reduce the liquid elsewhere. We knew that some dairy was important for a soft texture, but perhaps instead of milk we should be using half-and-half or cream, both of which contain less moisture and more fat. We tested them and decided that heavy cream made the eggs too rich and heavy; half-and-half, however, was perfect. These eggs were substantial, soft, and able to accept most of the ingredients we threw at them. Among the ingredients that were consistently successful were drier leafy greens, crunchy vegetables, and breakfast meats; there was nary a puddle on our breakfast plate. But we found it best to avoid very watery ingredients, such as mushrooms or ham steaks, which are often full of brine.

SCRAMBLED EGGS WITH BACON, ONION, AND PEPPER JACK CHEESE
SERVES 4 TO 6

12	large eggs
³/₄	teaspoon table salt
¹/₄	teaspoon ground black pepper
6	tablespoons half-and-half
4	bacon slices (about 4 ounces), halved lengthwise, then cut crosswise into ¹/₂-inch pieces
1	medium onion, chopped medium (about 1 cup)
1	tablespoon unsalted butter
1¹/₂	ounces Pepper Jack or Monterey Jack cheese, shredded (about ¹/₂ cup)
1	teaspoon minced fresh parsley leaves (optional)

1. Crack eggs into medium bowl; add salt, pepper, and half-and-half. Beat with dinner fork until thoroughly combined.

2. Cook bacon in 12-inch nonstick skillet over medium heat, stirring occasionally, until browned, 4 to 5 minutes. Using slotted spoon, transfer bacon to paper towel–lined plate; discard all but 2 teaspoons bacon fat. Add onion to skillet and cook, stirring occasionally, until lightly browned, 2 to 4 minutes; transfer onion to second plate.

3. Thoroughly wipe out skillet with paper towels, add butter, and set over medium heat. When

TASTING: Egg Substitutes

BEST EGG SUBSTITUTE **DON'T BE FOOLED BY FROZEN**

Of the five brands tested, Egg Beaters—the only one without unpleasant "off" flavors—was the clear favorite, although its "fake-o color" and "spongy" texture remained problems. Do not confuse with frozen Egg Beaters, which our tasters found watery.

SCIENCE: How Scrambled Eggs Work

Cooking causes profound changes in the structure of egg proteins. Heat encourages these proteins to unfold, stick together, and form a latticed gel (compare illustrations 1 and 2). As a result, eggs transition from a liquid to a semisolid that you can pick up with a fork.

Most scrambled egg recipes call for some sort of dairy. Both the water and the fat in dairy ingredients keep the eggs from becoming tough by getting in between the protein strands, preventing them from joining too tightly (illustration 3). The water also helps to incorporate pockets of air and steam into the eggs as they are gently folded. This translates into fluffy scrambled eggs.

When we added hearty ingredients (each containing some water) to our scrambled egg recipe, however, the eggs became watery and weepy. That's because eggs can hold only a limited amount of water—too much and they weep as they coagulate (illustration 4). Our solution to the problem of weepy eggs was to reduce the amount of liquid we had been using by 50 percent and to make our liquid of choice half-and-half rather than milk. While these scrambled eggs are not quite as fluffy as those made with milk, the extra fat in the half-and-half made for a pleasing texture, and the added heaviness of the eggs was imperceptible once sausage, bacon, and vegetables were folded in just before serving. —John Olson, Science Editor

BAD, WEEPY EGGS **GOOD, MOIST EGGS**

The scrambled eggs on the left were made with milk, which added enough extra moisture to cause puddles of unappetizing liquid to form on the serving plate. The eggs on the right were made with half-and-half, and they shed nary a tear.

RAW EGGS
1 Protein strands fold over on themselves.

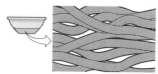

SCRAMBLED EGGS
2 Protein strands unfold and stick to each other.

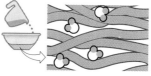

FLUFFY EGGS: Just enough liquid
3 Water and fat separate protein strands.

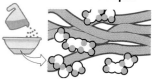

WET EGGS: Too much liquid
4 Protein strands are saturated and shed excess water.

butter foams, swirl to coat bottom and sides of skillet, then pour in eggs. With heatproof rubber spatula, stir eggs constantly, slowly pushing them from side to side, scraping along bottom of skillet and then around sides, and lifting and folding eggs as they form curds. Do not over-scramble, as curds formed will be too small. Cook eggs until large curds form but eggs are still very moist, 2 to 3 minutes. Off heat, gently fold in onion, cheese, and half of bacon until evenly distributed; if eggs are still underdone, return skillet to medium heat for no longer than 30 seconds. Divide eggs among individual plates, sprinkle with remaining bacon and parsley, and serve immediately.

SCRAMBLED EGGS WITH SAUSAGE, SWEET PEPPERS, AND CHEDDAR
SERVES 4 TO 6

- 12 large eggs
- ¾ teaspoon table salt
- ¼ teaspoon ground black pepper
- 6 tablespoons half-and-half
- 1 teaspoon vegetable oil
- 8 ounces sweet or hot Italian sausage, casing removed, sausage crumbled into ½-inch pieces
- 1 medium red bell pepper, cut into ½-inch cubes (about 1 cup)
- 3 medium scallions, white and green parts separated, both sliced thinly on bias
- 1 tablespoon unsalted butter
- 1½ ounces sharp cheddar cheese, shredded (about ½ cup)

1. Crack eggs into medium bowl; add salt, pepper, and half-and-half. Beat with dinner fork until thoroughly combined.

2. Heat oil in 12-inch nonstick skillet over medium heat until shimmering. Add sausage and cook until beginning to brown but still pink in the center, about 2 minutes. Add red bell pepper and scallion whites; continue to cook, stirring occasionally, until sausage is cooked through and peppers are beginning to brown, about 3 minutes. Spread mixture in single layer on medium plate; set aside.

3. Thoroughly wipe out skillet with paper towels, add butter, and set over medium heat. When butter foams, swirl to coat bottom and sides of skillet, then pour in eggs. With heatproof rubber spatula, stir eggs constantly, slowly pushing them from side to side, scraping along bottom of skillet and then around sides, and lifting and folding eggs as they form curds. Do not over-scramble, as curds formed will be too small. Cook eggs until large curds form but eggs are still very moist, 2 to 3 minutes. Off heat, gently fold in sausage mixture and cheese until evenly distributed; if eggs are still underdone, return skillet to medium heat for no longer than 30 seconds. Divide eggs among individual plates, sprinkle with scallion greens, and serve immediately.

SCRAMBLED EGGS WITH ARUGULA, SUN-DRIED TOMATOES, AND GOAT CHEESE
SERVES 4 TO 6

- 12 large eggs
- ¾ teaspoon table salt
- ¼ teaspoon ground black pepper
- 6 tablespoons half-and-half
- 2 teaspoons olive oil
- ½ medium onion, minced (about ½ cup)
- ⅛ teaspoon red pepper flakes

- 5 ounces arugula, stemmed and cut crosswise into ½-inch-wide strips (about 5 cups)
- 1 tablespoon unsalted butter
- 3 ounces drained oil-packed sun-dried tomatoes, rinsed, patted dry, and chopped fine (¼ cup)
- 3 ounces goat cheese, crumbled (⅓ cup)

1. Crack eggs into medium bowl; add salt, pepper, and half-and-half. Beat with dinner fork until thoroughly combined.

2. Heat oil in 12-inch nonstick skillet over medium heat until shimmering. Add onion and pepper flakes and cook until softened, about 2 minutes. Add arugula and cook, stirring gently, until arugula begins to wilt, 30 to 60 seconds. Spread mixture in single layer on small plate.

3. Thoroughly wipe out skillet with paper towels, add butter, and set over medium heat. When butter foams, swirl to coat bottom and sides of skillet, then pour in eggs. With heatproof rubber spatula, stir eggs constantly, slowly pushing them from side to side, scraping along bottom of skillet and then around sides, and lifting and folding eggs as they form curds Do not over-scramble, as curds formed will be too small. Cook eggs until large curds form but eggs are still very moist, 2 to 3 minutes. Off heat, gently fold in arugula mixture and sun-dried tomatoes until evenly distributed; if eggs are still too runny, return skillet to medium heat for no longer than 30 seconds. Divide eggs among individual plates, sprinkle with goat cheese, and serve immediately.

COOK'S EXTRA gives you free recipes online. For Scrambled Eggs with Asparagus, Prosciutto, and Parmesan, visit www.cooksillustrated.com and key in code 7001. This recipe will be available until February 15, 2005.

Glazed Winter Root Vegetables

Could we turn "boring" turnips, celery root, and parsnips into exciting side dishes?

⇒ BY SANDRA WU ⇐

Ask most people how to cook turnips, celery root, and parsnips and you can expect some blank stares. This wan trio of root vegetables might not be as popular as some of its more colorful cousins, but that doesn't mean these vegetables couldn't hold their own as a side dish if prepared properly. Perhaps the secret was to find a way to enhance, rather than mask, their naturally bitter, earthy, and sweet flavors.

My goal was to produce root vegetables with a nicely browned exterior and a tender, creamy interior, coated with a lightly sweetened glaze. For the vegetables to cook evenly, the first step was to cut them into large pieces of equal size. For round vegetables such as celery root and turnips, 3/4-inch cubes made the most sense. Long roots such as carrots and parsnips were best sliced 1/2 inch thick on the bias: easy and attractive.

Roasting tended to dry out most root vegetables, leaving the exterior tough and leathery. Boiling washed away flavor. The most promising results were achieved using a large nonstick skillet and a basic method of steaming the vegetables and reducing the remaining liquid.

To avoid a drab appearance and to provide a deep, virtually roasted flavor, I found that these vegetables needed to be browned first in melted butter over moderately high heat. It was important to leave the vegetables alone for the first few minutes of cooking, as constant stirring hindered caramelization. To get the vegetables to a tender-but-not-mushy state, I then had to simmer them, covered, in a combination of broth, seasonings, and a small amount of sweetener. Once the vegetables were tender, it was easy to create a glaze out of the remaining liquid. All I had to do was remove the lid, increase the heat to high, and allow the sugar and broth to quickly reduce down to a slightly sticky, caramelized coating, stirring constantly to prevent burning.

With a simple technique that worked across the board and the addition of a few complementary ingredients, the most maligned of root vegetables finally got the respect they deserve. In the end, it was only the vegetables that were glazed over, not my tasters' eyes.

GLAZED PARSNIPS AND CELERY

SERVES 4 AS A SIDE DISH

When selecting parsnips, try to choose those with tops no larger than 1 inch in diameter. If they are larger, their fibrous core should be removed before cooking (see Kitchen Notes, page 31).

1 1/2	tablespoons unsalted butter
1	pound parsnips, peeled, tapered ends sliced 1/2 inch thick on bias, large upper portions halved lengthwise, then cut 1/2 inch thick on bias
3	large celery ribs, strings removed with vegetable peeler, sliced 1/2 inch thick on bias (about 1 1/2 cups)
1/2	cup low-sodium chicken or vegetable broth
1	tablespoon sugar
1/2	teaspoon table salt
1/8	teaspoon ground black pepper

1. Heat butter in 12-inch nonstick skillet over medium-high heat; when foaming subsides, swirl to coat skillet. Add parsnips in even layer; cook without stirring over medium-high heat until browned, 2 to 3 minutes. Stir in celery and cook, stirring occasionally, until well browned, about 2 minutes longer. Add broth, sugar, salt, and pepper; cover skillet, reduce heat to medium-low, and simmer until vegetables are tender, about 6 minutes.

2. Uncover, increase heat to high, and cook, stirring frequently, until liquid in skillet reduces to glaze, about 1 minute. Transfer to serving dish; serve immediately.

GLAZED CELERY ROOT WITH ONIONS, GRAPES, AND PISTACHIOS

SERVES 4 AS A SIDE DISH

Sliced almonds can be substituted for pistachios.

2	tablespoons chopped roasted unsalted pistachios
1 1/2	tablespoons unsalted butter
1/2	medium red onion, cut into 1/4-inch wedges
1	medium celery root (1 to 1 1/4 pounds), trimmed, peeled, and cut into 3/4-inch cubes (about 2 cups)
1/2	cup low-sodium chicken or vegetable broth
1 1/2	tablespoons sugar
2	teaspoons red wine vinegar
1/2	teaspoon table salt
1/8	teaspoon ground black pepper
1	cup seedless red grapes, halved lengthwise

1. Toast pistachios in 12-inch nonstick skillet over medium heat until lightly browned, stirring frequently, about 3 minutes. Transfer to small bowl; set aside.

2. Heat butter in now-empty skillet over medium-high heat; when foaming subsides, swirl to coat skillet. Add onion and celery root in even layer; cook without stirring until browned, about 3 minutes. Stir and continue to cook, stirring occasionally, until all sides are browned, about 3 minutes longer. Add broth, sugar, vinegar, salt, and pepper; cover skillet, reduce heat to medium-low, and simmer until vegetables are just tender, about 10 minutes.

3. Uncover, increase heat to high, add grapes, and cook, stirring frequently, until liquid in skillet reduces to glaze, about 1 minute. Transfer to serving dish and sprinkle with pistachios; serve immediately.

LEMON-THYME GLAZED TURNIPS AND CARROTS

SERVES 4 AS A SIDE DISH

When selecting turnips, choose the smallest available (about the size of plums), as they tend to be less fibrous and less bitter than their larger counterparts. Do not substitute yellow turnips for the white turnips called for in this recipe.

1 1/2	tablespoons unsalted butter
1	pound white turnips, peeled and cut into 3/4-inch cubes (about 2 cups)
3	medium carrots (about 9 ounces), peeled, tapered ends sliced 1/2 inch thick on bias, large upper portions halved lengthwise, then cut 1/2 inch thick on bias
2/3	cup low-sodium chicken or vegetable broth
1 1/2	tablespoons packed brown sugar
1/2	teaspoon table salt
1/8	teaspoon ground black pepper
1	teaspoon fresh thyme leaves
1	teaspoon grated zest plus 1 teaspoon juice from 1 lemon

1. Heat butter in 12-inch nonstick skillet over medium-high heat; when foaming subsides, swirl to coat skillet. Add turnips and carrots in even layer; cook without stirring until browned, about 4 minutes. Stir and continue to cook, stirring occasionally, until well browned on all sides, about 4 minutes longer. Add broth, brown sugar, salt, pepper, thyme, and lemon zest; cover skillet, reduce heat to medium-low, and simmer until vegetables are just tender, about 8 minutes.

2. Uncover, increase heat to high, and cook, stirring frequently, until liquid in skillet reduces to glaze, about 1 minute. Stir in lemon juice, transfer to serving dish, and serve immediately.

Perfecting German Chocolate Cake

This cake has made it into the dessert hall of fame, but a closer look reveals shortcomings: faint chocolate flavor, microsuede-like texture, and a complicated mixing process.

≽ BY DAWN YANAGIHARA ≼

German chocolate cake. Its imposing stature, sweetness, and blend of flavors and textures are, without question, alluring. Understandably, many bakeries, bakers, and cookbooks try to capitalize on its appeal; German chocolate brownies, cupcakes, pies, and even cookies are not uncommon. Be that as it may, their inspiration, the triple-decker German chocolate cake—filled with sticky pecans and coconut, and au naturel on the sides—is not without flaws.

Not surprisingly, a search yielded recipes that were similar, if not identical, to the one on the German's Sweet Chocolate box. Most called for 4 ounces (one box) of this chocolate, made by Baker's, separated eggs, and buttermilk. For the filling, most called for evaporated milk, butter, and egg yolks. To get my bearings, I prepared the recipe on the box and found many shortcomings. First, all the tasters felt that this is one dessert that is actually too sweet. Second, the chocolate is so mild that it may as well be absent. Third, the listless texture of the cake and the unctuousness of the filling ran together to form a soggy, sweet mush. And, for the baker making the cake, an easier, more streamlined technique was in order.

First, some history. German chocolate cake is not German. The genealogy of this classic American dessert dates back to 1852, when Samuel German created an eponymous chocolate for Baker's Chocolate Company. More than a century later, in 1957, a recipe calling for German's Sweet Chocolate reportedly made its debut in a Texas newspaper and, as a result, there was a boost in sales of German's Sweet Chocolate. General Foods, then owner of the German's Sweet Chocolate trademark, got hold of the recipe, tweaked it to add yet another General Foods product—Angel Flake Coconut—then bestowed upon it the name German Sweet Chocolate Cake before sending it off to be eaten up by the American public.

All Mixed Up

In all of the German chocolate cake recipes I encountered, the cake was baked in three round cake pans, irrespective of the fact that many kitchens are equipped with only two. In addition, three cakes usually do not bake evenly in standard home

This multilayered cake always looks impressive. Some test kitchen tweaks gave it the flavor to match.

ovens, much less fit on a single oven rack. The first order of business, then, before fiddling with ingredients, was to adjust the recipe to fit into two 9-inch round cake pans. It was a task easily accomplished; all I had to do was scale back the recipe by one-quarter. The finished cake, instead of being a triple-decker, would be a four-layer affair, as each cake was tall enough to be split in two.

Next I attacked the cake-making technique. It started off easy enough, with creamed butter and sugar; then egg yolks were beaten in, followed

German Chocolate: Yes or No?

Can you make German chocolate cake without "German" chocolate? Yes. In fact, we found Baker's German's Sweet Chocolate too sweet and lacking in chocolate flavor. We had better results using a combination of cocoa powder and good-quality semisweet or bittersweet chocolate.

by the chocolate. Dry ingredients (flour and baking soda) and wet ingredients (buttermilk) were added alternately (for more on this topic, see Cake Mixing 101, page 24). Finally, the annoying part: The egg whites were whipped in a separate bowl and folded in.

I made cakes using various mixing methods, and, lo and behold, cakes made with the "original" separated egg technique were the least favorite. These cakes had a supersoft, lightweight crumb and a tight, microsuede-like texture that was a poor match for the heavyweight filling. The best cakes were made with whole eggs and a straightforward creaming technique—basically, the original technique—but without separating the eggs and whipping the whites. Nearly all tasters preferred the sturdy, open crumb and more resilient texture of these cakes. It was a pleasant surprise that superior texture and easy method went hand in hand.

More Chocolate Flavor, Please

One taster lamented that the chocolate in German chocolate cake acts primarily as a crayon, offering nothing more than light brown color. I wanted to put a little more chocolate behind the cake's name, but not so much that the result would no longer be identifiable as a German chocolate cake. Though I had reduced all the ingredients by one-quarter to fit the recipe into two cake pans, in the interest of chocolate flavor, I found I could leave the chocolate alone at 4 ounces. Tasters, however, were not satisfied. They wanted more chocolate flavor.

I thought I'd try a more assertive chocolate and baked cakes with various brands of semisweet and bittersweet chocolate. All other chocolates tested were favored over the original German chocolate. For a bit more flavor, I tried adding more chocolate but found instead that just ¼ cup of Dutch-processed cocoa introduced the right degree of flavor without upsetting the texture.

1. With serrated knife, halve each cake evenly through equator.

2. Carefully lift off upper cake layer and set aside.

3. Evenly distribute about 1 cup filling on bottom cake layer.

4. Place next cake layer on top and repeat process.

Recipes were inconsistent as far as the type of flour used. Some called for cake flour, some all-purpose, and others were not so specific. Cake flour yielded cakes that were too soft and delicate, with a weak structure, owing to the low protein content of the flour. All-purpose flour made texturally superior cakes; they had a more satisfying tooth-sinking quality while still being light and tender. As for sweetener, granulated sugar is the norm for German chocolate cake, but I tried brown sugar as well. A full trade of light brown sugar contained too much moisture and weighed the cakes down (but it also added lots of flavor); 1 cup of granulated sugar and ⅔ cup of packed light brown solved the texture problem. I had also reduced the total amount of sugar to address tasters' complaints that the cake was "too sweet."

Buttermilk is standard in all German chocolate cake recipes. Nevertheless, I made cakes with milk and sour cream. The cakes made with milk had a peculiar color—a light poodle-brown. Between the sour cream and buttermilk, it was a close call, but the sour cream won out for its fuller, richer flavor.

Fiddling with the Filling

Ask German chocolate cake aficionados and they will tell you that the filling makes the cake. Here again, recipes hardly differed. A mixture of evaporated milk, sugar, yolks, and butter is cooked on the stovetop; sweetened shredded coconut and chopped pecans are added; then the lot is set aside to cool. As for cooking the filling, most recipes say "until slightly thickened"—an insufficient descriptor. After making a few sloppy, drippy cakes, I discovered that the filling had to foam and froth at a lively simmer if it was going to thicken properly when cooled.

I assumed—erroneously, it turned out—that the fresher flavor of half-and-half or heavy cream would be preferable to evaporated milk. I ended up opting for evaporated milk after all; it was the leaner as well as the "classic" choice. I tried to substitute brown sugar for white to boost flavor. One cup of granulated and ¼ cup of light brown sugar hit the mark without turning the filling brown.

Recipes called for either 8 or 12 tablespoons of butter. The greater amount made a rather soft, soupy filling that had a difficult time holding itself in place between the cake layers. Eight was an improvement, but with 6 tablespoons the filling had a nice, thick yet spreadable consistency.

Whereas toasting the coconut did not improve the filling, toasting the pecans did—vastly—by intensifying their sweet nuttiness and gently crisping their rich texture. I found that stirring them into the filling just before cake assembly better preserved their texture than adding them while still hot.

Although devotees of German chocolate cake might argue that this dessert needed no tinkering in the first place, I hope some may find it improved; it's definitely easier to make, and it has, to the test kitchen's way of thinking, better texture and flavor. Without "German" chocolate, that is.

GERMAN CHOCOLATE CAKE WITH COCONUT-PECAN FILLING
SERVES 12 TO 16

When you assemble the cake, the filling should be cool or cold (or room temperature, at the very warmest). To be time-efficient, first make the filling, then use the refrigeration time to prepare, bake, and cool the cakes. The toasted pecans are stirred into the filling just before assembly to keep them from becoming soft and soggy.

Filling

    4   large egg yolks
    1   can (12 ounces) evaporated milk
    1   cup (7 ounces) granulated sugar
    ¼   cup (1¾ ounces) packed light brown sugar
    6   tablespoons (¾ stick) unsalted butter, cut into
        6 pieces
    ⅛   teaspoon table salt
    2   teaspoons vanilla extract

Cake Mixing 101

The mixing method for German chocolate cake is a common one for butter cakes: Butter and sugar are creamed, the eggs are beaten in, then the flour and liquid components are added alternately to the batter, beginning and ending with the flour. Each time I make a cake using this method, I wonder if this alternation of dry and wet really makes a difference in the cake's texture or if good results could be had without it (and without the extra work).

To find out, I made German chocolate cakes and yellow cakes using four mixing methods: (1) following the standard dry/wet alternation technique, (2) mixing in the wet ingredients followed by the dry, (3) mixing in the dry ingredients followed by the wet, and (4) mixing in dry and wet simultaneously.

The worst cakes were made with the last two methods. These cakes were plagued by dark spots, large holes, and uneven crumbs (coarse in some patches, fine in others)—all signs that the ingredients had not been properly incorporated into the batter. Mixing wet ingredients followed by dry (technique #2) yielded better cakes with fewer and smaller holes and more tender and even textures. The standard dry/wet alternation technique (#1), however, made superior cakes. They had far fewer and smaller holes and evenly fine, soft, tender textures. There are good reasons why this cake-mixing method is widely practiced. –D.Y.

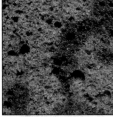 

MIXED UP **MIXED RIGHT**

The cake on the left was made by adding the wet and dry ingredients simultaneously to the batter. The ingredients were not well incorporated, as evidenced by the dark spots in this cake. The cake on the right was made by adding the dry and wet ingredients to the batter alternately; the batter was well combined.

Why the Pan Matters

NOT SO NICE

NICE AND NEAT

We discovered that our test kitchen cake pans, with their short, sloping sides, are not well suited to the German chocolate cake, with its unfrosted sides. The top layer pictured above, made in one of those pans, will produce a misaligned and unsturdy finished cake. Pans with straight sides will bake even cake layers, such as the bottom one pictured above. See "Cake Pans" below for recommendations.

2⅓ cups (7 ounces) sweetened shredded coconut
1½ cups (6½ ounces) finely chopped pecans, toasted on baking sheet in 350-degree oven until fragrant and browned, about 8 minutes

Cake

4 ounces semisweet or bittersweet chocolate, chopped fine
¼ cup Dutch-processed cocoa, sifted
½ cup boiling water
2 cups (10 ounces) unbleached all-purpose flour, plus additional for dusting cake pans
¾ teaspoon baking soda
12 tablespoons (1½ sticks) unsalted butter, softened
1 cup (7 ounces) granulated sugar
⅔ cup (about 4¾ ounces) packed light brown sugar
¾ teaspoon table salt
4 large eggs, room temperature
1 teaspoon vanilla extract
¾ cup sour cream, room temperature

1. **FOR THE FILLING:** Whisk yolks in medium saucepan; gradually whisk in evaporated milk. Add sugars, butter, and salt and cook over medium-high heat, whisking constantly, until mixture is boiling, frothy, and slightly thickened, about 6 minutes. Transfer mixture to bowl, whisk in vanilla, then stir in coconut. Cool until just warm, cover with plastic wrap, and refrigerate until cool or cold, at least 2 hours or up to 3 days. (Pecans are stirred in just before cake assembly.)

2. **FOR THE CAKE:** Adjust oven rack to lower-middle position; heat oven to 350 degrees. Combine chocolate and cocoa in small bowl; pour boiling water over and let stand to melt chocolate, about 2 minutes. Whisk until smooth; set aside until cooled to room temperature.

3. Meanwhile, spray two 9-inch-round by 2-inch-high straight-sided cake pans with nonstick cooking spray; line bottoms with parchment or waxed paper rounds. Spray paper rounds, dust pans with flour, and knock out excess. Sift flour and baking soda into medium bowl or onto sheet of parchment or waxed paper.

4. In bowl of standing mixer, beat butter, sugars, and salt at medium-low speed until sugar is moistened, about 30 seconds. Increase speed to medium-high and beat until mixture is light and fluffy, about 4 minutes, scraping down bowl with rubber spatula halfway through. With mixer running at medium speed, add eggs one at a time, beating well after each addition and scraping down bowl halfway through. Beat in vanilla; increase speed to medium-high and beat until light and fluffy, about 45 seconds. With mixer running at low speed, add chocolate, then increase speed to medium and beat until combined, about 30 seconds, scraping down bowl once (batter may appear broken). With mixer running at low speed, add dry ingredients in 3 additions, alternating with sour cream (in 2 additions), beginning and ending with dry ingredients, and beating in each addition until barely combined. After final flour addition, beat on low until just combined, then stir batter by hand with rubber spatula, scraping bottom and sides of bowl, to ensure that batter is homogenous (batter will be thick). Divide batter evenly between prepared cake pans; spread batter to edges of pans with rubber spatula and smooth surfaces.

5. Bake cakes until toothpick inserted into center of cakes comes out clean, about 30 minutes. Cool in pans 10 minutes, then invert cakes onto greased wire rack; peel off and discard paper rounds. Cool cakes to room temperature before filling, about 1 hour. (Cooled cakes can be wrapped in plastic wrap and stored at room temperature for up to 1 day.)

6. **TO ASSEMBLE:** Stir toasted pecans into chilled filling. Set one cake on serving platter or cardboard round cut slightly smaller than cake, and second cake on work surface (or leave on wire rack). With serrated knife held so that blade is parallel with work surface, use sawing motion to cut each cake into two even layers. Starting with first cake, carefully lift off top layer and set aside. Using icing spatula, distribute about 1 cup filling evenly on cake, spreading filling to very edge of cake and leveling surface. Carefully place upper cake layer on top of filling; repeat using remaining filling and cake layers. If necessary, dust crumbs off platter; serve or refrigerate cake, covered loosely with foil, up to 4 hours (if refrigerated longer than 2 hours, let cake stand at room temperature 15 to 20 minutes before serving).

GERMAN CHOCOLATE CAKE WITH BANANA, MACADAMIA, AND COCONUT FILLING

If you cannot find roasted unsalted macadamia nuts, substitute salted ones, but first remove excess salt by spreading them on a clean kitchen towel and giving them a good rub.

1. Follow recipe for German Chocolate Cake; in filling, reduce vanilla to 1 teaspoon, add 2 teaspoons dark rum with vanilla, and substitute roasted unsalted macadamia nuts for pecans.

2. Just before assembling, peel and cut 4 medium bananas into ⅜-inch-thick slices. Arrange one quarter of banana slices on first cake layer, then spread filling evenly over; repeat with remaining cake layers, bananas, and filling.

GERMAN CHOCOLATE CAKE WITH COFFEE, CASHEW, AND COCONUT FILLING

Follow recipe for German Chocolate Cake; in filling, add 2 teaspoons ground coffee with sugars; substitute roasted unsalted cashews for pecans.

TESTING EQUIPMENT: Cake Pans

When we tested 11 cake pans back in 1999, we proclaimed the cheapest pan—the Baker's Secret ($4)—the best. We noted that the pan had flared rather than straight sides, but we found that frosting covered up this minor problem. German chocolate cake, however, has no frosting on its sides. Also, splitting a flared cake creates two cakes of different diameters. As a result, the finished cake is less sturdy and somewhat homely. To make matters worse, we recently discovered that our Pineapple Upside-Down Cake (September/October 2004) barely fits into the rather

THE PAN TO PICK
Of the eight pans tested, the Chicago Metallic Professional Lifetime Non-Stick cake pan was the best choice for German chocolate cake—and more.

squat Baker's Secret pan, with sides that measure just 1½ inches tall. Clearly, it was time to find a better all-purpose cake pan—one with straight, 2-inch-high sides.

We baked génoise, German chocolate cake, and pineapple upside-down cake in eight pans that fit this description. All pans were passable, but the nonstick pans stood out. The dark coatings on these pans promoted better browning than shiny surfaces and yielded more attractive cakes.

The Chicago Metallic Professional Lifetime Non-Stick ($14.95) and Calphalon's Commercial Nonstick ($18.95) were testers' top choices. Both pans lack handles (a nice addition to the Baker's Secret), but they are better suited to a wide range of cakes, including German chocolate. —Garth Clingingsmith

Much Ado about Dutching

How is Dutch-processed cocoa different from "natural" cocoa? Does the home cook need both? After weeks of testing, we discovered a simple, surprising answer.

> BY JOLYON HELTERMAN <

Processed ham. Processed cheese food. The bureaucratic process. Suffice it to say that Dutch-processed cocoa already had a few strikes against it before our tasting panel took one bite—if only for its etymology. The idea that a product treated chemically to remove characteristic flavors might taste better than the original simply runs counter to the basic tenets of ingredient selection. Especially when that original is called "natural."

Of course, the natural advocates among us had already suffered a setback. In 1995, the magazine conducted a series of cocoa powder tastings, and the Dutched cocoas made a strong showing. Although tasters liked Dutched and natural cocoas equally in the baked preparation (a brownie), Dutch-processed cocoa was the clear favorite for a steaming mug of hot chocolate.

This time around, we were ready. On a hunch, we decided to cover the cups of hot chocolate with sip tops (like the ones used for takeout coffee) to keep tasters from seeing each sample. The logic was simple. The Dutching process—treating cacao beans with alkaline chemicals—has a striking effect on color: Natural cocoa looks beige; Dutch-processed cocoa boasts a deep, dark, rich-looking brown. Surely, the 1995 tasters had relied on their eyes as much as their taste buds in bestowing victory on the hot chocolates made with Dutched cocoas. This year's trials? All about taste, we reasoned.

So the sip tops went on, and the tasting began. To narrow the field, we tested five Dutched and five natural cocoas separately, first in hot chocolate and then in chocolate shortbread. The top two Dutched cocoas and the top two natural cocoas (see the chart on page 27) moved on to compete in a final showdown—an expanded series of tests that included not only hot chocolate and shortbread but also low-fat chocolate pudding, devil's food cake, and chocolate pudding cake. Unfortunately, the results were different from those of the 1995 tests, but not in the way we expected.

The winning shortbread? Dutched. The devil's food cake? Dutched. The pudding, the pudding cake, the hot chocolate tasted through a sip top? Dutched, Dutched, Dutched. Not quite ready to award Dutched cocoa the undisputed crown, we considered explanations other than Dutching itself.

Fudge Factors

Because makers of upscale cocoa powders often tout their product's high fat content, we first compared cocoa-butter percentages. After all, we could think of plenty of foods for which higher fat content equals more flavor. Our results told a different story. Although Dutched Callebaut, our top performer overall, was fairly high in fat (22 percent), Hershey's Dutched, our second-best performer, had the lowest fat content of the group, at just over 10 percent. A scan of the remaining fat values convinced us that fat had little to do with cocoa preference. Additional research confirmed our conclusion.

Next we considered price. Although years of blind tastings have taught us never to assume that price and quality are directly related, sometimes you do get only what you pay for. Once again, the data belied that hypothesis. The price ranges for the Dutched cocoas ($0.36 to $1.08 per ounce) and the natural cocoas ($0.29 to $1.37 per ounce) were very close. What's more, the only two cocoas priced at more than a dollar an ounce, the Dutched Valrhona and the natural Scharffen Berger, came in dead last in their respective categories.

A call to Hershey Foods, the only manufacturer represented by both Dutched and natural cocoas in our tasting, put to rest the possibility that Dutched cocoas simply begin with higher-quality beans. According to a Hershey spokesperson, the only difference between the company's Dutched and natural cocoas is the Dutching. Although Hershey's natural and Hershey's Dutched both made it to the finals, tasters preferred Hershey's Dutched in all five applications.

Basic Solution

That left Dutching itself as the source of preferred flavor. To figure out why, we brushed up on cocoa-making basics. Chocolate and cocoa come from chocolate liquor, a paste made from beans scooped from the pods of the tropical cacao tree. The beans are fermented, roasted, shelled, and ground into a paste. Half fat (cocoa butter) and half cocoa solids, the paste is hardened in molds. Some is sold as unsweetened baking chocolate. The rest is fed into hydraulic presses to remove up to three-quarters of its fat, then pulverized and called cocoa powder.

Beans destined for life as Dutched cocoa have one extra stop between shelling and grinding. The shelled beans (or nibs) are soaked in an alkaline (low-acid) solution, usually potassium carbonate. They're pressed, pulverized, and dried—and Dutch-processed cocoa powder is born.

There's nothing particularly Dutch about the Dutching process except for the person who thought it up: a 19th-century Dutchman named Coenraad J. van Houten. Van Houten had pioneered the use of the hydraulic press to defat chocolate liquor, prompted by his aversion to the greasy scum that rose to the top of his favorite beverage, hot chocolate. But van Houten still wasn't satisfied. The drink, now made with cocoa powder, tasted harsh and had an insipid color.

Van Houten's remedy lay in simple chemistry. Cocoa in its natural state is slightly acidic, as indicated by its pH value of around 5.4. By soaking the cocoa nibs in a basic (or alkaline) solution, he found he could raise the pH to 7 (neutral) or even higher. The higher the pH, the darker the color. What's more, the acids present in natural cocoa were neutralized, reducing its harshness.

The Bitter End

If tasters had described the Dutched samples as more mellow than the natural samples, all would be explained. But that wasn't the case. Tasters consistently perceived the Dutched cocoas as having a stronger chocolate flavor. How could neutralizing part of the cocoa flavor profile result in a more chocolatey taste? What flavor remained?

Plenty, said chocolate expert Gregory Ziegler, a food science professor at Penn State University. Like wine, chocolate has a complex flavor profile that consists of hundreds of attributes. The most common notes are sour, bitter, astringent, fruity, figgy, raisiny, floral, nutty, smoky, hammy, and even "chocolatey," the essence of cacao beans themselves. Dutching eliminates only the fundamentally acidic components—sour, bitter, astringent, fruity. The others remain intact.

Tasters' comments on the natural cocoas reflected that supposition. Bitterness and sourness were common complaints, as was an unexpected fruitiness. Two alert tasters even picked up on astringency in a few samples. The Dutched cocoas, by contrast, seldom lost points for bitter, sour, fruity, or astringent notes.

More intriguing was a phenomenon Ziegler called flavor masking. "If you bite into a spoiled peanut, you get this horrible, oxidized flavor. It

TASTING COCOA POWDER

Twenty *Cook's Illustrated* staff members tasted 10 cocoa powders in two simple preparations: a hot-chocolate beverage made with whole milk and sugar and a shortbread made with butter, flour, salt, and sugar. The Dutched and natural cocoas were tasted separately, with one control in each lineup to confirm the validity of tests. The two top cocoas in the Dutched and natural categories were then pitted against each other in five tests: hot chocolate, shortbread, pudding, devil's food cake, and pudding cake. The cocoas are listed below, in order of preference. Cocoa butter percentages and pH values were determined by independent lab tests.

DUTCH-PROCESSED COCOAS

BEST OVERALL COCOA: CALLEBAUT Cocoa Powder
- $20.00 for 2.2 pounds
- Cocoa butter 22%/pH 6.99

Our top performer overall won consistent raves for balance and rich chocolate flavor. Several tasters were impressed with the absence of bitterness and off-flavors compared with other samples. "Tastes perfect to me," noted one panelist.

BEST OVERALL VALUE: HERSHEY'S European Style Dutch Processed Cocoa
- $2.89 for 8 ounces
- Cocoa butter 10.06%/pH 7.42

Tasters appreciated the "full body" and "fudgy flavor" of this cocoa and praised its " toasty" flavor and "creamy, chocolatey goodness." But some complained of "chalky texture."

DROSTE Cocoa
- $3.99 for 8.8 ounces
- Cocoa butter 19%/pH 7.09

Complexity was not Droste's strong suit. "This is standard, Swiss Miss flavor," said one taster. Others compared it with "chocolate ice cream" and "warm chocolate milk—it totally falls flat."

SCHOKINAG Gourmet Cocoa Powder
- $16.50 for 2.2 pounds
- Cocoa butter 21.46%/pH 7.53

Our most alkalized cocoa, Schokinag lost points for an "overly sweet taste" and artificial flavors: "Tastes canned, metallic, fake." Three panelists—in separate tastings—detected "cheese," and accusations of "plastic" off-notes abounded.

VALRHONA Cacao
- $9.50 for 8.82 ounces
- Cocoa butter 20.93%/pH 7.49

In both hot chocolate and shortbread, tasters detected overtones of "hot dog" as well as "burnt, woody, smoky" flavors. As one taster put it, "Ham is good, but not in cocoa."

NATURAL COCOAS

MERCKENS Natural Cocoa
- $5.95 for 16 ounces
- Cocoa butter 21.99%/pH 5.44

Tasters noted "very dark chocolate overtones" and "an assertive flavor that lingers." Others detected "dark-roast coffee" and fruity notes, especially raspberry. There's a definite bitterness, said one panelist, "but in a good way."

HERSHEY'S Cocoa
- $2.95 for 8 ounces
- Cocoa butter 10.43%/pH 5.57

The most common supermarket cocoa for generations conjured up nostalgic comments. "Am I in a ski lodge sitting by the fire?" asked one taster. But there were complaints about astringency, bitterness, and off-flavors "like molasses."

NESTLÉ Toll House Cocoa
- $2.29 for 8 ounces
- Cocoa butter 10.38%/pH 5.47

"Sour" and "bitter" were common descriptors, and tasters detected fruity notes that seemed "artificial" and out of place.

GHIRARDELLI Premium Baking Cocoa
- $4.49 for 10 ounces
- Cocoa butter 21.85%/pH 5.75

This cocoa confounded tasters: "Fruity," "dusty," "chalky," "bitter," "metallic," "acidic," "insipid," "blah," "burnt," "smoky," "corn," and "strange horseradish" represent just a few of the panel's attempts to describe what they were tasting.

SCHARFFEN BERGER Natural Cocoa Powder
- $8.25 for 6 ounces
- Cocoa butter 20.4%/pH 5.69

"Nutty" was the most positive comment mustered for this cocoa. Tasters raised a red flag about "some sort of savory, vegetal element." One taster wrote, "It's more sour than bitter." The shortbread? "If I'd had my eyes closed, I might not have picked this out as having a chocolate flavor." Nutty, indeed.

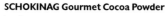

---

so overwhelms you that you're not thinking, 'But does it have good peanut flavor?' Similarly, if you taste cocoa that's particularly acidic or bitter, it's hard to say, 'How much chocolate flavor do I really sense beyond that?'" The removal of a cocoa's harshest notes lets us better appreciate the remaining flavors—the notes that recede into the background when forced to compete with acidic notes. And an acidic note, confirmed Ziegler, can be "a pretty dominating factor."

The only case remaining for choosing natural cocoa concerned leavening. Getting a baked good to rise properly depends on a delicate balance of acids and bases. Conventional wisdom thus dictates that Dutched cocoa and natural cocoa cannot be used interchangeably. Many cookbooks include cautionary notes about the dangers of substitution.

With these caveats in mind, we chose two recipes (for devil's food cake and hot pudding cake) that call for a particular type of cocoa—one Dutched, one natural. To our surprise, we noticed no difference in leavening among the four samples in either of these applications. And, across the board, the two Dutched cocoas beat out the two natural cocoas in terms of both flavor and texture.

So does the home cook need both Dutched and natural cocoas? Not based on our findings. If you're organized enough to arrange an Internet or telephone order, Callebaut is our enthusiastic recommendation. The supermarket Hershey's Dutched was a close second. And for those who buy only "natural," Merckens is the best choice, tying the second-place Hershey's Dutched in two of the tastings.

Do You Really Need a Saucier Pan?

Will a saucier make your risottos turn out better? Probably not. But it might make you turn them out more often.

≩ BY JOLYON HELTERMAN WITH GARTH CLINGINGSMITH ≲

The *Cook's Illustrated* test kitchen is divided fairly evenly into two distinct groups: Those who count sauciers among their most essential pans and those who never use them. As a de facto member of the latter camp, I was bemused by the breathless exuberance lavished by some of my normally skeptical colleagues on what appears to be no more than a souped-up saucepan. The two noticeable differences are a slightly wider mouth and rounded, flared sides—the latter designed expressly to accommodate wire whisks and to eliminate any distinct edge where a sauce might seek temporary "refuge" and overcook.

To better ascertain the potential benefits of the saucier, I conducted a survey of the test kitchen's most zealous saucier mavens. "I love cooking in my saucier," proclaimed one exuberant test cook. "It's used so frequently that it rarely gets put away." Tasks for which the saucier camp reported reaching for this pan rather than a saucepan included preparations demanding constant stirring—custards, risottos, sauces—as well as those requiring poaching (especially fruit) and braising. One staffer praised the saucier for combining the best qualities of a saucepan and a skillet: "It's got depth and capacity but also width and easy interior access."

Anecdotal enthusiasm was all well and good. But how would sauciers fare in objective kitchen tests? To find out, we brought seven leading brands into the kitchen to perform typical stovetop tasks.

Saucepan versus Saucier

A saucepan (left) has straight sides, and its diameter measures the same at the top and the bottom. A saucier (right) is bowl-shaped, with flared sides, making it narrower at the bottom than at the top.

Task Masters

We'll cut to the chase. Except for one model, every pan performed every task brilliantly, including the test kitchen's favorite saucepan, which we included for comparison. (See the chart on page 29.) Risotto after risotto, béchamel after tedious béchamel, our daily stovetop sessions spent hunting for illuminating signs of variation invariably ended with a tidy row of virtually identical preparations. "This third risotto may be a bit more watery," one of us would venture aloud. (It wasn't.) "Gravy No. 6—does it have a slightly darker hue?" (It didn't.) An extra minute of cooking time here, a more conspicuously caramelized piece of onion there, but the results were all safely within our protocols for "good" performance. Given that our trusty saucepan was among these good performers, these tests raised the question: Why purchase a saucier if you already have a good saucepan?

The quick (and honest) answer is that you don't have to, especially if you already have a large, high-quality saucepan such as the All-Clad, which won our test back in January/February 2002. Sauciers have their advantages to be sure: easy access to the corners (thanks to the rounded bottom), slightly easier stirring, and an extra-wide mouth that allows for wider, lazier circles with the whisk. But these are not deal breakers when it comes to using a traditional saucepan. If you don't have the ideal saucepan, however, you might consider purchasing a saucier instead. The question is, which one?

It's about the Journey

After several weeks of stirring and studying, we had developed some pretty clear preferences. First, we liked a lip around the edge to facilitate pouring. Although one of the lipless pans—the All-Clad—appeared to be deliberately curved to promote tidy pours, the others made a mess.

Second, the wider the pan, the easier and more luxuriant seemed the task at hand. The large diameters of the All-Clad, Viking, and Farberware sauciers allowed for loose, relaxed, forearm-powered rounds rather than tight circles directed mostly by the wrist—a notable difference between our saucepan and the best sauciers. One guest risotto stirrer, who'd missed the drama of the gravy and béchamel sessions, praised the open feel of the Sitram, which tied with the All-Clad

for widest diameter. By contrast, the KitchenAid saucier was only slightly wider than the saucepan, making the task of stirring a tighter operation.

Less subjective than "luxuriant whisk feel" was the direct relationship between the width of the bottom of the pan and the amount of heat that wafted up its sides during cooking. The narrower pans (such as the KitchenAid), which covered a smaller area of the gas burner, allowed more heat to escape. And this residual heat proved uncomfortable after about 10 minutes of cooking—a legitimate concern when using a saucier, which is designed primarily for tasks that demand a cook's constant proximity to the pan.

We also preferred long, substantial handles: After 15 minutes on moderate heat, most pans were plagued by about 4½ inches of unusable handle. The Viking, Farberware, and All-Clad each had plenty of cool handle to spare; the rest were all but untouchable. (The KitchenAid, with the shortest handle of the lot and the narrowest diameter, was the least touchable of all, as the handle heated up very quickly.)

Weight was also a significant factor. Cooking proceeded more evenly in the heavier pans, and their heft also gave us a greater sense of security at the stovetop. Four of the five heaviest sauciers—the Viking, then the All-Clad, Farberware, and Calphalon—all made it to the top of our chart.

Only one pan, the Sitram, stood out as "Not Recommended." Unlike our favorite pans, it does not have the benefit of cladding or anodization (both methods of protecting a pan's highly conductive but somewhat delicate aluminum core); it is instead reinforced by a thick aluminum disk bonded to the pan bottom. The problem with this construction is the gap created at the point where the disk ends and the rounded sides begin their curve upward. When we browned butter and flour for béchamel sauce and mirepoix (finely chopped vegetables) for gravy, a dark ring quickly formed around the Sitram's interior. The ring went from deep brown to smoking black minutes before the mirepoix was done, and the uneven heat produced gloppy béchamel with unsightly brown flecks. Thus, the Sitram didn't make the cut.

Wrapping Up

So, after weeks of testing, where did we come out? Four pans (the All-Clad, Farberware, Viking,

RATING SAUCIERS

We tested and evaluated seven medium-size sauciers (2½ to 3½ quarts), sufficient for a risotto dinner for four or multiple servings of sauce or gravy. Because manufacturers differ on nomenclature, our criterion for selecting pans was the mixing-bowl shape rather than the product name. Tests were performed over gas burners on the ranges in our test kitchen. The pans are listed in order of preference.

PRICE: Prices paid in Boston-area stores, in national mail-order catalogs, and on Web sites.

MATERIALS: Materials the pan is made from.

WEIGHT: Weight (as measured in the test kitchen) without the lid, rounded to the nearest ounce.

DIAMETER: Measured across the top of the pan, from rim to rim.

HANDLE: Length from its point of contact with the pan.

LIP: Does the pan have a flared lip on its rim to facilitate pouring?

PERFORMANCE: We boiled water; made béchamel sauce; cooked a basic risotto; sautéed chopped onions; and sautéed a mirepoix, then deglazed the pan and prepared gravy. For each test, both the quality of the end product and the factors contributing to it during cooking were important. These factors included ease of stirring, development of fond, evenness of cooking, and reduction time. Scores of good, fair, or poor were assigned for each test, and the composite of these scores constitutes the overall performance rating.

DESIGN: Factors evaluated included whether the pan's dimensions, shape, and handle design contributed to maneuverability and user-friendliness. Comfortable handle temperature was important, as were pan contour and ease of pouring.

RECOMMENDED

All-Clad Stainless 3-Quart Saucier Pan with Lid
PRICE: $145.00
MATERIALS: Stainless steel exterior and interior with complete aluminum core; stainless steel handle

WEIGHT: 2 lb. 10 oz.
DIAMETER: 9 15/16"
HANDLE: 8 3/8"
LIP: No
PERFORMANCE: ★★★
DESIGN: ★★★

Our favorite saucier lacked a pouring lip, but its ideal contours, heft, and maneuverability compensated for what would otherwise be a deficiency. We particularly liked the wide, generous distribution of the cooking area. As one tester put it, "It's awfully easy to look into the pan to see what's going on."

$$$ BEST BUY $$$

Farberware Millennium Clad Stainless Steel 2½-Quart Covered Saucier
PRICE: $36.30
MATERIALS: Stainless steel exterior and interior with complete aluminum core; hollow cast stainless steel handle

WEIGHT: 2 lb. 8 oz.
DIAMETER: 8 15/16"
HANDLE: 8 1/8"
LIP: Yes
PERFORMANCE: ★★★
DESIGN: ★★★

In every task, this low-priced saucier matched or outperformed the rest of the field. The lip was appreciated, and its handle stayed cooler than most. Were it not for its smaller (by ½ quart) capacity, which some testers found "slightly cramped," it might have bested the winning All-Clad.

Viking Professional Cookware 3½-Quart Reduction Sauce Pan
PRICE: $159.95
MATERIALS: Stainless steel exterior and interior with complete aluminum core; stainless steel handle

WEIGHT: 3 lb. 11 oz.
DIAMETER: 9 3/4"
HANDLE: 9 5/8"
LIP: No
PERFORMANCE: ★★★
DESIGN: ★★★

Our largest saucier won points for its roomy contours and gradual, deep fond development. Testers at first found the handle angle to be awkward but soon got used to it. Outweighing the other pans tested by more than 1 pound, the Viking made one-handed pours a challenge, but the extra-long handle remained cool enough to use both hands.

Calphalon Infused Anodized 3-Quart Chef's Pan with Lid
PRICE: $159.95
MATERIALS: Hard-anodized exterior and interior; stainless steel handle

WEIGHT: 2 lb. 7 oz.
DIAMETER: 9 1/2"
HANDLE: 8 1/8"
LIP: Yes
PERFORMANCE: ★★★
DESIGN: ★★★

The tight but deep contours of this pan seemed perfectly made for a whisk. "It's like an ultra-designed sports car," remarked one tester. The downsides were the pan's tendency to shake slightly at a full boil (it was the third-lightest pan) and a dark interior that made it difficult to evaluate browning.

RECOMMENDED WITH RESERVATIONS

KitchenAid Hard Anodized 2½-Quart Covered Saucier
PRICE: $145.00
MATERIALS: Hard-anodized exterior and stainless steel interior; stainless steel handle

WEIGHT: 2 lb. 9 oz.
DIAMETER: 8 15/16"
HANDLE: 7 1/8"
LIP: No
PERFORMANCE: ★★★
DESIGN: ★★

This saucier performed every task brilliantly. The undersized handle was its downfall: When cooking over high temperatures, testers couldn't touch it without a potholder. This saucier also has a rather small diameter, and testers complained about residual heat wafting up the pan's sides.

Anolon Commercial Clad 2½-Quart Covered Saucier
PRICE: $49.99
MATERIALS: Stainless steel exterior and interior with complete aluminum core; HollowCore stainless steel handle

WEIGHT: 2 lb. 6 oz.
DIAMETER: 9 15/16"
HANDLE: 8 1/8"
LIP: Yes
PERFORMANCE: ★★★
DESIGN: ★★

This saucier performed well in all the tasks, but testers found it too light and disliked the "slickness" of its ultra-polished cooking surface. Some testers liked the highly designed hollow-cast handle (one saying that it resembled "a car's parking brake"), but others found it bulky.

NOT RECOMMENDED

Sitram Cybernox2 3.3-Quart Saucier Pan with Cover
PRICE: $73.93
MATERIALS: Stainless steel exterior and interior with aluminum-steel stamp; stainless steel handle

WEIGHT: 2 lb. 5 oz.
DIAMETER: 9 15/16"
HANDLE: 8 1/2"
LIP: No
PERFORMANCE: ★★
DESIGN: ★

This pan's light weight and wide diameter were a recipe for trouble. The ring around the interior corresponding to the point at which disk-stamp reinforcement ended was prone to burning. The handle also heated up very quickly.

and Calphalon) are recommended. Among these $100-plus stars sits the Farberware (in second place), a pan that retails for less than $40. In fact, some testers picked this sturdy pan (with its lip for easy pouring and its protective long handle) as their favorite. At this price, the act of adding a saucier to your kitchen lineup no longer rings of culinary folly.

As a final test, I took the Farberware model home for the weekend to see if it moved me to greater heights of culinary endeavor. First I prepared an involved wild mushroom risotto that I hadn't bothered making in years. Next came a lobster Thermidor dinner for three guests, the requisite béchamel made easily. Three hours later, while whipping up a dessert of bananas

Foster, I noted how nicely the curved sides of the pan contained the rum-soaked flambé. A stir-fry, a balsamic reduction, and a rewarmed soup later, I was beginning to understand saucier fever. And for a mere $36 and change, the Farberware seemed a reasonable proposition, even if you already own the saucepan of your dreams.

> BY DAWN YANAGIHARA <

Salt Early or Salt Late?

Culinary students are taught to add salt to a pan of heating water only after it has reached a boil. Two explanations are offered: (1) Salt increases the time it takes for the water to boil, and (2) salt can cause pitting (the formation of tiny white spots on the pan) unless added after water has come to a boil.

Indeed, science says that salt will increase the boiling point of water. The generally accepted formula, put into easy-to-comprehend terms, says that 1½ tablespoons of salt in 1 quart of water will raise the boiling point by about 1 degree Fahrenheit. But those proportions yield a super-salty solution that is almost never used in cooking, so what are the real implications for the cook?

In the test kitchen, on the same burner and in the same pot, 4 quarts of water with and without 1 table-spoon of salt (the amounts we use to cook 1 pound of pasta) reached a boil, uncovered, in the same amount of time, about 17½ minutes. Our conclusion: Don't worry that adding salt to a pot of water will slow its progress toward a boil.

As for pitting, when we conducted the aforementioned tests, we did not witness an occurrence (we used a stainless steel pot; aluminum is also susceptible to pitting). Still, we have all seen it happen at home and in the test kitchen. Cookware manufacturers say pitting does not affect the performance, only the appearance, of cookware and that the quick dissolution of salt in boiling water helps to prevent it.

Cook's recipes almost always direct the cook to add salt to water after it has come to a boil. Because this practice complies with manufacturers' instructions, we'll continue to recommend it. However, if you tend to be an absent-minded cook for whom salting at the outset is the best way to ensure that it gets done, then go ahead and add salt at the outset. If pitting is a concern, stir the water until the salt dissolves.

Spatula Specifics

As a group, spatulas are under-appreciated but indispensable kitchen workers. There are a number of different kinds of spatulas, or "spats," as they are sometimes affectionately called in professional kitchens. Here's a quick explanation of the key spats used in our test kitchen.

Rubber spatula "Rubber" spatula is a bit of a misnomer because the best ones these days are made of heat-resistant silicone. We recommend equipping your kitchen with one medium-size rubber spatula (3 inches long by 2 inches wide) for scraping out the mayonnaise jar and one large one (4 inches long by 2½ inches wide) for everything else. Our favorite brands from a 2003 testing were Rubbermaid and Le Creuset.

Icing spatula These narrow, flexible metal spatulas, available with straight or offset blades, are used for icing cakes. A straight icing spatula is good for frosting the sides of cakes. An offset icing spatula is ideal for spreading fillings and frostings on horizontal surfaces. For cake decorators, both are a must, but for most other cooks, an offset icing spatula is all that's needed. It often comes in handy for flipping small or delicate foods, for removing that difficult first piece of lasagna, and for serving pies and cakes.

Fish spatula The blade of a fish spatula is angled and very thin, making it ideal for getting under delicate foods such as—no surprise—fish. The slots in the blade allow excess fat to drain away and reduce the chances of food sticking to the spat. A fish spat can also be useful for turning cutlets and omelets.

Metal spatula/turner These spatulas are almost always offset and are available in a variety of shapes and sizes. A large metal one can handle two burgers at a time, while a small one removes one cookie at a time from a baking sheet. We recommend owning an all-purpose medium-size metal spat.

RUBBER SPATULA

OFFSET ICING SPATULA

FLAT ICING SPATULA

FISH SPATULA

METAL SPATULA

KITCHEN SCIENCE: **A Few Sobering Thoughts**

It is a commonly heard refrain: "Cooking removes all the alcohol." But the truth is much more complex. To clarify things, we decided to address what readers say are their chief concerns.

I am not supposed to consume alcohol, but I do eat stews containing wine. How can they possibly have any alcohol left after cooking for so long?
We measured the alcohol content of the stew liquid in our Beef Burgundy recipe before it went into the oven. Every hour, we sampled the liquid to measure the alcohol concentration, and every time, it had dropped—but not as much as might be expected. After three hours of stewing (the recipe calls for two to three hours stewing), the alcohol concentration of the stew liquid had decreased by 60 percent. A major reason for the retention of alcohol in this dish

is the use of a lid. If the surface of the liquid is not ventilated, alcohol vapor will accumulate, reducing further evaporation. Because most stews and braises are cooked in lidded pots, significant alcohol retention is the rule rather than the exception, even after hours of cooking.

Some say a flambé burns off most of the alcohol, while others say it burns off hardly any at all. Who's right?
One way to quickly reduce the amount of alcohol in a liquid is to ignite the vapors that lie above the pan, a technique known as flambéing. But the degree to which a flambé will remove alcohol depends partly on the heat added to the liquid underneath. We found that brandy ignited over high heat retains 29 percent of its original alcohol concentration, while brandy flamed in a cold pan held 57 percent. In

the case of a flambé, the addition of heat (not just the flame from a match) can make a significant difference in the strength of the finished sauce. Practically, what does this mean? Steak Diane, which is cooked on the stovetop, will lose more alcohol than Cherries Jubilee, in which flaming liquid is poured over ice cream.

Conclusion: The chemistry of alcohol evaporation is no different from that which governs water evaporation; alcohol evaporation just occurs more readily. Factors that influence how much alcohol will be lost during cooking include the degree of ventilation (whether the pan is covered or uncovered) and the amount of heat added. The diameter of the pan is also a factor; the wider the pan, the more total evaporation. Though it is possible to remove the majority of alcohol in food through cooking, traces will almost always remain.

—John Olson, Science Editor

Recipe Conventions

Below is a list of conventions we observe in the test kitchen that apply to all of the recipes we develop. An expanded list is available on our Web site. Visit www.cooksillustrated.com and search for "frequently asked questions."

BLACK PEPPER For maximum flavor, black pepper should be freshly ground.

BUTTER Use unsalted butter unless salted butter is specified.

FLOUR Pillsbury, Gold Medal, or any other unbleached all-purpose flour with a protein content close to 10.5 percent will give you results like those we get in the test kitchen. When measuring flour, use the dip-and-sweep method: Dip the measure into the flour and level off the top with a flat edge.

FRESH HERBS AND GREENS Wash and dry thoroughly before using. When using herbs, pick or remove leaves from fibrous or woody stems before chopping. To measure, pack herbs or greens loosely into the measuring spoon or cup.

GRATED HARD CHEESES Weight is the most accurate measure for hard cheeses such as Parmesan because the volume of the grated cheese is affected by the grater used. For instance, a rasp-style grater yields fine, fluffy shreds, while the fine holes of a box or hand grater yield larger, coarser shreds. If you don't own a scale, you can account for the discrepancy as follows: If using a rasp grater, pack the cheese into the measuring cup; if using a box or hand grater, simply pile it into the cup without packing. Either way, 1 ounce of grated Parmesan should then equal about ½ cup.

OLIVE OIL Use regular olive oil unless extra-virgin is specified.

ONIONS Use yellow onions unless otherwise specified.

PAN SIZE Measure skillets and baking pans across the top, from one inside edge to the other. Saucepans are measured by volume. Depth is measured from the bottom inside of the pan to the top of the lip, with the measure being held perpendicular to the pan bottom.

PARSLEY More flavorful flat-leaf, or Italian, parsley is preferred to curly parsley.

SUGAR Use granulated white sugar unless otherwise specified.

ZEST Zest is the finely grated rind of a citrus fruit. Use only the outermost, colored part of the skin and none of the white pith, which tastes bitter. We recommend the Microplane grater for zesting.

A Hard-Core Issue

While developing the recipe for Glazed Parsnips and Celery (page 22), we encountered some aged parsnips that were gristly and fibrous at the core even when fully cooked. Those larger than an inch in diameter at the top tended to be the culprits, so we took to coring them before cooking. Should you wind up with big-top parsnips, here's how to core them.

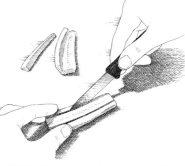

Divide the narrow tapered end from the bulky top end and halve the top end lengthwise (as directed in the recipe). Using a paring knife, remove the core by carefully cutting a V-shaped channel down the center of the parsnip.

A Sweet Something

Somewhere around the umpteenth batch of our All-Purpose Cornbread (page 11), we got it in our minds to make whipped honey butter for spreading on the warm cornbread. (If you're familiar with Marie Callender's restaurants, you know where this idea came from.) The combination was such a hit that we thought we'd pass along the recipe we devised.

WHIPPED HONEY BUTTER

In a standing mixer fitted with a whisk attachment, beat 8 tablespoons (one stick) of room-temperature unsalted butter at medium speed until smooth, about 30 seconds; stop the mixer and add 1 tablespoon of honey and a pinch of salt. Beat the mixture at medium speed until combined, about 15 seconds, then increase the speed to high and whip until very light and fluffy, about 2 minutes, scraping down the bowl with a rubber spatula as needed.

Sauce Reductions Part Two

The sauce in our recipe for **Steak Diane** (May/June 2004) relies on an intense sauce base (basically a quick demi-glace) for flavor and texture. Several readers asked if they could make the sauce base and freeze it for another use. We went back into the test kitchen and discovered that the answer is a resounding yes. Here's what to do.

Cubes of our quick demi-glace can be frozen and used to make an instant sauce for steaks or chops.

After straining the sauce base, portion the sauce into plastic ice cube trays and freeze. When the sauce has frozen, empty the trays into a zipper-lock bag for easy storage. Use these cubes to create a quick sauce for grilled, broiled, or pan-seared steaks or chops. To make a very potent sauce for two people, melt two demi-glace cubes in a small skillet and finish by whisking in ½ tablespoon unsalted butter. For a less rich sauce that can serve four, melt two demi-glace cubes with 2 tablespoons water and then finish with ½ tablespoon butter. Either way, the sauce base already has highly concentrated flavors, so you will probably not need to season this quick sauce with salt and pepper. **Cook's Extra:** To get our recipe for Sauce Base for Steak Diane, go to www.cooksillustrated.com and key in code 7002. The recipe will be available until February 15, 2005.

Cheese Bread Light?

In the test kitchen, we develop recipes using whole milk. Several readers wondered if they could use whatever milk they had on hand—usually low fat—in our recipe for **Cheese Bread** (May/June 2004). We baked three loaves—one with whole milk, one with 2 percent milk, and the last with skim milk—to find out.

The bread made with skim milk had a very soft, yielding texture owing to its higher percentage of water versus fat. The flavor of this loaf was unbalanced, more sharp than cheesy. With less milk fat in the recipe, the sour cream dominated in an unappealing way. The loaf made with 2 percent milk had a soft texture, but the flavor was fine. The original version made with whole milk had the most substantial texture and balanced flavors; it was tasters' favorite. Our cheese bread is best made with whole milk, but it will taste fine if you have only 2 percent milk on hand. If the only milk in the fridge is skim, take a trip to the market.

Taking Thai Chicken Indoors

We've been contacted by readers wanting to know how to make **Thai Grilled Chicken** (July/August 2004) indoors. Until the weather warms up, here are a few pointers for making this recipe without a grill.

Heat your oven to 450 degrees and adjust an oven rack to the lower-middle position, as food tends to brown more deeply and evenly toward the bottom of the oven. Set the brined, rubbed chicken on a flat wire roasting rack and place the rack over a baking sheet lined with foil. Roast the chicken for 15 minutes, rotate the pan, and then cook for an additional 15 minutes. The skin should be light golden brown, and an instant-read thermometer inserted into the thickest part of each breast (not touching any bone) should register 160 degrees. To get the same deep brown exterior that the grill provides, finish the chicken with a quick shot under the broiler (2 to 3 minutes, with the chicken 6 to 8 inches from the broiler element). This pass under the broiler will help to crisp the skin, but the skin will probably not be quite as crisp as it is in the grilled version. The flavors, however, will be just as good. –Compiled by Nina West

IF YOU HAVE A QUESTION about a recently published recipe, let us know. Send your inquiry, name, address, and daytime telephone number to Recipe Update, Cook's Illustrated, P.O. Box 470589, Brookline, MA 02447, or to recipeupdate@bcpress.com.

EQUIPMENT UPDATE
Electric Knives

Since 2000, when we first tested electric knives, some changes have occurred in this product category. Black & Decker no longer makes our favorite electric knife, the Ergo, but the company has replaced it with the EK800 Slice Right ($24.99). The Hamilton Beach 74250 Easy Slice Electric Knife ($25.99), which we downgraded in 2000 for an awkward, bulky handle, has been redesigned. And we found a new model from Cuisinart that retails for a whopping $60, more than twice the

BLACK & DECKER
EK800 Slice Right
A worthy replacement for our favorite electric knife.

price of the other two. We brought all three knives into the test kitchen.

The Black & Decker Slice Right is every bit as good as its predecessor. It executed all tasks perfectly. Hamilton Beach's loop-style handle has been made more comfortable, but now the power button needs to be both pressed and pulled, more like a trigger. The need to apply extra pressure quickly becomes tiring.

The handsome Cuisinart comes with two sets of blades: carving and bread. But both blades seem reluctant to bite into food, whether a brisket or a baguette, and the sleek-looking handle feels quite bulky. For half the price and better performance, we will reach for the new Black & Decker Slice Right.

DO YOU REALLY NEED THIS?
Cake Cutters

What's the best way to split a cake into two even layers? In the test kitchen, we always use a serrated knife, but we uncovered four gadgets designed specifically for this task and decided to try them out.

The most unusual is the Frieling Layer Cake Slicer ($6.99). This tool guides a thin wire around a cake that is then crossed and pulled through the cake. Think James Bond strangling an unlucky adversary. Wilton's Cake Leveler ($2.99) relies on a similar wire blade strung between two metal legs. In both cases, we found that dull wire blades left a rough surface and messy "exit wounds" on cakes. Wilton also makes a Large Cake Leveler ($19.99), which has a 19-inch serrated blade strung between two legs. This product, as well as the 14-inch Magic Line Torting Knife ($27.99), seemed better suited to a professional bakery. We found it awkward to use such lengthy blades on small 9-inch-round cakes.

Whether you are a cake-splitting novice or pro, we recommend a serrated knife. Oh, and it will also cut bread.

PRODUCT UPDATE
Plastic Wrap

Many brands of plastic wrap clutter supermarket aisles these days. Are they all created equal? We bought five to find out.

Stretch-Tite, Saran Premium, Saran Cling Plus, Glad Cling Wrap, and Glad Press'n Seal all survived a microwave test and kept guacamole from turning brown for 72 hours. The real differences came when we tried using these wraps to cover bowls made of glass, metal, and plastic. The Glad Press'n Seal stuck to all three—but only if the bowls were perfectly dry. A glass bowl kept in a refrigerator for a few minutes gathered enough condensation to render the Press'n Seal useless. We consider this a fatal flaw.

The other four wraps performed equally well when used on metal or on glass. Plastic was another story. None of the wraps could cling to the plastic bowl. In every case we had to wind extra wrap around the first sheet. This is where Stretch-Tite, the stickiest of all the wraps tested, really shines. Stretch-Tite is not as readily available as Saran or Glad products, but mail-ordering

big 500-square-foot rolls is an option. Also look for these rolls at warehouse clubs.

EQUIPMENT UPDATE
Pepper Mills

We have yet to find a pepper mill that can approach the Unicorn Magnum Plus, winner of our July/August 2001 test; it offers the ultimate in grind quality and speed. But it is expensive at $45. It turns out that the Magnum Plus is an overgrown version of the $31 Magnum, which seemed worth a try.

The 5¾-inch Magnum grinds just as quickly and effectively as the 9-inch Magnum Plus. In the test kitchen, we really appreciate the huge 15-tablespoon capacity of the Magnum Plus, but the Magnum's 7-tablespoon capacity is fine for home use. All in all, for cooks who want a less expensive option than the Magnum Plus, the unassuming Magnum is a great choice.

Sources

The following are mail-order sources for items recommended in this issue. Prices were current at press time and do not include shipping and handling unless indicated. Contact these companies to confirm up-to-date prices and availability.

page 19: INEXPENSIVE DUTCH OVEN
- Tramontina Sterling II 7-Qt. Dutch Oven: $56.95, item #TRA-6503-28, ABestKitchen.com (330-535-2811).

page 25: CAKE PAN
- Chicago Metallic Professional Lifetime Non-Stick 9" Round Cake Pan: $14.95, item #101457, Cooking.com (800-663-8810).

page 27: COCOA
- Callebaut Cocoa Powder: $20.00 for 35 ounces, item #CP, ChocolateSource.com (800-214-4926).

page 29: SAUCIERS
- All-Clad Stainless 3-Qt. Saucier Pan with Lid: $145.00, item #2743,

A Cook's Wares (800-915-9788; www.cookswares.com).
- Farberware Millennium Stainless Steel 2½-Qt. Covered Saucier: $36.60, item #B0000850X2, Amazon.com.

page 32: ELECTRIC KNIFE
- Black & Decker EK800 Slice Right: $24.99, EverythingHome.com (877-367-5189).

page 32: PEPPER MILL
- Unicorn Magnum: $31.00, Tom David (800-634-8881; www.peppergun.com).

page 32: PLASTIC WRAP
- Stretch-Tite Plastic Wrap: $9.95, item #7604, The Baker's Catalogue.

United States Postal Service
Statement of Ownership, Management, and Circulation

1. Publication Title	2. Publication Number	3. Filing Date
Cook's Illustrated	1 0 6 8 - 2 8 2 1	10/1/2004

4. Issue Frequency	5. Number of Issues Published Annually	6. Annual Subscription Price
Bi-Monthly	6	$35.70

7. Complete Mailing Address of Known Office of Publication (Not printer) (Street, city, county, state, and ZIP+4)
17 Station Street, Brookline, MA 02445
Contact Person
Telephone 617-232-100

8. Complete Mailing Address of Headquarters or General Business Office of Publisher (Not printer)
Same as Publisher

9. Full Names and Complete Mailing Addresses of Publisher, Editor, and Managing Editor (Do not leave blank)
Publisher (Name and complete mailing address)
Christopher P. Kimball, Boston Common Press
17 Station Street, Brookline, MA 02445

Editor (Name and complete mailing address)
Same as Publisher

Managing Editor (Name and complete mailing address)
Jack Bishop, Boston Common Press
17 Station Street, Brookline, MA 02445

10. Owner

Full Name	Complete Mailing Address
Boston Common Press	17 Station Street
Limited Partnership	Brookline, MA 02445
(Christopher P. Kimball)	

11. Known Bondholders, Mortgagees, and Other Security Holders Owning or Holding 1 Percent or More of Total Amount of Bonds, Mortgages, or Other Securities. If none, check box ▶ ☐ None

Full Name	Complete Mailing Address
N/A	

12. Tax Status (For completion by nonprofit organizations authorized to mail at nonprofit rates) (Check one)
PS Form 3526, October 1999

13. Publication Title	14. Issue Date for Circulation Data Below
Cook's Illustrated	September/October 2004

15. Extent and Nature of Circulation	Average No. Copies Each Issue During Preceding 12 Months	No. Copies of Single Issue Published Nearest to Filing Date
a. Total Number of Copies (Net press run)	787,187	790,064
b. Paid and/or Requested Circulation (1) Paid/Requested Outside-County Mail Subscriptions Stated on Form 3541	559,195	577,988
(2) Paid In-County Subscriptions Stated on Form 3541		
(3) Sales Through Dealers and Carriers, Street Vendors, Counter Sales, and Other Non-USPS Paid Distribution	91,303	92,509
(4) Other Classes Mailed Through the USPS		
c. Total Paid and/or Requested Circulation [Sum of 15b. (1), (2),(3),and (4)] ▶	650,497	670,497
d. Free Distribution by Mail (1) Outside-County as Stated on Form 3541	3,658	3,875
(2) In-County as Stated on Form 3541		
(3) Other Classes Mailed Through the USPS		
e. Free Distribution Outside the Mail (Carriers or other means)	3,531	4,680
f. Total Free Distribution (Sum of 15d. and 15e.) ▶	7,189	8,555
g. Total Distribution (Sum of 15c. and 15f) ▶	657,686	679,052
h. Copies not Distributed	129,502	111,012
i. Total (Sum of 15g. and h.) ▶	787,187	790,064
j. Percent Paid and/or Requested Circulation (15c. divided by 15g. times 100)	98.91%	98.74%

16. Publication of Statement of Ownership
☑ Publication required. Will be printed in the Jan/Feb 05 issue of this publication. ☐ Publication not required.

17. Signature and Title of Editor, Publisher, Business Manager, or Owner
Date 10/1/04

PS Form 3526, October 1999 (Reverse)

RECIPES
January & February 2005

Onion-Braised Beef Brisket, 14

Pasta with Chicken, Broccoli, and Sun-Dried Tomatoes, 12

Scrambled Eggs with Sausage, Sweet Peppers, and Cheddar, 21

Chicken Teriyaki, 9

Glazed Winter Root Vegetables, 22

Black Bean Soup, 19

Pork Chops with Vinegar and Sweet Peppers, 7

German Chocolate Cake, 24

All-Purpose Cornbread, 11

PHOTOGRAPHY: CARL TREMBLAY, STYLING: MARY JANE SAWYER

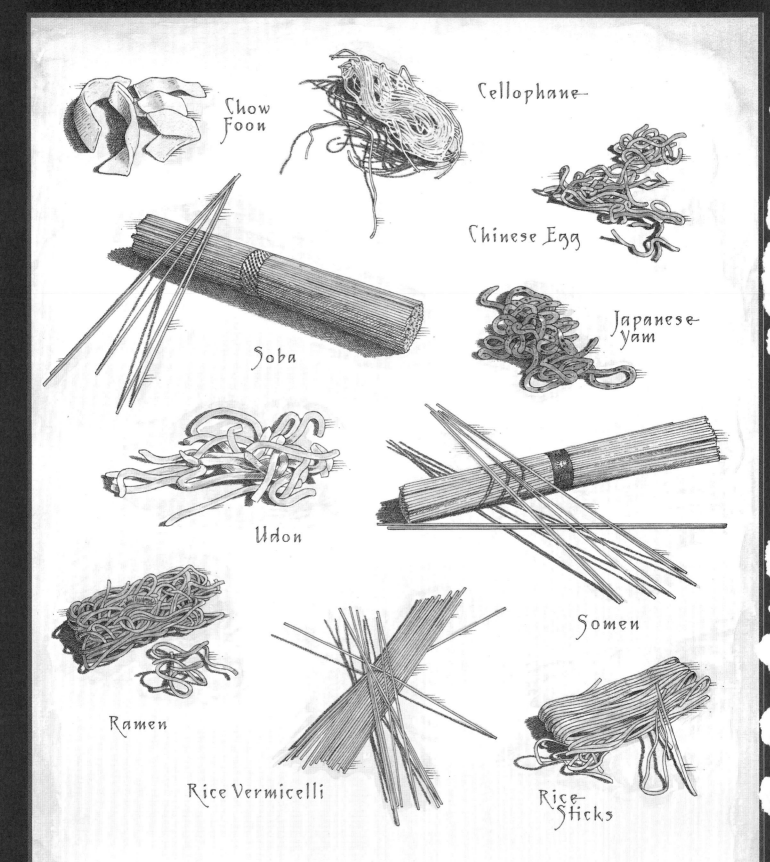

Chow Foon

Cellophane

Chinese Egg

Japanese Yam

Soba

Udon

Somen

Ramen

Rice Vermicelli

Rice Sticks

ASIAN NOODLES

NUMBER SEVENTY-THREE

MARCH & APRIL 2005

COOK'S
ILLUSTRATED

Stuffed Roast Chicken
Novel Method, Perfect Results

Italian Pot Roast
Forget the $40 Barolo

Pasta with Cherry Tomatoes

Tasting Swiss Cheese
Does It Have to Be Swiss?

Chocolate Cupcakes
Just Dump and Stir

Homemade Sourdough
Authentic Flavor in Only 24 Hours

Rating Measuring Cups
Can "Better" Designs Beat Pyrex?

Freezing Food 101
Easy Quesadillas
Fish Fillets with Quick Sauces
Tortilla Soup
Pan-Roasted Asparagus

www.cooksillustrated.com

$5.95 U.S./$6.95 CANADA

0 74470 62805 7

CONTENTS
March & April 2005

www.cooksillustrated.com

HOME OF AMERICA'S TEST KITCHEN

Founder and Editor Christopher Kimball
Executive Editor Jack Bishop
Senior Editors Jolyon Helterman
Dawn Yanagihara
Editorial Manager, Books Elizabeth Carduff
Test Kitchen Director Erin McMurrer
Senior Editors, Books Julia Collin Davison
Lori Galvin
Senior Writer Bridget Lancaster
Managing Editor Rebecca Hays
Associate Editor, Books Keith Dresser
Associate Editor Sandra Wu
Science Editor John Olson
Web Editor Lindsay McSweeney
Copy Chief India Koopman
Test Cooks Stephanie Alleyne
Erika Bruce
Sean Lawler
Jeremy Sauer
Rachel Toomey
Diane Unger-Mahoney
Sarah Wilson
Assistant Test Cooks Garth Clingingsmith
Charles Kelsey
Nina West
Editorial Assistant, Books Elizabeth Wray
Assistant to the Publisher Melissa Baldino
Kitchen Assistants Barbara Akins
Nadia Domeq
Maria Elena Delgado
Ena Gudiel
Editorial Intern Elizabeth Bomze
Contributing Editors Matthew Card
Elizabeth Germain
Consulting Editors Shirley Corriher
Jasper White
Robert L. Wolke
Proofreader Jean Rogers

Design Director Amy Klee
Designer Heather Barrett
Staff Photographer Daniel van Ackere

Vice President Marketing David Mack
Sales Director Leslie Ray
Retail Sales Director Jason Geller
Corporate Sponsorship Specialist Laura Phillipps
Sales Representative Shekinah Cohn
Marketing Assistant Connie Forbes
Circulation Director Bill Tine
Circulation Manager Larisa Greiner
Fulfillment Manager Carrie Horan
Products Director Steven Browall
Direct Mail Director Adam Perry
Customer Service Manager Jacqueline Valerio
Customer Service Representative Julie Gardner
E-Commerce Marketing Manager Hugh Buchan

Vice President Operations James McCormack
Senior Production Manager Jessica Lindheimer Quirk
Production Manager Mary Connelly
Book Production Specialist Ron Bilodeau
Production Assistants Jeanette McCarthy
Jennifer Power
Christian Steinmetz
Systems Administrator Richard Cassidy
WebMaster Aaron Shuman

Chief Financial Officer Sharyn Chabot
Controller Mandy Shito
Staff Accountant Maya Santoso
Office Manager Saudiyah Abdul-Rahim
Receptionist Henrietta Murray
Publicity Deborah Broide

PRINTED IN THE USA

TUBERS AND RHIZOMES Tubers are starchy, bulbous sections of underground plant stems whose function is food storage. The most common tubers are potatoes and sweet potatoes. Taro root, or dasheen, can be cooked like a potato. While fresh arrowroot, like other tubers, can be cooked, it is most commonly dried and ground. This white powder becomes clear when cooked and is used as a flavorless thickener for sauces and fruit fillings. Water chestnuts closely resemble regular chestnuts on the outside but have a firm, white, juicy interior and add a crisp texture to stir-fries. The lotus root forms the underwater tuberous root of the lotus water lily. Jerusalem artichokes, commonly known as sunchokes, are not artichokes at all but rather the tuber of a variety of sunflower. Rhizomes are similar to tubers, but they are not as starchy and grow horizontally underground. Ginger is used to flavor both sweet and savory dishes. Its more pungent cousin galangal is found primarily in Asian markets. Turmeric adds a brilliant yellow-orange color and a floral spiciness to Indian curries and is also a common ingredient in mustards.

COVER *(Asparagus & Turnips)*: Elizabeth Brandon, BACK COVER *(Tubers & Rhizomes)*: John Burgoyne

For list rental information, contact: ClientLogic, 1200 Harbor Blvd., 9th Floor, Weehawken, NJ 07087; 201-865-5800; fax 201-867-2450.
Editorial Office: 17 Station St., Brookline, MA 02445; 617-232-1000; fax 617-232-1572. Subscription inquiries, call 800-526-8442.
Postmaster: Send all new orders, subscription inquiries, and change of address notices to Cook's Illustrated, P.O. Box 7446, Red Oak, IA 51591-0446.

'WE HAE MEAT AND WE CAN EAT'

Over the Thanksgiving table this year, neighbors and family often traded graces. Charlie, our 10-year-old Bart Simpson act-alike, is particularly taken with "Rub-a-dub-dub, thanks for the grub." Emily likes to repeat the grace recited at school: "For what we are about to receive, may our hearts be truly thankful." Older, more traditional graces followed, such as, "Bless O Lord this food to our use and us to thy service." But the one that I found most compelling was *The Selkirk Grace* from Robert Burns: "Some hae meat and canna eat and some there are that want it; but we hae meat and we can eat, so let the Lord be thankit." I guess I found the plain-spoken manner and lack of flourish appealing. Perhaps that is just the nature of a people—be they Vermonters or Scotsmen—who are used to scratching a living from stony soil.

The next day, I got up before dawn and headed for my lower tree stand, the one that is set on the edge of a recently cleared field. Deer season runs through Thanksgiving weekend, but by this time many hunters have moved over to New York State, where the hunting is better, leaving Vermont to the die-hards. I got into the stand while the moon was still a bright, perfect circle over the ridge, reflecting off of standing puddles in the logging road and the skimcoat of ice on the pond. As it slowly sank out of sight, it soured yellow and silhouetted a row of trees on the ridgeline that stood out like a Marine's brushcut.

I went back for lunch and then headed out again, this time past the hunting cabin and up through the saddle to the top, where I looked down across the fields and rolling ridges of New York. All the colors of late fall were on display: gray oak, silver beech, chestnut brown, russet timothy, birch white, green moss, and the occasional sprinkle of brightly frosted leaves in the cooler spots. I consider spring, summer, and the tawdry colors of a tourist weekend no match for the subtle palette of late November.

It's a bit lonely this time of year, standing on a gusty, cold mountaintop, but it is the kind of loneliness that a hunter yearns for during the warmer months. It is momentary and reflective rather than a wasting condition. Indeed, a hunter is hardly alone in the woods; a giant crow lifts off of a stump with a huge flap of wings and a sharp "caw," the wind rattles reddish-brown leaves still attached high up in a red maple, and then the flash of a white tail startles as a deer bounds through the underbrush.

Years ago, Adrienne and I would drive with our two young daughters, Whitney and Caroline, to my mother's house in rural Connecticut. It was a farm of sorts, plenty of hens, a dog, and a large unkempt root cellar garden. My job upon arriving on Thanksgiving morning was to secretly turn up the stove; she was fond of roasting a 20-pound local bird at 200 degrees, a cooking method espoused by 1960s health guru Adelle Davis that never got the bird cooked on time. (On the subject of food safety, my mother justified this cooking method by pointing out that nobody in the family had yet died. I simply regarded this as unfinished business.) My mother lived alone by then and had little patience for small, unruly children, a sharp rebuke likely to explode into the fragile cease-fire at any moment. Or she would simply disappear up to her office over the garage when it all became too much.

Around the Thanksgiving table, she had her traditions: the beeswax candles, the proper setting of the table, the pillow on her chair, and, of course, the behavior of the children. Offering an opinion (almost always negative) on whether one liked a particular foodstuff was the height of bad manners, and the offending urchin was quickly set straight, almost to the point of tears. "Stop squirming!" was another common exclamation. I am quite sure that an invited guest might have sensed that he had been transported into one of the earlier scenes from *A Christmas Carol*, perhaps the moment when Bob Cratchit asked for a bit more coal. My view is altogether different and

Christopher Kimball

is based on closer observation: the moist eye upon our leaving; the children's videos rented and set out by the television; the unsteady walk, hand-in-hand, with a four-year-old to show her the different breeds of hens running around the backyard; and the proud countenance as our family was enthusiastically introduced to neighbors.

This year, on our farm in the Green Mountains, conversation around the Thanksgiving table was of a different sort. We told stories about Harry Skidmore, who was known to put up a roadblock on the town road, stopping motorists who looked like hippies, especially Karl Stuecklin, our resident artist. (Harry's wife, Jenny, however, was a kind soul, offering a free turkey or a weekly sauna and river bath to those in need.) Jean, our neighbor across the valley, brought her family's famous cream pie, the one that uses no eggs and takes half a day to bake. (This year, it was a great success, although last year Jean said that her aunt's pie did not set up properly.) Emily sang a Thanksgiving tune along the lines of "Frère Jacques" that began, "Cornbread muffins, chestnut stuffing, pudding and pie, three feet high…" The kids went off to play Stratego, and the rest of us were much too full to get up.

The fire reduces to embers. I finish off my last piece of maple pecan pie, and then Jack, a veteran fighter pilot from the North African campaign, sits up straight and states to nobody in particular, "This was the finest Thanksgiving dinner I have ever eaten." Then I remember what a neighbor once said about the old-time farmers, the ones who had to live off their wits and hands. A hard life brings out faith in others, while ready-made success is apt to encourage a bit too much self-reliance. In the words of Robert Burns, "We hae meat and we can eat." Simple enough to say, but the meaning is clear. For the food, the company, and for no more than a seat at the table, may our hearts be truly thankful.

FOR INQUIRIES, ORDERS, OR MORE INFORMATION:

www.cooksillustrated.com

At www.cooksillustrated.com, you can order books and subscriptions, sign up for our free e-newsletter, or renew your magazine subscription. Subscribe to the Web site and you'll have access to 12 years of *Cook's* recipes, cookware tests, ingredient tastings, and more.

COOKBOOKS

We sell more than 40 cookbooks by the editors of *Cook's Illustrated*. To order, visit our bookstore at www.cooksillustrated.com or call 800-611-0759 (or 515-246-6911 from outside the U.S.).

COOK'S ILLUSTRATED Magazine

Cook's Illustrated magazine (ISSN 1068-2821), number 73, is published bimonthly by Boston Common Press Limited Partnership, 17 Station Street, Brookline, MA 02445. Copyright 2005 Boston Common Press Limited Partnership. Periodicals postage paid at Boston, Mass., and additional mailing offices, USPS #012487. POSTMASTER: Send address changes to Cook's Illustrated, P.O. Box 7446, Red Oak, IA 51591-0446. For subscription and gift subscription orders, subscription inquiries, or change-of-address notices, call 800-526-8442 in the U.S. or 515-247-7571 from outside the U.S., or write us at Cook's Illustrated, P.O. Box 7446, Red Oak, IA 51591-0446.

≥COMPILED BY INDIA KOOPMAN AND SANDRA WU ≤

Decoding Produce Stickers

Are the numbers printed on the stickers of fruits and vegetables at the supermarket just an easy way for cashiers to scan in produce prices, or is there something more to them?

CASSIE KUO
ATLANTA, GA.

➤ The four- and five-digit numbers you see on the stickers of bulk produce items are known as PLU (price look-up) codes. These codes, assigned by the Produce Marketing Association through the Produce Electronic Identification Board, are indeed used by checkout clerks to identify and price fresh fruits and vegetables. But in addition to being used for inventory purposes, these sticky tags also indicate how the produce was grown: conventionally, organically, or through genetic modification.

Here's how to read the stickers: Items that are conventionally grown have four-digit PLU codes that begin with the number 3 or 4, while their organically grown counterparts have codes that are five digits long and begin with the number 9. For instance, a conventionally grown banana is labeled 4011, while an organic banana is labeled 94011. Genetically modified fruits and vegetables are rare finds but can be identified by five-digit PLU codes that begin with the number 8. For instance, genetically modified bananas would be labeled 84011.

The PLU code will tell you if an item has been grown organically or conventionally.

Don't Be Foiled

Recently, I found a recipe that read, "Cover the pan with foil, shiny side down." Does it really matter which side faces up or down?

ANN DOLYNIUK
SAN FRANCISCO, CALIF.

➤ A few people in the test kitchen admitted to wondering the same thing, so we contacted Erin Griffith at the Reynolds Kitchens News Bureau in Richmond, Va., for some clarification. According to Griffith, the foil-manufacturing process creates the dull and shiny sides. In the final rolling step, two layers of aluminum foil are passed through the rolling mill at the same time. The side coming in contact with the mill's highly polished steel rolls becomes shiny. The other side, not coming in contact with the heavy rolls, comes out with a dull finish. Griffith says there is little difference between the two sides when the foil is used to cook, freeze, or store food.

To confirm this statement, we conducted three tests. First, we baked two potatoes, each of exactly the same weight, in a 350-degree oven, one wrapped in foil with the shiny side facing out, and the other with the shiny side facing in. Although we don't recommend baking potatoes in foil, we wanted to see if the heat conduction was the same. After one hour, both potatoes reached an internal temperature of 198 degrees. Next, we filled two ovensafe beakers with 71-degree water and wrapped each in foil. After 30 minutes in a 350-degree oven, the water in the beaker wrapped in foil with the shiny side facing in was 2 degrees hotter. For the final test, we baked cold mashed potatoes for 45 minutes in two 8 by 8-inch glass baking pans covered with foil. The result? The same negligible 2-degree difference. So when it comes to foil, don't worry about the shiny and dull sides.

Fishy Substance

Why does my salmon sometimes ooze a white substance when I cook it? Am I under- or overcooking it?

MARIE CLAIRE TRAN
RANCHO PALOS VERDES, CALIF.

➤ We occasionally encounter this problem in the test kitchen when cooking salmon and guessed that the unattractive ooze had something to do with overcooking. But after we pan-seared a few salmon fillets, we were surprised to find that even perfectly cooked fillets (those with opaque exteriors and traces of bright orange inside) exuded a few strands of this white material along the unseared sides. Slightly more of this matter showed up on fillets that we overcooked intentionally.

We turned to Donald Kramer, professor of seafood science at the University of Alaska, Fairbanks, for an explanation. According to Kramer, this "white curd" is composed of fish albumin, soluble proteins that are squeezed out onto the surface of the fish and coagulate once they denature during the cooking process. Most often, this curd is seen when salmon is canned, smoked, or poached.

"There's nothing harmful in it," said Kramer. "There will always be a certain amount that comes out, and how you cook it is probably not going to affect that."

The best way to check for doneness is not to wait for albumin to appear on the surface but to peek inside the fillet with the tip of a paring knife. If the salmon is opaque all the way through, the fish is clearly overdone. A little translucency is a good sign. If the look of the albumin really bothers you, use a damp paper towel to gently blot it off.

How to Boil Pasta

A friend and I have a little gentleman's wager that we would like you to settle. Is it best to cook pasta with the lid off the pot or on the pot? He argues that if you reduce the heat under the pasta pot and put a lid on it you can produce the same quality pasta as when you leave the lid off and the water is at a rolling boil. I believe that leaving the lid on will create softer pasta, but he argues that checking the pasta for doneness takes care of it.

PETER DELONG
MINNEAPOLIS, MINN.

➤ In the test kitchen, we cook pasta over high heat with the lid off, but your friend's method intrigued us. To settle your bet, we brought 4 quarts of water to a rolling boil in each of two Dutch ovens. We added 1 tablespoon salt and 1 pound spaghetti to each pot, stirring to separate the strands. Both pots were covered and allowed to return to a boil. We continued to cook one batch over high heat at a rolling boil, uncovered, stirring occasionally until al dente. The other batch was cooked in a covered pot over medium heat (to prevent the water from boiling over). We lifted the lid periodically to stir the pasta and check for doneness. The pasta in the pot with the lid on required one more minute of cooking to get to the same al dente texture. The same test performed on rigatoni yielded identical cooking times. We also found no discernible difference between the batches of hot pasta when it came to taste.

Whether you cook your pasta covered or uncovered, then, is an entirely personal choice. Because both methods require stirring and tasting to reach the preferred degree of doneness, we still prefer cooking pasta uncovered. We'd rather not fuss with a hot lid. Because both you and your friend are at least partially correct, we haven't really settled your wager. Want to make it double or nothing with another question?

What Is 'Food Grade' Plastic?

A recent local restaurant inspection by the Thurston County, Wash., Health Department, as published in the *Daily Olympian,* noted an out-of-compliance issue based on the use of a "non-food grade" plastic bag to store flour. This got our attention because we store our flour in plastic containers and wonder about the concept of "food grade plastics." Could you describe the criteria that make plastics "food grade," and especially the length of time one may safely use food grade plastic containers before they should be replaced? For example, we store our flour in a Tupperware plastic bin that has been in use for several years and wonder about any possible leaching of chemicals from the plastic into the flour.

DAVID AND JUDITH KENNEDY
OLYMPIA, WASH.

➤ We turned to Mary Keith, an extension agent in food, nutrition, and health at the Hillsborough County Cooperative Extension Service, Seffner, Fla., for an answer to your question. She explained that food grade plastic is simply plastic that was manufactured with the intent of being used with food. The ingredients in the plastic must be approved by the U.S. Food and Drug Administration to ensure that they do not leach into the food under the intended circumstances of use. A garbage bag is not intended for storing food, but a zipper-lock plastic bag is. According to Keith, storing flour in Tupperware for long periods of time is usually not a problem.

Note that you can get into trouble if you don't follow manufacturers' recommendations on the proper use of products made with food grade plastic. For instance, excessive heat can promote the leaching of chemicals in plastics into food. Make sure to read labels to see if (and how) plastic containers can be heated.

Cleaning Baking Stones

We've moved residences four times in six years and in the process lost the instructions for our baking stone. It has charred-on bits of cheese and is really black. What's the best method for cleaning it?

CAROL AND LEE AGON
PASO ROBLES, CALIF.

➤ To answer your question, we burned shredded mozzarella cheese and a raspberry-sugar mixture (akin to what might bubble out of a pie or tart) onto multiple samples of our favorite baking stone, the 16 by 14-inch stone manufactured by The Old Stone Oven. After allowing the stones to cool completely, we scraped the surfaces with a metal bench scraper to remove as much of the

charred mess as possible before testing several cleaning methods.

We divided each stone into sections, leaving one section untouched, and cleaned the others using the following methods: sanding down the stains using sandpaper, scrubbing with a scouring pad using a paste of baking soda and water and rinsing off the subsequent mixture with hot water, rinsing with hot running water while scrubbing with a scouring pad, and cleaning with an S.O.S pad and hot water (even though a number of manufacturers advise against cleaning a stone with soap for fear that it will seep into the porous material). While the sandpaper got the stones fairly smooth, small patches of rough charred material still remained. The scouring pads did a good job of removing the raised soot, but it didn't seem to matter if we used the baking soda paste with the pads or just plain hot running water; the soap-laden S.O.S pad worked on a par with the scouring pads.

To make sure that no off flavors had been picked up by the cleaned stones, we baked pizza dough on them. While the smells of the residual burnt cheese and the raspberry-sugar mixture were evident when we opened the oven door,

they did not carry over to the baked pizza dough. Nor could tasters detect off flavors from the stone cleaned with soap.

Our advice: For regular cleaning, use a scouring pad and hot water. Avoid sandpaper and don't bother using baking soda or soap. They won't hurt, but they won't help, either.

None of the cleaning methods we tested were successful in returning the stone to its original appearance. Some discoloration over time is natural, but to alleviate this problem, use parchment paper when possible and bake high-fat items such as cookies on baking sheets. It's fine to store your stone in the oven, and leaving it there will help bake off stains over time.

One last note: Leaving your stone in the oven during the self-cleaning cycle might seem like a great way to blast it clean, but there have been reports of stones (especially those that have absorbed oil) catching fire when subjected to these extreme temperatures.

Quick Tips

⩾ COMPILED BY ERIKA BRUCE ⩽

Better Blending

Oil or melted butter added to dressings or sauces in a whirring blender can splatter back up through the opening in the lid and make a mess. Chuk Campos of Livermore, Calif., found he could eliminate this problem by placing a small funnel in the opening and pouring the liquid through it slowly and steadily.

Shower Caps as DustBusters

It makes sense to store the attachments for an electric mixer inside the bowl. But doing so can also expose them to dust. Valerie Kosubenko of Chicago, Ill., designates a clean shower cap as a portable cover for the bowl and the attachments stored inside. She uses the same trick to keep dust from collecting on utensils stored upright in a crock. Whenever she's cooking or has company, all she has to do is slip off the cap and stick it in a kitchen drawer.

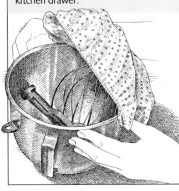

No More Sticky Garlic

Home cooks often shy away from hand-mincing garlic because it can be sticky stuff. But if a recipe leaves you no alternative, George Packard of Sherkin Island, Ireland, has a helpful tip.

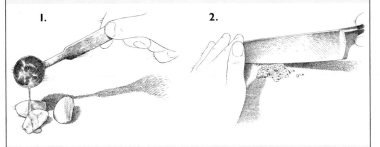

1. Sprinkle a few drops of olive or vegetable oil over the garlic.
2. Proceed to chop or mince; the oil coats the garlic and keeps it from sticking to both the knife and your hands.

Taco Tips

A. As someone who makes the *Cook's* taco recipe on a weekly basis, Courtney Humphrey of Swampscott, Mass., found a way to make the process more efficient by preparing the seasonings in packets ahead of time.

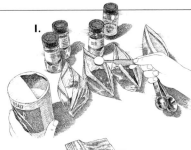

1. Combine each recipe portion of spices (2 tablespoons chili powder, 1 teaspoon ground cumin, 1 teaspoon ground coriander, ½ teaspoon dried oregano, ¼ teaspoon cayenne, and ½ teaspoon salt) in separate zipper-lock bags.
2. When it comes time to make tacos, just grab the spice mix and add it to the sautéed aromatics, with no wasted time measuring.

B. Meg van Meter of Ambler, Pa., discovered a clever way to avoid the mess of spilled taco filling, which occurs after the taco shell inevitably shatters. She lines the shell with a lettuce leaf, then adds filling and toppings. When the shell shatters, the lettuce contains the filling.

Handy Dispenser for Dishwashing Liquid

Appreciating the neatness and ease of dispensing hand soap from a small pump, Lois Lungaro of Orland Park, Ill., wanted the same ease of use for her dishwashing liquid. Her tip is especially helpful if you buy supersize bottles, which are usually a bargain but are also ungainly.

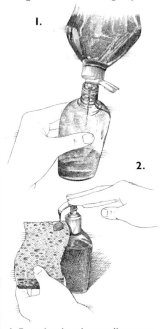

1. Recycle a hand-soap dispenser bottle by refilling it with dishwashing liquid.
2. When it comes time to wash the dishes, simply pump the desired amount of soap onto the sponge.

Extending Counter Space

Lacking the luxury of ample counter space, Linda Licker of Duncanville, Texas, often has a problem finding room for the cooling racks when baking cookies. To extend her counter space, she sets the racks directly over the sink, which has the added benefit of making it easy to clean up the crumbs that fall through the rack. (We don't recommend this tip for households with young children running about.)

Making Sure to Season Pasta

Audrey Hunter of Glendive, Mont., doesn't like to add salt to pasta water before it comes to a boil for fear of pitting her pots. But by the time it does come to a boil, she's often preoccupied with the rest of the meal and forgets to add the salt. Being no fan of unseasoned pasta, she came up with this clever solution: Add the salt to the opened box of pasta (we recommend 1 tablespoon of table salt per pound of pasta), then simply dump the contents into the boiling water.

Improving an Old Rice Cooker

Rice cookers can produce perfect rice, but they can be difficult to clean—especially as they age—whether nonstick or not. Susan Shisler of Felton, Calif., found a way to breathe some new life into her sticky old rice cooker.

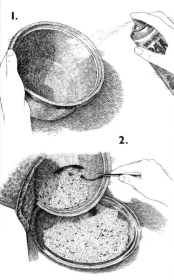

1. Spray the bottom and sides of the rice cooker bowl with cooking spray before adding the rice and water.
2. The oil will help keep the rice from sticking once cooked.

Keeping Eggs in Place

A. While assisting her mother in a baking project, 5-year-old Maura Shehan of Sherman, Texas, suggested the use of a recycled egg carton both as a container to keep the eggs from rolling off the counter and as a receptacle for the empty shells.

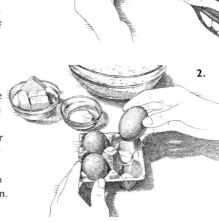

1. Trim the top and the flap from the carton, then cut the base into three sections, each able to hold up to four eggs.
2. While measuring the other ingredients of a recipe, safely store the eggs in one section and return the spent shells to the container as you use them.

B. Katherine Wong of Winnipeg, Manitoba, found a quicker fix when only one or two eggs need to be corralled. Simply nest the egg inside of a thick rubber band.

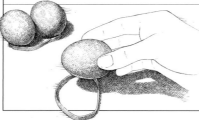

Peeling Hazelnuts

Jennifer Smiljanich of Linden, Mich., loves hazelnuts but hates to peel them. She found a way to make the process a little less painful.

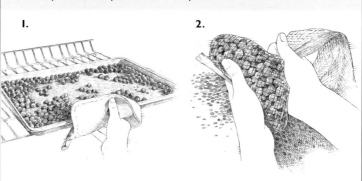

1. Toast the nuts on a rimmed baking sheet in a 350-degree oven for 10 minutes.
2. After letting the nuts cool slightly, place them in a recycled plastic mesh bag, such as the kind oranges are sold in. With both ends secured, roll the nuts between both hands over a sink or garbage can. The skins are rubbed off and dispensed with in one fell swoop.

Better Brownie Cutting

Neatly cutting brownies can be tricky because half the crumbs end up sticking to the knife, especially if the brownies are really fudgy. Callie Svenson of Tarpon Springs, Fla., found a neat remedy. Instead of using a serrated or chef's knife, she uses a sturdy plastic knife. It glides easily through even the stickiest brownies, picking up no crumbs.

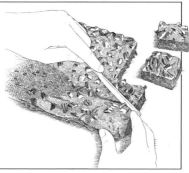

A New Use for Coffee Filters

Hazel Marx of Hubertus, Wis., found a clever use for the larger basket-type coffee filters. When she needs to blind-bake a pie shell, she uses a filter to contain the pie weights.

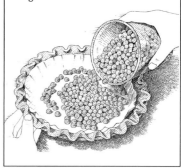

Storing Ginger

In a September/October 2004 quick tip, reader Susan Brown suggested storing fresh ginger in the freezer to extend its shelf life. Grace Stevens of San Mateo, Calif., offered an alternate method.

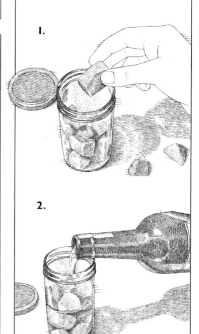

1. Peel and cut the ginger into 1-inch pieces and place in a canning or other glass jar.
2. Fill the jar with sherry, cover with an airtight lid, and store in the refrigerator for up to six months. This technique not only preserves the ginger but gives you ginger-flavored sherry to use in Asian recipes.

Reconstructing Stuffed Roast Chicken

Could kitchen shears and some aluminum foil origami eliminate overcooked meat, stingy amounts of undercooked stuffing, and the need for trussing?

> BY SANDRA WU

Stuffed roast chicken should be the culinary equivalent of a power couple. Each partner brings a lot to the table, and this marriage represents the ultimate symbiotic relationship—at least in theory. The stuffing elevates the roast chicken beyond common everyday fare, while the chicken lends flavor and moisture to what would otherwise be dry bread crumbs. And, unlike roast turkey, its bigger and more complicated cousin, stuffed roast chicken should be simple. But stuffed roast chicken often doesn't deliver. What you get instead is either a perfectly cooked bird filled with lukewarm stuffing (hello, salmonella!) or safe-to-eat stuffing packed in parched poultry. I also wanted more than a few tablespoons of stuffing per person, a problem given the small cavity of a roasting chicken, even one weighing in at more than 5 pounds. No wonder most home cooks ask for a trial separation when it comes to this everyday recipe.

We've roasted literally thousands of chickens in the test kitchen and made more than our fair share of stuffing. It will come as no surprise, then, that I immediately decided to brine the bird before stuffing and roasting it. This was the only way to ensure moist, flavorful white meat. Next I was on to the stuffing, and my initial tests revolved around the traditional stuff 'n truss method used in turkey preparation. This technique was an abject failure. When I packed the chicken loosely with stuffing, I ended up with a miserly 1½ cups. I then packed the chicken until it nearly burst (about 3 cups), first heating the stuffing to 145 degrees in a microwave to give it a head start. But the stuffing still did not reach the safe temperature of 165 degrees by the time the meat was done. Apparently, fully cooked stuffing meant overcooked breast meat.

Our unorthodox method for "stuffing" a big chicken cuts the roasting time in half.

Switching Gears

A few years back, the test kitchen developed a method for high-roast chicken that started with a butterflied bird. (The backbone is removed and the bird is flattened and then roasted at 500 degrees.) I figured it was worth a try. I began with a flattened, brined bird and placed it on top of a broiler pan with 3 cups of stuffing directly beneath the chicken and another 5 cups in the bottom of the pan. After an hour, the skin on the chicken was crisp and evenly browned and the meat mostly moist. Finally, I had enough stuffing (at a safe 165 degrees) to feed a crowd, but now it suffered from a dual identity. The stuffing underneath the cavity was cohesive, while its counterpart in the bottom of the pan was dry and crunchy. When I tried placing all of the stuffing in the bottom of the pan (not directly beneath the chicken), it became greasy. In addition, the chicken (technically speaking) was not stuffed.

For my next test, I replaced the broiler pan with a traditional roasting pan and piled a mound of stuffing into it before placing a splayed butterflied chicken on top. After about an hour at 500 degrees, the chicken was slightly dry and the stuffing had many burnt bits. At 425 degrees, the chicken skin browned less evenly, but the stuffing was moist and cohesive. Tasters agreed that 450 degrees yielded the best results, although the stuffing was still charred in some areas and was greasy from the rendered fat.

To solve these two problems, I began a series of tests that eventually culminated in a strange version of culinary origami. First, I placed the stuffing inside an 8-inch square baking dish upon which the butterflied chicken perched; the whole thing then went into a roasting pan. Because the splayed chicken extended partially over the top of the baking dish, I hoped most of the fat from the skin would drip into the roasting pan rather than into the stuffing, but this was not the case. Next, I turned to aluminum foil, creating a packet around the stuffing that I poked with holes so the chicken juices could irrigate the dry contents. Sure, this stuffing was moist, but it lacked color and texture because it was shielded from the oven's dry heat. Finally, I made an aluminum foil bowl, mounded the stuffing into it, and placed the chicken on top, snugly encasing the stuffing. After about an hour of roasting, with a single pan rotation in between, the stuffing was browned and chewy on the bottom as well as moist and flavorful throughout from the juices. The fat from the skin was deposited directly into the roasting pan, never even touching the stuffing. Even though the roasting pan was hot, I could easily grab the foil bowl with my bare hands and dump the stuffing in one fell swoop into a serving bowl. Good technique and cleanup, all in one!

The Right Stuff

It was time to get serious about stuffing. An informal poll in the test kitchen revealed that most people wanted a jazzed-up version of a traditional bread stuffing. I obliged by replacing the typical onion with thinly sliced leek, adding the requisite celery, and throwing in some chopped mushrooms for additional texture and substance. A dose of minced garlic, fresh sage and parsley, and chicken broth finished my recipe.

With a roasting technique and stuffing recipes now in place, I had finally managed to turn stuffed roast chicken into a successful marriage.

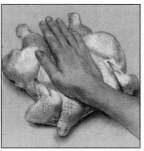

1. Cut through bones on either side of backbone, then remove and discard backbone.

2. Flip chicken over and use heel of hand to flatten breastbone. Tuck tips of wings behind back.

3. Stack two 12-inch squares of foil on top of each other. Fold edges to construct 8 by 6-inch bowl.

4. Coat inside of foil bowl with nonstick cooking spray and pack stuffing into bowl.

5. Position chicken over stuffing. Adjust edges of foil bowl to fit shape of chicken cavity.

"STUFFED" ROAST BUTTERFLIED CHICKEN
SERVES 4

Use a traditional (not nonstick) roasting pan to prepare this recipe; the dark finish of a nonstick pan may cause the stuffing to overbrown. If using a kosher chicken, skip step 1.

- ½ cup table salt
- 1 whole chicken (5 to 6 pounds), trimmed of excess fat, giblets discarded
- 1 teaspoon vegetable or olive oil
  Ground black pepper
- 1 recipe stuffing (recipe follows)

1. Dissolve salt in 2 quarts cold water in large container. Immerse chicken and refrigerate until fully seasoned, about 1 hour.

2. Adjust oven rack to lower-middle position; heat oven to 450 degrees. Remove chicken from brine and rinse under cold running water; pat dry with paper towels. Butterfly chicken, flatten breastbone, and tuck wings behind back (see illustrations 1 and 2). Rub skin with oil and sprinkle with pepper.

3. Following illustrations 3 through 5, construct foil bowl, spray inside of bowl with nonstick cooking spray, and place bowl in roasting pan. Gently mound and pack stuffing into foil bowl and position chicken over stuffing (chicken should extend past edges of bowl so that most of fat renders into roasting pan, not into foil bowl). Roast chicken until just beginning to brown, about 30 minutes. Rotate pan and continue to roast until skin is crisped and deep golden brown and instant-read thermometer registers 160 degrees in thickest part of breast, 175 degrees in thickest part of thigh, and 165 degrees in stuffing, 25 to 35 minutes longer. Using tongs, transfer chicken to cutting board; let rest 10 minutes.

4. While chicken rests, transfer stuffing from foil bowl to serving bowl; fluff stuffing with spoon. Cover stuffing with foil to keep warm. Carve chicken and serve with stuffing.

MUSHROOM-LEEK BREAD STUFFING WITH HERBS

The dried bread cubes for this stuffing can be stored in an airtight container for up to 1 week.

- 6 ounces white sandwich bread (about 6 slices), cut into ¼-inch cubes (about 5 cups)
- 2 tablespoons unsalted butter
- 1 small leek, halved lengthwise, rinsed thoroughly, white and light green parts cut crosswise into ⅛-inch slices (about 1 cup)
- 1 small celery rib, chopped fine (about ¾ cup)
- 8 ounces button mushrooms, cleaned and chopped medium (about 2½ cups)
- 1 large garlic clove, minced or pressed through garlic press (about 1½ teaspoons)
- ½ teaspoon minced fresh sage leaves (or ¼ teaspoon dried)
- ½ teaspoon minced fresh thyme leaves (or ¼ teaspoon dried)
- ¼ cup minced fresh parsley leaves
- 1 large egg
- ½ cup plus 2 tablespoons low-sodium chicken broth
- ½ teaspoon table salt
- ½ teaspoon ground black pepper

1. Adjust oven rack to middle position; heat oven to 250 degrees. Spread bread cubes in single layer on baking sheet; bake until thoroughly dried but not browned, about 30 minutes, stirring once halfway through baking time.

2. Meanwhile, heat butter in 12-inch skillet over medium-high heat; when foam subsides, add leek, celery, and mushrooms and cook, stirring occasionally, until vegetables begin to soften, about 4 minutes. Add garlic and continue to cook, stirring frequently, until vegetables begin to brown, 2 to 3 minutes. Stir in sage, thyme, and parsley and cook until fragrant, about 1 minute.

3. Whisk egg, broth, salt, and pepper in large bowl until combined. Add bread cubes and leek/mushroom mixture; toss gently until evenly moistened and combined. Set aside.

TASTING: **Roaster Chickens**

When tasting broiler/fryer chickens (weighing 3 to 4 pounds), we have found that spending a little more for a "premium" or kosher bird pays off. Does the same hold true for roasting chickens, which are older birds that tip the scales at 5 to 7 pounds? To find out, we gathered a representative selection. Because kosher birds are salted during processing, we brined the three other chickens to level the playing field.

Tasters did not like the mass-market roaster (from Perdue) or the supermarket sample (from Shaw's). Both birds were lacking in chicken flavor and were mushier than our favorites: the kosher bird (from Empire) and the premium bird (from Bell & Evans). These were praised for their authentic chicken flavor and superior texture. Our advice: If your market sells a kosher or premium roaster, buy it. –Garth Clingingsmith

RECOMMENDED

➤EMPIRE Kosher Frozen Roasting Chicken $1.99/lb.
The overwhelming favorite was deemed the juiciest and most flavorful. Tasters liked its "roasted flavor." Don't brine this bird.

➤BELL & EVANS Large Roaster $2.29/lb.
Tasters praised this juicy, "buttery" bird, which has a milder flavor than our top choice. Brine this bird for best results.

NOT RECOMMENDED

➤SHAW'S (Supermarket) Whole Young Chicken $1.59/lb.
This nearly flavorless "plain Jane" chicken offended no one, but some tasters disliked the "mushy," "prechewed" texture.

➤PERDUE Oven Stuffer Fresh Whole Roaster $1.79/lb.
Tasters objected to "metallic" flavors and "spongy" breast meat, which seemed to "crumble."

Pan-Roasted Asparagus

Is it possible to get great grilled flavor from a simple stovetop recipe?

⇒ BY SEAN LAWLER ⇐

Although I consider grilling to be the ultimate method for cooking asparagus, there are plenty of rainy Tuesday nights when asparagus is on the menu. Rather than waste time heating a finicky broiler, I was hoping that a simple stovetop method might deliver crisp, nicely browned spears.

I turned up several promising recipes, but the results were disappointing. In most cases, the spears were indeed browned but also limp, greasy, and shriveled. Equally daunting was the logistics of cooking enough asparagus to feed four people. All the recipes I consulted suggested laying the spears out in a single layer, then individually rotating them to ensure even browning. This seemed like a lot of meticulous fuss for one measly bunch of asparagus, which, with these restrictions, was all I could fit into a 12-inch pan.

After testing different-sized spears, heat levels, pan types, and cooking fats, a few things became clear. As in grilling, the thinner spears would have to be eliminated. They overcooked so quickly that there was no way to get a proper sear. Selecting thicker spears helped to solve this problem, but I was still a long way from getting them to brown properly. Over moderate heat, the spears took so long to develop a crisp, browned exterior that they overcooked. But cranking up the burner was not a good alternative—the spears skipped brown altogether and went straight to spotty and blackened.

I knew that in restaurants line cooks blanch off pounds of asparagus before service, then toss them into the pan or onto the grill to order for a quick sear. They do this primarily to save time, but I wondered if parcooking would also enhance browning. I tried searing some asparagus spears that had first been quickly blanched in boiling water. Sure enough, they quickly developed a crisp, golden brown crust.

Our science editor explained that the exterior of raw asparagus is dry and waxy, and the sugars necessary for browning reactions are locked up inside the plant's tough cell walls. Some cooking is required to release these sugars, as is the case with sliced onions, which need to sweat before they caramelize. I was reluctant to call for this extra step, but what if covering the pan at the start of the cooking would have the same effect?

I cooked two more batches, covering the skillets for the first five minutes and adding a few tablespoons of water to one of them. The latter batch was definitely steamed, but the extra moisture inhibited its browning after I removed the lid. The asparagus in the other skillet, which had contained nothing besides olive oil, steamed very little. When I replaced the oil with butter, however, the results were quite different: A small cloud of steam escaped the pan when the lid was lifted, and the asparagus had softened and turned bright green. Evidently, the small amount of moisture in the butter (while olive oil is 100 percent fat, butter is roughly 20 percent water) was enough to start steaming the asparagus, which then began to release its own moisture to help the process along. Tasters eventually agreed that a mixture of olive oil and butter provided the best combination of flavor and browning.

Once the lid was removed, however, it was a race against the clock to try to get all the spears turned and evenly browned before they overcooked and turned limp. Even with very thick asparagus, it was a race I almost always lost. In the course of this round of tests, however, I made a fortunate discovery. Citing the pleasing contrast of textures, tasters actually preferred the spears that were browned on only one side and remained bright green on the other—and these half-browned spears never went limp.

This finding also helped to solve the problem of how to fit more asparagus into the skillet. The rationale behind not crowding the pan—it causes the food to steam and brown unevenly—no longer applied. In fact, it was precisely the result I was after. Carefully positioning the asparagus in the pan also helped. A better fit and better browning were possible with half of the spears pointed in one direction and the other half pointed in the opposite direction. Now just an occasional toss was enough to ensure that all the spears became partially browned.

PAN-ROASTED ASPARAGUS

SERVES 3 TO 4

This recipe works best with asparagus that is at least ½ inch thick near the base. If using thinner spears, reduce the covered cooking time to 3 minutes and the uncovered cooking time to 5 minutes. Do not use pencil-thin asparagus; it cannot withstand the heat and overcooks too easily.

- 1 tablespoon olive oil
- 1 tablespoon unsalted butter
- 2 pounds thick asparagus spears (see note), ends trimmed

Kosher salt and ground black pepper
- ½ lemon (optional)

1. Heat oil and butter in 12-inch skillet over medium-high heat. When butter has melted, add half of asparagus to skillet with tips pointed in one direction; add remaining spears with tips pointed in opposite direction. Using tongs, distribute spears in even layer (spears will not quite fit into single layer); cover and cook until asparagus is bright green and still crisp, about 5 minutes.

2. Uncover and increase heat to high; season asparagus with salt and pepper. Cook until spears are tender and well browned along one side, 5 to 7 minutes, using tongs to occasionally move spears from center of pan to edge of pan to ensure all are browned. Transfer asparagus to serving dish, adjust seasonings with salt and pepper, and, if desired, squeeze lemon half over spears. Serve immediately.

PAN-ROASTED ASPARAGUS WITH TOASTED GARLIC AND PARMESAN

Heat 2 tablespoons olive oil and 3 medium garlic cloves, sliced thin, in 12-inch skillet over medium heat; cook, stirring occasionally, until garlic is crisp and golden but not dark brown, about 5 minutes. Using slotted spoon, transfer garlic to paper towel–lined plate. Follow recipe for Pan-Roasted Asparagus, adding butter to oil in skillet. After transferring asparagus to serving dish, sprinkle with 2 tablespoons grated Parmesan, toasted garlic, and lemon juice; adjust seasonings and serve immediately.

PAN-ROASTED ASPARAGUS WITH WARM ORANGE-ALMOND VINAIGRETTE

Heat 2 tablespoons olive oil in 12-inch skillet over medium heat until shimmering; add ¼ cup slivered almonds and cook, stirring frequently, until golden, about 5 minutes. Add ½ cup fresh orange juice and 1 teaspoon chopped fresh thyme; increase heat to medium-high and simmer until thickened, about 4 minutes. Off heat, stir in 2 tablespoons minced shallot, 2 tablespoons sherry vinegar, and salt and pepper to taste; transfer vinaigrette to small bowl. Wipe out skillet; follow recipe for Pan-Roasted Asparagus. After transferring asparagus to serving dish, pour vinaigrette over and toss to combine; adjust seasonings and serve immediately.

The Problem with Sautéed Fish Fillets

A sautéed fish fillet needs a pan sauce to turn it into a satisfying main course.
The problem is coordinating the cooking so that both are done perfectly.

⇒ BY BRIDGET LANCASTER ⇐

I had always thought of sautéed fish as a slam-dunk supper: A hot skillet, a squeeze of lemon, and dinner is served. After further examination, I realized there is a lot to consider. First of all, there's the daunting task of fish selection. With the myriad choices of fillets versus steaks, thick versus thin, and endless species, fish shopping is akin to choosing an insurance policy. Next—let's face it—fish without a pan sauce can be boring. But getting a hot pan sauce and hot fish on the table at the same time isn't so easy. The fish (especially thin fillets) cools down quickly. All of this sounded like a case of swimming upstream, but, in typical test kitchen style, I decided to start at the beginning.

What's the Catch?

I headed to the seafood counter at my local supermarket to view the offerings. The grouper looked good, so I ordered four fillets, which seemed like a reasonable amount to fit into my large skillet. Maybe my eyes shouldn't have wandered off to the two-for-one sale on baked beans, because what I got wasn't what I ordered. Instead of four individual fillets, I unwrapped four 18-inch pieces of grouper (perhaps the large size and weight of the package should have been a tip-off). After calling the market to complain, I was told that four fillets was, in fact, exactly what I got. Evidently, in the fishmonger's lingo, "fillet" means just about any cut section from a whole side of fish. Lesson learned.

Apparently, I hadn't been clear enough, so next time I wrote down exactly what I wanted, mustered a bit of confidence, and marched back to the supermarket. "Four 5-ounce haddock fillets," I said to the man at the counter (haddock was on sale). He reached for a huge piece of fish that was nearly 1 inch thick at one end and thin as a pancake at the other. That wouldn't do. "Nope. I want only fillets that are around ½ inch thick, small enough to fit four in a skillet." So

To keep fish from falling apart, always use a wide offset spatula to remove fillets from the pan. A slotted plastic spatula lets excess fat drip away and won't scratch nonstick surfaces.

guess what? He cut four ½-inch fillets from the center section of the haddock and wrapped them up. What's the moral of the story? Know what you want, and don't be afraid to ask for it.

However, if your market sells only whole sides that vary in thickness, there's no need to panic (or walk away), especially if the fish looks fresh. Ask the fishmonger to cut the fish into pieces that are roughly the same weight (or do this yourself; see "Downsizing a Large Fillet," page 10). To even out the cooking time between the thick and thin pieces, fold the thinner piece (which invariably comes from the tail end) in half. I found that a simple nick and tuck (see "Tucking the Tail," page 11) could turn a too-thin tail into a meaty fillet thick enough to cook right alongside the center-cut fillets.

Gone Fishin'

Getting the fish you want is no easy task. Fish may be sold in small pieces and called "fillets," or they may be sold by the whole side and still be referred to as "fillets." Armed with a little knowledge, you can pick out the right catch of the day with ease. Here are descriptions of the white fish (appropriate for our recipe) that you are likely to encounter at the market, along with tips for buying them.

The Cut If possible, have the fishmonger cut out the fillets from the whole side. Usually, the center part of the side will yield at least 4 fillets. Most markets will cut and weigh fillets to your specifications.

The Thickness To ensure evenly cooked fillets, order and buy fillets that are the same thickness. A panful of thin fillets will cook more evenly than a pan containing a mix of thick and thin.

About Thin Fillets If the fish selection is limited, you can "cheat" by folding paper-thin fish fillets (often flounder or sole) in half. Their larger girth will cook more evenly alongside thicker fillets.

Flavor Key Flavor can run from mild to downright fishy. Here's how to buy fish that matches your personal preference.

mild	🐟
medium	🐟🐟
assertive	🐟🐟🐟

FISH	THICKNESS	FLAVOR
Catfish	1 – 1 ½"	🐟🐟🐟
Cod	¾ – 1 ½"	🐟🐟
Flounder	¼ – ½"	🐟
Grouper	¾ – 1 ¼"	🐟🐟
Haddock	¾ – 1 ½"	🐟🐟
Hake	¾ – 1 ½"	🐟🐟
Monkfish	1 – 1 ½"	🐟🐟🐟
Orange Roughy	¾ – 1 ½"	🐟🐟🐟
Perch	¼ – ¾"	🐟
Red Snapper	¾ – 1"	🐟🐟🐟
Sea Bass	¾ – 1 ½"	🐟🐟🐟
Sole	¼ – ½"	🐟
Tilapia	¾ – 1"	🐟🐟🐟

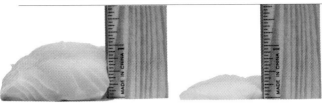

THICK   THIN

Depending on the thickness of the fillet, you will need to adjust the cooking time. We recommend that you get out a ruler before you cook. The fillet on the left is nearly 1 inch thick and will need 5 to 7 minutes of cooking time. The fillet on the right is just over ¼ inch thick and will need only 2½ to 4 minutes of cooking time.

Casting Tradition Aside

Back in the kitchen, I began working on the sauté. Wanting a bit of a browned crust on the fish, I tried sautéing it with and without a coating of flour. The flour added just the right amount of crust (not too tough) and color, but it didn't always adhere properly. I discovered that by seasoning the fish with salt and pepper and then letting it sit for a few moments before flouring, moisture in the fish would bead to the surface, helping the flour to adhere.

As for size, I found that anything thinner than ¼ inch would fall apart and should not be sautéed. I also found that fillets between ¼ inch and 1 inch thick could be cooked in the same way (a bit longer on the first side, less on the second side). (Very thick fillets—more than 1 inch—require a different cooking method, including some oven time, so I excluded them from further testing.)

Most recipes for sautéed fish with pan sauce call for slightly undercooking the fish, removing it from the pan, making the sauce, and then tossing the fish back into the sauce to finish cooking. This method bordered on acceptable; the tender fish began to flake apart around the edges by the time it was reheated, and the crisp outer layer was history. Next I followed the same procedure but finished with the fillets and sauce in a hot oven. Once again, the fish fell apart as soon as it was served, and the whole dish was a mess.

Out of necessity comes invention, or so I reasoned. What if I had the pan sauce waiting on the fish instead of the other way around? Unlike a steak, for example, the fish was not creating a *fond* (browned bits on the bottom of the pan) that was going to contribute a lot of flavor. (Because I was using a nonstick skillet, the fond

formation would be minimal even with beef or pork.) I made a sauce in a separate saucepan and kept it on a low burner while I cooked the fish. As soon as the last side was sautéed, I placed the fish on a plate, spooned the sauce over it, and proceeded to enjoy juicy, hot-from-the-skillet fish. Ta-da!

Deduce and (Lightly) Reduce

Another benefit of making the sauce first was that I could take a bit more time (up to five minutes or so) to reduce liquids (such as wine) to concentrate flavors. Because I didn't have to worry about the fish cooling off, I could give the sauces a bit more attention. Brightness was added via vinegar and citrus, and garlic and shallots added bite and depth. But I had one more surprise ahead of me. During one test, I neglected to reduce the liquids to a classic, thick consistency. Still full of concentrated flavor, these lighter, brothy sauces were much better suited to thin, delicate fish fillets. All that was left to do was please my tasters by making plenty of sauce—enough for the fish and whatever else was served on the side.

In addition to three reduction sauces (one with white wine, one with orange juice and cream, and one with coconut milk), I also developed a simple grapefruit vinaigrette, which is perhaps the easiest sauce of all, as it requires no cooking.

SAUTÉED WHITE FISH FILLETS
SERVES 4

When it comes to the size of a fish fillet, there are generally two categories: thick and thin. Thickness determines in part how long the fillet must be cooked. For the purpose of this recipe, we are putting fillets ⅝ inch to 1 inch thick in the thick category. To serve four, try to select four 6-ounce fillets; alternatively, use six 4-ounce fillets. In the thin category are fillets ¼ inch to ½ inch thick. If the fillets are small (about 3 ounces each), use eight; if they are slightly larger (about 4 ounces each), use six. Do not use fillets thinner than ¼ inch, as they will overcook very quickly. Note that the sauce recipes are meant to be prepared before the fish fillets are cooked. The sauce is then held until serving.

½ cup all-purpose flour
4–6 boneless, skinless thick fish fillets (4 to 6 ounces each; see note)
OR
6–8 boneless, skinless thin fish fillets (3 to 4 ounces each; see note)
Table salt and ground black pepper
3 tablespoons vegetable oil

1. Place flour in baking dish or pie plate. Pat fish fillets dry with paper towels. Season both sides of each fillet with salt and pepper; let stand until fillets are glistening with moisture, about 5 minutes. If using any tail-end fillets, score and tuck tail under, following illustrations on page 11. Coat both sides of fillets with flour, shake off excess, and place in single layer on baking sheet.

2. Heat 2 tablespoons oil in 12-inch nonstick skillet over high heat until shimmering but not smoking; place half of fillets in skillet in single layer and immediately reduce heat to medium-high. *For thick fillets:* Cook, without moving fish, until edges of fillets are opaque and bottoms are golden brown, 3 to 4 minutes. *For thin fillets:* Cook, without moving fish, until edges of fillets are opaque and bottoms are lightly browned, 2 to 3 minutes.

3. Using spatula, gently flip fillets. *For thick fillets:* Cook on second side until thickest part of fillets is firm to touch and fish flakes easily (see page 11), 2 to 3 minutes. *For thin fillets:* Cook on second side until thickest part of fillets is firm to touch and fish flakes easily (see page 11), 30 to 60 seconds.

4. Transfer fillets to serving platter and tent with foil. Add remaining 1 tablespoon oil to skillet, increase heat to high, and heat until oil is shimmering but not smoking; repeat steps 2 and 3 to cook remaining fillets.

5. Place second batch of fillets on platter with first batch; tilt platter to discard any accumulated liquid. Serve fish immediately with sauce.

WHITE WINE–SHALLOT SAUCE WITH LEMON AND CAPERS
MAKES ABOUT 1 CUP

One tablespoon of lemon juice is cooked into the sauce; an additional tablespoon can be added later, if desired, for a bright, tart flavor.

2 teaspoons vegetable oil
2 large shallots, minced (about ½ cup)
½ cup dry white wine
1–2 tablespoons juice from 1 lemon (see note), plus lemon wedges for serving
4 tablespoons cold unsalted butter
1 tablespoon capers, rinsed and drained
1 tablespoon chopped fresh parsley leaves
Table salt and ground black pepper

Fish fillets are sold in a range of sizes, and you may need to cut them down to fit into the pan. Use a sharp chef's or boning knife to cut the fillet into pieces of equal weight. Or ask your fishmonger to cut the fillet for you. At home, tuck the thin tail piece according to the illustrations on page 1

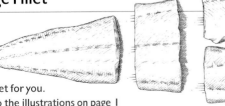

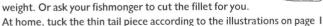

1. Heat oil in medium saucepan over medium heat until shimmering but not smoking; add shallots and cook, stirring frequently, until softened and beginning to color, about 1½ minutes. Add wine and 1 tablespoon lemon juice, increase heat to high, and bring to boil; boil until reduced to ¾ cup, 3 to 5 minutes. Remove saucepan from burner, whisk in butter, capers, parsley, and, if desired, remaining 1 tablespoon lemon juice until combined; season to taste with salt and pepper. Cover to keep warm and set aside, stirring once after about 1 minute.

2. To serve, stir sauce to recombine and spoon ½ cup over fish. Serve immediately with lemon wedges, passing remaining sauce separately.

ORANGE-TARRAGON SAUCE WITH CREAM
MAKES ABOUT I CUP

We like the delicate, fruity flavor of champagne vinegar in this sauce, but white wine vinegar can also be used.

- 2 teaspoons vegetable oil
- I medium shallot, minced (about 3 tablespoons)
- I cup juice from 2 medium oranges
- 3 tablespoons champagne vinegar
- ¼ cup heavy cream
- 2 tablespoons cold unsalted butter
- I tablespoon chopped fresh tarragon leaves
  Table salt and ground black pepper
  Orange wedges for serving

1. Heat oil in medium saucepan over medium heat until shimmering but not smoking; add shallot and cook, stirring frequently, until softened and beginning to color, about 1½ minutes. Add orange juice and vinegar, increase heat to high, and bring to boil; boil until reduced to ¾ cup, 4 to 6 minutes. Add heavy cream and continue to cook until slightly reduced, about 1 minute. Remove saucepan from burner, whisk in butter and tarragon until combined; season to taste with salt and pepper. Cover to keep warm; set aside, stirring once after about 1 minute.

2. To serve, stir sauce to recombine and spoon ½ cup over fish. Serve immediately with orange wedges, passing remaining sauce separately.

GRAPEFRUIT-LIME VINAIGRETTE WITH MINT AND CHIVES
MAKES ABOUT ½ CUP

Make sure to remove all white pith and membranes from grapefruit sections destined for garnishing the fish.

- 2 tablespoons juice from ½ pink grapefruit, remaining half cut into sections for serving
- 2 tablespoons juice from I to 2 limes
- I medium shallot, minced (about 3 tablespoons)
- I teaspoon honey

- 6 tablespoons extra-virgin olive oil
- I tablespoon chopped fresh mint leaves
- I tablespoon chopped fresh chives
  Table salt and ground black pepper

1. Combine grapefruit and lime juices, shallot, and honey in medium bowl. Whisking constantly, gradually add olive oil; add mint and chives and season to taste with salt and pepper. Set aside while cooking fish.

2. To serve, whisk vinaigrette to recombine; drizzle vinaigrette over fish fillets and serve immediately with grapefruit sections.

COCONUT–RED CURRY SAUCE
MAKES ABOUT I CUP

For those who like assertive flavors, the amount of red curry paste can be doubled; in this case, be conservative when seasoning with salt and pepper.

- 2 teaspoons vegetable oil
- I small garlic clove, minced or pressed through garlic press (about ¾ teaspoon)
- 2 teaspoons minced fresh ginger
- 2 teaspoons red curry paste (see note)
- ½ teaspoon light brown sugar
- I cup coconut milk
- I½ tablespoons juice from I lime
- 2 teaspoons fish sauce
- 3 tablespoons water
- I tablespoon chopped fresh cilantro leaves
  Table salt and ground black pepper
  Lime wedges for serving

1. Heat oil in medium saucepan over medium heat until shimmering but not smoking; off heat, add garlic, ginger, curry paste, and sugar and cook, stirring constantly, until fragrant, about 30 seconds. Add coconut milk, lime juice, fish sauce, and water; increase heat to high and bring to boil;

TECHNIQUE
TUCKING THE TAIL

I. With sharp knife, cut halfway through flesh crosswise 2 to 3 inches from tail end. This will create seam to fold tail under.

2. Fold tail end under to create fillet of relatively even thickness.

boil until sauce is reduced to about 1 cup, about 3 minutes. Off heat, stir in cilantro and season to taste with salt and pepper. Cover to keep warm and set aside; stir once after about 1 minute.

2. To serve, stir sauce to recombine and spoon ½ cup over fish. Serve immediately with lime wedges, passing remaining sauce separately.

When Is It Done?

HALF-COOKED   **PERFECTLY COOKED**   **OVERCOOKED**

To make sure that the fish is cooked just right, use a paring knife to peek inside. If the flesh is still translucent (left), the fish is not yet done. If the flesh is opaque and flaky but still juicy (middle), the fish is ready to come out of the pan. If the flesh looks dry and falls apart (right), the fish has been overcooked.

Simplifying Tortilla Soup

An 'authentic' tortilla soup requires a trip to a Latin market and an afternoon in the kitchen.
We had just one hour and limited our grocery shopping to the local Price Chopper.

≥ BY REBECCA HAYS ≤

During my last trip to Mexico, I ate *Sopa de Tortilla* nearly every night. A meal in a bowl, this spicy chicken-tomato broth overflowing with garnishes (fried tortilla strips, crumbled cheese, diced avocado, and lime wedges) always satisfied with intensely rich flavors and contrasting textures. In essence, it's a turbocharged, south-of-the-border chicken soup. Returning home, I quickly rounded up some recipes only to find my enthusiasm fading as fast as my tan. *Cotija? Epazote? Crema?* Authentic recipes called for at least one, if not several, uniquely Mexican ingredients, none of which I was going to find at my local market in Boston. In addition, this recipe demanded a major investment of time; making homemade chicken stock and frying tortilla strips seemed beyond the pale for a weeknight soup.

Just to get my bearings, I did make a few of these authentic recipes (after a long hunt for ingredients). They tasted great, but the preparation was arduous at best. Yet when I cooked up a few "Americanized" recipes, I ended up with watery brews of store-bought chicken broth and canned tomatoes topped with stodgy, off-the-shelf tortilla chips. Quick, but definitely not what I would call great-tasting.

Crisp strips of oven-fried corn tortillas add crunch and heft to a bowl of potent Mexican chicken soup flavored with chiles, tomatoes, and fresh herbs.

Back to Basics

I started anew and broke the soup down into its three classic components: a flavor base made with fresh tomatoes, garlic, onion, and chiles; chicken stock; and an array of garnishes, including fried tortilla strips. I zeroed in on the flavor base first, recalling that the best of the soups I had made called for a basic Mexican cooking technique in which the vegetables are charred on a *comal*, or griddle, then pureed and fried to create a concentrated paste that flavors the soup.

Without a *comal* in the test kitchen, I used a cast-iron skillet for charring, and the results were superb, even with mediocre supermarket tomatoes. The downside was that it took 25 attentive minutes to complete the task. I wondered if I could skip charring altogether by adding smoke-flavored dried chiles to a puree of raw tomatoes, onion, and garlic. (I used *guajillo* chiles, which are often used

to spice up tortilla soup.) The answer was yes, but toasting and grinding these hard-to-find chiles didn't bring me any closer to a quick and easy recipe. Chipotle chiles (smoked jalapeños) seemed like a more practical choice. Canned in a vinegary tomato mixture called adobo sauce, chipotles pack heat, roasted smoky flavor, and, more important, convenience. I also found that aggressively frying the raw tomatoes, onion, and chipotle puree over high heat forced all of the water out of the mixture and further concentrated its flavor.

Taking Stock

With the vegetable-charring step eliminated, I moved on to the chicken stock. Yes, the test kitchen does have an excellent recipe for homemade stock, but I was hoping to move this recipe into the express lane. The obvious alternative was

to "doctor" low-sodium canned chicken broth, especially since this soup is awash with so many other vibrant flavors. I tried cooking chicken in canned broth bolstered with onion and garlic, reasoning that the chicken would release and take on flavor while it poached. (I chose bone-in chicken as it has more flavor than boneless.) Split chicken breasts poached in just 20 minutes and could then be shredded and stirred back into the soup before serving. (Rich-flavored chicken thighs are an equally good choice, but, if poorly trimmed, they can turn the soup greasy.) Cooked this way, the chicken retained its juiciness and tender texture and the broth was nicely flavored.

Every authentic recipe for tortilla soup calls for fresh epazote, a common Mexican herb that imparts a heady, distinctive flavor and fragrance to the broth. Unfortunately, while epazote is widely available in the Southwest, it is virtually nonexistent in the Northeast. Still, I managed to track some down for testing purposes. Its wild, pungent flavor is difficult to describe, but after careful tasting I decided that it most closely resembles fresh cilantro, mint, and oregano. Using a broth steeped with epazote as a control, I sampled broths made with each of these herbs. The winner was a pairing of strong, warm oregano with pungent cilantro. It was not identical to the flavor of epazote, but it scored highly for its intensity and complexity. I now had deeply flavored broth that when stirred together with the tomato mixture made for a soup that was starting to taste like the real thing.

Last but Not Least

Flour tortillas, whether fried or oven-baked, tasted fine on their own but quickly disintegrated in hot soup. That left me with corn tortillas. The classic preparation is frying, but cooking up two or three batches of corn tortilla strips took more time and attention than I wanted to muster. Tasters flatly rejected the notion of raw corn tortillas—a recommendation I found in more than one recipe—as they rapidly turned gummy and unpalatable when added to the hot soup. Corn tortillas require some sort of crisping.

After much testing, I came across a technique in a low-fat cookbook that was both fast and easy: Lightly oiled tortilla strips are simply toasted in the oven. The result? Chips that are just as crisp, less greasy, and much less trouble to prepare than their fried cousins.

As for the garnishes, I worked through the list one ingredient at a time. Lime added sharp, fresh notes to an already complex bowl, as did cilantro leaves and minced jalapeño. Avocado was another no-brainer. Thick, tart Mexican *crema* (a tangy, cultured cream) is normally swirled into individual soup bowls, too. If it's unavailable, sour cream is a natural stand-in. Crumbled cotija or queso fresco cheese is great but hard to find. *Cotija* (the test kitchen favorite) is sharp and rich, while *queso fresco* is mild and milky. If you can't find cotija, use Monterey Jack, which melts nicely.

At last, I had managed to create a bowl of reasonably authentic tortilla soup using common supermarket ingredients. Best of all, I could make the soup in less time than it takes to get to the airport.

TORTILLA SOUP
MAKES ABOUT 9 CUPS, SERVING 6

Despite its somewhat lengthy ingredient list, this recipe is very easy to prepare. If you desire a soup with mild spiciness, trim the ribs and seeds from the jalapeño (or omit the jalapeño altogether) and use the minimum amount of chipotle in adobo sauce (1 teaspoon, pureed with the tomatoes in step 3). Our preferred brand of low-sodium chicken broth is Swanson's Natural Goodness.

If advance preparation suits you, the soup can be completed short of adding the shredded chicken to the pot at the end of step 3. Return the soup to a simmer over medium-high heat before

TASTING: **Corn Tortillas**
We tasted six brands of corn tortillas and found that thicker tortillas did not brown as well in the oven and became more chewy than crisp. Thin tortillas, either white or yellow, quickly became feather-light and crisp when oven-fried. Flavor differences between brands were slight, but locally made tortillas did pack a bit more corn flavor than national brands. Our advice? Purchase the thinnest tortillas you can find and choose a locally made brand, if possible.

THICK:
TOO CHEWY

THIN:
JUST RIGHT

---

proceeding. The tortilla strips and the garnishes are best prepared the day of serving.

Tortilla Strips
- 8 (6-inch) corn tortillas, cut into ½-inch-wide strips
- 1 tablespoon vegetable oil
  Table salt

Soup
- 2 bone-in, skin-on split chicken breasts (about 1½ pounds) or 4 bone-in, skin-on chicken thighs (about 1¼ pounds), skin removed and well trimmed of excess fat
- 8 cups low-sodium chicken broth
- 1 very large white onion (about 1 pound), trimmed of root end, quartered, and peeled
- 4 medium garlic cloves, peeled
- 2 large sprigs fresh epazote, or 8 to 10 sprigs fresh cilantro plus 1 sprig fresh oregano
  Table salt
- 2 medium tomatoes, cored and quartered
- ½ medium jalapeño chile
- 1 chipotle chile in adobo, plus up to 1 tablespoon adobo sauce
- 1 tablespoon vegetable oil

Garnishes
- 1 lime, cut into wedges
- 1 Hass avocado, diced fine
- 8 ounces cotija cheese, crumbled, or Monterey Jack cheese, diced fine
  Cilantro leaves
  Minced jalapeño
  Mexican crema or sour cream

1. **FOR THE TORTILLA STRIPS:** Adjust oven rack to middle position; heat oven to 425 degrees. Spread tortilla strips on rimmed baking sheet; drizzle with oil and toss until evenly coated. Bake until strips are deep golden brown and crisped, about 14 minutes, rotating pan and shaking strips (to redistribute) halfway through baking time. Season strips lightly with salt; transfer to plate lined with several layers paper towels.

2. **FOR THE SOUP:** While tortilla strips bake, bring chicken, broth, 2 onion quarters, 2 garlic cloves, epazote, and ½ teaspoon salt to boil over medium-high heat in large saucepan; reduce heat to low, cover, and simmer until chicken is just cooked through, about 20 minutes. Using tongs, transfer chicken to large plate. Pour broth through fine-mesh strainer; discard solids in strainer. When cool enough to handle, shred chicken into bite-sized pieces; discard bones.

3. Puree tomatoes, 2 remaining onion quarters, 2 remaining garlic cloves, jalapeño, chipotle chile, and 1 teaspoon adobo sauce in food processor until smooth. Heat oil in Dutch oven over high heat until shimmering; add tomato/onion puree and ⅛ teaspoon salt and cook, stirring frequently, until mixture has darkened in color, about 10 minutes. Stir strained

INGREDIENTS:
Translating Tortilla Soup
Authentic tortilla soup is chock-full of hard-to-find Mexican ingredients. We tested dozens of widely available substitutes. Here are our favorites.

EPAZOTE

FRESH CILANTRO & OREGANO

Cilantro and oregano replicate the pungent flavor of fresh epazote better than dried epazote.

COMAL-ROASTED CHILE

CHIPOTLES IN ADOBO SAUCE

Smoked jalapeños in a tomato-vinegar sauce take the place of skillet-charred chiles and tomatoes.

COTIJA

MONTEREY JACK

Monterey Jack doesn't crumble like cotija, but it melts better than other choices, such as feta.

CREMA MEXICANA

SOUR CREAM

Sour cream is milder than cultured Mexican cream, but it's close enough.

broth into tomato mixture, bring to boil, then reduce heat to low and simmer to blend flavors, about 15 minutes. Taste soup; if desired, add up to 2 teaspoons additional adobo sauce. Add shredded chicken and simmer until heated through, about 5 minutes. To serve, place portions of tortilla strips in bottom of individual bowls and ladle soup into bowls; pass garnishes separately.

Rescuing Pasta with Cherry Tomatoes

Have you ever tried to make a great sauce with off-season supermarket tomatoes?
Cherry tomatoes are your best bet, but even then the resulting sauce can be uninspired.

> BY ERIKA BRUCE

Nothing is better on pasta than a bright fresh tomato sauce, heady with garlic and basil. But in late winter, when my cravings for summer tomatoes start to kick in, the supermarket options are limited to vibrantly red specimens that deliver mealy texture and almost no discernible flavor. Yes, one can start with canned tomatoes for a quick sauce, but the promise of a really good fresh tomato sauce in March is a worthy goal indeed. When I want to find an off-season tomato with at least some positive attributes, I usually turn to cherry tomatoes. But my hopes have too often been dashed by mediocre results.

This time, I decided to sample both no-cook and quick sauté recipes. The no-cook concept is simple enough: Toss halved cherry tomatoes in a little olive oil, fresh herbs, and salt; allow them to sit and give off their juices; then toss with pasta. This method works with sweet, tender, summertime tomatoes, but with tart off-season varieties the sauce was flat, watery, and completely segregated from the pasta. The quick sauté method, which exposes the halved tomatoes to just enough high heat to warm them through, was equally disappointing. Not only does it require precision timing to avoid overcooking, but it failed to improve the meager flavor of the tomatoes. The obvious place to turn was roasting, a method that would concentrate and sweeten their flavor.

Oven to the Rescue

I found plenty of recipes that called for two to three hours of roasting, an amount of time that seemed absurd for a quick tomato sauce. In addition, these recipes produced tomatoes with a leathery texture that seemed more oven-dried than slow-roasted. I wanted a quicker recipe and a juicier end result.

Roasting the tomatoes in high heat (400 to 450 degrees) took considerably less time, but the high oven temperature caused the tomatoes to explode out of their skins, something that did not translate into a palatable sauce. They were juicy, yes, but they were also mushy and quickly disintegrated when mixed with the pasta. I needed to

To create a winter sauce with summertime flavor, toss halved tomatoes with salt, sugar, and seasonings (here garlic, capers, and red pepper flakes) and then roast everything in the oven.

test lower oven temperatures. In the end, the best choice was 350 degrees. These tomatoes became sweet and concentrated in just 35 minutes.

Once these moderately roasted cherry tomatoes were mixed into pasta, however, they released a tremendous amount of liquid, making the sauce watery. One thing I did not want to do was to extend the cooking time. Then I noticed something that might help me avoid this: The tomatoes had been forming a double layer in the medium-size baking dish I had been using, and I guessed that this arrangement might be deterring the evaporation of moisture. When I switched to a large rimmed baking sheet, the tomatoes fit in a single layer,

and voilà!—enough liquid cooked off in the oven to give me a viscous sauce.

The Sauce Comes Together

Garlic was a must, but I wanted to add it the easy way, roasting it along with the tomatoes. Normally, I enjoy the convenience of a garlic press, but the flavor of pressed garlic in this case was overwhelming. (By crushing the cell membranes, a garlic press maximizes garlic flavor.) Minced garlic was also too strong, but garlic cut into slivers was just right. Although onions added a harsh flavor, delicate shallots were sweet enough to complement the tomatoes. But when I mixed the admittedly larger slices of shallot in with the tomatoes, as I had done with the garlic slivers, they didn't cook quickly enough. Simply sprinkling the slices on top of the tomatoes helped them to roast more quickly.

By the time I reached the twentieth batch of pasta, I noticed the sweetness level of the tomatoes tended to vary. Sometimes leaning to the sweeter side (much like in-season cherry tomatoes or their cousins, grape tomatoes), most were exceedingly tart. I added a small amount of sugar to the recipe to adjust for this tartness (it can be easily reduced or even omitted when using sweeter tomatoes). Two other ingredients that boosted flavor were a modest tablespoon of balsamic vinegar and a pinch of crushed red pepper, both added to the tomatoes before roasting. Fresh basil and Parmesan cheese, added just before serving, completed the sauce.

In the end, then, is a fresh tomato sauce in late winter a good idea? Yes. This relatively quick and simple roasting method guarantees rich tomato

Roasting Tomatoes

TOO MUCH
Overroasted tomatoes are too dry to create an ample sauce, and they turn into hard lumps that fail to mingle with the pasta.

JUST RIGHT
Tomatoes roasted to the perfect degree look slightly wrinkled but still hold juicy flesh within their skins.

flavor, even with third-rate supermarket tomatoes. Now when it comes to fresh tomato sauce, I no longer have to fear the Ides of March.

PENNE WITH CHERRY TOMATOES, GARLIC, AND BASIL

SERVES 4 TO 6

Grape tomatoes can be substituted, but because they also tend to be sweeter, you will want to reduce or even omit the sugar. Do likewise if your cherry tomatoes are very sweet, but this is less likely when using winter cherry tomatoes.

1	medium shallot, sliced thin
1/4	cup olive oil
3	pints (2 pounds) cherry tomatoes, each tomato halved pole to pole
	Table salt
1/4	teaspoon red pepper flakes
1/4	teaspoon ground black pepper
1 1/2	teaspoons sugar, or to taste
1	tablespoon balsamic vinegar
3	large garlic cloves, sliced thin
1	pound penne
1/4	cup chopped fresh basil leaves
2	ounces grated Parmesan cheese (about 1 cup)

1. Adjust oven rack to middle position; heat oven to 350 degrees. In small bowl, toss shallots with 1 teaspoon oil; set aside. In medium bowl, gently toss tomatoes with remaining oil, 1/2 teaspoon salt, pepper flakes, black pepper, sugar, vinegar, and garlic. Spread in even layer on rimmed baking sheet (about 17 by 12 inches), scatter shallots over tomatoes; roast until edges of shallots begin to brown and tomato skins are slightly shriveled (tomatoes should retain their shape), 35 to 40 minutes. (Do not stir tomatoes during roasting.) Remove tomatoes from oven and cool 5 to 10 minutes.

2. While tomatoes cook, bring 4 quarts water to boil in large stockpot. Just before removing tomatoes from oven, stir 1 tablespoon salt and pasta into boiling water and cook until al dente. Drain pasta and return to pot. Using rubber spatula, scrape tomato mixture into pot on top of pasta. Add basil and toss to combine. Serve immediately, sprinkling cheese over individual bowls.

SPAGHETTI WITH CHERRY TOMATOES, OLIVES, CAPERS, AND PINE NUTS

SERVES 4 TO 6

3	pints (2 pounds) cherry tomatoes, each tomato halved pole to pole
1/4	cup olive oil
	Table salt
1/2	teaspoon red pepper flakes
1/4	teaspoon ground black pepper
1 1/2	teaspoons sugar, or to taste
3	large garlic cloves, sliced thin

1/4	cup drained capers
1	pound spaghetti
1/4	cup chopped kalamata olives
3	tablespoons chopped fresh oregano leaves
1/4	cup pine nuts, toasted
2	ounces grated Pecorino Romano cheese (1 cup)

1. Adjust oven rack to middle position; heat oven to 350 degrees. In medium bowl, gently toss tomatoes with oil, 1/2 teaspoon salt, pepper flakes, black pepper, sugar, garlic, and capers. Spread in even layer on rimmed baking sheet (about 17 by 12 inches) and roast until tomato skins are slightly shriveled (tomatoes should retain their shape), 35 to 40 minutes. (Do not stir tomatoes during roasting.) Remove tomatoes from oven and cool 5 to 10 minutes.

2. While tomatoes cook, bring 4 quarts water to boil in large stockpot. Just before removing tomatoes from oven, stir 1 tablespoon salt and pasta into boiling water and cook until al dente. Drain pasta and return to pot. Using rubber spatula, scrape tomato mixture into pot on top of pasta. Add olives and oregano; toss to combine. Serve immediately, sprinkling pine nuts and cheese over individual bowls.

FARFALLE WITH CHERRY TOMATOES, ARUGULA, AND GOAT CHEESE

SERVES 4 TO 6

1	medium shallot, sliced thin
1/4	cup olive oil
3	pints (2 pounds) cherry tomatoes, each tomato halved pole to pole (2 pounds)
	Table salt
1/4	teaspoon red pepper flakes
1/4	teaspoon ground black pepper
1 1/2	teaspoons sugar, or to taste
1	tablespoon sherry or red wine vinegar
3	large garlic cloves, sliced thin
1	pound farfalle
1	large bunch arugula, leaves torn into bite-sized pieces (about 4 cups loosely packed)
4	ounces goat cheese, crumbled (about 1/2 cup)

1. Adjust oven rack to middle position; heat oven to 350 degrees. In small bowl, toss shallots with 1 teaspoon oil; set aside. In medium bowl, gently toss tomatoes with remaining oil, 1/2 teaspoon salt, pepper flakes, black pepper, sugar, vinegar, and garlic. Spread in even layer on rimmed baking sheet (about 17 by 12 inches), scatter shallots over tomatoes; roast until edges of shallots begin to brown and tomato skins are slightly shriveled (tomatoes should retain their shape), 35 to 40 minutes. (Do not stir tomatoes during roasting.) Remove tomatoes from oven and cool 5 to 10 minutes.

2. While tomatoes cook, bring 4 quarts water to boil in large stockpot. Just before removing tomatoes from oven, stir 1 tablespoon salt and

pasta into boiling water and cook until al dente. Drain pasta and return to pot; add arugula and toss until wilted. Using rubber spatula, scrape tomato mixture into pot on top of pasta and toss to combine. Serve immediately, sprinkling cheese over individual bowls.

Getting to Know Your Freezer

Is your freezer an overstocked warehouse for aging mystery meat? Learn to get more out of your icebox. BY SEAN LAWLER

Overly thrifty cooks treat their freezers like subzero trash cans, packing them full of whatever scraps cross their cutting board, then promptly forgetting the items as soon as they close the freezer door. For others, the freezer is no more than an oversized icemaker. Putting a little thought into your freezer philosophy will save you time and money. Here are some tips about what to freeze, how to freeze it, and why.

FREEZER BASICS

The most commonly asked question about freezers is, "How long can I freeze [fill in the blank]?" It's always a difficult question to answer. From a safety standpoint, food that is frozen properly (that is, kept at a constant temperature of 0 degrees Fahrenheit or lower) will be safe to eat for a long, long time. In our experience, however, "safe to eat" is not the same as "edible." The activity of enzymes and other chemical processes that are slowed, but not stopped, by freezing causes the quality of frozen food to diminish over time, usually a matter of months. Exactly how much time depends on the freshness of the food when frozen; the age, efficiency, and type of freezer (and how full it is); the frequency with which the freezer door is opened; and various other factors.

While we cannot give a precise answer to the question of how long any particular item will keep, we can tell you two things you can do to extend the life of your frozen foods: Keep your freezer as cold as possible and wrap foods for freezer storage properly.

DEFROSTING

The safest way to defrost frozen meat and poultry is in the refrigerator, never at room temperature. Frozen meat left on the kitchen counter can begin to grow microorganisms in as little as two hours. When defrosting multiple items, separate them for faster defrosting. Refrigerator defrosting requires planning ahead, however. In a pinch, smaller quantities of frozen food can be defrosted using the microwave, set on low (30 percent) power. (Large items, such as whole frozen turkeys and chickens, which can take days to defrost in the refrigerator, should never be defrosted in the microwave.) The defrosting meat should be loosely covered with plastic wrap and rotated occasionally. For best results, do not defrost completely in the microwave, as the meat will start to cook. Defrost only until softened—not warm. The meat will continue to defrost as you prep it for cooking.

Approximate Refrigerator Defrosting Times

Thin steaks, chops, chicken breasts	8–12 hours
Thick steaks, chops, bone-in chicken parts, 1 pound ground beef	24 hours
Frozen casseroles (let defrosted casserole sit at room temperature for 1 hour before baking)	24 hours
Whole chickens, turkeys, roasts	5 hours/pound

Temperature: Many freezers can be too warm. Keep tabs on the temperature of your freezer with an inexpensive refrigerator/freezer thermometer. According to food safety experts, your freezer should register 0 degrees Fahrenheit or colder at all times.

Air flow: Keep foods away from the vent in the back wall of the freezer; this allows the cold air to circulate more efficiently.

The coldest spot: The rear center is the coldest spot in a freezer. This is the best place to store the canister for an ice cream maker, which must be thoroughly frozen if the freshly made ice cream is to set up. Don't crowd the canister and give it plenty of time to freeze (overnight is best).

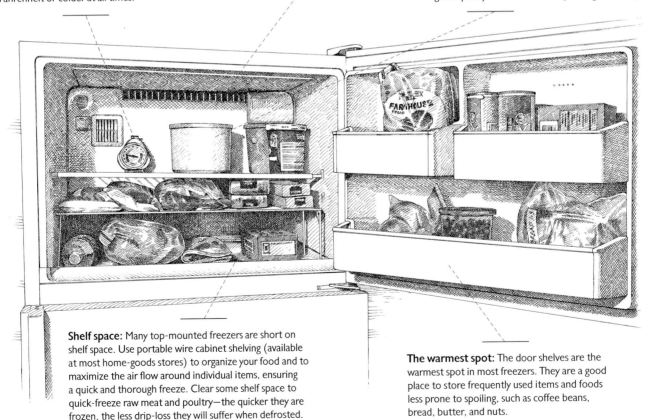

Shelf space: Many top-mounted freezers are short on shelf space. Use portable wire cabinet shelving (available at most home-goods stores) to organize your food and to maximize the air flow around individual items, ensuring a quick and thorough freeze. Clear some shelf space to quick-freeze raw meat and poultry—the quicker they are frozen, the less drip-loss they will suffer when defrosted.

The warmest spot: The door shelves are the warmest spot in most freezers. They are a good place to store frequently used items and foods less prone to spoiling, such as coffee beans, bread, butter, and nuts.

THE RIGHT WRAP

There are three rules for freezer storage. First, wrap food tightly. This prevents the moisture loss that causes frozen foods to become dry and discolored, a condition known as freezer burn. Second, wrap the food again—this time in a thicker layer of foil or plastic. (We use zipper-lock freezer bags.) Frozen foods easily pick up off odors and flavors, and this second wrap will help to keep them out. Third, wrap individual portions separately. They will freeze more quickly and can then be defrosted individually.

Steaks, Chops, and Chicken Cutlets: Don't store these items in their supermarket packaging. Wrap each piece securely in plastic wrap, place inside a gallon-sized freezer bag, and press out the air. Freeze the items in a single layer. Once they are frozen, fold the bag over to save space.

Burgers: Separate individual hamburger patties with squares of parchment, then place the meat in a freezer bag. This technique also works with tortillas and crêpes.

Bread: Freshly baked bread will keep, frozen, for several months when wrapped first in aluminum foil then placed in a large, plastic freezer bag.
To reheat: Remove the foil-wrapped loaf from the bag and place it on the center rack of a 450-degree oven for 10 to 15 minutes. Carefully remove the foil and return the loaf to the oven for a few minutes to crisp the crust.

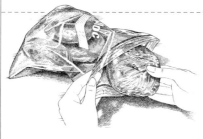

Bagels: Frozen bagels go straight from freezer to toaster, but it's easier to slice them before freezing. Wrap each bagel in plastic, slipping the wrap between the two halves as well as around them. Then place in a freezer bag.

Stock: Pour the stock into a coffee mug lined with a quart-sized zipper-lock bag. Seal the bag, place it on a cookie sheet, and freeze. Once the stock is frozen, you can remove the bags from the cookie sheet and store them wherever there is room.

Labeling: Use a permanent marker to label freezer bags and plastic containers; its waterproof ink won't run if exposed to moisture from frost or condensation. Write on strips of masking tape or directly on the plastic. Remove ink from empty plastic containers with rubbing alcohol.

PORTION CONTROL

One of the most efficient ways to use your freezer is to divide foods into individual portions before freezing, thus avoiding having to defrost a large block of food and refreeze or discard the rest. There are countless applications of this idea—here are some of our favorites.

Bacon: Roll up the bacon in tight coils, each with two to four slices. Put the coils in a zipper-lock freezer bag and place the bag flat in the freezer.

Canned Chipotle Chiles: It can be difficult to use up a whole can of chipotle chiles—a little goes a long way. To freeze the leftovers, spoon out the chiles, each with a couple teaspoons of adobo sauce, onto different areas of a cookie sheet lined with parchment. Freeze the chiles, then transfer them to a zipper-lock freezer bag. This technique also works with canned tomato paste.

Cookie Dough: To freeze cookie dough, divide it into balls and arrange the balls on a cookie sheet lined with parchment or waxed paper. Place the cookie sheet in the freezer. When the dough balls are frozen, place them in a zipper-lock freezer bag or small airtight container. Bake without defrosting.

Egg Whites: Freeze leftover egg whites (but never yolks) in an ice cube tray.

WHAT'S IN THE TEST KITCHEN FREEZER?
The freezer is not just for pork chops and ice cream. While there are some items that should not be frozen—whole eggs, most cheeses (except mozzarella), raw vegetables, and most fruits (unless prepared for freezing in a sugar syrup)—some of the staples in your pantry or refrigerator can be better preserved in the freezer. Here's a list of some of the more unusual items we store in the test kitchen freezer.

Ripe or overripe bananas: Great for making banana bread or muffins, or drop them into a blender while still frozen for fruit smoothies. Peel bananas before freezing.

Nuts: Sealed in a zipper-lock freezer bag, nuts stay fresh tasting for months. And there's no need to defrost; frozen nuts chop just as easily as fresh.

Herbs: Dried bay leaves retain their potency much longer when stored in the freezer. Chopped fresh herbs such as parsley, sage, rosemary, and thyme can be covered with water in an ice cube tray and then frozen indefinitely. Keep the frozen cubes in a zipper-lock freezer bag until needed for sauces, soups, or stews. Homemade pesto can also be frozen in ice cube trays, and there's no need to add water.

Butter: When stored in the refrigerator, butter picks up off odors and eventually turns rancid. You can prolong its life by storing it in the freezer. Transfer it to the refrigerator one stick at a time, as you need it.

Dry goods: Stored in the freezer, flour, bread crumbs, cornmeal, oats, and other grains are protected from humidity, bugs, and rancidity.

Beef in Barolo

Beef in Barolo can be the ultimate pot roast. Or it can be an expensive mistake that wastes a $30 bottle of wine and produces tough, stringy meat.

⇒ BY SANDRA WU ⇐

A s cashmere cannot be confused with acrylic, neither can beef in Barolo be mistaken for the standard workaday pot roast. Featuring tender, moist beef enveloped in a rich, silky red wine sauce—rather than the beefy gravy and vegetal bits characteristic of its down-home American cousin—beef in Barolo appears in countless Italian cookbooks. Most recipes utilize a tough cut of meat that is slowly braised in the famed Piedmontese wine. So what's the problem? For starters, Barolo isn't Chianti; most bottles start at a whopping $30. For that kind of investment, I wanted a lot more than a glorified pot roast. Cheap meat cooked in expensive wine? I had my doubts, but given that Italian cooking is usually about practical home cooking, not silly showmanship, I put them aside.

Bring on the Beef

Prior test kitchen efforts to perfect pot roast revealed chuck roast as the overwhelming favorite cut of meat for its moistness and flavor. Initial tests of several beef in Barolo recipes confirmed these results. A boneless sirloin yielded what one taster called "insanely dry" meat and a watery, raw-tasting wine sauce. Perhaps it would be wiser to stick with a chuck roast after all. But which one?

In a side-by-side comparison of three classic chuck roasts—a boneless chuck-eye roast, a seven-bone roast, and a top-blade roast—tasters praised each for being moist, tender, and beefy. In the end, the decision boiled down to aesthetics and convenience. The center of the top-blade roast sported an unappealing strip of partially melted connective tissue that was reminiscent of meat-flavored gummy bears. The seven-bone roast was hard to carve and even harder to find in the supermarket. The chuck-eye roast won by default.

My recipe was beginning to take shape, but after four long hours of braising, the meat was precariously close to being shredded and overdone and contained unsightly pockets of squishy fat and connective tissue. While this might be acceptable in a more rustic pot roast, beef in Barolo demands a more refined presentation. The fat would have to go.

This elegant Italian pot roast calls for cutting a chuck roast in two, removing the fat, and then tying each piece back together before braising.

I wondered what would happen if I split the large cylindrical roast into two sleeker halves. Dividing the roast into two fairly equal pieces was easy, as the seam of fat that runs down the center of the roast acts as a built-in guide. I trimmed out the obvious wads of fat from each lobe, leaving a thin layer of fat cap, and seasoned and tied each piece to keep it from falling apart during braising. With less extraneous fat and a shortened cooking time to boot (the meat was now done in three hours), these two roasts were definitely better than one.

Brown, Barolo, Braise

Following Italian custom, I began this recipe by searing the roasts in olive oil, but the sauce needed pizzazz. I remembered seeing pancetta in some recipes and decided to brown the meat in the fat rendered from this Italian bacon instead. This helped immensely in developing flavor. Putting the browned roast aside, I then sautéed onions, carrots, and celery, adding a tablespoon

of tomato paste to create a deep roasted flavor. After stirring in minced garlic, a bit of sugar, and a tablespoon of flour to help thicken the sauce during the final reduction, I was ready to add the wine.

Made from Nebbiolo grapes grown in the northern region of Piedmont, Barolo is a bold, full-bodied, often tannic and acidic red wine that is hailed as Italy's "king of wines and wine of kings." The price alone makes it the "wine of kings." Unlike its lighter, fruitier Italian counterparts, such as Chianti, which are often better off quaffed from a glass than used in vigorous cooking, Barolo is very hardy and can carry the day, even after being simmered for hours. We found that in a pinch, several other, cheaper "big reds" can be substituted (see page 19), but this dish calls out for its namesake. Luckily, an $11 Barolo (below) was tasters' top choice.

Unfortunately, the robust flavor also added unexpected difficulties. This "king" of wines was more out-of-control despot than temperate monarch—harsh and generally disliked. First, I focused on how and when to add the wine. Should it be reduced first to concentrate its flavors, added in two parts (at the beginning and the end), or simply dumped in with the meat? Much to my surprise and delight, dumping the whole bottle into the pot won out.

But I still needed to find an ingredient to counterbalance the harsh flavors in this big wine. Broth did not

Finding the Best Barolo

We tasted four bottles of Barolo, ranging in price from $11 to $40, in our recipe. There was surprising unanimity in the test kitchen. Almost everyone preferred the least expensive wine, the 1997 Argento ($10.99), available at Trader Joe's markets. Tasters praised its "tart" and "tangy" flavors, which were offset by a "sweet roundness." So you can spend like a pauper and eat like a king.

CHEAPEST WINE WINS

work; neither did water. Eventually, I discovered that drained diced tomatoes did the trick. The meatiness of the tomatoes produced the balance of sweet, salty, and hearty flavors this dish needed.

I then gently placed the browned roasts back into the pot along with a few fresh herbs, brought everything back up to a simmer, covered the pot with foil to prevent moisture loss, replaced the lid, and let the beef braise in a 300-degree oven for three hours. (When given less time, the meat was too resilient; given more, it fell apart.) Flipping the meat every 45 minutes helped to achieve perfect tenderness without dry patches.

A Silky, Suave Finish

Once the meat was tender, I removed it from the pot to rest while I concentrated on the sauce, which I felt ought to be a far cry from the typical pot roast liquid. After all, why use Barolo to start with if the sauce isn't grand? After skimming off the top layer of fat to remove as much grease as possible, I reduced the liquid over high heat to concentrate and intensify the multiple layers of flavor. Pureeing the liquid, vegetables, and herbs yielded a weak sauce that eventually separated into watery and mealy components. Straining out the vegetables proved to be key. Boiled down to 1½ cups, the sauce was dark and lustrous, with the body and finesse of something you might serve over a fine steak.

Better than pot roast? You bet. And you don't need to dip into a trust fund to put this dish on the table. I admit it: The Italians do know something about pot roast after all.

BEEF BRAISED IN BAROLO
SERVES 6

Purchase pancetta that is cut to order, about ¼ inch thick. If pancetta is not available, substitute an equal amount of salt pork (find the meatiest piece possible), cut it into ¼-inch cubes, and boil it in 3 cups of water for about 2 minutes to remove excess salt. After draining, use it as you would pancetta.

This braise can be prepared up to 2 days in advance; complete the recipe through step 2. When you're ready to serve, skim off the fat congealed on the surface and gently warm until the meat is heated through. Continue with the recipe from step 3.

- 1 boneless chuck-eye roast (about 3½ pounds), prepared according to illustrations above
      Table salt and ground black pepper
- 4 ounces pancetta, cut into ¼-inch cubes (see note)
- 2 medium onions, chopped medium (about 2 cups)
- 2 medium carrots, chopped medium (about 1 cup)
- 2 medium celery ribs, chopped medium (1 cup)
- 1 tablespoon tomato paste
- 3 medium garlic cloves, minced or pressed through garlic press (about 1 tablespoon)

1. Pull roast apart at its major seams (delineated by lines of fat) into two halves. Use knife as necessary.

2. With knife, remove large knobs of fat from each piece, leaving thin layer of fat on meat.

3. Tie three pieces of kitchen twine around each piece of meat to keep it from falling apart.

- ½ teaspoon sugar
- 1 tablespoon unbleached all-purpose flour
- 1 bottle (750 milliliters) Barolo wine
- 1 can (14½ ounces) diced tomatoes, drained
- 1 sprig fresh thyme, plus 1 teaspoon minced leaves
- 1 sprig fresh rosemary
- 10 sprigs fresh parsley

1. Adjust oven rack to middle position; heat oven to 300 degrees. Thoroughly pat beef dry with paper towels; sprinkle generously with salt and pepper. Place pancetta in 8-quart heavy-bottomed Dutch oven; cook over medium heat, stirring occasionally, until browned and crisp, about 8 minutes. Using slotted spoon, transfer pancetta to paper towel–lined plate and reserve. Pour off all but 2 tablespoons fat; set Dutch oven over medium-high heat and heat fat until beginning to smoke. Add beef to pot and cook until well browned on all sides, about 8 minutes total. Transfer beef to large plate; set aside.

2. Reduce heat to medium; add onions, carrots, celery, and tomato paste to pot and cook, stirring occasionally, until vegetables begin to soften and brown, about 6 minutes. Add garlic, sugar, flour, and reserved pancetta; cook, stirring constantly, until combined and fragrant, about 30 seconds. Add wine and tomatoes, scraping bottom of pan with wooden spoon to loosen browned bits; add thyme sprig, rosemary, and parsley. Return roast and any accumulated juices to pot; increase heat to high and bring liquid to boil, then place large sheet of foil over pot and cover tightly with lid. Set pot in oven and cook, using tongs to turn beef every 45 minutes, until dinner fork easily slips in and out of meat, about 3 hours.

3. Transfer beef to cutting board; tent with foil to keep warm.

Allow braising liquid to settle about 5 minutes, then, using wide shallow spoon, skim fat off surface. Add minced thyme, bring liquid to boil over high heat, and cook, whisking vigorously to help vegetables break down, until mixture is thickened and reduced to about 3½ cups, about 18 minutes. Strain liquid through large fine-mesh strainer, pressing on solids with spatula to extract as much liquid as possible; you should have 1½ cups strained sauce (if necessary, return strained sauce to Dutch oven and reduce to 1½ cups). Discard solids in strainer. Season sauce to taste with salt and pepper.

4. Remove kitchen twine from meat and discard. Using chef's or carving knife, cut meat against grain into ½-inch-thick slices. Divide meat between warmed bowls or plates; pour about ¼ cup sauce over and serve immediately.

TASTING: Barolo Substitutes

Not everyone has a bottle of Barolo lying around the house. Could a moderately priced wine-cabinet staple really take the place of this king of wines? We tested our recipe using five inexpensive red wines to see which was best suited to wear the crown. We found that it takes a potent wine to withstand three hours in the oven and still have much character. Our one Italian entrant, the Chianti, fell flat, as did the Merlot and Côtes du Rhône, the other medium-bodied wines in our tasting. These fruity wines lacked the potency of a heady Barolo. We had better luck with Zinfandel, but Cabernet Sauvignon was the most commanding and was, therefore, the better substitute.

–Garth Clingingsmith

GOOD STAND-INS:
Cabernet Sauvignon, Zinfandel

NOT SUITED FOR THE JOB:
Merlot, Côtes du Rhône, Chianti

Quick and Easy Quesadillas

Sports bars have hijacked this modest Mexican grilled-cheese sandwich. Could we rescue it?

> BY SEAN LAWLER

A truly "authentic" quesadilla is just a humble kitchen snack: a fresh, handmade tortilla folded around a mild melting cheese, quickly fried or crisped on a griddle, then devoured just as quickly. As the quesadilla migrated north of the border, however, it evolved into a greasy happy hour spectacle for beer and burger joints, becoming nothing more than bad Mexican pizza: stale and soggy supermarket tortillas filled with "buffalo chicken" or "Cajun shrimp" and sliced into big, floppy triangles.

My quest focused on a quesadilla that would be authentic in spirit, if not quite in substance—that is, a quick and casual but still satisfying snack, ready at a moment's notice from supermarket staples. I tested a half-dozen techniques for cooking the quesadillas, including a deep fry, a shallow fry, a lightly oiled skillet, and a completely dry one. The lightly oiled nonstick skillet produced the best—though not perfect—results. While the exterior of the tortillas was nicely crisp and browned, the interior had a raw, doughy texture, and the cheese was not entirely melted.

What I needed was a way to preheat the tortillas so that I could assemble the quesadilla while it was still warm. I could then crisp it up quickly over fairly high heat without worrying that the filling would not be sufficiently heated. Some cookbooks suggest passing the tortillas over the flame of a gas burner to lightly char and soften them. This idea worked, but it excluded electric cooktops and demanded close attention to keep the tortillas from going up in flames. I got better results by simply toasting the tortillas in a hot dry skillet. As a tortilla heated up, it released its own steam, causing the tortilla to puff up and its layers to separate. Once filled and returned to the oiled skillet, this batch of tortillas made for quesadillas with a pleasing contrast in texture—their outer layer thin and crispy, their inner layer warm and soft, with just a little bit of chew.

I knew I didn't need much, but even a few drops of oil tended to bead up and puddle in the nonstick skillet, resulting in uneven browning. A better approach, I found, was to brush the tortillas with oil before adding them to the skillet. I

COOK'S EXTRA gives you free recipes online. For Cubano Quesadillas and Quesadillas with Queso Fresco and Roasted Peppers, go to www.cooksillustrated.com and key in code 4052. These recipes will be available until April 15, 2005.

sprinkled the tortillas lightly with kosher salt after brushing them with oil, and tasters agreed that this made them seem crispier.

My quesadillas were tasty, but they still suffered from a few design flaws. My working recipe called for sandwiching cheese between two 10-inch flour tortillas. These were tricky to flip without spilling the fillings and oozed melted cheese all over the cutting board when cut into wedges. I switched to smaller 8-inch tortillas and began folding them in half around the filling, fitting them into the skillet two at a time. Cut in half instead of into multiple wedges, these "half moon" quesadillas were much sturdier and easier to eat, and, thanks to the folded edges, they kept their filling inside, where it belonged.

QUESADILLAS
MAKES 2 FOLDED 8-INCH QUESADILLAS

Cooling the quesadillas before cutting and serving is important; straight from the skillet, the cheese is molten and will ooze out. Finished quesadillas can be held on a baking sheet in a 200-degree oven for up to 20 minutes.

- 2 (8-inch) flour tortillas
- ⅔ cup (3 ounces) shredded Monterey Jack or cheddar cheese
- 1 tablespoon minced pickled jalapeños (optional)
  Vegetable oil for brushing tortillas
  Kosher salt

1. Heat 10-inch nonstick skillet over medium heat until hot, about 2 minutes. Place 1 tortilla in skillet and toast until soft and puffed slightly at edges, about 2 minutes. Flip tortilla and toast until puffed and slightly browned, 1 to 2 minutes longer. Slip tortilla onto cutting board. Repeat to toast second tortilla while assembling first quesadilla. Sprinkle ⅓ cup cheese and half of jalapeños, if using, over half of tortilla, leaving ½-inch border around edge. Fold tortilla in half and press to flatten. Brush top generously with oil, sprinkle lightly with salt, and set aside. Repeat to form second quesadilla.

2. Place both quesadillas in skillet, oiled sides down; cook over medium heat until crisp and well browned, 1 to 2 minutes. Brush tops with oil and sprinkle lightly with salt. Flip quesadillas and cook until second sides are crisp, 1 to 2 minutes. Transfer quesadillas to cutting board; cool about 3 minutes, halve each quesadilla, and serve.

CHEDDAR, BACON, AND SCALLION QUESADILLAS

Cut 2 strips bacon crosswise into ½-inch pieces; fry in 10-inch nonstick skillet over medium heat until crisp, about 5 minutes. Using slotted spoon, transfer bacon to paper towel–lined plate; pour fat into small bowl and reserve, if desired. Wipe out skillet with paper towels. Follow recipe for Quesadillas, using cheddar cheese and sprinkling bacon and 1 tablespoon thinly sliced scallions over cheese in each quesadilla. If desired, substitute reserved bacon fat for oil and omit salt.

CORN AND BLACK BEAN QUESADILLAS WITH PEPPER JACK CHEESE

1. Heat 10-inch nonstick skillet over medium-high heat until hot. Add ⅓ cup thawed frozen corn and cook, stirring occasionally, until kernels begin to brown and pop, 3 to 5 minutes; transfer corn to bowl. Heat 2 teaspoons vegetable oil in now-empty skillet over medium heat until shimmering; add ⅓ cup minced red onion and cook until softened, about 3 minutes. Add 1 teaspoon minced garlic and ½ teaspoon chili powder and cook until fragrant, about 1 minute; stir in ⅓ cup canned black beans and cook until heated through, about 1 minute. Return corn to skillet; gently press mixture with spatula to lightly crush beans. Transfer mixture to now-empty bowl, stir in 2 teaspoons lime juice, and season with salt.

2. Wipe out skillet with paper towels and return pan to medium heat until hot. Follow recipe for Quesadillas, using Pepper Jack cheese and dividing corn and bean filling between quesadillas.

TECHNIQUE | TWO IN A PAN

To cook two quesadillas at once, arrange folded edges toward center of skillet.

Sleuthing Sourdough

Could we take the most difficult bread recipe and turn it into a foolproof, one-day affair?

⋛ BY ERIKA BRUCE ⋚

Before the advent of commercial yeast, bakers depended on sourdough starters to leaven their bread. Truly the staff of life, these starters were handed down from generation to generation and passed from Old World to New. While today there are easier and more convenient means of making bread, sourdough remains on the table; but now it's consumed more for its thick and crunchy crust, chewy interior, and deliciously sour tang than for the need to sustain life. In fact, sourdough bread has become as much a benchmark of a good artisanal bakery as the French baguette.

For the home baker with aspirations of rivaling the artisans, there are endless dissertations to be found on the art of baking with sourdough. But start to read through this pile of weighty tomes and you'll find that no two say the same thing and that all sound equally intimidating. Some recipes instruct the home baker on how to make starter from scratch (a process that takes several weeks), using anything from organic grapes to potatoes to rye flour. Upon accomplishing this feat, you then can look forward to another four to five days spent making the bread. Now, if you ask me, this is borderline compulsive, especially when my local bakery produces an excellent loaf. But I enjoy baking other breads at home, and I was keen on climbing the peak of bread baking: homemade sourdough. I had only two stipulations: The recipe could take days but not weeks, and, more important, it had to taste and chew like real sourdough, not some mediocre imitation.

I placed great hopes on beginning the process with commercial yeast and then somehow "flavoring" the bread to achieve a quick, easy, and acceptable loaf (see "Searching for a Fast Start," page 22). This would eliminate the need for a starter, which is rife with complications. A half-dozen recipes later, I had to abandon this path, as none of the loaves (all of them decent rustic breads, to be sure) were even the least bit sour. Now I had to go back to the start—to the starter—and there was no way around it.

COOK'S EXTRA gives you free recipes online. For a sourdough starter recipe, visit www.cooksillustrated.com and key in code 4053. This recipe will be available until April 15, 2005.

We spent three months on a bread-baking odyssey before we understood the secrets to real sourdough flavor and texture at home.

Bread Primer

The production of rustic breads typically involves a sponge—a mixture of commercial yeast, flour, and water—left overnight to develop flavor. The sponge is then combined with additional flour, water, salt, and, occasionally, more yeast to create the dough. After a period of mixing or kneading (which serves to develop gluten), the dough is allowed to rise, or ferment. During fermentation, the yeast breaks down starches in the flour and feeds on the resulting sugars. Byproducts of this process are carbon dioxide and alcohol, which cause the dough to rise and develop flavor. Next the dough is shaped before undergoing another rising period. This second rise, also called the proof, produces the crumb structure of the final loaf as the small pockets of air formed during mixing and fermentation fill with more carbon dioxide. Finally, the bread is slashed and put into the oven, where it rises for the third and last time, demonstrating an effect known as ovenspring. When the crust fully develops and colors, and the interior reaches a temperature of around 200

degrees, the bread is, at long last, done.

The first thing that sets the making of sourdough bread apart from this process is the use of a starter instead of commercial yeast. A starter is basically made up of wild yeasts living happily in a mixture of flour and water. Sour starters (not all starters are "sour") have in addition bacteria that produce acid and thus contribute a sour flavor to the bread (see "The Secrets of Starter," page 23). I began my quest by trying to cultivate my own wild yeasts and bacteria. Over the next month, I tested a variety of recipes, and only one produced a viable starter as well as very good bread. The bad news is that the recipe took 15 days to complete, with the starter requiring three feedings per day (much like a child). Even in our test kitchen, this was considered beyond the pale. The good news is that starters are readily available by mail order and, if fed properly, will last forever. For all but the most devoted home baker, then, a purchased starter is the way to go.

Now that I had a starter, I turned my attention to other factors that contribute to the unique flavor of sourdough—among them, time. Most sourdough recipes take at least three days, not including the making of the starter. On the first day, the sponge is made and allowed to sit overnight on the counter. On the second day, water, flour, and salt are added to make the dough, which is then refrigerated overnight. On the third, the dough is shaped, proofed, and baked. Why so slow? Well, to put it simply, for flavor development. Bread-making mavens agree that for any bread—including sourdough—a long, cool rise is crucial to flavor development. When it comes to sourdough in particular, this slow, cool fermentation helps to maintain a balance between the activity of the yeast and the bacteria. Remember that these bacteria are crucial to the particular flavor of sourdough.

Keeping My Cool

Desperate for any shortcut or technique that might make this process more manageable for home bakers, I started out by simply eliminating the sponge altogether. I mixed the starter directly with the flour, water, and salt to make the dough, and then I proceeded to ferment, shape, proof, and bake it. This bread tasted sour all right—too sour. Rather than starting out subtle and building

to a nice tang, the flavor was sharp and pungent. Apparently, the sponge stage could not to be avoided. Now I wondered if I could speed it up. I tested various shorter rising times at room temperature and was pleasantly surprised to find that the bread made from a sponge that sat at room temperature until it doubled (about three hours) was just as flavorful as the bread made with a sponge that sat overnight.

The next big chunk of time that I wanted to reduce was the fermentation period. Challenging the mandate for a long refrigerated fermentation, I added warm water when mixing the dough and set it in a toasty corner of the kitchen. The dough doubled in less than three hours, but the bread tasted more boozy than sour. So it seems that the experts are right when they say that warm temperatures are not conducive to the development of sour flavor. A compromise, however, was in the offing. I tried using cool water to mix the dough and setting it to rise at cool room temperature. This combination made for a slightly longer fermentation (four to five hours) and produced a bread with more balanced flavor; in fact, it held its own against the bread made with dough that had undergone an overnight fermentation in the fridge.

Same-Day Service?

So where was I? I was using a mail-order starter, I had skipped the overnight rise sponge method in favor of a three-hour rise, and I had opted for a five- to six-hour, cool room-temperature fermentation of the dough. So far, I was still on day one, but the tyrannical gods of bread making were about to intervene.

Some bakers believe that the shaped loaves should be proofed not at room temperature but in the refrigerator overnight. Happy that I was now producing sourdough bread in just one day, I was loath to consider this a necessary step. So, with more skepticism than curiosity, I prepared enough dough

for two loaves and baked one loaf that night and the other the next morning (allowing it to finish proofing at room temperature that day). My same-day loaf was humbled by its slower, cooler twin; the relatively tight crumb and lackluster flavor paled next to the wonderfully irregular crumb and a deep, nutty sourness. This overnight loaf was the closest I had come to bakery sourdough thus far, especially when it came to the crust, which was now well developed and thick, improving my overall experience of texture and flavor when I bit into a slice. Waiting an extra day for this bread was—I hated to admit—worth it.

Yet another complication came my way. If I did not bake the loaves at just the right time, my payoff was much compromised. Underproofed loaves—those not given enough time to stretch and relax—had a dense crumb and split open while baking. Overproofed loaves were overstretched—to the point where the cell walls weakened and the bread couldn't rise to full capacity. During the course of all of this proofing, I eventually figured out a couple of reliable ways to determine when just the right amount of time had passed. One, of course, was size; once the loaves had about doubled, they baked beautifully. The second involved a gentle knuckle poke into the top and sides of the loaf. The speed with which the dough filled back out told me how inflated it was; a sluggish rate of recovery told me that it was ready.

To promote crust development and oven spring, I used a spray bottle filled with water to spritz the loaves once before putting them in the oven and then a couple of times more during the first five minutes of baking. I had the best results when I heated the oven to 500 degrees (baking stone included) and then reduced it to 450 degrees once I added the loaves; this initial high temperature compensated for any heat lost during spritzing. A fairly high internal temperature of 210 to 212 degrees produced the best crumb surrounded by a dark, flavorful crust. Cooling the

bread thoroughly was important to get the best texture; if during a moment of weakness I cut into a hot loaf, a steaming, gummy interior awaited.

At the end of it all, I had not achieved my goal of a same-day loaf that used commercial yeast and no starter. That path led to sourdough ruin: lousy flavor and texture. Yes, I had to concede that a real starter and a certain amount of time were necessary to achieve the perfect sour flavor, rustic crumb, and thick, crunchy crust. But the swell of pride I felt when sharing this bread with my colleagues reminded me of my original purpose. Baking sourdough bread at home did not have to be complicated or take weeks, as some recipes suggest. A couple of days, a properly sour starter, a cool dough, and an overnight proof—this was just basic bread making, not rocket science.

SOURDOUGH STARTER REFRESHMENT

If you do not already have a starter, dried starter packets (sold by mail and in some natural foods stores) or fresh mail-order starters (see Sources, page 32) work well. Follow the package directions to get the starter going, then follow the directions below for feeding once the starter is going strong. No matter where you get your starter and how carefully you maintain it, you should refresh it according to the instructions below before using in the Sourdough Bread recipe. Use King Arthur, Hodgson Mill, Heckers, or Ceresota all-purpose flour or Gold Medal or Pillsbury bread flour. Use filtered or bottled water; chlorinated tap water may affect the development of the culture.

> Sourdough starter
> Filtered or bottled water, 75 to 80 degrees
> Unbleached flour with 11 to 13 percent
> protein content (see note)

Begin in the evening, two days before you intend to use the starter:

1. Stir starter well to recombine, measure out 1 cup (9 ounces), and discard remaining starter (or give it to a friend). Place measured starter in glass bowl or container with at least 1½-quart capacity. Stir in 1 cup (8 ounces) water until combined, then stir in 1½ cups (7½ ounces) flour until evenly moistened (mixture will be lumpy). Cover with lid or plastic wrap.

2. Let stand at room temperature 8 to 12 hours; repeat, pouring off all but 1 cup starter and feeding with 1 cup water and 1½ cups flour, in the morning of the following day, and, finally, once again in the evening, letting it stand at room temperature for the entire time. The starter will be fully refreshed and ready to use the next morning, 8 to 12 hours after the last feeding.

Long-term starter maintenance:

To keep a starter alive over a long period of nonuse, store it in the refrigerator. It's best to feed it weekly, according to the instructions in step 1;

let it stand at room temperature for 4 to 6 hours after feeding, then return it to the refrigerator.

24- HOUR SOURDOUGH BREAD
MAKES TWO 1½-POUND ROUND LOAVES

Once you have a healthy, refreshed starter (see "Sourdough Starter Refreshment" on page 22), the bread will take about 24 hours (over the course of two days) before it is ready for baking. It is best to start the recipe in the morning, no more than 12 hours after the last feeding of the starter. For the sponge, use the lower amount of water if you live in a humid climate, the higher amount in an arid climate. During kneading, this dough should not exceed a temperature of 80 degrees. If your kitchen is very warm or very cold, use water a few degrees cooler or warmer, respectively. A few pieces of equipment are highly recommended: digital scale, baking stone, parchment paper, instant-read thermometer, and spray bottle filled with water. A baking peel and razor blade are also handy but not essential. The dough can be kneaded by hand, but the kneading times must be doubled. When spritzing the loaves in the oven, be careful to avoid spraying water on the oven light.

Sponge
4½	ounces (½ cup) refreshed starter
3–4	ounces (³⁄₈–½ cup) filtered or bottled water, 80 degrees
5	ounces (1 cup) unbleached flour with 11 to 13 percent protein content

Dough
12	ounces (1½ cups) filtered or bottled water, 70 degrees
24	ounces (about 4 ¾ cups) unbleached flour with 11 to 13 percent protein content
2½	teaspoons table salt

Follow instructions and photos at right.

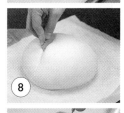
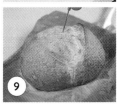

Making Sourdough Bread in 24 Hours

1. **MAKE THE SPONGE:** In bowl or container with at least 1-quart capacity, use rubber spatula to stir together starter and water until fully combined. Stir in flour until combined; mixture should resemble thick pancake batter. Cover with plastic wrap and let rise at room temperature (about 72 degrees) until doubled in bulk, 2 to 3 hours.

2. **MAKE THE DOUGH:** Measure water into bowl of standing mixer; add sponge to water. Fit mixer with dough hook; with mixer running on lowest speed, add flour ½ cup at a time. Once all flour has been added, continue kneading until dough forms ball, about 1 minute longer. Cover bowl with plastic wrap and let dough rest 20 minutes.

3. **KNEAD THE DOUGH:** Using fingers, create pocket in rested dough; add salt to pocket. Knead on low speed until dough is soft, smooth, and moist (dough should not be sticky), about 5 minutes. Transfer dough to clean work surface and knead by hand until dough forms firm ball, about 30 seconds.

4. **LET THE DOUGH RISE:** Lightly spray container or bowl with at least 4-quart capacity with nonstick cooking spray; place dough in container and lightly spray surface of dough. Take internal temperature of dough; then cover tightly with plastic wrap. If temperature registered below 78 degrees, set container at room temperature (about 70 degrees) in draft-free spot; if warmer than 78 degrees, set container at cool room temperature (about 65 degrees) in draft-free spot. Let stand until dough doubles in bulk, 3 to 5 hours.

5. **STRETCH THE DOUGH:** Scrape dough out onto clean work surface. Gently stretch dough (to redistribute and refresh yeast) as far as possible without tearing, then fold it into thirds like a letter.

6. **DIVIDE AND SHAPE THE DOUGH:** Using bench scraper or chef's knife, divide dough in half, each piece weighing about 1½ pounds. Form each half into rough ball, cover loosely with plastic wrap or damp kitchen towel, and let rest 15 minutes. To shape dough, use one hand to push dough against unfloured work surface, using other hand as guide. Goal is to make taught ball without ripping surface. Pinch bottom seam and set each round, seam side down, on separate sheets of parchment paper on dinner plates, rimless cookie sheets, or inverted rimmed baking sheets.

7. **REFRIGERATE THE ROUNDS OVERNIGHT:** Spray rounds lightly with nonstick cooking spray and cover loosely but completely with plastic wrap. Refrigerate overnight 8 to 12 hours.

8. **PROOF AND SLASH THE ROUNDS:** Remove rounds from refrigerator and gently slide onto room-temperature surface where they can rise undisturbed for several hours; space them at least 6 inches apart. Loosen plastic wrap to allow rounds to rise; let rise until at least doubled in bulk and dough barely springs back when poked with your knuckle, 3 to 4 hours. Meanwhile, after about 2 hours, adjust oven rack to lower-middle position, place baking stone on rack, and heat oven to 500 degrees. Working one at a time, carefully slide rounds on parchment onto baking peel, rimless cookie sheet, or inverted rimmed baking sheet. Using sharp razor blade or knife held at 45-degree angle to work surface, slash surface of rounds ½ to ¾ inch deep.

9. **BAKE THE BREAD:** Working quickly, spray loaves with water, slide onto baking stone, and immediately reduce oven temperature to 450 degrees. During first 5 minutes of baking, spray loaves with water 2 additional times; bake until deep golden brown and instant-read thermometer inserted into center of loaves registers about 210 degrees, about 30 minutes total. Transfer loaves to wire rack, discard parchment, and cool loaves to room temperature on wire rack, about 2 hours.

Rediscovering Chocolate Cupcakes

Why settle for faint flavor from a mix when homemade cupcakes are not much more work?

⇒ BY DAWN YANAGIHARA ⇐

No knives, no forks, no sharing: three good reasons why adults and kids alike love cupcakes. But whereas kids go gaga for confetti sprinkles and a mountain of sugary icing, adults are (or should be) seeking quality—rich, buttery flavor; light, moist, cakey texture; and just a little sugar. This is precisely why, to the adult palate, cake mixes cannot deliver. It is also why most homemade cupcakes don't deliver. Factor chocolate into the equation and the situation is even more glum. Mixes and most recipes really choke when it comes to offering rich chocolate flavor.

My foray into chocolate cupcakes began with a search not only for chocolate cupcake recipes but also for chocolate cake recipes; after all, cupcakes are just pint-sized cakes. What followed was a cupcake-baking marathon. I made all manner of chocolate cupcakes (well over 150): chocolate mayonnaise cupcakes, devil's food cupcakes as black as night, cocoa-only cupcakes, cupcakes with vegetable oil, cupcakes with buttermilk, cupcakes with sour cream, and so on.

Some were OK. None were great. Solid chocolate flavor and moist, tender texture seemed not to coincide; where there was one, the other was not. Well-textured recipes seemed to use a light hand with chocolate, while those with flavor seemed to be weighed down by the chocolate. It would take more than a few tries to create the consummate chocolate cupcake, with ideal texture and flavor.

Causing a Stir

It made sense to first determine the best mixing method, as this would probably influence the amounts of ingredients to be determined in later tests. I had three options. I could use the typical cake-making method of creaming the butter and sugar in a standing mixer until light and fluffy, adding the eggs, and then finally the wet and dry ingredients. Or I could use an easy dump-and-stir method in which the ingredients are unceremoniously combined in a mixer. The last option was the melted-butter method, a simple mixer-free method that we often use in making muffins, quick breads, and brownies.

Dump-and-stir was a failure. Unevenly textured, crumbly, undermixed cupcakes were the result. Creaming wasn't ideal, either. The batter, fluffy with air, was so voluminous that the muf-

Perfect but not complicated, these cupcakes have big chocolate flavor and a buttery, creamy frosting.

fin cups were nearly filled to overflowing. And when baked, the cupcakes' caps spread too far and wide.

Cupcakes made by the melted-butter method had a light, cakey texture with a tender, fine crumb. That they were incredibly easy and quick to make was a bonus—no mixer to haul out, no butter to slowly soften. This method entailed whisking the eggs and sugar, adding the melted butter and chocolate, and then stirring in the dry ingredients in two additions, with buttermilk (deemed the best liquid in early tests) added in between. It couldn't be much easier. If it was, it would be a cake mix.

Take Two

Next: chocolate. Cocoa powder, unsweetened chocolate, bittersweet or semisweet chocolate, and combinations thereof were the candidates. Sorting it all out required more than a half-dozen batches. What I found was that cocoa and unsweetened chocolate alone could each provide blunt flavor (because of their

high percentages of cocoa solids), but both came up short in the nuance department. Bittersweet and semisweet chocolate could supply nuance and complexity but not assertive chocolate flavor. Obviously, it was going to take two forms of chocolate to achieve the balanced flavor that I sought. Ultimately, ½ cup of cocoa powder (Dutch processed was preferred over natural for its fuller, deeper flavor) and 2 ounces of bittersweet chocolate were the winning combination. The cupcakes were now deep, dark, and terrifically chocolaty. As a quick side note, I found that instead of treating the cocoa as a dry ingredient and combining it with the flour, it was better to mix it with the butter and chocolate as they melted, a technique that made the chocolate flavor stronger and richer.

I tried sour cream and whole milk in place of the buttermilk in my working recipe. It was nearly unanimous: Tasters found the cupcakes made with sour cream to be richer and moister (but not at all greasy).

Then came the tricky part: the leavening. Baking soda, which reacts with the acidic sour cream, was the obvious choice, but I could add only so much before it was too much. A small amount of baking soda fully neutralizes the sour cream; any excess is ineffective at leavening and can be detected as an "off" flavor that some describe as soapy. One-half teaspoon was the baking soda ceiling, but because that amount didn't provide adequate lift, I enlisted the aid of baking powder. Three-quarters of a teaspoon of powder in addition to the baking soda encouraged the cupcakes to dome ever so slightly, the result I was looking for.

Oven Temperature Really Matters

BAKED AT 375 DEGREES   **BAKED AT 350 DEGREES**

Just 25 degrees makes a difference in this recipe. Baked at 375 degrees, the cupcakes form odd peaks. Baked at 350 degrees, they form domed tops that are much easier to frost.

The Icing on the (Cup)Cake

My fellow cooks and I agreed that the sort of icing that comes out of a grocery-store bakery would be in keeping with the cupcake spirit, but we also agreed that an icing that tasted of real butter, not shortening, would be better. The solution was a confectioners' sugar buttercream—basically, butter and confectioners' sugar whipped together until light and fluffy. Sometimes a little egg yolk or milk is added for a silkier texture, but I found that a bit of heavy cream was even better.

What's more is that a simple buttercream is a canvas for a vast array of variations: vanilla and chocolate were compulsory offerings, but I also developed coffee and peppermint buttercreams, and each had ardent fans. Underneath it all, however, was a succulent, super-chocolaty chocolate cupcake that was not much more difficult to assemble and bake than a boxed cake mix. Finally, we can have our cake and eat it, too.

DARK CHOCOLATE CUPCAKES
MAKES 12 CUPCAKES

This recipe does not double very well. Cupcakes made from a doubled batch and baked side by side in the oven yield a slightly compromised rise. It's best to make two separate batches and bake each separately. Store leftover cupcakes (frosted or unfrosted) in the refrigerator, but let them come to room temperature before serving.

- 8   tablespoons unsalted butter, cut into 4 pieces
- 2   ounces bittersweet chocolate, chopped
- ½   cup (1½ ounces) Dutch-processed cocoa
- ¾   cup (3¾ ounces) unbleached all-purpose flour
- ½   teaspoon baking soda
- ¾   teaspoon baking powder
- 2   large eggs
- ¾   cup (5¼ ounces) sugar
- I   teaspoon vanilla extract
- ½   teaspoon table salt
- ½   cup (4 ounces) sour cream

1. Adjust oven rack to lower-middle position; heat oven to 350 degrees. Line standard-sized muffin pan (cups have ½-cup capacity) with baking-cup liners.

2. Combine butter, chocolate, and cocoa in medium heatproof bowl. Set bowl over saucepan containing barely simmering water; heat mixture until butter and chocolate are melted and whisk until smooth and fully combined. Set aside to cool until just warm to touch.

3. Whisk flour, baking soda, and baking powder in small bowl to combine.

4. Whisk eggs in second medium bowl to combine; add sugar, vanilla, and salt and whisk until fully incorporated. Add cooled chocolate mixture and whisk until combined. Sift about one-third of flour mixture over chocolate mixture and whisk until combined; whisk in sour cream until com-

bined, then sift remaining flour mixture over and whisk until batter is homogenous and thick.

5. Divide batter evenly among muffin pan cups. Bake until skewer inserted into center of cupcakes comes out clean, 18 to 20 minutes.

6. Cool cupcakes in muffin pan on wire rack until cool enough to handle, about 15 minutes. Carefully lift each cupcake from muffin pan and set on wire rack. Cool to room temperature before icing, about 30 minutes. (To frost: Mound about 2 tablespoons icing on center of each cupcake. Using small icing spatula or butter knife, spread icing to edge of cupcake, leaving slight mound in center.)

EASY VANILLA BEAN BUTTERCREAM
MAKES ABOUT 1½ CUPS, ENOUGH TO FROST 12 CUPCAKES

If you prefer to skip the vanilla bean, increase the extract to 1½ teaspoons. Any of the buttercream frostings can be made ahead and refrigerated; if refrigerated, however, the frosting must stand at room temperature to soften before use. If using a handheld mixer, increase mixing times significantly (by at least 50 percent).

- 10   tablespoons unsalted butter, softened
- ½   vanilla bean, halved lengthwise
- I¼   cups (5 ounces) confectioners' sugar
-      Pinch table salt
- ½   teaspoon vanilla extract
- I   tablespoon heavy cream

In standing mixer fitted with whisk attachment, beat butter at medium-high speed until smooth, about 20 seconds. Using paring knife, scrape seeds from vanilla bean into butter and beat mixture at medium-high speed to combine, about

15 seconds. Add confectioners' sugar and salt; beat at medium-low speed until most of sugar is moistened, about 45 seconds. Scrape down bowl and beat at medium speed until mixture is fully combined, about 15 seconds; scrape bowl, add vanilla extract and heavy cream, and beat at medium speed until incorporated, about 10 seconds, then increase speed to medium-high and beat until light and fluffy, about 4 minutes, scraping down bowl once or twice.

EASY CHOCOLATE BUTTERCREAM

Follow recipe for Easy Vanilla Bean Buttercream, omitting vanilla bean and heavy cream and reducing sugar to 1 cup. After beating in vanilla extract, reduce speed to low and gradually beat in 4 ounces melted and cooled semisweet or bittersweet chocolate.

EASY COFFEE BUTTERCREAM

Follow recipe for Easy Vanilla Bean Buttercream, omitting vanilla bean and dissolving 1½ teaspoons instant espresso in vanilla extract and heavy cream.

EASY PEPPERMINT BUTTERCREAM

Follow recipe for Easy Vanilla Bean Buttercream, omitting vanilla bean, reducing vanilla extract to ¼ teaspoon, and adding ¾ teaspoon peppermint extract along with vanilla extract.

COOK'S EXTRA gives you free recipes online. For three more frostings, visit www.cooksillustrated.com and key in code 4054. These recipes will be available until April 15, 2005.

Is the Best Swiss Cheese Swiss?

Genuine Swiss Emmenthaler should easily best supermarket Swiss imposters, right?
After weeks of testing, we discovered a few holes in that theory.

⇒ BY JOLYON HELTERMAN ⇐

It's not that hard to find willing tasters for a story on chocolate cupcakes (see page 24). But try rounding up 20 volunteers a day for supermarket Swiss and desks suddenly go empty, schedules suddenly become full, food "allergies" suddenly take a turn for the worse.

Why such an unenthusiastic attitude toward an American sandwich standard? Mostly because the pallid slices sold at supermarkets often pale by comparison with the real deal: genuine Emmenthaler from Switzerland. The original cheese with the famous holes (called "eyes"), imported Emmenthaler is prized for a subtle flavor profile of sweet, nutty, fruity, and slightly pungent notes, as well as a texture that's firm but gently giving. By contrast, Swiss cheese—the generic name for Emmenthaler-style cheese sold in the United States—gets a bad rap for being little more than a bland, rubbery layer of dairy that takes up space in uninspired ham sandwiches.

A preliminary tasting convinced us that the varieties called "baby Swiss" and "lacey Swiss" are too different from regular Swiss cheese to be included in the main tastings (see "A Slice of Confusion," right). In the end, our panel sampled eight nationally distributed supermarket Swiss cheeses: five domestic brands (Heluva Good, Kraft, Sara Lee, Sargento, and Tillamook); Jarlsberg, a popular brand of Emmenthaler-style cheese made in Norway; and two Finnish imports (the deli brands Finlandia and Boar's Head). Finally, we included a genuine imported Emmenthaler. Tasters tried the cheeses raw and cooked in grilled-cheese sandwiches. The results? Unexpected.

A Heated Discussion

But not in the raw tasting. As anticipated, the imported Emmenthaler handily bested the competition. Even though we served julienne slices to keep tasters from distinguishing the block of Emmenthaler from the presliced samples, there was no disguising the flavor. Tasters roundly praised the imported Swiss original for its buttery, nutty, and fruity flavor profile. Three supermarket brands—Sargento, Boar's Head, and Tillamook—also received high marks, but none of them could match the well-balanced subtlety of Emmenthaler. What's more, true to stereotype, several samples were indicted for rubbery texture and flavor profiles that amounted to "bland nothingness."

Next came the grilled-cheese tasting, and that's where surprises began. Jarlsberg, which had clocked an unremarkable seventh place in the raw tasting, was suddenly the grilled-cheese champ. Puzzled, I compared tasters' comments with the numerical data. Because Jarlsberg was the only cheese not to elicit a panicked "desperately needs salt!" from tasters, I zeroed in on sodium content. Sure enough, it contained twice the sodium of the other brands: 120 milligrams per ounce, compared with 50 to 65 milligrams. The results now seemed less far-fetched. Because grilled cheese is traditionally made with much saltier cheeses—such as American (400 milligrams per ounce) or cheddar (180 milligrams)—Jarlsberg came closest to this norm.

More curious than Jarlsberg's second-round rise was Emmenthaler's precipitous fall. After an easy triumph in the raw tasting, Emmenthaler finished the grilled-cheese round not second, not third, but ninth out of nine samples. Tasting sheets overflowed with sour invective: "I spit this out—it's like rubbing alcohol," complained one taster. "Way too gamey," said another. The same panel that had found raw Emmenthaler nutty and nicely balanced now deemed it too funky, chemical, and "moldy." How could the same Swiss have dropped from first place to dead last?

It's all about temperature, says Mark Johnson, a cheese expert at the Wisconsin Center for Dairy Research. "Typically, we prefer eating cheese at about 65 degrees or a little warmer—room temperature, if you will—just to bring out flavors." But go from a little warmer to a lot warmer, and you risk amplifying some of the flavor notes that might best remain faint voices in the background. "Certain volatile flavors [come out] that wouldn't if you just ate the cheese at 65 or 70 degrees," he says.

That explained how interesting, balanced complexity could bloom into gamey, over-the-top pungency once heated. Still puzzling, however, was why Emmenthaler had made such a steep drop when heated while the rest of the samples (other than Jarlsberg) barely shuffled order. To find out, I needed a better grasp on how Emmenthaler-style cheeses get their flavor in the first place.

The Eyes Have It

Swiss-cheese making is a complex process, but it very roughly breaks down like this: Starter bacteria are added to partially skimmed milk (about 2.8 percent milk fat, compared with whole milk's 3.6 percent), which is cooked, worked, then placed

---

A Slice of Confusion: Baby, Lacey, and Reduced-Fat Swiss

Be careful which Swiss you toss into your shopping cart—and not just which brand. One false move could send you home with a package of "baby Swiss," "lacey Swiss," or "reduced-fat Swiss." How different are these cheeses from the genuine article? A lot more than their deceptively similar packaging would indicate. In a blind tasting, not one taster had trouble identifying the type.

When baby Swiss is made, the milk's whey is replaced with water to remove sugars and acids that would lead to flavor development. The result is a mild, creamy cheese that some tasters likened to Muenster or provolone. Reduced-fat Swiss starts off with slightly leaner milk than regular Swiss, and it's cured with less salt. There are two styles of reduced Swiss: One looks exactly like regular Swiss; the other, lacey Swiss, is completely strewn with tiny holes, giving it the appearance of translucent lace when sliced. To achieve this textural effect, cheesemakers add a bacteria strain that begins furiously making gas bubbles almost immediately.

How do they stack up to regular Swiss? We tasted all three varieties of our two "Recommended" brands, Sargento (regular, baby, and reduced) and Boar's Head (regular, baby, and lacey). To our surprise, the baby Swiss did as well as our regular recommended brand. But the dreadful taste of the lacey/reduced varieties was too high a price to pay for roughly 1 gram less fat per serving. –J.H.

BABY
Pretty good

LACEY
Awful

REDUCED FAT
Just as awful

RATING SUPERMARKET SWISS CHEESES

Twenty *Cook's Illustrated* staff members tasted nine Emmenthaler-style Swiss cheeses in raw strips and grilled-cheese sandwiches. To ensure validity, samples were tasted in different orders by different tasters, and one cheese served as a control (appearing twice in each plate of samples). Tasters were asked to rate each sample for flavor, saltiness, and texture, then give each an overall score of 1 to 10. The brands are listed in order of preference. Fat and sodium values given are per ounce.

BEST CHEESE FOR EATING RAW: **EMMENTHALER** (SWISS)

➤ **$10.49 for 1 lb. Fat: 9 g. Sodium: 50 mg.**
The hands-down raw-tasting winner shocked its admirers in the grilled-cheese tasting. "Mildly pungent with nutty overtones" quickly gave way to "chemical, funky" and "evil, evil cheese" when the heat was cranked up.

BEST CHEESE FOR GRILLED CHEESE: **JARLSBERG** (NORWEGIAN)

➤ **$3.99 for 8 oz. Fat: 7 g. Sodium: 120 mg.**
The grilled-cheese favorite won praise for creamy, salty mildness, but the raw tasting was a different story: "Bland," "generic tasting," and "rubbery" were tasters' descriptions of this sample in its uncooked state.

RECOMMENDED ALL-PURPOSE CHEESES

SARGENTO Deli Style Aged Swiss Cheese (DOMESTIC)

➤ **$3.79 for 8 oz. Fat: 7.5 g. Sodium: 60 mg.**
This ubiquitous dairy-shelf brand was good all-around. Its "buttery, tangy" flavors and creamy texture reminded some tasters of cheddar. Several liked the "pleasantly sour taste of buttermilk."

BOAR'S HEAD Gold Label Premium Imported Swiss Cheese (FINNISH)

➤ **$6.99 for 1 lb. Fat: 8 g. Sodium: 65 mg.**
This is "Swiss cheese for grown-ups," remarked one panelist. More strongly flavored than many of the others (the biggest eyes of the bunch), this deli standard maintained its balance even when cooked. "Lots of roasted, earthy sensations."

RECOMMENDED WITH RESERVATIONS

TILLAMOOK Swiss Cheese (DOMESTIC)

➤ **$4.39 for 12 oz. Fat: 8 g. Sodium: 60 mg.**
Panelists found this "tangy" Oregon brand to be more like cheddar than Swiss but were divided as to whether that was a plus.

HELUVA GOOD Aged Swiss Cheese (DOMESTIC)

➤ **$2.29 for 8 oz. Fat: 8 g. Sodium: 60 mg.**
Heluva Fair? Tasters had no major complaints about this upstate New York brand; they had no major compliments, either. "Does not stand out to me in any way," said one taster.

NOT RECOMMENDED

KRAFT Deli Deluxe Swiss (DOMESTIC)

➤ **$2.89 for 8 oz. Fat: 9 g. Sodium: 50 mg.**
This widely available brand won admirers for its "soft, uniform texture," but the negative comments outweighed the positive. Tasters criticized off-putting sour notes and an artificial aftertaste.

FINLANDIA Imported Swiss Cheese (FINNISH)

➤ **$7.29 for 1 lb. Fat: 8 g. Sodium: 60 mg.**
This deli brand's flavor was over-the-top—and not in a pleasant way. Tasters found the samples "gamey, almost rancid," with sour off-tastes. The dry, rubbery texture was also panned.

SARA LEE Swiss Cheese (DOMESTIC)

➤ **$3.79 for 8 oz. Fat: 8 g. Sodium: 58 mg.**
"Rubber city!" complained one taster. Others decried artificial overtones and "a plasticky, industrial bite." But patience may be rewarded: "There's a soapy off-flavor initially, ending with an almost Swiss cheese flavor."

---

in a temperature-controlled room to ripen. In Switzerland and Finland, cheesemakers generally use unpasteurized milk; in Norway (for Jarlsberg) and the United States, they use pasteurized milk to achieve a cleaner—though potentially less complex—flavor profile. Then there's the cow's diet: Some cheesemakers swear by particular combinations of grass and grain (or one or the other) to get their product's flavor profile just so.

Proprietary and regional differences aside, the bacteria responsible for flavor development in all Emmenthaler-style cheeses release carbon dioxide, which forms rounded air pockets in the gradually hardening cheese—the source of the trademark holes, or eyes. Longer aging leads to larger eyes, as does a warmer aging environment. Generally speaking, the larger the eyes, the more pronounced the flavor: It means the enzymes and bacteria have had more time to work their magic.

To ensure generous eye development, the Swiss government dictates that Emmenthaler cannot be exported until it has aged for at least 90 days. (The two Finnish brands in our lineup proudly advertise being aged "over 100 days" before reaching the deli display case.) But that's not the case in America, says Johnson. Not only do we require just 60 days' aging, but the aging temperature is much lower. "The cheese is held at a colder temperature—which limits the size of the eyes—so less flavor develops."

Do American cheesemakers imagine the U.S. cheese-eating public can't handle strong-tasting Swiss? Not necessarily. It's actually the big eyes they're trying to avoid, Johnson says, not the big flavors. The logic is simple. Because most Swiss cheese made in the United States is sold presliced, sturdiness is a major consideration. Cheese with large holes has a tendency to fall apart in high-speed, automated slicers. The more slices that must be discarded along the way, the costlier the process. So American manufacturers let the eyes grow to a certain limit, then they transfer the cheese to a cold environment to stifle further development.

Armed with this new knowledge—and a ruler and pen—I returned to our cheeses. Measuring dozens and dozens of cheese holes (the test kitchen life is a glamorous one), I calculated average eye diameter for each sample. Sure enough, the best-endowed cheeses were three of the European samples: Boar's Head (2.1 centimeters), Finlandia (1.8 centimeters), and Emmenthaler (1.7 centimeters), the ones aged longest. All were described as strongly flavored, and all but the Boar's Head tanked in the grilled-cheese round. The eyes of the U.S.-made cheeses hovered around 1 centimeter. The smallest eyes? Like clockwork: the very mild Jarlsberg, at 0.7 centimeter.

At the end of the day, then, what Swiss cheese do we recommend? For a plate of cheese and crackers, we think a genuine Emmenthaler (with large eyes) is the best bet. For grilled cheese and other simple cooked preparations, give Jarlsberg a try. If you want to buy one cheese for all applications, Sargento and Boar's Head performed consistently well—no matter what the temperature.

Disparate Measures

The cookware aisle is crowded with souped-up variations on the lowly liquid measuring cup. Is it time to trade in our classic Pyrex?

⇒ BY JOLYON HELTERMAN AND GARTH CLINGINGSMITH ⇐

For years, the term "liquid measuring cup" meant one thing: a flared, graded cup with a handle, usually made from Pyrex-brand glass. No longer. Nowadays, the ubiquitous Pyrex shares retail shelf space with cups sporting a dizzying array of newfangled options, including gleaming metals, angled consoles, laboratory-style beaker shapes, and gradations broken down to number of teaspoons.

Do these "innovations" go beyond bells and whistles? Is it finally time to upgrade from the classic Pyrex? We brought 11 models into the test kitchen to find out.

Reading Is Fundamental

There's a clear distinction between liquid measuring cups and dry. A liquid measuring cup has multiple gradation lines. Dry measuring cups have none—there's a different cup for every amount.

Dry ingredients and wet ingredients are also measured differently. The test kitchen measures the dry sort by dipping the cup into the ingredient, scooping a heaping cupful, then sweeping across the cup with a spatula (or the flat side of a knife) until the contents are level with the top of the cup—a method referred to as "dip and sweep."

We measure liquids by filling the cup until the surface of the liquid is even with the correct gradation line when viewed at eye level (which means stooping down to look). So far, so good—but be careful which part of the surface you're looking at. Liquids in a container have a tendency to form a *meniscus*, a slight curving of the surface. (The meniscus forms because water molecules are more attracted to the cup material than to one another, so they creep up the sides a bit.) When viewed from the side of the cup, the meniscus looks like a "cord" around the top of the liquid. To maximize accuracy, simply measure from the bottom of the cord, not the top.

The dry/liquid divide came to haunt a couple of the designs in our lineup. As we began our tests, it became obvious that metal is absolutely the wrong choice of material for liquid measuring cups: There's no way to view the gradation lines at eye level, much less spot the bottom of the meniscus.

Was it fair to dismiss metal cups based solely on our meniscus-reading theory? Not, we reasoned, if accuracy were only negligibly affected. So we had 12 test-kitchen staffers measure 1 cup of water from the sink with each model, then pour the water into a waiting bowl. As testers focused on making commentary about each model's design (ease of pouring, handle shape, etc.), we were busy weighing the amount of water they'd managed to transfer to the bowl. Now we had proof. The only two cups off by more than half an ounce were made of metal: All-Clad, which was an average of 0.73 ounce over, and Polder, which averaged a whopping 1.1 ounces over—that's 6.6 extra teaspoons per cup!

As we watched panelists measure water with each model, another pattern emerged: They seemed to be filling the plastic cups at a faster pace. Puzzled, we pored through the testing sheets. Comments of "nice, flat water line" and "easy-to-read meniscus" popped up repeatedly for the plastic cups but never for the glass. Additional research uncovered an interesting bit of physics: Water molecules are more attracted to glass than to plastic, so less surface curvature occurs with plastic cups—an enhanced clarity testers appreciated.

Sometimes lack of clarity affected accuracy; other times, it was simply irritating. For instance, testers were annoyed by the sheer number of markings on some of the models, with column after column obsessively delineating useless equivalent measures in cups, third-cups, quarter-cups, milliliters, cubic centimeters, tablespoons, and more. As one tester put it, "I've never made a recipe that calls for 78 teaspoons of *anything*."

Less may be more, but not if it's ridiculously less. The All-Clad had just three gradation lines (¼ cup, ½ cup, ¾ cup); nowhere except for the discarded packaging was there an indication that its full capacity was 1 cup. Other models, which performed well in every test, inexplicably had no ⅓-cup gradation markings.

The most innovative cup of the bunch, the Oxo Angled represents an attempt to eliminate stooping altogether. The gradation lines, printed both on the sides and on a diagonal plane that juts through the cup, are designed to be read from above rather than at eye level. However, the multiple planes created an awkward optical effect: The meniscus line on the interior of the cup seemed out of phase with the one on the side,

as though they were at different levels.

To minimize spillage, liquid measures should feature extra space between the uppermost gradation marking and the rim. Two of our models lacked this buffer zone, making liquid transfer a daunting task.

Measuring, then transferring, cups of honey with each model convinced us of the virtues of roomy, rounded interiors. The skinnier designs had us reaching for our smallest spatulas, while the wider models made honey transfer quick work even with a standard-size spatula. The Oxo Angled was the loser in this round: Its multiple planes provided numerous edges where honey could take refuge.

In the test kitchen, we often ladle hot chicken broth into a measuring cup before adding it to a simmering saucepan. It's a task that doesn't go so smoothly with a narrow-mouthed cup. Broth dribbled down the sides of the three narrowest cups: the Norpro Measuring Glass, the Catamount Flameware, and the All-Clad.

The broth test earned plastic cups some new fans by staying noticeably cooler than the glass. That said, many staffers still weren't ready to give up on the classic Pyrex, even though the plastic matched the glass in the dishwasher and microwave challenges. But little did we know that the plastic cups would soon win over a few more testers.

Good to the Last Drop

One afternoon, toward the end of testing, we were engrossed in a spirited debate of our tentative chart order (see page 29), and that's when the Catamount Flameware bit the dust. There it lay, glass shards strewn across the test kitchen's slip-resistant floors. A moment of panicked silence. Then eerie calm: "I think the Pyrex would have survived," one of us said, resuming the original debate.

That's all it took. We quickly cleared out a section of the test kitchen, donned safety goggles, and lined up the surviving models along the countertop. In front of a rapt crowd of onlookers ("I can't *not* look!" exclaimed one wide-eyed test cook), we dropped each cup three times from a height of 3 feet by tipping it off the countertop. The cups made of metal or plastic survived with mere scratches. The Norpro Measuring Glass lasted one drop before exploding into hundreds

RATING MEASURING CUPS

We tested 11 liquid measuring cups, with capacities as close to 2 cups as we could find in each manufacturer's line. The cups are listed in the chart in order of preference, based on our evaluation of performance, design, and durability.

MATERIAL: The material the cup is made from.

PRICE: Prices paid at Boston-area retail, national mail-order, or online outlets. You may encounter different prices.

DIAMETER: Measured across the mouth, from inside rim to inside rim. (For the Oxo, the only model with an elliptical mouth, we give major and minor axes.)

MICROWAVE-SAFE? Based on manufacturer recommendations.

PERFORMANCE: Twelve *Cook's Illustrated* staff members measured 1 cup of water and transferred it to a bowl; after each transfer, we weighed the transferred water and compared its weight with the standard for 1 cup. We ladled hot broth into each cup, then transferred it to a stockpot. We measured honey, then transferred it to a bowl. Scores of good, fair, and poor were assigned for each test, and the composite score constitutes the overall performance rating.

DESIGN: Factors evaluated included whether the cup's dimensions, shape, gradation markings, and materials contributed to or detracted from overall user-friendliness.

DURABILITY: We heated water in the cups in the microwave until boiling (if deemed microwave-safe by the manufacturer), ran them through 25 dishwasher cycles (with Heated Dry mode turned on), and dropped them on linoleum and tile floors. Cups were downgraded for breaking, for scratching, and/or for not being microwave-safe.

RECOMMENDED

	TEST CRITERIA		TESTERS' COMMENTS

Rubbermaid Measuring Cup
MATERIAL: Plastic
DIAMETER: 3¹⁵/₁₆ inches
MICROWAVE-SAFE? Yes

PRICE: $3.79
PERFORMANCE: ★★★
DESIGN: ★★★
DURABILITY: ★★★

The roomy, rounded interior made quick work of honey transfer, the wide mouth was optimal for ladling broth, and the plastic kept cool, survived our stress tests, and boasted a flat meniscus. Make sure to buy the model with ¹/₃-cup markings.

Pyrex Measuring Cup
MATERIAL: Glass
DIAMETER: 4¹/₄ inches
MICROWAVE-SAFE? Yes

PRICE: $4.95
PERFORMANCE: ★★★
DESIGN: ★★★
DURABILITY: ★★

Pyrex won praises for a wide mouth, comfortable handle, and readable markings. Residual honey was removed with one easy swipe of the spatula. A bit heavy, though; not for klutzes with tile floors.

Emsa Perfect Beaker
MATERIAL: Plastic
DIAMETER: 4⁵/₁₆ inches
MICROWAVE-SAFE? Yes

PRICE: $7.99
PERFORMANCE: ★★★
DESIGN: ★★
DURABILITY: ★★★

A spacious design with an excellent pour and a nice, shallow meniscus. On the downside, the concave base is a trap for dirty dishwasher water, and some testers complained about units-of-measure overkill.

Anchor Hocking
Liquid Measuring Cup
MATERIAL: Glass
DIAMETER: 4¹/₄ inches
MICROWAVE-SAFE? Yes

PRICE: $6.75
PERFORMANCE: ★★★
DESIGN: ★★
DURABILITY: ★★

The model we tested has raised, see-through markings that testers found hard to read, but the company does make one with flat colors. "This is just like the Pyrex but less balanced," said one panelist, referring to the heavy cup's disproportionately light handle.

RECOMMENDED WITH RESERVATIONS

Cambro Camwear 1-Pint
Measuring Cup
MATERIAL: Plastic
DIAMETER: 3⁵/₈ inches
MICROWAVE-SAFE? Yes

PRICE: $6.90
PERFORMANCE: ★★★
DESIGN: ★★
DURABILITY: ★★★

Thin gradation lines, raised and painted numbers, clean cylindrical shape, and shallow meniscus almost put this cup on top. Not until late in the testing did we notice a flaw: no ¹/₃-cup markings.

Oxo Angled Measuring Cup
MATERIAL: Plastic, with rubber handle grip
DIAMETER: 4³/₁₆ inches, 5 inches
MICROWAVE-SAFE? No

PRICE: $7.99
PERFORMANCE: ★★
DESIGN: ★★
DURABILITY: ★★

Testers questioned the merits of angled markings: "How much effort does it really save?" Having numbers both on the sides and down the diagonal was distracting, and the multiple planes created an irritating phasing effect—and waylaid plenty of honey. Best pour of the bunch.

Catamount Flameware
Liquid Measuring Cup
MATERIAL: Glass
DIAMETER: 3 inches
MICROWAVE-SAFE? Yes

PRICE: $9.95
PERFORMANCE: ★★
DESIGN: ★★
DURABILITY: ★

Flamesafe, ovensafe, dishwasher-safe, microwave-safe— but linoleum-floor-safe would have been a nice touch. The laboratory-style beaker handled most tasks well, but testers didn't trust its sturdiness. The narrow mouth made ladling broth a chore.

NOT RECOMMENDED

Amco See Thru Measuring Cup
MATERIAL: Stainless steel, with plastic window
DIAMETER: 3¹¹/₁₆ inches
MICROWAVE-SAFE? No

PRICE: $11.25
PERFORMANCE: ★★
DESIGN: ★
DURABILITY: ★★★

Why make a liquid measure that's only partially see-through? To read the numbers, you must position the handle directly away from you, and there are spouts on every side but the useful one (opposite the handle).

Norpro Measuring Glass
MATERIAL: Glass
DIAMETER: 2¹¹/₁₆ inches
MICROWAVE-SAFE? Yes

PRICE: $11.50
PERFORMANCE: ★
DESIGN: ★
DURABILITY: ★

Testers were unimpressed with the narrow, spoutless mouth, sloppy pour, and "shimmery" cursive markings. We needed a potholder to finish the hot broth test. Its relative accuracy saved this model from last place.

All-Clad 1-Cup Liquid Measure
MATERIAL: Stainless steel
DIAMETER: 3¹/₁₆ inches
MICROWAVE-SAFE? No

PRICE: $19.99
PERFORMANCE: ★
DESIGN: ★
DURABILITY: ★★★

The packaging says "liquid measure," but testers weren't convinced. Major spillage, sloppy pouring, and unclear markings were this cup's downfalls—not to mention the quick-heating material it's made from.

Polder 4-Cup Measure Cup
MATERIAL: Stainless steel
DIAMETER: 4⁷/₁₆ inches
MICROWAVE-SAFE? No

PRICE: $10.00
PERFORMANCE: ★
DESIGN: ★
DURABILITY: ★★

The 1-cup line was so deep down in this "clunky" behemoth that testers had trouble judging when to stop filling. During the broth test, excess steam made the task even harder, and the metal got piping hot.

---

of pieces. The thick-glass Pyrex and Anchor Hocking? Three drops, no mess.

The rubber surface victories were impressive, but how would these invincible glass cups fare with a tile kitchen floor? We moved our experiment to a tile-floored restroom. Using a 2½-foot-high shelf as a stand-in for the countertop, we dropped our nine intact cups once again. The metals and the plastics got a bit more banged up (the Polder suffered a dent). And, yes, *smash*—the Pyrex and the Anchor Hocking met their demise.

At the end of the day, then, which cup do we recommend? The fancy, stylish pretenders to the Pyrex throne failed to overthrow the king. But as we swept up the king's remains from the tile floor, we crowned the not-so-fancy Rubbermaid—with its wide mouth, flat meniscus, and stay-cool, sturdy plastic—as a worthy successor.

KITCHEN NOTES

⋛ BY DAWN YANAGIHARA ⋚

Scratching the Nonstick Surface

We've learned the hard way in the test kitchen: Metal utensils can easily scratch nonstick surfaces, sometimes even when the manufacturer promises otherwise. Scratches and gouges not only are unsightly but also reduce the effectiveness of the surface. We have since outfitted the kitchen with silicone-clad wire whisks and plastic-tipped tongs. If you're concerned about the longevity of your nonstick cookware, we recommend that you do the same.

Torn-tillas

When making quesadillas (page 20), the first serious problem we encountered was separating single flour tortillas from their tightly packed stacks. When peeled apart, the tortillas would tear, making them useless as containers for fillings. Eventually, we noticed that this was a problem only with tortillas that came straight from the refrigerator; room-temperature tortillas separated easily enough.

Here's the simple solution we came up with to unstick a stuck stack of refrigerated tortillas without causing the edges to become dry and brittle: Dampen a clean kitchen towel, then wring out the excess water. Remove the stack from the package and set it on the towel; fold the ends of the towel over so that the stack is completely enclosed. Microwave the wrapped tortillas at 30 percent power for about 20 seconds, then peel away as many tortillas as possible (the top and bottom ones will likely be the first that can be freed). If necessary, rewrap the tortillas and repeat.

Fish Storage

Because fish is so perishable, it's best to buy it the day it will be cooked. But that's not always possible, even here in the kitchen. Here's what to do if you need to hold fish beyond the day it's purchased.

As soon as the fish gets into the kitchen, unwrap it, pat it dry, put it in a zipper-lock bag, press out the air, and seal the bag. Then set the fish on a bed of ice in a bowl or other deep container (that can contain the water once the ice melts) and place the bowl in the back of the fridge, where it is coldest. If the ice melts before you use the fish, replenish it. Another option is to set the patted-dry fish in a container or bowl or on a plate, press plastic wrap directly against the surface, and place frozen reusable ice packs on top. Either way, the fish should keep for one day.

The Done Deal on Poultry

The doneness of poultry is determined by taking its temperature in the thickest part of the breast and/or thigh. Just where is the "thickest part," you ask? So did we. To find out, we took whole cooked chickens and bone-in breasts and legs and cut them into thin cross-sections so that we could examine the thickness of the meat.

On a breast, the thickest part is—no surprise—the area that appeared to be the thickest, basically, the widest and plumpest area. But the question remained as to how and where the thermometer should be inserted.

The tendency when inserting a thermometer straight down into the meat (which is not even 2 inches thick) is to push it down too far or not far enough. For this reason, we prefer to insert the thermometer horizontally from the top (neck) end down the length of the breast. The idea is to insert the thermometer well into the meat, then slowly withdraw it, looking for the lowest temperature that registers.

If you're taking the temperature

KITCHEN SCIENCE: Reusing Frying Oil

In the test kitchen, we regularly deep-fry potatoes, chicken, and more, so we like to reuse our frying oil. But there are some caveats. First of all, oil can transfer flavors from food to food. For instance, once a batch of oil has been used to fry fish, we discard it. We have found that you can fry multiple batches of chicken or potatoes in the same oil, but at some point the oil starts to break down and smoke. We wondered why.

The Role of Free Fatty Acids The principal component of frying oil is the triglyceride, which consists of three long fatty acid tails connected to a molecule called glycerol. When the fatty acids are released from glycerol, they are called "free" fatty acids. The amount of these free fatty acids in the oil is an indication of the suitability of the oil for high-temperature frying. When we measured peanut oil, our favorite frying oil, we found a very low concentration of free fatty acids.

Smoke Point A low concentration of free fatty acids translates to a high smoke point. Depending on the recipe, deep-frying usually occurs between 325 and 375 degrees Fahrenheit. When we tested the smoke points of four fats, we found peanut oil had the highest: 451 degrees. (Canola oil was the runner-up at 442 degrees.) This number will vary from brand to brand based on several factors, including how much the oil has been refined. For instance, unrefined peanut oil has a much lower smoke point than a refined peanut oil and is not suitable for frying. In general, refined oils are relatively tasteless.

Why Oil Breaks Down Even though peanut oil has a high smoke point, the oil will eventually start to smoke during normal use. That's because water from the food reacts with the oil to release the fatty acids. The more you use an oil, the lower the smoke point becomes. To demonstrate this, we fried three consecutive batches of chicken in 8 cups of peanut oil. We then filtered the used oil and heated it again to the smoke point. The smoke point had dropped 28 degrees. When we had the used oil analyzed for free fatty acid content, we learned that the total amount had jumped 37 percent. While patting food dry before frying can retard oil degradation, water is not the only enemy of oil. Heating to the smoke point also promotes decomposition, as can salt if it is added to food before frying. Keeping oil clean as you fry also helps to extend its life.

The Bottom Line Choose an oil with a smoke point well above normal frying temperatures so you have a built-in cushion against the effects of reusing the oil. (This is one reason we like to fry with peanut oil.) Make sure not to overheat the oil (monitoring the temperature of the oil with a thermometer is essential). Finally, limit contact with salt and water and skim bits of food from the oil.

– John Olson, Science Editor

CHOP   DICE   PRECISE DICE

In general, the recipe instruction "dice" (or "cube", depending on the recipe writer) denotes more precision than "chop." A *diced* carrot is cut into neat cubes, whereas a chopped carrot can consist of more irregularly shaped pieces. That said, "dice" can mean two things: relatively tidy and uniform pieces or painstakingly precise cubes. The latter involves squaring off rounded edges and, hence, a good deal of waste. We almost never require such fussy precision at *Cook's*: When appearance is of considerable importance, we use the less rigid dice, as in diced tomatoes for Fresh Tomato Salsa (July/August 2004). We chop on most other occasions (onions for potato salad, celery for stuffing, and the like).

Onions and tomatoes present unique cases in that the same technique is used for both dicing and chopping. One could argue, though, that when dicing an onion or tomato (as opposed to chopping it), special care should be taken to make evenly spaced cuts so that the pieces are as uniform as possible.

---

of the breast on a whole chicken, aim for the meat just above the bone by inserting the thermometer low into the thickness of the breast. Because the cavity slows the cooking, the coolest spot sits just above the bone (which is a poor conductor of heat). If you're taking the temperature of a single breast (bone in or boneless), aim for the dead center of the meat by inserting the thermometer at the midpoint of the thickness.

On a single thigh or leg quarter, the meat is relatively thin and of even thickness, which simplifies the task of taking the temperature. When the leg is part of a whole chicken, however, taking the temperature is more complicated because its musculature is not as apparent. We found that the best way to take the temperature of the thigh on a whole bird is to insert the probe down into the space between the tip of the breast and the thigh. Angle the probe outward

ever so slightly so that it pierces the meat in the lower part of the thigh. To get some idea of how deeply it's inserted—and to be certain that it isn't inserted too far—push the probe until it pokes through the bottom side of the chicken, then slowly withdraw it, looking for the lowest registered temperature.

The technique of overinserting the thermometer accommodates both digital and dial thermometers. The former have sensors located at the tip of the probe; the latter have sensors located about an inch up from the tip.

Yet even if you follow the above guidelines to the letter, the process of testing for doneness remains by and large one of trial and error. It's best to poke the bird a couple times to find the lowest temperature. Moving the probe just a few millimeters to the left or right or up or down can reveal a different temperature.

Taking an Accurate Temperature

THIGH: With the thermometer perpendicular to counter, insert probe between tip of breast and leg and into lower thigh. BREAST: With thermometer parallel to counter, slide probe into neck end just above bird's cavity.

RECIPE UPDATE: **READERS RESPOND**

Quick or Old-Fashioned Oats?

When we wrote that either rolled (or old-fashioned) oats or quick-cooking oats could be used in our recipe for **Oatmeal Scones (September/October 2003)**, some readers wondered if the quick oats would also work in our recipe for **Big Chewy Oatmeal-Raisin Cookies (January/February 1997)**, which listed only rolled oats.

After making and tasting two batches of the cookies, one with quick oats, the other with rolled oats, we came up with an answer: Yes. Judged on the basis of appearance alone, the cookies made with rolled oats came out on top. They were more attractive because we could actually see the oats. They also had a full oat flavor and a pleasing chew. The cookies made with quick oats were no slouches, though, even if we did have to peer long and hard to spot the oats. They were praised for being a bit more refined, lighter, and cakier while still retaining their chew and boasting full oat flavor. The verdict? For the best-looking cookies, use old-fashioned oats, but if the only oats you have in the cupboard are quick oats, rest assured that neither the flavor nor the texture of the cookies will suffer.

Rice of a Different Color

Many readers wrote in asking if they could use long-grain brown rice in place of the long-grain white rice called for in our **Mexican Rice (September/October 2004)**. Because brown rice absorbs more liquid and requires a longer cooking time than white, we knew a direct swap wouldn't work. But we did figure out how to modify the recipe so that it would work with brown rice. As for the liquid, we found that increasing the amount of chicken broth to $2\frac{1}{2}$ cups did the trick. As for cooking time, a longer period of $1\frac{1}{4}$ to $1\frac{1}{2}$ hours, with a good stir every 30 minutes, was sufficient. During testing, we also found it necessary to decrease the amount of time the rice was sautéed in oil to 3 to $3\frac{1}{2}$ minutes; any longer and the rice started to split and turn overly dark. At the end of testing, we sat back and enjoyed the nuttier, more healthful take on our recipe.

How Much Frying Oil Is Enough?

Several readers have expressed confusion over our recommendation to use "3 to 4 cups" of peanut oil or vegetable shortening when making our **Ultimate Crispy Fried Chicken (May/June 2001)**. They wanted to know which measurement they should go by and why there was such a range.

This range in volume takes different pan sizes into consideration. While the recipe specifies an 8-quart cast-iron Dutch oven with a diameter of about 12 inches, we realize that not every home cook has this type of pot at the ready. As a general guideline for pots ranging in size from 7 quarts to 8 quarts (one of which most cooks do have), we recommend that the amount of oil used should not exceed 1 inch when poured into an empty pot and should not exceed 2 inches once the chicken is added. The variable "3 to 4 cups" called for in the recipe recognizes the fact that pots with slightly different diameters will need more or less oil to reach this depth.

We also heard from readers who wanted to use a small 4-quart saucepan or large 16-quart stockpot to fry chicken. We don't recommend either, and here's why: Most 4-quart saucepans are much too narrow (just 8 inches in diameter) to accommodate even half of a cut-up chicken in a single batch. While a whole cut-up chicken would certainly fit in a 16-quart stockpot, the pot is so wide (at least 13 inches) that a lot more oil would be needed to attain a depth of 1 inch.

– Compiled by Nina West

IF YOU HAVE A QUESTION about a recently published recipe, let us know. Send your inquiry, name, address, and daytime telephone number to Recipe Update, Cook's Illustrated, P.O. Box 470589, Brookline, MA 02447, or to recipeupdate@bcpress.com.

COOK'S EXTRA To get our recipe for Mexican Brown Rice, go to www.cooksillustrated.com and key in code 4055. The recipe will be available until April 15, 2005.

≥ BY GARTH CLINGINGSMITH ≤

DO YOU REALLY NEED THIS?
Quesadilla Maker

While nobody wanted to believe that a glorified sandwich press could outperform a skillet, we had to acknowledge that the Sante Fe Quesadilla Maker by Salton neatly sequesters the cheesy fillings into six triangular sections and eliminates the need to flip the quesadilla. The problem was that the recipes that came with this device advised a paltry ¼ cup cheese for two 10-inch flour tortillas—not nearly enough, in our opinion. When we ignored these stingy instructions and added more cheese, the cheese flooded into the moat surrounding the heating plates. So for our quesadilla needs—which include healthy amounts of *queso*—we'll stick with a skillet.

QUESADILLA MAKER
Can a quesadilla maker outperform a skillet?

EQUIPMENT UPDATE
Cutting Boards

When we rated cutting boards for the May/June 2001 issue, our favorites were two dishwasher-safe designs: the handsome Bemis Dishwasher Safe Wood Large Cutting Board, made with a compressed-wood composite/phenolic resin base and a natural hardwood veneer, and the polyethylene Joyce Chen Spot'n Chop, which boasts a surface that cushions knife strikes much as wood does. A few years and thousands of knife strikes later, those recommendations need some adjustment.

The 15 by 11-inch Bemis board resisted staining and warping, but the heavy test-kitchen use eventually wore the side seal thin, allowing the veneer to peel. (Note that an identical board continues to survive perfectly well with more moderate use in a test cook's home kitchen.) The Joyce Chen board also avoided warping and discoloration, but its long narrow shape (17⅛ inches by 9¾ inches) left us reaching for wider boards.

Simply ordering a bigger model wasn't the answer. Most polyethylene cutting boards—the Joyce Chen included—increase in length and width while the thickness remains constant at ½ inch: a recipe for dramatic warping.

Our solution? Head to a restaurant supply outlet, which is stocked with plenty of polyethylene cutting boards whose thickness is proportionate to their length and width. The test kitchen's roomy 20 by 15-inch boards are a healthy 11⁄16 inch thick, and they're practically warp-free.

EQUIPMENT TEST
Baking Peels

The test kitchen is stocked with an assortment of metal and wood baking peels, and we generally just reach for whichever is handy. Then we wondered, is one peel really better than another? We tested five peels.

We found that a 14- to 16-inch peel will accommodate free-form bread loaves and is spacious enough for any pizza. Handle length should be a minimum of 8 inches to keep your hands a safe distance from the hot baking stone.

Wooden peels required less cornmeal or flour to keep dough from sticking, but the thickness of the wood sometimes made it difficult to slide the peel under a finished item. Storage can also be tricky. A wooden peel stored flat will not dry evenly and may warp. A better option is to hang it by the handle.

Dough is more likely to stick to a metal peel. On the other hand, the thin metal slides more easily than wood beneath finished items. Metal peels are also easier to clean and store.

THE SUPER PEEL
Think all peels are created equal?

What to buy? Wood is a favorite with traditionalists who have the space to hang it during storage. Metal is practical and easy to store. Both are easy to find for about $20.

We also tested one unconventional peel, the Super Peel, which is simply a regular wooden peel outfitted with a pastry cloth that's threaded through the board like a conveyor belt. The dough is placed on the cloth, and, as the board is pulled back, the cloth rotates and gently deposits the dough onto the stone. When well floured, the cloth proved to be essentially nonstick. The Super Peel requires one hand to hold the cloth, so you can't keep your hand out of the oven, but it practically guarantees a perfectly round pizza and has a gentle touch with bread loaves. The Super Peel ($33.95) is extremely versatile, but the extra $15 worth of benefits might be lost on the infrequent pizza cook.

EQUIPMENT TEST
Wine Keepers

A half-finished bottle of wine more than a couple of days old is generally relegated to "cooking wine" status. Does that have to be the case?

Taking five 25.4-ounce bottles of red wine, we removed 10 ounces from each, then "preserved" them using five different methods. Two of the gadgets, the Vacu Vin Vacuum Wine Saver ($9.99) and the EZ Vac Wine Saver ($10.95), are designed to remove air from the bottle to prevent oxidation (the reaction of oxygen with compounds in the wine that accounts for much flavor deterioration). Private Reserve's Wine Preserver ($9.99 for 120 uses) is sprayed on the surface of the leftover wine, depositing a "blanket" of inert gases meant to keep oxidation at bay. Haley's Corker ($5.99) is an airtight rubber replacement cork. The fifth method? We just shoved the original cork back in the bottle.

Ten days later, we tasted our "preserved" wines alongside a freshly opened bottle from the same case. As expected, tasters preferred the wine from the new bottle. The wines "protected" by the EZ Vac, the spray, the replacement cork, and the reused cork left tasters puckering. The only system that came close to fooling our panel was the Vacu Vin, which proved as convenient as it was effective. A small rubber plug acts as the cork; to it you attach a hand pump that quickly removes the air in the bottle to create a tight seal. Extra plugs ($4.49 for two) are a good idea.

VACU VIN
Can a simple gadget keep a good wine from going bad?

Sources

Prices were current at press time and do not include shipping. Contact companies directly to confirm prices and availability.

page 3: JAR OPENER
● Swing-A-Way Adjust-A-Grip Jar and Bottle Opener: $7.29, item #4175, Fante's (800-443-2683, www.fantes.com).

page 22: SOURDOUGH STARTER
● Classic Sourdough Starter: $6.95, item #1522, Baker's Catalogue (800-827-6836, www.bakerscatalogue.com).
● Goldrush Old Fashioned San Francisco Starter: $4.99; item M1001, Goldrush Products Company (800-729-5428, www.mccornbread.com).

page 25: MUFFIN PAN
● Wilton Ultra-Bake Non-Stick 12 Cup Muffin Pan: $7.99, product #2105-3525, Target Stores (800-591-3869).

page 29: MEASURING CUP
Rubbermaid Measuring Cup: $3.89, item #66261, Ace Hardware (866-290-5334, www.acehardware.com).

page 32: BAKING PEEL
● Super Peel: $33.95, Exoproducts (518-371-3173, www.superpeel.com).

page 32: WINE KEEPER
● Vacu Vin Vacuum Wine Saver: $9.99, item #97558. Vacu Vin Vacuum Stoppers: $4.49 for two, item #97559, Fante's.

RECIPES
March & April 2005

Corn and Black Bean Quesadillas with Pepper Jack Cheese, 20

"Stuffed" Roast Butterflied Chicken, 7

Spaghetti with Cherry Tomatoes, Olives, Capers, and Pine Nuts, 15

Sautéed White Fish Fillets with Coconut–Red Curry Sauce, 10

Beef Braised in Barolo, 19

www.cooksillustrated.com

Join the *Cook's* Web site and Get Instant Access to 12 Years of Recipes, Equipment Tests, and Tastings!

Web site members can also join the *Cook's* chat room, ask our editors cooking questions, find quick tips and step-by-step illustrations, maintain a private list of personal favorites (recipes, quick tips, tastings, and more), and print out shopping lists for all recipes.

Yours Free: As a paid Web site member, you will also receive our **2005 Buying Guide for Supermarket Ingredients.** Simply type in the promotion code **CB5IA** when signing up.

Here's Why More Than 60,000 Home Cooks Subscribe to Our Web Site:

Quick Search for "Best" Recipes: Quick access to each and every recipe published in *Cook's Illustrated* since 1993.

Cook's Extra Recipes: Continued access to the recipes that don't "fit" in each issue of the magazine, including many flavor variations.

Updated Cookware Ratings: Charts of all buying recommendations published in the magazine (you can download them) plus frequent updates on new models and price changes.

Tasting Results: Which chicken broth is best? How about chocolate? You'll have access to every tasting published in the magazine, plus tastings conducted only for Web members.

Questions for the Editors: Paid members can ask us a question by email and are guaranteed a response.

The Chat Room: Find out what other *Cook's* subscribers think about recipes, equipment, and cooking techniques. Or just meet the subscribers in your town.

Magazine/Book Customer Service: Pay invoices, give gifts, handle returns, check your subscription status, etc.

Visit Our Bookstore: Order any of our books online and also qualify for special offers.

AMERICA'S TEST KITCHEN TV SHOW

Join the millions of home cooks who watch our show, *America's Test Kitchen*, on public television every week. For more information, including recipes and a schedule of program times in your area, visit www.americastestkitchen.com.

Tortilla Soup, 13

Pan-Roasted Asparagus with Toasted Garlic and Parmesan, 8

Dark Chocolate Cupcakes, 25

24-Hour Sourdough Bread, 23

PHOTOGRAPHY: CARL TREMBLAY, STYLING: MARY JANE SAWYER

Turmeric

Taro Root

Ginger

Galangal

Sweet Potato

Arrowroot

Russet Potato

Lotus Root

Jerusalem Artichoke

Water Chestnut

TUBERS AND RHIZOMES

NUMBER SEVENTY-FOUR MAY & JUNE 2005

COOK'S
ILLUSTRATED

Grilling Flank Steak

Skillet-Roasted
Potatoes
Extra Crispy in Just 20 Minutes

Improving Stuffed
Pork Chops
Juicier Meat, Better Stuffing

Tasting Chicken
Broths
Can, Carton, or Concentrate?

Ultimate Oatmeal
Cookies

Rating Cookie Sheets
Should You Spend $10 or $90?

How to Substitute
Ingredients

New Salad Dressings
Making Paella at Home
Easy Raspberry Tart
Hearty Frittatas
Asian Orange Chicken

www.cooksillustrated.com
$5.95 U.S./$6.95 CANADA

06>
0 74470 62805 7

CONTENTS

May & June 2005

www.cooksillustrated.com

HOME OF AMERICA'S TEST KITCHEN

Founder and Editor	Christopher Kimball
Executive Editor	Jack Bishop
Senior Editors	Jolyon Helterman
	Dawn Yanagihara
Editorial Manager, Books	Elizabeth Carduff
Test Kitchen Director	Erin McMurrer
Senior Editors, Books	Julia Collin Davison
	Lori Galvin
Managing Editor	Rebecca Hays
Associate Editor, Books	Keith Dresser
Associate Editor	Sandra Wu
Web Editor	Lindsay McSweeney
Copy Chief	India Koopman
Test Cooks	Erika Bruce
	Garth Clingingsmith
	Sean Lawler
	Rachel Toomey
	Diane Unger-Mahoney
	Nina West
	Sarah Wilson
Assistant Editor, Books	Charles Kelsey
Editorial Assistant, Books	Elizabeth Wray
Assistant to the Publisher	Melissa Baldino
Kitchen Assistants	Maria Elena Delgado
	Nadia Domeq
	Ena Gudiel
Editorial Interns	Elizabeth Bomze
	Max Gitlen
Contributing Editors	Matthew Card
	Elizabeth Germain
Consulting Editors	Shirley Corriher
	Jasper White
	Robert L. Wolke
Proofreader	Jean Rogers
Design Director	Amy Klee
Designer	Heather Barrett
Staff Photographer	Daniel van Ackere
Vice President Marketing	David Mack
Sales Director	Leslie Ray
Retail Sales Director	Jason Geller
Corporate Sponsorship Specialist	Laura Phillipps
Sales Representative	Shekinah Cohn
Marketing Assistant	Connie Forbes
Circulation Director	Bill Tine
Circulation Manager	Larisa Greiner
Fulfillment Manager	Carrie Horan
Products Director	Steven Browall
Direct Mail Director	Adam Perry
Customer Service Manager	Jacqueline Valerio
Customer Service Representative	Julie Gardner
E-Commerce Marketing Manager	Hugh Buchan
Vice President Operations	James McCormack
Senior Production Manager	Jessica Lindheimer Quirk
Production Manager	Mary Connelly
Book Production Specialist	Ron Bilodeau
Production Assistants	Jeanette McCarthy
	Jennifer Power
	Christian Steinmetz
Systems Administrator	Richard Cassidy
Internet Technology Director	Aaron Shuman
Chief Financial Officer	Sharyn Chabot
Controller	Mandy Shito
Staff Accountant	Maya Santoso
Office Manager	Saudiyah Abdul-Rahim
Receptionist	Henrietta Murray
Publicity	Deborah Broide

FRESH HERBS

FRESH HERBS Many delicate herbs are best used raw or added at the end of cooking, including tarragon, dill, chives, and basil. Prolonged exposure to heat may dull the flavor, color, and texture of these herbs. Italian flat-leaf parsley has a slight peppery flavor, and we prefer it to curly parsley. Chervil is related to parsley and has a mild, delicate flavor. Along with parsley, tarragon, and chives, chervil is a key component in *fines herbes*, a classic mixture used commonly in French cooking. Mint's refreshing flavor complements many sweet preparations as well as savory ones. Heartier herbs, including thyme, oregano, rosemary, and sage, are more pungent and stand up well to cooking. Sprigs of thyme are used in *bouquet garni* (along with parsley stems and dried bay leaves) to flavor stocks and soups. Oregano is a key ingredient in slow-simmering tomato sauces. Piney rosemary must be used in moderation because its strong flavor can easily overwhelm a dish. The same can be said for sage, whose musty, earthy flavor can become bitter when used in large quantities.

COVER *(Carrots)*: James Harrington, BACK COVER *(Fresh Herbs)*: John Burgoyne

For list rental information, contact: ClientLogic, 1200 Harbor Blvd., 9th Floor, Weehawken, NJ 07087; 201-865-5800; fax 201-867-2450.
Editorial Office: 17 Station St., Brookline, MA 02445; 617-232-1000; fax 617-232-1572. Subscription inquiries, call 800-526-8442.
Postmaster: Send all new orders, subscription inquiries, and change-of-address notices to Cook's Illustrated, P.O. Box 7446, Red Oak, IA 51591-0446.

PRINTED IN THE USA

'HANDS ON THE PLOUGH'

Those of us of a certain age remember recipes that had real names: Marie's Nutmeg Doughnuts, Renny Powell's Blueberry Boy-Bait, Rena Scribner's Maple Fudge, and Mrs. Pope's Southern Pecan Bars, not to mention Clara Mae's Famous Pensacola Fried Chicken, Sweet Potatoes Georgian, and Dorothy's New England Cream Pie.

Looking at a map of our small Vermont town is a quick history lesson, each place named for a family or defining characteristic. Red Mountain, Egg Mountain, Bear Mountain, and Tate Mountain. Walnut Hill, Minister Hill, and then Swearing Hill right across from it. Our hollows: Skinner, Cook, Mears, Corbett, Kent, and Wilcox. The Green River runs through town, but there are also plenty of small brooks with names: Tidd, Baldwin, and Chunks. Plus names that appeal to a small boy's imagination: Snake Ridge, Pumpkin Hook, Chestnut Woods, The Notch, Goose Egg Ridge, and Eldridge Swamp.

People seem to have had better names back then, too. My favorites were Onie, Herbie, Cliff, Floyd, Harley, Willy, Sonny, and Mickey. Country stores were still called by their proper names: Wayside, Cullinan's, or Sherman's, for example. Decades after the original owners died or moved away, a house was still referred to as the Lomberg home and a farmhouse—like The Yellow Farmhouse—could never escape its color. Long after the Woodcocks moved out of their place up on the West Road (and their doghouse with the TV antenna on top had been bulldozed), everyone still called it the Woodcock place. That's just what it was.

When I walk up into our woods, I know where the old gravel pit used to be, where Harley Smith used to pasture his father's cows in the summer, where the sheep were kept up above the ledges, the place where Nate saw the bear coming by his tree stand during deer season, and the site of the old sugarhouse. I can see where the sheep fencing and barbed wire have grown into the tree trunks, becoming part of the historical record.

I know where to look to see the "40 smokes," where as a kid on a cold morning, Floyd Bentley might have looked up the mountain to see smoke curling up from 40 chimneys. And the one-room schoolhouse is still across from the church, where on one cold morning the kids locked the outhouse door and the teacher had to make do behind a snowbank. The dance halls have all burned to the ground, but we know where they used to be. After all, it happened only 100 years ago.

In those days, a place earned its name by means of either hard work or sheer determination. Today, however, places sell their names, as in Boston's Fleet Center (it is still the "Garden" to locals). Fenway Park has yet to follow suit—an act of marketing infamy that would cause a week of rioting. I grew up, like many of us, with Moxie, Nehi, and Mallo Cups and was thrilled to discover packs of Teaberry and Black Jack chewing gum on a back shelf at Sherman's store. The gum, I am sad to report, had seen better days.

At a recent local gathering, we swapped stories about other lost traditions. One neighbor remembers the bleach man, who did in fact sell bleach door-to-door, along with 100-pound bags of soap. There was the ragman and, of course, the musical hurdy-gurdy man—the one with the monkey. (You paid the monkey, not the musician.) My father loved to tell stories about the ice man, who delivered large blocks of ice for the aptly named ice box.

Today, we seem to have lost our belief in constancy, the unwavering good sense to follow a single path in life. I spent last Sunday rabbit hunting with Tom, the local president of the Old Rabbit Hunters' Association, and Teddy, a local carpenter and stonemason who goes out every weekend during the season. He has a half dozen dogs—we hunted that day with Tubby—and on

Christopher Kimball

Father's Day, when his kids asked him what he wanted to do, he said he wanted to take a walk with his dogs to scout for rabbits—even though rabbit season was long over. That's constancy for you.

And life is full of smaller bits of constancy that are comforting: the sight of a crisp winter sky chock-full of stars as I trudge back from the barn after dinner; the announcement by our 6-year-old, Emily, that she just had another baby (she has more than two dozen store-bought "children" at this point); the first taste of hot biscuits slathered with butter and homemade plum jam; the radiating warmth of a wood cookstove on a dark, cold morning; and the feel of a horse resting his head on your shoulder. But, of course, constancy has a higher purpose. Ossie Davis, the late, great American actor, once said, "We can't float through life—we must fix our gaze on a guiding star [and keep] our hands on the plough. It is the consistency of the pursuit . . . that gives you the constancy, that gives you the encouragement, that gives you the way to understand . . . why it is important for you to do what you can do."

Finding that star on a cold winter's night, knee-deep in snow, wrapped in a tattered long-coat, is not easy. I can hear the horses shifting in their stalls, and I see our farmhouse on a hill, lit modestly, as if by candle, underneath a canopy so brightly decorated that not one star stands out. It is the choice of a lifetime, one that seems oddly tightfisted against the startling breadth of the heavens. But before I reach the sudden warmth of home, I do indeed choose a star. It is not the brightest perhaps, nor part of a well-sketched constellation, but it is the one I will follow. With an eye toward the horizon, I aim to plough a straight furrow, encouraged by the notion that hard work and constancy will someday bear the sweet fruit of a job well done.

FOR INQUIRIES, ORDERS, OR MORE INFORMATION:

www.cooksillustrated.com

At www.cooksillustrated.com, you can order books and subscriptions, sign up for our free e-newsletter, or renew your magazine subscription. Subscribe to the Web site and you'll have access to 12 years of *Cook's* recipes, cookware tests, ingredient tastings, and more.

COOKBOOKS

We sell more than 40 cookbooks by the editors of *Cook's Illustrated*. To order, visit our bookstore at www.cooksillustrated.com or call 800-611-0759 (or 515-246-6911 from outside the U.S.).

COOK'S ILLUSTRATED Magazine

Cook's Illustrated magazine (ISSN 1068-2821), number 74, is published bimonthly by Boston Common Press Limited Partnership, 17 Station Street, Brookline, MA 02445. Copyright 2005 Boston Common Press Limited Partnership. Periodicals postage paid at Boston, Mass., and additional mailing offices, USPS #012487. POSTMASTER: Send address changes to Cook's Illustrated, P.O. Box 7446, Red Oak, IA 51591-0446. For subscription and gift subscription orders, subscription inquiries, or change-of-address notices, call 800-526-8442 in the U.S. or 515-247-7571 from outside the U.S., or write us at Cook's Illustrated, P.O. Box 7446, Red Oak, IA 51591-0446.

Spoonful of Sugar

Recently, I went down to our local food co-op, where the only options in bulk sugar are turbinado sugar and evaporated cane juice. I was told they stock these sugars instead of what I'm more familiar with (white, granulated sugar in a 5-pound bag) because they are more nutritious. Is there really a difference between these sugars, and does one type work better than others in recipes?

JO GARDINER
PORT TOWNSEND, WASH.

➤ First, a brief primer on these sugars: Granulated, or white, sugar is made from highly refined cane or beet sugar; its fine crystals make it a great all-purpose sweetening agent. Evaporated cane juice—made from filtered sugar cane juice that is evaporated into a syrup, then crystallized and dried—is slightly less processed than granulated sugar, has marginally coarser straw-colored granules, and tastes faintly of molasses. Turbinado sugar, which is actually a light brown sugar, has even larger dark blond crystals and a mild molasses flavor.

We tasted evaporated cane juice (using Florida Crystals Natural Cane Sugar, the most widely available brand) and granulated sugar in baking by making two batches each of our sugar cookies and pound cake, using cup-for-cup substitutions. In appearance, texture, and flavor, tasters found no differences between the cookies made with granulated sugar and those made with evaporated cane juice. As for the pound cake, several people felt the cake made with granulated sugar was slightly sweeter and moister, but most people strained to find any differences at all.

With its large grains, turbinado sugar (such as Sugar In The Raw) doesn't dissolve as readily as granulated. In fact, we found it should not be used in doughs and batters. It does a fine job of sweetening tea and coffee, however, and adds welcome texture when sprinkled on top of muffins, scones, and other baked goods.

Are either of these "natural" sugars as all-purpose as granulated?

While evaporated cane juice might have trace amounts of nutrients not found in granulated sugar, most nutritionists we spoke to agreed that any potential benefits are negligible. Sugar is sugar. So for recipes calling for granulated sugar, evaporated cane juice is a perfectly fine substitute. Just don't expect any health benefits. And save turbinado sugar for sweetening hot beverages and topping pastries.

Boil First, Then Simmer

Why do soup and braise recipes always call for bringing the liquid to a full boil before simmering? Why not just bring it up to a simmer slowly and continue?

HELEN MICARI
HIGHLAND PARK, ILL.

➤ Simmering—cooking foods over moderate heat—is an important technique in making soups, stews, braises, sauces, and stocks. But why boil first? It boils down to two major issues: time (and energy) efficiency and food safety. If you bring a stew or braise up to a simmer over low heat, the total cooking time will be considerably longer. In one recent test here in the kitchen, an osso buco recipe required an extra hour when we failed to bring the liquid to a boil before turning down the heat. Starting from a boil also ensures that all of the ingredients (proteins and starches as well as the liquid) in the pot get up to a safe temperature quickly and evenly. If you let foods come to a simmer very slowly, they are likely to spend more time in the so-called danger zone, between 40 and 140 degrees, which in certain foods promotes the growth of bacteria.

Cleaning a Cast–Iron Skillet, Revisited

Would you be able to tell me how to recondition my cast-iron frying pan? Years of use have created an impenetrable layer of grit all over my pan. How do I strip away the residue and get to the cast iron again?

ESTHER GILBERT
PHILADELPHIA, PA.

➤ When years of stubborn, sticky residue, rust, and who knows what else accumulate on a cast-iron pan, getting it all off (even with vigorous scrubbing) to restore the pan to its original state can be difficult. While we have been perfectly happy with our usual method of cleaning dirtied cast-iron cookware with a thick paste of warm vegetable oil and kosher salt, we wanted to find an alternate method for cases where the grime

isn't limited to the inside of the pan. We knew that throwing the pan into a wood fire would work, but we had also heard of a more contemporary technique and wanted to investigate. The technique? Putting the pan in an oven and running it through the self-cleaning function. After soliciting the staff for beyond-repair pans, we were offered the perfect specimen: a dusty, rusted skillet with a thick layer of charred detritus caked onto the interior cooking surface and firmly crusted on the bottom and sides.

After scrubbing off as much of the loose dirt and rusted bits from the dry skillet as we could, we allowed the pan to go through an oven's self-cleaning function. After giving the pan time to cool, we retrieved from the oven what appeared to be an item straight from a Bronze Age exhibit in a museum of natural history. The pan, which had turned dark gray, was covered in a layer of large rust-coated flakes and ash. We scrubbed the pan with hot water and steel wool to remove the remaining rust, allowed it to dry, and then reseasoned it according to the following procedure: Heat the pan on top of the stove until a bead of water evaporates on contact with the pan. Wipe the inside of the pan with a wad of paper towels dipped in vegetable oil (hold the paper towels with tongs to protect yourself). Wipe out the excess oil and repeat as needed until the pan is slick.

Cherry Sources

Do you know of a source for frozen sour cherries at a reasonable price?

ESTHER HANSEN
NORTH BRANFORD, CONN.

➤ We conducted a search for frozen sour cherries at our local Boston grocery stores during the off-season and were unsuccessful in finding any. While most stores carried bagged, frozen sweet cherries, they did not stock the tart Morello or Montmorency varieties.

A quick Web search, however, provided some good leads. The Cherry Marketing Institute, based in the prime cherry-growing state of Michigan, has a Web site (www.cherrymkt.org) with a searchable guide of cherry processors and wholesalers. Several of the companies listed sell individually quick frozen (IQF) tart cherries (containing no added sugars or preservatives) to

> **COOK'S EXTRA** For the results of our testing of preseasoned cast-iron pans, visit www.cooksillustrated.com and key in code 5051. This information will be available until June 30, 2005.

individual consumers, but at a hefty price after the cost of overnight shipping is factored in. For example, one producer sold the cherries at a mere $1.50 per pound, but the cost of shipping alone for 8 pounds of the fruit was $49.65. And that was considered the cheaper end of the scale.

Another option? After fresh tart cherries, we've found that jarred Morello cherries from Trader Joe's provide the truest cherry flavor and best texture. If there is a Trader Joe's near you, we suggest that you try this product.

Classifying Cream Cheese

What is Neufchâtel cheese? Does it really have less fat then regular cream cheese?

JERILYN YOUNG
AIEA, HAWAII

➤ Traditional Neufchâtel cheese is a soft, white, unripened cheese that originated in the French town of Neufchâtel in the region of Normandy. This creamy, delicate cheese is available in several shapes and sizes, including square, rectangular, cylindrical, and heart shaped (a version called Coeur de Bray). With a dry and velvety rind covered in a fine white mold and a mild, delicate flavor, this cheese pairs well with crusty bread.

Here in America, however, the product packaged and sold as Neufchâtel cheese in your local supermarket dairy case is worlds apart from the French variety. Neufchâtel cheese made in the United States is available in plastic tubs for spreading on bagels or in square blocks for use in recipes. Regular cream cheese—soft, unripened cheese made from milk and cream that often contains stabilizers such as carrageenan, xanthan, carob bean, or guar gums to increase firmness and shelf life—must contain at least 33 percent milk fat and no more than 55 percent moisture, according to the U.S. Food and Drug Administration. American Neufchâtel may have a moisture content of up to 65 percent and a milk fat content of 20 to 33 percent. That means that some brands of Neufchâtel do not have less fat then regular cream cheese, but most do. These brands are often labeled "one-third less fat."

A Squeeze of Herbs

Have you tried herbs in a tube, sold in the refrigerated shelves near the produce section of supermarkets? The brand is Gourmet Garden, made by Botanical Foods of Queensland, Australia.

JOAN WORLEY
MARYVILLE, TENN.

➤ Prior to receiving your letter, we had never seen or heard of this product, as it is not currently available in the Northeast, but after reading about it on the manufacturer's Web site (www.gourmetgarden.com), we were intrigued. Fresh herb taste out of a refrigerated squeeze tube without the hassle of washing, drying, and chop-

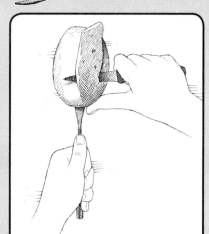
ping, no waste from leftovers, and a shelf life of three months in the refrigerator or six months in the freezer? Seemed too good to be true. We asked a friend on the West Coast to send us a few tubes.

Gourmet Garden Herbs and Spices, first sold in the United States in 2002 in six varieties—basil, chili, cilantro, garlic, ginger, and lemon grass—are now available in all but 13 states. All have salt, sugars, oil, and stabilizers added to prevent oxidation and maintain freshness. We decided to give the basil, cilantro, and lemon grass versions a try.

To taste the products, we used them in common recipe applications, comparing them side by side with fresh herbs. As per package instructions, we used teaspoon-for-teaspoon substitutions. For the basil, the difference was obvious to tasters in both appearance and in taste in a tomato-basil vinaigrette. The vinaigrette made with the Gourmet Garden product was noticeably more emulsified than the fresh herb version, perhaps because of the added oil and stabilizers. Interestingly enough, most tasters preferred the tubed herb version for its sweeter, more balanced flavors.

The results for the other two herbs were not as

Can herbs in a tube take the place of fresh?

favorable. We used the lemon grass to infuse plain chicken broth. While the flavor was much more pronounced using the tubed lemon grass, one taster complained that it tasted "like candy" and smelled "like Pledge." We also blended a small amount of cilantro with sour cream to make a simple dip. Comments for the tubed cilantro version ranged from "so fake, tastes like soap" to "disgusting and tastes stale." Used again in a salsa, the tubed cilantro tasted dull and looked "ugly as hell."

A Purple "Rose"

When buying garlic at the supermarket recently, I noticed that the skin was lavender rather than the usual white. In addition to the unusual skin coloring, the cloves seemed slightly sweeter than regular white garlic. Is this a different variety?

KAY STAUFFER
VIA E-MAIL

➤ When it comes to garlic, there are more varieties out there than you could possibly imagine. But when it comes to supermarket garlic, the choices can be narrowed down to just a few. You probably picked up Italian or Mexican garlic, two of the three major types of garlic available commercially in the United States (the other being white-skinned American garlic). Both Italian and Mexican garlic are tinged with purple and are slightly milder in flavor than white garlic.

SEND US YOUR QUESTIONS We will provide a complimentary one-year subscription for each letter we print. Send your inquiry, name, address, and daytime telephone number to Notes from Readers, Cook's Illustrated, P.O. Box 470589, Brookline, MA 02447, or to notesfromreaders@bcpress.com.

Quick Tips

⇒ COMPILED BY ERIKA BRUCE ⇐

Cool Tuna

Tuna fish salad sandwiches are quick and easy. But Zach Demuth of Newton, Mass., like most people, prefers his tuna on the cool side, and waiting for it to chill after opening a new can is not what he has in mind when he's hungry. His solution? Store cans of tuna fish in the fridge. (Recommended only for water-packed tuna.)

Easier Citrus Pressing

A citrus press can be a handy tool, but using one to press the juice from several lemons or oranges can be a pain—literally. Danielle Ramos of Saugus, Mass., found a way to ease the pressure on her hands by cutting the fruit into quarters rather than halves. Juicing a quarter is not only easier than juicing a half, but it also yields more juice.

Preserving Leftover Herbs

Stuck with a plethora of herbs growing in your garden? Mrs. Dorcas Unger of Wayland, Mass., was in the same position, just watching her herbs go to seed, until she found a quick, easy way to dry and store them.

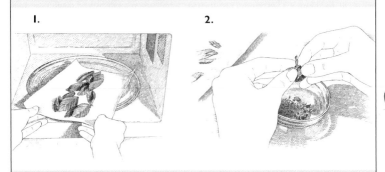

1. After washing and drying the herbs, place them on a clean paper towel and microwave on high power for 30 to 40 seconds.
2. Crumble the dried herbs and store in an airtight container (for up to three months, for best flavor).

Thermometer Holder for the Grill

Neil Macmillan of Nanaimo, British Columbia, is an avid griller, and he came up with a convenient holder for the thermometer he uses to monitor the temperature—an ordinary wooden clothespin. It has the benefit of staying cool to the touch while also protecting the head of the thermometer from the hot metal surface of the grill.

Organized Road Trips

A well-packed car usually means restricted access to snacks. To get to the food more easily without forfeiting organization, Jane Hsu of Chester, N.J., recycles the empty box from a case of wine. The cardboard insert (used to separate the bottles) creates compartments for holding soda cans, napkins, utensils, fruit, and the like. Now it's so easy to find the food that her kids can help themselves.

Orange Bowls for Sherbet

Cathy Cavaliere-Rossi of Bryn Mawr, Pa., found a clever way to use all of the spent orange halves left over after making our Fresh Orange Sherbet (May/June, 2004).

1.

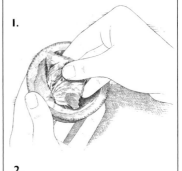

2.

1. After juicing the oranges, carefully peel out the remaining flesh by hand. If necessary, slice a thin section off the bottom of each half to keep the oranges upright.
2. After the sherbet has firmed up in the freezer, scoop it neatly into each orange half. Return to the freezer to store until ready to serve.

Measuring Guide for Butter

When you want to measure out only 1 or 2 tablespoons of butter from the butter dish, it seems silly to pull out a whole fresh stick just to use the marks on the wrapper as a measuring guide. Mary Stefani of Saline, Mich., makes things easier for herself by stapling a clean wrapper around an index card and using that to measure small portions of butter.

ILLUSTRATION: JOHN BURGOYNE

Wooden Skewers at the Ready

Not one for waiting around while skewers soak in water before he can use them on the grill, Scott Drake of Cambridge, Mass., soaks them ahead of time and then stores them in the freezer so they won't dry out.

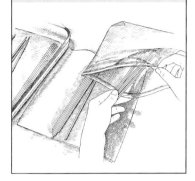

Getting Sausages Straight

Grilled sausages make a great summer sandwich, but fitting a curved link into a flat bun can be downright frustrating. After giving up on a search for curved buns, Mike Kincaid of Tulsa, Okla., came up with another solution.

1.

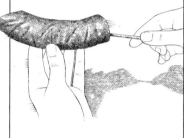

2.

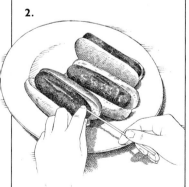

1. Insert bamboo skewers (that have first been soaked in water) lengthwise into each sausage prior to grilling. The skewers keep the sausages from curling during cooking.
2. When the sausages are done, pull out the skewers before fitting the straight links perfectly into their buns.

1.

2.

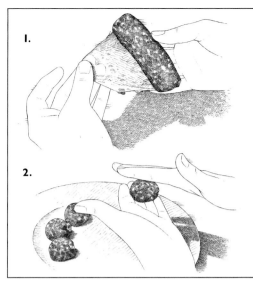

Emergency Meatballs

Need quick meatballs for that impromptu spaghetti dinner? Rich Hoxsey of Brooklyn, N.Y., shared his meatball shortcut, which uses sausages.

1. Remove all of the sausage filling from its casing.
2. Roll small sections of the filling into balls and fry them in a skillet. Make sure to cook thoroughly.

Novel Way to Serve Melon

Instead of serving plain wedges of cantaloupe or other melon, Dianne Panek of Fort Madison, Iowa, adds a handy touch to facilitate eating.

1.

2.

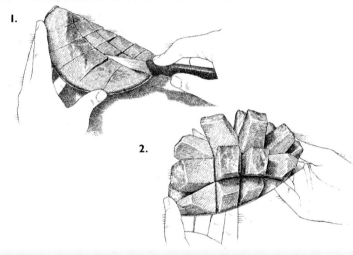

1. After cutting the melon into wedges and scraping out the seeds, cut the flesh lengthwise into strips and then crosswise into pieces.
2. Turn the wedge inside out and eat the pieces right off the rind.

Taking the Sting Out of Cutting Chiles

Tomer Gurantz of San Francisco, Calif., found a quick and clever way to protect his fingers from the sting of fresh chiles.

1. Coat one hand with oil (not the hand you use to hold the knife).
2. Cut the chiles, making sure to touch them only with your oiled hand. When done, wash your hands with hot soapy water.

1.

2.

Frostbite-Free Ice Cream Scooping

Spring and summer are packed with parties, and whether it's a birthday or a holiday that's being celebrated, ice cream is almost always involved. Tired of freezing her fingers while clutching tubs of ice cream as she serves it up, Ashley West of Friendswood, Texas, came up with a way to stave off frostbite.

Wrap a kitchen towel around the middle of the ice cream carton and twist the ends together. To scoop, grasp the twisted section of the towel firmly; this will give you a good grip—without the frostbite.

Extended Pantry Space

Stuck with a meager pantry in your kitchen? Laura Kaitz of Contoocook, N.H., was, too, until she extended her storage space by hanging an inexpensive plastic shoe rack over the inside of her pantry door. Racks with clear plastic pockets work best, providing quick visual access to all of the small items that might normally take up room on a shelf.

Grilled Marinated Flank Steak

So what's wrong with marinating steak in bottled Italian salad dressing? A lot.

⇒ BY ELIZABETH GERMAIN ⇐

America's love affair with flank steak marinated in a bottle of Italian-style salad dressing is both indisputable and curious. The flavor is often complex—or at least interesting—but the texture suffers terribly, the exterior turning mushy rather than tender. The culprit? It's the acid in the vinegar that ruins the texture and also turns the meat gray. (Yogurt, wine, and fruit juice can produce similarly distressing results.) The good news is that marinades do succeed in flavoring meat, even without the acid. So how could I develop a fresh, Mediterranean-style marinade that really boosts flavor without transforming this rough-and-ready piece of grilled meat into backyard baby food?

Before tackling the marinade, I first came up to speed on the cooking method. Prior work in the test kitchen gave me an excellent road map: Use a two-level fire, which lets you move the thin part of the steak to the cooler side of the grill once it is done and gives the thicker part more cooking time over higher heat. Cook the steak only to medium-rare to keep it from getting tough, and remember that carryover heat will continue to cook the meat once it comes off the grill. Let the steak rest for five to 10 minutes before slicing. (This reduces the loss of juices.)

Building a Better Marinade

Because fat carries flavor so well, I knew oil would be a key ingredient in my marinade. Without any vinegar or other acid, I also figured that my marinade would be more paste than liquid. Starting with those assumptions, I set out to determine the best method of infusing oil with standard Mediterranean flavors from ingredients such as garlic and rosemary. My working recipe contained 6 tablespoons of olive oil and 1 tablespoon each of garlic and rosemary.

I was pretty sure that heat would intensify the flavors, so I tested two marinades—one made with raw garlic and rosemary, the other a heat infusion I made by briefly cooking the garlic and rosemary in the oil. After trying the grilled steaks, tasters thought that the heat did improve the flavor, but only slightly. Cooking the garlic and rosemary in oil didn't seem worth the bother. Increasing the amounts of garlic and rosemary—to 2 tablespoons each—was far more effective. I tried adding many other ingredients to the marinade, but only shallots made the cut. Among the losers were parsley (too subtle), Worcestershire sauce and tomato paste (both toughened the

For maximum tenderness, hold the knife at a 45-degree angle and slice the meat across the grain.

meat), and anchovy paste (just plain fishy).

I had been mincing the piles of garlic, rosemary, and shallots by hand and then stirring them together with the oil. To save time, I wondered if I could just throw everything into the blender. Unfortunately, the blender failed to mince things finely enough; the rough bits just didn't contribute as much flavor as the fine mince. In the end, I chose to mince the garlic, rosemary, and shallots with a knife and then combine them with the oil in the blender. When rubbed into the meat, this extremely fine, well-blended paste flavored the steak in just one hour.

Two minor tests and one failure followed. First, I pricked the flank steak with a fork before rubbing on the paste, and this did boost the flavor. Second, I tried grilling the steak with the paste on (I had been wiping it off before cooking), and this turned out a blotchy, burnt-tasting piece of meat. Removing the paste just prior to grilling was clearly the way to go.

Deductive Seasoning

My recipe was good at this point, but I wanted to take a detour and explore the effects that salting might have on the meat. Our recipe for steak tips (May/June 2003) calls for marinating the beef in a mixture of oil and soy sauce. The salt in the soy

sauce in effect "brines" the meat, adding moisture and seeming to tenderize it. Of course, soy sauce isn't right in a Mediterranean paste. Could I get the benefits of salt without the soy?

I tried adding salt to the marinade, but the salt wouldn't dissolve in the oil. What if I just salted the meat, then rubbed on the paste? Sure enough, this technique made for a beefier flavor and an improved texture. (The total time required—for both salting and marinating—remained one hour.) Kosher salt, with its large crystals, was easier to apply than table salt and won a place in my recipe.

For a final series of tests, I developed two additional marinade recipes, one with sesame oil, ginger, scallions, and garlic and the other a spicier version with chipotle and jalapeño chiles and garlic. Now I was done—or at least I thought so. One colleague suggested that I

Marinating No-No

A bottle of Italian dressing is a quick route to flavoring flank steak, but our tests convinced us that one of its primary ingredients—the vinegar—turns the meat mushy and gray.

try marinating the meat the night before. Sliced and served, this steak was potently flavored, but so was the one-hour version. The good news is that the marinade can be made and applied to the steak well before you cook it, if you prefer, so you don't need to set aside an hour of marinating time before getting dinner on the table.

GRILLED MARINATED FLANK STEAK
SERVES 4 TO 6

Flank steaks smaller or larger than 2 pounds can be used, but adjust the amount of salt and pepper accordingly. We prefer flank steak cooked rare or medium-rare. If the steak is to retain its juices, it must be allowed to rest before being sliced.

If using a gas grill, cook the steak over high heat, following the times in step 3, but keep the cover down. If the meat is significantly under-done when tested with a paring knife, turn off one burner and position the steak so that the thinner side is over the cool part of the grill and the thicker side is over the hot part of the grill.

- 1 whole flank steak (about 2 pounds), patted dry with paper towels
- 2 teaspoons kosher salt
- 1 recipe wet paste marinade (recipes follow)
- ¼ teaspoon ground black pepper

1. Place steak on rimmed baking sheet or in large baking dish. Using dinner fork, prick steak about 20 times on each side. Rub both sides of steak evenly with salt and then with paste. Cover with plastic wrap and refrigerate at least 1 hour or up to 24 hours.

2. Using large chimney starter, ignite about 6 quarts (1 large chimney, or 2½ pounds) charcoal briquettes and burn until covered with thin coating of light gray ash, about 20 minutes. Empty coals into grill; build two-level fire by arranging coals to cover one half of grill. Position grill grate over coals, cover grill, and heat grate for 5 minutes; scrape grate clean with grill brush. Grill is ready when coals are hot (you can hold your hand 5 inches above grate for just 2 seconds).

3. Using paper towels, wipe paste off steak; season both sides with pepper. Grill steak directly over coals until well browned, 4 to 6 minutes. Using tongs, flip steak; grill until second side is well browned, 3 to 4 minutes. Using paring knife, make small cut into thickest part of meat; if meat is slightly less done than desired, transfer steak to cutting board (meat will continue to cook as it rests). If steak is significantly underdone, position so that thinner side is over cool side of grill and thicker side is over hot side; continue to

cook until thickest part is slightly less done than desired, then transfer steak to cutting board.

4. Loosely tent steak with foil; let rest 5 to 10 minutes. Using sharp chef's knife or carving knife, slice steak about ¼ inch thick against grain and on bias. Serve immediately.

GARLIC-SHALLOT-ROSEMARY
WET PASTE MARINADE

- 6 tablespoons olive oil
- 6 medium garlic cloves, minced or pressed through garlic press (2 tablespoons)
- 1 medium shallot, minced (about 3 tablespoons)
- 2 tablespoons minced fresh rosemary leaves

Puree all ingredients in blender until smooth, scraping down blender jar as needed.

GARLIC-GINGER-SESAME
WET PASTE MARINADE

- 4 tablespoons toasted sesame oil
- 2 tablespoons vegetable oil
- 1 piece (about 3 inches) fresh ginger, peeled and minced (about 3 tablespoons)
- 2 medium scallions, minced (about 3 tablespoons)
- 3 medium garlic cloves, minced or pressed through garlic press (1 tablespoon)

Puree all ingredients in blender until smooth, scraping down blender jar as needed.

GARLIC-CHILE WET PASTE MARINADE

- 6 tablespoons corn or vegetable oil
- 6 medium garlic cloves, minced or pressed through garlic press (2 tablespoons)
- 2 medium scallions, minced (about 3 tablespoons)
- 1 medium chipotle chile in adobo sauce, minced (about 1 tablespoon)
- 1 medium jalapeño chile, minced (about 1 tablespoon)

Puree all ingredients in blender until smooth, scraping down blender jar as needed.

Maximum Flavor in Minimum Time

PERFECT SLICING
Good carving knives, like this one from Forschner, have rounded tips.

UNEVEN SLICING
Carving knives with pointed tips, like this one from Forschner, can produce uneven slices.

MORE SHREDDING THAN SLICING
Better for pumpernickel than for poultry, this serrated Wüsthof knife shredded turkey breast.

Our novel "marinating" technique starts by pricking the steak with a fork to speed flavor absorption (left). Next, kosher salt is rubbed into the meat, followed by a garlic-herb wet paste (center). After an hour, the paste and salt are wiped off so the steak will brown nicely on the grill (right).

Thick and Hearty Frittata

More challenging to cook properly than a regular thin frittata, a thick, hearty frittata often ends up dry, overstuffed, and overcooked.

≥ BY ERIKA BRUCE ≤

When I order a frittata in a restaurant, it comes to the table as a towering wedge, with a pleasing balance of egg to filling. The eggs are cooked perfectly, firm yet moist, and are framed by a supportive browned crust. Back at home, I grab a handful of leftovers and whip up a frittata that ends up as a lackluster, open-faced omelet lacking in height, flavor, and visual appeal. Something, perhaps a great many things, was getting lost in the translation.

Unable to find a single cookbook version that I liked, I cobbled together a starter recipe. This required a bit of decision making about the size of the pan and the number of eggs. Ten eggs, believe it or not, produced an insubstantial frittata if serving six hungry people. That meant an even dozen was in order, and I had to try to fit them all into a 12-inch skillet. It quickly became clear that 3 cups of cooked vegetables and meat would provide the best balance of filling to eggs, but I decided to develop a cooking method before worrying about the exact composition of the filling.

A frittata loaded with meat and vegetables needs a special cooking technique that relies on the stovetop, the broiler, and residual heat.

Choosing a Cooking Method

Traditional thin frittatas are cooked on the stovetop over low heat, without stirring, to allow a bottom crust to develop. When the bottom has browned and the eggs are almost set, the top is briefly cooked by flipping the frittata over in the pan or running it under the broiler. Would one of these methods work with my decidedly un-thin frittata? As for the flip, I never dared to try it. After a full 15 minutes on the stovetop, the eggs in my frittata were still too runny on top. The broiler did a fine job on the top, but the bottom wasn't looking very good. The eggs had spent so much time on the stovetop that the bottom had developed a thick, tough crust. Less time on the burner and more under the broiler translated to an undercooked center or, worse, a blackened, blistery top.

I reasoned that so many eggs might require more moderate heat to cook evenly. This time around, after adding the eggs to the skillet, I transferred the pan to a moderate 350-degree oven. After 15 minutes, the frittata had puffed and was cooked through. But it was very dry and

had an anemic-looking surface. (I was serving this frittata top side up; flipping it onto a serving platter was awkward.) Higher oven temperatures added some color and, in reducing the cooking time, made for a more moist frittata, but the eggs were spongy, like an overcooked custard.

Frustrated, I stopped cooking and assessed my situation. Of all the methods I had tried, the most promising was the traditional stovetop-to-broiler method. To reduce the time on the stovetop (the bottom of the frittata had overcooked in my earlier test), I stirred the eggs over medium heat to cook them quickly yet evenly. Then, with the eggs still on the wet side, I slid the skillet under the broiler. Nicely puffed and brown, this frittata was light, not spongy. The stirring had both cooked the eggs evenly and kept them fluffy. The broiler finished the job without overcooking them.

Repeated tries with this method did turn up a flaw. If I left the skillet under the broiler for a minute too long, the eggs crossed the line from properly cooked to overdone. Because every broiler is slightly different, I felt the need to

install a failsafe step in the recipe. I decided to take the frittata out of the oven when the top had puffed and browned but the eggs in the center were still slightly wet. Then I let the frittata rest for five minutes in the skillet, allowing the residual heat to finish the cooking. Now I had perfectly cooked eggs every time.

Finessing the Filling

Most frittata recipes call for cheese. I tested shredded Parmesan, which tasted fine but was too dry. Gruyère, a higher-moisture cheese, was much better. I also had luck with cheddar, goat cheese, and fontina. A fellow test cook suggested cubing the cheese rather than shredding it. This was a nice touch; little pockets of melted cheese throughout the frittata meant a more varied texture. (The goat cheese was best crumbled.) Although adding dairy other than cheese to frittatas is not traditional, I tested small amounts of heavy cream, half-and-half, and whole milk. Half-and-half was the winner, adding a touch of creaminess. (Milk turned the frittata watery, and heavy cream was too rich.)

Most any vegetable or meat can be added to a frittata, with two caveats: The food must be cut into small pieces, and it must be precooked to drive off excess moisture and fat. The latter was easy enough to do in the same skillet that would eventually hold the eggs. While many recipes claim that frittatas can be eaten cold, I prefer mine on the hotter side; this keeps the cheese pleasantly gooey and the eggs from losing too much moisture.

ASPARAGUS, HAM, AND GRUYÈRE FRITTATA
MAKES ONE 12-INCH FRITTATA, SERVING 6 TO 8

An ovensafe nonstick 12-inch skillet is a must for this recipe and the variations that follow. Because broilers vary so much in intensity, watch the frittata carefully as it cooks.

12	large eggs
3	tablespoons half-and-half
	Table salt and ground black pepper
2	teaspoons olive oil
½	pound asparagus, trimmed of tough ends,

spears cut on the bias into ¼-inch pieces

1 medium shallot, minced (about 3 tablespoons)
4 ounces ¼-inch-thick deli ham, cut into ½-inch cubes (about ¾ cup)
3 ounces Gruyère cheese, cut into ¼-inch cubes (about ¾ cup)

1. Adjust oven rack to upper-middle position, about 5 inches from heating element; heat broiler. Whisk eggs, half-and-half, ½ teaspoon salt, and ¼ teaspoon pepper in medium bowl until well combined, about 30 seconds. Set eggs aside.

2. Heat oil in 12-inch nonstick ovensafe skillet over medium heat until shimmering; add asparagus and cook, stirring occasionally, until lightly browned and almost tender, about 3 minutes. Add shallot and ham and cook until shallot softens slightly, about 2 minutes. Stir Gruyère into eggs; add egg mixture to skillet and cook, using spatula to stir and scrape bottom of skillet, until large curds form and spatula begins to leave wake but eggs are still very wet, about 2 minutes. Shake skillet to distribute eggs evenly; cook without stirring for 30 seconds to let bottom set.

3. Slide skillet under broiler and broil until frittata has risen and surface is puffed and spotty brown, 3 to 4 minutes; when cut into with paring knife, eggs should be slightly wet and runny. Remove skillet from oven and let stand 5 minutes to finish cooking; using spatula, loosen frittata from skillet and slide onto platter or cutting board. Cut into wedges and serve.

LEEK, PROSCIUTTO, AND GOAT CHEESE FRITTATA
MAKES ONE 12-INCH FRITTATA, SERVING 6 TO 8

12 large eggs
3 tablespoons half-and-half
   Table salt and ground black pepper
2 tablespoons unsalted butter
2 small leeks, white and light green parts halved lengthwise, washed, and sliced thin (about 3 cups)
3 ounces very thinly sliced prosciutto, cut into ½-inch-wide strips
¼ cup chopped fresh basil leaves
4 ounces goat cheese, crumbled (about ½ cup)

1. Follow recipe for Asparagus, Ham, and Gruyère Frittata through step 1.

2. Heat butter in 12-inch nonstick ovensafe skillet over medium heat until foaming subsides. Add leeks and ¼ teaspoon salt; reduce heat to low and cook covered, stirring occasionally, until softened, 8 to 10 minutes. Stir prosciutto, basil, and half of goat cheese into eggs; add egg mixture to skillet and cook, using spatula to stir and

COOK'S EXTRA For a primer on egg cookery, go to www.cooksillustrated.com, and key in code 5053. This information will be available until June 30, 2005.

RECIPE SHORTHAND: **Three Steps to Cooking a Thick Frittata**

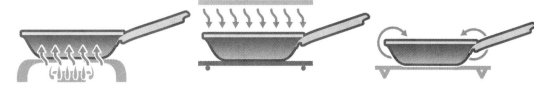

ON THE STOVETOP   **UNDER THE BROILER**   **ON A COOLING RACK**

1. Start frittata on stovetop, stirring eggs as they set. **2.** When eggs form large curds but top is still wet, slide skillet under broiler. **3.** Once top browns, move skillet to cooling rack, where residual heat gently completes cooking center of frittata.

scrape bottom of skillet, until large curds form and spatula begins to leave wake but eggs are still very wet, about 2 minutes. Shake skillet to distribute eggs evenly; cook without stirring for 30 seconds to let bottom set.

3. Distribute remaining goat cheese evenly over frittata; continue with recipe for Asparagus, Ham, and Gruyère Frittata from step 3.

BACON, POTATO, AND CHEDDAR FRITTATA
MAKES ONE 12-INCH FRITTATA, SERVING 6 TO 8

12 large eggs
3 tablespoons half-and-half
   Table salt and ground black pepper
8 ounces bacon (about 8 slices), cut crosswise into ¼-inch pieces
1 pound Yukon gold potatoes, peeled and cut into ½-inch cubes
4 ounces cheddar cheese, cut into ¼-inch cubes (about ¾ cup)
3 scallions, sliced thin on the bias (about ⅓ cup)

1. Follow recipe for Asparagus, Ham, and Gruyère Frittata through step 1.

2. Fry bacon in 12-inch nonstick ovensafe skillet over medium heat until crisp, about 9

RECIPE TESTING:
Two Flawed Cooking Methods
We tested recipes that called for cooking frittatas on the stovetop, in the oven, or under the broiler or for combinations of these methods. Here's how two common techniques fared.

STOVETOP ONLY
Flat and dense

OVEN ONLY
Souffléed but overcooked

minutes. Using slotted spoon, transfer bacon to paper towel–lined plate; pour off all but 1 tablespoon of bacon fat. Add potatoes to skillet and cook, stirring occasionally, until golden brown and tender, 15 to 20 minutes. Stir cheddar, scallions, and bacon into eggs; add egg mixture to skillet and cook, using spatula to stir and scrape bottom of skillet, until large curds form and spatula begins to leave wake but eggs are still very wet, about 2 minutes. Shake skillet to distribute eggs evenly; cook without stirring for 30 seconds to let bottom set.

3. Continue with recipe for Asparagus, Ham, and Gruyère Frittata from step 3.

FRITTATA WITH BROCCOLI RABE, SUN-DRIED TOMATOES, AND FONTINA
MAKES ONE 12-INCH FRITTATA, SERVING 6 TO 8

12 large eggs
3 tablespoons half-and-half
   Table salt and ground black pepper
2 teaspoons olive oil
8 ounces broccoli rabe, washed, trimmed, and cut into 1-inch pieces (about 3 cups)
1 medium garlic clove, minced or pressed through garlic press (about 1 teaspoon)
⅛ teaspoon red pepper flakes
3 ounces fontina cheese, cut into ¼-inch cubes (about ¾ cup)
3 ounces drained oil-packed sun-dried tomatoes, chopped coarse (about ¼ cup)

1. Follow recipe for Asparagus, Ham, and Gruyère Frittata through step 1.

2. Heat oil in 12-inch nonstick ovensafe skillet over medium heat until shimmering; add broccoli rabe and ¼ teaspoon salt and cook until beginning to brown and soften, 6 to 8 minutes. Add garlic and pepper flakes and cook until fragrant, about 30 seconds. Stir fontina and sun-dried tomatoes into eggs; add egg mixture to skillet and cook, using spatula to stir and scrape bottom of skillet, until large curds form and spatula begins to leave wake but eggs are still very wet, about 2 minutes. Shake skillet to distribute eggs evenly; cook without stirring for 30 seconds to let bottom set.

3. Continue with recipe for Asparagus, Ham, and Gruyère Frittata from step 3.

Paring Down Paella

Paella can be a big hit at restaurants but an unwieldy production at home. Could we re-create this Spanish classic in two hours without using any fancy equipment?

≥ BY SANDRA WU ≤

Despite its current reputation as a colorful Spanish restaurant staple, paella hasn't always been categorized as party food. Developed just outside the region of Valencia by agricultural workers as a means of cooking large quantities of rice, old-fashioned paella was anything but fancy. Cooked in flat-bottomed pans over an open wood fire and flavored with local, easy-to-find ingredients such as snails, rabbit, and green beans, this utilitarian dish was a far cry from what Americans define as paella today. A basic saffron-infused rice dish no longer, paella has evolved into a big production piece with a commanding list of ingredients and many complicated steps.

Modern recipes combine a broad spectrum of ingredients, ranging from artichokes, green beans, broad beans, bell peppers, peas, and pork to chorizo, chicken, lobster, scallops, calamari, fish, mussels, clams, and shrimp. And the list doesn't end there. I set out to create a simpler, less daunting recipe for the home cook that could be made in a reasonable amount of time, with a manageable number of ingredients, and without a special paella pan.

While none of the recipes I turned to for insight were perfect, some did offer important clues. One was that if the rice and proteins were to cook uniformly, they had to be arranged in a not-too-thick, relatively even layer. Crowding or mounding the ingredients in a pile was a surefire route to disaster, as a recipe for eight made in a 12-inch skillet quickly proved. So what was the best paella pan replacement? A Dutch oven held the same amount of ingredients as a 14- to 15-inch paella pan, fit perfectly on the stovetop, and offered the best distribution and retention of heat.

Looking over the various recipes, there seemed to be five key steps: browning the sturdier proteins, sautéing the aromatics, toasting the rice, adding liquid to steam the rice, and, last, cooking the seafood. As for proteins, I quickly ruled out lobster (too much work), diced pork (sausage would be enough), fish (flakes too easily and gets lost in the rice), and rabbit and snails (too

This streamlined paella can be prepared in a pot you probably own already—a Dutch oven.

unconventional). I was left with chorizo, chicken, shrimp (preferred over scallops or calamari), and mussels (favored over clams).

Meat and Sofrito Go First

I began by browning the chicken and chorizo, which would give the meat a head start and lend necessary flavor to the fat used to sauté the onion and garlic later on. While many recipes call for bone-in, skin-on chicken pieces, to save time I opted for boneless skinless thighs (richer in flavor and less prone to drying out than breasts). I seared both sides of some halved chicken thighs in a tablespoon of olive oil, not cooking them all the way through to make sure they would be tender and juicy once added back in with the rice to complete cooking.

Next I turned my attention to the sausage. Tasters preferred the firmer, saltier dry-cured Spanish chorizo for having "more bite" than the larger refrigerated Mexican-style chorizo, which faintly resembled supermarket smoked sausage. Slicing the chorizo on the bias was attractive, and the bigger surface area of the pieces made rendering the fat easier.

Whereas French cooking depends on a sautéed aromatic base of carrots, onions, and celery and Cajun cuisine relies on a trinity of bell peppers, onions, and celery, Spanish cuisine uses a trio of onions, garlic, and tomatoes—called *sofrito*—as the building block for its rice dishes. I began by sautéing one finely diced onion until soft and stirring in a large dose (2 tablespoons) of minced garlic. Traditionally, the final ingredient, tomato, is added in seeded, grated form. To avoid the mess (as well as skinned fingers), I used a can of drained diced tomatoes instead, mincing the pieces for a similarly fine consistency and cooking the resulting pulp until thick and slightly darkened.

The Rice Is Right

With the sofrito complete, I could now focus on the rice. Long-grain rice seemed out of place (a paella is not supposed to be light and fluffy), and medium-grain rice got a firm thumbs down for its one-dimensional, blown-out texture. Out of the short-grain varieties, Valencia was preferred for its creamy but still distinct grains, with Italian Arborio following closely behind (see "Shorties but Goodies," page 11). The more traditional (but harder to find and pricier) Bomba rice of Calasparra, Spain, yielded grains that were too chewy and separate for most tasters. One cup of rice was nowhere near enough for a small crowd; 2 cups was just right. Once the rice was sautéed in the sofrito just long enough to become slightly toasted and coated with the flavorful base, it was time to add the liquid.

Although most recipes use a liquid-to-rice ratio of 2 to 1, our test kitchen has found that less liquid is preferable to avoid soft, mushy grains. In this case, 3⅓ cups of liquid to 2 cups of rice was ideal. For its clean, full-bodied flavor, tasters

Recipes for this Spanish seafood and rice casserole run the gamut—from the ultra-convenient to the absurd. Here are three possibilities.

30 MINUTES

This boxed paella, with its own can of seafood, isn't worth the minimal bother.

TWO HOURS

Our recipe works in a pan you already own and relies on a reasonable shopping list.

FOUR HOURS

This ultimate recipe requires a paella pan and includes nine kinds of meat and seafood.

preferred rice cooked in straight chicken broth over clam juice or a combination of the two. Replacing some of the broth with a bit of white wine provided an additional layer of flavor.

Saffron gives paella its brilliant color and adds a distinctive earthy flavor. Most recipes call for steeping the saffron threads in a pot of simmering liquid, but, to save time and keep this a one-pot dish, I added cold liquid along with ½ teaspoon of saffron and a bay leaf (as well as the browned chicken and chorizo) to the rice and brought everything to a boil. After a few quick stirs to make sure sthe saffron was distributed evenly, I covered the pot and turned things down to a simmer, leaving the paella untouched until the rice had soaked up most of the liquid. Did it work? At first, I thought so. But this all-stovetop steaming method had a major flaw. While the rice in the middle of the pot was cooked perfectly, grains along the edges were partially undercooked.

We've had similar problems with our jambalaya and Mexican rice recipes, and our solution is simple: Transfer the pot to the oven to finish cooking. On my next try, then, after bringing the liquid to a boil and covering the pot to make sure none of the liquid would evaporate, I placed it in a 350-degree oven. Fifteen minutes later, the grains had evenly absorbed nearly all of the liquid. Once the seafood was added and the rice given more time to cook, there wasn't a raw grain to be seen.

Finish with Seafood

With the rice nearly done, the quick-cooking seafood was ready to make its appearance. The mussels, placed in the pot hinged end down so that they could open readily, cooked in about 10 minutes. When the shrimp were added raw along with the mussels, they were perfectly juicy but bland. Briefly searing the shrimp in a hot skillet improved their flavor but turned them tough and rubbery. The solution? I briefly marinated the raw shrimp in olive oil, salt, pepper, and minced garlic to boost the flavor.

Now all the paella lacked was vegetables. Peas and bell pepper were the most vibrant, least fussy choices. Adding the peas while the rice and broth came to a boil resulted in shriveled, gray, cafeteria-style pebbles, but scattering them over the rice toward the end of cooking (with the seafood) allowed them to retain their bright green hue. In paella, bell pepper often gets lost when mixed with the sofrito or when stirred into the rice. Wanting to showcase it, I decided to use strips of red bell pepper as a garnish. Before browning the

chicken and chorizo, I sautéed the pepper to give it a roasted flavor and then arranged the pieces over the rice once the seafood was in place.

At this point, I could easily have called it a day, but several people demanded *soccarat,* the crusty brown layer of rice that develops on the bottom of a perfectly cooked batch of paella (see photo, page 12). Curious to see if I could get this to work in a Dutch oven, I waited until the dish was completely cooked and then removed the lid and put the pot back on the stove. After only about five minutes, a spoon inserted into the depths of the rice revealed nicely caramelized grains. Before I let anyone dig in, I allowed the paella to rest, covered, so the rice could continue to firm up and absorb excess moisture. After adding a garnish of parsley and lemon, I was done.

My final recipe had all the flavor and sparkle of a restaurant-style paella minus the absurdly hefty workload. Now that I didn't have to spend all day in the kitchen, I could even afford to hang out with my dinner guests. Sangría, anybody?

PAELLA

SERVES 6

This recipe is for making paella in a Dutch oven (the Dutch oven should be 11 to 12 inches in diameter with at least a 6-quart capacity). With minor modifications, it can also be made in a paella pan (see instructions on page 12).

TASTING: **Shorties but Goodies**

When it comes down to it, a good paella is all about the rice: It's not just filler. Unfortunately, the rice you probably have in your pantry—the long-grain variety—just won't cut it. Long-grain rice is great for recipes in which light and fluffy grains are desirable (pilafs, for instance), but not for paella. Only short-grain rice retains distinct, individual grains while having the creamy-chewy texture that is so important in this dish. We tested three kinds of short-grain rice in our paella. Here's what we found.

BOMBA RICE

Grown in the Calasparra region of Spain, Bomba is the traditional choice for paella. Its short, round, fairly translucent grains are prized for their ability to absorb up to three times their volume in liquid while retaining a separate, distinct texture. Tasters liked the "nutty" flavor of this rice but disliked its firmness.

ARBORIO RICE

This Italian rice has larger, longer, and more opaque grains than Bomba and Valencia. Also creamier, more tender, and a bit stickier than either of the two Spanish grains, it is an acceptable choice for paella.

VALENCIA RICE

Like Bomba, this Spanish rice has grains that are short and round, though a bit larger than Bomba's. Tasters liked this rice best, praising its balance of textures: separate and chewy, but with a bit of creaminess. Use this rice if you can find it.

BOMBA RICE: TRADITIONAL BUT TOUGH
"Grains are too separate" and "not creamy enough."

ARBORIO RICE: GOOD BACKUP
"A little sticky" but "tender and chewy."

VALENCIA RICE: BEST CHOICE
"Perfect texture" and "chewy but still creamy."

Dry-cured Spanish chorizo is the sausage of choice for paella, but fresh chorizo or linguiça is an acceptable substitute.

Soccarat, a layer of crusty browned rice that forms on the bottom of the pan, is a traditional part of paella. In our version, soccarat does not develop because most of the cooking is done in the oven. We have provided instructions to develop soccarat in step 5; if you prefer, skip this step and go directly from step 4 to 6.

1	pound extra-large (21/25) shrimp, peeled and deveined
	Table salt and ground black pepper
	Olive oil
8–9	medium garlic cloves, minced or pressed through garlic press (2 generous tablespoons)
1	pound boneless skinless chicken thighs, each thigh trimmed of excess fat and halved crosswise
1	red bell pepper, seeded and cut pole to pole into ½-inch-wide strips
8	ounces Spanish chorizo, sliced ½ inch thick on the bias (see note)
1	medium onion, chopped fine (about 1 cup)
1	can (14½ ounces) diced tomatoes, drained, minced, and drained again
2	cups Valencia or Arborio rice
3	cups low-sodium chicken broth
⅓	cup dry white wine
½	teaspoon saffron threads, crumbled
1	dried bay leaf
1	dozen mussels, scrubbed and debearded
½	cup frozen peas, thawed
2	tablespoons chopped fresh parsley leaves
1	lemon, cut into wedges, for serving

1. Adjust oven rack to lower-middle position; heat oven to 350 degrees. Toss shrimp, ¼ teaspoon salt, ¼ teaspoon black pepper, 1 tablespoon oil, and 1 teaspoon garlic in medium bowl; cover with plastic wrap and refrigerate until needed. Season chicken thighs with salt and pepper; set aside.

2. Heat 2 teaspoons oil in large Dutch oven over medium-high heat until shimmering but

If You're Using a Paella Pan

A paella pan makes for an attractive and impressive presentation. Use one that is 14 to 15 inches in diameter. A 14-inch ovensafe skillet will work as well, but do not attempt to use anything smaller because the contents will simply not fit.

To use a paella pan or large skillet instead of a Dutch oven, follow the recipe for Paella, increasing the chicken broth to 3¼ cups and the wine to ½ cup. Before placing the pan in the oven, cover it tightly with foil. For soccarat, cook the paella, uncovered, over medium-high heat for about 3 minutes, rotating the pan 180 degrees after about 1½ minutes for even browning.

not smoking. Add peppers and cook, stirring occasionally, until skin begins to blister and turn spotty black, 3 to 4 minutes. Transfer peppers to small plate and set aside.

3. Add 1 teaspoon oil to now-empty Dutch oven; heat oil until shimmering but not smoking. Add chicken pieces in single layer; cook, without moving pieces, until browned, about 3 minutes. Turn pieces and brown on second side, about 3 minutes longer; transfer chicken to medium bowl. Reduce heat to medium and add chorizo to pot; cook, stirring frequently, until deeply browned and fat begins to render, 4 to 5 minutes. Transfer chorizo to bowl with chicken and set aside.

4. Add enough oil to fat in Dutch oven to equal 2 tablespoons; heat over medium heat until shimmering but not smoking. Add onion and cook, stirring frequently, until softened, about 3 minutes; stir in remaining garlic and cook until fragrant, about 1 minute. Stir in tomatoes; cook until mixture begins to darken and thicken slightly, about 3 minutes. Stir in rice and cook until grains are well coated with tomato mixture, 1 to 2 minutes. Stir in chicken broth, wine, saffron, bay, and ½ teaspoon salt. Return chicken and chorizo to pot, increase heat to medium-high and bring to boil, uncovered, stirring occasionally. Cover pot and transfer to oven; cook until rice absorbs almost all liquid, about 15 minutes. Remove pot from oven (close oven door to retain

heat). Uncover pot; scatter shrimp over rice, insert mussels hinged side down into rice (so they stand upright), arrange bell pepper strips in pinwheel pattern, and scatter peas over top. Cover and return to oven; cook until shrimp are opaque and mussels have opened, 10 to 12 minutes.

5. Optional: If soccarat (see note) is desired, set Dutch oven, uncovered, over medium-high heat about 5 minutes, rotating pot 180 degrees after about 2 minutes for even browning.

6. Let paella stand, covered, about 5 minutes. Discard any mussels that have not opened and bay leaf, if it can be easily removed. Sprinkle with parsley and serve, passing lemon wedges separately.

Searching for 'Soccarat'

Soccarat is the toasty, browned portion of rice that forms along the bottom of the pan. It is the hallmark of authentic paella. To create this crusty bottom layer of rice, return the Dutch oven to the stovetop for five minutes once the paella has finished baking.

Dressing Up Salad Dressings

We threw away the rulebook on vinaigrettes and used a host of unexpected ingredients.

≥ BY NINA WEST ≤

It's easy to pull some oil and vinegar off the shelf to adorn a handful of lettuce leaves. But it's a fine line between ease and boredom. We decided to think outside the bottle to give our dressings—and our salads—new life.

We built our recipes around ingredients not regularly used in dressings, including apples, raisins, carrot juice, and ruby port. We balanced these ingredients with fats such as cream, buttermilk, mayonnaise, nut oils, and yogurt and punctuated the dressings with condiments such as chili paste and orange marmalade. For more depth and intensity of flavor, we turned to the stovetop to reduce wine and juices and toast spices and sesame seeds.

SWEET SESAME-SOY VINAIGRETTE
MAKES 1½ CUPS

We like this vinaigrette on soft, tender greens such as Boston or Bibb lettuce, mâche, or a mixture of baby greens. Complementary salad garnishes include thinly sliced radishes or cucumbers, bean sprouts, slivers of red bell pepper, and scallions. Use about 2 tablespoons of this dressing per quart of greens, serving two.

- ⅓ cup rice vinegar
- 2½ tablespoons soy sauce
- ¼ cup packed light brown sugar
- ½ teaspoon grated fresh ginger
- 2 teaspoons Asian chili garlic paste
- 1 tablespoon toasted sesame oil
- ½ cup vegetable oil
- 2 teaspoons sesame seeds, toasted

Whisk vinegar, soy sauce, sugar, ginger, and chili garlic paste in medium bowl until sugar dissolves. Gradually whisk in oils; whisk in sesame seeds. (Can be refrigerated up to 3 weeks.)

FRESH APPLE AND PARSLEY DRESSING
MAKES ABOUT 1½ CUPS

If using a tart apple, add up to 1 tablespoon brown sugar. This dressing is nice on spicy greens like arugula and watercress, with garnishes such as shaved Parmesan, toasted nuts, and thin slices of apple or fennel. Use about 2 tablespoons of this dressing per quart of greens, serving two.

- 1 medium apple (about 7 ounces), unpeeled, quartered, cored, and cut into 1-inch cubes
- 2 tablespoons apple cider vinegar
- 1 teaspoon hot sauce, such as Tabasco
- 1 scallion, chopped coarse
- ¼ cup fresh parsley leaves
- ¾ teaspoon table salt
- ⅛ teaspoon ground black pepper
- 2–3 tablespoons water
- ½ cup vegetable oil

Combine apple, vinegar, hot sauce, scallion, parsley, salt, and pepper in blender; pulse, scraping down blender jar and adding water as needed, until very finely chopped. With machine running, gradually add oil, scraping down blender jar as needed. (Can be refrigerated up to 1 week.)

CREAMY AVOCADO RANCH DRESSING
MAKES 1½ CUPS

Crisp lettuces like iceberg and romaine are a perfect match for this creamy dressing. Shaved red onion, grape tomatoes, and crumbled bacon make excellent garnishes for greens tossed with this dressing. Use about 2 tablespoons per quart of greens, serving two.

- 1 ripe Hass avocado, pitted, flesh scooped from skin
- ½ teaspoon hot sauce, such as Tabasco
- 1 tablespoon juice from 1 lime
- ½ cup buttermilk
- ¼ cup mayonnaise
- 1 tablespoon minced red onion
- 1 tablespoon minced fresh cilantro leaves
- 1 medium garlic clove, minced
- ½ teaspoon sugar
- ¾ teaspoon table salt
- ¼ teaspoon ground black pepper

In food processor, puree avocado, hot sauce, and lime juice until avocado is broken down, about 30 seconds. Add remaining ingredients and process until dressing is completely smooth. (Can be refrigerated up to 1 week.)

ORANGE-PORT DRESSING WITH WALNUT OIL
MAKES ABOUT 1 CUP

Use this sweet, smooth dressing on assertive bitter greens such as escarole, radicchio, and endive. Appropriate salad garnishes include toasted nuts and crumbled blue cheese. For two servings, start with 1 tablespoon of this dressing per quart of greens, adding more as desired.

- 1½ cups ruby port
- ½ cup orange juice
- 2 tablespoons red wine vinegar
- 2 tablespoons heavy cream, room temperature
- 2 tablespoons orange marmalade
- ½ teaspoon minced fresh thyme leaves
- ¼ teaspoon table salt
- ⅛ teaspoon ground black pepper
- 2 tablespoons walnut oil
- ¼ cup vegetable oil

1. Simmer port and orange juice in small saucepan over medium heat until reduced to ½ cup, 25 to 30 minutes. Transfer to medium bowl; cool to room temperature.

2. Whisk vinegar, cream, marmalade, thyme, salt, and pepper into cooled port reduction. Whisk in oils until incorporated. (Can be refrigerated up to 3 weeks.)

MOROCCAN-SPICED VINAIGRETTE
MAKES ABOUT 1 CUP

Mellow greens, such as leaf lettuces, as well as spinach, pair nicely with this vinaigrette. Olives, shredded carrots, and golden raisins are good garnish options. Use about 2 tablespoons of this dressing per quart of greens, serving two.

- 2 tablespoons golden raisins
- ¼ teaspoon ground coriander
- ⅛ teaspoon ground cumin
- ½ cup carrot juice
- 2 tablespoons red wine vinegar
- 4 sprigs cilantro
- 1 tablespoon plain yogurt
- 1 teaspoon honey
- ½ teaspoon red pepper flakes
- ½ teaspoon table salt
- ½ cup extra-virgin olive oil

1. Place raisins in small bowl. Toast coriander and cumin in small skillet over medium heat until fragrant, 2 to 3 minutes. Transfer spices to bowl with raisins. Wipe out skillet; add carrot juice to skillet and simmer over medium heat until reduced to ¼ cup, about 6 minutes. Pour carrot juice over raisins; cool to room temperature.

2. Process carrot juice/raisin mixture, vinegar, cilantro, yogurt, honey, pepper flakes, and salt in blender until thoroughly combined. With machine running, gradually add oil, scraping down jar as needed. (Can be refrigerated up to 1 week.)

How to Stuff a Pork Chop

Filling the wrong chop with the wrong kind of stuffing and then cooking it using the wrong method produces familiar but easily improved results.

≥ BY SEAN LAWLER ≤

Forget about traditional (and bland) bread stuffing. A pork chop does best with moist and assertive fillings, like this one made with red onions, port, orange juice, and dried fruit.

The mention of stuffed pork chops usually brings to mind those enormous oddities exhibited at the supermarket meat counter: dinosaur chops, split open and barely able to contain their soggy, softball-size portions of bread crumbs, sausage, and fruit, the sight of which always leaves me wondering how I would cook such a thing, let alone consume it.

Stuffing a pork chop is not a bad idea—today's lean pork needs all the help it can get—but it is rarely well executed, as the supermarket variety illustrates. Most recipes insist on treating the chops like a turkey, cramming them full of bulky bread stuffing. This type of stuffing does little for a chop besides take up space that is tight to begin with. What I was after was my favorite pork chop—thick and juicy, seared crusty brown on the outside—enhanced by a flavorful stuffing.

Choose Your Chops

Initial tests showed that tasters preferred their stuffed chops on the bone, both for the visual appeal and because the meat stayed juicier. But shopping for bone-in pork chops can be confusing since butchers—and supermarket labels—rarely agree on precisely what is called what. For example: While cuts of beef may come from either the "loin" or the "rib," butchers refer to these two sections of the pig collectively as the "loin." Therefore, the common label "pork loin chop," while technically accurate, is too broad to be of much use. The more precise "center-cut loin chop" should, but does not always, refer to chops cut right from the center of the loin. They are easily identified by the T-shaped bone running through the center, which separates the loin muscle from the adjacent tenderloin.

A much better choice for stuffing is a chop cut from the rib cage, which has a wide, unbroken "eye" of meat and a curved rib bone off to the side and out of the way. This is the chop to buy. We call it a rib chop, but markets often do not make that distinction. Another cut also sold as a "rib chop" (and one that you do not want) is taken from the blade end of the rib cage (near the head and shoulder of the pig) and has a smaller central eye, broken up by threads of tough connective tissue and surrounded by a thick cap of meat that contracts during cooking.

A common approach to stuffing chops is to butterfly them completely open, then stitch them back together with toothpicks or string. Toothpicks are easy enough to use, assuming the cook has some handy in the kitchen, but only marginally effective at holding the seam closed as the meat cooks. Sewing the chops is effective but also extremely tedious. I much prefer the less invasive technique in which a sharp paring knife is used to cut a wide pocket whose opening is actually quite small. Care must be taken not to poke straight through the edge of the chop when enlarging the pocket, however. After making this mistake half a dozen times, I learned to guard against it by leaving the thin layer of fat and connective tissue around the edge of the chop untrimmed.

Cook 'Em Fast

Some recipes suggested braising the chops, usually covered and with some stock or wine in the pan. I knew it was important to keep the chops moist, but simply adding liquid to the recipe was not the way to go about it. In the test kitchen, we frequently turn to brining (a simple saltwater soak) to keep lean, mild-flavored meat and poultry from turning out bland and dry, and this technique worked well in this recipe.

With my chops brined, I turned to high, dry heat to develop the crusty brown exterior I wanted. Roasting the chops in a hot oven failed to deliver the goods, and cooking the chops in a skillet from start to finish took quite a while thanks to the thickness of the chops and the rather crowded pan. Transferring the seared chops (still in the skillet) to the oven worked better, but the best results came from first searing the chops in a hot skillet to develop the crust and then transferring them to a preheated baking sheet in the hot oven.

SHOPPING: Buying the Right Chop

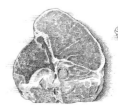

LOIN CHOP
The bone running through this chop makes it difficult to stuff.

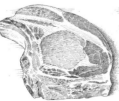

BLADE-END CHOP
This chop contracts during cooking and squeezes out the stuffing.

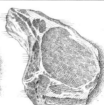

RIB CHOP
The unbroken eye of meat makes this chop perfect for stuffing.

Good Stuff Doesn't Happen by Chance

SUPERMARKET CHOP

OUR CHOP

Stuffed pork chops from the supermarket are typically overloaded with a bland bread stuffing that spills out before you even start to cook. We pack our chops with a moist, flavorful stuffing and seal the pocket with a citrus wedge. To do so, trim excess flesh from the juiced lemon or orange wedges and cut the wedges into 2-inch lengths that will fit snugly in the cavity. An added benefit: The citrus perfumes the stuffing.

Spread out on the hot baking sheet, the chops browned all over and cooked quickly.

Throughout my testing, I had experimented with different departures from a traditional bread-based stuffing. My priorities were to incorporate moisture, fat, and assertive flavors to enhance the lean, mild pork and to eliminate any bland, starchy fillers. Along the way, I discovered that consistency and texture were also important: Creamy, even sticky, stuffings were much easier to pack into a chop than dry, loose, crumbly ones. With these guidelines, I settled on a spinach and cheese stuffing, bound with ricotta and ground pine nuts, and a red onion and fruit jam stuffing with orange, pecans, and blue cheese.

STUFFED THICK-CUT PORK CHOPS
SERVES 4

Prepare the stuffing while the chops brine. (The stuffing can also be made a day in advance, but it must be microwaved just to room temperature before being packed into the chops.) One stuffed chop makes for a very generous serving. If desired, remove the meat from the bone and cut it into ½-inch slices to serve 6.

- 4 bone-in pork rib chops, 1½ inches thick (12 to 14 ounces each)
- ¾ cup packed light brown sugar
     Table salt
- 1 recipe stuffing (recipes follow)
     Ground black pepper
- 2 teaspoons vegetable oil

1. **TO BRINE THE CHOPS:** Using sharp paring knife, cut 1-inch opening into side of each chop, then cut pocket for stuffing (see illustrations at right). Dissolve sugar and ¼ cup salt in 6 cups water in large bowl or container; submerge chops, cover with plastic wrap, and refrigerate for 1 hour.

2. **TO STUFF AND COOK THE CHOPS:** Adjust oven rack to lower-middle position, place rimmed baking sheet or shallow roasting pan on rack, and heat oven to 450 degrees. Remove chops from brine and rinse under cool running water; pat dry with paper towels. Place one-quarter of stuffing in pocket of each chop. Trim reserved lemon or orange wedges from stuffing recipe to 2-inch lengths; insert one lemon or orange wedge into each pocket to contain stuffing. Sprinkle chops with salt and pepper.

3. Heat oil in heavy-bottomed 12-inch skillet over medium-high heat until just beginning to smoke. Arrange chops in skillet and cook without moving chops until well browned, about 3 minutes. Using tongs, flip chops and cook until well browned on second side, 2 to 3 minutes longer.

4. Using tongs, transfer chops to preheated pan in oven; cook until instant-read thermometer inserted into center of stuffing registers 135 degrees, 15 to 20 minutes, flipping chops halfway through cooking time. Transfer chops to platter, tent loosely with foil, and let rest 10 minutes (internal temperature will climb to 145 degrees); sprinkle chops with blue cheese if using Red Onion Jam Stuffing. Serve immediately.

SPINACH AND FONTINA STUFFING WITH PINE NUTS
MAKES ABOUT 1⅓ CUPS, ENOUGH TO STUFF 4 CHOPS

- 1 slice white sandwich bread, torn into quarters
- ¼ cup pine nuts, toasted
- 1 tablespoon olive oil
- 2 medium garlic cloves, minced or pressed through garlic press (about 2 teaspoons)
- 6 ounces spinach leaves, washed and stemmed (about 12 cups)
- 2 ounces shredded fontina cheese (about ½ cup)
- ¼ cup ricotta cheese
- 1 ounce Parmesan cheese, grated (about ½ cup)
- 1 medium lemon, cut into 4 wedges
- ¼ teaspoon table salt
     Pinch ground nutmeg
     Ground black pepper

1. In food processor, pulse bread and pine nuts until evenly ground, about ten 1-second pulses.

2. Heat oil in 12-inch skillet over medium-high heat until shimmering; add garlic and cook, stirring constantly, until fragrant, about 1 minute. Add spinach; using tongs, turn spinach to coat with oil. Cook, stirring with tongs, until spinach is wilted, about 2 minutes. Transfer spinach to colander in sink and gently squeeze to release excess moisture; cool spinach until just warm.

3. Mix together fontina, ricotta, and Parmesan in bowl. Add spinach and bread crumb mixture; using spatula, mix well to break up clumps. Squeeze juice from lemon wedges into small bowl; reserve juiced wedges for sealing stuffing pockets in chops. Stir 1 tablespoon lemon juice, salt, nutmeg, and pepper to taste into stuffing.

RED ONION JAM STUFFING WITH PORT, PECANS, AND DRIED FRUIT
MAKES ABOUT 1⅓ CUPS, ENOUGH TO STUFF 4 CHOPS

The blue cheese in the ingredient list is sprinkled over the pork chops just before serving.

- 1 tablespoon olive oil
- 1 large red onion, halved and sliced ⅛ inch thick (about 4 cups)
- 1 tablespoon sugar
- ⅓ cup chopped pitted dates
- ⅓ cup dried sour cherries
- ¾ cup ruby port
- 1 medium orange, cut into 4 wedges
- 2 teaspoons chopped fresh thyme leaves
- 3 tablespoons white wine vinegar
- ¼ teaspoon table salt
     Ground black pepper
- ⅓ cup pecans, toasted
- 3 ounces blue cheese, crumbled (about ¾ cup)

1. Heat oil in medium saucepan over medium heat until shimmering; add onion and sugar and cook, stirring occasionally, until beginning to color, 20 to 25 minutes. Meanwhile, combine dates, cherries, and port in microwave-safe bowl; cover with plastic and microwave on high until simmering, about 1 minute. Set aside until needed. Squeeze juice from orange wedges into small bowl; reserve juiced wedges for sealing stuffing pockets in chops.

2. When onions are soft, add dried fruit/port mixture, ¼ cup orange juice, thyme, 2 tablespoons vinegar, salt, and pepper to taste; continue to cook, stirring occasionally, until mixture is jamlike, 10 to 12 minutes. Stir in remaining 1 tablespoon vinegar and pecans; transfer to bowl and cool until just warm, about 15 minutes.

RECIPE SHORTHAND

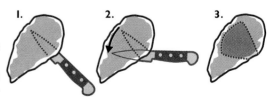

1.   **2.**   **3.**

Cutting the Pocket 1. Insert sharp paring or boning knife through side of chop until tip touches bone. Carefully cut opening to width of about 1 inch. **2.** Swing knife tip through chop to create pocket, being careful not to widen opening. Turn knife and swing blade in opposite direction. **3.** Finished pocket should be as large as possible.

How to Substitute Ingredients

Everybody does it (even though they shouldn't).
Here are some tips for doing it well. BY SEAN LAWLER

"Dear *Cook's Illustrated*: Your chocolate chip cookies are terrible! I followed the recipe exactly, except I made the following substitutions. . . ." We've received more than a few letters like this one over the years. We know that our carefully tested recipes are often subjected to abuse by our readers (and even by members of our staff), and we know the kinds of disasters that can result. For the record, we forgive you. No one wants to run out to the market for just one ingredient. Perhaps something you've got on hand will do the trick. With that in mind, we tested scores of widely published ingredient substitutions to figure out which ones work under what circumstances and which ones simply don't work. If you are going to substitute ingredients, you may as well do it better and smarter. Here's how.

DAIRY PRODUCTS

WHOLE MILK AND HALF-AND-HALF: Use the formulas below to substitute one dairy product for another.

TO REPLACE: **I cup whole milk**

- ⅝ cup skim milk + ⅜ cup half-and-half
- ⅔ cup 1% milk + ⅓ cup half-and-half
- ¾ cup 2% milk + ¼ cup half-and-half
- ⅞ cup skim milk + ⅛ cup heavy cream

TO REPLACE: **I cup half-and-half**

- ¾ cup whole milk + ¼ cup heavy cream
- ⅔ cup skim or low-fat milk + ⅓ cup heavy cream

HEAVY CREAM: Evaporated milk can be used in place of heavy cream to enrich soups and sauces.

TO REPLACE: **I cup heavy cream**

- I cup evaporated milk

NOT SUITABLE FOR: Whipping or baking recipes.

EGGS: All *Cook's Illustrated* recipes are tested with large eggs, but substitutions are possible. For half of an egg, whisk the yolk and white together and use half of the liquid.

Large		Jumbo	Extra-Large	Medium
I	=	I	I	I
2	=	I½	2	2
3	=	2½	2½	3½
4	=	3	3½	4½
5	=	4	4	6
6	=	5	5	7

CULTURED DAIRY PRODUCTS

BUTTERMILK: Regular milk can be "clabbered" with an acidic ingredient such as lemon juice, vinegar, or cream of tartar; the acid will react with baking soda to produce leavening and will approximate the tang of buttermilk in most pancake batters and baked goods.

NOTE: Lemon juice is our first choice; some sensitive tasters detected off flavors from vinegar and cream of tartar.

TO REPLACE: **I cup buttermilk**

- I cup milk + I tablespoon lemon juice
- I cup milk + I tablespoon white vinegar
- I cup milk + I teaspoon cream of tartar

Let stand to thicken, about 10 minutes

NOT SUITABLE FOR: Raw applications, such as a buttermilk dressing.

SOUR CREAM AND PLAIN, WHOLE MILK YOGURT: These can be swapped for each other in equal measure in most baking recipes with good results, but since sour cream has more than four times the fat, expect cakes and muffins baked with yogurt to have a slightly drier texture. Flavored yogurts such as lemon and vanilla can be substituted for plain in recipes where the flavors won't clash.

TO REPLACE: **I cup sour cream**

- I cup plain whole milk yogurt

TO REPLACE: **I cup plain yogurt**

- I cup sour cream

CAUTION: Nonfat and low-fat yogurts are too lean to use in place of sour cream.

FLOURS

The texture of baked goods depends on, among many other things, the protein content of the particular flour used to prepare them.

ALL-PURPOSE FLOUR: The kitchen workhorse and pantry staple, all-purpose flour has a protein content ranging between 10 and 12 percent. This staple has no substitute.

CAKE FLOUR: With just 6 to 8 percent protein, cake flour will impart a more tender, delicate, fine-crumbed texture to baked goods.

TO REPLACE: **I cup cake flour**

- ⅞ cup all-purpose flour + 2 tablespoons cornstarch

BREAD FLOUR: At the other end of the spectrum from cake flour, bread flour has close to 14 percent protein. This ensures strong gluten development and thereby a sturdy dough.

TO REPLACE: **I cup bread flour**

- I cup all-purpose flour

CAUTION: Breads and pizza crusts may bake up with slightly less chew, but results will be acceptable.

LEAVENERS

YEAST: Our favorite is instant yeast (also sold as rapid rise yeast and bread machine yeast) because it is fast acting and can be stirred directly into the other dry ingredients. Active dry yeast, on the other hand, must be dissolved in warm water (around 110 degrees) before being added to the rest of the ingredients. Other than the method of incorporation, instant and active dry yeast are interchangeable.

BAKING POWDER: All chemical leavening is based on the reaction of an acid and a base, or alkali (almost always baking soda), to produce the carbon dioxide gas that makes the baked good rise. Baking powder contains an acid along with baking soda and a small amount of cornstarch to absorb moisture and keep the mixture shelf-stable.

TO REPLACE: **I teaspoon baking powder**

- ¼ teaspoon baking soda + ½ teaspoon cream of tartar. Use right away.
- ¼ teaspoon baking soda + ½ cup of yogurt, buttermilk, or sour cream

NOTE: ¼ teaspoon of baking soda is the leavening equivalent of 1 teaspoon of baking powder.

SUGARS AND OTHER SWEETENERS

GRANULATED SUGAR: This staple has no substitute.

BROWN SUGAR: Granulated sugar and molasses make a close approximation.

TO REPLACE: I cup light brown sugar

- I cup granulated sugar + I tablespoon molasses

TO REPLACE: I cup dark brown sugar

- I cup granulated sugar + 2 tablespoons molasses

Pulse the molasses in a food processor along with the sugar, if desired, or simply add it along with the other wet ingredients.

SUPERFINE SUGAR: This is handy for cold drinks, as it dissolves more readily than granulated sugar.

TO REPLACE: I cup superfine sugar

- I cup granulated sugar ground in food processor for 15 seconds

POWDERED SUGAR: Because it contains cornstarch, powdered sugar should not be substituted for either brown or granulated sugar in most recipes.

TO REPLACE: I cup powdered sugar

- I cup granulated sugar + I teaspoon cornstarch ground together in blender (not food processor)

CAUTION: This works very well for dusting over desserts, less so in icings and glazes.

LIQUID SWEETENERS: Replacing some of the sugar in a recipe with honey, molasses, or maple syrup to add an extra dimension of flavor is a simple matter, provided you account for the extra moisture.

TO REPLACE: sugar with liquid sweetener

- Reduce liquid in recipe by ¼ cup for each cup of liquid sweetener added

CAUTION: As liquid sweeteners vary in moisture content, acidity, and even sweetness, it is usually not a good idea to replace more than half of the sugar in a recipe with a liquid sweetener.

SALT

For all intents and purposes, table salt is "saltier" than kosher salt or coarse sea salt. (Table salt has smaller individual crystals, so more crystals of table salt than kosher or coarse sea salt will fit into a measuring spoon.)

TO REPLACE: I tablespoon table salt

- I ½ tablespoons Morton Kosher Salt or fleur de sel
- 2 tablespoons Diamond Crystal Kosher Salt or Maldon Sea Salt

CAUTION: Kosher salt and coarse sea salt do not dissolve as readily as table salt; for this reason, we do not recommend using them in baking recipes.

HERBS

Dried herbs are more potent than fresh. They are best used in longer-cooking recipes like soups and stews, while fresh herbs are best added near the end of cooking.

TO REPLACE: I tablespoon fresh herbs

- I teaspoon dried herbs

CAUTION: Quite a few herbs should be avoided in dried form because they are tasteless; these include basil, chives, dill, parsley, and tarragon.

WINE

Vermouth makes an acceptable substitute for white wine in recipes that don't call for very much. Nonalcoholic substitutes are more difficult to come by. For soups and pan sauces, the best course of action is to use extra broth, adding wine vinegar (red or white, depending on the recipe) or lemon juice just before serving.

TO REPLACE: ½ cup wine

- ½ cup broth + I teaspoon wine vinegar
- ½ cup broth + I teaspoon lemon juice

CHOCOLATES

UNSWEETENED: Use this substitution in recipes that call for small quantities of chocolate or to replace the unsweetened chocolate in a recipe that calls for both unsweetened and bittersweet or semi-sweet chocolate.

TO REPLACE: I ounce unsweetened chocolate

- 3 tablespoons cocoa powder + I tablespoon vegetable oil
- I ½ ounces bittersweet or semisweet chocolate (remove I tablespoon sugar from recipe)

CAUTION: If making chocolate cake, brownies, or any other intensely chocolate-flavored baked good, do not replace all of the chocolate with cocoa powder; it will have a drastic effect on the texture.

BITTERSWEET/SEMISWEET: These are pure chocolates to which sugar, vanilla, and emulsifiers have been added. The terms themselves are not surefire indicators of relative sweetness. They can be freely interchanged in most recipes, but expect variations in flavor.

TO REPLACE: I ounce bittersweet chocolate or I ounce semisweet chocolate

- ⅔ ounce unsweetened chocolate + 2 teaspoons sugar

CAUTION: Unsweetened chocolate is starchier than sweetened chocolate, so while this substitution will work well with fudgy brownies, it could wreak havoc on a delicate custard or an airy cake.

CHIPS: These morsels of sweetened chocolate have added stabilizers to help them hold their shape when baked into cookies. As a result, we don't recommend using them in chocolate sauces or puddings, but they do produce acceptable results when substituted for bittersweet or semisweet chocolate in a simple brownie recipe.

ETHNIC INGREDIENTS

Supermarkets are getting better about stocking ethnic ingredients, but they can still be hard to find. Here are a few of the items that we stock in our pantry and suggestions for approximating their flavors if unavailable.

COCONUT MILK: Do not use canned cream of coconut, which is sweetened. If you have dried, shredded unsweetened coconut on hand, you can make a crude approximation of coconut milk. Bring equal parts whole milk and shredded coconut to a simmer and let steep, covered, for 15 minutes. Grind the mixture in a blender or food processor and let steep for another 15 minutes. Strain the mixture, pressing down on the coconut in the strainer to extract the most flavor. This will make an acceptable substitute for curries and stir-fry sauces, but it's less reliable in baked goods.

FISH SAUCE: One tablespoon of soy sauce mixed with I finely minced anchovy fillet will make a crude stand-in for I tablespoon of this salty, pungent Thai sauce.

MIRIN: To replace 2 tablespoons of this sweet, Japanese rice wine, substitute an equal amount of white wine or sake plus I teaspoon sugar.

PANKO: To make your own coarse Japanese bread crumbs, process some chunks of bread through the shredding disk of a food processor. Spread the crumbs out on a baking sheet and bake, shaking the sheet once or twice, in a 300-degree oven until dry but not toasted, about 6 minutes.

TAHINI: To replace this sesame paste, grind up an equal amount of sesame seeds in a blender with just enough peanut or vegetable oil to make a fairly smooth mixture. Add I teaspoon toasted sesame oil, or to taste, if you have some on hand. Another option is to blend 3 parts peanut butter with I part sesame oil, then use half the quantity of tahini called for in the recipe.

TAMARIND: To replace 2 tablespoons of tamarind paste soaked in ¾ cup hot water and strained, mix ⅓ cup lime juice and ⅓ cup water.

Crispy Skillet-Roasted Potatoes

Greasy potatoes, burnt crusts, and uneven cooking were just three of the problems we had to solve to resurrect this classic method of roasting spuds on the stovetop.

≥ BY ELIZABETH GERMAIN ≤

Before ovens were common in home kitchens, potatoes were roasted in a heavy skillet on the stovetop. The promise of this time-honored but old-fashioned method is extraordinarily crisp texture, something that is not always easily achieved in an oven. Thinking that this classic method deserved to be resurrected, I prepared a handful of recipes, most of them found in French cookbooks. Some required peeling and cutting, while others left the skin on and/or used whole potatoes. Olive oil, vegetable oil, butter, and clarified butter were all suggested, as were a variety of methods to facilitate crisping and cooking. The result? Six batches of stovetop-roasted potatoes that failed to impress. Uneven cooking, browned but soft exteriors, pale exteriors, dry insides, and greasy outsides were just a few of the problems. So why bother?

Many years ago I was served skillet-roasted potatoes that were truly outstanding: extra-crisp on the outside and moist and creamy on the inside. Hope sprang eternal. And, I admit, the notion of doing all of this on the stovetop—freeing up the oven and saving time—was also appealing. So back into the test kitchen I went to discover what had gone wrong with my half-dozen plates of disappointing spuds.

Mastering Technique

Initial tests convinced me that if the potatoes were to brown evenly, they would have to cook in a single layer without being crowded. I also noted that the best browning occurred when the potatoes were left undisturbed before turning. Without making any final decisions about potato type, I started with Red Bliss—a low-starch, high-moisture variety that we use for oven-roasting. I wanted to cook as many potatoes as possible, so I chose a hefty 12-inch skillet, the largest in most households.

Tasters preferred the appearance, texture, and flavor of potatoes cooked with the skin on. Potato size and cut became an obsession. It was obvious that the pieces had to be uniform for even cooking. Ten test batches later, I came to the conclusion that quartered medium potatoes (lemon sized)

Red Bliss potatoes become especially crisp when roasted in a skillet on the stovetop—and in just 20 minutes.

were best, as they offered two cut sides for crisping and one beautifully rounded side. Halved small potatoes were another good option.

Up until now, I had been using a traditional skillet, but occasionally a potato would stick. I switched to nonstick and was pleased that this rare problem disappeared completely and that the roasting results were equally good. In terms of fat for browning, butter proved problematic given its tendency to burn. I ruled out clarified butter (less

prone to burning, but too much effort to make). Next I pitted vegetable oil against olive oil, and the latter won for extra flavor. As for the amount, 1 tablespoon was serviceable, while 2 tablespoons produced a much crispier crust; 3 tablespoons were too much, making for greasy spuds.

My biggest remaining challenge was getting the interiors to cook through completely within the time it took for the exteriors to crisp and brown. I wondered if precooking the potatoes might help. I scrubbed and cut a batch, placed them in a saucepan with cold water, and brought them to a boil. Immediately, I drained the potatoes and put them in a hot skillet. The insides were cooked but mushy, and the outsides did not brown well. Much like precooking, adding some water to the pan failed. I thought maybe the cover could trap moisture and help solve this problem. I browned both cut sides of the potatoes uncovered over medium-high heat and then covered the skillet and finished cooking over medium-low. This technique, combined with the rinsing and drying of the cut potatoes before cooking (a common step when frying potatoes that removes surface starch), turned out crisp skillet potatoes that were also cooked through.

Reverting to Type

Now it was time to revisit potato type. I had been using the dense, high-moisture Red Bliss, the type of "waxy" potato one might use in a typical potato salad. At the other end of the spectrum are russets. These dry, low-starch potatoes turn out light and fluffy when baked but were a poor choice for this recipe: Dry interiors and poor browning were their downfall. Yukon Golds sit in the middle of the potato scale—neither dense and moist nor light and dry—but when skillet-roasted, they were judged on the dry side as well. So Red Bliss it was.

RECIPE TESTING: **Skillet Potatoes**

We uncovered several recurring problems when testing other recipes for skillet potatoes.

WRONG CUT
Thinly sliced potatoes cook unevenly. Some are browned, some are pale.

TOO MUCH FAT
Potatoes roasted with 1 ½ sticks of butter taste fried and fatty.

ADDED LIQUID
Adding broth to the skillet makes the potatoes soggy.

The Right Cut for the Right Potato

Small or medium potatoes can be used in our recipe, but they must be cut differently. Large potatoes are a poor choice; the cut pieces will be uneven and won't cook at the same rate.

SMALL
Small potatoes (1 ½ to 2 inches in diameter) should be cut in half.

MEDIUM
Medium potatoes (2 to 3 inches in diameter) should be cut into quarters.

A sprinkle of pepper was most welcome, and table salt lost out to kosher salt and sea salt (added just before serving), which provided bigger, more interesting hits of flavor. With a great crust, a moist interior, and a nicely salted and peppered outer layer, these were hands down the best oven-roasted potatoes I had ever eaten.

SKILLET-ROASTED POTATOES
SERVES 3 TO 4

For even cooking and proper browning, the potatoes must be cooked in a single layer and should not be crowded in the pan, so be sure to use a heavy-duty 12-inch skillet. A nonstick skillet simplifies cleanup but is not essential.

- 1½ pounds small or medium Red Bliss potatoes, scrubbed and unpeeled
- 2 tablespoons olive oil
- ¾ teaspoon kosher salt
- ¼ teaspoon ground black pepper

1. If using small potatoes (1½- to 2-inch diameter), halve each potato. If using medium potatoes (2- to 3-inch diameter), quarter each potato to create ¾- to 1-inch chunks. Rinse potatoes in cold water and drain well; spread on clean kitchen towel and thoroughly pat dry.

2. Heat oil in heavy-bottomed 12-inch nonstick skillet over medium-high heat until shimmering. Add potatoes cut side down in single layer; cook, without stirring, until golden brown (oil should sizzle but not smoke), 5 to 7 minutes. Using tongs, turn potatoes skin side down if using halved small potatoes or second cut side down if using quartered medium potatoes; cook, without stirring, until deep golden brown, 5 to 6 minutes longer. Stir potatoes, then redistribute in single layer. Reduce heat to medium-low, cover, and cook until potatoes are tender (paring knife can be inserted into potatoes with no resistance), 6 to 9 minutes.

3. When potatoes are tender, sprinkle with salt and pepper and toss or stir gently to combine; serve immediately.

SKILLET-ROASTED POTATOES WITH GARLIC AND ROSEMARY

Combine 1½ teaspoons minced or pressed garlic and 2 teaspoons minced fresh rosemary in small bowl. Follow recipe for Skillet-Roasted Potatoes; after seasoning potatoes with salt and pepper in step 3, clear center of skillet and add garlic and rosemary mixture. Cook over medium-low heat, mashing with heatproof rubber spatula, until fragrant, about 45 seconds, then stir mixture into potatoes.

SKILLET-ROASTED POTATOES WITH LEMON AND CHIVES

Combine 2 teaspoons grated lemon zest and 2 tablespoons minced fresh chives in small bowl. Follow recipe for Skillet-Roasted Potatoes; after seasoning potatoes with salt and pepper in step 3, stir lemon zest and chives into potatoes.

SPICY SKILLET-ROASTED POTATOES WITH CHILI AND CUMIN

Stir together 1 teaspoon chili powder, 1 teaspoon sweet paprika, ½ teaspoon ground cumin, and ¼ teaspoon cayenne in small bowl. Follow recipe for Skillet-Roasted Potatoes, substituting chili mixture for black pepper and cooking seasoned potatoes over medium-low heat until spices are fragrant, about 30 seconds.

SCIENCE: Is Nonstick Cookware Dangerous?

We regularly get questions from readers about the safety of nonstick cookware, particularly when used over high heat. Fumes released from the nonstick coatings applied to cookware have indeed been known to cause a temporary, flu-like condition known as polyfume fever in human beings and can kill birds.

According to DuPont, manufactorer of Teflon, nonstick cookware can be used safely until the surface temperature exceeds 500 degrees. At this point, the coating begins to break down—that is, particles, but not fumes, are released; emission of fumes occurs at temperatures above 600 degrees. DuPont recommends using the cookware only over low and medium heat and argues that 500 degrees is well beyond the temperature at which most "normal cooking" takes place. But is this realistic? To find out, we tracked the temperature of two skillets—a lightweight $15 aluminum pan from the hardware store and our favorite $140 heavy-duty nonstick skillet from All-Clad—while preparing our Skillet-Roasted Potatoes, a chicken stir-fry, and a frittata.

For the potatoes, which call for up to 13 minutes of cooking over medium-high heat, the highest temperature reached by the heavy-duty pan was 368 degrees; the light pan, 485 degrees. For the stir-fry, which calls for

high heat during the entire 10 to 11 minutes of cooking, the heavier pan rose to a high of 572 degrees; the other pan, 546 degrees. Our frittatas on pages 8–9 are finished under the broiler for a few minutes—another use not recommended by DuPont. The highest temperature we recorded for the pan directly after its removal from the broiler was 250 degrees.

We also decided to abuse the pans by heating them empty over high heat—something we would never rec-

TOO HOT? We used an infrared gun to measure skillet temperature as we prepared a number of recipes. In several cases, the temperature reached the zone in which the nonstick coating starts to break down.

ommend but which might happen by mistake. When left to sit over high heat, the high-quality pan passed 500 degrees in three minutes and passed 600 degrees in five minutes. The lighter pan passed 500 degrees in two minutes and 600 degrees in three minutes.

Where, then, does this leave you and your nonstick skillet? Our tests indicate that normal cooking applications can push nonstick skillets close to—or into—the danger zone. Clearly, placing an empty nonstick skillet over high heat is a mistake. We recommend that you always place oil in the pan as it heats—it will smoke long before the nonstick surface reaches a dangerous temperature and should remind you to add food to the pan. When stir-frying, use a fan and/or keep the window open and limit the time the pan spends over high heat. Finally, while the heavy-duty pan was a bit slower to heat up than the cheaper pan, it did ultimately reach unsafe temperatures, so caution should be taken even when using a more expensive pan. The best and safest substitute for a nonstick pan is a well-seasoned cast-iron pan.
–India Koopman

COOK'S EXTRA For more insight into nonstick coatings, visit www.cooksillustrated.com and key in code 5054. This information will be available until June 30, 2005.

Rescuing Orange-Flavored Chicken

This Chinese restaurant standard—battered and fried chicken drenched in a saccharine, neon-colored sauce—leaves us cold. Could we upgrade this dish from third class to first class?

≥ BY REBECCA HAYS ≤

When Americans order Chinese takeout, a container of orange-flavored chicken is often delivered with the egg rolls, fried rice, and egg drop soup. While it's far from authentic Chinese fare, it's not difficult to understand why this dish is so popular: The chicken is deep-fried, and the sauce is sticky and sweet. Sounds like a winning, if decadent, combination. But it's never as good as I hope it will be. While a quick taste of a candy-coated chicken nugget might have some appeal, my culinary satisfaction goes sharply downhill with successive bites.

Never was this more apparent than during the afternoon I spent strolling the neighborhoods surrounding the test kitchen (where there are a number of Chinese restaurants), ordering orange chicken at every turn. Faced with mouthful after mouthful of ultra-thick breading wrapped around scraps of greasy, gristly, tasteless chicken bathed in "orange" sauce (perhaps a mixture of corn syrup and orange food coloring?), my appetite waned. But my soft spot for this dish was not entirely squelched. Pushing back the last plate of sub-par chicken in favor of a steaming cup of black tea, I dreamed wistfully about the possibilities.

I wanted chicken that I could actually swallow—and that meant substantial, well-seasoned chunks with a crisp, golden brown crust. Puny scraps of chicken and heavy globs of breading need not apply. A perfect coating would be moderately crunchy and maintain its texture beneath a blanket of sauce. As for the sauce, I'd have to modulate the typical Chinese-American sweet/tart flavor profile, which generally leans much too far to the sweet side. But above all I wanted the sauce to offer a clear hit of fresh orange flavor, with balanced sweet, sour, and spicy background notes, plus a pleasing consistency.

Top Coats

Back in the test kitchen, I decided to tackle the chicken coating first, jotting down every coating/breading possibility I could think of, then ticking them off my list following kitchen tests. A fried chicken coating (a buttermilk dip followed by a flour/baking powder dip) was somewhat tough and shatteringly crisp. Panko (Japanese bread crumbs) tasted great but weren't right

Forget about takeout. Homemade orange chicken is much better.

for this recipe, a cake flour batter slipped off the chicken once fried, and a beer batter coating turned spongy and doughy beneath the sauce. I kept going and tried flour and a whole egg, flour and egg whites, cornstarch and sherry, and even flour and seltzer water. All failed.

Some of the recipes I tested early on called for "velveting" the chicken, a process used in some stir-fries in which the chicken is coated in a thin batter of foamy egg whites mixed with some cornstarch. While this approach wasn't quite the ticket when it came to deep-frying (the coating was insubstantial and turned soggy), when I separated the ingredients and dunked the chicken first in egg white, then in cornstarch, it worked. This chicken was perfect! I cornered our science editor to find out why. He explained that when egg whites and cornstarch are combined, the starch absorbs water from the whites and creates a sort of glue that, not surprisingly, turns soggy after frying. My successful two-step (egg white and then cornstarch) coating created a thin sheath of protein (the egg white) beneath plenty of dry cornstarch, which never got the opportunity to swell and absorb water. This dry coating browned

and crisped much more readily than a wet, gluey one.

So I now had just what I wanted—a coating that was tender and yielding in some spots and delicately crunchy in others, falling somewhere between fast-food fried chicken and tempura. Tasters couldn't get enough and gobbled it down, unsauced.

I made some minor refinements. A pinch of cayenne gave the chicken some zip, and baking soda was called in to help develop a golden color. (In baking and frying, baking soda has been shown to aid in browning.) The contest between light and dark meat was easily won—thigh meat has richer flavor and is more apt to remain moist when deep-fried (or cooked just about any other way) than drier breast meat. (Surprisingly, not one of the published recipes I found suggested dark meat for this dish, while every restaurant version I tried was made with boneless chicken thighs.) I also wondered if oil choice mattered much and ran a quick test, pitting peanut oil against vegetable oil. Peanut oil was unanimously preferred, producing chicken that was noticeably cleaner and fresher tasting than chicken fried in vegetable oil.

Having selected the oil, I fiddled with frying temperatures between 325 and 375 degrees and settled right in the middle. At 350 degrees, the chicken was crisp but not greasy in just 5 minutes, requiring one quick flip halfway through cooking.

Special Sauce

We know from developing stir-fry recipes that a salty marinade works wonders toward developing flavor and maintaining juiciness in chicken. To marinate chicken for this recipe, soy sauce was a natural choice—it would serve as a brine, seasoning the meat and locking in moisture. Garlic, ginger, measures of sugar (brown, for its gentle sweetness) and vinegar (white, for its unobtrusive acidity), plus plenty of orange juice and some chicken broth rounded out the recipe.

I also decided to make extra marinade, putting some in service as a sauce for the deep-fried chicken. I added some cornstarch to the extra marinade and then tasted it as a sauce. Truth be told, it had not even a hint of orange flavor. Luckily, I had a few more tricks up my sleeve: orange marmalade, frozen orange juice concentrate, reduced fresh orange juice, fresh orange zest, and dried orange zest. The marmalade was bitter, orange juice concentrate and reduced orange juice tasted "fake" and "exceedingly bright," and bottled dried zest was gritty and pithy. In the end, a combination of fresh orange juice and zest lent deep, pronounced orange flavor. The slightly bitter, floral taste of the zest plus a healthy dose of cayenne helped the sauce to grow up in a hurry, transforming it from sweetly one-dimensional and boring to complex, spicy, and savory.

Finishing the dish was a snap: I just tossed the fried chicken into the sauce and garnished with strips of orange peel and whole dried red chiles. Left whole, the chiles don't lend much flavor, but they almost always show up in this dish for visual appeal. Now I can look forward to savoring an entire serving (maybe even two) of orange-flavored chicken rather than forcing down just one bite.

ORANGE-FLAVORED CHICKEN
SERVES 4

We prefer the flavor and texture of thigh meat for this recipe, though an equal amount of boneless skinless chicken breasts can be used. It is easiest to grate the orange zest and remove the strips of orange peel before juicing the oranges; use a sharp vegetable peeler to remove the strips. For extra spiciness, increase the cayenne added to the sauce to ½ teaspoon. The whole dried chiles are added for appearance, not for flavor, and can be omitted. To fry the chicken, use a Dutch oven or a straight-sided sauté pan (with at least 3-quart capacity); do not use a 12-inch skillet with sloped sides, as it will be too small to contain the oil once the chicken is added. White rice and steamed broccoli are good accompaniments.

Marinade and Sauce
- 1½ pounds boneless, skinless chicken thighs, trimmed and cut into 1½-inch pieces
- ¾ cup low-sodium chicken broth
- ¾ cup juice, 1½ teaspoons grated zest, and 8 strips orange peel (each about 2 inches long by ½ inch wide) from 2 oranges (see note)

We purchased takeout Asian orange chicken from a half-dozen local restaurants. Tasters had two common complaints, which our homemade recipe addresses.

PROBLEM: DOUGHY COATING Chicken pieces are shrouded in a heavy, thick, greasy coating.
SOLUTION: DOUBLE DIP For a thin, crispy coating, dip the chicken first in egg white, then in cornstarch.

PROBLEM: SCARY SAUCE Sauce is gloppy and candy-sweet, with zero orange flavor.
SOLUTION: THINK FRESH Add fresh orange juice and zest for bold orange flavor, balance the vinegar/sugar ratio, and use a generous hand with garlic, ginger, and cayenne. Thicken the sauce with a modest amount of cornstarch.

- 6 tablespoons distilled white vinegar
- ¼ cup soy sauce
- ½ cup (3½ ounces) packed dark brown sugar
- 3 medium garlic cloves, minced or pressed through garlic press (1 tablespoon)
- 1 piece (about 1 inch) fresh ginger, grated (1 tablespoon)
- ¼ teaspoon cayenne
- 1 tablespoon plus 2 teaspoons cornstarch
- 2 tablespoons cold water
- 8 small whole dried red chiles (optional)

Coating and Frying Medium
- 3 large egg whites
- 1 cup cornstarch
- ¼ teaspoon cayenne
- ½ teaspoon baking soda
- 3 cups peanut oil

1. **FOR THE MARINADE AND SAUCE:** Place chicken in 1-gallon zipper-lock bag; set aside. Combine chicken broth, orange juice, grated zest, vinegar, soy sauce, sugar, garlic, ginger, and cayenne in large saucepan (with at least 3-quart capacity); whisk until sugar is fully dissolved. Measure out ¾ cup mixture and pour into bag with chicken; press out as much air as possible and seal bag, making sure that all pieces are coated with marinade. Refrigerate 30 to 60 minutes, but no longer.

2. Bring remaining mixture in saucepan to boil over high heat. In small bowl, stir together cornstarch and cold water; whisk cornstarch mixture into sauce. Simmer sauce, stirring occasionally, until thick and translucent, about 1 minute. Off heat, stir in orange peel and chiles (sauce should measure 1½ cups); set sauce aside.

3. **FOR THE COATING:** Place egg whites in pie plate; using fork, beat until frothy. In second pie plate, whisk cornstarch, cayenne, and baking soda until combined. Drain chicken in colander or large mesh strainer; thoroughly pat chicken dry with paper towels. Place half of chicken pieces in egg whites and turn to coat; transfer pieces to cornstarch mixture and coat thoroughly. Place dredged chicken pieces on wire rack set over baking sheet; repeat with remaining chicken.

4. **TO FRY THE CHICKEN:** Heat oil in 11- to 12-inch Dutch oven or straight-sided sauté pan with at least 3-quart capacity over high heat until oil registers 350 degrees on instant-read or deep-fry thermometer. Carefully place half of chicken in oil one piece at a time; fry until golden brown, about 5 minutes, turning each piece with tongs halfway through cooking. Transfer chicken to large plate lined with paper towels. Return oil to 350 degrees and repeat with remaining chicken.

5. **TO SERVE:** Reheat sauce over medium heat until simmering, about 2 minutes. Add chicken and gently toss until evenly coated and heated through. Serve immediately.

Secrets to Great Orange Chicken

1. Soy-orange marinade keeps chicken juicy.

2. Patting marinated chicken dry helps coating adhere.

3. Beaten egg white acts as "glue," securing coating to chicken.

4. Cornstarch and baking soda coating fries up golden and crisp.

5. Frying in peanut oil produces chicken with fresh, clean flavor.

The Ultimate Oatmeal Cookie

What could be better than an oatmeal cookie crammed with dozens of ingredients? How about an oatmeal cookie with just the right ingredients.

⪰ BY ERIKA BRUCE ⪯

Oatmeal cookies—graced with earthy oat flavor and hearty, chewy texture—can serve as the perfect vehicle for almost any addition, be it spices, chocolate, nuts, or dried fruit. But many recipe writers in pursuit of the "ultimate" oatmeal cookies lapse into a kitchen-sink mentality, overloading the dough with a crazy jumble of ingredients. Peanut Butter-Chocolate-Coconut-Cinnamon-Raisin-Brazil Nut Oatmeal Cookies are a good example. Rather than create yet another cookie monster, my goal was to become a cookie editor—to delete the unnecessary ingredients and arrive at a perfect combination of oats, nuts, chocolate, and fruit.

A taste test of overloaded oatmeal cookie recipes revealed another problem: poor texture. To my mind, the ideal oatmeal cookie is crisp around the edges and chewy in the middle. Initial recipe tests produced dry, tough cookies. In addition to trimming the ingredient list, I would have to take a close look at the formula for the dough itself. The ultimate oatmeal cookie—even with just the right amount of added ingredients—would require an ultimately forgiving cookie dough.

Oat Cuisine

I focused first on ingredient selection, and chocolate was at the top of my list. When I pitted semisweet chips against both chopped dark and milk chocolates, the bitter edge of the hand-chopped dark chocolate, as well as its irregular distribution in the cookie, gave it the upper hand.

Nuts and oats are natural complements. After sampling pecans, walnuts, hazelnuts, almonds, and peanuts, tasters professed some distinct preferences. Pecans were first for their sweetness and walnuts second for their meatiness, while hazelnuts were liked for their richness and crunch. Almonds were considered bland when paired with the oats, while peanuts overpowered them. Toasting the nuts first deepened their flavor and added more crunch.

Raisins are a familiar addition to oatmeal cookies, but they seemed too sweet in a cookie loaded with chocolate. Tasters felt the same way about flaked coconut and the rest of the tropical gang,

Great oatmeal cookies have a chewy texture and a balance of extra ingredients like chocolate, nuts, and dried fruit.

including dried pineapple, mango, and papaya. I had better luck with sour cherries and tart cranberries, which offered an assertive tang that stood out against the other additions.

All of the flavor components I wanted were now in place: sweet, tangy, nutty, and chocolaty. But using equal amounts of each (1 cup) did not translate to equal representation. The strong, rich flavor of the chocolate dominated the cookies. Reducing the amount of chocolate to ¾ cup brought the flavors into balance. In a final adjustment, I opted to omit all ground spices (common to most oatmeal cookies), which paired poorly

with the chocolate and dried cherries. Cinnamon, nutmeg, and the like were doing more harm than good—and the cookies had plenty of flavor without them.

One Tough Cookie

Cramming almost 3 cups of filling into the test kitchen's favorite oatmeal cookie recipe was taking its toll. Tasters complained about the dry, doorstop-like texture of my supposedly ultimate oatmeal cookies—the same problem I had run into with the test recipes. Reducing the oats was a first step in bringing back the chew: The batter was softer and the cookies less dry.

Still looking to add moisture, I turned to the sweetener. Because brown sugar is more moist than white sugar, I thought it might help (see "Why Brown Sugar Makes Chewy Cookies," page 23). My working recipe called for a mixture of light brown and granulated sugars. After testing a half-dozen combinations, I found that all dark brown sugar was best; all light brown was next best. Cookies made with brown sugar were much more moist and chewy than cookies made with granulated, and the brown sugar also gave the cookies a rich, dark color and deep caramel flavor.

Fewer oats and all brown sugar—these changes had altered the texture in my favor. But the next modification sealed the deal. The baking powder that I had been using in the recipe was making the cookies crisp from the inside out—a problem, since I wanted a chewy interior and a crisp exterior. When I switched the baking powder for baking soda, the cookies puffed in the oven and then collapsed, losing their shape and yielding not a hint of crispy exterior. Because I wanted a combination of crisp edges and chewy centers, I thought that a combination of baking powder

Loading Up the Flavor

The best oatmeal cookies contain a mix of chocolate, nuts, and fruit. Here's how to make the most of each ingredient and get the right balance of flavors.

CHOCOLATE
Irregular, hand-chopped chunks are better than chips. Use bittersweet chocolate to reduce overall sweetness.

NUTS
Pecans are our top choice, followed by walnuts. Toast nuts in 350-degree oven to maximize their flavor.

DRIED FRUIT
Choose something tart, such as cherries or cranberries, and chop coarse.

and soda might work. Sure enough, this pairing produced cookies that were light and crisp on the outside but chewy, dense, and soft in the center. Because of all the additional ingredients, these cookies require a lot more leavener than regular oatmeal cookies. In the end, I used ¾ teaspoon baking powder and ½ teaspoon baking soda—about twice the leavening power found in a typical oatmeal cookie recipe.

A couple of finishing touches: First, when I was portioning these cookies, I found out that size does matter. Tasters preferred a larger cookie (more contrast between crisp edges and chewy centers), and a spring-loaded ice cream scoop (see photo, above) made quick work of this thick dough. Second, though I am normally loath to rotate trays of cookies during baking and usually opt to bake one tray at a time, waiting 40 minutes to bake two batches of cookies seemed a waste of time. Baking both trays at once and rotating the pans made for a small inconvenience, but it also got me out of the kitchen 20 minutes earlier.

In the end, a moderate hand with ingredients, fewer oats, brown sugar instead of white, and good amounts of baking powder and soda produced a fully loaded—not overloaded—cookie with good chew. It's the ultimate oatmeal cookie, one that downloads lots of flavor but delivers on texture, too.

Worth the Dough

BIG DIPPER
For our large ultimate oatmeal cookies, we use a #16 scoop, which neatly portions out ¼ cup of dough.

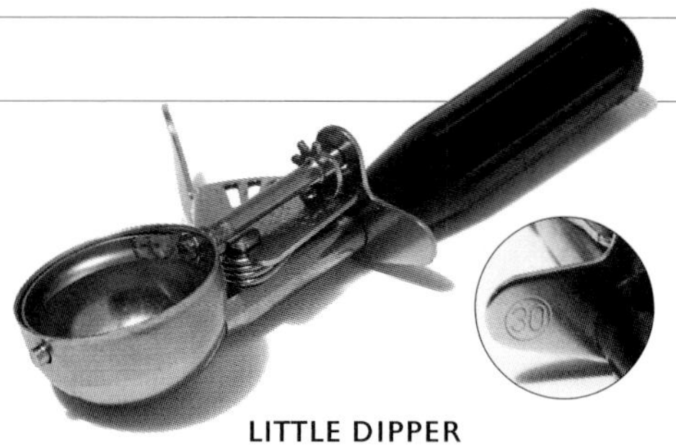

LITTLE DIPPER
For standard-size cookies that call for heaping tablespoons of dough, we reach for a #30 or #40 scoop.

Spring-loaded ice cream scoops don't make the job of scooping ice cream any easier, but we found a better use for them: portioning out cookie dough and muffin batter. These scoops are sized according to how many scoops will yield a quart. For example, a #8 scoop will render eight scoops per quart of ice cream (or dough or batter).

CHOCOLATE-CHUNK OATMEAL COOKIES WITH PECANS AND DRIED CHERRIES
MAKES SIXTEEN 4-INCH COOKIES

We like these cookies made with pecans and dried sour cherries, but walnuts or skinned hazelnuts can be substituted for the pecans, and dried cranberries for the cherries. Quick oats used in place of the old-fashioned oats will yield a cookie with slightly less chewiness. If your baking sheets are smaller than the ones described in the recipe, bake the cookies in three batches instead of two. These cookies keep for 4 to 5 days stored in an airtight container or zipper-lock plastic bag, but they will lose their crisp exterior and become uniformly chewy after a day or so.

1¼ cups (6¼ ounces) unbleached all-purpose flour
¾ teaspoon baking powder
½ teaspoon baking soda
½ teaspoon table salt
1¼ cups (3½ ounces) old-fashioned rolled oats
1 cup pecans (4 ounces), toasted and chopped
1 cup (5 ounces) dried sour cherries, chopped coarse
4 ounces bittersweet chocolate, chopped into chunks about size of chocolate chips (about ¾ cup)
12 tablespoons (1½ sticks) unsalted butter, softened but still cool
1½ cups (10½ ounces) packed brown sugar, preferably dark
1 large egg
1 teaspoon vanilla extract

1. Adjust oven racks to upper- and lower-middle positions; heat oven to 350 degrees. Line 2 large (18 by 12-inch) baking sheets with parchment paper.

2. Whisk flour, baking powder, baking soda, and salt in medium bowl. In second medium bowl, stir together oats, pecans, cherries, and chocolate.

3. In standing mixer fitted with flat beater, beat butter and sugar at medium speed until no sugar lumps remain, about 1 minute. Scrape down sides of bowl with rubber spatula; add egg and vanilla and beat on medium-low speed until fully incorporated, about 30 seconds. Scrape down bowl; with mixer running at low speed, add flour mixture; mix until just combined, about 30 seconds. With mixer still running on low, gradually add oat/nut mixture; mix until just incorporated. Give dough final stir with rubber spatula to ensure that no flour pockets remain and ingredients are evenly distributed.

4. Divide dough evenly into 16 portions, each about ¼ cup, then roll between palms into balls about 2 inches in diameter; stagger 8 balls on each baking sheet, spacing them about 2½ inches apart. Using hands, gently press each dough ball to 1 inch thickness. Bake both baking sheets 12 minutes, rotate them front to back and top to bottom, then continue to bake until cookies are medium brown and edges have begun to set but centers are still soft (cookies will seem underdone and will appear raw, wet, and shiny in cracks), 8 to 10 minutes longer. Do not overbake.

5. Cool cookies on baking sheets on wire rack 5 minutes; using wide metal spatula, transfer cookies to wire rack and cool to room temperature.

Getting the Texture Right

If you want cookies that are chewy in the middle, take them out of the oven before they look done. Trust us—the cookies will set up as they cool.

PROPERLY BAKED
When the cookies are set but still look wet between the fissures, take them out of the oven. Once cooled, the cookies will bend, not snap.

BAKED TOO LONG
Cookies that look matte (rather than shiny) have been overbaked. Once cooled, their texture will be crumbly and dry.

Baked Raspberry Tart

Tart raspberries, rich custard, and a buttery crust are a classic, white-tablecloth combination.
We were seeking a more rustic, casual approach.

⇒ BY DAWN YANAGIHARA ⇐

Tarts composed of plump, ruby-red raspberries lolling about on a dreamy layer of satiny pastry cream are a call to action. The crisp crust, the cool cream, and the bright berries invite the downward slice of a fork to cut through all three and unite them. The components of a baked raspberry tart—in which the fragrant berries are baked in, not arranged on, a rich, custardy layer—are united in the oven, not at the table—but less beautifully so. The heat of the oven brings together the buttery shell, rich custard, and tart raspberries into an earthy, rustic tart that beckons by taste rather than appearance.

When I sought recipes for baked raspberry tarts, I included tarts with classic custard fillings made with just egg and dairy (milk or cream) as well as tarts with clafouti-like fillings that also contained butter and flour. Most recipes that I tried yielded disappointing results: soft, soggy crusts; bleak, overcooked raspberries; heavy, unctuous, eggy, and sometimes even curdled custards. A recipe from Alice Waters, however, stood out. The tart shell was baked prior to filling, then loaded with fresh raspberries. A simple butter, egg, sugar, and flour batter was poured on top. The filling set into a creamy but sliceable berry-studded custard layer that was the perfect complement for the fresh raspberries. I used this as my working recipe and systematically tested each component.

Pastry Case

For the pastry, there were two obvious options: a *pâte brisée* and a *pâte sucrée*. The former is a delicate flaky pastry, much like a well-made pie crust. The latter is a cookielike crust with a distinct sweetness and crisp, sandy texture. Of the two, tasters preferred the tart made with the pâte sucrée, declaring its flavor and texture better suited to the filling. Fortunately for me, an excellent pâte sucrée recipe already existed in the *Cook's* repertoire. I was certain that prebaking the tart shell would be critical to the formation of a browned

Secret to Silky Custard

Wondra flour is better known as a thickener for sauces and gravies than as a baking ingredient, but the filling for our raspberry tart relies upon its quick-dissolving properties for a smooth, silky texture.

This rustic raspberry tart mixes the berries right into the buttery custard filling.

and crisped crust for the finished tart. Testing confirmed this. When instead baked beneath the filling, the tart shell was really only semibaked, and its texture was doughy and pasty.

Regarding the raspberries, there wasn't much to consider. Once the tart shell was baked and cooled, in went the berries in a single layer. What did need reviewing was the butter-egg-sugar-flour mixture that I poured over them. I wanted to eliminate extraneous steps and ingredients and to finesse the flavor and texture.

The working recipe enlisted a standing mixer for the filling, but I found that a bowl and a whisk worked equally well. The procedure now was embarrassingly simple: Whisk the eggs and sugar; add butter, lemon juice, flour, and a spot of cream; pour over the raspberries; and bake.

Custard Consistency

With two whole eggs the custard filling was rather heavy and eggy, but with only one it failed to set well enough to slice cleanly. A whole egg plus a yolk was barely an improvement. A whole egg plus a white, however, did the trick, as the filling set into a nicely firm but creamy texture. I tried various amounts of sugar and settled on a sort of odd measure—½ cup plus 1 tablespoon—as the ideal amount with moderately tart berries.

At a full melted stick (8 tablespoons), butter figured prominently in the filling. I added more and I added less and decided on 6 tablespoons for richness without greasiness. As the working recipe called for browning the butter (cooking it gently until the fragrance turns nutty and the milk solids turn brown), I made tarts with plain melted butter and browned butter. The filling made with browned butter did not taste distinctly of browned butter (nutty and toasty, that is), but the flavor was richer, fuller, and more complex. It was certainly worth the modest extra effort.

Next, the cream. The working recipe called for just 2 tablespoons, which I thought might be superfluous, but without cream the filling was stiff and waxy. I also thought the flour—also just 2 tablespoons—might be unnecessary (or even unwanted; several tasters detected a gritty, starchy taste). Wrong again. The filling clearly needed a starch to hold it together.

But was flour the best choice? I tried cornstarch and got a filling with a heavy, pasty texture. On a whim, I next tried Wondra, a flour formulated to dissolve quickly and a common choice for thickening sauces and gravies. This effected quite an improvement: The starchiness and coarseness were gone, and the filling was now smooth and velvety. A dose of salt, some lemon juice and lemon zest, and small measures of vanilla and framboise (kirsch worked well, too) enhanced the flavor.

Et voilà. A simple, humble raspberry tart—the perfect marriage of fruit, custard, and pastry.

BAKED RASPBERRY TART
MAKES ONE 9-INCH TART, SERVING 8 TO 10

To minimize waste, reserve the egg white left from making the tart pastry for use in the filling. If your raspberries are either very tart or very sweet, adjust the amount of sugar in the filling by a tablespoon or so. Wondra flour is sold in small canisters in the baking aisle alongside all-purpose flour. All-purpose can be used in place of Wondra, but it will give the filling a slightly starchy, gritty feel. The tart is best eaten the day it is made.

Tart Pastry (Pâte Sucrée)
- 1 large egg yolk
- 1 tablespoon heavy cream
- 1/2 teaspoon vanilla extract
- 1 1/4 cups (6 1/4 ounces) unbleached all-purpose flour
- 2/3 cup (about 2 3/4 ounces) confectioners' sugar
- 1/4 teaspoon salt
- 8 tablespoons (1 stick) very cold unsalted butter, cut into 1/2-inch cubes

Filling
- 6 tablespoons unsalted butter
- 1 large egg plus 1 egg white
- 1/2 cup plus 1 tablespoon sugar
- 1/4 teaspoon table salt
- 1 teaspoon vanilla extract
- 1 teaspoon framboise or kirsch (optional)
- 1/4 teaspoon grated zest plus 1 1/2 teaspoons juice from 1 lemon
- 2 tablespoons Wondra flour
- 2 tablespoons heavy cream
- 2 half-pint containers fresh raspberries (about 10 ounces total), picked over

1. **FOR THE TART PASTRY:** Whisk together yolk, cream, and vanilla in small bowl. Combine flour, sugar, and salt in food processor with four 1-second pulses. Scatter butter pieces over flour mixture; pulse to cut butter into flour until mixture resembles coarse meal, about twenty 1-second pulses. With machine running, add egg mixture and process until dough comes together, about 12 seconds. Turn dough onto sheet of plastic wrap and press into 6-inch disk; wrap with plastic wrap and refrigerate at least 1 hour or up to 48 hours.

2. Remove dough from refrigerator (if refrigerated longer than 1 hour, let stand at room temperature until malleable). Unwrap and roll out between large, lightly floured sheets of parchment paper or plastic wrap to 11-inch round.

(If dough becomes soft and sticky, slip onto baking sheet and refrigerate until workable.) Transfer dough to tart pan by rolling dough loosely over rolling pin and unrolling over 9-inch tart pan with removable bottom. Working around circumference of pan, ease dough into pan by gently lifting dough with one hand while pressing dough into corners and sides of pan with other hand. Press dough into fluted sides of pan, patching breaks or cracks if necessary. (If some edges are too thin, reinforce sides by folding excess dough back on itself.) Run rolling pin over top of tart pan to remove excess dough. Set dough-lined tart pan on baking sheet or large plate and freeze 30 minutes. (Frozen dough-lined tart pan can be wrapped tightly in plastic wrap and frozen up to 1 month.)

3. Meanwhile, adjust oven rack to middle position and heat oven to 375 degrees. Set dough-lined tart pan on baking sheet; lightly spray one side of 18-inch square heavy-duty extra-wide foil with nonstick cooking spray. Press foil greased side down inside frozen tart shell, folding excess foil over edge of pan; fill with metal or ceramic pie weights. Bake until pastry appears dry and pale gold under foil and edges have just begun to color, 20 to 25 minutes, rotating halfway through baking. Remove from oven and carefully remove foil and weights by gathering edges of foil and pulling up and out. Return baking sheet with tart shell to oven and bake until sides are medium golden brown, about 5 minutes; set on wire rack to cool.

4. **FOR THE FILLING:** While tart shell is cooling, heat butter in small saucepan with light-colored interior over medium heat; cook, swirling or stirring occasionally, until butter smells nutty and milk solids at bottom are golden brown, about 7 minutes. Transfer butter to small heatproof bowl to stop cooking; cool butter until just warm to touch. Whisk egg and egg white in medium bowl until combined; add sugar and salt and whisk vigorously until light colored, about 1 minute. Whisk in warm browned butter until combined; then whisk in vanilla, framboise (if using), and lemon zest and juice. Whisk in Wondra flour, then whisk in cream until combined.

5. **ADD BERRIES AND BAKE:** Distribute raspberries in single tightly packed layer in bottom of cooled tart shell. Pour filling mixture evenly over raspberries. Place tart on baking sheet in oven. Bake until fragrant and filling is set (does not jiggle when shaken), bubbling lightly around edges, and surface is puffed and deep golden brown, about 30 minutes, rotating sheet pan after about 20 minutes for even browning. Cool on wire rack to room temperature, at least 1 1/2 and up to 6 hours. Remove tart pan ring; slide thin-bladed spatula between tart pan bottom and crust to loosen, then slide tart onto serving platter. Cut into wedges and serve.

TESTING EQUIPMENT: **Rolling Pin Guides**

Rolling out dough to a precise, uniform thickness can be an intimidating task. Lately, however, we've noticed some gadgets meant to make uneven crusts a thing of the past. Do they really work?

Rubber Rolling Pin Rings ($7.99 for a set of four) slide onto the end of a rolling pin to serve as guides; you simply roll out the dough until the rings reach the surface on which you're rolling. A nice idea, but not without problems. The rings appear to be one-size-fits-all, but many failed to fit a single roller in the test kitchen. In addition, the rings shortened the usable length on tapered, French-style rolling pins (our favorite) by almost half.

The Dobord LTD Pastry Board ($59.95) is a wooden pastry board with an adjustable frame, along which the straight rolling pin included in the package glides. The Dobord lets you focus simply on rolling the dough into a round shape; the smooth surface helps to prevent sticking, and the frame keeps the mess contained. On the downside, the 14-square-inch work area is cramped for some tasks, and adjusting frame height is somewhat tedious. And, in case you hadn't noticed, this board is expensive.

Perfection Strips ($8.00 for a set of three) consist of broad lengths of wood of varying thicknesses. They are placed alongside the dough, and the pin is rolled on top of them. The strips do not impede the rolling pin, but you may want to use them only as you start to approach the desired thickness (keeping them oriented correctly as you turn the dough early on can be frustrating). Novice rollers were surprised at the flawless uniformity they achieved with the help of these guides. However, we encountered the same problem using French-style pins here as with the rings.

In the end, then, we found that nothing replaces old-fashioned patience and practice. But an inexpensive set of strips (when used with an untapered pin) offers an effective set of training wheels, providing a boost of confidence for the apprehensive roller. –Garth Clingingsmith

SILLY RINGS
These rubber rings shorten the usable length of many rolling pins by half.

PRICEY BOARD
This wooden pastry board can be tedious to use and costs too much.

SUITABLE STRIPS
These wooden strips are inexpensive insurance for perfectly even dough.

Preferred Stock

Most commercial chicken broths are dreadful, 'fowl' concoctions. So what is the time-pressed home cook to do?

⇒ BY JOLYON HELTERMAN ⇐

In a perfect world, of course, there would be no commercial chicken broth. Home cooks would always reach into softly gurgling pots of long-simmered homemade stock—heady with rich chicken and aromatics—just to ladle out the single quarter-cupful required for Tuesday night's fricassee.

Here in harsh reality, though, rare is the cook who has the time for slowly simmered perfection. The rest of us head to the soup aisle of the local supermarket to make do with some permutation of commercially prepared chicken broth. But truth be told, it could take nearly as long just to choose from the confusing array of offerings: Alongside the standard metal cans of broth and the dehydrated bouillon powders sit dozens of broths sporting "aseptic" packaging (resealable paper cartons) and glass jars filled with gloppy "base" (chicken broth reduced to a concentrated paste). Add organic, low-sodium, and gourmet-shop varieties to the mix, and the number of options quickly becomes overwhelming.

So many choices, but was there a single decent stand-in among them for homemade stock? I brought a shopping cart full of chicken broth products into the test kitchen to see what it all boiled down to.

Homemade versus Prepared

Homemade chicken stock should beat the prepared stuff hands down, right? There was only one way to find out. We pitted our four recommended brands—Swanson Certified Organic, Better Than Bouillon, Swanson Natural Goodness, and Imagine—against the *Cook's* chicken stock recipe to see if tasters would choose homemade in a blind test of hot broth. Sure enough, the homemade was the clear favorite. Tasters praised its forward chicken flavor compared with the prominent vegetable notes of the supermarket broths. But tasters were surprised by how close our top store-bought broths came.

So when should you go through the trouble of making chicken stock from scratch? It's a worthwhile investment if stock is a featured ingredient in the recipe (as in chicken noodle soup) or if the ingredient list is short on strong flavors. For most dishes, though, we think our top four brands make convincing substitutions. –J.H.

A Saline Solution

As I surveyed the 40-odd products I'd gathered during my soup-aisle sojourn, one thing was clear: I had to narrow the field. A quick comparison of nutritional information convinced me to zero in on sodium content, which ranged from 140 milligrams to 1,350 milligrams per serving.

How much salt was ideal? A preliminary tasting reconfirmed our historical preference for lower-sodium broths (around 700 milligrams per serving and below). Although the high-salt varieties fared well when tasted at regular strength (simply warmed up as soup), reducing them by even one-third—for preparing, say, a pan sauce—rendered them virtually inedible.

Discarding broths with sodium contents above 700 milligrams per serving quickly cut my list in half. But I still couldn't ask colleagues to make in-depth comparisons of 18 broth samples in one sitting. The solution, I decided, was to make the first tasting—plain, warmed broth—an elimination round: Tasters would simply weed out the truly bad ones. The nine best would then advance to the finals, which would include tastings of plain broth (again) and simple gravy reductions. Finally, in both plain-broth rounds, we would make the samples' sodium levels roughly equivalent by adding appropriate amounts of salt, so tasters could focus on the flavor profiles. Saltiness would be tackled in the gravy round.

Fowl Brews

As tasters pried the lids off 18 steaming samples, nothing prepared them for the wretched sensory assault to follow. Suffice it to say the qualities separating these broths were far from subtle. Some were actually startling in their rancid, sour flavors; others were tough to smell, let alone taste. Panelists took to the tasting sheets to vent their disgust. "Did you get this out of a dumpster?" complained a taster about one boutique organic broth (which didn't make the final cut). "It smells like a rotten carcass," said another. The most consistently negative remarks were saved for Herb Ox, a powdered bouillon product several staffers confessed to keeping on hand in case they run out of their favorite broth.

What could possibly account for such a varied spectrum of dreadful tastes and aromas? To find out, a behind-the-scenes peek at chicken broth manufacturing was in order.

In the test kitchen, we use 4 pounds of chicken to produce 2 quarts of stock—a ridiculously expensive formula for broth makers planning to charge less than $2 a quart at retail. So factories use much less. That explained why several broths in the lineup were described as "bland" and "insipid." But what about the horrible rancidity, which so vexed the panel of tasters?

According to Brian Sheldon, a poultry science professor at North Carolina State University, rancid off-tastes are caused by one thing: oxidation of fats. Just a few hours of air exposure are enough to cause minor spoilage that, while not unsafe, is wildly unpalatable. Occasional oxidation is an inevitable part of the broth production game, and the only way for manufacturers to combat it is with vigilant quality control. "Smaller firms would be expected to have fewer financial resources and therefore smaller quality control staffs and programs," he said. Although Sheldon warns he's only speculating, our tasting data support such a hypothesis. The worst offenders in terms of rancidity were products made by smaller companies.

Label Sleuthing

To compensate for using less chicken, most manufacturers opt to add flavor enhancements, especially salt, vegetables, and monosodium glutamate (MSG). A comparison of label ingredient lists proved telling: Our favorite broths were those whose list of ingredients included most or all of the components of the standard *mirepoix* chefs use to make sauces—that is, carrots, celery, and onions. In fact, you can almost predict how good-tasting a commercial chicken broth will be by counting the number of mirepoix elements listed.

Why wouldn't all broth makers jump onto the mirepoix bandwagon? Because it's very expensive, said Sheldon. "Every additional ingredient means additional cost."

Based on past tastings, I expected the most flavorful brands to include MSG, a traditional but controversial flavor enhancer. So I was puzzled to find that only two of the 18 broths in the initial tasting included "monosodium glutamate" in the list of ingredients—College Inn and Herb Ox. Had the controversy surrounding MSG convinced most manufacturers to buck tradition? Not so fast. Additional research uncovered an interesting loophole in labeling laws. The U.S. Food and Drug Administration requires manufacturers to

TASTING SUPERMARKET CHICKEN BROTHS

Twenty *Cook's Illustrated* staff members tasted 18 brands of lower-sodium chicken-broth products (between 140 milligrams and 690 milligrams per serving) as plain soup, with sodium adjusted to the same level. The top nine finalists were tasted once again as plain soup (sodium levels adjusted), then cooked in a simple gravy reduction (sodium levels unadjusted). Tasters rated each sample. Brands are listed below in order of preference. Sodium levels given are per 1-cup serving, based on package information.

RECOMMENDED

SWANSON Certified Organic Free Range Chicken Broth
➤ **$2.79 for 32-ounce carton SODIUM: 570 mg.**
We're not ones to jump on the organic bandwagon for its own sake; the proof's in the taste. Swanson's newest broth won tasters over with "very chickeny, straightforward, and honest flavors," a hearty aroma, and restrained "hints of roastiness."

BETTER THAN BOUILLON Chicken Base
➤ **$4.99 for 8-ounce jar of concentrate (makes 38 cups) SODIUM: 690 mg.**
Fairly salty, but tasters were fond of its "straightforward" flavor profile. Though it does take about 5 minutes to reconstitute the concentrated paste in water, the 18-month refrigerator shelf life means it's a good replacement for dehydrated bouillon.

SWANSON "Natural Goodness" Chicken Broth
➤ **$2.19 for 32-ounce carton SODIUM: 570 mg.**
Swanson's standard low-sodium broth tasted almost as good as the winner, though some panelists found it "overly roasted." Very full chicken flavor, but several tasters noted an out-of-place tartness reminiscent of lemon.

IMAGINE Organic Free Range Chicken Broth
➤ **$1.99 for 32-ounce carton SODIUM: 570 mg.**
A "decent flavor of chicken that lingers." This broth had very prominent onion notes, which some tasters loved and others disliked. Some panelists weren't fond of the pale yellow color.

RECOMMENDED WITH RESERVATIONS

COLLEGE INN Light & Fat Free Chicken Broth
➤ **$1.99 for 32-ounce carton SODIUM: 450 mg.**
Some tasters were sold on this broth's "nice, mild chicken flavors," deeming its "understated" profile as optimal for blending into recipes. Others found it "blah and boring—nothing offensive, though."

ORRINGTON FARMS Chicken Flavored Soup Base and Food Seasoning
➤ **$2.99 for 16-ounce jar of powdered concentrate (makes 91 cups) SODIUM: 680 mg.**
The only dehydrated bouillon product in the top 10, we discovered, got flavor from a chicken *and* a cow. Beef tallow helped give this product "nice, rich flavors."

NOT RECOMMENDED

TRADER JOE'S Free Range Chicken Broth
➤ **$1.99 for 32-ounce carton SODIUM: 570 mg.**
Tasters couldn't make up their minds whether this broth tastes more like "bad takeout Chinese soup" or the "cardboard" container it comes in. The "wretched odor" earned it no extra points.

KITCHEN BASICS Natural Chicken Stock
➤ **$2.89 for 32-ounce carton SODIUM: 480 mg.**
Not one taster believed this brand really was chicken broth. "Medicinal and beefy—are you sure this is chicken?" asked one worried taster. "Tastes like Vegemite tea." Beads of oil floated on top.

PACIFIC Organic Free Range Chicken Broth
➤ **$2.49 for 32-ounce carton SODIUM: 570 mg.**
One taster noticed an "interesting mushroom smell," but that's as positive a comment as tasters could muster. "Watery," "chemical," "dirty," and "like an entire vegetable drawer gone bad" were more-representative observations.

EVEN LESS RECOMMENDED

These products—listed in order of preference—were deemed not good enough to make the final cut: TELMA Reduced Sodium Consomme Stock (cube), CARMEL Kosher Chicken Soup Base (powder), SHELTON'S 100% Organic Chicken Broth Original Recipe (can), HEALTH VALLEY Fat Free Chicken Broth (can and carton), CAMPBELL'S Low Sodium Chicken Broth Soup (can), NATURE'S PROMISE Organic Chicken Broth (carton), SHARIANN'S Organic Chicken Broth (can), HERB OX Very Low Sodium Chicken Granulated Bouillon (powder).

---

list MSG only if it's added in its pure form. But several food additives that contain the offending glutamic acid may be included without special labeling—among them, autolyzed yeast, yeast extract, dried whey, hydrolyzed soy protein, and disodium inosinate. A second look at the labels revealed that five of the top six broths in our lineup contain one or more of these compounds (the exception is Imagine). And a few of them trumpet "No MSG" across their packaging.

Because no canned broths made our top nine, we wondered if the relatively new aseptic cartons were responsible for maintaining fresh flavors without off-tastes. Only two of our broths, Swanson Natural Goodness and College Inn, are available in both types of packaging, and a head-to-head test revealed the flavor differences to be negligible. What's more, some of our worst-performing brands are packaged only in aseptic cartons.

So what chicken broth product should you reach for when you haven't got time for homemade? We recommend choosing a mass-produced, lower-sodium brand—and check the label for evidence of mirepoix ingredients. (The best-tasting brands get help from vegetables, a glutamic compound, or both.) Swanson Certified Organic was our clear favorite, but the less expensive, third-place Swanson Natural Goodness was solid as well. And if you don't mind adding water, Better Than Bouillon chicken base came in a very close second—and was the favorite of several tasters.

COOK'S EXTRA For our homemade chicken stock recipe and a quick pressure cooker variation, visit www.cooksillustrated.com and key in code 5056. The recipes will be available until June 30, 2005.

The Problem(s) with Cookie Sheets

You can pay anywhere from $10 to a whopping $90 for a single cookie sheet.
Does it matter? We baked 2,900 cookies to find out.

≥ BY JOLYON HELTERMAN AND GARTH CLINGINGSMITH ≤

For such a simple-looking piece of equipment, the cookie sheet is rife with complex problems. Warping, sticking, overbrowning, underbrowning—it's a miracle that edible, attractive cookies get made at all on these temperamental squares of metal.

Bakeware manufacturers have heard the call, trotting out redesign after snazzy redesign. But these "solutions" tend to offer little more than temporary displacement, solving one problem only to exacerbate another. Is it really too much to ask for one cookie sheet that browns evenly, refuses warping, resists sticking, *and* transfers to and from the oven with ease?

The ultimate pan had to be out there somewhere, we reasoned. But should we spend just a few dollars or fork over more than 10 times as much? We came up with 10 varied cookie sheets close in size to the test kitchen's favorite all-purpose baking sheet (technically, a four-sided "jellyroll" pan that measures 16 by 12 inches), which we added to our list for comparison. Then the baking marathon began.

Sticking Points

First, we had to tackle the respective merits of regular and nonstick sheets. In the past, we've been partial to regular surfaces for their tendency to brown more uniformly, lining the pans with parchment paper to compensate for the higher incidence of sticking. In the seven years since our last cookie-sheet testing, however, several new players have entered the bakeware arena. We were willing to give nonstick another go.

We baked 11 batches each of lemon cookies, walnut lace cookies, chocolate chip cookies, and spritz cookies, once with parchment paper, once without. During the unlined round, the cookies clung tenaciously to the uncoated surfaces (breaking into pieces when we pried them off), while the nonstick sheets released their contents effortlessly. No surprises there. But one uncoated sheet, the Chicago Metallic, released cookies almost as well as the nonstick models. The difference? This was the only traditional sheet with a matte rather than a shiny, slick surface, making it harder for the cookies to form a tight seal.

The cookies baked on the darker nonstick sheets browned more quickly than we wanted, but at least they were intact. When we repeated the tests using parchment paper, however, the traditional sheets came out on top, browning evenly and at a comfortable pace—and without any release issues. Even with parchment paper, the nonstick sheets overbrowned the cookies.

Why such a difference? In baking, cooking occurs primarily through convection: heat transferred indirectly to the food via air currents. Since food can't float in midair—it has to sit on bakeware—additional heat is transferred directly from the pan. Dark-colored surfaces absorb more heat than light-colored surfaces (which reflect it), so more heat gets transferred to the food.

If only it were possible to make a cookie sheet with a light-colored nonstick coating. A call to the Cookware Manufacturers Association left us scratching our heads. "You can tint nonstick coatings any color you want," explained a CMA spokesperson. "At one point, there were even white nonstick coatings." So why do bakeware companies today insist on making dark coatings? It turns out the preference for dark coatings is a relic of 1960s marketing; that's when DuPont began tinting its Teflon-brand coating to differentiate it from the competition—inferior-quality nonstick coatings made with clear silicone. The misconception that equates a dark finish with higher quality persists to this day.

Since overbrowning is unacceptable, we prefer a cookie sheet with a regular rather than a nonstick surface—at least until the nonstick-coating industry lightens up. Besides, keeping parchment paper on hand is easy enough.

Not all regular surfaces are created equal, however. We dismissed texturized surfaces fairly quickly. The Emerilware's diamond-shaped grooves, designed to let hot air circulate beneath the food, did little but retard browning—unnecessary with light-colored sheets. The AirBake insulated pans had similar problems: The two-layer sheets, unsealed to allow air to fill the interior, slowed browning.

With the nonstick, texturized, and insulated sheets eliminated, only four cookie sheets remained in the game: Chicago Metallic, All-Clad, Kaiser, and the generic jellyroll pan.

Side Issues

Most cookie sheets have at least one perfectly flat side to allow batches of cookies to be whisked from sheet to cooling rack unhindered. After breaking one too many cookies in transit, we were convinced that a good cookie sheet can't have four raised sides. But what was the optimal number? Several models had just one raised side, which proved awkward when rotating them midway through baking, a necessary step for most recipes. (The side with the "handle" always ended up in an awkward position: either facing toward the back of the oven or on the left side, if the baker was right-handed.) For that reason, we recommend cookie sheets with two handles—positioned at the short sides.

Unfortunately, three of our four final contestants fell short in the handle department, either having four sides (the jellyroll pan) or just one side (the Kaiser and the All-Clad). That left us with just one contender, the Chicago Metallic, and that brings us to the subject of warping. The thinner and lighter the sheet, the greater the tendency to warp at higher temperatures. Beyond the disturbing sound of struggle emanating from the oven, warping is undesirable because of the tendency for delicate cookies to break or spread unevenly at the site of the temporary bend. The Chicago Metallic sheet was on the light side and evidenced warping when used at high oven temperatures. It's a good cookie sheet, but not a perfect one.

You've Got Mail (Order)

After weeks of testing, then, where were we? We hadn't found the cookie sheet of our dreams—ideally, a heavy sheet with a light-colored matte finish and handles on the two short sides. We headed back to department stores, kitchenware shops, and bakeware Web sites in search of our elusive sheet, but to no avail. Then, during a visit to a restaurant supply store, we found the Holy Grail of cookie sheets. Made by Vollrath, the sheet boasted every one of our choosy preferences. After confirming that industry outsiders can order the sheet by mail (see Sources, page 32), we brought it back to the test kitchen to see how it negotiated our battery of trials.

Sure enough, the Vollrath handled every task brilliantly. We repeated the tests with our reigning favorites—our four flawed-but-solid sheets—just to make sure the Vollrath was truly the top choice. But 16 more batches of cookies later, the conclusion was clear: no warping, two well-positioned handles, and minimal sticking, even unlined. For the Ultimate Cookie Sheet, then, our money's on the Vollrath.

RATING COOKIE SHEETS

We tested 12 cookie sheets, as close to 16 inches by 12 inches as we could find in each manufacturer's line, baking several styles of cookies on each model. The sheets are listed below in order of preference, based on our evaluation of performance, design, and durability.

MATERIAL: Material the sheet is made from.

COOKING SURFACE: Dimensions of the cooking surface.

WEIGHT: Rounded to the nearest ounce.

PRICE: Prices listed are what we paid at Boston-area retail, national mail-order, or online outlets. You may encounter different prices.

PERFORMANCE: Factors evaluated included cooking speed as well as evenness and degree of browning. Sheets that browned cookie bottoms to the appropriate shade consistently and within the recipes' recommended cooking times were rated good. Browning that was moderately darker or lighter, that was inconsistent from cookie to cookie, or that proceeded slightly too fast or slow meant a fair rating. Extreme differences in browning, cooking times, or consistency earned a poor rating.

DESIGN: Factors evaluated included whether the sheet's dimensions, shape, material, and handle design contributed to or detracted from overall user-friendliness.

DURABILITY: Sheets were rated good, fair, or poor based on how well they resisted warping and scratching after repeated sessions of washing, stacking, utensil use, and oven heat.

HIGHLY RECOMMENDED

Vollrath

MATERIAL:	Steel
COOKING SURFACE:	17" x 14"
WEIGHT:	2 lb. 8 oz.
PRICE:	$19.95
PERFORMANCE:	★★★
DESIGN:	★★★
DURABILITY:	★★★

TESTERS' COMMENTS: "This is the one we've been waiting for," remarked one tester. Roomy and sturdy, with handles on the short sides (where we like them). Minimal sticking, even when unlined.

RECOMMENDED

Chicago Metallic Commercial

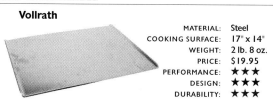

MATERIAL:	Aluminized steel
COOKING SURFACE:	14⅛" x 13⅛"
WEIGHT:	1 lb. 11 oz.
PRICE:	$21.95
PERFORMANCE:	★★★
DESIGN:	★★★
DURABILITY:	★★

TESTERS' COMMENTS: Not until near the end of testing did we realize this pan wasn't nonstick. Cookies released easily even without a liner, and the handles are right where they should be. Some warping at higher temperatures.

WearEver Commercial Jellyroll Pan

MATERIAL:	Tinned steel
COOKING SURFACE:	16⁹/₁₆" x 11⅝"
WEIGHT:	1 lb. 14 oz.
PRICE:	$10.99
PERFORMANCE:	★★★
DESIGN:	★★
DURABILITY:	★★★

TESTERS' COMMENTS: Our old standby handled tasks well, but some cookies broke on one of the four raised sides as we whisked parchment paper from sheet to cooling rack.

Kaiser Bakeware

MATERIAL:	Tinned steel
COOKING SURFACE:	15³/₁₆" x 12³/₁₆"
WEIGHT:	1 lb. 15 oz.
PRICE:	$10.99
PERFORMANCE:	★★★
DESIGN:	★★
DURABILITY:	★★★

TESTERS' COMMENTS: It's a solid pan, but we'd rather have two raised sides and a slightly duller finish. The curved shape of its one raised side meant sticking your hand fairly far into the oven to remove the pan.

All-Clad

MATERIAL:	Stainless steel with aluminum core
COOKING SURFACE:	16³/₁₆" x 12⅛"
WEIGHT:	3 lb. 1 oz.
PRICE:	$89.95
PERFORMANCE:	★★★
DESIGN:	★★
DURABILITY:	★★

TESTERS' COMMENTS: This beautiful sheet turned ruddy after weeks of constant use. Perfect browning, but the handle placement made rotating this heavy pan awkward. Without a liner, cookies and sheet became one.

RECOMMENDED WITH RESERVATIONS

Calphalon Commercial Bakeware

TESTERS' COMMENTS: Good handle placement, but the dark nonstick coating browned cookies too quickly.

MATERIAL:	Aluminum with nonstick coating
COOKING SURFACE:	15¼" x 13"
WEIGHT:	1 lb. 12 oz.
PRICE:	$12.99
PERFORMANCE:	★★
DESIGN:	★★
DURABILITY:	★★

WearEver AirBake Nonstick

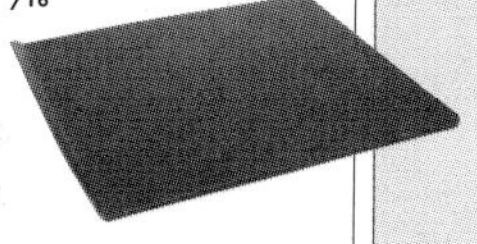

TESTERS' COMMENTS: We're not fans of the insulated pan style—a two-layer sheet with hollow interior—but the insulation compensated for this dark pan's tendency to overbrown. Special pains must be taken to keep the interior from getting wet.

MATERIAL:	Two-layer (insulated) aluminum with nonstick coating
COOKING SURFACE:	15⅝" x 13¹⁵/₁₆"
WEIGHT:	1 lb. 5 oz.
PRICE:	$12.49
PERFORMANCE:	★★
DESIGN:	★★
DURABILITY:	★★

NordicWare Pro-Form Nonstick

TESTERS' COMMENTS: Unsurprisingly, the darkest pan in the lineup produced the most egregious overbrowning. Cookies placed near the raised sidewall suffered most.

MATERIAL:	Aluminized steel with nonstick coating
COOKING SURFACE:	14⁵/₁₆" x 13³/₁₆"
WEIGHT:	1 lb. 12 oz.
PRICE:	$13.99
PERFORMANCE:	★★
DESIGN:	★★
DURABILITY:	★★

Anolon SureGrip Bakeware

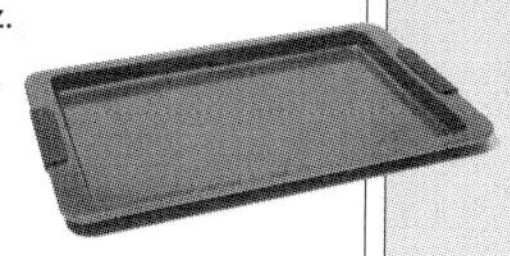

TESTERS' COMMENTS: This behemoth was unwieldy, the dark surface browned too quickly, and the four-sided design was less than ideal for whisking parchment sheets to the cooling rack.

MATERIAL:	Carbon steel, with silicone handles and nonstick coating
COOKING SURFACE:	16¾" x 10⅝"
WEIGHT:	3 lb. 10 oz.
PRICE:	$20.00
PERFORMANCE:	★★
DESIGN:	★★
DURABILITY:	★★★

NOT RECOMMENDED

Emerilware

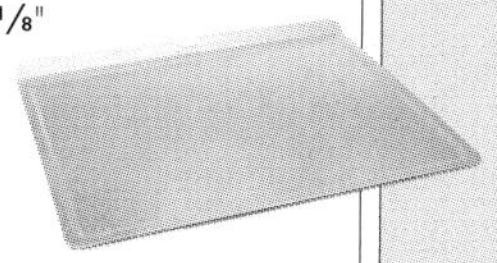

TESTERS' COMMENTS: The texturized surface slowed browning, the handle is on the wrong side, cookies stuck horribly when unlined, and warping was a serious problem.

MATERIAL:	Aluminum
COOKING SURFACE:	16⅛" x 12⅛"
WEIGHT:	1 lb. 8 oz.
PRICE:	$24.99
PERFORMANCE:	★
DESIGN:	★★
DURABILITY:	★★

WearEver AirBake

TESTERS' COMMENTS: The insulation retarded browning drastically, and there was no dark nonstick surface to make up for it. Special pains must be taken to keep the interior from getting wet.

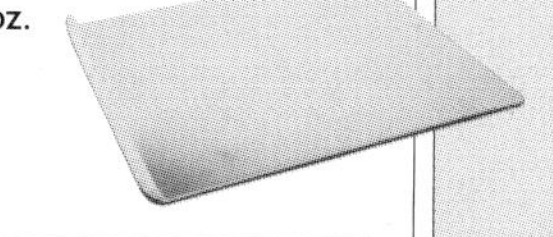

MATERIAL:	Aluminum
COOKING SURFACE:	15⅝" x 13¾"
WEIGHT:	1 lb. 4 oz.
PRICE:	$9.99
PERFORMANCE:	★
DESIGN:	★★
DURABILITY:	★★

KitchenAid

TESTERS' COMMENTS: Design flaws—wide borders and a gimmicky slanted end (meant to help cookies slide off)—robbed this already-small sheet of precious cooking area. The dark surface made for the usual browning problems.

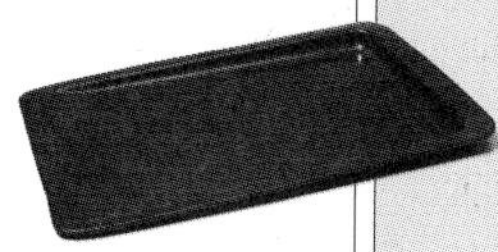

MATERIAL:	Carbon steel with nonstick coating
COOKING SURFACE:	13¼" x 9"
WEIGHT:	1 lb. 8 oz.
PRICE:	$19.99
PERFORMANCE:	★★
DESIGN:	★
DURABILITY:	★★

≥ BY DAWN YANAGIHARA ≤

Convection Ovens: Hype or Help?

In addition to the usual *bake* and *broil*, many new ovens now offer convection settings. Readers have asked when and how to use the convection option, so we decided to make a dozen of our recipes in the test kitchen's Wolf and KitchenAid ovens using both the convection setting and the regular bake setting.

How does a convection oven work? A built-in fan circulates the hot air, which helps to maintain a constant temperature and eliminate hot spots. This should translate to even browning and faster cooking because the hot air fully engulfs the food and conveys the heat more efficiently than it does in a standard oven, where the hot air does not circulate.

Most ovens with a convection feature are equipped with at least two convection settings: *convect bake* and *convect roast*. In the former, a majority of the heat is generated from the lower heating element to mitigate surface browning. In the latter, heat is generated from both the upper and lower heating elements to promote the surface browning desired in most roasted preparations. In our tests, we used the convection setting appropriate for the preparation and in some cases tested both. Manufacturers recommend reducing the oven temperature by 25 to 50 degrees when using a convection setting, and we incorporated these temperature adjustments into our tests.

The following is a review of our findings. Of course, these tests represent just the tip of the iceberg; we intend to make convection oven tests an ongoing project.

CAKES We found no advantage to baking yellow layer cakes on the convect bake setting. In the convection mode, the cakes required a 25-degree temperature reduction to prevent the surfaces from becoming dry and leathery. This temperature adjustment slowed baking by several minutes, with no improvement in the cakes.

COOKIES With the oven temperature reduced 25 degrees, cookies baked up nicely on the convect bake setting, but the baking sheets still required top-to-bottom shuffling. (When we lowered the temperature by 50 degrees and extended the baking time, we found that the cookies browned evenly without switching the position of the baking sheets. We are, however, hesitant to recommend a universal 50-degree temperature reduction when baking cookies on a convection setting. Attempt this at your own risk.) We found that cookies that are better baked one sheet at a time in a standard oven—such as our Molasses Spice Cookies (January/February 2002)—can be baked two sheets at a time on the convect bake setting.

ROAST CHICKEN Chickens roasted on the convect roast setting were done 10 to 15 minutes ahead of those roasted in a standard oven, and the skins were darker and more evenly browned. Chickens roasted on the convect bake setting also cooked faster, but they did not brown any better than in a standard oven. Stick with convect roast. No temperature adjustment is necessary.

YEASTED BREAD When we baked free-form rustic loaves on preheated baking stones, the convect bake setting yielded a loaf with a slightly thicker, crispier crust. The loaves browned and rose on par with each other, indicating that no time and temperature adjustments are necessary.

PREBAKED TART SHELL With the oven temperature reduced 25 degrees, tart shells lined with foil, filled with pie weights, and prebaked on the convect bake setting browned a bit more quickly than tart shells baked on the standard bake setting. Once the foil and weights were removed and the shells returned to the oven, the bottom of the convection-baked tart shells browned better and more evenly.

TO SUMMARIZE: Convection settings do promote even browning and work well for preparations in which browning and crisp surfaces are desired. Temperature reduction is necessary for more delicate and sugary baked goods such as cookies and tart shells but not for sturdier, more savory foods such as roast chicken and yeasted breads.

BETTER BROWNING
In most tests, food cooked in convection ovens showed better, more even browning, as did this tart shell.

Cookie Re-Crisper

With storage, chewy cookies like our Chocolate-Chunk Oatmeal Cookies (page 23) lose some of the textural contrast that makes them so appealing fresh out of the oven. They lose their crispness around the edges and become uniformly soft. Faced with a plethora of leftover cookies from testing, we decided to see if we could restore some of their fresh-baked allure by re-crisping them.

After testing several possibilities (including the microwave), we got the cookies almost as good as fresh by putting them into a 425-degree oven for four to five minutes. Make sure to let the cookies cool on the baking sheet for a couple of minutes before removing them, and consume them while they're warm.

Smart Cookies

We often hear from readers that their cookies don't bake properly in the allotted time. If that's the case in your home, we think we know

---

Choosing the Right Fontina

Fontina cheese is one of our favorites to use in cooking because it has excellent melting properties and a mild, nutty, earthy flavor. But caveat emptor: There are different types of fontina, and, for most cooking purposes, we recommend the middle ground. Fontina Val d'Aosta is the Italian fontina par excellence. It has small irregular holes, a rather elastic texture, and a natural brown rind. At about $15 a pound, it also has a nice price tag. For serving with crackers, this is the cheese to buy.

On the other end of the spectrum is Swedish or Danish fontina. Coated in red wax, this inexpensive cheese has a generic, unremarkable flavor. Between the two is an Italian-made fontina that costs about $8 a pound; it has a waxy brownish coating and a semi-soft, super-creamy texture. This is the fontina that we recommend using in our recipe for Frittata with Broccoli Rabe, Sun-Dried Tomatoes, and Fontina (page 9), as well as in the spinach and fontina stuffing for our pork chops (page 15). We purchase it from our local supermarket; it is also available in most good cheese shops.

FONTINA VAL D'AOSTA

ITALIAN FONTINA

SWEDISH OR DANISH FONTINA

Pan-frying stirs fear in many home cooks. But for really crisp fried chicken or breaded pork cutlets, it's a technique worth mastering. Here are some guidelines:

- **USE A HEAVY PAN** Think cast iron or enameled cast iron, which will distribute heat evenly.
- **USE A PAN WITH HIGH SIDES** A Dutch oven is ideal.
- **USE A FAT WITH A HIGH SMOKE POINT** Peanut oil is a good example.
- **USE ENOUGH OIL** Fat should come halfway up the sides of the food.
- **DO NOT OVERCROWD THE PAN** For instance, do not allow chicken pieces to touch one another or overlap. Cook food in small batches.
- **MAINTAIN THE FRYING TEMPERATURE** Most frying takes place between 325 and 375 degrees (see specific recipes). Check the temperature with a thermometer.
- **TURN FOOD JUST ONCE** Use tongs, not a fork, to avoid piercing food.
- **KEEP FOOD WARM** Place fried food on a rack set over a baking sheet in a 200-degree oven while cooking subsequent batches. – Nina West

---

the reason. Assuming that your oven is properly calibrated (and that's assuming a lot), we bet that improper portioning is the culprit. When it comes to dough mounds, size does matter. Cookies portioned out larger or smaller than the recipe directs bake differently and may not yield the intended texture.

In the test kitchen, for recipes with relatively small yields (two dozen or fewer), we portion all the dough into the correct number of mounds before baking the first sheet. That's why our recipes always give an exact number, not an approximate yield. We then examine the mounds, stealing bits from larger ones to bulk up puny ones. Finally, we shape the evenly sized mounds, arrange them on baking sheets, and bake as directed. Sounds a bit compulsive, but if you want cookies with a texture that's just so, it's worth the extra step.

And what about recipes that yield several dozen cookies? It's not practical to portion 48 balls of dough at one time. In this case, pay special heed to the size of each portion of dough. Our recipes tell you how much dough to use (in tablespoons) and then indicate the diameter of each shaped dough ball (in inches).

Browned Butter

Browned butter, or *beurre noisette* (hazelnut butter), as it is called in French, gives the filling of our Baked Raspberry Tart (page 25)

a deep, rich flavor. It is called hazelnut butter in French because as the butter browns, it takes on the flavor and aroma of toasted nuts. Browned butter is used in both baked goods and savory preparations; brightened with lemon juice, it makes a classic, simple "sauce" for Fish Meunière (January/February 2004) as well as for vegetables such as asparagus and green beans.

When making browned butter, use a saucepan or skillet with a light-colored interior; the dark color of nonstick or anodized aluminum cookware makes it difficult to judge the color of the butter as it browns. Use medium to medium-high heat, and stir or swirl the butter occasionally so that the milk solids brown evenly; depending on the heat setting and the amount of butter, the process may take as few as three minutes if browning just a couple of tablespoons or as long as 10 minutes if browning a full cup. Finally, if not using the browned butter immediately, transfer it to a bowl; if left in the saucepan or skillet, residual heat can cause it to continue cooking . . . and then it becomes *beurre noir*.

NOT QUITE READY

PROPERLY BROWNED

Quicker Stuffed Potatoes

When developing our recipe for **Stuffed Baked Potatoes** (September/October 2004), it was a given that we would bake the potatoes twice: once whole and again once they'd been hollowed out and stuffed. But a few readers wondered if the initial hour-long baking time could be cut short by using the microwave.

Although the skin on the microwaved potatoes was flabby, this wasn't much of an issue, as the potato shells are broiled to crisp them before stuffing. The microwave cuts about 50 minutes off the prep time. So here's how to do it: Place four potatoes in a shallow baking dish, puncture the skin with a fork, and microwave the spuds, rotating them every three minutes, until a skewer can be inserted and removed with little resistance, nine to 12 minutes. Once the microwaved potatoes have cooled for 10 minutes, simply continue with the now much shorter recipe by halving the potatoes, hollowing them out, making the filling, and broiling the shells before stuffing them and broiling again.

Berry Good Pancakes?

Readers wanted to know if other berries could be used in our recipe for **Blueberry Pancakes** (July/August 2003). It seemed like a logical assumption, as the pancakes need to cook only about 1 minute on the side with the berries. But it was not to be. Fresh strawberries and raspberries simply broke down too much, exploding and burning onto the pan despite the short cooking time. If you want to add other fresh berries to your pancakes, serve them as a garnish once the pancakes make it out of the hot pan.

SOFT BERRIES RUIN PANCAKES

Tomato Tart

Waiting for tomato season to hit before making our **Tomato and Mozzarella Tart** (July/August 2003)? So were many other readers, who wondered if we could find a way to make this simple, savory tart at any time of year. Replacing the plum tomatoes with cherry tomatoes (which are pretty reliably sweet year-round) and roasting the cherry tomatoes with some additional flavorings helped concentrate their flavor. But for an even quicker substitution, drain a jar of sun-dried tomatoes, rinse them to remove the dull flavor of the oil and herbs, and then mince.

Orange Ice

Our recipe for **Lemon Ice** (July/August 2003) is a test kitchen favorite, but several readers wondered if it was possible to make a less mouth-puckering version with orange juice. A straight substitution of fresh-squeezed orange juice for lemon juice produced an ice that was candy-sweet. Reducing the sugar from 1 cup to ½ cup got the sweetness right but harmed the texture and made the orange ice, well, too icy. We solved this problem by boosting the acidity of the orange juice with 2 tablespoons of lemon juice. We really liked this flavor combination; it was fresh, orangey, and acidic. The lemon juice also allowed us to increase the sugar—back up to ¾ cup—and thereby give our Orange Ice a satisfyingly smooth texture. – Compiled by Nina West

---

COOK'S EXTRA To get the recipes mentioned above, go to www.cooksillustrated.com and key in the following codes: Microwave-Baked Potatoes for Twice-Baked Potatoes (5057), Cherry Tomato and Mozzarella Tart (5058), Sun-Dried Tomato and Mozzarella Tart (5059), Orange Ice (6050). These recipes will be available until June 30, 2005.

IF YOU HAVE A QUESTION about a recently published recipe, let us know. Send your inquiry, name, address, and daytime telephone number to Recipe Update, Cook's Illustrated, P.O. Box 470589, Brookline, MA 02447, or write to recipeupdate@bcpress.com.

WEAR AND TEAR
Colanders

The winner of our 2001 rating of colanders, the 5-quart Precision Pierced Endurance Stainless Steel Colander, remains a reliable test-kitchen workhorse. We still like its "mega-perforated" bowl (almost more perforation than bowl). Just one problem: Those soldered-on, loop-shaped side handles have started popping off in the dishwasher.

We shopped around for colanders of similar design in hope of replacing our winner. But after testing several likely contenders, we found that none could take down the champ. This somewhat misleadingly named colander is still the best-performing model out there—even without the handles. Grudgingly, we vowed to ignore the Endurance's "dishwasher-safe" instructions and begin washing our intact colanders by hand. After all, how dirty does a colander really get?

ENDURANCE COLANDER
Time for a new name?

EQUIPMENT TEST
Nonstick Baking-Pan Liners

With so many brands of reusable baking-pan liners available, we wondered if any could replace the countless rolls of parchment paper the test kitchen blows through every week.

We pitted five liners against plain old parchment by baking cookies on our two favorite cookie sheets, made by Vollrath and Chicago Metallic. Sticking was never an issue, and browning was unaffected as long as the liner lay flat. However, when used on the Chicago Metallic pan, the liner edges bowed upward, leaving a portion of the liner without direct pan contact—and us with several pale, unevenly browned cookie bottoms per batch. This problem affects about half the cookie sheets tested on page 29, so it's a big deal. The lightweight liners, KatchAll's Cook-Eze ($13.95) and Chef's Planet Half Size Sheet Pan Liner ($14.95), can be cut to fit cookie sheets of any size, but these liners were less durable in our tests, creasing slightly after just a few washes. The heavy-duty, fiberglass-weave liners—Silpat ($19.99), Exopat ($19.99), and Tupperware's Wonder Mat ($30)—are designed to fit only standard half-sheet pans (about 16 by 12 inches), and cutting to fit isn't an option.

So what to buy? If your baking sheet is exactly the right size, the heavy-duty mats we tested work fine, and they're not that hard to clean. Frankly, though, we're not sold on any of them. In the long run, parchment paper may be the most expensive option, but its versatility and disposability make it worth the dough.

DO YOU REALLY NEED THIS?
Food Injectors

One test cook, perhaps a tad too well versed in late-night infomercials, mused aloud on the syringe-type food injectors designed to simplify the process of stuffing multiple pork chops (see the story on page 14). A round of snickering—and a few easy payments later—we had a sampling of these gadgets in the test kitchen.

The wide needle of the Flavor Express Marinator ($39.95, below left) choked on the spinach stuffing we developed for the pork chops. The opening of the Ronco Solid Flavor Injector ($17.99 for a set of two, below right) was ample enough to deliver items as large as olives.

THE RIGHT STUFF?
These solid-food injectors flunk the test.

Unfortunately, packing the stuffing into the injector was more difficult than filling the chop itself. The blunt expanding tip is not easy to jab into a slab of meat, and who wants olive-size items injected into a chop, anyway? We recommend simply stuffing the pork chops by hand.

EQUIPMENT UPDATE
Digital Kitchen Scale

Our tests of digital kitchen scales in March/April 2000 brought us to the Soehnle Cyber Electronic Kitchen Scale (model 8048), which we've found to be well worth the hefty $125 price tag. Unfortunately, this product has been difficult to find over the past few years. A few phone calls identified the likely culprit: business restructuring. Soehnle's kitchen-scale unit was recently acquired by Leifheit Housewares, which has since renamed the product the Soehnle Futura. Happily, the transition seems to be complete, and our favorite scale isn't nearly as hard to get. Or as expensive: The price has fallen to a much more reasonable $79.99.

EQUIPMENT UPDATE
Sauciers

During testing for our January/February 2005 story on sauciers, we put together an exacting profile of the ultimate design for this rounded, flared saucepan. Our recommended (fourth-place) Calphalon Infused Anodized 3-Quart Chef's Pan came close. Its downfall was a dark matte interior that made it tricky to judge how much fond had developed. It was also a bit cramped. So we were intrigued when Calphalon announced its latest cookware line, which has a shiny, stainless steel cooking surface and a roomy design.

We ran the new 3½-quart Calphalon Contemporary Stainless Sauce Pan ($135) through our original tests, putting our winning All-Clad Stainless 3-Quart saucier ($145) and the anodized Calphalon Chef's Pan ($159.95) through the trials as well. All three turned out perfect béchamel, risotto, and gravy. But, as in our original testing, what separates these pans is design. The roomier Calphalon Contemporary contained splashing from even a vigorous whisk better than its competition, its extra-long handle stayed cool, and the surface developed fond as well as the All-Clad did.

Our verdict? This new Calphalon pan is definitely on par with the winning All-Clad, and we enthusiastically recommend it as an alternative.

Sources

Prices were current at press time and do not include shipping and handling. Contact companies directly to confirm prices and availability.

page 3: MANGO FORKS
- Mango Forks (set of 2): $39.95, item #1071, **Melissa Guerra** (877-875-2665, www.melissaguerra.com).

page 7: SLICING KNIFE
- Forschner 10" x 1½" Slicer, Round Tip: $40.55, item #F40644, **The Knife Merchant** (800-469-4834, www.knifemerchant.com).

page 12: PAELLA PAN
- La Ideal Enameled Paella Pan, 34 cm: $27.99, **Amazon** (www.amazon.com).

page 25: ROLLING PIN GUIDES
- Perfection Strips: $8, **Country Kitchen SweetArt** (800-497-3927, www.countrykitchensa.com).

page 29: COOKIE SHEET
- Vollrath Cookie Sheet (17" x 14"): $19.95, item #895200, **Broadway Panhandler** (800-266-5927, www.broadwaypanhandler.com).

page 32: COLANDER
- Endurance Precision Pierced Stainless Steel 5-Quart Colander: $26.99, item #7061, **Fante's Kitchen Wares Shop** (800-443-2683, www.fantes.com).

page 32: DIGITAL KITCHEN SCALE
- Soehnle Futura Digital Food Scale: $79.99, model #66524, **Amazon** (www.amazon.com).

page 32: SAUCIER
- Calphalon Contemporary Stainless 3½-Quart Sauce Pan: $135, **Macy's** (800-289-6229, www.macys.com).

RECIPES
May & June 2005

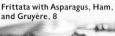

Frittata with Asparagus, Ham, and Gruyère, 8

Chocolate-Chunk Oatmeal Cookies with Pecans and Dried Cherries, 23

Grilled Marinated Flank Steak, 7

Skillet-Roasted Potatoes, 19

www.cooksillustrated.com

Join the *Cook's* Web Site and Get Instant Access to 12 Years of Recipes, Equipment Tests, and Tastings!

Web site members can also join the *Cook's* chat room, ask our editors cooking questions, find quick tips and step-by-step illustrations, maintain a private list of personal favorites (recipes, quick tips, tastings, and more), and print out shopping lists for all recipes.
Yours Free: As a paid Web site member, you will also receive our **2005 Buying Guide for Supermarket Ingredients.** Simply type in the promotion code **CB53A** when signing up.

Here's Why More Than 70,000 Home Cooks Subscribe to Our Web Site

Quick Search for "Best" Recipes: Quick access to each and every recipe published in *Cook's Illustrated* since 1993.
Cook's Extra Recipes: Continued access to the recipes that don't fit in each issue of the magazine, including many flavor variations.
Updated Cookware Ratings: Charts of all buying recommendations published in the magazine (you can download them) plus frequent updates on new models and price changes.
Tasting Results: Which chicken broth is best? How about chocolate? You'll have access to every tasting published in the magazine, plus tastings conducted only for Web members.
Questions for the Editors: Paid members can ask us a question by e-mail and are guaranteed a response.

Salad Dressings, 13

The Chat Room: Find out what other *Cook's* subscribers think about recipes, equipment, and cooking techniques. Or just meet the subscribers in your town.
Magazine/Book Customer Service: Pay invoices, give gifts, handle returns, check your subscription status, and more.
Visit Our Bookstore: Order any of our books online and also qualify for special offers.

AMERICA'S TEST KITCHEN TV SHOW

Join the millions of home cooks who watch our show, *America's Test Kitchen*, on public television every week. For more information, including recipes and a schedule of program times in your area, visit www.americastestkitchen.com.

Baked Raspberry Tart, 25

Orange-Flavored Chicken, 21

Thick-Cut Pork Chops with Red Onion Jam Stuffing, 15

Paella, 11

PHOTOGRAPHY: CARL TREMBLAY, STYLING: GEORGE SIMONS

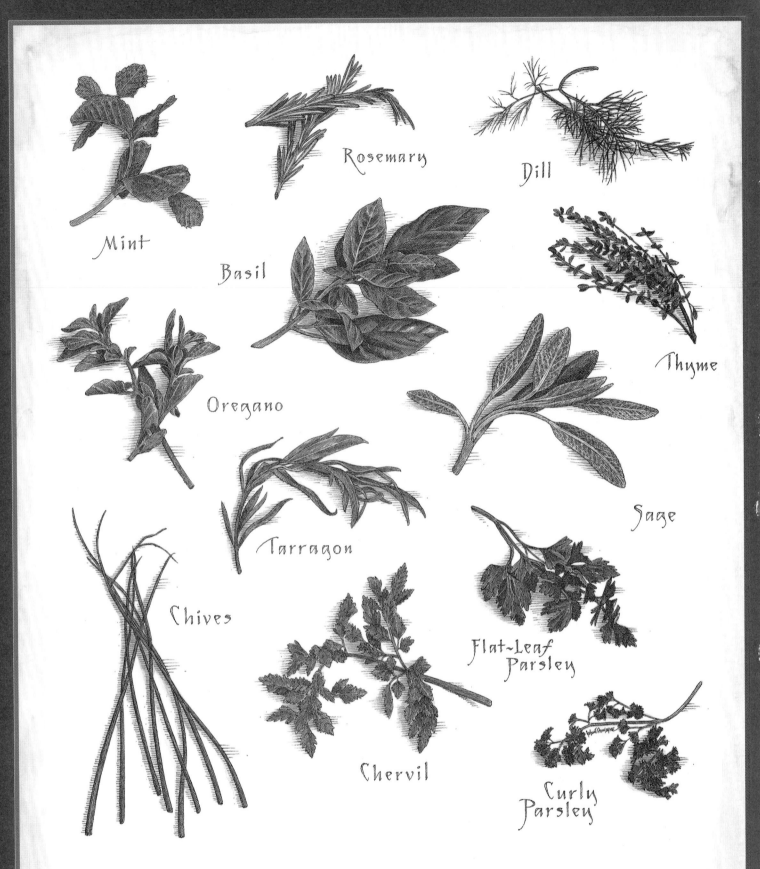

Mint

Rosemary

Dill

Basil

Thyme

Oregano

Sage

Tarragon

Chives

Chervil

Flat-Leaf Parsley

Curly Parsley

FRESH HERBS

NUMBER SEVENTY-FIVE

JULY & AUGUST 2005

COOK'S
ILLUSTRATED

BBQ Pulled Chicken

Backyard Grilled
Pizza
Crisp, Chewy, and Easy

Grilling Pork Loin

Blueberry Buckle
Buttery Cake, Crunchy Streusel

Tasting White
Wine Vinegars
Best Brands for Cooking, Salads

Illustrated Guide to
Essential Cookware

Rating Oven Mitts
Are High-Tech Designs Worth $60?

Best Blondies
Thai Chile Beef
Summer Fruit Salsas
Ultimate Veggie Burger
Perfect Aïoli

www.cooksillustrated.com

$5.95 U.S./$6.95 CANADA

08>

0 74470 62805 7

CONTENTS

July & August 2005

www.cooksillustrated.com

HOME OF AMERICA'S TEST KITCHEN

Founder and Editor Christopher Kimball
Executive Editor Jack Bishop
Senior Editors Jolyon Helterman
Dawn Yanagihara
Editorial Manager, Books Elizabeth Carduff
Test Kitchen Director Erin McMurrer
Senior Editors, Books Julia Collin Davison
Lori Galvin
Managing Editor Rebecca Hays
Associate Editor, Books Keith Dresser
Associate Editor Sandra Wu
Web Editor Lindsay McSweeney
Copy Chief India Koopman
Test Cooks Erika Bruce
Garth Clingingsmith
Sean Lawler
Rachel Toomey
Diane Unger-Mahoney
Nina West
Sarah Wilson
Assistant Editor, Books Charles Kelsey
Editorial Assistant, Books Elizabeth Wray
Assistant to the Publisher Melissa Baldino
Kitchen Assistants Maria Elena Delgado
Nadia Domeq
Ena Gudiel
Editorial Interns Elizabeth Bomze
Max Gitlen
Contributing Editors Matthew Card
Elizabeth Germain
Consulting Editors Shirley Corriher
Guy Crosby
Jasper White
Robert L. Wolke
Proofreader Jean Rogers

Design Director Amy Klee
Marketing Designer Julie Bozzo
Designer Heather Barrett
Staff Photographer Daniel van Ackere

Vice President Marketing David Mack
Retail Sales Director Jason Geller
Corporate Sponsorship Specialist Laura Phillipps
Retail Sales Specialist Shekinah Cohn
Marketing Assistant Connie Forbes
Circulation Director Bill Tine
Circulation Manager Larisa Greiner
Fulfillment Manager Carrie Horan
Circulation Assistant Elizabeth Dayton
Products Director Steven Browall
Direct Mail Director Adam Perry
Customer Service Manager Jacqueline Valerio
Customer Service Representative Julie Gardner
E-Commerce Marketing Manager Hugh Buchan

Vice President Operations James McCormack
Senior Production Manager Jessica Lindheimer Quirk
Production Manager Mary Connelly
Project Manager Anne Francis
Book Production Specialist Ron Bilodeau
Production Assistants Jeanette McCarthy
Jennifer Power
Christian Steinmetz
Systems Administrator Richard Cassidy
Internet Technology Director Aaron Shuman

Chief Financial Officer Sharyn Chabot
Controller Mandy Shito
Staff Accountant Maya Santoso
Office Manager Saudiyah Abdul-Rahim
Receptionist Henrietta Murray
Publicity Deborah Broide

CUCUMBERS The familiar garden (or American) cucumber has a thick, dark green skin and is most often used in salads and crudités. Mild, sweet English (or hothouse) cucumbers are cultivated to produce thinner skins and fewer seeds. Japanese cucumbers are long and slender; used peel-on, they add crunch and flavor to rolled sushi. The small, thin Mediterranean cucumber is fairly straight and is juicy rather than watery. Even smaller are fresh cornichons, which are almost always seen in their pickled form. The most commonly used pickling cucumber is the Kirby, easily recognizable for its squat, warty appearance. Lemon cucumbers, colored and shaped like their namesake, are very seedy yet delicately flavored.

CUCUMBERS

COVER (Corn): Elizabeth Brandon, BACK COVER (Cucumbers): John Burgoyne

For list rental information, contact: ClientLogic, 1200 Harbor Blvd., 9th Floor, Weehawken, NJ 07087; 201-865-5800; fax 201-867-2450.
Editorial Office: 17 Station St., Brookline, MA 02445; 617-232-1000; fax 617-232-1572. Subscription inquiries, call 800-526-8442.
Postmaster: Send all new orders, subscription inquiries, and change-of-address notices to Cook's Illustrated, P.O. Box 7446, Red Oak, IA 51591-0446.

PRINTED IN THE USA

ON THE ROAD TO MOROCCO

Many of our family vacations are best remembered through a glass darkly, years after the fact, when the family album fails to remind us of the moments best forgotten. But every once in a while, one of our family vacations actually bears fruit—the sweet variety, not an unripe tropical specimen. In March, we flung caution to the wind and decided to trek through the Sahara Desert in Morocco, near the Algerian border. Three planes and 24 hours after leaving Boston, we ended up in the streets of Marrakech, trailing the donkey cart that held our luggage through the narrow streets of the old city on the way to our *riad,* a small hotel that was once a private home.

I am not one to tour palaces and other architectural monuments—just give me something good (and unusual) to eat. This, of course, is no mean feat when you are traveling with young children and local guides who prefer to steer their clients to the most European eateries. (Yes, you can order spaghetti Bolognese and pizza in a tourist café fronting the major plaza in the old city.) But Marrakech did eventually come through in the food department. Fresh-squeezed local oranges; yogurt lightly sweetened with rose water; the local flatbreads; coconut cookies; lamb tagine with fresh almonds; skewers of ground, spiced lamb; and *pastilla*, a thick pancake-style pastry filled with ground meat, spices, and nuts.

The next day we piled into two Land Rovers and headed southeast, through the High Atlas and down toward Ouarzazate. By the afternoon, we had left the paved road behind and were on a track that wound around old mud and wattle towns built into the sides of bleak mountains, with serpentine river valleys, lush and green, below. (Locals take the bus to the end of the line, where they switch to donkeys. The animals are arranged in a stand much like taxis.) The day is a confused memory of fiercely handsome Berber children, goatherds and shepherds, and

donkeys fitted out with metal "roof racks" that let them transport huge loads of forage.

The next day, at the tail end of sunset, we finally made our way into the desert and to our campsite. El Hussein, the sprightly 72-year-old camel driver, was waiting (he had walked three days to meet us) along with his four camels. (As warm-blooded creatures go, by the way, camels are quite intelligent. They drool rather than spit, their legs fold up like lawn chairs when they sit, they enjoy a good rub behind the ears, and their huge feet spread out like yeast dough as they plop them on the sand.) The next morning, after a breakfast of flatbread, oranges, and coffee, we set out over the dunes, mostly walking, with rest periods taken on camelback.

The desert is not just a sandbox. The landscape varies wildly from the classic dunes of *Lawrence of Arabia* to towering black mountains, parched white lakebeds, scrub, thousands of small white and blue flowers (which, owing to my inaccurate translation of our guide's conversational French, I erroneously call "Monkey's Onion"), and seas of rock and thorn. Far on a mountainside, we see dozens of goats grazing and a goatherd standing still in a dark *djellaba* (robe) on top of a ridge. Two young boys cross our path in the middle of nowhere and stop to chat. We come across an abandoned Berber beehive oven used to make bread. (The bread is cooked over coals on top of a perforated metal shelf.)

That evening, I sit on the top of the largest dune near our campsite and watch the sun dissolve into a far haze. On the next peak, a man is kneeling and praying to Allah. A small village is visible off to the east, toward Algeria. I count 17 hand-sketched trees in and around the swirl of dunes. I can hear the murmur of

Christopher Kimball

the local Berber dialect spoken by the cook, Hussein, and our guide, Muhammed, punctuated by exuberant expressions of "Inshallah." An hour passes, the sun is ebbing, and I sense that I am sitting above a vast pool of time, as if the days and weeks have fled the rest of the world, swirling to a stop on this flat sun-drenched landscape where there are no shadows. I was told that the Berbers are still a nomadic people. How else does one live in this timeless landscape?

And then, on the third day, it happens. The simple, well-prepared food. The loose robes and headdresses. The hours of walking and storytelling. The front-and-back rhythm of the camels. The hot, sweet mint tea. The intense flavor of a cool, sliced orange after lunch. There is so little here that each thing becomes important. Each gesture, each bite of food, and each sip of water matters. A fig, a date, a handful of nuts . . . we learn to enjoy the small things.

We make our way to Fez, a city more cosmopolitan than Marrakech. We spend a day walking the bazaar and discover live snails, a camel's head, brightly colored vats of soap, dyed silk, fruit, mint, fish, live poultry, leather goods, brass and copper pots, sweets, street food, hole-in-the-wall bakeries . . . the senses are overwhelmed. We depart before sunrise, hefting duffel bags through dark, narrow streets. I leave with the taste of perfumed oranges, rose water, mint, almonds, saffron, preserved lemon, cinnamon, cumin, and coconut still lively on the tongue. But it's the vast, unfiltered memory of the desert that beckons, as if I were leaving home for a foreign land. The sun is rising, but, in my mind's eye, it is sinking, there is a call to prayer, men in hooded djellabas face Mecca, and there is finally time to consider every grain of sand.

FOR INQUIRIES, ORDERS, OR MORE INFORMATION:

www.cooksillustrated.com

At www.cooksillustrated.com, you can order books and subscriptions, sign up for our free e-newsletter, or renew your magazine subscription. Subscribe to the Web site and you'll have access to 12 years of *Cook's* recipes, cookware tests, ingredient tastings, and more.

COOKBOOKS

We sell more than 40 cookbooks by the editors of *Cook's Illustrated*. To order, visit our bookstore at www.cooksillustrated.com or call 800-611-0759 (or 515-246-6911 from outside the U.S.).

COOK'S ILLUSTRATED Magazine

Cook's Illustrated magazine (ISSN 1068-2821), number 75, is published bimonthly by Boston Common Press Limited Partnership, 17 Station Street, Brookline, MA 02445. Copyright 2005 Boston Common Press Limited Partnership. Periodicals postage paid at Boston, Mass., and additional mailing offices, USPS #012487. POSTMASTER: Send address changes to Cook's Illustrated, P.O. Box 7446, Red Oak, IA 51591-0446. For subscription and gift subscription orders, subscription inquiries, or change-of-address notices, call 800-526-8442 in the U.S. or 515-247-7571 from outside the U.S., or write us at Cook's Illustrated, P.O. Box 7446, Red Oak, IA 51591-0446.

Battle of the Paring Knives

What is the purpose of a curved paring knife?

MICHAEL HASS
CENTRAL CITY, IOWA

➤ A variation on the standard paring knife, a "bird's beak," or "tournée," paring knife has a 2- to 3-inch blade and a forward-curving, hooked tip. It is typically used for peeling, cutting, and removing surface blemishes from rounded fruits and vegetables and for carving tournéed (seven-sided, football-shaped) vegetables as well as intricate garnishes.

An informal poll taken in the test kitchen indicated that most of our test cooks do not own a bird's beak paring knife. Most of those who do said they use it rarely and own it only because it came as part of a set. Still, we wondered if this knife offers any advantages.

We timed four test kitchen staffers as they peeled pearl onions, peeled and sliced apples, and tournéed potatoes using our top-rated Forschner (Victorinox) paring knife as well as a Forschner bird's beak paring knife. We also asked testers to rate the two knives. Peeling onions was a toss-up, and testers preferred a traditional paring knife when peeling apples. When it came to the tournée test, however, most did prefer the bird's beak knife.

BIRD'S BEAK
Does your paring knife need a beak?

Our conclusion? Despite having a slight advantage over a traditional paring knife when it comes to tournéeing, the bird's beak knife failed to generate much support from the kitchen staff. Everyone felt that a regular paring knife was more than adequate even for this delicate (and rarely called for) task.

To Halve or Halve Not

In your May/June 2003 issue, after tasting various tomato pastes, you selected Amore as the winner. Is it correct to assume that because it is double concentrated, the amount used in recipes can be halved?

TODD CARLSON
ARLINGTON, TEXAS

➤ When you use ultra-concentrated liquid laundry detergent in place of the regular variety, it takes less product to wash the same amount of clothing.

Unfortunately, the same principle doesn't apply to tomato paste. Based on our experience, Amore-brand tube tomato paste, though labeled "double concentrated," is not twice as potent as regular canned tomato paste. In the tasting you mention, conducted for our Weeknight Pasta Bolognese recipe (May/June 2003), we used the same amount of each brand of tomato paste.

We revisited the issue by conducting a couple of visual tests with Amore and one of the canned brands, Hunt's, to see if the Amore was drier (and thus more concentrated). Side-by-side spoonfuls of Amore and Hunt's were both thick and stiff, each one sticking to the spoon even when turned upside down. The Amore was slightly thicker and a more vibrant red than the muted, darker Hunt's, which also had a few liquidy pockets. Next we placed five level 1-tablespoon samples of each brand on sheets of single-ply paper towel and let them sit for an hour. Neither the tubed nor the canned sample exuded much liquid—only perhaps a millimeter could be detected extending beyond the borders of the pasty blobs.

While we don't recommend using half as much Amore when tomato paste is called for in a recipe, we still recommend Amore over the other six brands we tested (including Hunt's) for its fresher, fuller tomato flavor. And because it's packaged in a tube, Amore lacks the tinny aftertaste that plagues many canned tomato pastes. Just ignore the "double concentrated" labeling and use the amount called for in the recipe.

Cheese with an Ashy Disposition

I've often seen ash-covered goat cheese behind the cheese counter at my local gourmet supermarket. What is the source of the ash? Is it edible, or should it be scraped off?

TODD VANADILOK
CHICAGO, ILL.

➤ The light layer of ash that covers some goat cheeses (both aged and fresh) is indeed edible and should not be scraped off. The ash is made from burnt vegetal growth (such as white pine, juniper wood, eggplant, bell peppers, vine cuttings, and leaves) that is pounded until it achieves a fine, powdery consistency.

According to Ihsan Gurdal, cheesemaker and owner of Formaggio Kitchen, a fine-foods purveyor with stores in Boston and Cambridge, Mass., the French developed this method of covering goat cheese, and the Spaniards followed shortly thereafter. The ash, said Gurdal, is used for aesthetic purposes rather than to flavor the

ASH-COVERED GOAT CHEESE
Sooted for human consumption?

cheese. Similar to goat cheeses covered in spices such as curry powder or cayenne pepper, the ash doesn't delay or speed up rind development or act as a barrier against mold.

Famous French ash-covered goat cheeses include the cylindrical Saint-Maure and the disk-shaped Selles-sur-Cher of the Loire Valley. Domestically, there is Humboldt Fog, an aged, ash-covered goat cheese defined by an additional fine layer of ash dividing the top and bottom hemispheres of the cheese.

Nick, Don't Slash

When checking to see if a cut of meat is sufficiently cooked, you have suggested the "nick-and-peek" method. On the other hand, you also call for letting meat rest after cooking to prevent the loss of juice that will occur if it's cut into right away. Doesn't the nick-and-peek method negate or diminish the potential benefit of allowing the meat to rest?

JONATHAN LOONIN
STAMFORD, CONN.

➤ The most accurate method of testing meat for doneness is to check its internal temperature using an instant-read thermometer. When cooking a particularly thin piece of meat, however, it's difficult to use a thermometer, so nicking the meat with a paring knife is our recommended alternative.

Curious as to whether this method results in any significant moisture loss, we prepared two samples each of 1¼-inch-thick pan-fried strip steaks (cooked to medium-rare, or 130 degrees), pan-seared oven-roasted pork tenderloins (cooked to medium, or 140 degrees), and pan-roasted chicken breasts (cooked until well done, or 160 degrees). We used both methods—thermometer and paring knife—to test for doneness and measured the amount of liquid expelled after each sample had rested for about 10 minutes. Both strip steaks exuded equal amounts of liquid (2 teaspoons), while the pork tenderloin checked using the nick-and-peek method lost ¼ teaspoon more juices, and the nicked chicken breast lost ¾ teaspoon more.

Why the difference? Because the pork and the chicken were more fully cooked than the medium-rare steaks, it was necessary to make a relatively deep cut to determine doneness. In these cases, then, there is more moisture loss, so we recommend the thermometer method. Save nicking and peeking for fish and thinner cuts of meat where a shallow slash will work just fine.

Storing Celery
What's the best way to store celery? I never manage to finish a whole bunch before it goes bad.

CAROL PAI
PITTSBURGH, PA.

➤ To answer your question, we took five bunches of celery (with the outermost stalks removed), each wrapped in a different way, and stored them in the refrigerator. We placed one bunch in a paper bag, wrapped another in aluminum foil, wrapped another in plastic wrap, returned another to its original perforated plastic sleeve, and placed the last one upright in a container holding about 2 inches of water.

At the end of one week, the celery in the paper bag was still green but slightly limp, the celery in the original plastic packaging was slightly more bendable and faded in color, and the bunch in the water even more dried out—these methods all allowed too much moisture to escape; the celery became limp as it dehydrated. The plastic- and foil-wrapped celery, however, remained amazingly green and firm. Given another week,

only the foil-wrapped celery was still mostly green and crisp.

Why did the foil work so well while the plastic wrap eventually failed? Celery continues to respire after it is harvested and produces small amounts of the ripening hormone *ethylene*. This gas activates enzymes that break down and soften the cell walls in celery, creating moisture loss. Ethylene easily gets trapped when celery is wrapped tightly in plastic, causing the vegetable to go limp and spoil faster than when wrapped in aluminum foil, which is not "gas tight."

In a pinch, you can always revive wayward celery stalks by cutting off about an inch from both ends and submerging the stalks in a bowl of ice water for 30 minutes. But to prolong freshness, we recommend wrapping celery in foil.

Alternative Milks
Can lactose-free or nonrefrigerated boxed milk be substituted for regular milk in recipes?

KATHY SCHOENE
NORTH ANDOVER, MASS.

➤ Initially, several members of the test kitchen staff made faces at the prospect of cooking with these untraditional milks, but ultimately they admitted to being curious about the potential results. We pitted Hood whole milk (our local "regular" brand) against whole milk versions of Lactaid and Parmalat in three applications: scones, a yellow layer cake, and a béchamel sauce.

GOT MILK?
Can either of these milk substitutes compete with the real thing?

Straight from the carton, Lactaid tends to have a slightly sweeter flavor than regular milk. This is because of the added lactase, an enzyme that breaks down lactose (the sugar found in milk) into two sweeter-tasting simple sugars that lactose-intolerant individuals can easily digest. Not surprisingly, the scones and yellow cake made with Lactaid tasted sweeter than those made with regular milk, and some tasters preferred them. On the other hand, the béchamel made with Lactaid was booed for having an "odd flavor" that one taster described as "kind of rank" and several others simply found "too sweet."

Parmalat, a shelf-stable boxed milk that can be kept for up to six months unopened and unrefrigerated because of treatment with a special ultra-high-heat pasteurization process, lacks the fresh taste of regular milk and has a flavor profile closer to that of cooked milk. Nonetheless, tasters found that scones and cake made with Parmalat were very similar in flavor to those made with regular whole milk. A few people noticed a slightly off flavor in the béchamel made with Parmalat, calling it "funky," "musty," and "tangy." Most tasters, however, thought the béchamel made with Parmalat was just fine.

To sum up, sweet baked goods made with lactose-free or boxed milk are just as good as—and some think even better than—those made with fresh milk. In savory applications, boxed milk is OK if fresh milk isn't available, but avoid using lactose-free milk unless a sweet-salty result is your intended goal.

Juicers on the Web
Following publication of the 'What Is It?' item in the January/February 2005 issue, many readers wrote in to praise the virtues of their own Wear-Ever juicers, which several people dubbed as being their favorite juicer. Although this item is no longer being manufactured, a search revealed that it is available for sale on several Web auction sites, eBay among them.

SEND US YOUR QUESTIONS We will provide a complimentary one-year subscription for each letter we print. Send your inquiry, name, address, and daytime telephone number to Notes from Readers, Cook's Illustrated, P.O. Box 470589, Brookline, MA 02447, or to notesfromreaders@bcpress.com.

WHAT IS IT?

I came across several of these utensils one day while digging around in my grandmother's old silverware set. Is it a spoon or a fork?

JESSICA BACHAR
CLYDE, N.C.

With its fork-like edges, this old-fashioned ice cream spoon digs into even the iciest ice cream.

➤ After scratching our heads trying to guess what your monogrammed utensil was used for, we walked a few blocks from our offices to see antique dealer and appraiser Toby Langerman of the Antique Company in Brookline, Mass., for a consultation.

According to Langerman, this utensil—with a 3-inch handle and a shallow head, or bowl, about 2 inches long and 1¼ inches across its widest point—is a spoon produced in the early 1900s for the sole purpose of eating ice cream. Langerman speculates that ice cream may have been icier or harder than most of the commercial varieties that exist today and so the spoon's forked edges could have been useful for digging into the icy confections.

We were slightly wary of those sharp-looking edges before trying the spoon, but it ended up being just about as dangerous as a fork. The spoon did a good job of cutting through a scoop of hard, fresh-from-the-freezer ice cream, but we wouldn't recommend using it with looser or softer desserts like granita, sorbet, or gelato. Its bowl isn't deep enough to capture the melted, dribbly bits.

Quick Tips

⇒ COMPILED BY ERIKA BRUCE ⇐

Picking More Than One Pepper

Running out to the store each time you need a tiny chile pepper can be a pain. Susan Pierson of Doylestown, Pa., buys large bags of peppers and stores them in the freezer. When she needs a chopped or minced pepper for a recipe, she takes it straight from the freezer to a cutting board.

Reaching Beyond Your Grasp

To grasp lightweight items that are just out of reach, Jennifer Hellwig of Bradenton, Fla., sidesteps her stepstool in favor of another kitchen tool—a pair of tongs. They're great for grabbing things like bags of pasta, cereal boxes, or spices from the top shelves of the cupboard or pantry.

Seedless Jalapeño Rings

To make neat rings of jalapeños without the seeds or spicy ribs when garnishing nachos and the like, Nate Cobb of Jamaica Plain, Mass., employs a vegetable peeler.

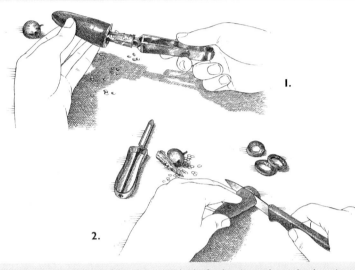

1. Cut off the stem end of the jalapeño with a knife, then insert the peeler down into the chile. Using a circular motion, core the pepper and pull out the ribs and seeds.
2. Shake any remaining seeds out of the chile, then slice it into rings.

Homemade Ice Packs

Katherine Connell of Skowhegan, Maine, got tired of filling and emptying ice cube trays when stocking up on the ice she uses to chill beverages when having a party. Now she makes her own ice packs with zipper-lock bags—and they keep things cool a lot longer than ice cubes do.

1. Fill quart- or gallon-sized zipper-lock bags to within 2 inches of the top with water. (That way the bags won't burst when the water expands as it freezes.)

2. Place the bags in the freezer, letting them lie flat so they can be stacked, thereby making the most economical use of freezer space.

Corn Husking Made Easier

Husking corn is no one's favorite job, but it's one that Sharon Guditis of Kalispell, Mont., has made much easier.

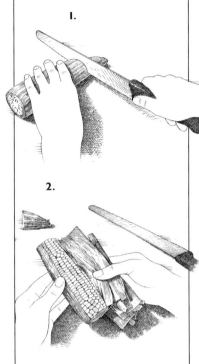

1. With the husk still attached, cut off both ends of an ear of corn (a serrated knife works best).
2. Roll the ear on the counter, and the husk comes right off. Finish by removing any remaining threads of silk.

Smoothie Pops

Instead of letting any of the smoothie left behind in the blender melt and go to waste, Marya Skrypiczajko of Nelson, British Columbia, freezes it in Popsicle molds (or 3-ounce waxed paper cups). She lets the "pops" freeze partway before placing a Popsicle stick in the middle, then freezes them till firm and someone wants a quick snack.

Send Us Your Tip We will provide a complimentary one-year subscription for each tip we print. Send your tip, name, and address to Quick Tips, Cook's Illustrated, P.O. Box 470589, Brookline, MA 02447, or to quicktips@bcpress.com.

ILLUSTRATION: JOHN BURGOYNE

Handy Garbage Disposal

To keep her work area clean and save herself a few trips to the garbage can, Kate Takahashi of San Diego, Calif., puts a supermarket plastic bag in one half of her sink when preparing recipes. When she is finished putting scraps in the bag, she seals it to eliminate odors, then tosses it into the garbage can.

Yogurt with the Fruit on Top

Ann Frenningkossuth, of Allston, Mass., found an attractive way to serve yogurt with the fruit on top instead of hidden at the bottom.

1.

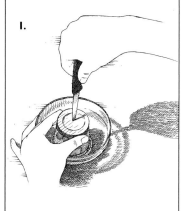

2.

1. Open the yogurt container and flip it upside down in a serving bowl. Punch a small hole in the bottom with a paring knife to release the vacuum.
2. Lift the container straight off, leaving the yogurt and fruit behind.

Shaker for Spice Rubs

Todd H. Dittrich of Fort Thomas, Ky., found a clever use for empty store-bought spice jars.

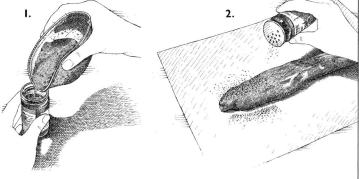

1. Gently pry the perforated lid off the jar, refill with your favorite homemade spice rub, and snap the lid back in place.
2. The spices can now be applied more evenly on the meat.

Disposable Basting Brush

While barbecuing chicken on a recent camping trip, Lizy Moromisato of Los Angeles, Calif., found herself without a brush to neatly apply the sauce. Relying on ingenuity, she made good use of the cornhusks at her disposal.

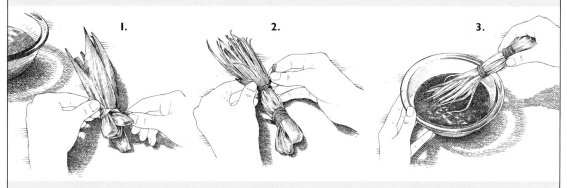

1. Gather a fistful of husks and tie them together at one end with an additional husk.
2. To make the brush bristles, fray the loose husks at the opposite end. Tie the middle with another husk to secure.
3. Dip the cornhusk brush into your sauce and apply to the food; when finished, you can just toss out the brush.

Quicker Tomato Coring

A. Dawn Jacobson of Vallejo, Calif., found another use for the large star tip she gets out just once a year when using a pastry bag to make spritz cookies: coring tomatoes. She pierces the tomato at the stem scar with the pointed end of the tip, gives it a twist, and uses the tip to cut out and remove the core.

B. Tanya Seifert of Howell, Mich., employs a similar technique with an apple corer, which she inserts halfway into the tomato.

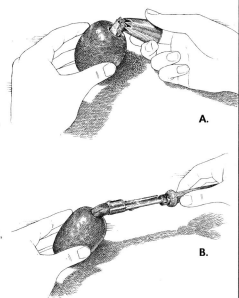

Easier Herb Washing

Leslie Mackenzie of Santa Clara, Calif., uses a salad spinner to wash herbs. Once the herbs are clean, she simply lifts the basket with the herbs out of the dirty water, discards the water, fits the basket back into its base, and spins the herbs dry.

Mixing Natural Peanut Butter

Doris Lancaster of Lakenheath, Suffolk, UK, found a way to reincorporate the layer of oil that separates from natural peanut butter. Use only one wire beater attachment on your hand-held mixer; carefully mix on low until the peanut butter is homogenous.

Grill-Roasted Pork Loin

Inexpensive and easy to find, a boneless pork loin roast seems nicely suited to grilling. Why, then, is it so often dry and flavorless?

≥ BY ELIZABETH GERMAIN ≤

The affordable and widely available pork loin roast is a popular cut to grill. The obvious problem, however, is that today's leaner pork dries out considerably when cooked with this dry-heat method. Salsa is the culinary scoundrel's solution, but I wanted to investigate the heart of the matter and produce an aromatic roast with a deep brown crust and succulent, smoke-flavored meat.

What is a loin roast? Two muscles run along the back of a pig. The larger, longer muscle is simply referred to as the loin and the smaller, shorter one, the tenderloin, which is more tender and less flavorful.

Butchers typically cut and merchandise a loin roast in three sections. Closest to the shoulder is the blade end (*blade* refers to the shoulder blade). Moving down the back of the pig you find the center cut, which is the most expensive—comparable to a beef prime rib when sold bone-in. The third and last section is called the sirloin. Here the loin muscle tapers off and rests above the tenderloin. When the sirloin section is cut into roasts or chops, part of the tenderloin is included. The tenderloin muscle can be purchased separately as a boneless roast, but it should not be confused with the larger loin roast, the roast that is the subject of this article.

I wondered if one of these three roasts—the blade end, the center cut, or the sirloin—was better suited to grilling than the others, so I bought all three cuts and put them to the test. The sirloin roast was quickly eliminated. Its two relatively large muscles cooked at vastly different speeds. I thought the center-cut roast, with its one attractive large muscle, would be the favorite, but tasters found its meat pale, dry, and bland, especially when compared with the meat from the blade roast, which was richer in flavor and relatively moist. Containing small parts of various shoulder muscles that are redder and more fibrous than the center cut, the blade roast was favorably likened to the dark meat of chicken. The fatty pockets that separate the different muscles added moistness and flavor. It was the hands-down winner.

Brining ensures a juicy roast, while a generous dose of coarse-ground pepper helps create a flavorful crust.

Grilling It Right

First I tried to grill a blade roast directly over a hot fire, but the outside scorched before the inside was cooked through. The result was the same when I tried to grill the meat directly over a moderate fire. I quickly moved on to grill-roasting, an indirect-heat approach in which a covered grill creates an oven-like environment. I banked the lit coals on one side of the kettle, leaving the other side empty, then placed the loin roast over the empty side, covered the grill, and left the roast to cook. Now it lacked a crisp crust, and the side closest to the coals cooked faster.

I tried again, this time searing all sides directly over the hot coals before moving the roast to the coal-free side of the grill. Then, halfway through cooking, I flipped it so that both long sides of the loin spent time close to the coals. Forty minutes into cooking, the crust was well browned and the meat was done.

I was well on my way to success, but my tasters kept complaining about dry meat, a common problem with today's lean pork. In the test

kitchen, we find that lean pork roasts and chops should display a hint of pink when sliced. A final internal temperature of 150 degrees is ideal. Because the temperature continues to climb as a roast rests, I found it best to take the meat off the grill when it hit 140 degrees. This step helped to alleviate the dryness—but not enough.

Adding Moisture and Enhancing Flavor

I tried the test kitchen's favorite approach to improving texture: brining. Sure enough, brined roasts produced rave reviews. The meat was juicy, moist, and even more flavorful.

Up until now, I had been simply seasoning the outside of the roast with pepper (the brine contributed enough salt), but perhaps I could up the ante a bit. Keeping things simple, I tried using a coarser grind to create a pepper crust. (I also developed two spice rub variations on this theme.) Finally, I had found the grill-roasted pork loin I was searching for. A deep brown, peppery crust perfectly balanced the sweet, juicy meat.

GRILL-ROASTED PORK LOIN FOR CHARCOAL GRILL
SERVES 4 TO 6

If only "enhanced" pork is available (it will be stated on the label), do not brine the roast. Instead, simply add 2 tablespoons kosher salt to the black pepper seasoning.

With minor recipe adjustments, a roast larger than the one called for can be cooked using the same method. For each additional pound of meat over 3 pounds (do not use a roast larger than 6 pounds), increase the salt in the brine by ¼ cup and the water by 1 quart; also increase the oil and pepper by 1 teaspoon each (if using a spice rub, increase the recipe by one-third). Because the cooking time depends more on the diameter of the loin than its length, the cooking time for a larger roast will not increase significantly. After rotating the roast in step 5, begin checking the internal temperature after 30 minutes of cooking.

¾ cup table salt
1 boneless blade-end pork loin roast, 2½ to 3 pounds, tied with kitchen twine at 1½-inch intervals (see illustration on page 7)
2 tablespoons olive oil
1 tablespoon coarsely ground black pepper or 1 recipe spice rub (recipes follow)

BLADE-END ROAST
Our top choice, this cut is
moist and flavorful.

CENTER-CUT ROAST
Our second choice, this mild
cut can dry out on the grill.

SIRLOIN ROAST
With two kinds of muscle,
this cut cooks unevenly.

TENDERLOIN ROAST
Don't be fooled by two
tenderloins tied together.

1. Dissolve salt in 3 quarts water in large container; submerge roast, cover with plastic wrap, and refrigerate until fully seasoned, 3 to 4 hours. Rinse roast under cold water and dry thoroughly with paper towels.

2. Rub roast with oil; sprinkle with pepper or spice rub and press into meat. Let roast stand at room temperature 1 hour.

3. Meanwhile, soak two 3-inch wood chunks in water to cover for 1 hour; drain. About 25 minutes before grilling, open bottom grill vents. Using large chimney starter, ignite about 5 quarts charcoal, or about 90 individual briquettes, and burn until fully ignited, about 15 minutes. Empty coals into grill; build modified two-level fire by arranging coals to cover one-half of grill, piling them about 3 briquettes high. Place soaked wood chunks on coals. Position grill grate over coals, cover grill, and heat until hot, about 5 minutes; scrape grill grate clean with grill brush.

4. Grill pork directly over fire until browned, about 2 minutes; using tongs, rotate one-quarter turn and repeat until all sides are well browned, about 8 minutes total. Move loin to cool side of grill, positioning roast parallel with and as close as possible to fire. Open grill lid vents halfway; cover grill so vents are opposite fire and draw smoke through grill. (Internal grill temperature should be about 425 degrees.) Cook 20 minutes.

5. Remove cover; using tongs, rotate roast 180 degrees so side facing fire now faces away. Replace cover and continue cooking until instant-read thermometer inserted into thickest part of roast registers 140 degrees, 10 to 30 minutes longer, depending on thickness.

6. Transfer roast to cutting board; tent loosely with foil and let rest 15 minutes. Internal temperature should rise to 150 degrees. Remove twine; cut roast into ½-inch-thick slices and serve.

GRILL-ROASTED PORK LOIN FOR GAS GRILL

1. Follow recipe for Grill-Roasted Pork Loin for Charcoal Grill through step 2. Soak 2 cups wood chips in water to cover for 30 minutes; drain. Place chips in small disposable aluminum pan.

2. About 20 minutes before grilling, place wood-chip pan on primary burner (burner that will remain on during cooking); position cooking grate. Ignite grill, turn all burners to high, cover, and heat until very hot, about 15 minutes. (If chips ignite, use water-filled spray bottle to extinguish.) Scrape grate clean with grill brush.

3. Continue with recipe from step 4, keeping lid down except as needed to check progress of pork.

CHILI-MUSTARD SPICE RUB
MAKES ABOUT 2 TABLESPOONS

2	teaspoons chili powder
2	teaspoons powdered mustard
1	teaspoon ground cumin
½	teaspoon cayenne

Combine all ingredients in small bowl.

SWEET AND SAVORY SPICE RUB
MAKES ABOUT 2 TABLESPOONS

1	tablespoon cumin seeds
1½	teaspoons coriander seeds
1	teaspoon fennel seeds
½	teaspoon ground cinnamon
¼	teaspoon ground allspice

Combine cumin, coriander, and fennel in small skillet; toast over medium heat until fragrant, about 2 minutes, shaking skillet occasionally. Cool to room temperature; grind coarse. Transfer to small bowl; stir in cinnamon and allspice.

TECHNIQUE

TYING PORK LOIN

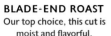

No fancy knots needed—just use double knots to secure pieces of kitchen twine at 1½-inch intervals. For information on buying twine, see page 31.

TESTING EQUIPMENT:

Remote Meat Thermometers

The only way to ensure a well-cooked roast is through constant temperature monitoring, but repeatedly lifting the lid off the grill wreaks havoc on cooking times. Could a remote thermometer—which transmits the temperature from a probe inserted in the food to a cordless console—solve this problem? To find out, we rounded up four models.

What separated the best from the worst were the transmission range and the temperature-setting options. Some models transmitted up to 200 feet, while the shortest range was a mere 30 feet. Our favorite models clearly indicated when we had moved out of transmission range (sounding a series of warning beeps); the others simply ceased flashing a display light—a bit too subtle.

More important is that some models are restricted to factory-determined temperature settings. For instance, if you want to pull off a turkey at 165 degrees (which we recommend) using the Weber Barbecue Beeper Digital Thermometer, the best you can do is set it to "Beef—Medium" (160 degrees) or "Beef—Well Done" (170 degrees). It can't be set to 165. We urge you not to use the "Turkey" setting (programmed at a parchingly dry 180 degrees).

In the end, we liked the Taylor thermometer best. The provided temperature guidelines can be overridden to set any temperature, the range is ample (up to 150 feet), and the clippable pager is small enough not to hinder an impromptu game of catch. –Garth Clingingsmith

FAVORITE THERMOMETER
➤**TAYLOR** Wireless Oven
Thermometer with Remote
Pager $34.99

A decent range, and there's a clear indication when you move out of it. Plus, you can set it to any temperature.

BETTER FOR BARBECUE
➤**MAVERICK** Remote Smoker
Thermometer $39.99

The range (advertised at 100 feet, 30 feet in testing) limits its usefulness, but a second probe measures ambient grill temperature.

RUNS TOO HOT
➤**WEBER** Barbecue Beeper
Digital Thermometer $34.95

Great range, but it's not obvious when you've left it. Preset temperature alerts are limiting.

ALL TALK
➤**BROOKSTONE** Grill Alert
Talking Remote Thermometer
$75.00

Same problems as the Weber. For the extra $40, a computerized voice says, "Your entrée is ready." Creepy.

Perfect Aïoli

When making this French condiment, the key is to avoid a bitter garlic aftertaste.

⇉ BY SARAH WILSON ⇇

The term *aïoli* is derived from the French words *ail*, meaning "garlic," and *oli*, which is Provençal for "oil." Aïoli is an emulsion sauce that by tradition is the centerpiece of a simple supper served with cooked vegetables and potatoes and steamed fish. Consisting of only a few ingredients—olive oil, garlic, egg yolk, and lemon juice—aïoli can be delightfully smooth and simple when made properly. When it's made badly, however, the overwhelming impression is one of garlic: bitter, sharp, and long-lasting.

After making multiple batches, I was more than familiar with this common complaint. Aïoli traditionally makes use of raw minced garlic (it is from garlic that it proudly gets its defining flavor), but imperfectly minced garlic ruined the texture and left oversized pieces that exploded in the mouth like garlic bombs. I needed a finer mince and a more reliable system for producing it. The answer turned out to be a good garlic press or a rasp-style zester/grater. I also discovered that it is important to remove the bitter green germ (if there is one) that runs down the center of the clove.

Now the sauce was smooth and the garlic well distributed, but the flavor of the raw garlic still seemed overwhelming. Why not, I thought, cook it first? I roasted, toasted, and simmered cloves in oil, but tasters criticized every batch for being bland. I tried cooking half of the garlic and leaving the rest raw, but this didn't work either. Forced back to tradition, I tried far less garlic than most recipes suggest. A single minced clove gave the aïoli pleasant heat without the shock value.

Most recipes use lemon juice to cut through the cloying richness of the oil and egg yolk, but the lemon can add sour notes, too. I added a bit of sugar to offset the bitterness and found that I now had a clean, bright, and balanced sauce.

The biggest ingredient by volume in aïoli is the oil. Of the different oils tested, I was shocked to find that regular (not extra-virgin) pure olive oil was the tasters' favorite. It gave the sauce body and a slightly fruity flavor that complemented the lemon and garlic. Extra-virgin olive

Getting the Garlic Right

For a smooth aïoli, it is essential to mince the garlic very finely, almost to a paste. We rely on a garlic press or rasp grater.

Garlicky aïoli perks up blanched green beans and boiled new potatoes.

oil, usually preferred in raw sauces because of its stronger, fruitier flavor, imparted too much of its own distinct character and was ruled out as overpowering. Vegetable oil, to my great surprise, was liked for its pure clean flavor, but the sauces made with it lacked both the depth and character one expects from aïoli. Supplemented with some extra-virgin olive oil, however, vegetable oil was just as good as regular olive oil.

I focused next on the mixing method. In the blender, the emulsion became so thick it seized the blades. Whisking by hand worked beautifully, but after four minutes, my arm was very tired. The food processor, which pulled the sauce together in just 30 seconds, was my top choice.

AÏOLI

MAKES ABOUT ¾ CUP

Use this sauce as a condiment for meats, fish, and vegetables or spread it on sandwiches. If necessary, remove the green germ (or stem) in the garlic before pressing or grating it; the germ will give the aïoli a bitter, hot flavor. If you do not have regular olive oil, use a blend of equal parts extra-virgin olive oil and vegetable oil. Ground white pepper is preferred because it's not as visible in the finished aïoli as black pepper, but either

can be used. The aïoli will keep refrigerated in an airtight container for up to 3 days.

- 1 medium garlic clove, peeled
- 2 large egg yolks
- 1 tablespoon plus 1 teaspoon juice from 1 lemon
- ⅛ teaspoon sugar
- ¼ teaspoon table salt
  Ground pepper, preferably white
- ¾ cup olive oil

1. Press garlic through garlic press or grate very finely on rasp-style grater. Measure out 1 teaspoon garlic; discard remaining garlic.

2. In food processor, combine garlic, yolks, lemon juice, sugar, salt, and pepper to taste until combined, about 10 seconds. With machine running, gradually add oil in slow steady stream (process should take about 30 seconds); scrape down sides of bowl with rubber spatula and process 5 seconds longer. Adjust seasoning with additional salt and pepper and serve.

ROSEMARY-THYME AÏOLI

Serve this robust aïoli with roasted and grilled meats or grilled vegetables.

Follow recipe for Aïoli, adding 1 teaspoon chopped fresh rosemary and 1 teaspoon chopped fresh thyme to food processor along with garlic.

SAFFRON AÏOLI

Powdered saffron (see page 30) releases its flavor more quickly than saffron threads. If using powdered saffron, stir only ⅟₁₆ teaspoon into the finished aïoli, allow it to stand for at least 20 minutes, then stir again before serving. Saffron aïoli is a nice accompaniment to fish and shellfish.

In small bowl, combine ⅛ teaspoon saffron threads, crumbled, and 1 teaspoon boiling water; let steep 10 minutes. Follow recipe for Aïoli, adding saffron to food processor along with garlic; transfer finished aïoli to bowl, cover with plastic wrap, and refrigerate at least 2 hours to allow saffron flavor to bloom. Stir before serving.

COOK'S EXTRA gives you free recipes online. For our Basil-Dill Aïoli recipe, visit www.cooksillustrated.com and key in code 7051. This recipe will be available until August 31, 2005.

Restaurant-Style Grilled Pizza at Home

Burnt or bland, most homemade versions of this restaurant classic can't come close.
Could we make grilled pizza a success for the backyard cook?

≥ BY MATTHEW CARD ≤

My first grilled pizza set the bar impossibly high for those that followed. My wife was a graduate student in Providence, R.I., and, despite being flat broke, we had our hearts set on dinner at Al Forno, the restaurant famed for its rustic Italian cooking. After pinching our pennies for weeks, we made reservations and even splurged on a taxi to take us there. We ordered their trademark grilled pizza for our first course, but it wasn't much to look at when it arrived—vaguely shaped and stingily topped with a scattering of cheese, tomatoes, and herbs. I wondered if we had just thrown away $15. But the first bite dispelled my doubts: The lightly charred, cracker-thin crust was packed with flavor, and the toppings were perfectly balanced. Since then, I have had grilled pizza in many restaurants and backyards, but none has measured up. What was Al Forno doing so right that everyone else was doing so wrong?

I've made hundreds of oven-baked pizzas and consider myself a pretty skilled pizzaiola, but my first attempt at grilled pizza was a nightmare. The crust burned fast to the grill in the middle but remained raw around the rim, and sauce and cheese dripped onto the coals, causing arm-singeing flare-ups. And what was edible didn't taste very good. Abject failure taught me an important lesson: Grilled pizza is not baked pizza—leave all preconceptions behind. The demands placed on both the pizza and the cook are far different, far more challenging.

Crust

I wanted to make a simple tomato and cheese pizza, and I knew that grilled pizza was nothing without a great-tasting crust—it's much more than just a vehicle for toppings. The dough has to be manageable, too. The batch I had made for my trial run clung tenaciously to everything it touched.

Dough for grilled pizza has to be slack enough to be stretched thin—thinner than baked pizza, so that it can cook through quickly on the grill—yet strong enough not to rip. High-protein bread flour generally makes a stronger dough than all-

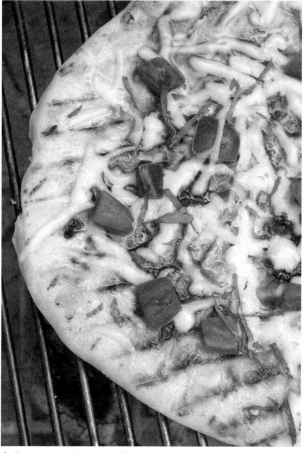

Grilled pizza is all about perfect choreography and a light hand with potently flavored toppings.

purpose flour, and a head-to-head test proved it. As for the ratio of water to flour, the wetter the dough, the easier it was to stretch and the crispier the crust, but at a cost: The dough was intractably sticky. I backed off on the water a little at a time until the dough, though still pretty wet, could be worked without clinging too firmly to my hands or the countertop.

Kneading develops gluten in dough; the longer it is kneaded, the stronger the dough. I thought slowly kneaded dough made in a standing mixer would be the best bet for grilling, but, to my surprise, once grilled it was indistinguishable from dough made in a food processor in a fraction of the time. I experimented with different processing times and settled on 1½ minutes—time enough for the dough to become smooth and supple. It

was a breeze to work with and shape, more elastic and rip resistant than most of the baked pizza doughs I had tried.

Olive oil adds flavor and richness to a lean dough. In this case, a tablespoon was noticeable, but twice that better yet. The dough seemed smoother, suppler, and less sticky. But then I noticed something else. The dough with the higher amount of oil seemed impervious to sticking to the grill. Within 30 seconds over the fire, the crust easily released. Other recipes slicked the dough with oil before grilling to the same effect, but I found this method caused flare-ups as oil dripped onto the hot coals. Better to bake the protective oil right into the dough.

Now that I had the texture of the dough right, I realized that the flavor was still too meek for grilling; the toppings and the char from the hot fire overpowered it. I'd seen a recipe or two in which whole wheat, rye, or buckwheat flour was added to the dough, an idea I thought promising. The smallest addition translated into a surprising amount of flavor. I settled on a scant tablespoon of whole wheat flour; any more made it taste like an Indian *chapati*. A little sugar further improved flavor and also helped to color the blond crust. (Cooked less than baked pizza, grilled pizza tends to be a tad pale.) The last touch was to increase the amount of salt. To compensate for the skimpier gloss of topping, I wanted this crust to be more highly seasoned than a baked crust.

Fire

For the sake of testing, I had been following the grilling method collectively embraced by most of the recipes I had researched. The crust is cooked on one side over a medium-hot, two-level fire until crisp, then flipped, topped, and finished on the cool side of the fire. This method worked, but I found it limited the number of pizzas I could top and cook to one at a time, leaving me stranded grill-side while everybody else tucked into hot pizza (like pancakes, grilled pizzas are best eaten ASAP).

I tried a single-level hot fire but soon realized that this was too risky an approach. Sure, I could cook all four crusts at once, but it took all my rusty line-cook skills to keep them from burning.

Troubleshooting Grilled Pizza

Here are three problems we encountered when making grilled pizza—and the steps we now take to avoid them.

MISSHAPEN

PROBLEM: Crust is amoeba shaped.
SOLUTION: Stretching the dough by hand may be traditional, but rolling it out with a rolling pin keeps it much more symmetrical. Rolling also presses out air pockets and reduces bubbling when the dough is grilled.

BURNT

PROBLEM: Crust burns in center.
SOLUTION: The dough stretches easily and can get very thin at the center. Using a pizza peel or baking sheet to slide the pizza onto the grill keeps the weight of the dough from overstretching the center.

SOGGY

PROBLEM: Crust is soggy.
SOLUTION: Mounds of sliced tomatoes (or sauce) and cheese make for a mushy mess. Modest amounts of cheese and diced tomatoes (salted to draw off moisture) add flavor without weighing down the pizza.

Lowering the temperature of the fire made the technique safer, but the texture of the crust was now more dense and less crackery. After trying several different arrangements of coals, I found that a single-level, medium-hot fire spread over three-quarters of the grill bottom gave me enough heat and real estate to cook two pizzas at once and a safety zone onto which I could slide any crusts that were at risk of burning—a rare but real threat. And instead of finishing the first two pizzas immediately, I opted to grill the other two crusts—the half-baked crusts held well—and then top and finish the pizzas two at a time. Covering the topped pizzas with the grill lid for a few minutes trapped enough heat to make the toppings sizzle, and, in a matter of minutes, I had four hot pizzas ready to serve.

Toppings

From my first sorry attempt at grilled pizza, I knew that a standard pairing of tomato sauce and mozzarella wouldn't work; the sauce would simply soak through the thin crust, and the cheese would ooze off into the fire. The toppings had to be drier and more potently flavored so a smaller amount could be used. Sliced fresh, meaty plum tomatoes were the easiest substitution for sauce,

but they, too, turned the crust soggy. Seeded and coarsely chopped tomatoes fared better but were still too wet. I finally tried salting the chopped tomatoes to draw off excess juices, and the results were the best yet. I set the tomatoes in a colander and allowed them to drain for 30 minutes before blotting them with paper towels. The tomatoes were firmer, drier, and, most important, more flavorful.

As for cheese, full-bodied, soft cheeses like fontina, Montasio, Bel Paese, smoked mozzarella, and Taleggio all proved better than plain mozzarella, with fontina finding the most fans. To round out its ripe, earthy flavor, tasters suggested a hard grating cheese. Pecorino and Asiago came on a little strong, but nutty Parmesan added just the right note. Mixing it with the fontina simplified the job of topping the pizzas and made the sticky fontina easier to work with.

Just about any herb tasted good, but a scattering of torn basil leaves added the classic touch and flavor. It might be grilled, but it was still pizza, after all.

Control

My pizzas were finally tasting almost as good as what I remembered, but they were frightful to

look at: misshapen, char splotched, and bloated with large bubbles. Al Forno's amorphous pies were rustic; mine were monstrous. Shaping the dough outside by the grill, with everything else going on, was simply too much. I brought it back into the kitchen and shaped the rounds all at once, finding that I could sandwich them between flour-dusted sheets of parchment paper, stack them like tortillas, and shuttle them out to the grill.

But there was still the mad bubbling. When I tried pressing the dough flat with my hands after stretching it, things did improve, but not by much. I revisited the recipes I had collected and saw that some employed a rolling pin to shape the crust—a technique I dislike when baking pizza because it makes the dough too flat, leveling the puffy outer corona. But that was baking; this was grilling. Rolling the dough effectively forced out the larger bubbles and made the dough more uniform. The crust bubbled when grilled, but only enough to lightly pucker the surface—just the right amount for an ideally crisp yet chewy texture. Now I had all the flavor of the restaurant pizza in my own backyard, with a manageable method and without the stiff price tag.

GRILLED TOMATO AND CHEESE PIZZAS FOR CHARCOAL GRILL
MAKES FOUR 9-INCH PIZZAS

The pizzas cook very quickly on the grill, so before you begin grilling them, be sure to have all the equipment and ingredients you need at hand. Equipment includes a pizza peel (or a rimless baking sheet), a pair of tongs, a paring knife, a large cutting board, and a pastry brush; ingredients include all the toppings and a small bowl of flour for dusting. Timing and coordination are crucial; if you are unsure of your skill level, try cooking the first two pizzas one at a time, then work up to cooking the final two in tandem.

The pizzas are best served hot off the grill but can be kept warm for 20 to 30 minutes on a wire rack in a 200-degree oven. Hardwood charcoal and charcoal briquettes work equally well. Whichever you use, it is important that the coals be spread in an even layer over three-quarters of the grill bottom; coals placed any higher will scorch the crust.

STEP BY STEP: GRILLED PIZZA 101

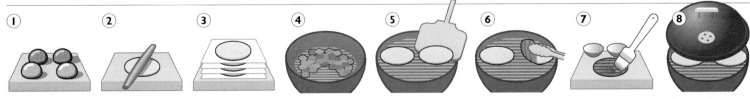

1. Shape dough into 4 smooth, tight balls. **2.** With pin, roll each dough ball on parchment paper to form 9-inch round. **3.** Stack dough rounds, separated by parchment. **4.** Arrange lit coals in even layer over three-quarters of grill. **5.** Invert dough round onto floured peel, remove parchment, and slide onto grill. Cook 2 dough rounds at once. **6.** Using tongs, lift up dough round and peek to make sure it's not scorching. If it's cooking too fast, slide pizza to cool part of grill. **7.** Transfer dough round to cutting board, browned side up. Brush dough round with garlic oil and top with cheese mixture and tomatoes. **8.** Return pizza to grill and cover grill to help cheese melt.

Dough

2	tablespoons extra-virgin olive oil
1	cup (8 ounces) water, room temperature
2	cups (11 ounces) bread flour, plus more for work surface
1	tablespoon whole wheat flour (optional)
2	teaspoons sugar
1¼	teaspoons table salt
1	teaspoon instant yeast

Topping

1½	pounds plum tomatoes (5 to 6 medium), cored, seeded, and cut into ½-inch dice
¾	teaspoon table salt
6	ounces fontina cheese, shredded (about 2 cups)
1½	ounces Parmesan cheese, finely grated (about ¾ cup)
1	recipe Spicy Garlic Oil (recipe follows)
½	cup chopped fresh basil leaves
	Coarse salt

1. **FOR THE CRUST:** Combine oil and water in liquid measuring cup. In food processor fitted with plastic dough blade or metal blade, process bread flour, whole wheat flour, sugar, salt, and yeast until combined, about 5 seconds. With machine running, slowly add liquid through feed tube; continue to process until dough forms tacky, elastic ball that clears sides of workbowl, about 1½ minutes. If dough ball does not form, add more flour 1 tablespoon at a time and process until dough ball forms. Spray medium bowl lightly with nonstick cooking spray or rub lightly with oil. Transfer dough to bowl and press down to flatten surface; cover tightly with plastic wrap and set in draft-free spot until doubled in volume, 1½ to 2 hours.

2. When dough has doubled, press down gently to deflate; turn dough out onto work surface and divide into 4 equal-sized pieces. With cupped palm, form each piece into smooth, tight ball. Set dough balls on well-floured work surface. Press dough rounds with hand to flatten; cover loosely with plastic wrap and let rest about 15 minutes.

3. **FOR THE TOPPING:** Meanwhile, toss tomatoes and table salt in medium bowl; transfer to colander and drain 30 minutes (wipe out and reserve bowl). Shake colander to drain off excess liquid; transfer tomatoes to now-empty bowl and set aside. Combine cheeses in second medium bowl and set aside.

4. Gently stretch dough rounds into disks about ½ inch thick and 5 to 6 inches in diameter. Working one piece at a time and keeping the rest covered, roll out each disk to ⅛-inch thickness, 9 to 10 inches in diameter, on well-floured sheet of parchment paper, dusting with additional flour as needed to prevent sticking. (If dough shrinks when rolled out, cover with plastic wrap and let rest until relaxed, 10 to 15 minutes.) Dust surface of rolled dough with flour and set aside. Repeat with remaining dough, stacking sheets of rolled dough on top of each other (with parchment in between) and covering stack with plastic wrap; set aside until grill is ready.

5. **TO GRILL:** Ignite 6 quarts (1 large chimney) hardwood charcoal or briquettes in chimney starter and burn until fully ignited, 15 to 20 minutes. Empty coals into grill and spread into even layer over three-quarters of grill, leaving one quadrant free of coals. Position cooking grate over coals and heat until grill is medium-hot, about 5 minutes (you can hold your hand 5 inches above grill grate for 4 seconds); scrape grate clean with grill brush.

6. Lightly flour pizza peel; invert 1 dough round onto peel, gently stretching it as needed to retain shape (do not stretch dough too thin; thin spots will burn quickly). Peel off and discard parchment; carefully slide round onto hot side of grill. Immediately repeat with another dough round. Cook until tops are covered with bubbles (pierce larger bubbles with paring knife) and bottoms are grill marked and charred in spots, 1 to 2 minutes; while rounds cook, check undersides and slide to cool area of grill if browning too quickly. Transfer crusts to cutting board browned sides up. Repeat with 2 remaining dough rounds.

7. Brush 2 crusts generously with Spicy Garlic Oil; top each evenly with one-quarter of cheese mixture and one-quarter of tomatoes. Return pizzas to grill and cover grill with lid; cook until bottoms are well browned and cheese is melted, 2 to 4 minutes, checking bottoms frequently to prevent burning. Transfer pizzas to cutting board; repeat with remaining 2 crusts. Sprinkle pizzas with basil and coarse salt to taste; cut into wedges and serve immediately.

GRILLED TOMATO AND CHEESE PIZZAS FOR GAS GRILL

1. Follow recipe for Grilled Tomato and Cheese Pizzas for Charcoal Grill through step 4.

2. Light all burners and turn to high heat, cover grill, and heat grill until hot, about 15 minutes; scrape cooking grate clean with grill brush.

3. Continue with recipe from step 6, cooking pizzas with lid down in both steps 6 and 7 and increasing cooking times in steps 6 and 7 by 1 to 2 minutes, if needed.

SPICY GARLIC OIL
MAKES ENOUGH FOR 4 PIZZAS

4	medium garlic cloves, minced or pressed through garlic press (4 teaspoons)
½	teaspoon red pepper flakes
⅓	cup extra-virgin olive oil

Cook all ingredients in small saucepan over medium heat, stirring occasionally, until garlic begins to sizzle, 2 to 3 minutes. Transfer to small bowl.

Just Give Me the Dough

Many cuisines offer up some take on grilled flatbread. It can be eaten almost plain, merely slicked with our Spicy Garlic Oil, or dressed with any number of simple toppings other than tomatoes and cheese. Flatbread can serve as a quick appetizer or a light accompaniment to a meal—once it's been cooked the coals should still be hot enough to grill meat or fish. For the best flavor and texture, grilled flatbread should be served as soon as possible. Sprinkle with coarse salt before serving.

GRILLED FLATBREAD
MAKES FOUR 9-INCH FLATBREADS

1	recipe Grilled Pizza Crust prepared through step 6
1	recipe Spicy Garlic Oil
1	topping (see Topping Choices), optional Coarse salt

Brush grilled sides of 2 crusts generously with garlic oil; top each evenly with one-quarter of topping, if using. Return flatbreads to grill; cook uncovered until bottoms are well browned and toppings are heated through, 1 to 3 minutes. Transfer flatbreads to cutting board; repeat with remaining 2 crusts. Sprinkle flatbreads with salt to taste; cut into pieces and serve immediately.

TOPPING CHOICES
- 2 ounces Parmesan, finely grated (about 1 cup)
- ½ cup coarsely chopped mixed herbs, such as thyme, parsley, basil, marjoram, and oregano
- 3 tablespoons sesame seeds mixed with 1 tablespoon chopped fresh thyme leaves; sprinkle flatbreads lightly with lemon juice before serving
- ½ cup coarsely chopped fresh oregano leaves and 6 ounces crumbled feta
- 2 tablespoons chopped anchovies mixed with 6 tablespoons chopped black or green olives
- ½ cup prepared tapenade or pesto

For a great appetizer or accompaniment to dinner, skip the tomatoes and simply grill the dough to make flatbread.

Best Barbecued Pulled Chicken

Most recipes stick with boneless breasts and bottled sauce. How about a barbecue sandwich that rivals pulled pork in a fraction of the time?

⇒ BY SEAN LAWLER ⇐

The pulled chicken sandwich is a lesser staple of Dixieland barbecue shacks, where the ribs and pulled pork usually take center stage. But from a business standpoint, it's a very practical choice for the pitmaster, who no doubt has plenty of extra barbecued chicken on hand. The tender, smoky meat is simply pulled off the bone in moist, soft shreds, tossed with tangy, sweet sauce, and piled high on soft white bread with pickle chips and coleslaw. To me, this is the ultimate example of taking leftovers to another level. I'll sometimes try it at home, but not being a pitmaster (and a Yankee to boot), my leftover chicken is more often merely boneless and bland, and a bottle of barbecue sauce offers little help. If I wanted some great pulled chicken barbecue, I'd have to start from scratch.

Most of the recipes I researched were no more than footnotes to recipes for barbecued chicken that treated pulled chicken sandwiches as mere leftovers. The few exceptions were pale, "quick and easy" imitations of the ideal, instructing me to grill a few boneless chicken breasts and then toss them with sauce. This approach was so inferior to the real thing—no smoke or fall-apart texture, just pasty bottled sauce—that it reminded me of the crimes committed every day by Northerners in the name of Southern cornbread. I wanted, at the very least, to take the pulled chicken sandwich seriously. And, like most Northerners, I didn't have all day.

Choosing Chicken

Tasters loved the smoky flavor of a whole chicken, which spent about an hour on the grill, but there were two problems. First, coordinating the doneness between breasts and legs seemed like overkill for pulled chicken. Also, there was something heartbreaking about taking a whole grill-roasted chicken with crisp, mahogany skin and chopping it down into a sandwich. Using parts would solve both problems: It would give me more control over cooking, and I would avoid having to deconstruct the perfect barbecued bird.

I tried grilling both whole leg quarters and bone-in breasts; the latter tended to dry out, so I went with the legs. These quarters, when cooked

A smoky grill, a tangy sauce, and a quick shredding technique turn meaty chicken legs into classic barbecue fare.

over direct heat, didn't develop much smoky flavor in only 30 minutes, so I turned to indirect heat and a "low and slow" grill temperature. During this longer cooking time, the meat turned deliciously smoky and was moist and tender as well. (Unlike breast meat, dark leg meat can cook for more than an hour without drying out.) I tested various setups for the charcoal and finally settled on two piles of coals on either side of the grill, with the legs in the middle and a drip pan underneath. (Putting all of the coals on one side of the grill produced uneven heat, cooking the legs closest to the coals too quickly.)

Without any direct heat to sear the meat, there was no need to flip the legs during cooking. In fact, there were advantages to keeping the legs skin side up for the duration: The rendered fat from the skin basted the meat, keeping it juicy and preventing it from turning dry and leathery from the heat and smoke. With two moderate piles of charcoal (about 40 briquettes each) and

two good-sized chunks of hickory or mesquite, the legs cooked gently but thoroughly in about an hour and absorbed plenty of smoke flavor along the way.

Pulling My Legs

Whole chicken legs (thighs and drumsticks attached) have great flavor, they are dirt cheap (especially when purchased in giant supermarket "family packs"), and the dark meat is nearly impossible to overcook. On the downside, they are riddled with connective tissue, blood vessels, and interior veins of fat, none of which are appetizing. And while the breast is basically one big muscle, the leg is made up of a dozen or so smaller muscles, with fibers running every which way. Also, pulling and shredding breast meat is a snap; handling leg meat is a chore.

I discovered a partial solution to this problem when I accidentally overcooked the chicken one afternoon. The internal temperature had shot up to around 185 degrees (15 degrees past "done" for legs), but the meat was still moist. In addition, more of the connective tissue had dissolved, so the meat now fell off the bone in large pieces with only a gentle tug. More fat had rendered out as well, making the chicken less greasy.

Always impatient, I wanted a shortcut to the shredding work once the meat was off the bone, so I tried pulsing the meat in the food processor. This raised a few eyebrows in the test kitchen. "I prefer to chew my own food," quipped one colleague when I placed a bowl of the sauced, machine-chopped chicken in front of her. It may have looked like cat food, but tasters liked the flavor, and this "processed" chicken was able to absorb more sauce than the hand-pulled. While

A Leg Up

Chicken legs are our top choice for this recipe. They are inexpensive, nearly impossible to overcook, and have a rich, meaty flavor that stands up to smoke and barbecue sauce.

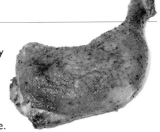

packing up the leftovers from this test, I tossed together the hand-pulled and machine-processed batches of chicken. Right away, I noticed that the combination of the two textures looked better than either of the two alone—it looked, in fact, just like pulled pork. In addition to the flavor boost, the chopped chicken helped to bind the mixture and made it stiffer, so it piled nicely on the bun instead of sliding off onto the plate.

The next day, with this 50/50 mixture in mind, I began separating the chicken into two piles as I pulled it off the bones. The intact larger pieces were set aside for hand shredding, while the smaller, crustier bits went into the food processor for a few quick pulses. Not only did this result in the perfect texture, but it also saved me some preparation time.

Sizing Up the Sauce

I experimented with different types of barbecue sauce, including thin vinegar- and mustard-based "Carolina-style" sauces—the traditional complements for the rich, full flavor of pulled pork. Tasters, however, found these sauces too overpowering for relatively lean, mild chicken. They much preferred *Cook's* existing recipe for quick barbecue sauce, which has a base of ketchup and juice from pureed onions and can be made in less than 30 minutes. I made just a few adjustments to the consistency, as the existing sauce was too thick to properly coat the finer shreds of chicken.

My last problem was that the pulled chicken had cooled to room temperature once all the shredding work was done. When I tossed the pulled chicken back into the pan with the sauce to heat it up, the meat also softened nicely in the steam generated by the sauce. At last, I had barbecued pulled chicken that was bun-worthy. Not bad for a Northerner!

BARBECUED PULLED CHICKEN FOR CHARCOAL GRILL

SERVES 6 TO 8

Chicken leg quarters consist of drumsticks attached to thighs; often also attached are backbone sections that must be trimmed away. Supermarkets may also sell chicken legs, which are chicken leg quarters with the backbone sections already removed; they require less trimming and may weigh less than leg quarters. When trimming the fat from the chicken legs, try to leave the excess skin intact, as it will keep the meat moist on the grill. For equipment, you will need two 3-inch wood chunks (we like hickory or mesquite) and a 16 by 12-inch disposable aluminum roasting pan to catch the fat as the chicken cooks.

If you would like to hold the dish once the chicken and sauce are combined and heated through, transfer the mixture to a 13 by 9-inch glass baking dish, cover with foil, and place in a 250-degree oven for up to an hour. Serve the

Adjusting the Texture

Shredding pulled chicken with forks yields attractive strips (left), but the meat doesn't hold together very well on a bun. Pulsing the chicken in a food processor produces soft shreds that soak up lots of sauce but are visually unappealing (center). For best results, use an even mix of shredded and pulsed chicken (right).

| SHREDDED | PULSED | HALF SHREDDED/HALF PULSED |

pulled chicken with hamburger rolls or sandwich bread, pickles, and coleslaw.

Chicken

- 8 bone-in, skin-on chicken leg quarters (about 7 pounds total), trimmed of backbone (see illustrations on page 14) and excess fat
  Table salt and ground black pepper

Sauce

- 1 large onion, peeled and quartered
- ¼ cup water
- 1½ cups ketchup
- 1½ cups apple cider
- 3 tablespoons Worcestershire sauce
- 3 tablespoons Dijon mustard
- ¼ cup molasses
- ½ teaspoon ground black pepper
- 4 tablespoons apple cider vinegar
- 1 tablespoon vegetable oil
- 2 medium garlic cloves, minced or pressed through garlic press (2 teaspoons)
- 1½ tablespoons chili powder
- ½ teaspoon cayenne
  Hot pepper sauce, such as Tabasco

1. **FOR THE CHICKEN:** Soak two 3-inch wood chunks in cold water to cover for 1 hour; drain.

2. Using large chimney starter, ignite about 4½ quarts charcoal, or about 80 individual briquettes, and burn until fully ignited, about 15 minutes. Empty coals into grill; divide coals in half, creating piles on opposite sides of grill. Place 16 by 12-inch disposable aluminum roasting pan in center, between coal piles. Nestle one soaked wood chunk on top of one pile (reserve remaining wood chunk). Position cooking grate over coals, cover grill, and heat until hot, about 5 minutes; scrape grate clean with grill brush.

3. Meanwhile, sprinkle both sides of chicken legs with salt and pepper. Place chicken legs skin side up in single layer on center of grill over roasting pan. Cover and cook 30 minutes (internal grill temperature should register about 325 degrees after 30 minutes).

4. Working quickly to prevent excess heat loss, remove cover, and, using tongs, rotate each leg so

that side facing inward now faces coals; do not flip chicken pieces. Add second wood chunk to either pile of coals; cover and cook until instant-read thermometer inserted into thickest part of thighs registers about 185 degrees, 30 to 40 minutes longer (internal grill temperature should register about 310 degrees). Transfer chicken to cutting board; let rest until cool enough to handle.

5. **FOR THE SAUCE:** While chicken is cooking or cooling, process onion and water in food

---

TESTING EQUIPMENT:

Rethinking Roasting Racks

Our recipe calls for barbecuing eight chicken legs, the maximum number that can fit comfortably on our grill grate. Could we use some sort of rack to hold more than eight chicken legs and make barbecued pulled chicken for a crowd?

Our first thought was a rib rack. It works by tilting a rack of ribs on its side and "filing" it into one of four slots. We hoped that sliding three legs into each slot would do the same for our chicken. But the legs were awfully cramped, and the cooking time for the middle four legs lagged behind that of the legs "on the aisles." Two legs in each slot worked better, but that put us back where we started—cooking just eight legs in total.

Then an ingenious test cook pondered the use of our favorite roasting rack, the Norpro Nonstick Roasting Rack ($9.75). With six "slots," it is the perfect tool for this job. Two legs in each slot means all 12 fit (and finish cooking) at once—plenty to feed a hungry crowd. – Garth Clingingsmith

This roasting rack can be put to work on the grill during the roasting "off season."

---

processor fitted with steel blade until pureed and mixture resembles slush, about 30 seconds. Pass mixture through fine-mesh strainer into liquid measuring cup, pressing on solids with rubber spatula; you should have ¾ cup strained onion puree. Discard solids in strainer.

6. Whisk onion puree, ketchup, apple cider, Worcestershire, mustard, molasses, pepper, and 3 tablespoons cider vinegar together in medium bowl. Heat oil in large nonreactive saucepan over medium heat until shimmering; add garlic, chili powder, and cayenne and cook until fragrant, about 30 seconds. Stir in ketchup mixture; increase heat to medium-high, bring to boil, reduce heat to medium-low, and simmer, uncovered, until flavors meld and sauce is slightly thickened, about 15 minutes. You should have scant 4 cups sauce. Transfer about 2 cups sauce to serving bowl; leave remaining sauce in saucepan.

7. Remove and discard skin from chicken legs. Using fingers, pull meat off bones, separating larger pieces (which should fall off bones easily) from smaller, drier pieces into two equal piles.

8. Place smaller chicken pieces in food processor and pulse until just coarsely chopped, three to four 1-second pulses, stirring chicken with rubber spatula after each pulse. Transfer chicken to sauce in saucepan. Using fingers or two forks, pull larger chicken pieces into long shreds and add to saucepan. Stir in remaining tablespoon cider vinegar; cover saucepan and heat chicken over medium-low heat, stirring occasionally, until heated through, about 10 minutes. Add hot sauce to taste and serve, passing remaining barbecue sauce separately.

TECHNIQUE | TRIMMING LEG QUARTERS

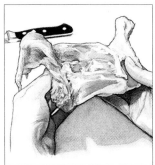 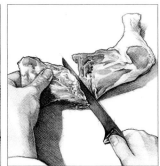 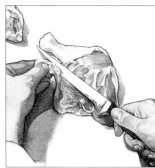

1. Carefully grasp leg and bend backbone section to pop joint.

2. Using a sharp boning knife, cut backbone section from leg.

3. Trim away any large pockets of fat.

BARBECUED PULLED CHICKEN FOR GAS GRILL

1. Soak 2 cups wood chips in water to cover for 30 minutes; drain. Place chips in small disposable aluminum pan; set pan on primary burner (burner that will remain on during barbecuing); position cooking grate. Ignite grill, turn all burners to high, cover, and heat until very hot and chips are smoking, about 15 minutes. (If chips ignite, use water-filled spray bottle to extinguish.) Scrape grate clean with grill brush. Turn off all burners except primary burner.

2. Follow step 3 of recipe for Barbecued Pulled Chicken for Charcoal Grill, placing chicken legs skin side up in single layer on cool side of grill. Proceed as directed, omitting wood chunks and extending cooking time in step 3 to 35 minutes and cooking time in step 4 to 45 minutes.

BARBECUED PULLED CHICKEN FOR A CROWD

This technique works well on a charcoal grill but not so well on a gas grill. If your gas grill is large and can accommodate more than 8 legs, follow the recipe at left, adding as many legs as will comfortably fit in a single layer. You may need to increase the cooking time.

Follow recipe for Barbecued Pulled Chicken for Charcoal Grill, igniting 6 quarts charcoal briquettes, using 12 chicken legs, and slotting them into V-shaped roasting rack set on top of cooking grate over disposable roasting pan (see page 13). Increase cooking time in step 3 to 45 minutes and cooking time in step 4 to 45 to 55 minutes. In step 6, remove only 1 cup of sauce from saucepan. In step 8, process chicken in food processor in 2 batches.

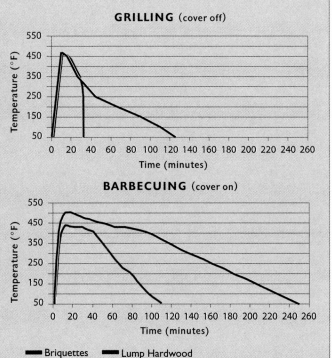

ILLUSTRATION: RANDY GLASS

Simple Fruit Salsas

Mushy and bland or just plain weird, most fruit salsas miss the mark. So how do you make a simple one with clear, refreshing flavor?

≥ BY MATTHEW CARD ≤

Salsa with crisp, sweet fruit offset by the tart, spicy kick of lime and chile is my favorite answer to the sultry heat of summer. But the bowlful of mushy fruit awash in watery slurry that restaurants often serve with grilled meat or fish doesn't come close to my ideal. After all, how hard can it be to throw together this tropical version of relish?

My search started on the Internet, where I found thousands of fruit salsas, each a little wilder than the last. Curry-Spiced Citrus? Balsamic Berry? Holiday Cranberry? Despite their differences, each included a basic trinity: fruit, acid, and onion. When tested, many of these recipes were unbalanced, overly harsh, or too saccharine. And most swamped the fruit with dissonant levels of competing flavors. The challenge was clear: Pick a fruit, let its flavor dominate, and support it with a judicious selection of flavorings.

The first step was to determine which fruits worked best as a foundation. Mango, pineapple, nectarine, and, surprisingly enough, melon, all readily absorbed other flavors without renouncing their own. Very ripe fruit was crucial to the salsa's flavor and texture; tasteless, crunchy fruit made for tasteless, crunchy salsa. Our test cooks preferred a tiny, tidy dice, as larger pieces created an unappealing salad-like consistency.

The second key ingredient was an acid, but vinegars tasted harsh. That is one reason most recipes call for lime juice, but a light hand was deemed best in this department. One tablespoon or less per cup of fruit—depending on the fruit—was all that was needed to boost each fruit's own tartness and tone down its sweetness.

The last item in the trinity, onion, appeared in most recipes, but tasters found that its harsh flavor quickly dominated. The more refined flavor and delicate texture of shallots proved a better match. I first sliced the shallots crosswise into thin rings for visual and textural contrast, but this made for too much shallot per bite. I switched to a fine mince so that it would vanish into the salsa's other ingredients as it softened in the lime and salt. As for garlic, slivered, minced, or even when pounded to a paste, it tasted out of place.

Things were going well, but perhaps the flavors were still a bit one-dimensional. Adding a second, complementary vegetable or fruit with a contrasting flavor and texture was the simple solution. Mango received a boost from crunchy red bell pepper; nectarine tasted sweeter mixed with a handful of crunchy raw corn kernels. Other ingredients were easily added to the mix, including most any fresh herb, a handful of toasted seeds, and pinches of sugar or spice.

As I made batch after batch of salsa, I noticed that they improved in flavor and consistency if allowed to sit for half an hour (15 minutes in a pinch). The salt and acid seemed to "cook" and mellow the ingredients, much as they do in ceviche. Clean tasting and quick to make, these recipes make the perfect summer condiment.

MANGO AND SWEET PEPPER SALSA WITH TOASTED PEPITAS
MAKES ABOUT 3 CUPS

Pepitas, or pumpkin seeds, are available in most supermarkets and natural foods stores. This salsa pairs well with pork, chicken, or firm white fish. See page 30 for tips on preparing the mango.

- 1 large ripe mango, peeled, flesh cut from pit into ¼-inch dice (1¾ to 2 cups)
- ½ large red bell pepper, cored, seeded, and cut into ¼-inch dice (about ½ cup)
- 1 small shallot, minced (about 2 tablespoons)
- 2–3 tablespoons juice from 1 to 2 limes
- 2 tablespoons chopped fresh cilantro leaves
  - Table salt
  - Cayenne
- ¼ cup unsalted pepitas, toasted in small skillet over medium heat until lightly browned, 3 to 5 minutes

In medium bowl, toss together mango, red bell pepper, shallot, 2 tablespoons lime juice, cilantro, ½ teaspoon salt, and ⅛ teaspoon cayenne; let stand at room temperature to blend flavors, 15 to 30 minutes. Adjust seasoning with additional lime juice, salt, and cayenne; stir in pepitas and serve.

PINEAPPLE AND CUCUMBER SALSA WITH MINT
MAKES ABOUT 3 CUPS

This salsa can be made spicier by mincing and adding the chile's seeds and ribs. It's a nice match with lamb, tuna, or salmon.

- ½ large pineapple, peeled, cored, and cut into ¼-inch dice (about 2 cups)
- ½ medium cucumber, peeled, seeded, and cut into ¼-inch dice (about 1 cup)
- 1 small shallot, minced (about 2 tablespoons)
- 1 medium serrano chile, seeds and ribs removed, then minced (about 2 teaspoons)
- 2 tablespoons chopped fresh mint leaves
- ½ teaspoon very finely grated ginger
- 1–2 tablespoons juice from 1 lime
  - Table salt
  - Sugar

In medium bowl, toss together pineapple, cucumber, shallot, chile, mint, ginger, 1 tablespoon lime juice, and ½ teaspoon salt; let stand at room temperature to blend flavors, 15 to 30 minutes. Adjust seasoning with additional lime juice and salt, and add sugar as needed if pineapple is tart; serve.

SPICY NECTARINE AND CORN SALSA
MAKES ABOUT 3 CUPS

It's a good idea to wear rubber gloves when working with spicy habanero chiles. This salsa is excellent with pork, chicken, shrimp, or scallops.

- 3 medium ripe nectarines, pitted and cut into ¼-inch dice (about 2½ cups)
- 1 ear fresh corn, husks and silk removed, and kernels cut from cob (about ⅔ cup)
- ½ small shallot, minced (about 1 tablespoon)
- 1 small habanero chile, seeds and ribs removed, then minced (about 1 teaspoon)
- 1–2 tablespoons juice from 1 lime
  - Table salt
  - Sugar
- 2 tablespoons chopped fresh chives

In medium bowl, toss together nectarines, corn, shallot, chile, 1 tablespoon lime juice, and ½ teaspoon salt; let stand at room temperature to blend flavors, 15 to 30 minutes. Adjust seasoning with additional lime juice and salt, and add sugar if nectarines are tart; stir in chives and serve.

COOK'S EXTRA gives you free recipes online. For our Honeydew Peach Salsa recipe, visit www.cooksillustrated.com and key in code 7052. This recipe will be available until August 31, 2005.

A Guide to Essential Cookware

To outfit your kitchen without breaking the bank, invest in cookware that is durable and versatile. Here's our master list of what to buy and why. BY SEAN LAWLER

In any cluttered kitchen (ours included), there are pots and pans that gather dust and others that rarely get put away. After a decade of careful testing, we've identified the true multitaskers, the "must-have" pots and pans that we reach for time and again. We think every cook should own these eight pieces of cookware.

THE BEST OF BOTH WORLDS:
Constructing "Clad" Cookware
Few pans on the market today are made from a single material. Manufacturers are constantly inventing new ways to bond materials together to take advantage of their different properties. "Clad" cookware comes in two varieties. "Fully clad" pieces have a complete core of conductive material (aluminum or copper) that extends up the sides of the pan. In a "disk-bottom" pan, the core is a conductive disk of aluminum added to the bottom exterior of the pan. Our tests have shown that disk-bottom pans often perform just as well as fully clad pans: With some exceptions, the thickness of the core is more important than whether or not it covers the sides of the pan.

TRADITIONAL SKILLET
ALTERNATE NAMES: Frypan, Omelet Pan

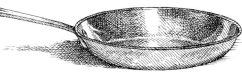

What We Use It For: This is the pan we reach for when pan-searing steaks, chops, and cutlets and when pan-roasting chicken parts. The traditional (that is, not nonstick) finish develops *fond*—the crusty, brown bits that collect on the pan bottom and are deglazed to make pan sauces.

Why We Like It: The flared, shallow sides encourage the rapid evaporation of moisture, so pan sauces reduce quickly and foods sear rather than steam.

TEST KITCHEN TIPS:
➤ Consider weight carefully. The pan should be heavy enough to retain heat, but it also needs to be easily maneuverable (even when loaded with 3 pounds of chicken parts).
➤ Look for a comfortable handle that can safely go under the broiler.
➤ A 12-inch diameter (measured across the top) is the best choice to accommodate four large chops or a whole, cut-up chicken.

And the Winner Is . . .
★ **ALL-CLAD** Stainless 12-Inch Frypan, $125
★ **BEST BUY: WOLFGANG PUCK** Bistro 12-Inch Open Omelet Pan, $30

NONSTICK SKILLET
ALTERNATE NAMES: Frypan, Omelet Pan

What We Use It For: This is our favorite pan for searing delicate items that have a tendency to stick or break apart, such as fish fillets. We also favor it for stir-fries, pancakes, omelets, and other egg dishes.

Why We Like It: The nonstick finish means no *fond* for pan sauces, but the foods themselves still get nicely browned provided the pan is large enough to avoid overcrowding. The flared sides allow for the quick redistribution of food by jerking and sliding the pan over the burner. Easy cleanup, of course.

TEST KITCHEN TIPS:
➤ Nonstick bonding technology has improved by leaps and bounds, meaning that it's worth investing in a nonstick skillet with a thick base that distributes heat evenly.
➤ A 12-inch nonstick skillet can handle a batch of fish fillets or a stir-fry serving four. Smaller nonstick skillets (8 or 10 inches) are a good choice for omelets and snacks like quesadillas or grilled-cheese sandwiches.

And the Winner Is . . .
★ **ALL-CLAD** Stainless Nonstick 12-Inch Frypan, $125
★ **BEST BUY: WOLFGANG PUCK** Bistro 12-Inch Nonstick Omelet Pan, $35

Traditional versus Nonstick
There are advantages to both traditional and nonstick pans. The latter are easy to clean and require very little cooking fat, while traditional surfaces excel at developing *fond*, those crusty, stuck-on bits of food that add deep flavor and color to pan sauces. In the test kitchen, we reach for a nonstick pan when cooking delicate foods that are prone to sticking, such as eggs, seafood, and stir-fries. For searing steaks, chops, or chicken or making any other recipe that favors browning over frequent stirring, we prefer a traditional pan, preferably one with a light-colored interior finish that makes it easy to watch for signs of burnt drippings.

CAST-IRON SKILLET
ALTERNATE NAME: Frypan

What We Use It For: Cast iron is just the thing for searing or blackening food quickly over very high heat. When we're after a really dark, even crust on steaks, chops, or even cornbread, there's nothing better.

Why We Like It: In our lineup of winning pans, this is the placekicker. We may not use it every day, but it's almost essential to have on hand when the right recipe comes along. Why? For the simple reason that no other metal in the cookware arena retains heat as well as cast iron. With its slow response time and tremendous heft, this pan is the wrong choice for delicate sauté work, but it's dirt cheap and will outlast any other pan.

TEST KITCHEN TIPS:
➤ This pan's tiny, scorching-hot handle tells you something: It's not designed to be moved around while in use. So heavier is better, within reason.
➤ Look for a pouring lip for easier disposal of used oil.
➤ A 12-inch skillet is the best all-purpose size.

And the Winner Is . . .
★ **LODGE** 12-Inch Skillet, $20

SAUTÉ PAN
ALTERNATE NAME: None

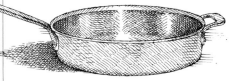

What We Use It For: A good choice for pan-frying. Also good for dishes in which you want to brown meat and vegetables and then add liquid, such as smothered chops, fricassees, and meaty pasta sauces.

Why We Like It: With its high, straight sides, this pan has a greater capacity for liquid than a skillet and a slightly wider cooking surface. Does well in the oven, too.

TEST KITCHEN TIPS:
➤ Handles should be long, comfortable, and ovensafe, and they should stay cool on the stovetop—some phenolic (heat-resistant plastic) handles are oven-worthy only to about 350 degrees.
➤ A 3-quart pan, 10 to 11 inches in diameter, is best.

And the Winner Is . . .
★ **ALL-CLAD** Stainless 3-Quart Covered Sauté Pan, $195

SAUCEPAN

ALTERNATE NAME: None

What We Use It For: Rice, sauces, vegetables, gravy, pastry cream, and poached fruit, to list just a few.

Why We Like It: Just the right size and shape for a thousand and one common kitchen tasks. A true work-horse: It's easy to maneuver and stays out of your way on a crowded cooktop.

TEST KITCHEN TIPS:

➤ A comfortable, stay-cool handle is a must, and the handle should also be long enough for two-handed carrying when the pan is full.

➤ Larger saucepans should be able to handle some sauté work, so good heat conduction is a must.

➤ Every kitchen should be equipped with a large saucepan with a capacity of 3 to 4 quarts.

➤ Consider a nonstick finish when choosing smaller saucepans, which are useful for cooking oatmeal and reheating leftovers.

And the Winner Is . . .

★ **ALL-CLAD** 3-Quart Stainless Saucepan, $150

★ **BEST BUY: SITRAM** Profiserie 3.3-Quart Sauce Pan, $50

SAUCIER

ALTERNATE NAMES: Chef's Pan, Reduction Saucepan

What We Use It For: Does anything a saucepan can do—and does a few things better. A good choice for sauces, risotto, pastry cream, or anything else that requires constant attention and frequent stirring.

Why We Like It: A saucier's wide mouth and rounded, flared sides easily accommodate whisks and spatulas and eliminate tight corners where food can stick and burn.

TEST KITCHEN TIPS:

➤ We like the wider, shallower pans in this category for easy access and visibility. A saucier should be weighty enough to distribute heat evenly yet still be maneuverable. Its bottom should be wide enough to cover the burner and prevent excess heat from wafting up the sides.

➤ Also look for a stay-cool handle that's long enough to keep hands clear of heat during constant stirring.

➤ Avoid "disk-bottom" sauciers, which are prone to burning.

And the Winner Is . . .

★ **ALL-CLAD** Stainless 3-Quart Saucier, $145

What about a Stockpot?

Just about the only thing we don't use our Dutch oven for is boiling water for pasta, corn on the cob, or the occasional lobster. Our favorite enameled cast-iron pot is a bit slow in bringing water to a boil and simply too heavy to carry over to the sink and drain. For these tasks, we employ an inexpensive stockpot, the sort you can find at your local hardware store for about $30. When it comes to actually making stock, which often involves browning meat and sweating vegetables, we reach for the Dutch oven instead.

DUTCH OVEN

ALTERNATE NAMES: French Oven, Casserole

What We Use It For: Our choice for soups and stocks, a Dutch oven is also ideal for frying, stewing, and braising.

Why We Like It: Built for both oven and stovetop use, a Dutch oven is generally wider and shallower than a conventional stockpot. This makes it accessible (that is, easy to reach and see into) and provides a wider surface area for browning (at least a 2:1 ratio of diameter to height is ideal). Its tremendous heft translates into plenty of heat retention, which is perfect for keeping frying oil hot or maintaining a very low simmer.

TEST KITCHEN TIPS:

➤ Looping handles should be extremely sturdy and wide enough to grab with thick oven mitts.

➤ Lids should be tight fitting and heavy enough not to clatter when the pot contents are simmering below.

➤ We find the most useful sizes to be 6 to 8 quarts.

And the Winner Is . . .

★ **LE CREUSET** 7¼-Quart Round French Oven, $215

ROASTING PAN

ALTERNATE NAME: Roaster

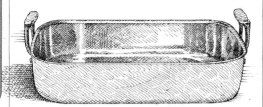

What We Use It For: As its name suggests, this pan is for roasting, especially poultry and other large cuts of meat. It can also be used to deglaze drippings for gravies and sauces on the stovetop.

Why We Like It: This pan's low sides and open design provide roasts with maximum exposure to the oven's hot air for even browning. (High-sided covered roasters cook faster and hotter but cause meat to steam and inhibit browning.) Deglazing is the key to great sauces and gravies, so if it's not flameproof, forget it.

TEST KITCHEN TIPS:

➤ A roaster should be heavy enough to handle large birds and roasts without buckling but not so heavy as to be backbreaking.

➤ Look for handles that are sturdy, upright (not perpendicular to the sides), and large enough to accommodate thick oven mitts.

➤ A light-colored interior finish makes it easier to spot burning drippings.

➤ Oval-shaped models may not accommodate roasting racks.

➤ Measure your oven before shopping for a roasting pan; it should fit with about 2 inches of clearance on all sides. Most of the large roasters we tested were between 16 and 18 inches long and would hold a turkey weighing up to 25 pounds.

And the Winner Is . . .

★ **CALPHALON** Contemporary Stainless Steel Roasting Pan, $100

METAL SHOP: **The Big Four**

COPPER conducts heat extremely well, but it is also expensive and heavy, tarnishes easily, and is reactive, leaching into many foods to produce off colors and flavors. For this reason, it is almost always lined with tin or stainless steel. **Not worth the expense.**

ALUMINUM is second to copper in conductivity among the metals used for cookware, but it is also light and inexpensive and retains heat well, provided it is of sufficient thickness. But aluminum is also reactive, and the soft metal dents and scratches easily. To compensate for these drawbacks, manufacturers have developed anodized aluminum cookware, in which the pans undergo electrolytic processing that makes the outer surface both harder and less reactive. The dark color of anodized aluminum can make it tricky to monitor the development of *fond* for pan sauces. **Unless anodized, best used in combination with other metals.**

CAST IRON heats up slowly but retains heat very well. Cast iron is inexpensive and lasts a lifetime (or several!), but it is very heavy, is mildly reactive, and must be seasoned before use. Enameled cast iron is nonreactive and need not be seasoned, but the exterior can chip and scratch. **Useful in limited applications.**

STAINLESS STEEL is a poor heat conductor. Inexpensive cookware made entirely of thin-gauge stainless steel is prone to hot spots and warping over high heat. Stainless steel is, however, nonreactive, durable, and attractive, making it an excellent choice for coating, or "cladding," aluminum or copper. **Great with other metals.**

Thai Chile Beef at Home

This dish offers an exotic change of pace from Chinese stir-fries. But who has shrimp paste, tamarind pulp, galangal, and palm sugar, plus three hours to make dinner?

≥ BY REBECCA HAYS ≤

Based on a sophisticated combination of four flavors—spicy, sweet, sour, and salty—Thai chile beef promises to be vastly more interesting than most everyday stir-fries. According to my recipe research, this simple transformation would be built on a foundation of just four ingredients: chiles, sugar, lime juice, and fish sauce.

I set out with high hopes, rounding up and testing cookbook recipes and even ordering Thai chile beef from three neighborhood restaurants. The net result of all this tasting and testing, however, was disappointment—with one notable exception. One "authentic" Thai recipe produced a wonderful dish. It contained no vegetables (restaurants frequently add vegetables to reduce the cost per serving), and the meat was sauced in a thick, complex, well-balanced chile jam. The problem? For starters, the ingredient list, which contained dried prawns, shrimp paste, tamarind pulp, galangal, and palm sugar. And then there was the three-hour prep time, which involved deep-frying many of the ingredients separately. While I had tasted the ultimate Thai chile beef, I had to wonder how I could possibly re-create it for an American home kitchen.

An Exceptional Cut

I started with the key ingredient: the beef. I stir-fried four easy-to-find cuts (filet, sirloin steak, strip steak, and blade steak) and compared them with our usual choice, flank steak.

The flank steak fared well, as expected. Mild filet, the choice in several recipes, could not stand up to the assertive Thai flavors. Sirloin and strip steaks both fared poorly because stir-fried meats tend to end up thoroughly cooked, making these cuts chewy and dry. The cheapest cut of all, the blade steak, was the surprise winner of the tasting. Generally, beef with the biggest flavor is tough, but blade steak is an exception. Cut from the chuck—the forequarter of the animal—this inexpensive, well-marbled cut delivered more than enough flavor to stand up to its spicy competition yet was more tender than flank steak when thoroughly cooked.

Peanuts, fresh mint, and fresh cilantro give this stir-fry a last-minute blast of flavor.

'Tis the Seasoning

Here in the test kitchen, we marinate beef for Chinese stir-fries in soy sauce, a practice that seasons and tenderizes the meat. For this recipe, salty soy sauce would be replaced with the salty, fermented fish sauce that is traditional in Thai chile beef. The fish sauce simulated the briny flavors of the dried shrimp and shrimp paste listed in the original recipe, but something was missing. I dug deeper into a few Thai cookbooks and discovered that white pepper is a key ingredient—and for good reason. It is deeply spicy and penetrating, with a somewhat gamey flavor. I added a smidgen (a little goes a long way) to the marinade, along with citrusy coriander. This was a huge hit with tasters and substantially boosted the complexity and sophistication of the dish, even though the meat was marinated for a mere 15 minutes. (White pepper has such a distinct flavor that it's worth purchasing some just for this recipe. See page 30 for more information.)

I also added some of the sweet element in this dish to the marinade as a strategy for developing extra caramelization on the beef. Palm sugar is the traditional sweetener used in Thai cooking, but I found light brown sugar to be a perfect substitute. A mere teaspoon was just the right amount; any more caused scorching.

Too Hot to Handle

Tiny, narrow Thai bird chiles are the classic choice for this recipe, but I'm not about to hunt down exotic peppers for a Wednesday-night stir-fry. A taste test suggested that moderately hot serranos or milder jalapeños are the best stand-ins. (Insanely hot habanero chiles, tasting of tropical fruit, were admired by some but panned by most, who found the heat level punishing.)

After settling on the chiles, a new problem emerged: wild inconsistency in heat levels. Using a constant number of jalapeños, some stir-fries were flaming hot, while others didn't even send up sparks (see "Sizing Up Chile Heat," page 19). I came up with a straightforward solution that can be used in any recipe calling for chiles. The trick is to use not one but two sources of heat, one of which is easily controlled (unlike fresh chiles). I tested cayenne and hot red pepper flakes, and both produced likeable results, but the winner was Asian chili-garlic paste, which provided a complex mix of flavors—spicy, toasty, and garlicky.

The Best Cut for Thai Chile Beef

BLADE STEAK

We tested five cuts of beef—blade steak, filet, strip steak, sirloin steak, and flank steak—for this stir-fry. Blade steak was the clear winner, flank steak the runner-up. Tasters liked blade steak for its generous fat marbling, which gives this cut its tenderness and its "very beefy flavor." At just $3.69 per pound, blade steak was also the cheapest option tested. One minor inconvenience: The line of gristle running down the center should be removed (see page 19).

The last step in a stir-fry is to deglaze the hot pan with sauce ingredients. After many trials, I realized the importance of reintroducing every member of the Thai quartet at this stage. Adding fish sauce and brown sugar to the marinade boosted flavor, but the inclusion of both in the sauce really punched up the finished dish. For the sour component, both rice vinegar and tamarind paste fared better than lime juice—less acidity and more sweetness brought me closer to my goal of balanced flavors. I settled on rice vinegar because I usually keep it in my pantry.

The only remaining considerations were the fresh, raw ingredients added just before serving. Thai basil is traditional, contributing freshness and adding a cooling counterpoint to the chiles. Unfortunately, this herb can be hard to find (it was often out of stock at a large Asian supermarket here in Boston), so I made a substitution that I've used successfully in other recipes: fresh mint and cilantro. Used in tandem, they carry a complexity similar to that of Thai basil. The sweet basil that's readily available in most supermarkets is not a good substitute; Thai basil is tangier and spicier. I also added chopped peanuts for crunch. A fresh squirt of lime juice at the table was the final touch.

STIR-FRIED THAI-STYLE BEEF WITH CHILES AND SHALLOTS
SERVES 4 WITH RICE

If you cannot find blade steaks, use flank steak; because flank steak requires less trimming, you will need only about 1¾ pounds. To cut a flank steak into the proper-sized slices for stir-frying, first cut the steak with the grain into 1½-inch strips, then cut the strips against the grain into ¼-inch-thick slices. White pepper lends this stir-fry a unique flavor; black pepper is not a good substitute. Serve the stir-fry with steamed jasmine rice.

1. Halve each steak lengthwise, leaving gristle on one half.

2. Cut away gristle from half to which it is still attached.

3. Slice meat on angle into ¼-inch-thick strips.

Beef and Marinade

¾	teaspoon ground coriander
⅛	teaspoon ground white pepper
1	teaspoon light brown sugar
1	tablespoon fish sauce
2	pounds blade steaks, trimmed and cut into ¼-inch-thick strips (see illustrations, above)

Stir-Fry

2	tablespoons fish sauce
2	tablespoons rice vinegar
2	tablespoons water
1	tablespoon light brown sugar
1	tablespoon Asian chili-garlic paste
3	medium garlic cloves, minced or pressed through garlic press (1 tablespoon)
3	tablespoons vegetable oil
3	serrano or jalapeño chiles, halved, seeds and ribs removed, chiles cut crosswise ⅛ inch thick
3	medium shallots, trimmed of ends, peeled, quartered lengthwise, and layers separated
½	cup fresh mint leaves, large leaves torn into bite-sized pieces
½	cup fresh cilantro leaves
⅓	cup roughly chopped roasted unsalted peanuts Lime wedges for serving

1. **FOR THE BEEF AND MARINADE:** Combine coriander, white pepper, brown sugar, and fish sauce in large bowl. Add beef, toss well to combine; marinate 15 minutes.

2. **FOR THE STIR-FRY:** In small bowl, stir together fish sauce, vinegar, water, brown sugar, and chili-garlic paste until sugar dissolves; set aside. In small bowl, mix garlic with 1 teaspoon oil; set aside. Heat 2 teaspoons oil in 12-inch nonstick skillet over high heat until smoking; add one-third of beef to skillet in even layer. Cook, without stirring, until well browned, about 2 minutes, then stir and continue cooking until beef is browned around edges and no longer pink in the center, about 30 seconds. Transfer beef to medium bowl. Repeat with additional oil and remaining meat in 2 more batches.

3. After transferring last batch of beef to bowl, reduce heat to medium; add remaining 2 teaspoons oil to now-empty skillet and swirl to coat. Add chiles and shallots and cook, stirring frequently, until beginning to soften, 3 to 4 minutes. Push chile-shallot mixture to sides of skillet to clear center; add garlic to clearing and cook, mashing mixture with spoon, until fragrant, about 15 seconds. Stir to combine garlic with chile-shallot mixture. Add fish sauce mixture to skillet; increase heat to high and cook until slightly reduced and thickened, about 30 seconds. Return beef and any accumulated juices to skillet, toss well to combine and coat with sauce, stir in half of mint and cilantro; serve immediately, sprinkling individual servings with portion of peanuts and remaining herbs, and passing lime wedges separately.

Asian Chili-Garlic Paste

Made with a mix of dried red chiles, garlic, vinegar, salt, and sometimes sugar, this complex condiment is moderately spicy and slightly acidic. Once opened, jars of chili-garlic paste (also called *sriracha*) can be refrigerated for several months.

SCIENCE: Sizing Up Chile Heat

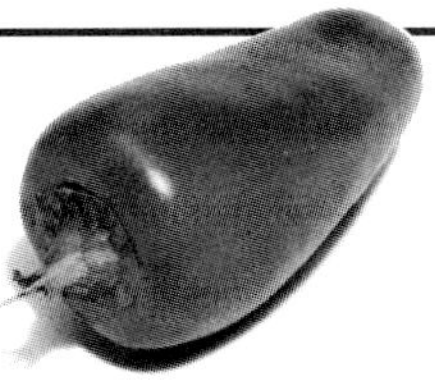

In the test kitchen, we've noticed that some jalapeños are searingly hot, while others are mild as bell peppers. We tracked down a number of theories to explain this great variation—and size kept popping up. According to this theory, a small chile will be hotter than a larger one.

But when we arranged a tasting of jalapeños of various sizes, there seemed to be no correlation between size and heat. To investigate the matter further, we sent five similarly sized jalapeños to the lab, requesting levels of capsaicin and dihydrocapsaicin (the compounds responsible for the majority of the perception of "heat"). Sure enough, some chiles were nearly 10 times hotter than others—even though they all looked alike.

One burning question remained: Are there any visual indicators of pungency? No, says Danise Coon of the Chile Pepper Institute, who explained that capsaicin production is tied to the environment. Chiles grown in sunny, arid weather undergo a lot of stress, and stressed chiles produce more capsaicin than chiles grown in temperate climates. (Hot, dry New Mexico is known for producing very hot chiles.)

Until someone comes up with a procedure for diagnosing stressed-out chiles, then, the only surefire way to judge the heat level of a chile is to taste it. If you want more control over the heat when you're cooking with chiles, start with an easy-to-measure heat source such as cayenne, red pepper flakes, or chili-garlic paste, then layer on modest amounts of fresh chiles, removing the ribs and seeds if you want less heat. –R.H.

CHILE ROULETTE
Do small chiles pack more punch?

Veggie Burgers Worth the Trouble

Store-bought veggie burgers border on inedible, but most homemade renditions are a lot of work. Could we develop a recipe that was really worth the effort?

≥ BY SARAH WILSON ≤

When a vegetarian friend was coming to visit one weekend, I knew that my barbecue menu needed a meat-free offering, and veggie burgers immediately came to mind. Store-bought veggie burgers are terrible (see page 21), so I knew I would have to make my own. Unfortunately, homemade veggie burgers are much more work than their beefy brethren. Truthfully, veggie burgers are a labor of love, so they'd better taste great.

My first step was to make a bunch of burgers, guided by a variety of vegetarian cookbooks. What I learned after making a dozen or so was pretty clear. No veggie burger was going to taste like a hamburger—a foolish goal, I decided. But tasters wanted these burgers to "act" like hamburgers. They wanted a patty with a modicum of chew, a combination of savory ingredients that did not taste specifically of any one thing (nobody wanted a "black bean burger," for example), and the ability to go from grill to bun without falling apart.

From TVP to Umami

Many veggie burgers start with soy-based products to boost the protein content and achieve a meaty texture. It didn't take long, however, for the meat substitutes I tested to disappoint, even when used as only one of several ingredients. Textured vegetable protein, or TVP, has the appearance and texture of ground beef but little flavor of its own. It produced bland burgers. I also tried tempeh, a soybean cake made by fermenting cooked soybeans. Although tempeh has a rich, meaty texture, its sour flavor made for awful burgers. I also tried seitan, a wheat gluten product, resulting in overly soft patties that tasters described as "gummy" and "fishy." Not quite what I had in mind.

Next on my list were legumes. During my first round of recipe testing, tasters had rated lentil burgers best in terms of flavor but not texture; they were soggy and hard to grill. To get rid of some of this moisture, I drained the cooked lentils thoroughly in a sieve and then laid them out on a thick layer of paper towels. As many recipes for veggie burgers pair legumes with a grain,

Lentils, bulgur, mushrooms, and cashews are key ingredients in a grill-worthy veggie burger.

I decided to follow suit. Rice was too soft and pasty, whereas barley was too hard. The grains of bulgur wheat, however, were small enough to incorporate easily into the mix and married well with the lentils in terms of flavor.

With a base of lentils and bulgur, it was time to turn to vegetables. Sautéed onions, garlic, celery, and leeks proved the best choices, delivering depth of flavor without being overwhelming.

So far so good, but tasters kept telling me that the burgers needed some "meat." Certain foods, such as mushrooms, nuts, and seaweed, are rich in the taste sensation called *umami*, which, though roughly translated from the Japanese as "delicious," actually imparts a flavor that taste experts refer to as "meaty." Not ready to take someone else's word for it, I tried cremini mushrooms and cashews and found that they did provide the meaty flavor everyone had been looking for.

(Seaweed proved unnecessary.) Because uncooked mushrooms are more than 80 percent water, I had to be sure to cook them thoroughly.

From Soggy to Toothsome

Pulsing everything together in the food processor made for a more cohesive and even-textured mix, but the burgers still didn't hold together as well as I wanted. I tried various binders, including sour cream, cheese, egg, and mayonnaise, and finally settled on the latter. It provided the necessary fat and binding qualities along with good flavor.

To soak up excess moisture, I tried adding flour and bread crumbs. Flour made the burgers taste pasty. Plain bread crumbs worked reasonably well, but some tasters complained that these "heavy" burgers reminded them of meatloaf. The solution was to reduce the amount of bread crumbs and to use panko, Japanese bread crumbs that are especially flaky, light, and crunchy. While they did not remain crunchy in the veggie burger mix for long, they did absorb residual moisture and remained virtually undetectable in terms of flavor.

Because the ingredients in these veggie burgers are already cooked, my goal was to achieve a golden crust while just heating them through. A clean, well-oiled grill and plenty of heat did the trick. Paired with buns and all the fixin's, this labor of love was much appreciated not only by my vegetarian friend but by the meat eaters at my barbecue as well.

Getting the Texture Right

For a consistent, cohesive texture that makes veggie burgers easier to form and that's similar to the texture of hamburgers when cooked, pulse the burger ingredients in a food processor.

Secrets to Better Veggie Burgers

Removing moisture from ingredients ensures firmer patties.

1. Spread lentils between layers of paper towels and blot dry.

2. Once softened, drain bulgur in sieve and press with spatula.

3. Sauté mushrooms and vegetables until caramelized and dry.

ULTIMATE VEGGIE BURGERS
MAKES TWELVE 4-INCH BURGERS

Canned lentils can be used, though some flavor will be sacrificed. Use a 15-ounce can, drain the lentils in a mesh strainer, and thoroughly rinse under cold running water before spreading them on paper towels and drying them, as directed in step 1 below. If you cannot find panko, use 1 cup of plain bread crumbs. For tips on freezing uncooked patties, see page 30.

¾	cup dried brown lentils, rinsed and picked over
2½	teaspoons table salt
¾	cup bulgur wheat
2	tablespoons vegetable oil
2	medium onions, chopped fine (2 cups)
1	large celery rib, chopped fine (about ½ cup)
1	small leek, white and light green parts only, chopped fine (about ½ cup)
2	medium garlic cloves, minced or pressed through garlic press (2 teaspoons)
1	pound cremini or white mushrooms, cleaned and sliced about ¼ inch thick (about 6½ cups)
1	cup raw unsalted cashews
⅓	cup mayonnaise
2	cups panko (Japanese bread crumbs)
	Ground black pepper
12	burger buns for serving

1. Bring 3 cups water, lentils, and 1 teaspoon salt to boil in medium saucepan over high heat; reduce heat to medium-low and simmer, uncovered, stirring occasionally, until lentils are just beginning to fall apart, about 25 minutes. Drain in fine-mesh strainer. Line baking sheet with triple layer paper towels and spread drained lentils over. Gently pat lentils dry with additional paper towels; cool lentils to room temperature.

2. While lentils simmer, bring 2 cups water and ½ teaspoon salt to boil in small saucepan. Stir bulgur wheat into boiling water and cover immediately; let stand off heat until water is absorbed, 15 to 20 minutes. Drain in fine-mesh strainer; use rubber spatula to press out excess moisture. Transfer bulgur to medium bowl and set aside.

3. Heat 1 tablespoon oil in 12-inch nonstick skillet over medium-high heat until shimmering. Add onions, celery, leek, and garlic; cook, stirring occasionally, until vegetables begin to brown, about 10 minutes. Spread vegetable mixture on second baking sheet to cool; set aside. Add remaining 1 tablespoon oil to now-empty skillet; heat over high heat until shimmering. Add mushrooms and cook, stirring occasionally, until golden brown, about 12 minutes. Spread mushrooms on baking sheet with vegetable mixture; cool to room temperature, about 20 minutes.

4. Process cashews in food processor until finely chopped, about fifteen 1-second pulses (do not wash food processor blade or bowl); stir into bowl with bulgur along with cooled lentils, vegetable-mushroom mixture, and mayonnaise. Transfer half of mixture to now-empty food processor and pulse until coarsely chopped, fifteen to twenty 1-second pulses; mixture should be cohesive but roughly textured (see photo on page 20). Transfer processed mixture to large bowl; repeat with remaining unprocessed mixture and combine with first batch. Stir in panko, 1 teaspoon salt, and pepper to taste. Line baking sheet with paper towels. Divide mixture into 12 portions, about ½ cup each, shaping each into tightly packed patty, 4 inches in diameter and ½ inch thick; set patties on baking sheet; paper towels will absorb excess moisture. (Patties can be covered with plastic wrap and refrigerated up to 3 days.)

TO COOK ON THE GRILL: Build medium-hot charcoal fire or preheat gas grill on high. Using tongs, wipe grate with wad of paper towels dipped lightly in vegetable oil. Grill burgers, without moving them, until well browned, about 5 minutes; flip burgers and continue cooking until well browned on second side, about 5 minutes. Serve.

TO COOK ON THE STOVETOP: Heat 2 tablespoons vegetable oil in 12-inch nonstick skillet over medium-high heat until shimmering; cook burgers, 4 at a time, until well browned, about 4 minutes per side, lowering heat to medium if browning too quickly. Repeat with additional oil and burgers. Serve. (Cooked burgers can be kept warm in 250-degree oven for up to 30 minutes.)

Improving Blueberry Buckle

How can a simple yellow cake batter support an entire quart of blueberries without turning heavy and soggy? Think cookie dough.

≥ BY DAWN YANAGIHARA ≤

Just what is a blueberry buckle? It's an American classic, in case you've forgotten or never really knew: a streusel-topped blueberry coffee cake. To call it a mere coffee cake, however, is to sell it short. The substance of a blueberry buckle is the blueberry, not the cake. This rustic confection starts with blueberries held together in a buttery cake batter and is then topped with a crisp, sugary streusel. And the name? The cake, burdened as it is with fruit and topping, is said to buckle on the surface as it bakes.

I collected a score of recipes and baked off six. They were a ragtag collection of cakes, running the gamut from dense and greasy to lean and dry. Oh, and don't forget bland. The problem? The overwhelming berry-to-cake ratio threw things out of whack. The moisture released from the berries during baking often added a disagreeable sogginess and density.

Buckle Down

I cobbled together a working recipe made in the manner of a cake or cookie: The butter and sugar were creamed, the eggs beaten in, the flour added, the blueberries folded in. A melted butter variation had a less fulsome rise, the result of lack of aeration, which provides lift.

Determining the amount of blueberries seemed paramount—recipes ranged from 1½ cups to as many as 5 cups. According to tasters, even 2 cups weren't enough, giving the cake, berries, and streusel equal billing. Three cups? Better. Four? Bingo. The blueberries were the headliner; the cake and streusel were the supporting cast.

Next was the problem of the soggy cake. I hunted for a solution, starting with the type of flour. Buckles made with cake flour (which is low in protein) were structureless, pasty, and sodden. An all-purpose flour buckle was drier and cakier, and its sturdier texture could contend with all the fruit; this buckle was far superior.

A buckle is a yellow cake loaded with berries and crowned with crisp and crumbly streusel.

Dairy—milk or sour cream—often appears in buckle recipes and is almost always used in regular cakes and muffins. But a buckle has to be stiff to hold up all those berries, and milk and sour cream loosen up the mixture so much that the berries sink during baking. Evidently, the batter for a buckle should be more like a cookie dough: You need structure and plenty of it to deal with a full quart of moist berries plus a streusel topping.

Sugar was a simple matter. Only a modest amount was needed to sweeten the cake and counter the tartness of the berries: ⅔ cup. (This was, after all, a coffee cake, not dessert.)

Air incorporated into the batter by creaming the butter and sugar provided some leavening. But the heavy batter required the assistance of baking powder—1½ teaspoons—for a nice lift and texture.

The final additions were salt and vanilla and a little grated lemon zest to freshen up the flavors. The best oven temperature was 350 degrees; the cake baked through and the streusel browned perfectly in about 55 minutes.

Buckle Up

The streusel formula consisted of flour, sugar, butter, and a pinch of salt. One-half cup of flour moistened with 4 tablespoons butter topped the cake generously. More flour made the topping powdery and dry, while more butter made it greasy and insubstantial.

With all light brown sugar (dark brown made the streusel too dark and bitter), the streusel had an overly assertive molasses flavor; with all granulated sugar, it lacked character. The solution was a mix of light brown (½ cup) and granulated (2 tablespoons). A hint of cinnamon lent fragrance and warm flavor. I had been using melted butter to make the streusel, but when I attempted a softened butter version, I struck upon a superior streusel. It was crisp and crumbly, not hard and pebbly.

The Buckle Family

Buckle is one of many classic American fruit desserts with a funny name. Here are some other close relations.

BETTY
Fruit layered with buttered bread.

CRISP
Fruit sprinkled with streusel.

COBBLER
Fruit topped with tender biscuits.

Secrets to a Better Buckle

STIFF BATTER must be spread into pan with rubber spatula.

CHUNKY STREUSEL must be squeezed into pea-sized pieces.

So there it was. A cake that was a cookie dough in disguise, strong enough to support a full quart of blueberries. In fact, this buckle didn't really buckle during baking; it could hold its own. Now do we have to change its name?

BLUEBERRY BUCKLE
MAKES ONE 9-INCH CAKE, SERVING 8 TO 10

The batter will be extremely thick and heavy, and some effort will be required to spread it into the prepared pan. This buckle is best made with fresh blueberries, not frozen ones, which are too moist. If you'd like to serve the buckle as dessert, consider a vanilla ice cream or whipped cream accompaniment. Leftovers can be wrapped in plastic and stored at room temperature for up to 2 days.

Streusel
- 1/2 cup (2 1/2 ounces) unbleached all-purpose flour
- 1/2 cup (3 1/2 ounces) packed light brown sugar
- 2 tablespoons granulated sugar
- 1/4 teaspoon ground cinnamon
  Pinch table salt
- 4 tablespoons (1/2 stick) unsalted butter, cut into 8 pieces, softened but still cool

Cake
- 1 1/2 cups (7 1/2 ounces) unbleached all-purpose flour
- 1 1/2 teaspoons baking powder
- 10 tablespoons (1 1/4 sticks) unsalted butter, softened but still cool
- 2/3 cup (about 4 3/4 ounces) granulated sugar
- 1/2 teaspoon table salt
- 1/2 teaspoon grated zest from 1 lemon
- 1 1/2 teaspoons vanilla extract
- 2 large eggs, room temperature
- 4 cups (about 20 ounces) fresh blueberries, picked over

1. **FOR THE STREUSEL:** In standing mixer fitted with flat beater, combine flour, sugars, cinnamon, and salt on low speed until well combined and no large brown sugar lumps remain, about 45 seconds. Add butter and mix on low until mixture resembles wet sand and no large butter pieces remain, about 2½ minutes. Transfer streusel to small bowl and set aside.

2. **FOR THE CAKE:** Adjust oven rack to lower-middle position; heat oven to 350 degrees. Spray 9-inch round cake pan with 2-inch sides with nonstick cooking spray, line bottom with parchment or waxed paper round, and spray parchment; dust pan with flour and knock out excess.

3. Whisk flour and baking powder in small bowl to combine; set aside. In standing mixer fitted with flat beater, cream butter, sugar, salt, and lemon zest at medium-high speed until light and fluffy, about 3 minutes; using rubber spatula, scrape down bowl. Beat in vanilla until combined, about 30 seconds. With mixer running at medium speed, add eggs one at a time; beat until partially incorporated, then scrape down bowl and continue to beat until fully incorporated (mixture will appear broken). With mixer running on low speed, gradually add flour mixture; beat until flour is almost fully incorporated, about 20 seconds. Disengage bowl from mixer; stir batter with rubber spatula, scraping bottom and sides of bowl, until no flour pockets remain and batter is homogenous; batter will be very heavy and thick. Using rubber spatula, gently fold in blueberries until evenly distributed.

4. Transfer batter to prepared pan; using rubber spatula in a pushing motion, spread batter evenly to pan edges and smooth surface (see photo, above). Squeeze portion of streusel in hand to form large cohesive clump; break up clump with fingers and sprinkle streusel evenly over batter (see photo, above). Repeat with remaining streusel. Bake until deep golden brown and toothpick or wooden skewer inserted into center of cake comes out clean, about 55 minutes. Cool on wire rack 15 to 20 minutes (cake will fall slightly as it cools).

5. Run paring knife around sides of cake to loosen. Place upside-down plate (do not use serving platter) on top of cake pan; invert cake to remove from pan, lift off cake pan, then peel off and discard parchment. Invert cake onto serving platter. Cool until just warm or to room temperature, at least 1 hour. Cut into wedges and serve.

Pan Prep 101
Our buckle recipe calls for a multistep pan-prep process—grease the pan, line with parchment, grease the parchment, dust the pan and parchment with flour. Are all of these steps really necessary? Yes. The moisture in the berries keeps the cake from forming a thick crust in the oven. As a result, greasing the pan is not enough. The parchment offers added insurance that the cake will release. And the flour is there to wick up moisture from the batter.

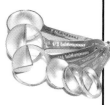

Building a Better Blondie

Had a chewy, full-flavored blondie lately? No? Well, neither had we.

⋛ BY MATTHEW CARD ⋜

A fashion editor once said that style lies in the ability to walk across a room without having anyone notice you. What speaks for fashion, I believe, also holds true for food. Brownies, with their brash, full-frontal chocolate flavor, are the plunging necklines of baking, whereas the more subtle, butterscotch-flavored blondies have real style. Of course, subtle elegance in baking is hard to come by, and that's why blondies are often greasy, cakey, and bland. Nobody said style was easy.

Despite these differences, brownies and blondies are cut from similar cloth. Each includes a simple list of ingredients: flour, eggs, butter, sugar (light brown sugar for blondies), vanilla, and salt. Brownies add melted chocolate, whereas blondies include nuts and chocolate chips. I collected a slew of remarkably similar recipes, baked them, and quickly learned my first lesson about blondies: Proportions make all the difference. Cloyingly sweet, bland, crumbly, greasy—all these ills were readily apparent with only slight variations in ingredients. I also discovered that producing great chewy texture along with good flavor was no mean feat; having one seemed to preclude the other.

Blondies are prepared in two very distinct styles. The first calls for melted butter that is mixed with sugar and eggs before the dry ingredients are folded in. The second requires creaming (beating) butter and sugar until fluffy and then adding the eggs and dry ingredients. Tests proved that the melted butter versions were, on the whole, preferred for their dense, chewy texture (the creamed versions were too cakey). As the baker, I gave this approach my vote as well, preferring its utter simplicity.

Batter Matters

Most blondie recipes have close to a 1:1 ratio of light brown sugar to all-purpose flour—much more flour than is typically included in brownie recipes. The reason? Chocolate. Chocolate, like flour, contains starch, and it also acts as an emulsifier, helping to hold the batter together. When I reduced the flour in blondies to the proportions common in brownie recipes (closer to a 3:1 ratio of sugar to flour), the blondies turned into a greasy puddle. Additional testing simply left me back

Some of our tasters preferred white chips, while others liked semisweet chips. Some of each was a happy compromise.

where I had started: equal parts sugar and flour.

Mixing and matching sugars—adding portions of dark brown sugar or granulated sugar to the light brown sugar—did not improve the recipe. Neither did adding liquid sugars like molasses or caramel-flavored dark corn syrup. (The latter severely altered the blondies' texture for the worse.) Light brown sugar, the choice in most recipes, worked best.

I had been using two sticks of butter (melted and briefly cooled) in my working recipe because this amount helped to produce a pleasant chewy texture. But it also made the blondies greasy, a problem common to many blondies recipes. I reduced the butter a tablespoon at a time in subsequent tests until I reached the tipping point—12 tablespoons—below which flavor and texture were compromised. Blondies tend to use fewer eggs than brownies, and I soon found out why. More than two eggs put the texture into the "rubbery" category.

I had made some progress, but my blondies were still squat and dense, in dire need of a lift.

Baking powder was the obvious answer. One teaspoon provided the lift and also contributed to the elusive chewiness I was after.

Timing, as with so much in life, appeared to be crucial. I was baking the blondies at 350 degrees—no other temperature between 300 and 400 degrees worked as well. When I removed them from the oven even a moment too soon, they had the pale, sticky sweetness and gummy texture of cookie dough. Removed a few moments too late, the blondies dried out and became boring. The usual signifiers of an adequately baked bar cookie—the cooked dough pulls away from the sides of the pan, a toothpick comes out clean—did not apply to blondies. Better indicators were color and texture: a light golden brown top that looked shiny and cracked. The chewy texture, then, was as much about the baking as the ingredients.

Odds and Ends

Now that my blondies had the proper texture, it was time to tweak their flavor. My recipe was largely improved by a stiff shot of vanilla. Most recipes include a token teaspoon or two, but I found that the flavor improved with each teaspoon I added; I stopped at 4 teaspoons. Most recipes favor walnuts, although pecans are not unusual. Tasters liked both and were ultimately split in making a choice, so I've left it up to you—the baker. Either way, everyone agreed that browning the nuts before adding them to the dough boosted flavor. A simple thing, perhaps, but blondies, as I was finding, are a study in subtlety. I also found that stovetop toasting (in a dry skillet) produced only faint coloring with spotty singeing; a more thorough oven toasting was the better approach.

RECIPE COMPARISON: **Raising the Bar**

BROWNIE

BLONDIE

Chocolate adds more than just flavor to brownies. It contains a fair amount of starch that also helps brownies hold their shape. Because blondies contain just chips (no melted chocolate), this recipe requires a lot more flour than a brownie recipe.

As with the choice of nuts, the test kitchen was split on the addition of chocolate chips. Half of the tasters thought that chips muddied the waters—one taster referred to this variation as a "dirty blond"—while the rest preferred a bit of culinary counterpoint. I also tested butterscotch chips, a common addition, but one taste confirmed my suspicion that any flavor they added would be artificial—no thanks. While buying the butterscotch chips, I picked up a bag of white chocolate chips as well. A bit to my surprise, the white chips did indeed enrich the flavor and became a key component in the recipe that everyone in the test kitchen could agree on.

So here was my final batch of blondies: chewy without being dense, sweet without being cloying, and sufficiently interesting with the addition of nuts and white chocolate chips to hold one's attention beyond just one bar. That's the kind of culinary style I like.

BLONDIES

MAKES 36

Be very careful not to overbake the blondies; they dry out easily and will turn hard. Start checking the oven a couple of minutes before they will be done. If you can't find our recommended brand of white chocolate chips, coarsely chop a good-quality white chocolate bar.

1	cup (4 ounces) pecans or walnuts
1 1/2	cups (7 1/2 ounces) unbleached all-purpose flour
1	teaspoon baking powder
1/2	teaspoon salt
12	tablespoons (1 1/2 sticks) unsalted butter, melted and cooled
1 1/2	cups (10 1/2 ounces) packed light brown sugar
2	large eggs, lightly beaten
4	teaspoons vanilla extract
6	ounces good-quality white chocolate chips (1 cup) or chopped bar, or 3 ounces each white chocolate and semisweet chocolate chips

1. Adjust oven rack to middle position; heat oven to 350 degrees. Spread nuts on large rimmed baking sheet and bake until deep golden brown, 10 to 15 minutes. Transfer nuts to cutting board to cool; chop coarsely and set aside.

2. While nuts toast, cut 18-inch length foil and fold lengthwise to 8-inch width. Fit foil into length of 13 by 9-inch baking pan, pushing it into corners and up sides of pan; allow excess to overhang pan edges. Cut 14-inch length foil and fit into width of baking pan in same manner, perpendicular to first sheet (if using extra-wide foil, fold second sheet lengthwise to 12-inch width). Spray foil-lined pan with nonstick cooking spray.

3. Whisk flour, baking powder, and salt together in medium bowl; set aside.

4. Whisk melted butter and brown sugar together in medium bowl until combined. Add

eggs and vanilla and mix well. Using rubber spatula, fold dry ingredients into egg mixture until just combined; do not overmix. Fold in chocolate and nuts and turn batter into prepared pan, smoothing top with rubber spatula.

5. Bake until top is shiny, cracked, and light golden brown, 22 to 25 minutes; do not overbake. Cool on wire rack to room temperature. Remove bars from pan by lifting foil overhang and transfer to cutting board. Cut into 2-inch squares and serve.

CONGO BARS

Sweetened coconut is not a suitable substitute here because it will burn.

After toasting nuts in step 1 of recipe for Blondies, toast 1 1/2 cups unsweetened, shredded coconut on rimmed baking sheet, stirring 2 or 3 times, until light golden, 5 to 7 minutes. Follow recipe for Blondies, adding coconut with chocolate in step 4.

Great Whites

Is white wine vinegar a generic commodity? Or does brand matter? We discovered the answers in a bottle of nail-polish remover.

≥ BY JOLYON HELTERMAN ≤

White wine vinegar has never enjoyed the cachet of its red-hued brethren—at least in this country. Balsamic vinegar and red wine vinegar, as the condiment aisle's true stars, are the ones most often thrust into the spotlight for dramatic turns in rich pan reductions, bold salad dressings, and other full-flavored fare. Not so with white wine vinegar, which American cooks tend to relegate to backstage tasks: quietly punching up pickle brine, brightening butter-based sauces, providing unobtrusive (and untinted) foundation for delicate citrus vinaigrettes.

Of course, that's when we use it at all: According to the Vinegar Institute, an industry trade group, Americans buy a much higher percentage of distilled white vinegar (46 percent) than any other variety, including cider vinegar (22 percent), red wine vinegar (12 percent), balsamic (10 percent), and rice vinegar (5 percent). White wine vinegar? Lumped together with malt vinegar and obscure fruit vinegars (date vinegar, anyone?) as "Other Vinegars," a category comprising just 5 percent of total sales. (By contrast, every self-respecting French cook keeps *vinaigre de vin blanc* on hand for whisking up a classic vinaigrette.)

Does brand even matter? Or does white wine vinegar have more in common with distilled white vinegar (made by distilling grain rather than fermenting grapes), which trades on straightforward strength, not flavor-profile subtlety? To find out, I purchased 10 national supermarket white wine vinegars, which tasters sampled straight (sucking the liquid through sugar cubes, a trick experts use to minimize palate fatigue); whisked into a simple vinaigrette (with mild canola oil); and reduced in a beurre blanc. They also tasted 10 batches of pickled green beans, jarred for a month to give our acidic contenders time to work their magic.

Fermented Wisdom

After weeks of diligent puckering, one thing was clear: The vinegars differed dramatically. Some were quite aggressive in taste; some boasted floral or fruity notes; others had fermented, malty qualities. The notion of white wine vinegar as a brand-less, faceless commodity was duly put to rest.

Less clear was how to interpret the testing data. There seemed to be no discernible pattern, as the winning vinegars from one tasting ended up in the lower ranks of the next one. To figure it out, I first needed a better grasp on the basics of vinegar making.

All vinegar is the product of double fermentation. In the first round, yeast transforms a sugary or starchy substance (apples, grains, grapes) into alcohol (cider, malt, wine). In the second, the bacteria *Acetobacter aceti* transform the alcohol into acetic acid, and vinegar (cider vinegar, malt vinegar, wine vinegar) is born. Nowadays, yeast and *Acetobacter* are strategically introduced, but once upon a time the organisms arrived naturally from the air. (The word *vinegar* comes from the French *vin aigre*, which translates as "sour wine"—originally, wine spoiled accidentally via this process.) After the second fermentation, the liquid's acidity level has reached 10 to 12 percent, a bit too harsh for consumption. So the vinegar is diluted with water almost by half. European wine vinegars are legally obligated to have 6 percent acidity or higher; in the United States, the minimum is just 4 percent.

White wine vinegar manufacturers today generally handle only the second fermentation first-hand, purchasing pre-made "wine stock" (wine blends of slightly lesser quality than drinking wine) from local vineyards. Which varietals? All kinds. Manufacturers maintain flavor-profile consistency from batch to batch by adjusting the proportions of wine stock of differing characters, just the way a winemaker would. Some stocks may be chosen for color, some for fruitiness, others for depth. (Single-varietal white wine vinegars are specialty items that tend to be more expensive and less standardized; see "Tasting Upscale White Wine Vinegars," below.)

Clue Sniffing

Back to the results, I first zeroed in on acid levels, which ranged from 5 percent to 7.5 percent. Any hopes that such an obvious clue would bring order to the proceedings were quickly dashed: In every test, the high-acid and low-acid brands were evenly distributed from the top of the ranks to the bottom. Even in the beurre blanc tasting, where I expected higher acidity to be an advantage (to cut through two full sticks of butter), it was clear that acidity had little bearing on taster preference.

Likewise, attempts to divine a pattern based on national origin proved a dead end. It wasn't until I took a closer look at tasters' comments that I found my first important clue. In the plain tasting, the losing vinegars were indicted consistently for artificial fruit flavors and harsh, chemical off-notes. What caught my eye, however, were the repeated references to "nail-polish remover." (Ethyl acetate, the solvent that gives nail-polish remover its characteristic smell, is often used in confectionery to manufacture artificial fruit flavors.)

In the test kitchen, when one taster comes up with a quirky association, chances are it's just a fluke. When several tasters independently make the same association, it's worth investigating. So I concocted another experiment. Pouring helpings of each of our vinegars, I persuaded 10 test-kitchen staffers to take a whiff from a bottle of nail-polish remover, then indicate the samples that most resembled it in smell or

In the Tasting Room

Why do some vinegars smell like nail-polish remover? Our tasters sniffed out the truth.

> **Tasting Upscale White Wine Vinegars**
>
> The white wine vinegars in our lineup all sell for less than $5. So what do you get if you spend $10 to $30 for a high-end bottle? For that kind of cash, you'll usually get three things that you won't get with the supermarket brands: longer aging (a few years rather than a few months), single varietals (just Chardonnay or Champagne grapes rather than a blend of wine stocks), and breathtaking packaging. But how do they taste?
>
> Test-kitchen staffers sampled five high-end brands plain and whisked in a beurre blanc, tasting our top three supermarket brands as well. In the plain tasting, the pricey vinegars were noticeably more mellow and complex. (Our panelists, it turns out, have very expensive tastes: The $30 Gegenbauer Brauerei Chardonnay Vinegar won them over with its deep-aged, "grapey" sweetness.) But in the beurre blanc, such mellow complexity proved a handicap, as the brighter supermarket brands cut right through the richness. Save the pricey stuff for vinaigrettes. –J.H.

This Chardonnay vinegar makes great vinaigrette, but is it worth $30?

taste—if at all. Sure enough, several brands set off tasters' makeshift ethyl acetate alarms.

Were some manufacturers adding ethyl acetate to their vinegars to ramp up the fruity notes? Not quite. According to Sylvain Norton, a vinegar-industry expert, a white wine vinegar's flavor profile can be adjusted through wine-stock blending alone. But vinegar makers have another trick up their sleeves: adjusting fermentation times. "If you stop fermentation before all the alcohol gets converted to acetic acid, you end up with a more pungent solvent-y flavor." Why? The excess alcohol reacts with the newly formed acetic acid to create a new compound: ethyl acetate. Vinegar makers weren't adding it to their brews; they were letting it occur naturally.

The Raw and the Cooked

It was time to call in the experts. I poured the samples into vials labeled 1 through 10 and sent them off to a Boston-area laboratory. A week later, the results came back. Sure enough, ethyl acetate levels varied markedly—from trace amounts (less than 10 milligrams per liter) to a whopping 713 milligrams per liter!

Suddenly, the pieces were falling into place. The four vinegars with the highest concentrations of ethyl acetate—Carapelli (713 milligrams), Colavita (260), Laurent du Clos (191), and Monari Federzoni (123)—made up the lower ranks of the plain and vinaigrette tastings. Tasters liked the bright, fruity notes of these samples but decried their artificial off-tastes. The top-ranked vinegars in these two rounds—Acetaia Bellei (72), Spectrum Naturals (trace), and Maille (trace)—had low concentrations of ethyl acetate and were generally described as fermented, "malty," and rich.

For the cooked applications, the results were almost the reverse: The vinegars with more ethyl acetate carried the day in the pickle and beurre blanc tasting. And it didn't take much research to figure out why. Both recipes call for bringing the vinegar to a boil—at which point ethyl acetate would evaporate, leaving behind only the bright, clean notes that tasters liked in these vinegars. By contrast, the malty, fermented, darker notes of the vinegars with less ethyl acetate—which had proved such an advantage in the uncooked tests—lacked the brightness to cut the richness of the beurre blanc or to complement the pickle brine.

Given the fact that most Americans don't keep even *one* brand of white wine vinegar in the pantry, a bipartite recommendation may be overkill. Otherwise, we'd probably go with the fruity Colavita for cooking and the malty Maille—or even a high-end gourmet brand—for vinaigrettes. But for a white wine vinegar that works well in every application, we recommend either Acetaia Bellei or Four Monks: two well-made brands that contain only moderate amounts of ethyl acetate—but enough fruity brightness to stand up convincingly to even the most buttery beurre blanc.

TASTING WHITE WINE VINEGARS

Twenty *Cook's Illustrated* staff members tasted 10 brands of white wine vinegar four ways: straight up (sucked through sugar cubes to minimize palate fatigue), tossed with canola oil on lettuce leaves, cooked in a simple beurre blanc sauce, and in a brine for green-bean pickles. Tasters rated each sample for acidity, harshness, and complexity. Brands are listed below in order of preference. Acidity levels are based on package information. Ethyl acetate levels, given in milligrams per liter, were determined by independent lab tests.

RECOMMENDED

BEST ALL-PURPOSE
ACETAIA BELLEI Aceto di Vino Bianco "Oro"
➤ **$2.49 for 17 ounces**
Acidity: 6% Ethyl acetate: 72 mg/l
Tasters were impressed by this Italian vinegar's floral, fruity notes and "overtones of tart apples." The moderate ethyl acetate levels helped it maintain "an elegant balance" in all applications.

FOUR MONKS White Wine Vinegar
➤ **$1.89 for 12.7 ounces**
Acidity: 5% Ethyl acetate: 119 mg/l
This low-acid American brand was many tasters' favorite. The "extremely sweet and gentle" vinegar won high marks for "mellow but interesting herbaceous flavors" and "tart sour-apple" notes.

BEST FOR COOKING
COLAVITA Aged White Wine Vinegar
➤ **$2.99 for 16.9 ounces**
Acidity: 6% Ethyl acetate: 260 mg/l
"Nice and smooth, with the perfect level of tanginess," wrote one panelist. Several tasters noticed a "subtle sweetness" and fruity perfume in this Italian brand. The second-highest concentration of ethyl acetate bothered some tasters in the vinaigrette.

BEST FOR VINAIGRETTES
MAILLE Vinaigre de Vin Blanc
➤ **$2.99 for 8.5 ounces**
Acidity: 7% Ethyl acetate: trace
Won fans for its "deep, lingering, caramelized" notes and complex, "malty" flavors, but this French vinegar was intense. "It burns my throat, like Marsala," said one taster. Others noted "balsamicky" flavors.

SPECTRUM NATURALS Organic White Wine Vinegar
➤ **$4.69 for 16.9 ounces**
Acidity: 6% Ethyl acetate: trace
This Italian vinegar had the most diverse flavor profile in the lineup. The "dark, fermented-tasting, richness" and fruity overtones were enriched by flavors of "caramel," "oakiness," and "nutty, earthy mushrooms."

RECOMMENDED WITH RESERVATIONS

LAURENT DU CLOS White Wine Vinegar
➤ **$3.99 for 16.9 ounces**
Acidity: 6% Ethyl acetate: 191 mg/l
This fruity French contender was the green-bean-pickle champ, but the ethyl acetate levels sapped its charms in the vinaigrette. "Pleasant" overall, but with a "run-of-the-mill" flavor profile.

MONARI FEDERZONI 1912 White Wine Vinegar
➤ **$3.29 for 16.9 ounces**
Acidity: 7% Ethyl acetate: 123 mg/l
The "astringent," "box wine" notes in this Italian brand turned off some tasters, but others liked the "crisp, clean taste." The acidity was a tad on the strong side: "I taste a lot of wine here, but it's fairly harsh—makes my eyes blink."

NOT RECOMMENDED

CARAPELLI White Wine Vinegar
➤ **$3.19 for 17 ounces**
Acidity: 7.5% Ethyl acetate: 713 mg/l
This Italian vinegar was the most acidic of the bunch and had almost three times the ethyl acetate of any other brand tested. "Is this nail-polish remover?" complained one panelist. Tasters detected strong, artificial fruity notes.

MAITRE JACQUES White French Wine Vinegar
➤ **$3.19 for 16.9 ounces**
Acidity: 6% Ethyl acetate: trace
Sweet fruitiness was marred by "musty wine" flavors and an overpowering harshness that two tasters likened to "gasoline." This vinegar has a "bitterness that bites back," said one panelist.

REGINA White Wine Vinegar
➤ **$2.99 for 12 ounces**
Acidity: 5% Ethyl acetate: 24 mg/l
The "bland" flavor profile of this American brand tracked with its low acidity. "Like distilled white vinegar with a spoonful of fruit extract," said one taster.

Mitt Parade

Oven mitts once cost no more than the Sunday newspaper, but today a high-tech pair runs $60. We braved trials by fire, water, and grease to uncover the (very) painful truth.

≥ BY JOLYON HELTERMAN WITH GARTH CLINGINGSMITH ≤

As exacting as I get when shopping for skillets (fully clad, stainless steel, 2.6-millimeter-thick sides), such rigor has consistently escaped my oven-mitt-buying decisions (fuzzy, blue). And given the $5 price tags, I've been content to let kitchen décor, not performance, be my guiding light.

Lately, however, oven mitts have turned decidedly more ambitious. Competing with basic terry and cotton are mitts sporting fancy materials and features: leather, "treated" cotton, rubber, silicone, Nomex (a fireproof material used to make race-car-driver gear), and Kevlar (an even stronger synthetic, found in body armor and military helmets). There are flameproof suede gloves meant for welders, and the "melt"-resistant "Ove" Glove (as seen on TV!). These space-age products don't come cheap: The priciest sells for $30—and that's *per mitt*.

The 'Ouch' Factor

Bells and whistles aside, an oven mitt has two core requirements: enough heat resistance to keep hands from burning and enough pliability to keep cooks from inadvertently smashing food (or dropping pans). Because impressive dexterity is of zero importance if you can't pick up the hot pan in the first place, initial testing focused on heat protection.

We first measured the amount of time testers were able to lift and hold a Dutch oven filled with boiling water before the heat became unbearable. The silicone mitts were the winners, maxing out at an impressive 90 seconds; the Nomex/Kevlar mitts lasted a minute. Most of the rest clocked in at around 45 seconds, the leather model losing with a still-respectable 22. (How much longer does a Dutch oven need to be held in midair, anyway?)

Clearly, we'd have to brave the oven's high temperatures to separate the best mitt from the worst. But was merely recording how long it took a pan-laden test cook to start trembling nervously an objective enough measure of heat protection? I decided to outfit the interior of each mitt with a thermocouple—a wire probe that feeds temperature data to an attached console—with the probe strategically positioned at the point of contact. Testers would take turns holding a pan of lasagna (heated in a 400-degree oven) for as long as possible. Meanwhile, I would stand nearby—in a purely observational role—duly recording temperature readings from the console.

The sleek-lined LamsonSharp leather glove was the first contestant. I barely had time to get my clipboard situated comfortably when the tester emitted a piercing "*Owww!*" and slammed the bubbling batch of lasagna back onto the oven rack. Luckily, I kept my cool long enough to jot down the data: The LamsonSharp had risen to 109.9 degrees in just four seconds.

The rest of the mitts fared better, screams of pain were rare, and we were making clear progress. First, we had quantified the "ouch" factor: Like clockwork, testers faltered at 110 degrees. What's more, we had established a pecking order based on the number of seconds the mitts kept our hands below that threshold of pain: heavy silicone (90 seconds); heavy quilted cotton (65); padded Nomex/Kevlar and thin quilted cotton (40); rubber, treated cotton, and quilted terry (30); non-padded Nomex/Kevlar (the "Ove" Glove) (20); suede (15); and leather (4).

Until now, we had been careful to keep the mitts dry, as per manufacturer warnings. But such a caveat seemed a cop-out for a product meant for settings in which insidious liquids lurk at every turn. So we soaked each mitt for five seconds in room-temperature water, then repeated the Dutch Oven Lift Test. The waterproof silicones and rubbers again kept their cool beyond a minute, but the rest faltered much sooner.

Manipulating Data

As testers braved the heat-resistance trials, disdain abounded for the Orka mitts, made from heavy silicone. ("I can't even tell the pan handles are there!" complained one panelist.) The thick silicone—so effective for protecting hands—was also inhibiting dexterity. So I devised three new experiments.

First, 12 *Cook's* staffers, using each pair of mitts, took turns transferring a baking sheet full of cookies and an empty skillet from the oven to a cooling rack. Afterward, we headed outside to a hot charcoal grill, where we flipped 24 rounds of eggplant with medium-sized tongs. Testers rated each design on how well it negotiated the thin sides of the baking pan, the skinny skillet handle, and the precision movement of the tongs.

Our tests taught us several lessons. First, there's an inverse relationship between heat protection and dexterity. The very attributes that gave some of our mitts such impressive heat resistance (bulky padding, stiff synthetic material) had us chasing eggplant rounds around the grill grate—and smashing cookies. By contrast, the highest marks for dexterity went to the leather, the two suedes, and the "Ove" Glove—three of the worst in terms of heat protection. For a satisfactory mitt overall, then, we'd have to choose from above-average but not top-rated performers in both arenas.

During the eggplant trials, we also developed clear mitt-length preferences. The mitt lengths ranged from 8½ inches to 17 inches. The 17-inchers provided more-than-adequate heat protection—even after several minutes over a hot grill—but smaller testers found this size awkward (there was a tendency for sleeves or elbows to bump the gloves forward). We found 15 inches (12 inches, for smaller testers) to be the ideal length for indoors and outdoors.

Damage Control?

A constant complaint about oven mitts is how to keep them clean—especially when they're used outdoors. So I grabbed a bottle of barbecue sauce and a skillet full of steak grease and returned to my mitts. I spooned a heaping tablespoon of each substance onto the mitts, let them sit overnight, and then washed each according to manufacturer instructions. While most cleaned up beautifully, the leather glove bled dye everywhere and the suedes and the terry were sullied beyond repair.

A common mishap is setting fire to an oven mitt while trying to juggle pans on the stovetop. So we re-created the situation. Armed with safety goggles, fire extinguisher, and galvanized metal bucket, we subjected each mitt to a five-second flame test over a gas burner turned to high. The terry, cotton, and treated cotton models suffered gaping holes. The rubber glove burned at the seam. The suedes and the leather gave off smelly fumes but remained unharmed. The silicone and Nomex/Kevlar models survived without a blemish.

After weeks of testing, then, had we found the perfect mitt? The padded Nomex/Kevlar model, made by Kool-Tek, came pretty close. In addition to providing good heat protection and excellent dexterity, it washed easily and refused to burn.

The Kool-Tek's only downfall is price—a hefty $24.95 per mitt. After so many years making do with $5 mitts, could I bring myself to plunk down that kind of cash for what's really just a souped-up potholder? Skeptics can give our runner-up a try: For eight bucks, the Parvin quilted-cotton mitt handled most tasks well; just keep it out of fire and water. But this is one cheapo-mitt veteran who has seen the light.

RATING OVEN MITTS

Our kitchen tests fell into the following three categories:

HEAT PROTECTION: Mitts were rated good, fair, or poor based on how well they maintained a comfortable temperature during tests, which included hooking the mitt up to a thermocouple and picking up a hot pan of lasagna (near right). "Pain Threshold" indicates the number of seconds before the mitt interior rose to an unbearable temperature (110 degrees).

DEXTERITY: Mitts were rated good, fair, or poor based on ease of manipulation while transferring pans to and from the oven and the stovetop and while using tongs during grilling.

DURABILITY: Mitts were rated good, fair, or poor based on how they resisted staining and/or structural damage after being soiled with barbecue sauce and grease; undergoing five rounds of cleaning; and being scorched over a gas flame for five seconds (far right).

HIGHLY RECOMMENDED

Kool-Tek Protective Apparel

MATERIALS:	Nomex, Kevlar, treated cotton
PRICE:	$21.95, 12" $24.95, 15"
HEAT PROTECTION:	★★★
DEXTERITY:	★★★
DURABILITY:	★★★
PAIN THRESHOLD:	40 seconds

TESTERS' COMMENTS: Everything we want in a mitt—except maybe the price. Mostly Nomex (heat resistant to 450 degrees) with a "racing stripe" of Kevlar (heat resistant to 1,000 degrees), the Kool-Tek won fans for its natural grip, easy dexterity, and stay-cool comfort.

BEST BUY

Parvin Flameguard Oven Mitt

MATERIALS:	Treated cotton exterior with cotton padding
PRICE:	$8.40, 17" pair
HEAT PROTECTION:	★★★
DEXTERITY:	★★★
DURABILITY:	★★
PAIN THRESHOLD:	40 seconds

TESTERS' COMMENTS: Almost as many fans as the winner—especially for its comfortable dexterity and "just the right amount of padding"—but some found the length "a bit cumbersome." Don't set this one on fire.

RECOMMENDED WITH RESERVATIONS

Duncan's Kitchen Grips

MATERIAL:	Synthetic rubber
PRICE:	$14.95, 11" pair $19.95, 15½" pair
HEAT PROTECTION:	★★
DEXTERITY:	★★
DURABILITY:	★★
PAIN THRESHOLD:	30 seconds

TESTERS' COMMENTS: The "weird flatness" was annoying, and testers with small hands disliked the 2 to 3 inches of useless space at the top. The stylized shape made one tester feel like "a gingerbread man" (and not in a good way).

Ritz Quilted Oven Mitt

MATERIALS:	Padded cotton, with terry interior
PRICE:	$13.95, 12"
HEAT PROTECTION:	★★★
DEXTERITY:	★
DURABILITY:	★★
PAIN THRESHOLD:	65 seconds

TESTERS' COMMENTS: The bulky padding that made for awesome heat protection also made the task of maneuvering pans "a major pain."

NOT RECOMMENDED

Orka Oven Mitt

MATERIAL:	Silicone
PRICE:	$19.99, 11" $29.99, 17"
HEAT PROTECTION:	★★★
DEXTERITY:	★
DURABILITY:	★★★
PAIN THRESHOLD:	90 seconds

TESTERS' COMMENTS: The heat-protection champ, but testers hated almost everything else about it. The raised grip on the mitt portion was too bulky, and the interior quickly got sweaty. "Falling! Falling!" warned one tester, who couldn't feel the edges of the cookie sheet.

Kitchen Supply Mitt Glove

MATERIALS:	Padded terry, with cotton interior
PRICE:	$13.95, 12"
HEAT PROTECTION:	★★
DEXTERITY:	★★
DURABILITY:	★
PAIN THRESHOLD:	30 seconds

TESTERS' COMMENTS: Overly insulated finger compartments sapped this design of dexterity. During the washing test, the steak grease stained permanently and some of the padding came out.

Charcoal Companion Suede Gloves

MATERIALS:	Suede with treated cotton interior
PRICE:	$12.95, 13" pair
HEAT PROTECTION:	★
DEXTERITY:	★★★
DURABILITY:	★★
PAIN THRESHOLD:	15 seconds

TESTERS' COMMENTS: Nice-looking, comfortable, and easy to manipulate, but these gloves got very hot—and quickly. The pair we tested has yet to recover from the barbecue-sauce test.

Lincoln Electric Welder's Gloves

MATERIALS:	Suede with cotton interior
PRICE:	$14.95, 12" pair
HEAT PROTECTION:	★
DEXTERITY:	★★★
DURABILITY:	★★
PAIN THRESHOLD:	15 seconds

TESTERS' COMMENTS: "Welders must be tougher than I am," said one tester once the heat made it through the suede exterior. The delayed penetration gave testers a false sense of comfort—then rudely disturbed it.

The "Ove" Glove Hot Surface Handler

MATERIALS:	Woven Kevlar/Nomex with cotton/polyester interior
PRICE:	$19.99, 10"
HEAT PROTECTION:	★
DEXTERITY:	★★★
DURABILITY:	★★★
PAIN THRESHOLD:	20 seconds

TESTERS' COMMENTS: Everyone was eager to try the famous mitt from the TV ad, but no one trusted it. "It looks like a child's snow glove," said one staffer. And it worked about as well. This Kevlar/Nomex mitt lacked the layer of padding that pushed our winner to the top.

LamsonSharp Oven Mitt

MATERIAL:	Leather
PRICE:	$23.95, 17"
HEAT PROTECTION:	★
DEXTERITY:	★★★
DURABILITY:	★★
PAIN THRESHOLD:	4 seconds

TESTERS' COMMENTS: The best-looking mitt of the bunch was the worst when it came to heat protection. Although in the past we've liked LamsonSharp leather potholders, they have a two-ply design—unlike the one-ply gloves.

⇒ BY DAWN YANAGIHARA ⇐

Freezing Veggie Burgers

Our Ultimate Veggie Burgers (page 21) are perfect candidates for freezing (before grilling), or so we thought. With freezing and defrosting, however, the patties increase in moisture content; it is therefore necessary to add more bread crumbs before freezing. For each burger to be frozen, add 1 teaspoon panko or ½ teaspoon plain bread crumbs to the mixture before shaping. Thaw frozen patties overnight in the refrigerator on a triple layer of paper towels covered loosely with plastic wrap. Before cooking, pat the patties dry with paper towels and reshape to make sure they are tightly packed and cohesive.

Pepper in Black and White

In French cuisine, black pepper is preferred over white, which is used only when the purity of a dish's appearance would be tainted by flecks of black. In many Asian cuisines, however, the distinctive flavor of white pepper is preferred over the piney, slightly resinous notes of black. We side with the French for our Aïoli recipe (page 8) but take the Asian approach with Stir-Fried Thai-Style Beef with Chiles and Shallots (page 19).

The pepper berries used to make white pepper are the same as those used to make black pepper, but they are harvested at a riper stage. The hulls are then removed, and with them goes the heat that is characteristic of black pepper.

While freshly ground white pepper is more fragrant than preground, we use white pepper so infrequently in the test kitchen that we can't justify purchasing a pepper mill for the sole purpose of grinding it, nor can we be bothered emptying and then refilling the black pepper mill. Instead, we opt for preground white pepper, replenishing the stock when the pepper loses its fragrance. Here's a shopping tip: Purchase white pepper from an Asian market if there's one nearby; you'll pay just a fraction of the supermarket price.

Sizing Up Saffron

Saffron is available in two forms—threads and powder. Conventional wisdom says that deep, dark red threads are better than yellow or orange threads. We held a small tasting of broths infused with different saffron samples, and the threads with considerable spots of yellow and orange did in fact yield the weakest-colored and flattest-tasting broths. The reddest threads yielded intensely flavorful, heady, perfumed broths—so much so that less ardent saffron fans would have been happier with a little less saffron.

Conventional wisdom also cautions against the use of powdered saffron. Some sources say that inferior threads are used to produce the powder and that coloring agents may be added. While this may be true, we found powdered saffron purchased from a reputable source to be just as flavorful and fragrant as even the highest-quality threads. What's more, powdered saffron offers a few advantages over threads. First, a smaller amount can be used (about one-third to one-half the volume measurement of threads);

POWDERED SAFFRON

SAFFRON THREADS

second, the powder is easier to measure and does not need to be crumbled before use; finally, it releases its flavor much more rapidly (a boon for quick recipes such as the Saffron Aïoli on page 8 but not so important for simmered dishes such as paella and bouillabaisse).

In conclusion, when shopping for saffron, look for dark red threads without any interspersion of yellow or orange threads. Or, to save money, choose a good-quality powdered saffron. (See page 32 for a mail-order source.)

Pretend Panko

Coarser, flakier, and fluffier than standard bread crumbs, Japanese bread crumbs, called panko, give fried foods an unparalleled crispness. They are available in Asian markets and in the international section of well-stocked supermarkets, but in the event that you cannot find them, there is a way to make a close approximation from firm, good-quality sandwich bread. Here's what to do.

Fit a food processor with a medium or coarse shredding disk. Trim the crusts off the bread slices (5 slices will make about 1 cup of crumbs) and cut the slices in half. Drop a stack of three or four pieces (or as many as will fit comfortably) into the feed tube. Put the feed tube plunger in place and turn on the machine, allowing the weight of the plunger to push the bread through the shredding disk (do not apply additional pressure by pushing down on the plunger). Spread the crumbs in a thin, even layer on one or two rimmed baking sheets and let them dry at room temperature overnight.

If you can't wait that long, you can bake the crumbs in a 300-degree oven until dry to the touch, about 8 minutes; stir intermittently, but do not allow them to brown. The crumbs tend to clump in the oven; when the crumbs are cool, break up the clumps by rubbing them gently between your fingers. Once dried, the homemade panko can be stored in an airtight container or zipper-lock

---

KNIFE TECHNIQUE | REMOVING MANGO MEAT

Our Mango and Sweet Pepper Salsa with Toasted Pepitas (page 15) requires a diced mango. What is the best way to remove the meat from a mango, with its hulking pit concealed within? Here's the technique we often use in the test kitchen.

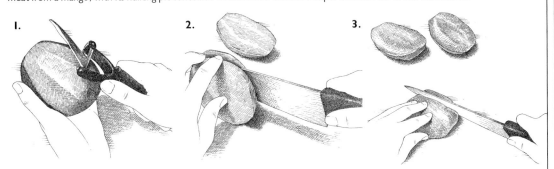

1. Slice off stem end from mango. Peel mango, using cut end as starting point. **2.** Stand peeled mango on its cut end. Slice along one flat side to remove meat. Turn mango around and remove meat from other flat side. **3.** Cutting around the pit, remove remaining meat.

Extra-virgin olive oil is often called for in uncooked recipes, such as vinaigrettes, where its rich, assertive, fruity flavor can be fully appreciated. An exception: our Aïoli (page 8), where we preferred the more restrained and subtle flavor of extra-virgin's lesser cousin, known plainly as olive oil. "Olive oil" is produced by combining a chemically refined and very neutral olive oil with virgin or extra-virgin olive oil to boost its color, aroma, and flavor. Olive oil contains only some of the fullness of flavor of virgin and extra-virgin. It is also less expensive. And because heat tampers with the flavor of costly extra-virgin olive oil, plain olive oil is a good candidate for use in cooked applications.

We gathered seven supermarket brands of plain olive oil in the test kitchen and held a blind tasting. One was a standout. DaVinci ($10.49 for 34 ounces) was lauded for its resemblance to extra-virgin olive oil. It was described as "fruity and herbaceous," "grassy," "slightly peppery," and "nice" overall, with a "good color." Incidentally, DaVinci was the winner of our March/April 2001 tasting of supermarket extra-virgin olive oils.

Colavita ($4.79 for 8.5 ounces) and Filippo Berio ($5.79 for 25.5 ounces) trailed DaVinci by a significant margin. They were deemed perfectly acceptable but unremarkable; Colavita had bolder flavor than the mild Filippo Berio.

Tasters were tepid when it came to Star ($5.29 for 17 ounces) and Rienzi ($5.99 for 34 ounces), the next finishers. "Bland," "mild," and even "boring" were common comments. Bringing up the rear were Carapelli ($6.29 for 25.5 ounces) and Bertolli ($10.99 for 34 ounces), both of which were likened to flavorless vegetable oil.

For a more detailed description of our olive oil tasting results, visit **Cook's Extra** at www.cooksillustrated.com and key in code 7055. The results will be available until August 31, 2005.

DAVINCI
The best "plain" olive oil.

---

bag for two to three weeks at room temperature or for several months in the freezer.

It's about Twine

A recipe calls for kitchen twine, but the only twine you have is a skein from the hardware store. Should you use it? Probably not. Because it's not intended for use with food, it's probably not foodsafe. Still, we thought we'd give it a try, pressing into service some nylon twine from the hardware store. Although it didn't melt or burn, the Day-Glo

FIT TO BE TIED
We tied a pork roast with dental floss and six kinds of twine to find the best choice.

yellow colorant leached onto the pork roast we had tied with it.

A common recommended alternative to kitchen twine is unwaxed dental floss, but it is so thin that while being tied on to a piece of meat it often cuts through it. After cooking, this whitish, almost translucent filament is all but invisible and so can be difficult to remove. We also found that dental floss is particularly ill suited to grilling because it easily singes and then breaks.

As for bona fide kitchen twine, you can buy cotton or linen. We found linen twine easier to tie, as it holds a nice tight overhand knot on its own. In addition, it pulls away from the cooked meat easily, taking a minimum amount of seared crust with it. That said, cotton twine worked nearly as well as linen and is a more economical choice. Look for a midweight cotton twine (of the four weights we tested, we liked 16-ply best). See page 32 for a mail-order source.

Cheesecake Encounters of the Frozen Kind

Can you freeze cheesecake? To find out, we made our **New York–Style Cheesecake** (March/April 2002). We suspected that the cake, with its dense texture, would hold up well to freezing and thawing but that the crust, made with graham crackers, would lose some crispness. We were right. Soggy crust notwithstanding, a cheesecake that had spent three to four weeks in the freezer was almost as good as fresh baked.

Here's how to freeze leftover cheesecake: Return the remaining cake to the springform pan it was baked in, with the sides in place for protection; wrap the pan twice in plastic wrap and then once in aluminum foil. To serve, pull the cake from the freezer and let it defrost in the refrigerator 8 to 12 hours or overnight. About an hour before serving, let the cake sit out at room temperature to shake off the last of the deep-freeze chill. To freeze a whole cheesecake, wrap the cooled cake, still in its springform pan, then freeze and thaw as described.

Crème Brûlée, Family Style

Can you make our **Crème Brûlée** (November/December 2001) if you don't own eight individual ramekins? After some trial and error, we figured out how to make a family-style version of this dessert in a 1½-quart casserole or 11 by 7-inch baking dish (we like the models with handles, which are easy to remove from the water bath). Instead

For easy maneuverability, bake crème brûlée in a casserole dish with handles.

of portioning the custard into eight ramekins, strain it into one of these large casseroles. The custard should reach about two-thirds of the way up the sides of the pan and have a depth of 1 to 1¼ inches. The cooking time will increase by about 10 minutes, to 40 to 50 minutes. Before removing the custard from the oven, make sure the temperature at the center has reached 170 to 175 degrees.

Chicken Teriyaki, Stovetop Style

Our **Chicken Teriyaki** (January/February 2005) recipe was developed to work in an in-oven broiler, but we recently figured out a way to make the recipe on the stovetop for those readers who have drawer-type broilers.

Whereas extra-crisp skin—a must for chicken teriyaki—is easily accomplished in an in-oven broiler, it's hard to get the same results by simply browning the thighs in a skillet. By weighting the thighs as they cooked, we were able to ensure maximum contact of skin with skillet, which in turn ensured that the fat rendered and the skin turned brown and crisp. To weight the chicken we used a Dutch oven filled with 28-ounce cans of tomatoes.

With this new stovetop method, we cut two steps from the process of preparing the chicken thighs for cooking: boning them and slashing the skin. Keeping the bone in helped the thighs to fit compactly inside the skillet, while weighting them helped enough with rendering the fat to make slashing unnecessary.

Cautionary note: This approach has the potential to produce a lot of smoke, so make sure to turn on your overhead oven fan and/or open a window.

–Compiled by Nina West

COOK'S EXTRA gives you free recipes online. Go to www.cooksillustrated.com and key in code 7056 for Stovetop Chicken Teriyaki and code 7057 for Family-Style Crème Brûlée. These recipes will be available until August 31, 2005.

IF YOU HAVE A QUESTION about a recently published recipe, let us know. Send your inquiry, name, address, and daytime telephone number to Recipe Update, Cook's Illustrated, P.O. Box 470589, Brookline, MA 02447, or write to recipeupdate@bcpress.com.

≥ BY GARTH CLINGINGSMITH ≤

DO YOU REALLY NEED THIS?
Burger Press

We have no qualms about patting out four patties by hand. But 12? Perhaps we'll take some help. And the best help came from the Fox Run Craftsmen's Hamburger Press ($5), which forms flawlessly shaped beef patties. The press proved especially useful for constructing veggie burgers (page 21), whose texture makes them a bit harder to shape than ground beef. The burger press cut burger-shaping time by 50 percent, and we found that it helped the cooking process, too: Flatter patties touch more of the pan, yielding better browning and a crispier crust.

MEET THE PRESS
Can a burger shaper outdo the freehand method?

EQUIPMENT UPDATE
Roasting Pan

During our 1999 rating of roasting pans, we decided that the upright handles, roomy interior, and sturdiness of All-Clad's Stainless Steel Roti ($275) justified its hefty price. Since then, however, we've noticed that our top-rated pan has a tendency to warp slightly on the stovetop while browning roasts or deglazing *fond*. (The Roti lacks the clad construction—an aluminum core sandwiched between layers of steel—that makes other All-Clad cookware so reliable.) So when we saw that Calphalon's fully clad Contemporary Stainless Roasting Pan features a similar design—and for a mere $100—we brought it in for the challenge.

To our delight, the Calphalon did not warp on the stovetop, and its lighter weight made it more responsive to burner adjustments than the All-Clad pan. This new Calphalon roasting pan has everything we want, including a reasonable price.

EQUIPMENT UPDATE
Chef's Knife

Our 2002 rating of chef's knives divided the test kitchen into two camps: those who like lighter, modern knives and those who prefer heavier, more traditional models. For the latter group, the 8-inch Wüsthof Grand Prix Chef's Knife has become the test-kitchen standard. When we found out the Grand Prix was being phased out to make way for its second-generation model, the Grand Prix II ($79.99), we were anxious to see how it compared.

The handle of the new knife is bulkier (and thus awkward for small-handed cooks), and that added bulk throws the center of balance closer to the handle, which makes the "rock and chop" technique most test cooks use feel somewhat less natural than it does with the "bouncier" design of the original.

Despite misgivings about the tweaked design, the Grand Prix II gets our stamp of approval. It earned high marks for its sharp blade and excellent performance in tests.

DO YOU REALLY NEED THIS?
Thermometer Whisk

Making custard takes three hands: one for the pan, one for the whisk, and another for the thermometer—essential for keeping custard below egg-curdling temperatures. Williams-Sonoma's Thermometer Whisk ($25) is designed to make custard construction a two-handed task. The tines on this high-tech whisk transmit temperatures (from −40 degrees to 400 degrees) to the digital display at the end of the handle. Intrigued, we gave one a whirl in the test kitchen.

The nicely contoured whisk worked well and the temperature registered quickly. So far, so good.

THERMOMETER WHISK
Ingenious tool with flawed calibration.

While double-checking the thermometer's accuracy, however, we discovered that the calibration was off by seven degrees, registering boiling water at 219 degrees! To make sure we hadn't simply tested a defective model, we purchased a second one and repeated the test. Once again, the calibration was off by seven degrees. Under normal circumstances, such egregious accuracy issues would guarantee a negative verdict, but we're so sold on the gadget's ingenuity that we're willing to do the subtraction—until a more accurate model comes along.

EQUIPMENT TESTING
Nonstick-Friendly Tongs

Tongs are one of the most versatile tools in the kitchen, but the bare-metal business ends have inflicted quite a few battle wounds on our nonstick cookware over the years. In an effort to preserve the test kitchen's trusty fleet of skillets, we introduced three types of nonstick-friendly tongs (nylon, silicone coated, and wood) to a pristine pan to see which ones got along best.

BEST TONGS FOR NONSTICK
These nylon Oxo tongs keep nonstick coatings out of harm's way.

None of the models damaged the nonstick coating—despite deliberate attempts to scratch the pans. So preferences came down to ease of manipulation. We had a hard time adjusting to the stiff wooden tongs, which one tester likened to "oversized, blunt chopsticks." The tongs with the silicone coating were broad, flat, and straight edged, making the grip difficult to gauge—and precision work a chore. Nylon is sleek enough to mimic the movement of traditional metal tongs. The 12-inch Oxo Good Grips Tongs with Nylon Heads ($8.95) can be locked shut and have a span ample enough to grab a large roast with ease.

Sources

These mail-order sources are for items recommended in this issue. Prices were current at press time and do not include shipping and handling. Contact companies to confirm prices and availability.

page 7: REMOTE THERMOMETER
• Taylor Wireless Oven Thermometer with Remote Pager: $34.99, model #1474, **Amazon.com.**

page 13: ROASTING RACK
• Norpro Nonstick Roasting Rack (13" x 10"): $9.75, item #103249, **Cooking.com** (800-663-8810; www.cooking.com).

page 23: MEASURING SPOONS
• Cuisipro Stainless Steel Oval Measuring Spoons (Set of 5): $10.95, item #137556, **Cooking.com.**

page 29: OVEN MITTS
• Kool-Tek Oven Mitt (12"): $21.95, item #114561; (15"): $24.95, item #114568, **Cooking.com.**
• Parvin Flameguard Oven Mitt (17"): $8.40 (for 2), item CFG2-17, **Parvin Mfg.** (800-648-0770; www.parvinmfg.com).

page 30: SAFFRON
• Powdered Saffron: $21.95, item #S303R, Vanilla, **Saffron Imports** (415-648-8990; www.saffron.com).

page 31: COOKING TWINE
• Cotton Cooking Twine (16-ply): $10.99 (for 1 pound), item #5221, **Fante's Kitchen Wares Shop** (800-443-2683; www.fantes.com).
• Linen Kitchen Twine (300'): $5.99, item #1762, **Fante's Kitchen Wares Shop.**

page 32: BURGER PRESS
• Fox Run Craftsmen Hamburger Press: $5.00, item FR5434, **Golda's Kitchen** (866-465-3299; www.goldaskitchen.com).

page 32: ROASTING PAN
• Calphalon Contemporary Stainless Steel Roasting Pan: $100.00, (www.calphalon.com).

page 32: CHEF'S KNIFE
• Wüsthof-Trident Grand Prix II 8" Chef's Knife: $79.99, item #38712, **A Cook's Wares** (800-915-9788; www.cookswares.com).

page 32: THERMOMETER WHISK
• Thermometer Whisk: $25.00, item #17-6441380, **Williams-Sonoma** (877-812-6235; www.williams-sonoma.com).

page 32: NONSTICK TONGS
• Oxo Good Grips Nonstick Locking Tongs (12"): $8.95, item #212624, **Cooking.com**

RECIPES

July & August 2005

Grill-Roasted Pork Loin, 7

Fruit Salsas, 15

Aïoli, 8

Barbecued Pulled Chicken, 13

Grilled Pizza, 10

www.cooksillustrated.com

Join the *Cook's* Web Site and Get Instant Access to 12 Years of Recipes, Equipment Tests, and Tastings!

Web site members can also join the *Cook's* bulletin board, ask our editors cooking questions, find quick tips and step-by-step illustrations, maintain a private list of personal favorites (recipes, quick tips, tastings, and more), and print out shopping lists for all recipes.
Yours Free: As a paid Web site member, you will also receive our **2005 Buying Guide for Supermarket Ingredients.** Simply type in the promotion code **CB53A** when signing up.

Here's Why More Than 78,000 Home Cooks Subscribe to Our Web Site

Quick Search for "Best" Recipes: Quick access to each and every recipe published in *Cook's Illustrated* since 1993.
Cook's Extra Recipes: Continued access to the recipes that don't fit in each issue of the magazine, including many flavor variations.
Updated Cookware Ratings: Charts of all buying recommendations published in the magazine (you can download them), plus frequent updates on new models and price changes.
Tasting Results: Which chicken broth is best? How about chocolate? You'll have access to every tasting published in the magazine, in addition to tastings conducted only for Web members.
Questions for the Editors: Paid members can ask us a question by e-mail and are guaranteed a response.
The Bulletin Board: Find out what other *Cook's* subscribers think about recipes, equipment, and cooking techniques. Or just meet the subscribers in your town.

Stir-Fried Thai-Style Beef with Chiles and Shallots, 19

Ultimate Veggie Burger, 21

Magazine/Book Customer Service: Pay invoices, give gifts, handle returns, check your subscription status, and more.
Visit Our Bookstore: Order any of our books online and also qualify for special offers.

AMERICA'S TEST KITCHEN TV SHOW

Join the millions of home cooks who watch our show, *America's Test Kitchen*, on public television every week. For more information, including recipes and a schedule of program times in your area, visit www.americastestkitchen.com.

Blueberry Buckle, 23

Blondies, 25

PHOTOGRAPHY: CARL TREMBLAY, STYLING: MARIE PIRANO

Kirby

Japanese

Fresh
Cornichon

Lemon

Garden

Mediterranean

English

CUCUMBERS

NUMBER SEVENTY-SIX

SEPTEMBER & OCTOBER 2005

COOK'S
ILLUSTRATED

Great Cheap Steaks
Taste Test Uncovers Best Buys

Rating Food Storage Bags
Twist, Slide, or Zip?

Deep-Dish Apple Pie
Crisp Crust, Perfect Fruit

Best Chicken Fajitas
Secrets of Marinating

Foolproof Alfredo
Guaranteed Creamy

Best Raspberry Bars
Fresh Berries Plus Jam

Tasting Canned Tomatoes

Flakiest All-Butter Pie Dough

Summer Vegetable Torta

Cheese Shopping 101

Butternut Squash Risotto

Chicken Francese

www.cooksillustrated.com

$5.95 U.S./$6.95 CANADA

10>

0 74470 62805 7

CONTENTS
September & October 2005

COOK'S
ILLUSTRATED
www.cooksillustrated.com
HOME OF AMERICA'S TEST KITCHEN

Founder and Editor	Christopher Kimball
Executive Editor	Jack Bishop
Deputy Editor	Jolyon Helterman
Senior Editors	Adam Ried
	Dawn Yanagihara
Editorial Manager, Books	Elizabeth Carduff
Test Kitchen Director	Erin McMurrer
Senior Editors, Books	Julia Collin Davison
	Lori Galvin
Managing Editor	Rebecca Hays
Associate Editor, Books	Keith Dresser
Associate Editors	Erika Bruce
	Sean Lawler
	Sandra Wu
Web Editor	Lindsay McSweeney
Copy Chief	India Koopman
Test Cooks	Garth Clingingsmith
	Rachel Toomey
	Diane Unger-Mahoney
	Nina West
	Sarah Wilson
Assistant Editor, Books	Charles Kelsey
Editorial Assistant, Books	Elizabeth Wray
Assistant to the Publisher	Melissa Baldino
Kitchen Assistants	Maria Elena Delgado
	Nadia Domeq
	Ena Gudiel
Editorial Intern	Elizabeth Bomze
Contributing Editor	Matthew Card
Consulting Editors	Shirley Corriher
	Guy Crosby
	Jasper White
	Robert L. Wolke
Proofreader	Jean Rogers
Design Director	Amy Klee
Marketing Designer	Julie Bozzo
Designer	Heather Barrett
Staff Photographer	Daniel van Ackere
Vice President Marketing	David Mack
Circulation Director	Bill Tine
Circulation Manager	Larisa Greiner
Fulfillment Manager	Carrie Horan
Circulation Assistant	Elizabeth Dayton
Direct Mail Director	Adam Perry
Products Director	Steven Browall
E-Commerce Marketing Manager	Hugh Buchan
Customer Service Manager	Jacqueline Valerio
Customer Service Representative	Julie Gardner
Vice President Sales	Demee Gambulos
Retail Sales Director	Jason Geller
Retail Sales Specialist	Arthur Barbas
Corporate Sponsorship Specialist	Laura Phillipps
Marketing Assistant	Connie Forbes
Vice President Operations	James McCormack
Senior Production Manager	Jessica L. Quirk
Production Manager	Mary Connelly
Project Manager	Anne Francis
Book Production Specialist	Ron Bilodeau
Production Assistants	Jeanette McCarthy
	Jennifer Power
	Christian Steinmetz
Systems Administrator	Richard Cassidy
Internet Technology Director	Aaron Shuman
Chief Financial Officer	Sharyn Chabot
Controller	Mandy Shito
Staff Accountant	Maya Santoso
Office Manager	Saudiyah Abdul-Rahim
Receptionist	Henrietta Murray
Publicity	Deborah Broide

PRINTED IN THE USA

SWEET PEPPERS Crisp and juicy bell peppers (so named for their shape) start out green in color and have a bittersweet, vegetal, and sometimes metallic flavor. As with many other varieties of both hot and sweet peppers, bell peppers change color as they mature on the vine. Depending on the variety, bell peppers can be red, yellow, orange, ivory, purple, or chocolate when they ripen. Red, yellow, and orange bell peppers are very sweet; ivory bell peppers are mild; purple and chocolate bell peppers taste more like green peppers and lose their exotic color when cooked. Elongated Italian frying peppers, also known as *cubanelles*, are thin skinned and sweet, with a color ranging from greenish yellow to red. They are most often stuffed with ground meat and roasted. Also excellent for stuffing, curvy bullhorn peppers can be either green or red. Diminutive sweet cherry peppers, not to be confused with their hot cherry pepper cousins, are attractive additions to antipasti or salads, whether they are green or red. Banana peppers are colored and shaped like their namesake; they are tangy as well as sweet.

COVER (*Cantaloupe*): Elizabeth Brandon, BACK COVER (*Sweet Peppers*): John Burgoyne

For list rental information, contact: ClientLogic, 1200 Harbor Blvd., 9th Floor, Weehawken, NJ 07087; 201-865-5800; fax 201-867-2450.
Editorial Office: 17 Station St., Brookline, MA 02445; 617-232-1000; fax 617-232-1572. Subscription inquiries, call 800-526-8442.
Postmaster: Send all new orders, subscription inquiries, and change-of-address notices to Cook's Illustrated, P.O. Box 7446, Red Oak, IA 51591-0446.

ON THE ROAD AGAIN

I have been riding motorcycles since I was 12, my first "ride" being a burgundy French moped that was purchased second-hand. It got me as far as the barn for milking or the Yellow Farmhouse for noon dinner, but going home, which was mostly uphill, was a chore. The moped was heavy, and its motor had significantly less power than our Sears push lawnmower.

My wife, Adrienne, and I spent our honeymoon on a Gold Wing, touring her childhood town of Earlville, N.Y. Then we made the rounds of the great Victorian white-tablecloth restaurants, with waitresses wearing starched-white uniforms and heavy white shoes with thick rubber soles, popovers in the bread basket, and the main course always a roast or chop.

Since then, four children have dampened our enthusiasm for motorcycle getaways, although a 1948 Indian Chief with the trademark suicide shift sits in our barn, used mostly for morning outings to the local diner. It suits me better than newer bikes because it seems to need my attention: starting it requires a graduate degree. (Choke down, key off, three strokes with kick-starter. Choke up three clicks, ignition on, retard timing, then one kick to start. Open oil filler cap, check flow, replace cap, return choke to top position.)

I like to ride bikes, but Lee, a friend of mine from Shushan, N.Y., rebuilds bikes (mostly Harleys) and owns a rare lemon yellow 1953 K Model (a stripped-down racing bike), the same bike he rode 9,000 miles across country and back. He told me that on one hot day, he was stuck behind a large truck and about 20 cars going up into the mountains of Arizona. They were at 6,000 feet so nobody was getting enough acceleration to pass the truck. Well, Lee had customized the bike with a cylinder of nitrous oxide that was activated by the right turn signal. (Injected into the cylinders, it about doubles the horsepower.) He told his girlfriend to hang on, moved out into the other lane, and pushed the button. Well, they were doing about 130 miles an hour as they got up to the truck and noticed

that the car just behind it was a cop. About an hour later, up in the mountains, the officer finally found him and signaled Lee over. Did he get arrested? Nope. The officer just wanted to see firsthand how Lee had tricked up his bike.

Most people would agree that anyone over 50 (count me in) has no business going fast. It seems self-evident that speed and youth are made for each other, so when a grandfather hops on a 115 horsepower V-Rod, the natural reaction is, "What's wrong with him?" He ought to be driving a Ford 350 towing a horse trailer or heading south with his RV for the winter.

In our town, the midlife crisis is almost an institution. Two years ago, Gerald, a talented, hard-working local carpenter, started to miss a day of work here and there, having decided to hang out by the Battenkill River or to show up one day, barefoot, to work with the road crew getting paid minimum wage. His final act of defiance was to purchase a '67 Camaro with a custom air scoop, which he proudly drove in the Fireman's Parade, beaming like a kid and racing the motor.

If my kids are listening, I'd like to say a word or two on behalf of Gerald, Lee, and the rest of us who are on the other side of 50. Maybe we look silly in our leather jackets astride a Fat Boy or vintage Indian. Maybe we're too old to do that cross-country bike trip one last time (although we think about it every night as we try to fall asleep). Maybe it's sheer stupidity to saddle up a horse and take off at a full gallop on a newly discovered logging road (as I did last weekend). Maybe we ought to preserve our last shreds of dignity and go along quietly, dressed in warm country tweeds and a nice pair of comfortable shoes. The problem is that we all know someone who died happily in the saddle.

So one of these days, I'm going to close the

Christopher Kimball

choke, prime the engine, kick-start it to life, and then head toward the diner for breakfast. And once I get there, I'll keep right on going, throttle open, face into the wind. I'll be thinking about Jack Kerouac, Hunter Thompson, Ken Kesey, and the Merry Pranksters. I'll remember the last time I saw Jerry playing "China Cat" at Winterland, Grace Slick belting out "White Rabbit" at a Halloween concert at Filmore East, and my 1970 visit to the Hog Farm just south of Taos, which, back then, seemed like the promised land. (Note to Wavy Gravy: It wasn't. I spent a weekend cleaning your filthy kitchen and doing the cooking. Oh, and nobody knew the first thing about farming.)

I admit that as a philosophy of life, the open road is pretty thin stuff in light of those who have given their lives to defend this country or have sacrificed everything for no more than a simple ideal. And it turned out there was a lot more to life than we thought; we lost friends who didn't make the curve or who couldn't figure a way to get off the road before it was too late. Yet our children deserve parents who still have their dreams, no matter how threadbare. My kids ask about my travels and I tell them stories, most of them true, about the ride down to the bluegrass festival on the Stanley Brothers farm in West Virginia or the time I drove 22 hours straight from San Bernardino to Santa Fe. I want my kids to know that the next time they hear the Indian start up in the barn, there is at least a possibility that I may not be back after breakfast. It's good for them to imagine that their father can still muster a bit of wanderlust, even though it's a pretty good bet that I'll be home by suppertime. It's taken half a century to realize that the song was only half right. Sure, it's been a long strange trip, but the surprise, the truth that we never expect, is that this is one trip that never really ends.

FOR INQUIRIES, ORDERS, OR MORE INFORMATION:

www.cooksillustrated.com

At www.cooksillustrated.com, you can order books and subscriptions, sign up for our free e-newsletter, or renew your magazine subscription. Join the Web site and you'll have access to 12 years of *Cook's* recipes, cookware tests, ingredient tastings, and more.

COOKBOOKS

We sell more than 40 cookbooks by the editors of *Cook's Illustrated*. To order, visit our bookstore at www.cooksillustrated.com or call 800-611-0759 (or 515-246-6911 from outside the U.S.).

COOK'S ILLUSTRATED Magazine

Cook's Illustrated magazine (ISSN 1068-2821), number 76, is published bimonthly by Boston Common Press Limited Partnership, 17 Station Street, Brookline, MA 02445. Copyright 2005 Boston Common Press Limited Partnership. Periodicals postage paid at Boston, Mass., and additional mailing offices, USPS #012487. POSTMASTER: Send address changes to Cook's Illustrated, P.O. Box 7446, Red Oak, IA 51591-0446. For subscription and gift subscription orders, subscription inquiries, or change-of-address notices, call 800-526-8442 in the U.S. or 515-247-7571 from outside the U.S., or write us at Cook's Illustrated, P.O. Box 7446, Red Oak, IA 51591-0446.

⇉ COMPILED BY SANDRA WU ⇇

Soaking Potatoes

How long can I keep peeled potatoes sitting in cold water in the refrigerator before I use them? I like to prep as much as possible well in advance when I know I'm having company.

MARCIA FRARY
FRAMINGHAM, MASS.

➤ To find out how long peeled potatoes could survive a stay in cold water, we peeled and sliced several batches for french fries, potato salad, and mashed potatoes and let them soak in the refrigerator for varying lengths of time.

When making french fries, we have found it best to soak cut potatoes for at least 30 minutes before cooking them. That's because soaking leaches out some of the starch and promotes a crisper exterior. But can you soak potatoes for too long? Potatoes soaked for two, six, and 12 hours yielded fries with equally soft, creamy interiors and crispy, golden brown exteriors. Potatoes soaked for 24 hours were slightly less crisp but still acceptable once fried. A two- or three-day soak, however, was beyond the pale. "They taste like old fries that have been sitting under the heat lamp for too long," said one taster, noting the paler, soggier exteriors and drier, mealier interiors.

Meanwhile, cubed potatoes for potato salad were tested three ways: boiled right away and left in cold water for four hours and 24 hours. The longer the potatoes soaked, the softer and mealier they became once cooked, but tasters agreed that none of the samples were undesirable. As for the mashed potatoes, we found that soaking the potatoes up to 24 hours made no noticeable changes in texture or flavor.

The lesson here? Preparing potatoes ahead of time is fine, but not by more than 24 hours if you plan to mash them or make potato salad and not by more than 12 hours if you plan to fry them.

Light Butter

Have you tried the new light butter from Land O' Lakes? I know you've rated regular Land O' Lakes highly in tastings. How does this new product compare?

SARAH SINDIAN
WALNUT, CALIF.

➤ While "regular" butter has 100 calories, 11 grams of fat, and 30 milligrams of cholesterol per tablespoon, each tablespoon of Land O' Lakes Light Butter has 50 calories, almost 6 grams of fat, and 15 mg of cholesterol. Unlike regular Land O' Lakes butter, made only from cream and natural flavoring, Land O' Lakes Light Butter (only available salted) contains additional water, stabilizers, and preservatives. Lighter in color, noticeably less smooth, and softer than regular butter, it is in terms of appearance and texture more like margarine. We doubted this reduced-fat butter would offer the same flavor and baking properties as regular butter but decided to run it through a few tests just to make sure.

LAND O' LAKES LIGHT BUTTER
Less fat, less flavor, more additives.

We tested it against the original in three applications: sautéed fish with browned butter sauce, sugar cookies, and pound cake, adjusting salt levels in these recipes as necessary. Used in the fish recipe, the light butter evaporated much more quickly in the pan than the regular butter, leaving us with unevenly browned fish fillets and a skimpy amount of browned butter that seized up almost immediately once plated. We don't recommend light butter for this recipe.

How about baked goods? While the dough in our standard sugar cookie recipe is firm enough to roll into balls, the version made with Land O' Lakes Light Butter was gloppy and difficult to handle. Instead of baking up into tender, chewy cookies with rich, buttery flavor, the reduced-fat cookies lacked strong butter flavor and spread into flat, tough disks with crispy edges. As for the pound cake, the light butter yielded a cake that was more dense and less flavorful than one made with regular butter.

While Land O' Lakes' regular unsalted butter is a favorite in the test kitchen, we can't say the same of its light butter. The two products are not interchangeable. In our opinion, the reduction in fat and calories is simply not worth the trade-off in taste and texture.

Indian Sugar

In one of my New England cookbooks, I noticed a recipe that calls for Indian sugar. What is it and where can I get it?

ELLY MILLER
PITTSFIELD, MASS.

➤ Indian sugar is none other than granulated maple sugar: not exactly an exotic ingredient but not exactly a mainstream one either. It is made by heating maple syrup to about 260 degrees

---

WHAT IS IT?

I found this tool at a flea market and thought it might be used for sweeping excess flour from a cutting board or work surface. Am I right?

LEE WILMETH, CAVE CREEK, ARIZ.

➤ Your flea market find is a *visp*, a 12-inch-long Swedish whisk made of thin birch branches bound together by additional strips of pliable birch. Believe it or not, this tool is used to whisk gravies and sauces.

We were initially doubtful that this flimsy-looking contraption could whisk anything, but it was surprisingly effective at whisking gravy and béchamel. The pliable, almost brush-like branches were able to get into the corners of the saucepan, an area hard to reach with most traditional stainless steel whisks. In addition, the less abrasive natural material posed little risk of damaging delicate nonstick surfaces. Cleaning the visp entailed swirling it vigorously in hot soapy water, rinsing it under hot running water, and letting it air-dry.

Although the Swedish visp is sturdier than it looks, it still isn't an all-around replacement for a stainless steel whisk. You could never get it to beat egg whites or whip cream properly. But it doesn't hurt to have a visp around for sauces—it certainly makes an interesting conversation piece. You can order a visp (item #2640) from Hemslöjd (800-779-3344, www.hemslojd.com) for $6.50.

What looks like a miniature broom but works as a whisk? The Swedish visp.

Fahrenheit, removing it from the heat source, and stirring continuously until all of the moisture is gone, leaving behind light brown granules of sugar.

The origin of maple sugar production has been attributed to Indian tribes in the Northeast, thus giving "Indian sugar" its name.

Indian sugar is also called *maple powder, maple sprinkles,* and *maple granules* and can be found at most natural foods stores as well as online. Brown sugar, while lacking in maple flavor, is similar in texture and makes a decent substitute in recipes, cup for cup.

To Sift or Not to Sift

I hate to sift flour. Is it really necessary? Can I just use a whisk to remove lumps?

FELICIA DONNOLO
MANALAPAN, N.J.

> Sifting removes lumps and aerates the flour so it can be incorporated more easily into batters. When we tested equal weights of sifted versus whisked flour in recipes, we noticed that both methods delivered similar results. Cakes made with sifted flour were a tad taller (sifting does aerate the flour more than whisking), but the differences were quite small.

Sifting does make a significant difference, however, in a way you might not anticipate. Sifted flour weighs 20 to 25 percent less per cup than unsifted flour, and we've found that just one additional ounce of flour can cause a normally moist and level cake to bake up drier and with a domed top. That's why we always weigh flour when baking.

If you are not going to weigh flour, you must pay special attention to recipe directions regarding sifting. For recipes that read "1 cup sifted flour," sift the flour directly into a measuring cup set on top of parchment paper and then level off the excess. For recipes reading "1 cup flour, sifted," measure the flour first (we use the dip-and-sweep method in the test kitchen, dipping a dry measure into a canister and then sweeping off the excess) and then sift it.

Pressure Cooker Chicken Stock

Your Quick Chicken Stock recipe is a lot faster to make than a traditional stock, but it still requires a decent amount of time hovering over the stove. Would this recipe work in a pressure cooker?

SID DANIELS, JR.
ELVERSON, PA.

> As you've probably discovered, if you're willing to use meat in your stock rather than sticking to just bones and scraps, you can have a rich, full-flavored stock in about an hour. Our "quick" recipe employs the basic methods of sautéing and sweating onions and chicken pieces, simmering them in water, and straining and defatting the resulting stock. We figured it couldn't get any

easier than that until you raised the question of the pressure cooker. We decided to investigate by developing a recipe for Pressure Cooker Chicken Stock (see Cook's Extra, below).

It also takes about an hour to prepare this recipe, but less active cooking time is involved. For 3 quarts of chicken stock, you'll need 1 onion, 6 pounds of chicken legs, and a couple of bay leaves. Once the onion is sautéed, the chicken can go directly into the pressure cooker with the water and bay leaves: no additional sautéing or sweating is necessary. While this version was a bit cloudier than our Quick Chicken Stock, we also found it more fully flavored.

Our conclusion? Unless you need more than 3 quarts of stock (not possible in even the largest capacity pressure cooker) or want a stock with a pristine appearance for something like consommé, the pressure cooker method is fine.

Wheat Three Ways

I have found conflicting information about whole wheat, cracked wheat, and bulgur. For instance, I've seen something called "cracked wheat bulgur," but I thought bulgur and cracked wheat were different. Please help clarify these terms.

JEANNE WEHMAN
DES PLAINES, ILL.

> Wheat berries (what you refer to as "whole wheat"), cracked wheat, and bulgur are all forms of wheat; the difference lies in the degree to which they are processed. Wheat berries are whole, unprocessed kernels of wheat. Cracked wheat consists of wheat berries that have been broken into coarse, medium, and fine pieces. Bulgur goes a step further: The wheat kernels have been steamed, dried, and ground.

Wheat berries must be cooked for an hour, while cracked wheat is done after 15 minutes on the stovetop. Bulgur, because it has been partly cooked, is ready after five minutes of simmering or a 15-minute soak in hot water. Even after an hour of cooking, wheat berries retain a chewy, al dente texture. Cracked wheat is still chewy but more tender than wheat berries, and bulgur is even finer in texture than cracked wheat and very tender.

WHEAT BERRIES

CRACKED WHEAT

BULGUR

While cracked wheat is similar to bulgur, the two products are not the same. We would assume that anything labeled "cracked wheat bulgur" is, in fact, just plain old bulgur.

Errata

> In the May/June 2005 issue, we reported our attempts to use the Flavor Express Marinator to stuff pork chops with spinach and cheese. We should have indicated that this product is primarily intended to inject liquid into food. We regret the confusion.

> Step 3 of Grill-Roasted Pork Loin for Gas Grill (July/August 2005, page 7) should have directed the cook to continue with the Grill-Roasted Pork Loin for Charcoal Grill recipe from step 4, *turning off all burners except the primary burner after browning the pork.*

Quick Tips

≽ COMPILED BY ERIKA BRUCE ≼

No-Skid Cutting Board

Lisa Grant of Providence, R.I., found a clever use for all the rubber bands taking up space in her kitchen drawers. She sprinkles a handful on the counter and places her cutting board on top, thereby preventing any slipping or sliding while she chops. If the bands get contaminated with juices from meat or poultry, she just throws them out.

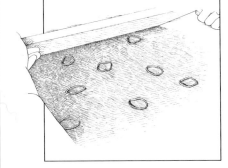

Securing Kitchen Garbage Bags

Most kitchen garbage bags tend to slip down inside the trash can, inviting an unpleasant mess to clean up later. Judith Howard of North Truro, Mass., suggests securing the bags to the receptacle with a lightweight bungee cord. Just make sure you don't throw out the cord along with the trash when you change the bag!

Impromptu Bread Mold

Barbara Hermansen of Winnetka, Ill., figured out a way to keep her loaves of bread in their long, narrow shape as they proof without using a mold.

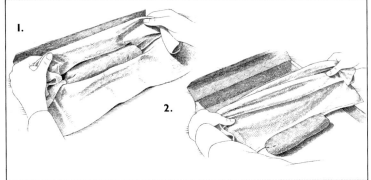

1. Save the cardboard box from a spent roll of parchment paper or extra-wide aluminum foil or plastic wrap. Line the box with a lightly floured kitchen towel and place the shaped loaf inside, seam side down.
2. When the loaf has proofed, gently roll it over onto a baking sheet or peel (seam side down again), then slash it and bake it.

No-Waste Salad Dressing

Elyse Boule of Greenwood Village, Colo., not only prepares vinaigrettes in her children's "sippy" cups but uses the cups as a tool for dressing her salads as well. The dressing is released slowly from the small spout, making it nearly impossible to waste vinaigrette or overdress a salad.

1. Add all the dressing ingredients to the cup and secure the lid.
2. While holding one finger securely over the spout, shake the cup vigorously to incorporate. Remove your finger from the spout and sprinkle the dressing over the salad.

Small Strainer Stand-In

If you don't happen to have a small enough strainer for small jobs (such as straining the juice of one or two lemons) and would rather not haul out your larger strainer, Andrea King of Quincy, Mass., has a tip for you.

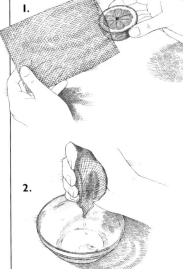

1. Save the leftover mesh bags from small produce items (such as shallots or new potatoes). After cleaning the bag well, drop in a lemon half.
2. Squeeze as much juice as needed. All of the seeds and pith will be trapped in the mesh bag.

Foil for Overheated Pan Handles

When testing skillets for the November/December 2004 issue, we noticed a drawback in the design of several pans: Over gas heat, their hollow handles heated up enough to require potholders. Peter Hofer of McCormick, S.C., wrote in to offer his solution to this problem: stuffing the handle with aluminum foil. The foil interrupts the heat flow from the burner up through the handle, keeping it cool enough to be grabbed without a potholder.

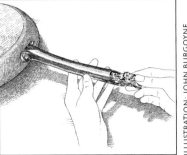

Send Us Your Tip We will provide a complimentary one-year subscription for each tip we print. Send your tip, name, and address to Quick Tips, Cook's Illustrated, P.O. Box 470589, Brookline, MA 02447, or to quicktips@bcpress.com.

ILLUSTRATION: JOHN BURGOYNE

Pastry Toolbox

Baking buffs know how quickly all the necessary tools of the trade can overtake the limited space in their kitchen drawers. Janeen Rojas of Baltimore, Md., avoids this problem by storing her baking gadgets (cookie cutters, icing spatulas, measuring cups, and the like) in an inexpensive plastic toolbox, purchased from a hardware store.

Lump-Free Polenta

One way to prevent lumpy polenta is to pour the cornmeal into boiling water in a fine steady stream while slowly whisking, a process many cooks are tempted to rush. Charles Gehring of Altamont, N.Y., found a method that's practically foolproof.

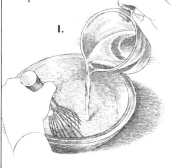

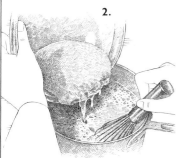

1. Using a basic recipe of 1 part cornmeal to 4 parts water, whisk one-quarter of the cold water into the cornmeal until it is well incorporated.
2. Bring the remaining water to a boil, remix the cornmeal mixture, then add all at once, stirring well, and continue cooking according to the recipe instructions.

Makeshift Colander

To avoid dirtying a large colander for a small cleaning job, Christine Brown of Castle Rock, Colo., reuses the perforated plastic containers in which small produce items such as cherry tomatoes and berries are packaged.

1. Place the items to be cleaned in an empty container and rinse, letting the water drain out through the holes.
2. Once thoroughly cleaned, transfer the items to paper towels to dry.

'Re-Bagging' Frozen Produce

Savvy cooks often keep bags of frozen fruit and vegetables on hand in case they need something in a pinch. The question is, what's the best way to store the leftovers from a large bag? Brenda Rossini of Bucyrus, Kan., came up with this efficient trick.

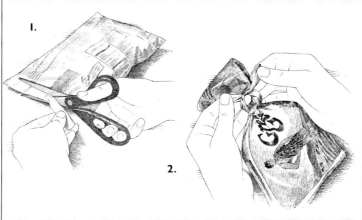

1. Using scissors, cut a thin strip from the top of the bag to open it.
2. After removing the desired amount of fruit or vegetables, twist the bag shut to remove excess air and secure by tying the cut strip of plastic at the base of the twist.

Cinnamon Stir Stick

Ingrid Hoff of North Vancouver, B.C., discovered a way to add honey to her cup of tea—and add a hint of cinnamon at the same time.

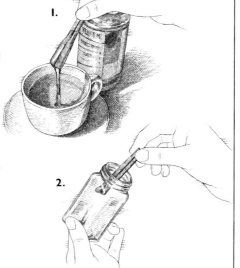

1. Twirl a cinnamon stick in a jar of honey to pick up the desired amount, then transfer to the cup of tea. Use the stick to stir and dissolve the honey.
2. To get more than one use out of each cinnamon stick, rinse, dry well, and store in an airtight container.

Keeping Tabs on Labels

It's always a good idea to label and date containers of leftover food stored in the refrigerator or freezer, and using masking tape is a great way to avoid marking up your Tupperware. But these pieces of tape can be tricky to pry off. Joy Vander Kolk of Lansing, Mich., employs a simple trick to keep her labels easy to remove.

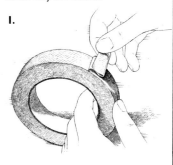

1. Fold over a small section at the end of the roll of masking tape to create a tab; then tear off a piece of tape and label the container.
2. Once the leftovers have been used up, just grab the tab and pull; the tape comes right off.

Windproof Chimney Lighting

Anyone who enjoys grilling well into autumn knows how frustrating it can be to light a chimney full of charcoal on a blustery fall day. Instead of using a match or lighter, Drew Kovash of Dickinson, N.D., gets the fire going with a small butane torch (the kind used for caramelizing crème brûlée).

Better Chicken Fajitas

Dry, stringy chicken breasts and limp, tasteless vegetables desperately need a truckload of toppings. How about chicken fajitas that taste great on their own?

⇒ BY SANDRA WU ⇐

With or without the sizzling cast-iron skillet, what passes for chicken fajitas in most restaurants these days is about as authentic as Belgian toaster waffles. Guacamole, sour cream, and salsa are slathered on in a weak attempt to mask the bland, soggy flavors of the underlying ingredients. We wanted to go back to the basics, a simple combination of smoky grilled vegetables and strips of chicken, wrapped up at the table in warm flour tortillas.

Meat Management

While the skirt steak in classic beef fajitas has no need for a marinade to add juiciness or flavor, boneless chicken breasts need all the help they can get. Starting with a mixture of lime juice, vegetable oil, garlic, salt, and pepper as my base, I tried several marinating methods. Grilling the chicken plain and tossing the cooked strips into the marinade (now really a sauce) left the chicken with only superficial flavor. Brining—soaking in a saltwater solution—seasoned the chicken and kept it juicy, but tasters found the meat too moist—waterlogged, even. "It might as well have been poached," said one. Making a "brinerade" (a cross between a brine and a marinade) by adding the marinade to a concentrated 2-cup brine only weakened the final flavors. Up to this point, soaking the chicken breasts directly in the marinade yielded the best results: tender browned chicken with bright, unadulterated tang. The high-acid mixture (⅓ cup lime juice and 4 tablespoons oil) not only added fresh citrus flavor notes but also reduced the marinating time to a mere 15 minutes—any longer and the meat started to "cook" in the acid, like a "chicken ceviche" of sorts.

Although moving in the right direction, the marinade still lacked smokiness and depth. After trying numerous (and unsuccessful) flavor additions, I finally hit upon Worcestershire sauce, an unlikely candidate for chicken but one that has some of the characteristics of *umami*, an overused and little-understood culinary term that refers to a fifth taste sensation beyond the familiar sweet, sour, bitter, and salty. (Some simply liken it to "meaty," while many think of umami as an unusual, sophisticated juxtaposition of flavors that provides a unique taste experience. I think it's like great art: You just know it when you taste it.) A mere tablespoon of Worcestershire was plenty to add another layer of saltiness and smoke without revealing its true identity. A bit of brown sugar helped round out the salty flavors, and minced jalapeño and cilantro added freshness.

Grill Work

Both green and red bell peppers gave the fajitas some needed contrast, not just in terms of color but in their bitter and sweet flavors. Quartering the peppers allowed them to lie flat on the grill and cook evenly on both sides. Onion wedges cooked unevenly,

Fajitas are a complete meal from the grill, but each component needs special handling.

while rounds were both pretty and practical. I quickly discovered that whereas the chicken needed blazing-hot coals, the vegetables, which are more prone to burning, required more moderate heat. Placing them over medium-hot coals helped them brown nicely as well as cook through without burning.

To allow the chicken and vegetables to cook side by side at slightly different heat levels, I created a simple two-level fire. I started with a full chimney of ignited coals spread in a single layer on the bottom of the grill, then added another 20 unlit coals to just one side of the grill, and waited until that side became hot (the coals on the other half of the grill were just medium-hot). Once the grill grate was in place, the chicken cooked for 8 to 10 minutes on the hotter side of the grill, while the vegetables cooked safely on the cooler side.

It's a Wrap

As for the flour tortillas, 8- to 10-inch rounds yielded too much excess tortilla; small (but not dainty) 6-inch tortillas were the perfect size. Heating each side of the tortillas for 20 brief seconds on the cooler end of the grill allowed them to puff up and lose their raw, gummy texture. Quickly wrapping the warmed tortillas in a clean kitchen towel or foil prevented them from becoming dry and brittle.

With the warm tortillas steaming in the wrapper and the requisite toppings ready to go, all that was left to do was separate the onion into rings and

Keys to a Better Marinade

Our marinade transforms bland chicken in just 15 minutes. We found that a generous dose of lime juice and a shot of Worcestershire sauce were key. The lime juice adds bracing acidity, while the Worcestershire (made with molasses, anchovies, tamarind, onion, garlic, and other seasonings) lends smoky, salty depth.

TANGY   **SMOKY, SALTY**

We tested dozens of fajita recipes and found most to be disappointing. Here are three of the worst offenders.

BIG AND BLAND **SOUTHWESTERN STIR-FRY** **GRITTY AND CRUNCHY**

One recipe with large strips of roasted chicken, huge chunks of bell pepper, and thick onion wedges was nearly impossible to eat and awfully bland (left). Another coated everything with a thick, goopy sauce that reminded tasters of a bad stir-fry (center). Chicken breasts coated with a spice rub and paired with undercooked onions and peppers were a recipe for overseasoned chicken and bland, raw-tasting vegetables (right).

slice the bell peppers and chicken breasts into strips. But something was still missing. By tossing just a small amount of unused reserved marinade back in with the chicken strips and vegetables, I was able to give them a burst of fresh flavor. It wasn't until I'd eaten my way through half of a chicken fajita that I realized I'd forgotten to add any condiments.

CHICKEN FAJITAS FOR CHARCOAL GRILL
SERVES 4 TO 6

The chicken and vegetables in these fajitas are only mildly spicy. For more heat, include the jalapeño seeds and ribs when mincing. When you head outside to grill, bring along a clean kitchen towel or a large piece of foil in which to wrap the tortillas and keep them warm as they come off the grill. Although the chicken and vegetables have enough flavor to stand on their own, accompaniments (guacamole, salsa, sour cream, shredded cheddar or Monterey Jack cheese, and lime wedges) can be offered at the table. For our recipes for salsa and guacamole, see Cook's Extra (below). The chicken tenderloins can be reserved for another use or marinated and grilled along with the breasts.

- 1/3 cup juice from 2 to 3 limes
- 6 tablespoons vegetable oil
- 3 medium garlic cloves, minced or pressed through garlic press (1 tablespoon)
- 1 tablespoon Worcestershire sauce
- 1 1/2 teaspoons brown sugar
- 1 jalapeño chile, seeds and ribs removed, chile minced
- 1 1/2 tablespoons minced fresh cilantro leaves Table salt and ground black pepper
- 3 boneless, skinless chicken breasts (about 1 1/2 pounds), trimmed of fat, tenderloins removed, breasts pounded to 1/2-inch thickness
- 1 large red onion (about 14 ounces), peeled and cut into 1/2-inch-thick rounds (do not separate rings)
- 1 large red bell pepper (about 10 ounces), quartered, stemmed, and seeded
- 1 large green bell pepper (about 10 ounces), quartered, stemmed, and seeded
- 8–12 (6-inch) flour tortillas

1. In medium bowl, whisk together lime juice, 4 tablespoons oil, garlic, Worcestershire, brown sugar, jalapeño, cilantro, 1 teaspoon salt, and 3/4 teaspoon pepper. Reserve 1/4 cup marinade in small bowl; set aside. Add another teaspoon salt to remaining marinade. Place chicken in marinade; cover with plastic wrap and refrigerate 15 minutes. Brush both sides of onion rounds and peppers with remaining 2 tablespoons oil and season with salt and pepper.

2. Meanwhile, using large chimney starter, ignite 6 quarts charcoal briquettes and burn until coals are fully ignited, about 20 minutes. Empty coals into grill, spreading them in even single layer; place additional 20 unlit coals over lit coals on one side of grill to create two-level fire. Position grill grate over coals and heat grate 5 minutes; scrape clean with grill brush.

3. Remove chicken from marinade and place chicken smooth side down on hotter side of grill; discard remaining marinade. Place onion rounds and peppers (skin side down) on cooler side of grill. Cook chicken until well browned, 4 to 5 minutes; using tongs, flip chicken and continue grilling until chicken is no longer pink when cut into with paring knife or instant-read thermometer inserted into thickest part registers about 160 degrees, 4 to 5 minutes longer. Meanwhile, cook peppers until spottily charred and crisp-tender, 8 to 10 minutes, turning once or twice as needed; cook onions until tender and charred on both sides, 10 to 12 minutes, turning every 3 to 4 minutes. When chicken and vegetables are done, transfer to large plate; tent with foil to keep warm.

> **COOK'S EXTRA** gives you free recipes online. When you don't feel like grilling, try our Chicken Fajitas Indoors: Visit www.cooksillustrated.com and key in code 9052. For Fresh Tomato Salsa, key in code 9053, and for Chunky Guacamole, key in code 9054. These recipes will be available until November 1, 2005.

4. Working in 2 or 3 batches, place tortillas in single layer on cooler side of now-empty grill and cook until warm and lightly browned, about 20 seconds per side (do not grill too long or tortillas will become brittle). As tortillas are done, wrap in kitchen towel or large sheet of foil.

5. Separate onions into rings and place in medium bowl; slice bell peppers lengthwise into 1/4-inch strips and place in bowl with onions. Add 2 tablespoons reserved unused marinade to vegetables and toss well to combine. Slice chicken into 1/4-inch strips and toss with remaining 2 tablespoons reserved marinade in another bowl; arrange chicken and vegetables on large platter and serve with warmed tortillas.

CHICKEN FAJITAS FOR GAS GRILL

1. Follow recipe for Chicken Fajitas for Charcoal Grill through step 1.

2. Light all burners on gas grill and turn to high, cover, and heat grill until hot, about 15 minutes; scrape grill grate clean with grill brush. Leave one burner on high heat while turning remaining burner(s) down to medium. Continue with recipe from step 3, cooking chicken and vegetables covered.

3. When grill is empty, set all burners to medium. Working in batches, if necessary, place tortillas in single layer on grate and grill until warm and lightly browned, about 20 seconds per side. As they are done, wrap tortillas in kitchen towel or large sheet of foil. Proceed as directed in step 5 of Chicken Fajitas for Charcoal Grill.

TASTING:
Supermarket Flour Tortillas

It's no surprise that the best flour tortillas are freshly made to order. But those of us without a local *tortillería* must make do with the packaged offerings at the local supermarket. To find out which ones taste best, we rounded up every 6-inch flour tortilla we could find (usually labeled "fajita size") and headed into the test kitchen to taste them.

Tasters immediately zeroed in on texture, which varied dramatically from "doughy and stale" to "thin and flaky." The thinner brands were the hands-down winners. Most brands had a mild, pleasantly wheaty flavor, but two of the doughier brands, Olé and La Banderita (both made by the same company), were panned for off, sour notes. Our advice is simple: Get the thinnest tortillas you can find at your local market. –Garth Clingingsmith

YOU CAN NEVER BE TOO THIN
Thin, flaky Tyson Mexican Original Flour Tortillas, Fajita Style, were tasters' clear favorite.

The Ultimate Vegetable Torta

Could we turn bland and soggy piles of eggplant and zucchini into a rich, savory tart?

≥ BY SEAN LAWLER ≤

Pizza may be the one that went on to international superstardom, but there are numerous lesser-known savory Italian tarts and pies equally deserving of the spotlight. And in most of these tortas, or tarts, it is the region's seasonal vegetables that take center stage, while the basic pizza components—cheese and crust—play supporting roles. The version I find the most appealing is a crustless, late-summer torta made with eggplant, zucchini, tomatoes, and bell peppers. When well made, it is not just a vegetarian main course but one of those rare four-star make-ahead recipes that never fails to please.

Like many authentic regional Italian recipes, however, this one has traveled a rocky road to the American kitchen. My recipe research told me that the most promising approach consisted of layers of roasted vegetable slices and cheese baked in a springform pan and then unmolded. Many recipes included beaten eggs poured over the top of the vegetables prior to baking, which made them easier to slice, as the eggs held everything together. The glossy magazine photo that accompanied one of these recipes promised a showstopper: a neat, elegant wedge displaying a colorful cross-section of thinly sliced roasted vegetables, carefully layered and bound with a delicate egg custard. But neither that recipe nor any of the others produced anything close to that impressive ideal. Instead, I was faced with pile after pile of soggy vegetables, impressive only in their ability to elicit sympathy from my colleagues. They had watched me spend hours slicing, roasting, and layering vegetables only to end up with a bland, watery mess that squished instead of sliced.

Water, Water Everywhere

Washed-out flavor and a wet, mushy texture—these two problems shared a common cause: the high water content of the eggplant, zucchini, and tomatoes. Ridding the vegetables of as much moisture as possible before layering them into the pan would, I hoped, concentrate their flavors and produce firm, appealing slices. In many test kitchen recipes, eggplant slices are salted and pressed prior to cooking to tame bitterness and

With a crisp bread-crumb crust and alternating layers of vegetables, cheese, and custard, this summer tart combines the best elements of pizza and quiche.

draw out excess moisture. Although bitterness is not an issue, the technique works just as well with zucchini and tomatoes, and it was not until I applied it with all three vegetables that I began to turn out tortas that showed promise.

Salting and pressing were only half the battle, however. How best to precook the vegetables before assembling? A frustrating round of testing involving broiling, roasting, steaming, and sautéing revealed that aside from their high moisture content, my various summer vegetables didn't have much in common. After salting, each required a different approach to drive off the remaining moisture. The eggplant, for example, responded well to high-heat roasting. In a 450-degree oven, the spongy slices dried out and browned nicely, collapsing to a fraction of their original thickness and releasing clouds of steam whenever I opened the oven door.

Zucchini is more dense, however, and thus retains more of its moisture when oven-roasted. Roasted zucchini may be fine for eating as is, but after a second trip to the oven inside the torta, the slices were a soggy, seedy mess. A test bowl of thin zucchini slices microwaved on high turned out soft and soggy, as expected. But as I was preparing another batch of vegetables for the next round of tests, something occurred to me. The paper towels I used to dry the salted vegetables, if left in contact with them, continued to draw out moisture as they sat. What if I microwaved a whole stack of zucchini on paper towels? Would the towels absorb the steam, leaving the slices nice and dry? After 10 minutes on high power, the stack weighted with a heavy plate, the zucchini slices were bright green but tender and dry while the paper towels were soaked. Layered into the torta, these slices maintained the slightest bite, which tasters thought contrasted nicely with the softer roasted eggplant.

The red bell peppers were mercifully uncomplicated. I simply roasted them whole in the oven alongside the eggplant to save time, then they were peeled and ready to go. Finally, I reckoned with the tomato slices. Although they gave up much of their moisture when salted and gently pressed, they retained enough water to disintegrate when baked inside the torta. The solution was to place the tomato slices not in the torta but on top of it, where they dried out nicely in the gentle heat of the oven.

Torta Reform

My tortas were now coming out firm and neatly sliceable, with excellent flavor, but they needed some cosmetic help. The custard—beaten eggs and a little cream for richness—would stick to the sides of the springform pan and burn. And no matter how well I greased the pan, the bottom layer of vegetables tended to stick as well. Evidently, I would need some sort of crust, but I was determined to keep it simple. Dry bread crumbs sprinkled onto the greased pan were useless, as only a few of them would stick to the sides. Then I tried a technique used to make graham cracker crusts for pies: binding the crumbs with

A Wet Torta Is a Bad Torta

Why bother salting and pressing all those vegetables? Because our moisture removal techniques extract more than 4 cups of liquid from the vegetables, which otherwise would make a very soggy torta.

melted butter to form a moist, slightly sticky mixture that I could press into the bottom and sides of the pan in a thick, protective layer. This simple crust worked wonders for the edges of the torta, baking up crisp and dark brown and putting an end to leaking eggs.

All that was left to do was choose some complementary flavors to match the roasted vegetables. Tasters approved of lemon juice and fresh thyme and preferred the stronger, saltier Asiago cheese to Parmesan. They also demanded garlic, but as I hadn't yet turned on a burner to sauté anything, I was at a loss as to how to incorporate it. Back to the oven, I wrapped a whole head of garlic in foil and roasted it with the eggplant and peppers. The garlic flavor mellowed and the cloves turned so soft that they could be stirred into the custard.

All my torta needed now was a long bake at a relatively slow 375 degrees—any hotter and the edges burned long before the center was set. Cooled slightly and unmolded to oohs and ahhs, this torta was a stunner.

VEGETABLE TORTA
SERVES 6 TO 8 AS A MAIN DISH OR 8 TO 10 AS A SIDE DISH

To prevent sticking, the eggplant slices are roasted on wire racks set over baking sheets. Alternatively, they can be roasted directly on well-oiled baking sheets; after roasting, use a thin spatula to carefully remove the slices. Hard Italian Asiago is too mild for this recipe—use a domestic Asiago (available in supermarkets) that yields to pressure when pressed. The torta is best served warm or at room temperature.

TO MAKE AHEAD: The eggplant, garlic, and peppers can be roasted, cooled, wrapped in plastic, and refrigerated for up to 24 hours before assembly. Or the torta can be assembled, baked, cooled, removed from the springform pan, wrapped in plastic, and refrigerated overnight. Allow the torta to stand at room temperature for about 1 hour before serving.

Vegetables
- 3 medium eggplants (about 1 pound each), halved crosswise and cut lengthwise into 1/2-inch-thick slices, outer thin slices of skin from each half discarded
  Kosher salt

- 3 tablespoons olive oil, plus additional oil for brushing wire racks
- 1 medium garlic head, outer papery skins removed and top third of head cut off and discarded
  Ground black pepper
- 2 medium red bell peppers (about 8 ounces each)
- 2 large ripe tomatoes (about 8 ounces each), cored and cut into 1/4-inch-thick slices
- 4 medium zucchini (about 8 ounces each), cut on steep bias into 1/4-inch-thick slices

Crust
- 4 large slices (about 6 ounces) white sandwich bread, torn into quarters
- 3 tablespoons unsalted butter, melted, plus additional softened butter for greasing pan
- 2 ounces Asiago cheese, grated on fine holes of box grater (about 2/3 cup)

Custard and Garnish
- 3 large eggs
- 1/4 cup heavy cream
- 2 teaspoons minced fresh thyme leaves
- 2 tablespoons juice from 1 lemon
- 3 ounces Asiago cheese, grated on fine holes of box grater (about 1 cup)
- 2 tablespoons thinly sliced fresh basil leaves

1. **FOR THE VEGETABLES:** Sprinkle both sides of eggplant slices with generous 1 tablespoon kosher salt; transfer salted eggplant to large colander set over bowl. Let stand until eggplant releases about 2 tablespoons liquid, about 30 minutes. Arrange eggplant slices in single layer on double layer paper towels; cover with another double layer paper towels. Firmly press each slice to flatten and remove as much liquid as possible.

2. While eggplant drains, adjust oven racks to upper-middle and lower-middle positions; heat oven to 450 degrees. Set 2 wire racks on 2 rimmed baking sheets; brush both racks with oil. Place garlic cut side up on sheet of aluminum foil and drizzle garlic with 1 1/2 teaspoons oil; wrap foil tightly around garlic and set aside.

3. Arrange salted and pressed eggplant slices on oiled racks; brush slices on both sides with 2 tablespoons oil and sprinkle with pepper.

4. Brush peppers with remaining 1 1/2 teaspoons oil and place 1 pepper on each baking sheet with eggplant. Place baking sheets in oven; place foil-wrapped garlic on lower oven rack alongside baking sheet. Roast vegetables until eggplant slices are soft, well browned, and collapsed, and peppers are blistered and beginning to brown, 30 to 35 minutes, rotating baking sheets and turning peppers over halfway through baking time. Transfer peppers to medium bowl, cover with plastic wrap, and set aside; allow eggplant to cool on wire racks. Continue to roast garlic until cloves are very soft and golden brown, 10 to 15 minutes longer. Set garlic aside to cool. Reduce oven temperature to 375 degrees.

Maximizing the Flavor of the Vegetables

THE FIRST STEPS: Our torta calls for 3 pounds of eggplant, 2 pounds of zucchini, and 1 pound of tomatoes. Before these vegetables can be layered into the springform pan, some of their liquid must be removed. Slicing, salting, and pressing with paper towels are just the first steps.

1. SLICE   2. SALT   3. PRESS

EGGPLANT: ROAST   ZUCCHINI: MICROWAVE   TOMATOES: BAKE

THE SECOND STEPS: After slicing, salting, and pressing, each vegetable then requires a special technique to remove even more liquid.
EGGPLANT: Eggplant should be roasted in a 450-degree oven until browned and dry. (Garlic and red peppers don't have as much excess moisture, but their flavors benefit from roasting, too.)
ZUCCHINI: Zucchini will fall apart if roasted. We had better luck microwaving it between paper towels weighted with heavy plates.
TOMATOES: Tomatoes don't require precooking—they will continue to dry out if baked on top of the torta.

1. Press bread-crumb mixture into bottom of pan, then tilt pan upright over bowl and press crumbs against sides of pan.

2. Layer eggplant into pan without overlapping. Tear slices as needed to fill in gaps.

3. After adding custard, tilt pan from side to side and shake gently back and forth to ensure even distribution.

4. Arrange tomatoes in circular pattern on top of torta, partially overlapping.

5. While vegetables roast, arrange tomato slices on double layer paper towels; sprinkle with 1 teaspoon kosher salt. Let stand 30 minutes, then cover with another double layer paper towels; gently press tomatoes to remove moisture.

6. While vegetables roast and tomatoes stand, sprinkle both sides of zucchini slices with generous 1 tablespoon kosher salt; transfer salted zucchini slices to large colander set over bowl. Let zucchini stand until it releases about ⅓ cup liquid, about 30 minutes. Place triple layer paper towels on large, microwave-safe plate. Arrange a third of zucchini slices on paper towels; cover with another triple layer towels, pressing to remove moisture. Repeat, arranging remaining zucchini in two additional layers separated by triple layer paper towels, and placing triple layer paper towels on top of final zucchini layer. Place another heavy, microwave-safe plate on zucchini stack; press firmly to compress. Microwave stack on high power until steaming, about 10 minutes. Using potholders, carefully remove stack from microwave and let stand 5 minutes; remove top plate.

7. When peppers are cool, remove skins. Slit peppers pole to pole; discard stem and seeds. Unfurl peppers so they lie flat; cut each pepper lengthwise into 3 pieces.

8. **FOR THE CRUST:** Pulse torn bread in food processor until coarsely ground, about ten 1-second pulses. With machine running, pour butter through feed tube and process until combined, about 4 seconds. Add ⅔ cup Asiago and pulse to combine, about three 1-second pulses. Transfer mixture to bowl. Do not wash food processor.

9. Thoroughly grease 9-inch springform pan with softened butter. Measure out 1 cup bread-crumb mixture and sprinkle in bottom of springform pan; using flat bottom of measuring cup, press crumbs into even layer. Holding pan upright, press additional 1¼ cups bread-crumb mixture into sides of pan, forming thick, even layer that stops about ¼ inch from top of pan. Reserve leftover bread-crumb mixture.

10. **FOR THE CUSTARD:** Squeeze garlic head at root end to remove cloves from skins. In small bowl, mash cloves with fork and place in food processor; add eggs, cream, thyme, and lemon juice. Process until thoroughly combined, about 30 seconds.

11. **TO ASSEMBLE AND BAKE:** Arrange single layer of eggplant on top of bread-crumb crust, tearing pieces as needed to cover entire bottom surface. Sprinkle evenly with 2 tablespoons cheese. Arrange single layer of zucchini and sprinkle with 2 tablespoons cheese. Repeat with another layer of eggplant and cheese. Layer in all red pepper pieces; sprinkle with 2 tablespoons cheese. Pour half of custard over vegetables; tilt pan and shake gently from side to side to distribute evenly over vegetables and down sides. Repeat layering of eggplant and zucchini, sprinkling each layer with 2 tablespoons cheese (about 4 more layers). Pour remaining custard over vegetables; tilt and gently shake pan to distribute. Arrange tomato slices around perimeter of pan, overlapping to fit, then fill in center with remaining slices. Press tomatoes gently with hands. Sprinkle torta with 3 tablespoons reserved bread-crumb mixture; discard any remaining bread crumbs.

12. Set torta on baking sheet and bake on lower-middle rack until tomatoes are dry, bread-crumb topping is lightly browned, center of torta looks firm and level (not soft or wet), and torta registers internal temperature of 175 degrees on instant-read thermometer, 75 to 90 minutes. Cool torta for 10 minutes on wire rack; run thin-bladed knife around inside of pan to loosen, then remove springform pan ring.

13. **TO SERVE:** Slide thin metal spatula between crust and pan bottom to loosen. Let stand 20 minutes longer (to serve warm) or cool to room temperature, sprinkle with basil, and cut into wedges.

EQUIPMENT UPDATE: Springform Pans

Two pans rose to the top of our 2002 testing of springform pans: Kaiser Bakeware's Noblesse Round Nonstick Springform Pan ($20) and Frieling's Handle-It Glass Bottom Springform ($31.95). Neither suffered problems with sticking, and neither had a lip around the bottom edge to impede release or slicing or serving up with a spatula. And while every pan we tested leaked when immersed in a water bath, these two proved better than the rest. To break the tie, we chose the Kaiser, considering its smaller price tag as well as the Frieling's seemingly fragile glass bottom.

But three years of intensive use in the test kitchen have taken their toll on the Kaiser pans, many of which suffered extensive peeling of the nonstick coating, especially on the pan bottom. As we wore down the Kaiser fleet, we started dusting off our little-used Frieling pans. To our surprise, we developed a preference for them. The glass bottom came in handy while developing our recipe for Vegetable Torta. How else could we monitor the browning of the crust, which can make or break the dish? And it turns out the tempered-glass bottom is anything but fragile—a conclusion we came to after it survived several falls onto the test kitchen floor. We also like the fact that the Frieling has handles, which are helpful when removing the pan from a water bath or oven.

So it's time we revised our original recommendation and gave the glass-bottomed, two-handled Frieling the top berth.

—Garth Clingingsmith

THE 'CLEAR' WINNER
The Frieling's transparent, sturdy glass bottom and convenient handles are worth the extra cash.

NOT UP TO THE TEST OF TIME
The Kaiser was our top choice in a previous test, but its nonstick coating didn't hold up well with use.

Foolproof Fettuccine Alfredo

This quintessential Roman dish—fresh egg noodles, cheese, butter, and cream—requires few ingredients and little time. Why, then, does Alfredo so often fail?

⇒ BY SARAH WILSON ⇐

Fettuccine Alfredo should be a lovely reminder of what a few ingredients can achieve when handled well. Unfortunately, a trip to Rome, where the dish originated, may be necessary to experience the culinary beauty of these ingredients, as stateside Italian restaurants often produce gargantuan portions, overcooked pasta, and a sauce that quickly congeals in the bowl (or the stomach).

Traditional recipes call for homemade fettuccine, but store-bought dried or refrigerated fresh fettuccine would have to do for home cooks. A morning in the test kitchen proved that dried noodles don't "grab" the sauce the way the more absorbent fresh noodles do, instead letting it pool at the bottom of the bowl. Luckily, fresh noodles are widely available in supermarkets and hold on to the sauce perfectly. One 9-ounce package was sufficient for four to six first-course portions. (Alfredo is awfully rich as a main course.)

The sauce consists of cheese, butter, and cream. For the cheese, Parmigiano-Reggiano won for its distinctive flavor, although I quickly discovered that more is not better. Recipes call for anywhere from ½ cup to 2 cups grated cheese. I finally settled on ¾ cup, enough to provide a rich taste of Parmigiano without overwhelming the flavors of the other ingredients. Some recipes use as much as a stick of butter, but I found a relatively modest 2 tablespoons to be fine.

Heavy cream is the foundation for this sauce, and I found it impossible to use less than the standard 1½ cups. Many recipes simmer the cream to give the sauce body. When I simmered the cream until it reduced by half, the sauce was unpalatably thick. After a series of tests, I ended up reducing only 1 cup of the cream down to ⅔ cup and then added the remaining (unreduced) half cup of cream back into the mixture along with salt and pepper. This not only produced luxurious texture but also gave the sauce a fresher flavor.

Now I had a supple, velvety sauce—but only if it were consumed in 60 seconds or less! Before my tasters could finish even a small portion, the sauce congealed, becoming thick and gritty. Restaurants often solve this problem by adding flour to stabilize the sauce, improving its staying power. The downside, of course, is that this produces a thick, weighty sauce

Fettuccine Alfredo is all about perfect timing, so prepare the cream sauce while the pasta water is heating.

that is a continent removed from the delicate marriage of simple ingredients one would find in fettuccine Alfredo's hometown.

Since flour was a no-no, I wondered if there was some other trick I could employ. After some trial and error, I found that adding a little pasta water toward the end of cooking thinned the sauce just enough without compromising its body. Yes, it may appear a bit thin at first, but the sauce thickens as it is served and consumed, virtually before your eyes. My last discovery was the

Time and Temperature Matter

WARM BOWL
Still creamy after five minutes

COLD BOWL
Congeals in just 60 seconds

The texture of the sauce changes dramatically as the dish stands and cools. Serving the Alfredo in warmed bowls helps it retain its creamy texture.

necessity of heated serving bowls. The warmth significantly prolongs the brief magic of this dish before the clock sounds and the transformation into bad restaurant food begins.

FETTUCCINE ALFREDO
SERVES 4 TO 6 AS A FIRST COURSE

Fresh pasta is the best choice for this dish; supermarkets sell 9-ounce containers of fresh pasta in the refrigerator section (see page 30 for tasting results). When boiling the pasta, undercook it slightly (even shy of al dente) because the pasta cooks an additional minute or two in the sauce. Note that Fettuccine Alfredo must be served immediately; it does not hold or reheat well.

1½	cups heavy cream
2	tablespoons unsalted butter
	Table salt
½	teaspoon ground black pepper
9	ounces fresh fettuccine
1½	ounces Parmesan cheese, grated (about ¾ cup)
⅛	teaspoon freshly grated nutmeg

1. Bring 4½ quarts water to rolling boil, covered, in large stockpot or Dutch oven. Using ladle or heatproof measuring cup, fill each individual serving bowl with about ½ cup boiling water; set bowls aside to warm.

2. While water comes to boil, bring 1 cup heavy cream and butter to simmer in 3- to 4-quart saucepan over medium heat; reduce heat to low and simmer gently until mixture reduces to ⅔ cup, 12 to 15 minutes. Off heat, stir in remaining ½ cup cream, ½ teaspoon salt, and pepper.

3. Add 1 tablespoon salt and pasta to boiling water; cook pasta until just shy of al dente. Reserve ¼ cup pasta cooking water, then drain pasta. Meanwhile, return cream mixture to simmer over medium-high heat; reduce heat to low and add pasta, Parmesan, and nutmeg to cream mixture. Cook over low heat, tossing pasta with tongs to combine, until sauce coats pasta and pasta is just al dente and cheese is melted, 1 to 2 minutes. Stir in reserved pasta cooking water; sauce may look rather thin but will gradually thicken as pasta is served and eaten. Working quickly, empty serving bowls of water; divide pasta among bowls, tossing pasta to coat well with sauce. Serve immediately.

Great Cheap Steaks

Tired of paying $12 a pound for porterhouse or T-bone? We tested 12 'cheap' steaks to find out how to save money without skimping on flavor or texture.

⋛ BY SARAH WILSON ⋚

For my family, a quick and simple dinner is a pan-seared steak, boiled potatoes, and salad. An experienced but not adventurous carnivore, I tend to buy the same expensive cut every time, so when I was asked to make dinner on a budget, using only inexpensive cuts, I didn't know where to begin. Staring at the confusing array of steaks at the supermarket, I had several questions. What did the names mean? Where did these cuts come from? Which ones were best?

What to Buy

Before narrowing down the cuts, I needed to understand a bit more about what makes certain cuts of beef inexpensive. In simple terms, steak is muscle and cost is driven primarily by tenderness. As the animal grows and exercises, the fibers and connective tissues within each muscle grow, making the muscles bigger and tougher. Within each steer, the more tender meat comes from the least exercised part of the animal, the middle. This is why the cuts of beef from the rib and the loin are so tender compared with any cut from the chuck (shoulder/front arms) or the round (back legs). Another factor that affects the perception of tenderness is fat content. Marbled fat adds to the tenderness of meat. During cooking, this kind of fat (as opposed to exterior fat) melts into the muscle and helps separate fiber from fiber.

Armed with this knowledge, I went off to four grocery stores with an upper price limit of $6.99 per pound. I bought every cut within my price range and quickly found my first challenge was identifying them by name. While there are Uniform Retail Meat Identity Standards (URMIS)—a national identification system that assigns a number and specific name to every retail cut of red meat—regional nomenclature is still common. For example, top butt, a steak I grew up eating in New Jersey, is a boneless shell sirloin steak in New England and a top sirloin steak in northern California. Even within a small geographic area, the same steak can be called by various names. Once I figured out the naming conventions, I was left with a list of 12 different cheap steaks.

To ensure that the meat is tender, slice it against the grain and on the bias before saucing.

Back in the test kitchen, I discovered that most of these steaks were too tough and/or lacked beefy flavor; others were so livery and gamy that many tasters had trouble even swallowing them, let alone enjoying the experience. But a few showed tremendous potential. Tasters were particularly enthusiastic about boneless shell sirloin steak and flap meat steak. Both of these cuts come from the sirloin, which is right behind the middle of the steer. In fact, when we compared these steaks with porterhouse ($11.99 per pound), they held their own, especially the boneless shell sirloin. Not bad for a steak that retails here in Boston for $4.29 per pound.

How to Cook It

I wondered if some sort of preparation could improve the flavor and texture of my cheap steak. I tried salting the meat, dry aging, wet aging, soaking in vinegar, sprinkling with meat tenderizer, soaking in pineapple juice, and even cutting the meat in half horizontally to shorten the strands of protein that can make it tough to chew. None of these methods improved the texture noticeably. I also tried marinating the meat from one to 24 hours. While some of these methods worked to enhance the beef flavor, they made no significant impact on tenderness.

Now the trick was to fine-tune my cooking method. I was looking for good overall browning on both sides of the steak and a generous *fond*, the browned bits that cling to the bottom of the skillet after searing and are crucial to a flavorful pan sauce. Sounds easy, but the challenges here are the same as for any pan-seared steak, expensive or not. What's important is to obtain a nice sear on both sides without overcooking the steak or allowing the fond to burn.

PAN-SEARED INEXPENSIVE STEAK

SERVES 4

A pan sauce can be made while the steaks rest after cooking (recipes follow); if you intend to make a sauce, make sure to prepare all of the sauce ingredients before cooking the steaks. To serve two instead of four, use a 10-inch skillet to cook a 1-pound steak and halve the sauce ingredients. Bear in mind that even those tasters who usually prefer rare beef preferred these steaks cooked medium-rare or medium because the texture is firmer and not quite so chewy.

- 2 tablespoons vegetable oil
- 2 whole boneless shell sirloin steaks (top butt) or whole flap meat steaks, each about 1 pound and 1¼ inches thick
  Table salt and ground black pepper

1. Heat oil in heavy-bottomed 12-inch skillet over medium-high heat until smoking. Meanwhile, season both sides of steaks with salt and pepper. Place steaks in skillet; cook, without moving steaks, until well browned, about 2 minutes. Using tongs, flip steaks; reduce heat to medium. Cook until well browned on second side and internal temperature registers 125 degrees on instant-read thermometer for medium-rare (about 5 minutes) or 130 degrees for medium (about 6 minutes).

2. Transfer steaks to large plate and tent loosely with foil; let rest until internal temperature registers 130 degrees for medium-rare or 135 degrees

for medium, 12 to 15 minutes. Meanwhile, prepare pan sauce, if making.

3. Using sharp knife, slice steak about ¼ inch thick against grain on bias, arrange on platter or on individual plates, and spoon sauce (if using) over steak; serve immediately.

MUSTARD-CREAM PAN SAUCE
MAKES ¾ CUP

1	medium shallot, minced (about 3 tablespoons)
2	tablespoons dry white wine
½	cup low-sodium chicken broth
6	tablespoons heavy cream
3	tablespoons grainy Dijon mustard
	Table salt and ground black pepper

After transferring steaks to large plate, pour off all but 1 tablespoon fat from now-empty skillet. Return skillet to low heat and add shallot; cook, stirring frequently, until beginning to brown, 2 to 3 minutes. Add wine and increase heat to medium-high; simmer rapidly, scraping up browned bits on pan bottom, until liquid is reduced to glaze, about 30 seconds; add broth and simmer until reduced to ¼ cup, about 3 minutes. Add cream and any meat juices; cook until heated through, about 1 minute. Stir in mustard; season to taste with salt and pepper. Spoon sauce over sliced steak.

TOMATO-CAPER PAN SAUCE
MAKES ¾ CUP

If ripe fresh tomatoes are not available, substitute 2 to 3 canned whole tomatoes.

1	medium shallot, minced (about 3 tablespoons)
1	teaspoon all-purpose flour
2	tablespoons dry white wine
1	cup low-sodium chicken broth
2	tablespoons capers, drained
1	medium ripe tomato, seeded and cut into ¼-inch dice (about ¼ cup)
¼	cup minced fresh parsley leaves
	Table salt and ground black pepper

After transferring steaks to large plate, pour off all but 1 tablespoon fat from now-empty skillet. Return skillet to low heat and add shallot; cook, stirring frequently, until beginning to brown, 2 to 3 minutes. Sprinkle flour over shallot; cook, stirring constantly, until combined, about 1 minute. Add wine and increase heat to medium-high; simmer rapidly, scraping up browned bits on pan bottom, until liquid is reduced to glaze, about 30 seconds; add broth and simmer until reduced to ⅔ cup, about 4 minutes. Reduce heat to medium; add capers, tomatoes, and any meat juices, and cook until flavors are blended, about 1 minute. Stir in parsley and season to taste with salt and pepper; spoon sauce over sliced steak.

TASTING: Inexpensive Steaks

We taste-tested 12 inexpensive steaks (all priced at $6.99 per pound or less). We've listed the steaks by the name used in the Uniform Retail Meat Identity Standards (a national system for standardizing terminology for retail cuts of meat), but because supermarkets still often use regional or other names, we've listed the likely alternatives you'll find, too. The "hard-to-find cuts" in the chart are usually sold only at butchers' shops; all other cuts can be found in most supermarkets.

Boneless Shell Sirloin

Flap Meat

Flank Steak

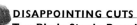
Skirt Steak

Top Blade

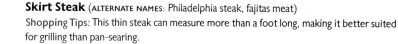

Shoulder Steak

Top Round

Bottom Round

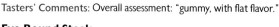

Eye Round

Tip Steak

Hanger Steak

Flat Iron

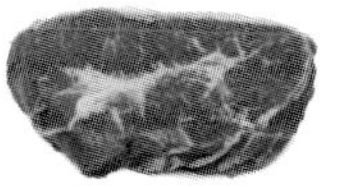

BEST CUTS FOR PAN-SEARING
Boneless Shell Sirloin Steak (ALTERNATE NAMES: Top butt, butt steak, top sirloin butt, top sirloin steak, center-cut roast)
Shopping Tips: One of the two main muscles from the hip. Can be quite large. Look for a 1-pound piece of uniform, 1¼-inch thickness.
Tasters' Comments: "Tremendous beef flavor" coupled with "very tender" texture make this steak a winner. "Just like butter."

Flap Meat Steak (ALTERNATE NAMES: Top sirloin tips, beef sirloin tips, sirloin tip steak, sirloin flap meat for tips)
Shopping Tips: Varies widely in size. Ask for a 1-pound steak of even thickness. Avoid small strips of meat or large steaks that taper drastically at one end.
Tasters' Comments: "Great beefy flavor" is the main selling point. Praised as "tender and fun to chew" and "never mushy."

CUTS BETTER FOR GRILLING
Flank Steak (ALTERNATE NAMES: Jiffy steak, London broil)
Shopping Tips: This wide, thin steak doesn't fit easily in a pan but works great on the grill.
Tasters' Comments: "Pleasant," "mild" flavor, with "just enough chew."

Skirt Steak (ALTERNATE NAMES: Philadelphia steak, fajitas meat)
Shopping Tips: This thin steak can measure more than a foot long, making it better suited for grilling than pan-searing.
Tasters' Comments: Tasters gushed with praise such as "wonderful" and "beefy heaven." The meat is "rich and fatty."

DISAPPOINTING CUTS
Top Blade Steak, Boneless (ALTERNATE NAMES: Blade steak, book steak, butler steak, lifter steak, petit steak, flat-iron steak, boneless top chuck steak)
Tasters' Comments: "Tender and juicy" but undependable. Often tastes "like liver." But "when it's good, it's really good." Watch out for vein that runs through center of steak.

Shoulder Steak, Boneless (ALTERNATE NAMES: Chuck for swissing, boneless clod steak, London broil, boneless shoulder cutlet)
Tasters' Comments: "Strong taste veers toward liver," but texture has "decent bite."

Top Round Steak (ALTERNATE NAME: Inside round cut)
Tasters' Comments: "Nice basic beef flavor," but texture is "like bubblegum."

Bottom Round Steak
Tasters' Comments: Overall assessment: "gummy, with flat flavor."

Eye Round Steak
Tasters' Comments: "Not much meat flavor"; also described as "tough" and "like sawdust."

Tip Steak (ALTERNATE NAMES: Sirloin tip steak, round tip steak, knuckle steak)
Tasters' Comments: "Spongy," "shallow" beef flavor. "Tough as shoe leather."

HARD-TO-FIND CUTS/BUTCHER'S SPECIALS
Hanger Steak (ALTERNATE NAMES: Hanging tenderloin, butcher's steak)
Shopping Tips: Usually a restaurant cut, but your butcher may be able to procure this thick steak that "hangs" between the last rib and the loin.
Tasters' Comments: "Bold, brash beef flavor," with a texture that's "moderately tender" and "a little chewy."

Flat Iron Steak (ALTERNATE NAME: Blade steak)
Shopping Tips: This restaurant cut comes from the same muscle as the top blade steak, but the muscle is cut in such a way that the vein is removed at the same time.
Tasters' Comments: "Great beef flavor" and "awesome combination of tender and chewy." Like blade steak, can be livery on occasion.

Butternut Squash Risotto

This classic Italian dish can be so sticky, starchy, and saccharine that just one bite is too much. We wanted a savory, well-balanced version that would keep us coming back for more.

⇒ BY SANDRA WU ⇐

Arborio rice and butternut squash are, at least theoretically, a perfect culinary couple. In reality, however, this pairing is more like a blind date gone bad.

Many recipes suggest roasting the squash ahead of time and then folding it into the finished rice. This was fine as far as it went, but the risotto and the squash never became properly intertwined. Somehow, I had to find a way to integrate the cooking of the two ingredients while preserving their individual personalities. I had high expectations for a recipe calling for pureed cooked squash added to the sautéed aromatics (usually onion and garlic) and cooked along with the rice, but my hopes were dashed when gluey squash paste emerged from the saucepan. The most obvious next step was to sauté the squash along with the aromatics and then leave it in the pan to cook down with the rice. But this approach was no winner, either, as the squash was reduced to mushy orange blobs.

What I sought was creamy, orange-tinged rice fully infused with deep (but not overly sweet) squash flavor, flecked with hints of broken-down squash as well as more substantial (but still soft) cubes. A quick, forced marriage wouldn't work; the results would be too jarring. A longer, multistep courtship would be necessary to wed these two disparate elements.

Squashing Tradition

To maintain the textural integrity of the squash pieces, I found that dicing and then cooking was better than roasting squash halves and then removing the flesh, which caused the squash to fall apart. As for the cooking method, roasting diced squash in a 450-degree oven worked fairly well, but most tasters found the concentrated sweetness that resulted from the dry, intense heat too distracting. The other obvious method, sautéing the squash pieces in a skillet, did not produce the color and flavor development I had hoped for. The solution? Tweak the sauté method by giving one side of the squash pieces enough time to caramelize slightly before gently and occasionally stirring them. This produced the color and flavor I was after without the overt sweetness

To make this dish work, we found that you must sauté the squash separately, cook half of it with the risotto, then fold in the remaining sautéed squash just before serving.

that was typical of the oven-roasting approach. I also found that olive oil was better than butter for sautéing here, as the latter caused the squash to darken more than I wanted.

Based on previous tests, I knew that the squash could not be added all at once to the rice. Added early on, the squash dissolved and lost its personality; added later in cooking, it never fully merged with the rice. My first idea was to mash half of the cooked squash pieces and add them to the pan along with the broth; once I had sautéed the aromatics and toasted the rice, I would fold in the remaining intact pieces. Although the rice now had a lot of squash flavor, it also had an unappealingly gummy texture, as the starches from the squashy paste stuck to the rice like glue. The solution was actually quite simple: I added half of the cooked squash pieces—this time intact—after toasting the rice, then gently folded the remaining pieces into the cooked risotto, as I had before. Now I had a perfect duo of harmonious equals.

Sauté, Simmer, and Stir

In keeping with risotto-making tradition, I began by sautéing the aromatics in some melted butter before adding short-grained Arborio rice, the test kitchen's grain of choice for achieving creamy, al dente risotto. While this is normally done in a saucepan or saucier, I knew I could probably get away with using the same nonstick skillet I had used to cook the squash. In addition to making one less pot to wash, this not-uncommon technique reduces sticking.

After the rice was toasted in the garlic-onion mixture, I added a cup of white wine (most basic risotto recipes call for half that) for extra acidity and brightness. Owing to the strong flavors of squash and cheese, however, the wine flavor was faint at best. The addition of lemon juice, apple cider vinegar, and white wine vinegar all lent unwelcome, off flavors to the dish, but increasing the wine to triple the standard amount—1½ cups—gave the rice the acidity and complexity needed to balance the sweetness of the squash. Once the rice grains had fully absorbed the wine, I stirred in half of the cooked squash.

Traditional risotto recipes are time-consuming, asking the cook to add only small amounts of stock or water to the pan at one time and to stir constantly for more than half an hour. The test kitchen had already discovered a more streamlined, quicker method, which calls

The Secret to Big Squash Flavor

IT TAKES GUTS

The seeds and stringy fibers have a surprising amount of flavor that can be imparted to risotto. We had the best results when we sautéed the squash scrapings and then simmered them with the chicken broth.

for preheating the chicken broth in a separate saucepan and then adding a whopping 3 cups to the rice once the wine has been absorbed. This speeds up the cooking and means less stirring at the outset. The remaining liquid is then added in smaller ½-cup increments and the rice stirred more frequently to prevent the bottom of the skillet from drying out.

In an effort to elevate the squash flavor further, I borrowed an unusual and surprisingly effective technique developed for our Butternut Squash Soup (November/December 2001). After sautéing the squash itself, I emptied the pan and sautéed the seeds and fibers, then added them to the saucepan with the broth (I would strain the broth later). A simple step, perhaps, but it yielded a complex and easy-to-detect boost in squash flavor without adding more sweetness.

At the Finish Line

As for other ingredients, tasters preferred the traditional sage to thyme. One tablespoon provided barely enough flavor; 2 tablespoons was perfect. As for cheese, a generous 1½ ounces of Parmesan was the overwhelming favorite. After stirring in ¼ teaspoon of freshly grated nutmeg for a hit of spicy warmth, I folded in the remaining squash.

I had finally achieved the balance I was looking for in both texture and flavor. As a culinary matchmaker, I had found this pairing of squash and rice difficult to pull off, but the hard work was well worth it. Now no one could be content with just one bite of this classic Italian dish.

BUTTERNUT SQUASH RISOTTO
SERVES 4 AS A MAIN COURSE OR 6 AS A FIRST COURSE

Infusing the chicken broth with the squash's seeds and fibers helps to reinforce the earthy squash flavor. We found that a 2-pound squash consistently yields a cup or so more than the 3½ cups needed in step 1; this can be added to the skillet along with the squash scrapings in step 2. To make this dish vegetarian, vegetable broth can

be used instead of chicken broth, but the resulting risotto will have more pronounced sweetness. See the illustrations on page 31 for tips on preparing the squash.

- 2 tablespoons olive oil
- 1 medium butternut squash (about 2 pounds), peeled, seeded (fibers and seeds reserved), and cut into ½-inch cubes (about 3½ cups)
- ¾ teaspoon table salt
- ¾ teaspoon ground black pepper
- 4 cups low-sodium chicken broth
- 1 cup water
- 4 tablespoons unsalted butter
- 2 small onions, chopped very fine (about 1½ cups)
- 2 medium garlic cloves, minced or pressed through garlic press (2 teaspoons)
- 2 cups Arborio rice
- 1½ cups dry white wine
- 1½ ounces finely grated Parmesan cheese (about ¾ cup)
- 2 tablespoons minced fresh sage leaves
- ¼ teaspoon grated nutmeg

1. Heat oil in 12-inch nonstick skillet over medium-high heat until shimmering but not smoking. Add about 3½ cups squash in even layer and cook without stirring until golden brown, 4 to 5 minutes; stir in ¼ teaspoon salt and ¼ teaspoon pepper. Continue to cook, stirring occasionally, until squash is tender and browned, about 5 minutes longer. Transfer squash to bowl and set aside.

2. Return skillet to medium heat; add reserved squash fibers and seeds and any leftover diced squash. Cook, stirring frequently to break up fibers, until lightly browned, about 4 minutes. Transfer to large saucepan and add chicken broth and water; cover saucepan and bring mixture to simmer over high heat, then reduce heat to medium-low to maintain bare simmer.

3. Melt 3 tablespoons butter in now-empty skillet over medium heat; when foaming subsides, add onions, garlic, remaining ½ teaspoon salt, and remaining ½ teaspoon pepper. Cook, stirring occasionally, until onions are softened, 4 to 5 minutes. Add rice to skillet and cook, stirring frequently, until grains are translucent around edges, about 3 minutes. Add wine and cook, stirring frequently, until fully absorbed, 4 to 5 minutes.

4. Meanwhile, strain hot broth through fine-mesh strainer into medium bowl, pressing on solids to extract as much liquid as possible. Return strained broth to saucepan and discard solids in strainer; cover saucepan and set over low heat to keep broth hot.

5. When wine is fully absorbed, add 3 cups hot broth and half of reserved squash to rice. Simmer, stirring every 3 to 4 minutes, until liquid is absorbed and bottom of pan is almost dry, about 12 minutes.

6. Stir in about ½ cup hot broth and cook, stirring constantly, until absorbed, about 3 minutes; repeat with additional broth 2 or 3 more times, until rice is al dente. Off heat, stir in remaining 1 tablespoon butter, Parmesan, sage, and nutmeg; gently fold in remaining cooked squash. If desired, add up to ¼ cup additional hot broth to loosen texture of risotto. Serve immediately.

BUTTERNUT SQUASH RISOTTO WITH SPINACH AND TOASTED PINE NUTS

1. Toast ¼ cup pine nuts in small, dry skillet over medium heat until golden and fragrant, about 5 minutes; set aside.

2. Follow recipe for Butternut Squash Risotto; in step 2, after transferring sautéed squash seeds and fibers to saucepan, add 1 teaspoon olive oil to empty skillet and swirl to coat. Add 4 ounces baby spinach and cook, covered, over medium heat, until leaves begin to wilt, about 2 minutes. Uncover and cook, stirring constantly, until fully wilted, about 30 seconds. Transfer spinach to mesh strainer; set aside. Proceed with recipe as directed.

3. Drain excess liquid from spinach and stir into risotto along with remaining squash in step 6. Top individual servings of risotto with toasted pine nuts.

RECIPE TESTING: Timing Matters

We found that adding the cooked squash to the rice in two batches—half once the rice has been toasted and half just before serving—was the key to proper texture. Other recipes don't follow this procedure. Here's what happened when we followed their lead.

AT THE BEGINNING
When all the squash is added at the beginning of the risotto-making process, the end result is gluey and starchy, with no cubes of squash in sight.

AT THE END
When all the squash is added just before serving, the squash and risotto remain too distinct, failing to form a cohesive dish in terms of either flavor or texture.

Shopping for Supermarket Cheeses

An opinionated guide to buying and using widely available 'cooking' cheeses. BY SEAN LAWLER

When we taste cheese in the test kitchen, it's usually to determine how it will behave in a particular recipe. Flavor certainly matters, but we are just as concerned with properties such as creaminess, melting ability, and stability at high temperatures. What's the best cheese for the best recipe? Some of our findings may surprise you.

ASIAGO

What It Is: This firm, aged cow's milk cheese is a common substitute for Parmesan.

Tasting Notes: Despite its credentials, authentic Asiago d'Allevo doesn't have the strength or complexity of flavor to stand in for Parmigiano-Reggiano. For the price (about $15 per pound), we'll pass. Domestic Asiago, especially Bel Gioioso brand, is a pleasant surprise: sharp, tangy, higher in moisture—and about half the price of the Allevo.

Cooking Tips: The texture of a good domestic Asiago (firm, but yielding to gentle pressure) makes it quite versatile: It is just soft enough to be eaten plain or with antipasto, broken into small chunks for a salad, or sliced thin and melted. It is also firm enough to be grated over pasta.

TEST KITCHEN WINNER
★ BEL GIOIOSO ASIAGO ($7.50/pound)

BLUE CHEESE

What It Is: Named for its streaks (called veins) of bluish-green mold, blue cheese may be made from goat's, sheep's, or cow's milk or a combination thereof.

Tasting Notes: At one extreme are pricey imports like Roquefort, a tangy, pungent sheep's milk cheese with a soft, almost spreadable texture, and Stilton, a crumbly English cow's milk cheese that is nutty and sharp. At the milder end of the spectrum is the inexpensive Danish Blue, which is sliceably firm and less complex tasting, though still tangy and assertive.

Cooking Tip: Most blue cheeses turn greasy and gritty when melted, so they are generally crumbled over salads or blended to make creamy dips and dressings.

TEST KITCHEN WINNERS
★ **For salads:** ROQUEFORT or STILTON (both about $18/pound)
★ **For dips and dressings:** DANISH BLUE ($4.99/pound) or STELLA ($5.69/pound)

CHEDDAR

What It Is: Depending on how it is aged, this cow's milk cheese ranges from "mild" to tangy "extra-sharp." This cheese is naturally yellow, but some are colored orange with annatto paste.

Tasting Notes: Tasters rejected a number of brands as bland and rubbery and dismissed a few of the more expensive organic cheddars as overly pungent and sour. The test kitchen favorites were balanced, tangy, and clean when tasted plain, smooth and buttery when melted.

Cooking Tips: When melted, cheddar can separate and turn greasy and grainy. This is especially true of extra-sharp varieties, which have less moisture. When both flavor and a smooth, creamy texture are important (think macaroni and cheese), we often use a mix of sharp cheddar and a smooth melter like Monterey Jack.

TEST KITCHEN WINNER
★ CABOT SHARP VERMONT CHEDDAR CHEESE ($4.60/pound)

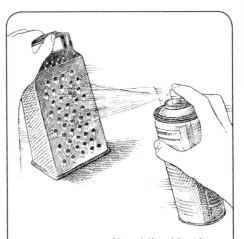

TEST KITCHEN TIP: Shredding Neatly
Semisoft cheeses such as cheddar and block mozzarella can become clogged in the holes of a box grater. Coating the large holes on the grater with nonstick cooking spray eliminates this problem.

CHÈVRE (GOAT CHEESE)

What It Is: Once strictly a French product, this soft, spreadable unripened goat's milk cheese has become a supermarket staple.

Tasting Notes: American goat cheeses are pleasantly tangy and clean tasting, with a creamy, faintly grainy texture. Imported French chèvres have a more assertive, gamy flavor and a chalkier texture.

Cooking Tips: Fresh goat cheese is excellent crumbled over salads or incorporated into spreads and dressings. It dissolves into a pasty mess when melted completely but is quite good when just warmed (sprinkled over hot pasta or grilled asparagus, for example) or formed into crusted rounds and baked.

TEST KITCHEN WINNER
★ VERMONT BUTTER AND CHEESE COMPANY CHÈVRE ($16/pound)

FETA

What It Is: Traditionally, this crumbly Greek cheese pickled in brine was made from sheep's milk, but most domestic versions come from pasteurized cow's milk.

Tasting Notes: Domestic cow's milk feta is uncomplicated: tangy, salty, moist, and creamy. Less important than brand name, we discovered, was packaging. Blocks of feta packed dry in Styrofoam trays and shrink-wrapped were found to be chalky and much less flavorful than cheese sold in tubs or vacuum-sealed along with a small quantity of brine.

Cooking Tips: Feta is not a smooth melter, but when crumbled and combined with a milder cheese, like ricotta, it will contribute some of its tangy flavor to fillings for ravioli, quiche, and other savory pies.

TEST KITCHEN WINNER
★ ATHENOS ($5.99/pound) or any brine-packed feta

FONTINA

What It Is: At any supermarket, you'll find squishy wedges of "fontina" covered with red wax and hailing from Denmark or Sweden. Italian and American cheesemakers also produce generic fontinas.

Tasting Notes: Real Fontina Val d'Aosta, made from high-quality raw cow's milk, has a barnyard aroma and a grassy, nutty flavor that can be overpowering in a frittata or spinach lasagna. At the opposite end of the spectrum, inexpensive Danish and Swedish fontinas, made from partially skimmed milk, are too bland for most recipes. For cooking, we prefer an American-made fontina or the generic Italian variety (look for a waxy, brownish rind), both of which are very creamy with a mildly tangy, nutty flavor.

TEST KITCHEN WINNERS
★ **For eating raw:** FONTINA D'AOSTA (about $16/pound)
★ **For cooking:** BEL GIOIOSO FONTINA ($7.50/pound) or generic Italian fontina (about $9/pound)

MONTEREY JACK

What It Is: One of only a handful of cheeses to originate in America, Jack cheese starts with pasteurized cow's milk and is ripened for only about a week.

Tasting Notes: Jack is a creamy cheese with a pronounced acidic tang that mellows considerably when the cheese is melted. Our winning supermarket cheese narrowly bested two artisanal Jacks from California, which tasters found slightly grainy.

Cooking Tip: Because of its mild flavor and good melting properties, Monterey Jack is often combined in recipes with a sharper cheese like cheddar.

TEST KITCHEN WINNER
★ CABOT MONTEREY JACK ($2.39/8-ounce block)

TESTING EQUIPMENT: Cheese Graters

BOX GRATER: Our first choice for quickly shredding or grating cheese is a box grater. It sits securely on the countertop and offers a variety of options: large holes for shredding soft cheeses like cheddar, smaller holes for grating harder cheeses like Parmesan, and a raised abrasive surface for grating ginger or zesting citrus. Of eight models tested, our favorite was the CUISIPRO 6-Sided Stainless Steel Grater ($24.95).

RASP GRATER: A MICROPLANE ($12.95) is an excellent supplement to a box grater. Besides breaking down hard cheese into feathery shreds, it handles shallots, garlic, ginger, nutmeg, horseradish, citrus zest, and chocolate.

ROTARY GRATER: Too slow and awkward for kitchen use, the rotary grater is a nice (and optional) purchase for the table, in part because it won't rake your knuckles. Of eight models tested, our favorite was the PEDRINI ($14.95).

MOZZARELLA

What It Is: Sold in firm, white blocks or already shredded in plastic bags, the stuff in the supermarket dairy case is officially "low-moisture" mozzarella, or, as the experts call it, "pizza cheese." It is a far cry from fresh Italian *mozzarella di bufala*, which is made from water buffalo milk, hand pulled, and extremely perishable. American cheesemakers also produce fresh mozzarella, almost always from cow's milk.

Tasting Notes: Tasters expected to dislike the preshredded pizza cheeses, which are coated with cellulose powder to prevent clumping, but these anti-caking agents actually aid smooth melting.

Cooking Tips: In its raw state, American mozzarella is dense and rubbery, so fresh mozzarella is the only sensible choice for eating plain. Some cookbooks say the high moisture content of fresh mozzarella will ruin a crisp pizza crust, but our tasters disagreed. Use it sparingly on a thin-crust pizza and add it near the end of cooking so it doesn't dry out.

TEST KITCHEN WINNERS
★ **Best block cheese:** DRAGONE WHOLE MILK MOZZARELLA ($3.79/pound)
★ **Best shredded cheese:** KRAFT SHREDDED PART-SKIM MOZZARELLA ($2.50/8-ounce bag)
★ **Best fresh cheese:** Locally made fresh mozzarella (about $8/pound)

PARMESAN

What It Is: A *grana*, or hard, grainy cow's cheese. The original and undisputed best in class is Parmigiano-Reggiano, made from unpasteurized milk in a specific region of Italy and aged for about two years. It is widely available in supermarkets, as are many imitators produced domestically and elsewhere around the world.

Tasting Notes: Freshly cut Parmigiano-Reggiano had a smooth texture and light crystalline crunch that was somewhat lacking in the precut, plastic-wrapped wedge of Parmigiano-Reggiano purchased at a supermarket. Both, however, had the winning flavor profile that this cheese is known for: spicy, nutty, and creamy. Tasters found domestic Parmesans, aged for only about 10 months, to be much more dense and salty, with a less complex flavor. The mass-produced powders tasted metallic and fishy—in short, entirely inedible. The grated "Parmigiano" sold in bags was dry and flavorless.

Cooking Tip: Once all of the cheese has been grated, the burnished, golden rind can be frozen and then used to flavor soups or stews.

TEST KITCHEN WINNERS
★ **Best choice:** PARMIGIANO-REGGIANO (about $14/pound)
★ **Budget choice:** DIGIORNO PARMESAN ($7.99/pound)

SWISS

What It Is: Supermarket cheeses labeled "Swiss," usually found sliced in packages or in blocks at the deli counter, are domestic imitations of Swiss Emmenthaler, the pressed cow's milk cheese famous the world over for its large holes, or "eyes."

Tasting Notes: Tasters loved the complex, nutty flavor of real Emmenthaler for a cheese plate but found that when melted it took on a much less appetizing, gamy flavor. For a toasted cheese sandwich, we prefer Jarlsberg, a widely available Norwegian brand of Emmenthal-style cheese with a mild, creamy flavor.

TEST KITCHEN WINNERS
★ **For eating raw:** EMMENTHALER ($10.49/pound)
★ **For melting:** JARLSBERG ($7.99/pound)

Reintroducing Chicken Francese

This fast-fading star of red-sauce Italian restaurants often features a rubbery coating and a puckery lemon sauce. Yet this quick dinner still holds promise for the home cook.

⇒ BY NINA WEST ⇐

You've probably never heard of chicken francese. This simple but refined dish consists of pan-fried chicken cutlets with a light but substantial eggy coating and a bright lemony sauce. Although its name hints at a rich pedigree—one account claims that Italians once made this dish for Napoleon Bonaparte—there is no classical French or Italian version. Instead, chicken francese is most strongly identified with Italian-American cooking in and around New York City. It's a humble dish with a fancy name.

Hazy background aside, I found that chicken francese was related to the familiar but loosely defined group of thin-cut chicken (and sometimes veal) dishes that includes scaloppine, parmigiana, Milanese, piccata, and Marsala. But francese also has much in common with a well-known egg-coated breakfast dish: French toast. While many of the other thin-cut chicken dishes are dusted with flour or shrouded in crisp bread crumbs, chicken francese has a soft, rich, eggy coating. The silky lemon sauce nestles into nooks in this soft coating so that each bite reveals just the right balance of chicken, coating, and sauce. Although this dish has fallen out of favor, it's simple, it's quick, and it's chicken—three things almost every home cook appreciates.

A soft, eggy coating on the chicken and a thick, lemony sauce are essential to the success of this quick recipe.

A Cut Above

For the chicken, I started with untrimmed and unpounded chicken breast halves. These proved too thick; the egg coating burned before the meat cooked through. Store-bought cutlets (roughly half the thickness of breast halves) were ragged and uneven, causing the edges of the cutlets and the coating to dry out by the time the chicken cooked through. I decided to trim and pound the breast halves into cutlets myself to get the evenness and thickness I wanted. By trimming off the tenderloins and slicing the breasts in half horizontally, I was able to get the thickness close to my desired ¼ inch. A few whacks with a meat pounder got me all the way there. Yes, this step did take five minutes, but the results were far superior to any I got with supermarket cutlets.

In all the recipes I could find, some combination of eggs and flour was used to create the soft coating. Although the ingredients were set, the method was not. Some recipes dredged the chicken in flour first, some in egg first, and still others combined the eggs and flour to create a batter. The batter approach seemed promising because it was simpler, but the resulting coating was tough and rubbery. Adding baking soda and/or baking powder to the mixture for lightness also added uncharacteristic crispness and an off flavor. Some batter recipes called for water or milk. Milk made the coating more tender, but the batter became too thin and dripped off the chicken.

I abandoned the batter approach and methodically tested the other options. In the end, dredging the cutlets in flour, dipping them in beaten egg, and then adding a second coating of flour worked best. This technique guaranteed that the coating would stay put and, because the last coating consisted of flour (as opposed to bread crumbs, for instance), the finished cutlets were delicate and soft. I wondered if the eggs would benefit from a little milk (something that had worked in my tests with a batter coating). Sure enough, just a couple of tablespoons all but guaranteed a tender—not rubbery—coating.

Getting Saucy

Sauces made with whole lemon slices were unbearably bitter because of the zest and pith. I quickly skipped over them in favor of fresh lemon juice, augmented with wine and chicken broth. Although not traditional in chicken francese, I also tested garlic, onion, and shallot. Only onion made the cut, providing a mellow, sweet background flavor that balanced the lemon while still letting the citrus lead the way.

Thin, watery sauces saturated the coating, making it peel right off; a thicker sauce, I reasoned, would cling to (but not penetrate) the coating I had worked so hard to attain. Reducing the wine, broth, and lemon juice was not sufficient. Finishing the sauce with butter or cornstarch helped to thicken it, but neither was perfect. The best solution was to make a classic roux of flour and butter cooked together. The roux was a more reliable thickener than either butter or cornstarch alone.

The Order of Things

Cutlets sautéed in butter tasted better than cutlets sautéed in oil, but the butter burned. Adding some oil to the butter raised its smoke point without diluting its flavor impact. By using a nonstick skillet, I could get away with just a tablespoon each of oil and butter for each batch of cutlets. To make sure that the second batch looked as nice as the first, I found it helpful to wipe out the pan between batches. Once the second batch was done and in the oven, I wiped out the pan again and finished my lemon sauce.

At this point, I thought I was done. Tasters loved my sauce and the chicken. Maybe they loved the sauce too much—they wanted more. At first I thought, no problem, just make more

THIN AND INSUBSTANTIAL **THICK AND EGGY** **JUST RIGHT**

A dusting of flour and a dip in beaten egg made a coating that was too thin (left). A batter coating (made by mixing flour and eggs) was too thick and rubbery (center). We obtained the best results by dusting cutlets with flour, dipping them in eggs beaten with milk, and coating them again with flour (right). This coating remained soft and tender but was sturdy enough to stand up to the lemon sauce.

sauce. But additional lemon juice, wine, and broth needed additional time to simmer and reduce. By the time the sauce was done, the cutlets in the oven had dried out. The solution was switching the recipe around and starting with the sauce, then cooking the chicken. Is it unconventional to make the sauce before cooking the chicken? You bet. But now I could deliver on the promise of this "lost" recipe—quick, fresh chicken cutlets with a soft, eggy coating and a generous amount of silky, well-balanced lemon sauce.

CHICKEN FRANCESE
SERVES 4

The chicken breasts will be easier to slice into cutlets if you freeze them for about 15 minutes until they are firm but not fully frozen. To slice in half, place one hand on top of a chicken breast to secure it, hold a chef's knife parallel to the cutting board, and slice through the middle of the breast horizontally. Note that just 1 tablespoon of the butter for the sauce is used in step 2; the remaining 2 tablespoons are used in step 5. The sauce is very lemony—for less tartness, reduce the amount of lemon juice by about 1 tablespoon.

Sauce
- 3 tablespoons unsalted butter
- 1 very small onion, minced (about ⅓ cup)
- 1 tablespoon all-purpose flour
- ½ cup dry white wine or vermouth
- ⅓ cup juice from 2 lemons
- 2¼ cups low-sodium chicken broth
    Table salt and ground black pepper

Chicken
- 1 cup all-purpose flour
    Table salt and ground black pepper
- 2 large eggs
- 2 tablespoons milk
- 4 boneless skinless chicken breast halves (6 to 8 ounces each), tenderloins removed, breasts trimmed of excess fat, halved horizontally (see note), and pounded to even ¼-inch thickness
- 2 tablespoons unsalted butter
- 2 tablespoons olive oil
- 2 tablespoons minced fresh parsley leaves

1. Adjust oven rack to middle position; heat oven to 200 degrees. Set wire rack on rimmed baking sheet and place sheet in oven.

2. **FOR THE SAUCE:** Heat 1 tablespoon butter in medium nonreactive saucepan over medium heat. When foaming subsides, add onion and cook, stirring occasionally, until translucent, 2 to 3 minutes. Add flour and stir until light golden brown, about 1 minute. Whisk in wine, lemon juice, and broth; increase heat to high and bring to boil, whisking constantly. Lower heat to medium-high and cook, whisking occasionally, until mixture is reduced to 1½ cups, 10 to 15 minutes. Strain sauce through mesh strainer, return to saucepan, and set aside.

3. **FOR THE CHICKEN:** Set second wire rack on second rimmed baking sheet on counter. Whisk together flour, 1 teaspoon salt, and ¼ teaspoon pepper in pie plate. In second pie plate, whisk eggs and milk until combined. Season both sides of each cutlet with salt and pepper. Using tongs and working with 2 cutlets at a time, coat cutlets in seasoned flour; shake off excess flour. Transfer cutlets to egg mixture; coat evenly and let excess run off. Return cutlets to seasoned flour; coat evenly and shake off excess flour. Place coated cutlets on wire rack on counter.

4. Heat 1 tablespoon each butter and oil in 12-inch nonstick skillet over medium-high heat; when foaming subsides, place 4 cutlets in skillet. Cook until well browned, 1½ to 2 minutes. Carefully flip cutlets and continue to cook until lightly browned on second sides, 30 to 60 seconds. Transfer chicken to wire rack in oven. Wipe out skillet with paper towels. Repeat, using remaining 1 tablespoon each butter and oil to cook remaining cutlets in now-empty skillet. After transferring chicken to oven, wipe out skillet with paper towels.

5. **TO FINISH SAUCE AND SERVE:** Transfer sauce to now-empty skillet and set over low heat; cook until sauce is heated through, about 1 minute. Whisk in remaining 2 tablespoons butter; adjust seasoning with salt and pepper. Remove baking sheet with chicken from oven; transfer 4 cutlets to skillet, turn to coat with sauce, then transfer each serving (2 cutlets) to individual plates. Repeat with remaining cutlets. Spoon 2

SHOPPING GUIDE:
Boneless Chicken Breasts
There's more than one way to buy boneless chicken breasts at the supermarket. Here are the options you are likely to encounter. The first three are acceptable; the last one is not. Prices for all of the options are similar.

Whole Boneless Chicken Breasts
➤ 12 to 16 ounces each
WHAT IT IS: The entire breast in one piece. Although some heavy butchering is required, some premium brands are sold this way and are worth the effort.
HOW TO PREPARE: Cut the breast in half, remove the cartilage that connects the breast halves, remove the tenderloins, trim the fat, slice each piece horizontally, and pound lightly.

Boneless Chicken Breast Halves
➤ 6 to 8 ounces each
WHAT IT IS: Half of a whole chicken breast. The most widely available choice, breast halves require a modest amount of work.
HOW TO PREPARE: Remove the tenderloin, trim the fat, slice in half horizontally, and pound lightly.

Chicken Fillets
➤ 4 to 6 ounces each
WHAT IT IS: Breast halves with the tenderloins and fat removed (sometimes called chef's trim). The easiest choice—buy them if they are available.
HOW TO PREPARE: At home, just slice each piece horizontally and pound lightly.

Chicken Cutlets
➤ 2 to 3 ounces each
WHAT IT IS: Breast halves that have been trimmed and sliced for you. Usually ragged and poorly butchered, cutlets are ready to use but cook very unevenly.
HOW TO PREPARE: Not worth buying.

tablespoons additional sauce over each serving and sprinkle with parsley. Serve immediately, passing extra sauce separately.

CHICKEN FRANCESE WITH TOMATO AND TARRAGON

Follow recipe for Chicken Francese, adding 1 sprig fresh parsley and 1 sprig fresh tarragon to sauce along with wine, lemon juice, and broth in step 2. Discard herbs after sauce is reduced. Add 1 medium tomato, seeded and cut into ¼-inch dice (about ¾ cup), to sauce before spooning additional sauce over each serving in step 5. Substitute 1 tablespoon minced fresh tarragon for equal amount of minced fresh parsley.

Foolproof All-Butter Pie Pastry

All-butter pie doughs tout great flavor, but they often fail to be flaky and are notoriously difficult to work with. Could we get everything right?

≥ BY ERIKA BRUCE ≤

The art of making American pie dough is full of mystery and suspense—even an accomplished baker often goes astray. A high proportion of fat (necessary for optimal flavor and texture) must be cut into the flour to the perfect degree and then just the right amount of water added: too little and a crumbly, hard-to-roll-out dough lies ahead; too much and it's sticky city. And the more difficult a dough is to handle, the more likely it is to be overworked. All this translates into a stubbornly tough pastry—an unhappy reward for a fair amount of labor.

In the past, we have made sure that our pie crusts would turn out both tender and flaky by using a combination of butter and vegetable shortening, as the latter makes for a more forgiving, easy-to-work-with dough. But what to do when the rich flavor of an all-butter crust beckons or when the idea of using hydrogenated vegetable oil (think Crisco) becomes unappealing? To find out, I took our American Pie Dough recipe and made it with butter alone—no shortening. The results were disastrous: I was faced with a forlornly greasy mass of dough that was difficult to roll out and that baked up into a stiff, dense shell—a far cry from the light and flaky layers of pastry the recipe usually produces.

Pastry Primer

Let's start with how fat, flour, and water can produce a flaky pie pastry. Cold fat is cut into flour until the mixture forms pea-sized crumbs (most easily achieved in a food processor); then ice water is gently mixed in with a spatula until the dough just forms a cohesive mass. (A common mistake among home bakers is not processing the butter and flour properly. While some small pieces of butter ought to remain intact, it is better to overprocess the butter to coat the flour thoroughly than to leave large chunks of butter in the mix.) The dough is chilled and then rolled out, flattening the pea-sized crumbs into longer, flaky layers.

During baking, the pockets of fat melt and the water in the dough turns to steam, filling the spaces left behind by the melted fat. Finally, the proteins in the flour set up and become rigid, locking the flaky layers in place. The depth of the flakes is determined by the size of the original fat pockets; small pieces of fat equal short flakes—ideal for pie crusts. And while specific baking times and temperatures vary among recipes, a relatively hot oven is essential: High heat ensures optimal steam release before the flour proteins set up and stiffen.

Why the difference in performance between an all-butter dough and one that contains vegetable shortening? Vegetable shortening is 100 percent fat, and it does not completely melt until it reaches 110 to 125 degrees Fahrenheit. Its fat content helps to tenderize pie crusts, and its melting point—well above body temperature—makes it easy to work with: It won't melt when handled. Butter, on the other hand, has a fat content of around 80 percent (the remaining 20 percent is mostly water) and a final melting point of 94 degrees—below the average body temperature. This means that simply handling an all-butter dough can cause a major meltdown: As the butter softens, the small pieces essentially melt into the flour, greatly diminishing the size of those all-

Pie-Pastry Troubleshooting Guide

There are three key steps for pie dough: cutting the fat into the flour, adding the liquid, and rolling out the dough.

COMBINE THE FLOUR AND FAT. Ideally, small lumps of butter should be evenly distributed throughout the dough. In the oven, these lumps will promote the formation of flaky layers. If the butter pieces are too large, the dough will be difficult to roll out. If the butter pieces are completely incorporated into the flour, the crust will be crumbly and cookie-like. When the butter has been properly incorporated into the flour, the largest pieces will be about the size of a pea.

BUTTER IS TOO LUMPY   **BUTTER IS JUST RIGHT**   **BUTTER IS TOO SMALL**

ADD THE RIGHT AMOUNT OF WATER.
Our recipe begins with a minimum of water. You will probably need to add more water, depending on the brand of flour and the humidity in your kitchen. Take a small handful of dough out of the food processor and pinch it together. If the dough seems at all floury or won't hold together, it needs more water. When the dough is properly hydrated, it will form large clumps and no dry flour will remain. The dough can be tacky but not sticky or gluey.

NEEDS MORE WATER   **PERFECTLY MOISTENED**

ROLL OUT THE DOUGH. The goal here is to shape a perfect circle. To view a free online video from our TV show that shows this process, go to www.cooksillustrated.com. Here are some key points to keep in mind:

• **Keep it cold.** If the dough is too warm, the butter will melt and causing sticking. Chill the dough thoroughly (at least 1 hour) before attempting to roll it out. If the dough is chilled for several hours, let it warm slightly before rolling it out.

• **Keep it covered.** A floured counter will keep dough from sticking, but the extra flour can make the dough tough. We prefer to roll dough between sheets of parchment paper or plastic wrap.

• **Keep it turning.** Misshapen dough is hard to fit into a pie plate and often has thinner edges. For a perfectly round dough of even thickness, don't keep rolling over the same spot or in the same direction. Starting at the center of the dough, roll away from yourself two or three times, then rotate the disk one-quarter turn and repeat.

TESTING EQUIPMENT: Rolling Pins

Once upon a time, rolling pins fell into two camps: standard wooden pins with dowel-style, ball-bearing handles and French rolling pins, also wooden, which are basically solid cylinders with tapered ends. Not anymore. These days, the old standbys compete for space in the bakeware aisle with newfangled models. Made from fancy materials and souped up with ergonomic designs and "deluxe" features, do these new pins make traditional wooden rolling pins passé? We rolled out pie crust and pizza and tart doughs with 10 different pins to find out.

Dough has a tendency to stick to rolling pins, an issue usually blamed on overwarm dough. Marble and metal pins (refrigerated before rolling) and a hollow pin made of laboratory glass (filled with ice) try to tackle the problem from a temperature perspective. A nylon pin (and one of the metal designs) opts for the nonstick-surface approach.

But at the end of the day, we hold that gimmick-free wooden pins are still the way to go. Dirt cheap and durable (unlike the accidentally smashed glass pin), they will also handle any task. Tapered pins should be around 20 inches long, with a diameter of at least 1½ inches—otherwise, there's not enough flat surface to ensure a level roll. You handled-pin fans should look for pins at least 12 inches long and with the largest diameter you can manage. –Garth Clingingsmith

OUR WINNER
Fante's French Rolling Pin with Tapered Ends ($7.99) is easy to use and offers maximum control.

RUNNER-UP
Fante's Handled Maple Rolling Pin ($11.99) is great for bakers who want a little extra leverage.

HANDLE WITH CARE
The Bennington Flameware Glass Rolling Pin ($19.99) seems like a bright idea—until you drop it.

NO COMFORT HERE
The Comfort Rolling Pin ($39.95) is molded to fit someone's hands—just not ours.

PRICEY PIN
The Matfer Nylon Rolling Pin ($64.95) offers the same performance as a wooden pin, at 8 times the price.

---

also a good idea to roll the dough between sheets of parchment paper, again minimizing the need for more flour.)

What's the formula for successful all-butter pie dough? For a double-crust pie, it's 2½ cups flour plus 16 tablespoons butter and 3 tablespoons sour cream. This combination makes the dough easier to mix, handle, and roll out than a traditional all-butter dough, and the acidity provided by the sour cream contributes to tenderness. Finally, a recipe for an all-butter pie dough without all the usual mystery and suspense—a happy ending is just about guaranteed.

FOOLPROOF ALL-BUTTER PIE PASTRY
MAKES ONE 9-INCH DOUBLE-CRUST PIE SHELL

If preparing the pastry in a warm kitchen, refrigerating all of the ingredients for 30 minutes before preparing the recipe will help to keep the dough cool during preparation. Disks of dough wrapped tightly in plastic wrap can be frozen for up to a month; before rolling the dough, thaw it in the refrigerator and then let it soften at room temperature for about 15 minutes.

- 2½ cups (12½ ounces) unbleached all-purpose flour, plus additional flour for work surface
- 1 teaspoon table salt
- 1 tablespoon sugar
- 16 tablespoons (2 sticks) cold unsalted butter, cut into ½-inch cubes and frozen for 10 minutes
- 3 tablespoons sour cream
- ⅓ cup ice water, or more if needed

1. Process flour, salt, and sugar together in food processor until combined, about 3 seconds. Add butter and pulse until butter is size of large peas, about ten 1-second pulses.

2. Using fork, mix sour cream and ⅓ cup ice water in small bowl until combined. Add half of sour cream mixture to flour mixture; pulse for three 1-second pulses. Repeat with remaining sour cream mixture. Pinch dough with fingers; if dough is floury, dry, and does not hold together, add 1 to 2 tablespoons ice water and process until dough forms large clumps and no dry flour remains, three to five 1-second pulses.

3. Turn dough out onto work surface. Divide dough into 2 balls and flatten each into 4-inch disk; wrap each disk in plastic and refrigerate until firm but not hard, 1 to 2 hours, before rolling. (Dough can be refrigerated for up to 24 hours. Let thoroughly chilled dough stand at room temperature for 15 minutes before rolling.)

COOK'S EXTRA gives you free recipes online. Visit www.cooksillustrated.com and key in code 9055 for Foolproof All-Butter Pie Pastry for Prebaked Pie Shell (for making single-crust pies such as pecan or pumpkin). To read a full account of our rolling pin testing, key in code 9056. The test results and recipe will be available until November 1, 2005.

---

important fat pockets. The result is a very crumbly pie crust that's more like shortbread or a cookie.

Bettering the Butter
Now, back to the abysmal results of my test using all butter in our American Pie Dough recipe. At first I thought there might be too much butter in the dough, making it difficult to handle and, therefore, easy to overwork. To test this hypothesis, I reduced the total amount of fat from 20 tablespoons to 16. While this dough did not suffer from being overworked (the crust wasn't tough), the missing fat was apparent in the crust's bland flavor and dry texture.

If more butter was a bad idea, what about some other form of fat, perhaps heavy cream, cream cheese, or sour cream? Sour cream beat the others in terms of flavor and tenderness. I wondered if the acid in the sour cream was the key factor in contributing to tenderness. To find out, I made an all-butter crust with lemon juice and compared it with the crust made with sour cream. Both were perfectly tender and flaky, but the crust made with sour cream, with its slightly nutty tang, outdid the one made with lemon juice. Because acid slows or reduces the development of gluten (the structure-forming protein in flour), it made sense that a more acidic dough would lead to a more tender crust.

But because sour cream also contains a lot of moisture, adding it along with the butter to the flour was problematic: The dough became a bit damp, making it difficult to cut in and disperse the small bits of butter properly. To remedy this, I tried mixing the butter and flour first and then adding the sour cream, which I had mixed with the ice water. Once again, though, I was disappointed, this time because it was hard to mix the dough in a bowl with a spatula; I could never get the water and flour to blend evenly. The food processor solved this problem, bringing the ingredients together quickly and evenly, with no harm done to the final texture. (The danger in using a food processor is overworking the dough and making it tough. Short pulses are best; the dough is done when it forms large clumps. If it doesn't clump, the best thing is to add a little more water. A dry dough is impossible to roll out.)

As with other doughs, this one needed sugar to enhance browning; 1 tablespoon did the trick. Glazing the crust also promotes browning; a brush of egg white followed by a sprinkle of sugar yielded the right color and crunch.

The last safeguard against an unworkable pie dough is proper chilling. After mixing, unless your kitchen is as cold as a refrigerated boxcar, the small butter pieces need to harden up before being rolled out (hard, cold butter will remain distinct from the flour, thereby maximizing flakiness). And once the dough has been rolled out, it may need another stay in the fridge if it becomes difficult to work with. It's always better to firm up dough by chilling it than by rolling it in more flour, which will only toughen the dough. (It's

The Problem with Deep-Dish Apple Pie

We wanted mounds of tender, juicy apples in our deep-dish pie, but first we had to wade through half-baked apples, soupy fillings, and sodden crusts.

≥ BY ERIKA BRUCE ≤

Deep-dish pies were traditionally baked crustless in casserole dishes, the generous filling blanketed with a layer of thick, flaky pastry. Nowadays, it is more common to find double-crust deep-dish apple pies, with the apples nestled between two layers of pastry. Unfortunately, these pies often bear little resemblance to their name, instead looking suspiciously like your standard apple pie. But I didn't want a thin slice of plain old apple pie; I wanted a towering wedge of tender, juicy apples, fully framed by a buttery, flaky crust.

After foraging for recipes that met my specifications for deep-dish—a minimum of 4 pounds of apples as opposed to the meager 2 pounds in a standard pie—I realized why most recipe writers stick with pies of modest size: While your standard apple pie may have a juicy filling, most deep-dish pies are downright flooded, with the apples swimming in an ocean of liquid. As a result, the bottom crust becomes a pale, soggy mess. In addition, the crowd of apples tends to cook unevenly, with mushy, applesaucey edges surrounding a crunchy, underdone center. Less serious—but no less annoying—is the gaping hole left between the apples (which shrink considerably) and the arching top crust, making it impossible to slice and serve a neat piece of pie.

After a week of rescue efforts, I had made little progress. My failed attempts included slicing the apples into thick chunks to prevent overcooked edges, cutting large vents in the crust to promote steam release, and baking the pies at different temperatures. Chunky apples were unattractive and even more unevenly cooked; both larger vents and varied oven temperatures proved, well, fruitless. Next I tried cutting the apples into thin slices (no good) and moving the pie to the very bottom rack of the oven (a feeble attempt at a burnished bottom crust). No matter what I tried, I was in the end confronted with the same two problems: soupy filling and soggy crust. To sop up the copious amount of liquid expunged by 4 pounds of apples, I added a thickening agent. But so much thickener (flour or cornstarch) was required to dam the flood that it muddied the bright flavor of the apples.

The Pectin Problem

Desperate times call for desperate measures: During my research, I had come across recipes that called for sautéing the apples before assembling them in the pie, the idea being to both extract juice and cook the apples more evenly. Although this logic seemed counterintuitive (how could cooking the apples twice cause them to become anything but insipid and mushy?), I went ahead with the experiment. After browning the apples in a hot skillet (in two batches to accommodate the large volume), I made yet another pie, then crossed my fingers. As expected, the apples were disappointingly mealy and soft, especially the exteriors, which had been seared in the hot pan. But this pie did deliver on a few counts: Aside from the absence of juice flooding the bottom of the pie plate, it offered a nicely browned bottom crust.

Could I keep the apples from disintegrating if I tried this method with a gentler hand? I dumped the whole mound into a large Dutch oven along with some granulated sugar (to flavor the apples and extract moisture), then covered the pan to promote more even cooking. With frequent stirring over a medium flame for 15 to 20 minutes, the apples were tender yet still held their shape. After cooling and draining the apples (so the butter in the crust would not melt immediately), I baked the pie, which was again free of excess juice and sported the same browned bottom as before. This time, however, the apples weren't mealy or blown out—they were miraculously tender.

After some digging, I discovered that apples undergo a significant structural change when held at low-to-moderate temperatures for 20 to 30 minutes. Between 120 and 140 degrees Fahrenheit, pectin is converted to a more heat-stable form. (While pectin provides structure in the raw fruit, it breaks down under the high heat of sautéing.)

A perfect deep-dish pie consists of evenly cooked apples coated (not drenched) in syrupy juice sitting on a well-browned (not soggy) bottom crust.

Variety Makes a Better Pie

A combination of sweet and tart apples works best in pie. These six varieties, all of which retain their shape when cooked, were our favorites in kitchen tests.

Sweet

GOLDEN DELICIOUS
Sweet with buttery undertones.

BRAEBURN
Takes on a pear-like flavor when baked.

JONAGOLD
Similar to Golden Delicious, but more intense.

Tart

GRANNY SMITH
Vibrantly tart. Held shape best.

EMPIRE
Strong, complex, cider-like flavor.

CORTLAND
Similar to the Empire, but more tart than complex.

Once an adequate amount of pectin has been stabilized at low heat (as it apparently was on the stovetop), the apples can tolerate the heat from additional cooking (in the oven) without becoming excessively soft.

This treatment allowed each slice of apple to retain its distinct half-moon shape after baking, stacking up neatly with its brethren. To top it off, because the apples were shrinking before going into the pie rather than after, I had inadvertently solved the problem of the maddening gap! The top crust now remained united with the rest of the pie, and slicing was a breeze.

Getting in Deep

Finally, with a cooking technique that produced picture-perfect results, it was time to adjust flavors. To start, I snuck in another pound of apples (bringing the total to 5 pounds) to compensate for the raw bulk lost during stovetop cooking. Tart apples, such as the Granny Smith and the Empire, were well liked for their brash flavor, but it was a one-dimensional profile. To achieve a fuller, more balanced flavor, I found it necessary to add a sweeter

The Incredible Shrinking Apple

When raw apples are used in a deep-dish pie, they shrink to almost nothing, leaving a huge gap between the top crust and filling. Precooking the apples eliminates the shrinking problem and actually helps the apples hold their shape once baked in the pie.

PROBLEM: Raw apples shrink away from crust.

SOLUTION: Pre-cook the apples.

This seems counterintuitive, but here's what happens: When the apples are gently heated, their pectin is converted to a heat-stable form that prevents the apples from becoming mushy when cooked further in the oven. The key is to keep the temperature of the apples below 140 degrees during this precooking stage. Rather than cooking the apples in a skillet (where they are likely to become too hot), it's best to gently heat the apples and seasonings in a large covered Dutch oven.

STEP-BY-STEP | FORMING THE CRUST

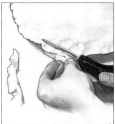
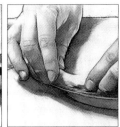

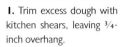

1. Trim excess dough with kitchen shears, leaving ¾-inch overhang.

2. Fold dough under itself so that edge of fold is flush with outer rim of pie plate.

3. To seal pie, flute edges using thumb and forefinger or press with fork.

4. Using sharp paring knife, cut four 2-inch-long slits in top of dough.

---

variety, such as Golden Delicious or Braeburn. Another important factor in choosing the right apple was texture. Even over the gentle heat of the stovetop, softer varieties such as McIntosh broke down readily and turned to mush.

With the right combination of tart and sweet apples, heavy flavorings were gratuitous. I added some light brown sugar along with the granulated sugar to heighten the flavor of the apples, as well as a pinch of salt and a squeeze of lemon juice (added after stovetop cooking to retain its bright flavor). Lemon zest was liked by most, but only when used modestly. After sampling the gamut of cinnamon, nutmeg, allspice, and cloves, tasters were content with just an unimposing hint of cinnamon. Now, at long last, the perfect slice was no longer a deep-dish apple pie in the sky but a reality, sitting up nice and tall on my plate.

DEEP-DISH APPLE PIE
MAKES ONE 9-INCH PIE, SERVING 8 TO 10

Use a combination of tart and sweet apples for this pie. Good choices for tart are Granny Smiths, Empires, or Cortlands; for sweet, we recommend Golden Delicious, Jonagolds, or Braeburns. Wrap leftovers tightly in plastic wrap and store at room temperature for up to 24 hours. To reheat, remove the wrap and warm the pie in a 350-degree oven for 15 to 20 minutes. See page 30 for our testing of apple peelers.

½	cup (3½ ounces) plus 1 teaspoon granulated sugar
¼	cup (1¾ ounces) packed light brown sugar
¼	teaspoon table salt
1	tablespoon juice and ½ teaspoon grated zest from 1 lemon
⅛	teaspoon ground cinnamon
2½	pounds firm tart apples (about 5 medium), peeled and cut into ¼-inch-thick slices (see note)
2½	pounds firm sweet apples (about 5 medium), peeled and cut into ¼-inch-thick slices (see note)
1	recipe Foolproof All-Butter Pie Pastry (page 21)
1	egg white, beaten lightly

1. Mix ½ cup granulated sugar, brown sugar, salt, zest, and cinnamon in large bowl; add apples and toss to combine. Transfer apples to Dutch oven (do not wash bowl) and cook, covered, over medium heat, stirring frequently, until apples are tender when poked with fork but still hold their shape, 15 to 20 minutes. (Apples and juices should gently simmer during cooking.) Transfer apples and juices to rimmed baking sheet and cool to room temperature, about 30 minutes. While apples cool, adjust oven rack to lowest position, place empty rimmed baking sheet on rack, and heat oven to 425 degrees.

2. Remove 1 disk of dough from refrigerator and roll out between 2 large sheets of parchment paper or plastic wrap to 12-inch circle, about ⅛ inch thick. (If dough becomes soft and/or sticky, return to refrigerator until firm.) Remove parchment from one side of dough and flip onto 9-inch pie plate; peel off second layer of parchment. Working around circumference, ease dough into plate by gently lifting edge of dough with one hand while pressing into plate bottom with other hand. Leave dough that overhangs plate in place; refrigerate until dough is firm, about 30 minutes.

3. Meanwhile, roll second disk of dough between 2 large sheets of parchment paper or plastic wrap to 12-inch circle, about ⅛ inch thick. Refrigerate, leaving dough between parchment sheets, until firm, about 30 minutes.

4. Set large colander over now-empty bowl; transfer cooled apples to colander. Shake colander to drain off as much juice as possible (cooked apples should measure about 8 cups); discard juice. Transfer apples to dough-lined pie plate; sprinkle with lemon juice.

5. Remove parchment from one side of remaining dough and flip dough onto apples; peel off second piece of parchment. Pinch edges of top and bottom dough rounds firmly together. Following illustrations 1 through 4, trim and seal edges of dough, then cut four 2-inch slits in top of dough. Brush surface with beaten egg white and sprinkle evenly with remaining teaspoon sugar.

6. Set pie on preheated baking sheet; bake until crust is dark golden brown, 45 to 55 minutes. Transfer pie to wire rack and cool at least 1½ hours. Cut into wedges and serve.

The Best Raspberry Bars

'Sandy,' 'crumbly,' and 'bland' shouldn't be the words used to describe a raspberry bar. 'Tender,' 'fruity,' and 'crunchy'—that's more like it.

⇒ BY ERIKA BRUCE ⇐

What you look for in a raspberry bar is neither refined flavor nor stately appearance but the homey comfort of a triple-decker: sturdy base, jam center, and crisp streusel on top. The secret of this bar cookie's simplicity is the dough, which serves as both bottom crust and—with a modification or two—pebbly topping. But a great-tasting raspberry bar requires just the right balance of bright, tangy fruit filling and rich, buttery shortbread.

Unfortunately, I've had my fair share of raspberry squares that were more crumb sandwich than bar cookie, landing on the floor rather than in my mouth. Worse than the loose crumbs was the meager layer of raspberry jam attempting feebly to hold it all together—so overcooked and leathery that the fruit flavor was gone.

One Dough, Many Problems

The first thing I discovered was that the economical use of a single dough for both the top and bottom crust was, unfortunately, problematic. The same dough responsible for a firm and sturdy bottom layer yielded a topping that was sandy and dry, refusing to cohere to the filling. Some recipe writers get around this problem by making two separate mixtures for the top and bottom layers, but I was loath to make more work for myself. My goal was to create a plain and simple shortbread-like bottom crust, then somehow customize a portion of this dough to end up with a successful streusel topping.

For the bottom crust, I started with a basic

To create neat edges, trim ¼ inch off the borders around the baked block before cutting it into bars.

shortbread recipe—a simple mixture of flour, sugar, salt, and what I thought was a "healthy" dose of softened butter (12 tablespoons for a batch that would fill a 13 by 9-inch pan). But this crust was dense and chewy. I tried chilling the butter before mixing it with the flour (as with biscuit or pie dough); this did little to lighten the dough but rather made it powdery and difficult to press

into the pan. Finally, I tested every other tenderizer I could think of, including baking powder, lemon juice, and cornstarch. All produced botched batches of dry and gritty crust with a texture more sandy than tender. Ignoring concerns about my waistline (which I believed was becoming more substantial with each batch), I had no choice but to return to the best tenderizer of all: pure butter. It was not until the butter in the recipe reached 16 tablespoons that I bit into a shortbread crust worth eating.

But even this butter-rich dough wasn't up to the task of forming a neat-crumbed topping for the jam. While streusel is generally on the loose side (it means "to sprinkle" in German), I wanted a more cohesive topping for these bars. I could hardly be surprised when an extra 2 tablespoons of butter (rubbed into the dough with my fingers) produced small hazelnut-sized crumbs that melded in the oven yet remained light and crunchy. All I had to do now was add sugar and spices. Light brown sugar lent a distinct sweetness, but spices were deemed unnecessary for these fruity bars. Instead, tasters opted for a few oats and chopped nuts for more interesting dimensions of flavor and texture.

Raising the Bar

Regardless of my buttery, shortbread crust and crisp, sweet streusel, these bars were still lacking. To live up to their potential, they needed a fresh-tasting fruity filling. Plain old raspberry jam was the filling of choice for most recipes. After sampling six brands, our tasters proclaimed Smucker's Red Raspberry Preserves the winner. Yet even these very good preserves (made simply by cooking the berries with high-fructose corn syrup) lost significant flavor when cooked again in the raspberry bars. Thinking this was just a symptom of overcooked jam, I tried baking the bars for less time (at a higher temperature to brown the topping); this only made the jam wet and runny, with no flavor improvement.

Resigned to a more moderate cooking time and temperature, I added a dash of lemon juice to brighten the filling. This worked against the deadening heat of the oven, but it didn't fool a single taster into believing there were fresh berries any-

RECIPE TESTING: The Problem with Raspberry Bars

We tested dozens of raspberry bar recipes and uncovered several recurring problems.

SANDY, DRY STREUSEL
Using the same dough for both the top and bottom layers resulted in a crumbly topping.

SKIMPY JAM
Tasters felt cheated by a skimpy, overcooked layer of jam, which got lost between thick, cookie-like layers.

TOO OATY
Too many oats and not enough flour created a streusel topping that melted right into the filling.

1. Press bottom crust firmly and evenly into foil-lined pan.

2. Spread fruit filling over hot bottom crust with spatula.

3. Sprinkle streusel evenly over filling, but resist urge to press it in.

where near these bars. The logical solution? Use fresh berries to get fresh berry flavor. But berries alone produced a sodden, mouth-puckeringly tart raspberry bar. Clearly, there's a reason why all recipes for raspberry bars call for jam or preserves—their viscous, sweet nature is essential to the filling. I found success with a combination of preserves and fresh berries (lightly mashed for easier spreading), which produced a well-rounded flavor and perfectly moist consistency.

RASPBERRY STREUSEL BARS
MAKES TWENTY-FOUR 2-INCH SQUARES

This recipe can be made in a standing mixer or a food processor. Frozen raspberries can be substituted for fresh; be sure to defrost them before combining with the raspberry preserves. If your fresh raspberries are very tart, add only 1 or 2 teaspoons of lemon juice to the filling. The bars are best eaten the day they are baked but can be kept in an airtight container for up to 3 days (the crust and streusel will soften slightly with storage).

2½   cups (12½ ounces) unbleached all-purpose flour
⅔   cup (about 4¾ ounces) granulated sugar
½   teaspoon table salt
16   tablespoons (2 sticks) plus 2 tablespoons unsalted butter, cut into ½-inch pieces and softened to cool room temperature
¼   cup (1¾ ounces) packed light or dark brown sugar
½   cup (1½ ounces) old-fashioned rolled oats
½   cup (2 ounces) pecans, chopped fine
¾   cup (8½ ounces) raspberry preserves
¾   cup (3½ ounces) fresh raspberries
1   tablespoon juice from 1 lemon

1. Adjust oven rack to middle position; heat oven to 375 degrees. Cut 18-inch length foil and fold lengthwise to 8-inch width. Fit foil into length of 13 by 9-inch baking dish, pushing it into corners and up sides of pan; allow excess to overhang pan edges. Cut 14-inch length foil and fit into width of baking pan in same manner, perpendicular to first sheet. (If using extra-wide foil, fold second sheet lengthwise to 12-inch width.)

Spray foil-lined pan with nonstick cooking spray.

2. In bowl of standing mixer fitted with flat beater, mix flour, granulated sugar, and salt at low speed until combined, about 5 seconds. With machine on low, add 16 tablespoons butter one piece at a time; then continue mixing on low until mixture resembles damp sand, 1 to 1½ minutes. (If using food processor, process flour, granulated sugar, and salt until combined, about 5 seconds. Scatter 16 tablespoons butter pieces over flour mixture and pulse until mixture resembles damp sand, about twenty 1-second pulses.)

3. Measure 1¼ cups flour mixture into medium bowl and set aside; distribute remaining flour mixture evenly in bottom of prepared baking pan. Using hands or flat-bottomed measuring cup, firmly press mixture into even layer to form bottom crust. Bake until edges begin to brown, 14 to 18 minutes.

4. While crust is baking, add brown sugar, oats, and nuts to reserved flour mixture; toss to combine. Work in remaining 2 tablespoons butter by rubbing mixture between fingers until butter is fully incorporated. Pinch mixture with fingers to create hazelnut-sized clumps; set streusel aside.

5. Combine preserves, raspberries, and lemon juice in small bowl; mash with fork until combined but some berry pieces remain.

6. Spread filling evenly over hot crust; sprinkle streusel topping evenly over filling (do not press streusel into filling). Return pan to oven and bake until topping is deep golden brown and filling is bubbling, 22 to 25 minutes. Cool to room temperature on wire rack, 1 to 2 hours; remove from baking pan by lifting foil extensions. Using chef's knife, cut into squares and serve.

Fresh Fruit Makes the Difference

We added fresh raspberries to preserves to get a cohesive filling that remained bright and full of raspberry flavor, even after baking.

TASTING: Raspberry Preserves

What's the difference between jellies, jams, preserves, and fruit spreads? To find out, we gathered six samples and tasted them on toast and in our raspberry bars.

In most markets, jellies have been almost completely replaced by fruit spreads (made with juice concentrates, usually pear and white grape). These spreads lack a strong, recognizable raspberry flavor and are one-dimensionally sweet. Based on our tasting, only a jam or preserve will do. The difference between the two is minor; the term "preserve" implies the presence of large pieces of fruit, while a jam should have a smooth and uniform consistency. Their flavor should speak loudly of raspberry, without too much tartness or cloying sweetness. Seedless versions came across as artificial and overprocessed. –Garth Clingingmith

OUR FAVORITE
➤ **SMUCKER'S** Red Raspberry Preserves, $2.99 for 18 ounces
Best of the bunch, preferred in bars and on toast. "Classic, clean" flavor, with an appropriate amount of seeds, is "exactly what this should be," one taster noted.

SEEDY SECOND
➤ **TRAPPIST** Red Raspberry Jam $3.49 for 12 ounces
Flavor-wise, very similar to our favorite, but a few complaints of "too thick" or "too seedy" knocked it to second place.

NOT FOR KIDS
➤ **AMERICAN SPOON FOODS** Red Raspberry Preserves $6.95 for 9.5 ounces
This very thick, reduced preserve is on the tart side; some tasters found it "deep and complex"; others, "burnt."

ON THE SWEET SIDE
➤ **BONNE MAMAN** Raspberry Preserves, $3.29 for 13 ounces
Less thick and "more spreadable" than the higher-rated preserves, but some tasters found it "toothachingly sweet."

NO MORE SEEDS
➤ **SMUCKER'S** Seedless Red Raspberry Jam, $2.69 for 18 ounces
This seedless option is a smoother, sweeter version of our winner. But even self-proclaimed "seed haters" liked at least a few to "add authenticity."

MYSTERY FRUIT
➤ **POLANER** Raspberry All-Fruit Spreadable Fruit $1.79 for 10 ounces
This spread reminded tasters of apples, strawberries, and grapes, but not raspberries. The "Jell-O-like texture" was no help.

Sleuthing Canned Whole Tomatoes

The worst canned tomatoes are mushy, bland, and bitter. How do you keep them out of your pantry? The clues are right on the label.

⇒ BY JOLYON HELTERMAN WITH GARTH CLINGINGSMITH ⇐

When a cookbook calls for canned tomatoes, it often smacks of a last resort: "If ripe, seasonal tomatoes are unavailable…" the recipe invariably begins. But in my kitchen, they're never available—not for cooking, at least. Juice-drenched seasonal tomatoes, available only a few weeks a year, are for eating raw on mayonnaise-slathered bread or straight off the cutting board—not cooking down into sauce.

Fortunately, good canned whole tomatoes always deliver better flavor than the neon-red orbs sold at the supermarket during the off-season. Unfortunately, for every can of fresh-tasting firm tomatoes with a pleasant balance of acidity and fruity sweetness, there's a disappointing tin of stale, bitter mush. The question was, is there a strategy for avoiding the bad ones?

To find out, I brought 10 brands into the test kitchen for a series of blind tastings. (Later, I pitted our supermarket winners against six upscale brands from a gourmet store.) Tasters sampled the tomatoes straight from the can, drained and cooked simply in a quick tomato sauce, and long-simmered in a more complex sauce (undrained) with herbs and wine.

Pureed Route

The first surprising discovery was the utter defeat of the four Italian brands in our lineup—all of which landed at the bottom of our chart. In every tasting, panelists found these samples bitter and stale tasting, and the textures were consistently on the mushy side. The American brands, by contrast, were generally deemed bright, fresh, and well-balanced.

For decades, Italy has been synonymous with superior tomato quality, so these results were puzzling. (So entrenched is the Italian cachet that several U.S. tomato canners go by Italian-sounding brand names.) First, we checked the tomato variety used for each brand, in case the difference was as simple as plum versus round. All of the Italian samples were plums, while the American samples (our top five brands) were split down the middle between plum and round. But tomato variety proved to have little to do with taster preference. While tasters found the round tomatoes milder than the plums, both types were well liked.

The stale taste of the Italian brands in our lineup, it turns out, has more to do with trade laws than crop differences. In 1989, the United States imposed debilitating punitive tariffs on imported European fruits and vegetables—from 13.6 percent to an exorbitant 100 percent. Unsurprisingly, Italian tomato prices went through the roof, and sales of imported tomatoes dropped off dramatically. To avoid paying the steep duty, Italian tomato canners eventually began packing their tomatoes in tomato puree rather than juice. The loophole? When packed in juice, tomatoes are considered a "vegetable"; when packed in puree, they're a "sauce," which carries a much lower customs duty. Sure enough, the Italian brands were all packed in a thick puree (even though two brands inaccurately call it "juice" on the label).

A clever strategy, but not without its downside. Tomato puree, which is made by pulverizing and then cooking tomatoes, imparts a "cooked" flavor to the fresh, uncooked tomatoes packed in it; tomato juice, by contrast, is uncooked. Taster comments fell in line with that hypothesis. The Italian brands were indicted repeatedly for metallic off-notes and "overcooked, stale" qualities, among other faults. By contrast, most of the domestic brands were packed in a thin juice. (For the generally well-liked Redpack, the one domestic exception, tasters had but one complaint: a somewhat processed taste reminiscent of "ketchup.")

Acid Redux

But there's more to the story than just puree versus juice. Tomato packers have to process hundreds of thousands of specimens, in and out of season, so they need to find ways of ensuring consistency, including the level of acidity. Consequently, most brands in our lineup include citric acid, added during processing to correct flavor-profile imbalances. Only Pastene and Rienzi, two low-scoring Italian brands, omit this step, and tasters took notice, complaining of dull, bitter notes and overripe profiles.

None of the brands listed the amount of citric acid added, but taster comments suggested it differed vastly. The best-performing American brands were praised for "refreshing, clean acidity," while the Italian brands were consistently faulted for lack of brightness. To see what was really going on, I decided to measure the pH (an indicator of relative acidity) of every sample. Sure enough, the levels ranged from a moderately acidic pH 4.48 to a more acidic pH 3.93, and all of the American brands were more acidic than the Italians. (The difference between pH 4.48 and pH 3.93 is more dramatic than it looks: It means that the most acidic tomatoes in our lineup were more than three times as tart as the least acidic brand.) Even more fascinating was how perfectly the pH values aligned with taster preference: Like clockwork, the top eight brands in our lineup were ranked in precise descending order from lowest pH (most acidic) to highest. The more acidic the canned tomato, the better.

TASTING: **Supermarket, Gourmet Tomatoes Face Off**

Most of the tomatoes in our lineup can be purchased for less than two bucks a can. But, as with most items, a few extra dollars can get you a fancier version from the gourmet store. In the canned-tomato world, "fancy" generally means one thing: The tomatoes hail from the San Marzano region of Italy, known for its fertile soil, optimal growing climate, and rigid regional quality control (similar to that practiced for sparkling wine in the Champagne region of France).

But how do they taste? We brought in four brands of San Marzano tomatoes, plus two other "San Marzano–style" imports (which ranged in price from $2.99 to $4.50 a can), and made a batch of quick tomato sauce with each one. For comparison, we cooked up two more batches, with Progresso and Redpack, our two favorite supermarket brands. In a blind tasting, panelists remained loyal to Progresso, which beat out all the upscale brands. But two San Marzano brands proved that Italy hasn't completely lost its tomato touch: La Regina and Pastene (the San Marzano tomatoes, not the regular stuff—see the chart on page 27) just edged out Redpack with a tie for second place. While tasters missed the American-style firmness, they praised the rich tomato flavor of these two Italian brands. That said, we still wouldn't bother spending the extra cash. –J.H.

Are these pricey San Marzano tomatoes worth a hefty premium?

TASTING CANNED WHOLE TOMATOES

Twenty *Cook's Illustrated* staff members tasted 10 supermarket brands of canned whole tomatoes straight out of the can; cooked into a quick, simple sauce with olive oil (drained); and slowly simmered in a more complex sauce along with herbs and wine (undrained). Brands are listed below in order of preference. Drained weights and pH levels were determined by our own tests. For each brand, we list origin (domestic or Italian), tomato type (plum or round), and packing medium (juice or puree). The labels for two brands indicate that they were packed in juice, but the thick, grainy consistency and cooked taste said otherwise; here, we have designated that possible discrepancy as "puree-style 'juice.'"

RECOMMENDED

PROGRESSO Italian-Style Whole Peeled Tomatoes with Basil
- $1.89 for 28 ounces; drained weight 11.6 ounces
- pH: 3.93 (domestic, plum, juice)

The winner in all three tastings. "Mmmm—bright, lively flavor and silky texture," said one taster. "The perfect balance of acidic and fruity notes," said another. Some disliked the basil, but all were impressed with the firm, fresh texture. Fairly salty.

REDPACK Whole Peeled Tomatoes in Thick Puree
- $1.29 for 28 ounces; drained weight 12.6 ounces
- pH: 3.95 (domestic, round, puree)

Were it not for the slightly "processed-tasting ketchup quality" of the puree, this "bright, sweet, and balanced" brand might have come out on top. Tasters liked the bold acidity and the full flavor, but some noted minor "metallic off-tastes."

HUNT'S Whole Tomatoes
- $1.39 for 28 ounces; drained weight 10.3 ounces
- pH: 3.97 (domestic, round, juice)

On tasting the quick sauce, one panelist said, "This one tastes the most like ripe, fresh tomatoes." But a few tasters found Hunt's too mild in the long-simmered sauce.

RECOMMENDED WITH RESERVATIONS

TUTTOROSSO Italian-Style Peeled Plum Tomatoes with Natural Basil Flavor
- $1.19 for 28 ounces; drained weight 12.8 ounces
- pH: 3.97 (domestic, plum, juice)

"Basil—with just a hint of tomato," joked one taster, referring to the prominent herbal notes. But even those distracted by the "vegetal, perfumey" overtones had to admit that the tomatoes underneath were bright and nicely balanced, "like freshly picked garden tomatoes."

MUIR GLEN Organic Whole Peeled Tomatoes
- $2.59 for 28 ounces; drained weight 12.3 ounces
- pH: 4.15 (domestic, round, juice)

The sweet flavor was pleasantly "mild and nourishing," but most tasters craved fuller flavor. The real downfall, though, was texture: "Waterlogged," "chewy," and "stringy" were recurring complaints.

RECOMMENDED WITH RESERVATIONS (continued)

RIENZI Peeled Tomatoes
- $1.29 for 28 ounces; drained weight 10.8 ounces
- pH: 4.36 (Italian, plum, puree-style "juice")

The best-scoring Italian brand had fine tomato flavor, but the dull, "stale" taste of the puree was distracting. Several tasters detected "metallic, tinny" off-tastes, and the lack of calcium chloride made for tomatoes that were "too broken down" when cooked.

CENTO Italian Peeled Tomatoes with Basil Leaf
- $2.20 for 35 ounces; drained weight 11.0 ounces
- pH: 4.37 (Italian, plum, puree)

Tasters complained about overcooked, "canned" flavors and a broken-down texture. Strong tomato flavor, but one tinged with "tinny" flavors and out-of-place herbal notes.

NOT RECOMMENDED

PASTENE Italian Peeled Tomatoes with Basil Leaf
- $1.69 for 28 ounces; drained weight 8.5 ounces
- pH: 4.44 (Italian, plum, puree-style "juice")

"All I taste is the can—it's like sucking on aluminum," said one participant. "Tastes like overripe tomato paste," said another. The "stringy, waterlogged," mushy texture did nothing to mitigate the rancid, "icky" off-notes.

MUIR GLEN Organic Fire Roasted Whole Tomatoes
- $1.99 for 28 ounces; drained weight 12.1 ounces
- pH: 4.10 (domestic, round, juice)

"Not good for spaghetti—but maybe for enchiladas?" ventured one polite taster, but that's as genteel as the comments got. The texture was fine, but no one thought that this charred, smoky variation was a good idea.

SCLAFANI Italian Peeled Tomatoes
- $2.39 for 35 ounces; drained weight 8.8 ounces
- pH: 4.48 (Italian, plum, puree)

The least acidic tomato in the lineup elicited grimaces across the board. "Bitter, plastic tasting—I would never voluntarily eat this!" complained one taster (who apparently felt coerced). The low drained weight cost this brand tomato-flavor-fullness points.

Solid Judgment

The only missing piece of the puzzle was why textures differed so substantially, and (once again) I found the answers listed on the label. The top five brands—the five American brands—contain calcium chloride, an additive manufacturers use to maintain tomato firmness. None of the Italian brands contained calcium chloride, and all were indicted for mushy, mealy texture. In the raw tasting, some panelists objected to the pronounced sturdiness of the American brands. But as soon as the tomatoes were cooked, those with this additive were preferred unanimously over the ones without, which quickly lost even the meager structure they had to begin with.

Finally, because some recipes call for drained whole tomatoes, I drained one 28-ounce can of each of the brands, then weighed the solids. The results were shocking. The drained weights of our top seven brands ranged between 10.3 ounces (Hunt's) and 12.8 ounces (Tuttorosso). But the two Italian brands in our "Not Recommended" category yielded a measly 8.8 ounces—or less! What wasn't shocking is that the drained-weight

values correlated directly with the scores tasters gave each sample for "Fullness of Tomato Flavor." Less tomato meat means less tomato flavor.

So where did we come out? For canned whole tomatoes, some extra processing goes a long way toward making a better product. Let the label be your guide: Check for evidence of domestic origin, citric acid, calcium chloride, and tomato juice rather than puree (the one exception was the puree-packed Redpack). Progresso was tasters' clear favorite, while the few who disliked the addition of basil preferred Redpack.

Bag Check

Plastic-bag makers are forever rolling out the 'next great advance' in food storage technology. But how far have we come from the simple twist-tied baggie?

≥ BY JOLYON HELTERMAN ≤

If the U.S. Patent and Trademark Office ever goes out of business, it won't be the fault of the food storage industry. A stroll down the plastic-bag aisle reveals an array of brightly colored boxes beckoning shoppers with breathless claims, coined terminology, and more circled R's than a conservative voter's ballot.

Just in case weighing the respective merits of FreshProtect®II (Glad's patented "pocketing" texture), Ziploc with FreezeGuard® (a patented zipper), and Hefty OneZip®'s Easy Grip® Slider (a patented sealing mechanism) wasn't dizzying enough, manufacturers have divided their product lines into bags for the freezer and bags for general storage. But how meaningful are these fancy-sounding features and designations? Could the simple baggie that our mothers used offer just as much protection—for a fraction of the price?

To find out, I tested 10 different 1-gallon bags from the three national brands—Glad, Hefty, and Ziploc—including four "storage" bags and five "freezer" bags. Within these categories, the bags also varied by seal design: regular zipper (a raised ridge that fits into a groove on the opposite flap) and slider zipper (same groove setup, but sealed by sliding a tab down the length of the opening). We also included a twist-tied baggie.

Film Studies

Storage bags have three core functions: keeping moisture in and keeping air and odor out. The first line of defense is the plastic film itself. So I sent the bags to a lab that uses a specialized machine to measure how fast moisture travels through a material—called the water vapor transmission rate, or porosity. The lower (or slower) the rate, the greater the protection.

The lab results arrived, and I made three important discoveries. First, porosity did vary significantly. The plastic film in the old-fashioned baggie had let through nearly six times more moisture than the next least porous bag. Second, forget FreshProtect II and all those other fancy-sounding features. A plastic bag's relative moisture protection springs from one thing and one thing alone: the thickness of the film. (In fact, all the bags were made from the exact same material—polyethylene.) The thicker the plastic, the better its moisture protection. Most bags ranged between 45 and 72 micrometers thick, which correlated inversely with porosity. (The poor, porous baggie was a flimsy 20 micrometers!)

Finally, the results suggested that the freezer bag/storage bag divide is little more than marketing. In general, freezer bags are thicker, but only 5 micrometers separated our thickest storage bag from our thinnest freezer bag—a suspiciously arbitrary difference.

Performing Seals

If the plastic film were the only route for moisture, air, and odor, testing would be done; the winner would simply be the thickest bag (Hefty Freezer). But moisture can also escape past the seal. To find out which bags were airtight, I placed five water-filled bags of each type in an airtight container with a half-dozen desiccant packs (those moisture-absorbing packets you find in boxes of new shoes), which I weighed before closing the containers.

A week later, I reweighed the packets to see how much moisture they had absorbed. In general, bags with zipper seals proved more airtight than those with slider seals. Three of the five zipper bags (Ziploc Freezer, Glad Freezer, and Ziploc Storage) exuded just 2 grams of total moisture—in line with the expected loss through the plastic film. By contrast, only one of the four slider bags (Hefty Storage) suffered no leakage through the seal. Two slider bags failed miserably: After a week, the desiccant packets were floating in a pool of water 2 inches deep. To make sure the seals had not been compromised by faulty sealing, I repeated the test. Second try, same results.

The problem? As the mechanism slides down the length of the bag's opening, the seal it creates along the way is essentially the same as the regular zipper seal. But the part of the opening directly beneath where the slider tab comes to rest is sealed only by its contact with the tab—and most weren't designed well enough to fit precisely.

Choosing a Winner

It was time to test how bag thickness and seal effectiveness worked in tandem in real applications. First, to evaluate odor protection, I placed bread-packed bags in airtight containers, along with freshly cut onions and garlic. The containers went into the refrigerator. Two weeks later, I roped in a dozen staffers for what may be the test kitchen's least popular tasting to date: comparing 10 samples of 14-day-old bread for onion-garlic contamination. The clear results, however, were worth my colleagues' grumblings: The bags with airtight seals were the odor-protection champs—regardless of film thickness.

Next, I stored bread slices in bags placed directly in the fridge and the freezer. For the next 21 days, my drill never wavered: Arrive at the office, bring 40 packets of bread to room temperature, then reweigh the slices for moisture loss. The slices stored in baggies lost the most weight (and were well on their way toward crouton consistency). Ziploc Freezer and Glad Freezer emerged as the moisture protection champs. Even after three weeks, the bread was soft and fairly fresh.

As testing drew to a close, I realized I needed to break a few ties. So I divided 15 gallons of spaghetti sauce among 20 bags (two samples each), then sealed the bags. Which contender was bag enough to survive an accidental plummet from the counter to the floor? Twenty drops later, the floor was a virtual bloodbath. Tiptoeing through the carnage in search of survivors, I spied only two bags with their entire two-member team still intact: Hefty Storage and Glad Freezer.

Which bag should you buy? Glad Freezer—with its trusty seal, low water vapor transmission rate, thick plastic film (the second thickest of the bunch), and break resistance—is our top recommendation. Based on our findings, the only reason to buy a "storage" bag rather than a "freezer" bag is price; freezer bags tend to cost more. But given that our winning freezer bag is at the cheaper end of the price spectrum, why clutter the kitchen with multiple products? The extra protection can't hurt.

Seeking Closure

| ZIPPER | SLIDER | TWIST TIE |

Some seals sacrificed airtightness for ease of use. We wanted both.

RATING FOOD STORAGE BAGS

We tested ten 1-gallon plastic food storage bags, five designed for use in the freezer and five designed for general food storage. Bags are listed in order of preference.

PRICE: Prices paid at Boston-area retail outlets.
THICKNESS: Of the plastic film, measured to the nearest micrometer ($^1/_{1000}$ of a millimeter).
WVTR: Water vapor transmission rate, as measured by the Mocon Permatran at the Guelph Food Technology Centre in Ontario. Calculated as grams per meters squared per day (the rate at which moisture passes through the plastic film). A small square sample of the plastic film was mounted onto

the machine, with water vapor positioned on one side of the film. An infrared sensor tabulated the amount of time it took for the water vapor to pass through to the other side. The lower the number, the better.
PERFORMANCE: Bags were rated good, fair, or poor based on how well they kept moisture from escaping—and odor and air from entering—in a series of tests. For the stinky bread test, five bread-filled bags were refrigerated for two weeks in an airtight container with onion and garlic; tasters sampled the bread, awarding a "good" for undetectable off tastes or odors. For the watertightness test, five bags filled with water were stored in an airtight container with

five weighed desiccant drying packets for one week; bags that exuded fewer than 10 grams of moisture were rated good. For the bread storage test, bread was stored in four bags (two in the freezer, two in the refrigerator) for three weeks, with weights recorded daily; bags that lost fewer than 0.4 gram of weight (on average) were rated good.
DESIGN: Bags were rated good, fair, or poor based on seal design, mouth width, and other features.
DURABILITY: Bags three-quarters full of spaghetti sauce were dropped from a height of 3 feet onto a plastic tarp; bags that survived two drops were rated good. (This parameter was factored in as a tie breaker only.)

RECOMMENDED

Glad Freezer Zipper Bags
PRICE: $3.69 for 30 bags (12 cents each)
THICKNESS: 68 micrometers
WVTR: 7.14

PERFORMANCE: ★★★
DESIGN: ★★★
DURABILITY: ★★★

TESTERS' COMMENTS: Our second-thickest bag won for its airtight double-groove seal, which held fast even through two rounds of the spaghetti-sauce-drop test. Testers hated the blue tinting ("looks like it belongs in a hospital, not a kitchen"), but we'll take performance over aesthetics any day.

Ziploc Freezer Bags
PRICE: $4.29 for 30 bags (14 cents each)
THICKNESS: 62 micrometers
WVTR: 7.79

PERFORMANCE: ★★★
DESIGN: ★★★
DURABILITY: ★★

TESTERS' COMMENTS: Sturdy, slick, and airtight, but the single-groove seal was not quite sturdy enough to withstand our stress test. (Our winner, Glad, has a double-groove seal that withstood this test.) The wide opening facilitates mess-free filling.

Hefty OneZip Storage Bags
PRICE: $2.50 for 17 bags (15 cents each)
THICKNESS: 47 micrometers
WVTR: 10.14

PERFORMANCE: ★★★
DESIGN: ★★★
DURABILITY: ★★★

TESTERS' COMMENTS: The highest-rated "storage" bag usually performed as well as (or better than) the thicker "freezer" bags, and the slider seal was watertight. But the higher water vapor transmission rate caught up with it about 12 days into the bread storage test.

Ziploc Storage Bags
PRICE: $2.69 for 20 bags (13 cents each)
THICKNESS: 45 micrometers
WVTR: 11.35

PERFORMANCE: ★★★
DESIGN: ★★
DURABILITY: ★★

TESTERS' COMMENTS: Classic zipper design with an airtight seal, which helped it perform remarkably well—especially given the thin film it's made of (the thinnest except for Hefty Baggies). The flimsy gauge made ladling sauce into this bag a chore.

RECOMMENDED WITH RESERVATIONS

Hefty OneZip Freezer Bags
PRICE: $3.79 for 25 bags (15 cents each)
THICKNESS: 72 micrometers
WVTR: 6.62

PERFORMANCE: ★★
DESIGN: ★★
DURABILITY: ★★

TESTERS' COMMENTS: The thickest bag of the bunch would likely have been the champ but for its (consistently) leaky seal. The slider mechanism, identical to the one on the lighter-gauge Hefty Storage, simply seemed ill-equipped to handle the heavier film.

Glad Storage Zipper Bags
PRICE: $3.79 for 40 bags (9 cents each)
THICKNESS: 54 micrometers
WVTR: 9.44

PERFORMANCE: ★★
DESIGN: ★★
DURABILITY: ★★

TESTERS' COMMENTS: The same double-groove seal design as its freezer counterpart, but not as thick—which led to odor-leaching woes in the stinky bread test. Some leakage.

NOT RECOMMENDED

Ziploc Easy Zipper Storage Bags
PRICE: $2.69 for 15 bags (18 cents each)
THICKNESS: 50 micrometers
WVTR: 10.76

PERFORMANCE: ★★
DESIGN: ★
DURABILITY: ★★

TESTERS' COMMENTS: The leaky seal on this bag let water and odor right in, but not as badly as its freezer-bag counterpart (see below). The slider mechanism had a tendency to unlock gradually during transport.

Ziploc Double Guard Freezer Bags
PRICE: $2.29 for 13 bags (18 cents each)
THICKNESS: 59 micrometers (outer layer, 45; inner layer, 14)
WVTR: 8.22

PERFORMANCE: ★★
DESIGN: ★
DURABILITY: ★★

TESTERS' COMMENTS: We assumed this two-ply bag was double the thickness of other bags. We were wrong. It was actually the thinnest freezer bag of the bunch. A bad choice for storing liquids (the chamber between layers gets waterlogged).

Ziploc Easy Zipper Freezer Bags
PRICE: $2.50 for 10 bags (25 cents each)
THICKNESS: 63 micrometers
WVTR: 8.52

PERFORMANCE: ★★
DESIGN: ★
DURABILITY: ★

TESTERS' COMMENTS: Impressive WVTR (which helped it do a passable job in the bread storage test), but the chintzy slider seal allowed water and odor to flow right in.

Hefty Baggies Storage Bags
PRICE: $2.79 for 75 bags (4 cents each)
THICKNESS: 20 micrometers
WVTR: 39.11

PERFORMANCE: ★
DESIGN: ★
DURABILITY: ★

TESTERS' COMMENTS: The twist-tie seal was surprisingly airtight—*if* you remembered to follow the twisting-bending-twisting sequence printed on the box. But moisture, air, and the aromas of onion and garlic all had no trouble penetrating the ultra-thin film.

⇒ BY SANDRA WU ⇐

Buying Fresh Pasta

While developing our Fettuccine Alfredo recipe (page 11), we wondered how "fresh" fettuccine from the supermarket would compare with both fresh pasta from a local Italian market and fresh home-made pasta. We headed into the test kitchen to find out, testing dried fettuccine from the super-market as well.

Tasters immediately recognized the bowl of dried fettuc-cine—it was swimming in the Alfredo sauce. Dried pasta is extruded through dies that leave a perfectly smooth, vir-tually impenetrable sur-face. By contrast, fresh pasta has a rough, porous surface that is better able to absorb sauce. All three fresh pastas, including Buitoni (from the supermarket refrig-erator case), received high marks from tast-ers. All had an "eggy" flavor and firm but yielding texture. The pasta we purchased from a local Italian market had the "wheatiest" flavor and chewiest texture. It was made with a mixture of durum flour and semolina. Durum-only Buitoni and our homemade pasta (made with all-purpose flour) were more bland and soft but still very good.

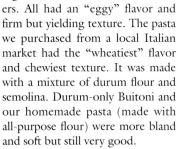

SUPERMARKET FRESH PASTA
As good as homemade?

Our advice? Buitoni is by far the most convenient option, and it can ably compete with homemade. But if you have access to locally made fresh pasta (especially one made with semolina), give it a try.

Nonstick Aluminum Foil

When developing our recipe for Raspberry Streusel Bars (page 25), we found that removing the alumi-num foil lining from the sides of the bars could be a pretty sticky proposi-tion if we'd forgotten to coat the foil with nonstick cooking spray before baking. Forget this all-important step and the raspberry jam will stick to the foil like glue.

But could we skip the spraying step if we used Reynolds Wrap Release Nonstick Aluminum Foil, which is coated on one side (the dull side) with a foodsafe nonstick material? We lined our pan with the foil, dull side up (the shiny side is not nonstick) before assembling and baking our raspberry bars. Once the bars had cooled, we peeled the foil away from the normally super-adhesive jammy edges with ease.

We also tested this nonstick foil in our Crisp-Skin High-Roast Butterflied Chicken and Potatoes (March/April 2000), which has a his-tory of sticking problems, even when the foil is well coated with cooking spray. Whereas the pota-toes normally have to be scraped off the spray-coated, foil-lined broiler pan, they slid right off a pan lined with nonstick foil: no spatula necessary. So for potentially sticky recipes, we now keep a roll of this special foil in the test kitchen.

Make-Ahead Deep-Dish Apple Pie

We tried two different methods for freezing our Deep-Dish Apple Pie (page 23): (1) fully assembled and ready to go directly from freezer to oven and (2) divided into separate components of crust and cooked apple filling to be thawed, assem-bled, and baked. Both versions were good, although the reassembled pie was deemed marginally better for its slightly flakier, more evenly browned crust. You'll probably want to choose one method or the other based on how long you expect to keep a pie (or its components) in the freezer.

Assembled pies kept well for up to two weeks in the freezer; after that, the texture of the crust and apples suffered. To freeze an assembled pie, follow the recipe all the way through sealing the pie crust, but do not brush with egg wash. Freeze the pie for two to three hours, then wrap it tightly in a double layer of plas-tic wrap, followed by a layer of foil, and return it to the freezer. To bake, remove the pie from the freezer, brush it with egg wash, sprinkle with sugar, cut slits in the top crust, and

place directly on the baking sheet in the preheated oven. Bake 5 to 10 minutes longer than normal.

For a longer freezer storage time of several months, freeze the crust and apples separately. Freeze individual batches of the cooked, drained apple filling in quart-sized freezer bags (this doubles as a great alternative to canning). Then make the pie dough, shape it into two 4-inch disks, wrap the disks tightly in a double layer of plastic wrap and foil, and freeze. When you're ready to make the pie, simply thaw the apples and crust in the refrigerator the night before, assemble as per the recipe instructions, and bake as directed. Of course, you can always just freeze the apples and make the crust fresh the day you bake the pie.

A Better Way to Peel Apples

Peeling 5 pounds of apples—let alone coring and slicing them—is a daunting task. If there was ever a recipe on which to test apple-processing gadgets (designed to handle all three tasks), our Deep-Dish Apple Pie (page 23) was it. So we rounded up five models—and a

---

COOKING WITH THE TEST KITCHEN: **When Is It Done?**

A great steak starts at the supermarket and ends with proper timing in the kitchen. Chefs who cook hundreds of steaks a week seem to know when a steak is done almost by intuition. Here are some of the more intriguing methods of determining doneness and our assessment of their practicality for home cooks.

THUMBS DOWN	LAST RESORT	TRIED AND TRUE
Press the meat. Rare meat feels like the flesh between your thumb and fore-finger. For medium meat, make a fist and touch the same part of your hand. Well-done meat feels like the tip of your nose. **OUR ASSESSMENT:** This method is too vague for most cooks.	**Nick and peek.** Slice into the steak with a paring knife and check the color. **OUR ASSESSMENT:** The steak has already been butchered once—why do it a second time in the pan and risk losing juices? Fine in an emergency, but not our first choice.	**Take the temperature.** Hold the steak aloft with a pair of tongs and slide an instant-read thermometer through the side, making sure to avoid bone. **OUR ASSESSMENT:** The most reliable method. Works the first time you try it—and every time thereafter.

KNIFE TECHNIQUE | DICING SQUASH

With its tough outer skin, bulbous base filled with seeds and fibers, and long, skinny neck, butternut squash can be a formidable foe when you approach it with a knife. But if you follow these steps, you'll have evenly diced pieces in no time.

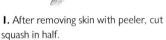

I. After removing skin with peeler, cut squash in half.

2. Cut bulb in half through base and remove seeds with spoon.

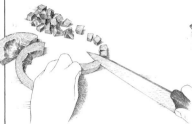

3. Cut each piece into ½-inch half-moons, then into into ½-inch dice.

4. Stand neck on end and slice into ½-inch planks. Cut planks into ½-inch strips, then into ½-inch dice.

---

bushel of apples—and headed into the test kitchen.

One by one, most peelers faltered, as testers found them to be more trouble than they were worth. The clamp-style models—too narrow for all but one of our countertops—lost out to those with a suction base, which also had the benefit of keeping the mess at the center (rather than the edge) of the work area. Once we'd managed to stabilize the models, performance of core tasks was hit-or-miss. When peeling, the gadgets either skimmed the apple's surface or removed a deep gouge of flesh along with the peel. Slicing and coring proved even rougher—literally: Crisp apples had a tendency to crack or break, while mushy apples were processed to, well, mush.

One model, however, surprised testers by peeling, coring, and slicing every apple we could throw at it. The Back to Basics Apple Peeler ($24.95)—with a noticeably sharper blade and sufficiently ample length to mount even extra-large apples—seemed primed to beat out even the handiest test cook. Of course, there was only one way to find out, and so we pitted this device against the test kitchen's best peeler (armed with a peeler, knife, and cutting board). Our test cook polished off 5 pounds of apples in 12 minutes. Not too shabby. The mechanized gadget? Just under four minutes. We're sold.

PLENTY OF APPEAL
If you make more than one pie a year, this gadget is worth every penny.

COOK'S EXTRA gives you free equipment-testing results online. For the results of our testing of apple peelers, visit www.cooksillustrated.com and key in code 9057. This information will be available until November 1, 2005.

Thai Chile Beef Variation

Some readers wondered if **Stir-Fried Thai-Style Beef with Chiles and Shallots** (July/August 2005) could be adapted to work with poultry or seafood. We initially thought chicken would pair well with the Thai flavors, but even dark meat from boneless thighs couldn't hold its own against the potent flavors in this recipe. We had better luck with shrimp; its briny sweetness played off the flavors in the marinade and the sauce. Extra-large shrimp remained juicy and cooked in just two minutes. (For this recipe and those that follow, see Cook's Extra, below.)

Whole-Wheat Biscuits

Several readers wondered if they could make our **Mile-High Biscuits** (July/August 2004) with whole-wheat flour. To find out, we tested four batches of biscuits, substituting varying amounts of whole-wheat flour for the all-purpose in the original recipe.

We noted a few changes as we incorporated whole-wheat flour. The flavor of the biscuits became sweeter and wheatier, the exterior softened, and the interior became drier and chewier. To remain sufficiently true to the original in terms of height, texture, and flavor, we recommend replacing only one-quarter of the all-purpose flour (½ cup) with an equal amount of whole-wheat flour.

WHOLE-WHEAT BISCUIT   **REGULAR BISCUIT**

Replacing just one-quarter of the all-purpose flour with whole-wheat flour produces a biscuit that rivals the original.

Chicken Biryani for a Crowd

Several readers asked if it was possible to double our recipe for **Chicken Biryani** (March/April 2004) to serve eight people. To find out, we started by doubling most of the recipe ingredients, but we soon realized we would have to make some adjustments. The cardamom and ginger were too potent and were better increased by half. Twice as much water made the dish too soupy, so we increased the water by a bit more than half. A double batch of sautéed onions steamed and barely browned. Cooking the onions in two batches ensured deep browning and rich caramelized flavor.

We found that with the increased volume of food, we needed to layer the chicken and rice into a larger cooking vessel and switched from a 4-quart saucepan to a Dutch oven. But now the rice burned on the bottom before it was cooked through. What to do? After layering everything into the pot, we simply changed the cooking venue from the stovetop to the oven. The rice now cooked evenly, and our super-sized recipe was as good as the original.

–Compiled by Nina West

IF YOU HAVE A QUESTION about a recently published recipe, let us know. Send your inquiry, name, address, and daytime telephone number to Recipe Update, Cook's Illustrated, P.O. Box 470589, Brookline, MA 02447, or write to recipeupdate@bcpress.com.

COOK'S EXTRA gives you free recipes online. Go to www.cooksillustrated.com and key in code 9058 for Stir-Fried Thai-Style Shrimp with Chiles and Shallots, code 9059 for Whole-Wheat Mile-High Biscuits, and code 90510 for Chicken Biryani for a Crowd. These recipes will be available until November 1, 2005.

≥ BY GARTH CLINGINGSMITH ≤

DO YOU REALLY NEED THIS?
Pie Crust Bag

The Pie Crust Maker—a round plastic pouch with a zipper—promises to make tidy, nonstick work of rolling out dough, and all for less than $4. Not bad, but could it beat out the two sheets of plastic wrap or parchment paper we normally use? We brought in a group of pastry professionals and novices to find out.

On the sticking front, it was a draw between the pouch and the wrap or parchment. But the pouch had a few distinct advantages. Testers had to readjust the plastic wrap as it stretched and creased (the parchment was moderately better), while the pouch was sturdy enough to resist wrinkling. The pouch also offers plenty of room to roll out a 12-inch crust; a typical roll of plastic wrap or parchment is barely wide enough. The round shape of the pouch helped its cause as well: Testers, especially novices, had a tendency to roll out rectangular crusts between the rectangular sheets of plastic and parchment. Finally, the pouch is washable; the wrinkled plastic and parchment must be discarded after every use.

PIE CRUST MAKER
Can the pouch beat the wrap?

EQUIPMENT UPDATE
Carving Knives

While carving our way through turkeys, roasts, and hams to test carving knives (May/June 2005), we developed some fairly specific design preferences, especially about what we don't like. Serrated slicers tend to shred the meat; pointed tips and narrow blades allow for too much agility (it's harder to maintain a steady, even stroke). In our tests, Forschner's 10-inch round-tipped slicer was our favorite because its broad, stiff blade easily

tracks a straight cut. However, the manufacturer has discontinued the model we tested (40644). Our second-place finisher—the same knife as our favorite, but with a longer, 12-inch blade (model 40645, $47.45)—is also good, but the longer blade makes it more difficult to avoid crooked cuts.

We cast our net a bit wider to come up with a few other knives that looked promising—at least on paper. Unfortunately, all were disappointing. We'll continue our search for the ultimate slicing knife; for now, at least, Forschner's 12-inch round-tipped slicer is the closest candidate.

EQUIPMENT UPDATE
Food Processor

The winning food processor from our November/December 2004 test, the KitchenAid Professional 670 (model KFP670, $279.99), has been discontinued. In its place are two larger models—and they cost less. We brought them into the kitchen for a test run.

Both the 12-Cup Ultra Wide Mouth Food Processor (model KTA KFP760, $229.95) and the 12-Cup Food Processor (model KTA KFP750, $199.95) performed as well as our discontinued winner—and better than our original runners-up—in core tasks such as chopping, pureeing, and making pie and bread dough. The difference came down to the size of the feed tube.

Ironically, the larger tube (that is, the Ultra Wide Mouth) was more limiting in terms of what we could process, thanks to the safety interlock system, a plastic "pusher" that guides the food down the tube and activates the power switch. For example, a large russet potato will fit into the large tube but must be laid on its side for the pusher to engage the slicer. Not a deal breaker,

KITCHENAID FOOD PROCESSOR
Our new favorite—and it's cheaper.

but the regular-size feed tube on the regular 12-Cup Food Processor (which is 2 inches by 3 inches) doesn't have that nagging safety feature; what's more, it costs less.

EQUIPMENT UPDATE
Pie Plates

Our favorite pie plate has been a simple Pyrex dish with a lip that sells for just $5. (Glass pie plates encourage browning and let us monitor it.) While developing our recipe for Deep-Dish Apple Pie (page 23), we came across a fancier version ($7) made by Pyrex—about half an inch deeper, with a fluted top edge rather than a lip. After making dozens of apple pies using both styles, we discovered some problems with the fancier plate. Although the contoured edge added decorative patterns to the sides of the crust, the absence of a broad, horizontal lip on which the crust's edge could rest precluded successful fluting by hand. We'll stick with our original recommendation.

EQUIPMENT TEST
Tortilla Warmers

A dinner out for fajitas wouldn't be complete without the insulated box that keeps the tortillas warm at the table. Why should homemade fajitas be any different? We gathered six tortilla warmers ranging from a $7 Styrofoam model to a ceramic beauty that cost $30 and headed for the test kitchen. Because tortillas heated in the microwave can become leathery and chewy, we developed a preference for ovensafe warmers.

TORTILLA WARMERS
Are they worth the dough?

Does that mean you need to blow $30 for your next fajita night? Not necessarily. We also tried a makeshift tortilla warmer: an ovensafe dinner plate covered with aluminum foil, heated in the oven for 15 minutes at 300 degrees, then kept warm during the meal with a kitchen towel. The results were just as good.

RECIPES

September & October 2005

www.cooksillustrated.com

Join the *Cook's* Web Site and Get Instant Access to 12 Years of Recipes, Equipment Tests, and Tastings!

Web site members can also join the *Cook's* bulletin board, ask our editors cooking questions, find quick tips and step-by-step illustrations, maintain a private list of personal favorites (recipes, quick tips, tastings, and more), and print out shopping lists for all recipes.

Yours Free: As a paid Web site member, you will also receive our **2005 Buying Guide for Supermarket Ingredients.** Simply type in the promotion code **CB53A** when signing up.

Here's Why More Than 80,000 Home Cooks Subscribe to Our Web Site

Quick Search for "Best" Recipes: Access to every recipe published since 1993.

Cook's Extra Recipes: Continued access to the recipes that don't fit in each issue of the magazine, including many flavor variations.

Updated Cookware Ratings: Charts of all buying recommendations published in the magazine (you can download them), plus frequent updates on new models and price changes.

Tasting Results: You'll have access to every tasting published in the magazine, in addition to tastings conducted only for Web members.

Questions for the Editors: Paid members can ask us a question by e-mail and are guaranteed a response.

Bulletin Board: Find out what other *Cook's* subscribers think about recipes, equipment, and cooking techniques. Or just meet the subscribers in your town.

Magazine/Book Customer Service: Pay invoices, give gifts, handle returns, check your subscription status, and more.

Visit Our Bookstore: Order any of our books online and also qualify for special offers.

AMERICA'S TEST KITCHEN TV SHOW
Join the millions of home cooks who watch our show, *America's Test Kitchen*, on public television every week. For more information, including recipes and a schedule of program times in your area, visit www.americastestkitchen.com.

Chicken Francese, 19

Vegetable Torta, 9

Fettuccine Alfredo, 11

Butternut Squash Risotto, 15

Chicken Fajitas, 7

Pan-Seared Inexpensive Steak, 12

Deep-Dish Apple Pie, 23

Foolproof All-Butter Pie Pastry, 21

Raspberry Streusel Bars, 25

PHOTOGRAPHY: CARL TREMBLAY, STYLING: GEORGE SIMONS

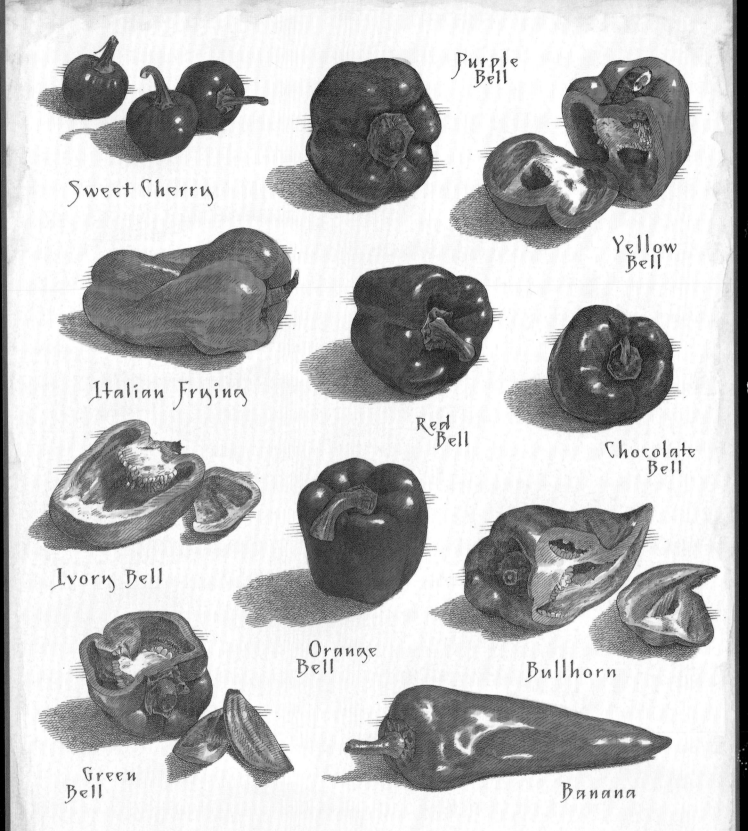

Sweet Cherry

Purple
Bell

Yellow
Bell

Italian Frying

Red
Bell

Chocolate
Bell

Ivory Bell

Orange
Bell

Bullhorn

Green
Bell

Banana

SWEET PEPPERS

NUMBER SEVENTY-SEVEN

NOVEMBER & DECEMBER 2005

COOK'S
ILLUSTRATED

Herbed Roast Turkey
New 4-Step Method

Tangy Buttermilk Mashed Potatoes

Supermarket Coffee Taste Test
Starbucks vs. Dunkin' Donuts

Chocolate Butter Cookies
Cocoa Powder Delivers Big Flavor

Rustic Beef Stew

Rating Mixers
$350 Model Beats
$1,500 Competitor

Roasted Green Beans

Hunter-Style Chicken
How to Buy and Use Chocolate
Perfect Linzertorte
Sweet Potato Casserole

www.cooksillustrated.com

$5.95 U.S./$6.95 CANADA

0   74470 62805   7

1 2>

CONTENTS

November & December 2005

COOK'S ILLUSTRATED

www.cooksillustrated.com

HOME OF AMERICA'S TEST KITCHEN

Founder and Editor	Christopher Kimball
Executive Editor	Jack Bishop
Deputy Editor	Jolyon Helterman
Senior Editor	Adam Ried
Editorial Manager, Books	Elizabeth Carduff
Test Kitchen Director	Erin McMurrer
Senior Editors, Books	Julia Collin Davison
	Lori Galvin
Managing Editor	Rebecca Hays
Associate Editor, Books	Keith Dresser
Associate Editors	Erika Bruce
	Sean Lawler
	Sandra Wu
Web Editor	Lindsay McSweeney
Copy Chief	India Koopman
Test Cooks	Garth Clingingsmith
	David Pazmiño
	Rachel Toomey
	Diane Unger-Mahoney
	Nina West
	Sarah Wilson
Assistant Editor, Books	Charles Kelsey
Editorial Assistant, Books	Elizabeth Wray Emery
Assistant to the Publisher	Melissa Baldino
Kitchen Assistants	Maria Elena Delgado
	Nadia Domeq
	Ena Gudiel
Editorial Interns	Elizabeth Bomze
	Lauren Oliver
Contributing Editor	Matthew Card
Consulting Editors	Shirley Corriher
	Guy Crosby
	Jasper White
	Robert L. Wolke
Proofreader	Jean Rogers
Design Director	Amy Klee
Marketing Designer	Julie Bozzo
Designer	Heather Barrett
Staff Photographer	Daniel van Ackere
Vice President Marketing	David Mack
Circulation Director	Bill Tine
Fulfillment Manager	Carrie Horan
Circulation Assistant	Elizabeth Dayton
Direct Mail Director	Adam Perry
Products Director	Steven Browall
E-Commerce Marketing Manager	Hugh Buchan
Customer Service Manager	Jacqueline Valerio
Customer Service Representative	Julie Gardner
Vice President Sales	Demee Gambulos
Retail Sales Director	Jason Geller
Retail Sales Specialist	Arthur Barbas
Corporate Sponsorship Specialist	Laura Phillipps
Marketing Assistant	Connie Forbes
Vice President Operations	James McCormack
Senior Production Manager	Jessica L. Quirk
Production Manager	Mary Connelly
Project Manager	Anne Francis
Book Production Specialist	Ron Bilodeau
Production Assistants	Jeanette McCarthy
	Jennifer Power
	Christian Steinmetz
Systems Administrator	Richard Cassidy
Internet Technology Director	Aaron Shuman
Chief Financial Officer	Sharyn Chabot
Controller	Mandy Shito
Staff Accountant	Maya Santoso
Office Manager	Saudiyah Abdul-Rahim
Receptionist	Henrietta Murray
Publicity	Deborah Broide

PRINTED IN THE USA

RUSTIC BREAD SHAPES Of all the rustic, freeform bread shapes that hail from Europe, the long, baton-like French baguette is the most familiar. The *epi*, or ear of wheat, is a decorative variation on this long, thin shape, achieved by cutting a series of diagonal slits partway through the loaf; alternating sections of dough are pulled out to create the classic wheat-stalk shape. The wreath is made either by joining a similarly thin log of dough at the ends or by punching a hole in the center of a dough round and gently widening it. The *ficelle* (French for "twine") is half the width of a regular baguette but just as long and can be used to make uniform rounds for hors d'oeuvres. Torpedo-shaped *batards* and rounded *boules* serve as the basis for a host of common breads, including sourdough and rye. *Ciabatta* is a traditional Italian freeform loaf, characterized by its squat shape and chewy, large-holed crumb. French *fougasse*—a cousin of Italian focaccia—is a flat bread scored with several holes to create the lattice shape.

COVER *(Apples)*: Elizabeth Brandon, BACK COVER *(Rustic Bread Shapes)*: John Burgoyne

For list rental information, contact: ClientLogic, 1200 Harbor Blvd., 9th Floor, Weehawken, NJ 07087; 201-865-5800; fax 201-867-2450.
Editorial Office: 17 Station St., Brookline, MA 02445; 617-232-1000; fax 617-232-1572. Subscription inquiries, call 800-526-8442.
Postmaster: Send all new orders, subscription inquiries, and change-of-address notices to Cook's Illustrated, P.O. Box 7446, Red Oak, IA 51591-0446.

CLOSE CALLS

A friend of mine owns a pair of Shire horses—each of which weighs in at a massive 2,400 pounds—that are used to pull mowers and other farm equipment. His wife, Annick, is an experienced equestrian and has taken to riding them, a notion that I have decried on many occasions as a uniquely hairbrained idea. After all, they haven't been schooled in pleasure riding, and arguing with more than a ton of stubborn horseflesh could be fatal. Well, you can guess the rest of the story. My wife, Adrienne, and I went down for a visit and Annick suggested we go for a ride. The other horses were ill-disposed, so she saddled up one of the Shires. One thing led to another and I soon found myself at a full lope, at which point the Shire, having had enough of this particular passenger, took a sharp left into a small stand of trees. I went from 20 miles per hour to zero in less than a second, having been swept out of the saddle by a set of thick branches. When I came to, my face was full of dirt, my ribs were bruised, my left leg was useless, and my neck was, well, stiff. It took about a month to mostly recover, and I still don't quite remember exactly what happened. It was a close call.

Many of our neighbors have had their own near-death experiences. A month ago, Nate was working next to an excavator, bent over as he was spraying a line on the grass. The operator swiveled the machine around just as Nate was standing up and caught him on the head with the back of the cab. It laid him out flat on the ground, his eyes were bloodshot for a week, and he still has a crease in his skull. Charlie Bentley had his own close call a few years ago when his head was caught between two disks in a harrow and was pulled 100 yards through a field face down by a runaway tractor. Tom, who works in construction, fell off of scaffolding above a concrete apron dotted with spikes of rebar. He landed on his feet in between the metal spikes and walked away without a scratch.

Nancy Tschorn runs the local country store with her husband, Doug, and she just wrote a book of stories, including her "close calls" with wily vendors. D-Wayne is one such salesman, and he phones her every few months to make her a special offer: 300 pounds of bubble wrap, a case of hammer heads (the handles got burned in a fire), Swedish (not Swiss) army knives for 99 cents apiece, and, on this one occasion, 10 pairs of socks for a dollar each. Socks sell well since the store is near the famous Battenkill River, which does a good job producing loads of wet socks. Knowing that acrylic socks are no bargain, she asked D-Wayne what material the socks were made from. After a long pause, he said in a southwestern drawl, "Well, let me see. They are 70 percent wool and 30 percent nylon." Nancy placed the order, as a combination of warm wool and strong nylon sounded like a good mix. A week later the shipment of 10 pairs arrived: Seven pairs were wool and three were nylon.

In the kitchen, of course, we have all had plenty of close calls as well as outright disasters. I recently put a baking sheet of individual chocolate bread puddings under the broiler with the timer set for a minute and left the kitchen. My 7-year-old, Emily, shouted out, "Daddy, the oven is on fire!" True enough. The chocolate had burned and the bread was indeed ablaze. Although I could not conceal my blunder, I did manage a bit of culinary surgery and topped each ramekin with plenty of whipped cream. Dessert was a close call.

Our closest calls, however, are often those times when we wisely opt to take a quiet path in the face of disaster. As a young farmhand, I was driving a tractor and baler down a steep hill when I pushed in the clutch and tried to downshift. Charlie Bentley (the farmer) was standing on the back of the tractor and said nothing. When we

Christopher Kimball

managed to get safely down the hill he said quietly, "Best not to shift a heavy load going downhill." I realized later that this had been a serious, potentially fatal mistake—a close call of the highest order. But Charlie knew that there was more at stake than his tractor. Instead of overreacting and shaking my confidence, he handled the situation quietly.

One summer night years ago, my oldest daughter, Whitney, decided to leave home on her bike, a green and white special with colored streamers on the handgrips. It was just the two of us home that evening, but I said nothing, leaving her to her preparations. She left (I peeked out of the living room window), bicycling down the long drive to the dirt road that runs through our small valley. I walked to the kitchen and set the timer for 30 minutes. When it went off, I went to the old Ford pickup and drove down the road toward New York State. I found her turned around, heading back home, just short of Harley Smith's farm. I turned the truck around and came up next to her, asking her if she might want a lift since it was mostly an uphill ride. She said, "Sure." I put the bike in the back of the truck, and we drove home without another word between us. We never spoke of it again, nor did I ever tell her mother. (That is, until now.)

Sometimes kids need their independence, need the freedom to head down the road on a hot July night. I guess I have learned something from the Vermont farmers I grew up with (although they might say otherwise). You stand by the stove, watching the timer count down slowly, dreaming of a little girl cycling purposefully toward the broad flatlands of New York State with a sandwich and marshmallows in her white vinyl saddlebag. You step back and take a chance, letting life fill in the future on its own, wondering just how close a call it will really be.

FOR INQUIRIES, ORDERS, OR MORE INFORMATION:

www.cooksillustrated.com

At www.cooksillustrated.com, you can order books and subscriptions, sign up for our free e-newsletter, or renew your magazine subscription. Join the Web site and you'll have access to 13 years of *Cook's* recipes, cookware tests, ingredient tastings, and more.

COOKBOOKS

We sell more than 40 cookbooks by the editors of *Cook's Illustrated*. To order, visit our bookstore at www.cooksillustrated.com or call 800-611-0759 (or 515-246-6911 from outside the U.S.).

COOK'S ILLUSTRATED Magazine

Cook's Illustrated magazine (ISSN 1068-2821), number 77, is published bimonthly by Boston Common Press Limited Partnership, 17 Station Street, Brookline, MA 02445. Copyright 2005 Boston Common Press Limited Partnership. Periodicals postage paid at Boston, Mass., and additional mailing offices, USPS #012487. POSTMASTER: Send address changes to Cook's Illustrated, P.O. Box 7446, Red Oak, IA 51591-0446. For subscription and gift subscription orders, subscription inquiries, or change-of-address notices, call 800-526-8442 in the U.S. or 515-247-7571 from outside the U.S., or write us at Cook's Illustrated, P.O. Box 7446, Red Oak, IA 51591-0446.

Reading Tea Leaves

Do white, green, oolong, and black teas come from the same plant? We have heard conflicting statements. Your expertise would be welcome.

RICHARD FLATOW
OAK CREEK, WIS.

➤ White, green, oolong, and black teas come from the same source: an evergreen plant in the *Camellia* family. The degree to which the leaves are processed determines the resulting forms of tea. Many historical experts and botanists believe green tea was the earliest type of tea produced in China, with black tea developed during the Ming dynasty (1368–1644) as a way to extend the leaves' keeping qualities as trade abroad increased.

All four varieties of tea require the same first step in processing: the withering stage, in which the water content of the leaves is reduced from 75–80 percent to 60–70 percent through exposure to sunlight or warm air. What happens next radically changes the nature of the leaves and the resulting cup of tea.

White tea is produced from new tea-leaf buds that are plucked before they open, allowed to wither, and dried. Because white tea is not rolled (a step that most teas undergo to release their aromatic juices) and is only slightly oxidized, its light gray leaves brew up a pale yellow liquid with a mild, slightly sweet flavor. For green tea, the leaves are withered, heat-treated, rolled, and heated once more until dry and dull green in color. The resulting tea is bright and grassy in flavor. The leaves destined to become black tea undergo the most processing.

WHITE
Brews up slightly sweet and mild

GREEN
Bright and grassy overtones

OOLONG
Moderately woody and floral

BLACK
Deep and smoky flavor notes

One Plant, Many Teas All four of these teas come from the same plant—an evergreen in the *Camellia* family. The difference is in the processing.

Like green tea leaves, black tea leaves are withered and rolled. Unlike green tea leaves, they are next fermented and dried, or "fired." This last step is necessary to stop the decomposition of the leaves, causing them to turn black and develop that familiar "tea" smell.

Oolong tea, which originated in the Fukien province of China, falls in between green and black teas in terms of both taste and processing method. Generally referred to as semi-fermented, it is withered and fermented, much like black tea, but for a shorter period of time, and its leaves are never broken by rolling.

Eggs, Sunny Side Down?

We noticed that cartons of eggs seem to come with the eggs placed pointed side down. When we transfer the eggs from the carton to the refrigerator egg holder, we turn them pointed side up. Does it matter which end is up?

CONAN AND TERESA COCALLAS
OAKHURST, CALIF.

➤ Some experts recommend storing eggs the way they are packaged, with the pointed side down. Why? The theory is that keeping eggs in their original configuration helps the yolks stay centered rather than shifting to one side when hard-cooked. We tested this theory by storing eggs both pointed side down and pointed side up for various lengths of time and then hard-cooking them. Guess what? No difference.

Our test kitchen has determined that eggs are best stored in their original cardboard (or Styrofoam) cartons on the top shelf of the refrigerator (not the door) to keep them from absorbing flavors from other foods and to maintain an ideal humidity level of 70 to 80 percent. Egg trays are typically located on refrigerator doors, where the temperature is often warmer than the recommended 40 degrees Fahrenheit.

Cocoa Update

➤ In the test kitchen, we prefer Dutch-processed cocoa powder—cocoa that's been treated with alkaline chemicals to temper its bitterness (see our January/February 2005 issue). When we found out that Hershey's European Style cocoa, our top-rated supermarket brand, had been discontinued to make room for a new version, Hershey's Special Dark, we

bought a box to give it a taste. Upon opening the lid, we immediately suspected the worst. Why? The more cocoa is "dutched" (or treated), the darker it gets—and this stuff was dramatically darker than the original. While moderate Dutching helps alleviate harsh notes, overzealously Dutched cocoa tends to take on a taste and consistency reminiscent of talcum powder.

Sure enough, in a blind tasting of Chocolate Butter Cookies (page 23) made with the original Hershey's European Style and the new Hershey's Special Dark, comments focused on the latter's dry, "hollow" texture, off-putting "black mud" color, and "chalky Oreo" flavor. Tasters much preferred the versions made with the moderately alkalized Callebaut cocoa (our mail-order favorite) and Droste, a widely available brand that is now our top-rated supermarket cocoa.

Hybrid Brown Sugar

What do you know about Splenda's Brown Sugar Blend? Can I use it the same way I would use regular brown sugar?

TESSA CARREON
HONOLULU, HAWAII

➤ Splenda is the trademarked name for an artificial sweetener made from sucralose, a chemically altered form of sugar that tastes sweet but isn't digested as calories or carbohydrates. Unfortunately, Splenda lacks the volume of real sugar—an important consideration in some baking recipes. So Splenda has come out with reduced-calorie spinoffs that split the difference, blending sucralose with the real stuff. Brown Sugar Blend is a mixture of sucralose and brown sugar that is twice as sweet as regular brown sugar, so you use half as much. (One teaspoon of brown sugar has 15 calories and 4 grams of carbs; the equivalent half-teaspoon of Brown Sugar Blend has 10 calories and 2 grams of carbs.)

We tested Brown Sugar Blend in three applications—chocolate chip cookies, blondies, and a streusel topping (sprinkled over a yellow cake)—tasting them side by side with versions prepared with regular brown sugar. Tasters detected a "bitter" and "soapy" aftertaste in the cookies and

BROWN SUGAR BLEND
Doesn't come out on top

I found what seems to be a large wooden fondue fork at a flea market. What is it really used for?

HUNTER THOMAS
GLENDIVE, MONT.

➤ The item you've found is a tool from Holland called a poffertjes fork. *Poffertjes* are small, puffy yeasted pancakes about the size of silver dollars that are served topped with butter and confectioners' sugar. They are cooked on the stovetop in a special cast-iron or nonstick pan featuring shallow rounded cavities. Once the batter is placed in the buttered cavities and the poffertjes have cooked on one side, the two-pronged wooden fork (about 10½ inches long, with 2-inch tines) is used to flip them so they can brown on the other side. Anyone keen on making this Dutch specialty would be well advised to purchase the fork (as well as a poffertjes pan; both fork and pan can be ordered from the source listed on page 32). The fork's long, thin, slightly curved tines cradle the bottom of the poffertjes in a way that a skewer or regular fork cannot, making the turning process a breeze.

This wooden fork is used to flip puffy little Dutch pancakes, or *poffertjes*, in a specially designed pan so they can brown on both sides.

blondies made with Brown Sugar Blend and also found them somewhat dry. The cause of the texture problem was clear. Real sugar has moisture-retaining (or *hygroscopic*) properties; because the Splenda blend contains less real sugar, it retains less moisture. Where Brown Sugar Blend really failed as a substitute, though, was in the streusel topping, which simply sank into the batter instead of crunching up into a recognizable streusel. Not much of a replacement in our book—even if you do save a few calories.

The Scoop on Synthetic Spoons

Do Exoglass cooking spoons have any advantages over traditional wooden spoons? What are they made from?

AMY RAO
NASHVILLE, TENN.

➤ Although they may look like they are made of meltable plastic, Exoglass cooking spoons, a product of France, are actually a blend of resin and fiberglass that makes them heat resistant up to 430 degrees. Unlike wooden spoons, which must be washed by hand, have a tendency to absorb odors and colors, and can split over time after repeated soaks in water, Exoglass spoons are quite durable and offer several advantages. First, they can be thrown into the dishwasher without melting or splintering. Second, being nonporous (unlike wood), they

EXOGLASS SPOON
Is this synthetic spoon superior to wood?

don't stain or retain food particles, odors, or bacteria, which makes them a good choice when melting or caramelizing sugar (food particles can cause the heating sugar to crystallize rather than liquefy) or when stirring slow-simmering, stain-prone foods such as chili, curry, and tomato sauce.

Such merits notwithstanding, the Exoglass spoon cannot entirely replace the wooden spoon, which we still find useful when trying to gauge the consistency of sauces via the "coating the back of the spoon" test (the slick surface of the Exoglass makes this more difficult) and to scrape up *fond* (browned bits) from the bottom of a pan (flat-bottomed spoons are the best choice here).

So we're holding on to our wooden spoons, but we wouldn't mind adding an Exoglass spoon or two to our utensil drawer—especially given that we found one for a modest $5.66. See Sources on page 32 to order.

Battle of the (Turkey) Sexes

Is there any way to figure out whether a supermarket turkey is a "tom" or a "hen," and is there a significant difference in flavor or texture?

PAMELA LOPEZ
BIRMINGHAM, ALA.

➤ When it comes to commercial turkeys, weight is the best indicator of whether a turkey is a tom (male) or a hen (female), as there are no obvious visual cues for distinguishing the two once they reach the market. Representatives from Butterball, Plainville Farms, and Empire Kosher Poultry all said that their smaller turkeys (10 to

A Better Stick of Butter?

When I moved to California, I noticed that the butter sticks are shorter and stubbier than the ones I grew up with back East. What's the history behind this difference? Is one style better than the other?

JILL OHLINE, REDWOOD CITY, CALIF.

➤ The Elgin, or Eastern-pack, style of packaging butter creates the long, skinny sticks available in most regions of the United States. They are 4¾ inches long by 1¼ inches wide and are stacked two by two in their boxy containers. The Western-pack style makes for the short, stubby sticks you noticed when you moved to California. They measure 3⅛ inches long by 1½ inches wide and are packed side by side in their flat, rectangular boxes. No matter what the style, one stick contains 8 tablespoons.

Elgin-style sticks (named for a once-prominent dairy in Elgin, Ill.) are the standard choice east of the Rockies. At some point, dairy farms in the West began using different butter printers (the machinery used to cut and package butter sticks) that produced shorter, wider sticks. We find both styles easy to use in the kitchen. The biggest difference may come down to your butter dish—most dishes are shaped to fit Elgin-style sticks.

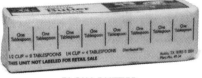

WESTERN BUTTER
Short and wide

ELGIN BUTTER
Long and thin

16 pounds) tend to be hens, while their larger birds (18 pounds and above) are typically toms. When in the 16- to 18-pound range, a turkey might be either a large hen or a small tom.

All of the turkey producers we spoke to agreed that there is no discernible difference in taste between toms and hens and that the age of the bird is what's most important when it comes to tenderness. Because the majority of supermarket turkeys are slaughtered when young (under 28 weeks of age), they are pretty tender—even the tom turkeys.

SEND US YOUR QUESTIONS We will provide a complimentary one-year subscription for each letter we print. Send your inquiry, name, address, and daytime telephone number to Notes from Readers, Cook's Illustrated, P.O. Box 470589, Brookline, MA 02447, or to notesfromreaders@bcpress.com.

Quick Tips

⊰ COMPILED BY ERIKA BRUCE ⊱

Make-Ahead Bread Crumbs

Cooks who like to plan ahead make more bread crumbs than called for in a single recipe and freeze them in a zipper-lock bag. But transferring the crumbs from food processor to bag—especially a small bag—can be tricky. Patrick Burgon of Ottawa, Ontario, removes the blade from the workbowl, lifts the workbowl from its base, and locks the lid in place. Next, he inverts the whole unit to funnel the crumbs through the feed tube into the bag.

Maximizing Oven Space

A large Dutch oven often leaves little room in the oven for anything else. Zag Hewell of Seattle, Wash., maximizes space by inverting the lid, covering it with foil, and roasting a side dish of potatoes or vegetables right on top.

A Better Way to Crack an Egg

Cracking an egg on the side of a mixing bowl is common kitchen practice. But Loretta Fisher of Anacortes, Wash., swears by another method, which is just as simple and more reliable.

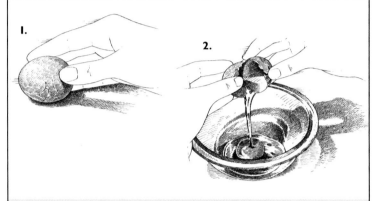

1. Tap the egg on a flat surface, such as the countertop, rather than the edge of a mixing bowl.
2. This results in a cleaner break through the shell and the inner membrane, which translates to fewer pieces of shattered shell in your bowl.

Press, Don't Pound, Chicken Breasts

After watching her tortilla press gather dust on the kitchen shelf, Patricia Jassir of Tampa, Fla., finally discovered another function for this sporadically used piece of equipment—flattening chicken breasts into cutlets.

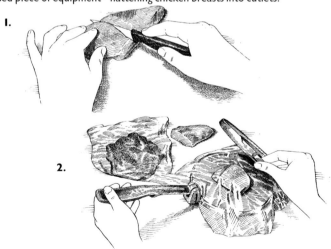

1. Start with small chicken breasts (3½ ounces or less) or cut a larger breast in half crosswise.
2. Wrap the breast in plastic (to keep the press plates clean), place it between the plates, and press.

Packaging Pies for Transport

Transporting freshly baked pies from home to a holiday party can be hazardous, as the pies slide every which way in the car. Virginia Rice of Philadelphia, Pa., solved the problem by getting a clean box from her local pizzeria. A small 10-inch-square pizza box is just the right size for keeping flat-topped pies, such as pecan and pumpkin, safe. (This tip won't work with domed pies, like lemon meringue.)

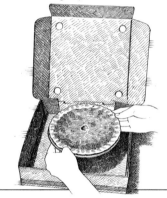

Tough Nut to Crack

Few nutcrackers are strong enough to crack the hard shells of many nuts, especially walnuts. Randy Czaplicki of Las Vegas, Nev., recommends using a hardware-store tool called a vise-grip, also known as curved-jaw locking pliers.

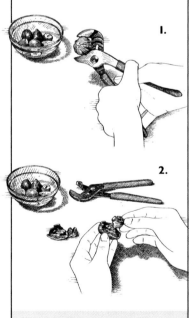

1. The adjustable rounded jaws can accommodate nuts of almost any shape or size.
2. The grip is strong enough to break through the hardest shell, leaving the tender flesh intact.

Send Us Your Tip We will provide a complimentary one-year subscription for each tip we print. Send your tip, name, and address to Quick Tips, Cook's Illustrated, P.O. Box 470589, Brookline, MA 02447, or to quicktips@bcpress.com.

Protecting Recipe Ingredients

After making repeated trips to the grocery store to replace recipe ingredients, Danielle L. Schultz of Evanston, Ill., finally got wise to her family's raids on the pantry. Now she places brightly colored stickers on any items reserved for use in a recipe as soon as she unpacks the groceries. Anything without a sticker is fair game.

Stuffed Mushroom Cups

For easier transport of her stuffed mushroom caps, Henny Hall of Edisto Island, S.C., uses mini muffin tins. Each mushroom perches neatly in a muffin cup, and not a single bread crumb is lost on the way to the party.

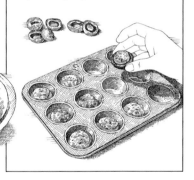

'Grilling' Buns Indoors

Hot dogs taste good any time of year and are even better when eaten on a warm, toasted bun. Throwing the buns on the grill is easy, but when cold weather keeps Saravuth Neou of Cambridge, Mass., from going outdoors, he uses a toaster, letting the buns lie on top of the slots, then flipping them over.

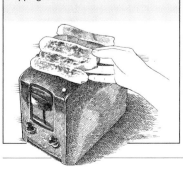

Rubber Bands as Labels

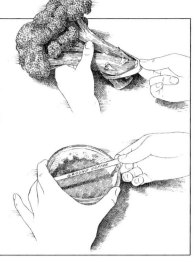

Broccoli and some other vegetables come neatly contained in thick rubber bands. Katja Patchowsky of Kew Gardens, N.Y., recycles the bands by using them to label items destined for the freezer. She stretches a band around the top and bottom of a container (which also helps keep a loose lid in place) and writes the container's contents on the band with a permanent marker. She even flips the band over to get one more use out of it.

Easier Bread Slicing

Slicing a loaf of rustic bread freshly heated in the oven can be a hot and messy proposition: It's hard to get a hold on the bread, and the crumbs tend to spray everywhere. Helene Jasper of Portland, Ore., came up with a practical way to solve the problem.

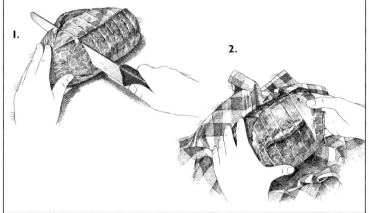

1. Cut slices of bread about ¾ of the way down to the bottom crust before crisping the loaf in the oven.
2. Because the loaf is still intact, it is easy to transfer to a serving basket, and the slices can be torn apart at the table with minimal mess.

Yogurt Containers for Cookie Decorating

After washing and drying them well, Meg van Meter of Ambler, Pa., uses yogurt containers with plastic snap-on lids to store cookie-decorating supplies such as colored sugars and sprinkles. She takes their use one step further by turning them into shakers.

1. Punch holes in the lids with a paper hole-punch.
2. Replace the lids and invert the containers to sprinkle decorations onto frosted cookies.

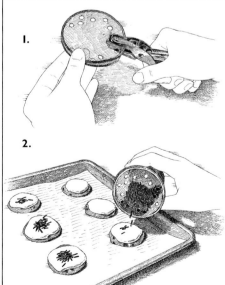

Gravy Carafe

To keep gravy warm at the table, as well as easy to pour, Gloria Anderson of Yorktown, Va., uses an insulated coffee carafe. It cuts down on spills and keeps gravy hot throughout the meal.

Pie-Dough Spritzer

Anyone who makes pie dough has faced the problem of dough that is too dry and crumbly when it's time to roll it out. Knowing that mixing in more water with a spoon or spatula can overwork the dough and make the crust tough, Ken Sinclair of Newton, Mass., relies on a spray-bottle full of ice water to distribute just the right amount of water needed.

Soundproof Coffee Grinder

Nothing is better than waking up to the smell of fresh-brewed coffee, but no one likes to be jolted from sleep by the loud whirring of the coffee grinder. To muffle the noise, Marshall King of Goshen, Ind., places an oven mitt over the grinder before turning it on.

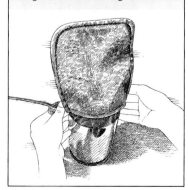

Beef Stew, Provençal Style

This beef stew from the south of France is country cooking at its best: bold, brash, and full-flavored. Could we translate the flavors of Provence to an American home kitchen?

⇒ BY SARAH WILSON ⇐

Daube Provençal, also known as daube Niçoise, has all the elements of the best French fare: tender pieces of beef, luxurious sauce, and complex flavors. Those flavors come from local ingredients, including olives, olive oil, garlic, wine, herbs, oranges, tomatoes, mushrooms, and anchovies.

But few of these ingredients made it into the large stack of "authentic" recipes I uncovered in my research. When tested, many of these recipes were one-note wonders—beef stew with olives or beef stew with oranges. One exception to this early testing was a recipe from Julia Child, which included most of the flavors I wanted. Although not without problems, her version inspired me to follow suit and led to my main challenge with this recipe: I would have to find a way to turn these strong, independent flavors of Provence into a robust but cohesive stew.

Food Fight

Over the years, the test kitchen has developed countless beef stews as well as a reliable set of techniques to turn tough beef into tender stew: Brown the beef (to ensure the richest, meatiest flavor); add the aromatic vegetables; sprinkle some flour in the pan (to thicken the braising liquid); deglaze with the predominant cooking liquid; add the meat back to the pot; and, finally, cover and cook in a low to medium oven until tender. Our choice of meat for stew is cut from the chuck, or shoulder, which is notoriously tough (the meat softens nicely during long, slow cooking) but also flavorful. While various chuck cuts are appropriate for this recipe, I found that the chuck-eye roast offered the best flavor and texture.

Most beef stews have a personality-defining ingredient, like the wine in beef Burgundy or the beer in carbonnade. In contrast, daube Provençal relies on a complex blend of ingredients, which I methodically began to test. Tasters loved the earthiness of dried cèpes (the mushroom known more commonly by its Italian name, *porcini*). Niçoise olives lent a briny and authentic local flavor, and tomatoes brought brightness and texture. Orange peel contributed a subtle floral element, while herbs, particularly thyme and bay, are

This rustic stew has especially large pieces of beef that can withstand the long cooking needed to meld the flavors in the braising liquid.

a natural addition in anything from Provence.

My tasters weren't enthusiastic about every authentic ingredient I tried. When I added anchovies, some tasters claimed that these pungent fish have no place in beef stew. Funny that no one noticed the two fillets that were already part of my working recipe. When I omitted the anchovies entirely, tasters claimed the stew lacked depth of flavor. Over the next couple of days, I quietly added the anchovies back in one at a time and stopped at three fillets, at which point tasters praised the rich, earthy flavors of the dish and noticed a complexity that had been missing without them. (They never knew the secret!)

Pig's trotters, a standard ingredient in many older recipes, contribute body to the sauce in the form of gelatin and flavor from the pork meat and fat. But the protests against a foot in the stew were too much, and this time I caved in. As a compromise, I substituted salt pork, a salt-cured cut from the pig's belly, and adjusted the amount of salt in the stew to accommodate it. Several tasters still

protested the extra fat on principle, but a side-by-side comparison made it clear that salt pork, like anchovies, added a richness of flavor that was unmistakably absent when not included. In any case, the salt pork was added in a single piece that I removed and discarded just before serving, once the pork had given up its flavor to the stew.

In the Thick of It

I had been following the French technique of adding a small amount of flour in the form of a *roux*, a butter and flour thickener, but up to this point I wasn't satisfied with the consistency of the sauce. The butter sometimes ended up floating to the top of the stew, making it look greasy, and the sauce was still too thin. I returned to our established technique and omitted the step of making a roux. Instead, I sprinkled flour into the pot to cook out with the vegetables and tomato paste. I also increased the amount of flour to ⅓ cup, which is a little more than most recipes contain. The result was immediately noticeable. The extra flour created a braising liquid that thickened to the consistency of a luxurious sauce.

What started as a key ingredient in daube Provençal, the red wine, had now been relegated to a mere afterthought, barely discernible amid the other ingredients. My recipe contained a half bottle. Could I add more? Conservatively, I began adding more wine, careful not to sacrifice the integrity of the other flavors. In the end, I discovered that this stew was bold enough to accommodate an entire bottle—at least in theory. The wine tasted a bit raw. So I put the stew back into the oven for additional 15-minute increments until the total cooking time approached three hours. The resulting sauce was gorgeous, with rich round flavors and a velvety texture.

What was good for the sauce wasn't so good for the meat. I had been cutting the chuck roast into 1-inch cubes, a standard size for beef stew. But with the longer cooking time, the meat was drying out and losing its distinct character. By cutting the chuck roast into 2-inch pieces, I was able to keep my longer braising time and create a truly complex sauce. The beef was now tender and flavorful, and the larger pieces added to the rustic quality of this dish.

DAUBE PROVENÇAL
SERVES 4 TO 6

Serve this French beef stew with egg noodles or boiled potatoes. If niçoise olives are not available, kalamata olives, though not authentic, can be substituted. Cabernet Sauvignon is our favorite wine for this recipe, but Côtes du Rhône and Zinfandel also work. Our favorite cut of beef for this recipe is chuck-eye roast, but any boneless roast from the chuck will work. Because the tomatoes are added just before serving, it is preferable to use canned whole tomatoes and dice them yourself—uncooked, they are more tender than canned diced tomatoes. Once the salt pork, thyme, and bay leaves are removed in step 4, the daube can be cooled and refrigerated in an airtight container for up to 4 days. Before reheating, skim the hardened fat from the surface, then continue with the recipe.

3/4 ounce dried porcini mushrooms, rinsed well
1 boneless beef chuck-eye roast (about 3 1/2 pounds), trimmed of excess fat and cut into 2-inch chunks
1 1/2 teaspoons table salt
1 teaspoon ground black pepper
4 tablespoons olive oil
5 ounces salt pork, rind removed
4 large carrots, peeled and cut into 1-inch rounds (about 2 cups)
2 medium onions, halved and cut into 1/8-inch-thick slices (about 4 cups)
4 medium garlic cloves, sliced thin
2 tablespoons tomato paste
1/3 cup all-purpose flour
1 bottle bold red wine (see note)
1 cup low-sodium chicken broth
1 cup water
4 strips zest from 1 orange, removed with vegetable peeler, each strip about 3 inches long, cleaned of white pith, and cut lengthwise into thin strips
1 cup pitted niçoise olives, drained well
3 anchovy fillets, minced (about 1 teaspoon)
5 sprigs thyme, tied together with kitchen twine
2 bay leaves
1 can (14 1/2 ounces) whole tomatoes, drained and cut into 1/2-inch dice
2 tablespoons minced fresh parsley leaves

1. Cover mushrooms with 1 cup hot tap water in small microwave-safe bowl; cover with plastic wrap, cut several steam vents in plastic with paring knife, and microwave on high power for 30 seconds. Let stand until mushrooms soften, about 5 minutes. Lift mushrooms from liquid with fork and chop into 1/2-inch pieces (you should have about 4 tablespoons). Strain liquid through fine-mesh strainer lined with 1 paper towel into medium bowl. Set mushrooms and liquid aside.

2. Adjust oven rack to lower-middle position; heat oven to 325 degrees. Dry beef thoroughly with paper towels, then season with salt and pepper. Heat 2 tablespoons oil in large heavy-bottomed Dutch oven over medium-high heat until shimmering but not smoking; add half of beef. Cook without moving pieces until well browned, about 2 minutes on each side, for total of 8 to 10 minutes, reducing heat if fat begins to smoke. Transfer meat to medium bowl. Repeat with remaining oil and remaining meat.

3. Reduce heat to medium and add salt pork, carrots, onions, garlic, and tomato paste to now-empty pot; cook, stirring occasionally, until light brown, about 2 minutes. Stir in flour and cook, stirring constantly, about 1 minute. Slowly add wine, gently scraping pan bottom to loosen browned bits. Add broth, water, beef, and any juices in bowl. Increase heat to medium-high and bring to full simmer. Add mushrooms and their liquid, orange zest, 1/2 cup olives, anchovies, thyme, and bay, distributing evenly and arranging beef so it is completely covered by liquid; cover partially and place in oven. Cook until fork inserted in beef meets little resistance (meat should not be falling apart), 2 1/2 to 3 hours.

4. Discard salt pork, thyme, and bay leaves. Add tomatoes and remaining 1/2 cup olives; warm over medium-high heat until heated through, about 1 minute. Cover pot and allow stew to settle, about 5 minutes. Using spoon, skim excess fat from surface of stew. Stir in parsley and serve.

SHOPPING: **Key Ingredients**
Here are some notes on buying the key ingredients in our daube.

SALT PORK
Cured (but not smoked) pork belly gives the stew richness and flavor. Buy a piece that's at least 75 percent meat, with a minimum of fat.

OLIVES
Use tiny, briny niçoise olives. Cook some of the olives with the stew, then add more just before serving to maximize their impact.

ANCHOVIES
No one will be able to detect their flavor, but anchovies add earthiness to this dish. Meaty Ortiz anchovies (in olive oil) won a test kitchen tasting.

RED WINE
Choose something bold, such as Cabernet, and simmer for at least 2 1/2 hours to cook off the raw flavors that an entire bottle contributes to the pot.

TOMATOES
Progresso whole tomatoes were the winner of a test kitchen tasting. To preserve their lively flavor, add the drained tomatoes just before serving.

Redefining Sweet Potato Casserole

More dessert than side dish, the typical recipe swamps this casserole in sugar, fat, and spices. We wanted to clear the way for the sweet potatoes.

⇒ BY MATTHEW CARD ⇐

Every Thanksgiving, without fail, millions of households across the country prepare the butter-laden, overspiced, marshmallow-topped side dish we all know and love as Sweet Potato Casserole. It's as much a side of nostalgia as it is a side dish, but with all of that fat, sugar, and spice, the flavor of the sweet potatoes gets lost. Very lost. Thinking that the supporting ingredients ought to play second fiddle to the potatoes, I set out to update this home-style classic.

Most of the recipes I researched for this story added a great deal of sugar, cream, butter, and eggs to mashed sweet potato. Toppings, I was pleased to find, ranged far beyond marshmallows to include everything from a simple scattering of nuts to such glorifications as canned pineapple rings, maraschino cherries, corn flakes, Rice Krispies, bread crumbs, and streusel. Some test recipes were prepared and tasted, and the streusel-topped casserole stole the show. The streusel's crisp texture and bittersweet flavor—dark brown sugar balanced by slightly bitter pecans—held the filling's richness at bay.

Hot Potato

Most of the recipes I found called for canned sweet potatoes. These have all the spunk of wet cardboard, so I ruled them out from the start. In terms of precooking the potatoes, the choices were boiling, microwaving, and roasting. The first two methods produced bland potatoes. Roasting was a different story. Although roasting took 1 to 1½ hours at 400 degrees, depending on the potatoes' girth, it produced a rich, earthy, intensely sweet flavor that was worth every minute. Once the potatoes cooled briefly, it was quick work to scrape the soft flesh free of the papery skins.

Like peanut butter, sweet potato casserole typically comes in two styles: chunky and smooth. A smooth-textured filling better complemented the crunchy streusel topping, but I couldn't get the potatoes smooth enough when mashing by hand. Both a handheld and a standing mixer were efficient, but I wanted to try one more option: the food processor. Expecting the worst (food processors turn regular potatoes into wallpaper paste in seconds), I tossed the roasted potatoes into the

A streusel topping with pecans is a more interesting option than the classic mini-marshmallows.

processor workbowl and let it rip. Instead of dissolving into a starchy mass, however, they quickly became silky smooth. (See "Sweet Potatoes and Starch," below, for details.)

But now the creamy filling proved a bit too smooth, so I tried a mix of potato chunks and smooth puree, reserving half of the roasted potatoes and folding them into the puree just before baking. Bites of dense potato were thus suspended throughout the puree. This amalgamated texture paired perfectly with the crunchy topping.

Sugar and Spice

Roasting had so intensified the flavor of the sweet potatoes that the excessive amounts of sugar traditionally added to the filling had become superfluous. Any more than a few tablespoons of white granulated sugar (brown sugar muddied the flavors) made the filling candy-sweet. Any cook knows that fat generally equals flavor, but in this case I found the opposite to be true. Heavy cream—usually added to the casserole's filling—muted the intensity of the potatoes. I thought I could simply reduce the volume, but this made the filling stiff and gummy. Switching to whole milk made the filling too lean, so I split the difference and chose half-and-half. It contributed richness without being cloying. Five tablespoons of butter (most recipes included a full stick or more) further smoothed things out.

Recipes typically add whole eggs to the filling, but I thought they made my casserole too stiff. Without any eggs, however, the filling was too loose and lacked depth of flavor. Yolks alone proved to be the solution. I tried as few yolks as one and as many as a half-dozen; four proved ideal, giving the casserole just enough body to scoop neatly with a serving spoon.

SCIENCE: Sweet Potatoes and Starch

After a disastrous experience making mashed potatoes in a food processor one Thanksgiving as a teenager (and still suffering gibes from my family about my "wallpaper paste"), I was reluctant to take the same tack with sweet potatoes. But the processor-pureed sweet potatoes—creamy and smooth—were everything the white potatoes hadn't been. Why? There seem to be two reasons.

First, sweet potatoes and white potatoes, which are from completely different plant families, have starches that are also very different. Sweet potato starch is similar to cornstarch. The starch granules are about half the size of those in white potatoes, and they are more stable during cooking. Second, sweet potatoes contain an enzyme that when heated converts some of the starches to sugars. With less starch that is more resistant to breakdown, cooked sweet potatoes are thus rendered creamy, not gluey, by the processor's whirling blade. –M.C.

GLUE FACTORY
When regular potatoes are pureed in a food processor, they form a gluey mess (above). In contrast, pureed sweet potatoes are creamy and light.

1. Instead of boiling sweet potatoes (as most recipes direct), roast them for a lighter, fluffier casserole.

2. As soon as sweet potatoes are finished cooking, cut them in half lengthwise so steam can escape.

Warm spices like cinnamon, ginger, and cloves made the casserole taste like pie. Nutmeg, however, in conjunction with a grind of black pepper, offset the rich sweetness of the potatoes. Vanilla—a stiff shot of it—contributed dimension by picking up floral undertones. Many recipes add orange juice or zest, but tasters found the flavors distracting. A splash of lemon juice delivered brightness without citrusy flavor.

Topping It Off

The winning streusel from my first round of tests was a simple blend of flour, brown sugar, pecans, and softened butter (melted butter made the streusel too hard). Although well liked, it was too sweet. I thought I could simply reduce the sugar, but this yielded a bland-tasting, sandy streusel. More butter failed to improve things, and more nuts did little good. Streusel may be a simple blend of ingredients, but, as I was finding out, they must be in perfect balance. After making a dozen batches in which I varied each ingredient by miniscule amounts, I finally arrived at an ideal ratio of 2 parts nuts to 1 part each of flour and brown sugar—very nutty and only lightly sweetened.

Between the roasted potatoes, a prudent use of sugar and seasonings, and a less sticky-sweet topping, the intense flavor of sweet potatoes was now the focus of this classic. Would I miss the marshmallows? Only until the first bite.

SWEET POTATO CASSEROLE
SERVES 10 TO 12

Because natural sugar levels in sweet potatoes vary greatly depending on variety, size, and season, it's important to taste the filling before adding sugar. If the filling is bland, add up to 4 tablespoons sugar; if the potatoes are naturally sweet, you may opt to omit the sugar altogether. When sweetening the filling, keep in mind that the streusel topping is quite sweet. If you can find them, Beauregard, Garnet, or Jewel sweet potatoes have the best texture for this recipe.

For even cooking, buy potatoes that are uniform in size. Avoid potatoes larger than 1½

pounds; they require a longer roasting time and tend to cook unevenly. The potatoes can be baked up to 2 days ahead. Scrape the flesh from the skins and refrigerate in an airtight container. To serve 4 to 6, halve all the ingredients and bake the casserole in an 8-inch-square baking dish for 35 to 40 minutes.

Sweet Potatoes

- 7 pounds (6–8 medium) sweet potatoes

Streusel

- 5 tablespoons unsalted butter, cut into 5 pieces and softened, plus additional for greasing pan
- ½ cup (2½ ounces) all-purpose flour
- ½ cup (3½ ounces) packed dark brown sugar
- ¼ teaspoon table salt
- 1 cup (4 ounces) pecans

Filling

- 5 tablespoons unsalted butter, melted
- 2 teaspoons table salt
- ½ teaspoon ground nutmeg
- ½ teaspoon ground black pepper
- 1 tablespoon vanilla extract
- 4 teaspoons juice from 1 lemon
  Granulated sugar
- 4 large egg yolks
- 1½ cups half-and-half

1. **FOR THE SWEET POTATOES:** Adjust oven rack to lower-middle position and heat oven to 400 degrees. Poke sweet potatoes several times with paring knife and space evenly on rimmed baking sheet lined with aluminum foil. Bake potatoes, turning them once, until they are very tender and can be squeezed easily with tongs, 1 to 1½ hours (or 45 minutes for small sweet potatoes). Remove potatoes from oven and cut in half lengthwise to let steam escape; cool at least 10 minutes. Reduce oven temperature to 375 degrees.

2. **FOR THE STREUSEL:** While potatoes are baking, butter 13 by 9-inch baking dish. Pulse flour, brown sugar, and salt in food processor until blended, about four 1-second pulses. Sprinkle butter pieces over flour mixture and pulse until

crumbly mass forms, six to eight 1-second pulses. Sprinkle nuts over mixture and pulse until combined but some large nut pieces remain, four to six 1-second pulses. Transfer streusel to medium bowl and return empty workbowl to processor.

3. Once potatoes have cooled slightly, use spoon to scoop flesh into large bowl; you should have about 8 cups. Transfer half of potato flesh to food processor. Using rubber spatula, break remaining potato flesh in bowl into coarse 1-inch chunks.

4. **FOR THE FILLING:** Add melted butter, salt, nutmeg, pepper, vanilla, and lemon juice to potatoes in food processor and process until smooth, about 20 seconds. Taste for sweetness, then add up to 4 tablespoons granulated sugar, if necessary; add yolks. With processor running, pour half-and-half through feed tube and process until blended, about 20 seconds; transfer to bowl with potato pieces and stir gently until combined.

5. **TO ASSEMBLE AND BAKE CASSEROLE:** Pour filling into prepared baking dish and spread into even layer with spatula. Sprinkle with streusel, breaking up any large pieces with fingers. Bake until topping is well browned and filling is slightly puffy around edges, 40 to 45 minutes. Cool at least 10 minutes before serving.

Are They Done Yet?

Sweet potatoes take longer to roast than you might think—up to 1½ hours in a 400-degree oven. Here are two ways to determine whether they are properly cooked.

SQUEEZE: Although the outside might be tender, the center can still be firm. Before removing sweet potatoes from the oven, squeeze them with a pair of tongs—they should give all the way to the center, without resistance.

PEEK: If you have doubts, cut sweet potatoes in half lengthwise. If you see whitish marbling (uncooked starches that are firm to the touch), press the halves back together, wrap the potatoes individually in foil, and continue roasting until the marbling disappears.

Roasting Green Beans

Is it possible to breathe new life into over-the-hill supermarket green beans?

⇒ BY REBECCA HAYS ⇐

Delicate and slender, garden-fresh *haricots verts* need only a few minutes of steaming, a pat of butter, and a sprinkle of salt and pepper to be ready for the table. In fact, they are so sweet, crisp, and tender that it's not uncommon to eat them raw. Take the same route with mature supermarket green beans, however, and you'll regret it. Unlike their lithe cousins, overgrown store-bought beans are often tough and dull, demanding special treatment.

Italians solve the problem with braising; gentle, moist cooking has a tenderizing effect. But the stovetop can get awfully crowded as dinnertime approaches—especially during the holidays. Roasting is commonplace for root vegetables like potatoes and carrots, and the technique is becoming popular for other vegetables, too. Would a stint in the oven have a positive effect on out-of-season green beans?

I had my answer when an embarrassingly simple test produced outstanding results. Roasted in a hot oven with only oil, salt, and pepper, an entire baking sheet of beans disappeared faster than french fries. Repeated tests confirmed that roasting consistently transforms geriatric specimens into deeply caramelized, full-flavored beauties. Here's why: As green beans mature, their fibers toughen and their sugars are converted to starch. The hot, dry heat of the oven helps to reverse the aging process. Fibers break down and an enzymatic reaction causes the starch to turn back into sugar, restoring sweetness. Roasting also encourages the Maillard reaction—a chemical response that creates flavor through browning—a benefit lost with moist cooking methods.

The technique needed a few refinements. Those rare roasted-green-bean recipes that I found called for at least 2 tablespoons of oil per pound of beans, but I favored a more restrained approach. A single tablespoon of oil encouraged browning without making the beans slick and greasy. And after testing multiple time and temperature combinations, 20 minutes (with a quick stir at the halfway point) in a 450-degree oven proved optimal. Finally, when I tested the recipe using a dark nonstick baking sheet and encountered scorching, I began lining the sheet with aluminum foil. The foil warded off burning and made cleanup so easy that I made it part of the recipe, regardless of the pan.

I now had beans that tasted great straight up, and it was time to experiment with recipe variations. But their development was not without missteps: Aromatics (garlic and ginger) added at the outset scorched. The solution wasn't to lower the heat (the beans didn't brown well enough) but rather to add these ingredients halfway through cooking. And when liquid seasonings like vinegar and sesame oil slid right off the beans onto the baking sheet, I included a spoonful of sticky sweetener (honey or maple syrup) to create an appealing glaze, a move that incidentally incited even more caramelization. Last, a smattering of raw ingredients (toasted nuts or seeds, fresh herbs, or crumbled cheese) when the beans finished cooking provided complexity and textural interest.

Shrivel Action

Wrinkles aren't always a sign of overzealous cooking. For roasted green beans, shriveled exteriors indicate a successful transformation from bland and stringy to tender and flavorful.

ROASTED GREEN BEANS
SERVES 4

An aluminum foil liner prevents burning on dark nonstick baking sheets. When using baking sheets with a light finish, foil is not required, but we recommend it for easy cleanup.

- 1 pound green beans, stem ends snapped off
- 1 tablespoon olive oil
  Table salt and ground black pepper

1. Adjust oven rack to middle position; heat oven to 450 degrees. Line rimmed baking sheet with aluminum foil; spread beans on baking sheet. Drizzle with oil; using hands, toss to coat evenly. Sprinkle with ½ teaspoon salt, toss to coat, and distribute in even layer. Roast 10 minutes.

2. Remove baking sheet from oven. Using tongs, redistribute beans. Continue roasting until beans are dark golden brown in spots and have started to shrivel, 10 to 12 minutes longer.

3. Adjust seasoning with salt and pepper, transfer to serving bowl, and serve.

ROASTED GREEN BEANS WITH RED ONION AND WALNUTS

Combine 1 tablespoon balsamic vinegar, 1 teaspoon honey, 1 teaspoon minced fresh thyme leaves, and 2 medium thin-sliced garlic cloves in small bowl; set aside. Follow recipe for Roasted Green Beans through step 1, roasting ½ medium red onion, cut into ½-inch-thick wedges, along with beans. Remove baking sheet from oven. Using tongs, coat beans and onion evenly with vinegar/honey mixture; redistribute in even layer. Continue roasting until onions and beans are dark golden brown in spots and beans have started to shrivel, 10 to 12 minutes longer. Adjust seasoning with salt and pepper and toss well to combine. Transfer to serving dish, sprinkle with ⅓ cup toasted and chopped walnuts, and serve.

ROASTED SESAME GREEN BEANS

Combine 1 tablespoon minced garlic (about 3 medium cloves), 1 teaspoon minced fresh ginger, 2 teaspoons honey, ½ teaspoon toasted sesame oil, and ¼ teaspoon hot red pepper flakes in small bowl; set aside. Follow recipe for Roasted Green Beans through step 1. Remove baking sheet from oven. Using tongs, coat beans evenly with garlic/ginger mixture; redistribute in even layer. Continue roasting until dark golden brown in spots and starting to shrivel, 10 to 12 minutes longer. Adjust seasoning with salt and toss well to combine. Transfer to serving dish, sprinkle with 4 teaspoons toasted sesame seeds, and serve.

ROASTED GREEN BEANS WITH SUN-DRIED TOMATOES, GOAT CHEESE, AND OLIVES

Follow recipe for Roasted Green Beans through step 2. While beans roast, combine 1 teaspoon extra-virgin olive oil, 1 tablespoon lemon juice, ½ cup drained oil-packed sun-dried tomatoes (rinsed, patted dry, and coarsely chopped), ½ cup pitted kalamata olives (quartered lengthwise), and 2 teaspoons minced fresh oregano leaves in medium bowl. Add beans; toss well to combine, and adjust seasoning with salt and pepper. Transfer to serving dish, top with ½ cup crumbled goat cheese (about 2 ounces), and serve.

Go to www.cooksillustrated.com
- Key in code 11051 for **Roasted Maple-Mustard Green Beans**.
- Recipe available until December 31, 2005.

Herbed Roast Turkey

How do you give a turkey herb flavor that's more than superficial? We rubbed, soaked, injected, poked, and operated on more than two dozen birds to find out.

⇒ BY SANDRA WU ⇐

This Thanksgiving, I decided to forgo the safe and reliable (aka boring) plain roasted bird for something riskier but potentially more flavorful and exciting: an herbed roast turkey. Now, let it be said that in prior years I have tried merely throwing a bunch of herbs into the cavity or rubbing the outside of the bird with a savory paste. These recipes were, at best, no better than the usual roasted bird and, at worst, just downright weird or blotched in appearance. I didn't want merely to flirt with the idea of great herb flavor, I wanted it in each and every bite.

At the outset, I knew I would stick to several of our established turkey-roasting procedures: brining the turkey, roasting it starting breast side down, and flipping it over to finish breast side up. (This technique, our testing has shown, is the one sure way to keep the white meat from overcooking before the rest of the bird is done.) Also, I wasn't exactly starting my quest for intense herb flavor at square one. Recently, the test kitchen developed a recipe that calls for applying a spice rub onto the skin, directly onto the flesh (under the skin), and onto the walls of the cavity. I knew that this three-pronged approach could provide worlds more herb flavor than simply garnishing the cavity with a sprig or two of unprocessed herbage, and it was a fine starting point. But to get the herbal intensity I was after—powerful, aromatic flavor that permeated well beyond the meat's surface—more hard-core measures were called for: I would have to go in deep.

Deep Impact

As I gathered an arsenal of excavation tools that might come in handy during my journey to the center of the bird, an idea hit. Was there a way to reach the turkey's depths without actually piercing the flesh? After all, brining had proved an effective method for infusing salt and moisture. Could I use this less invasive procedure to, well, kill two birds with one stone? Temporarily pushing aside my collection of knives, shears, and syringes, I set about creating an herb-infused brine. I boiled some fresh herbs in water, strained out the solids, stirred in the salt, then "herb-brined" the turkey

Most herbed roast turkeys lack noticeable herb flavor—a problem we solved by creating an interior pocket of fresh herbs well beneath the surface.

for six hours. But the experiment was a bust; the fresh herbs contributed hardly any additional flavor. Interestingly, I did get powerful results when I repeated the experiment using dried herbs—too powerful. This time, the meat had an overwhelming, perfumed flavor that tasters found more "pickled" than herb-infused. Brining good, pickling bad: I had to come up with a powerful herb infusion method, but one that I could control.

Taking a step back, I experimented with a poke-and-fill approach. I carefully made multiple incisions throughout the breast and thigh meat and spooned the herb paste into the slots. Instead of a beautiful Thanksgiving dinner centerpiece, however, I got a turkey with puncture wounds oozing green stuff. (Too bad Halloween had already come and gone.) But what if the points of insertion were not as large and ghastly? Reaching for a solid food injector, I pumped the paste into several key spots throughout the meat. While more attractive than my previous, slasher-film-ready turkey, this version left me with the same condensed blobs of over-

whelmingly strong, raw-tasting herbs. What's more, the deeper layers were still lacking in noticeable herb flavor.

Thus began my attempts at full-frontal bird surgery. To get a thin, even layer of herb paste within the meat, I butterflied each breast, applied the paste to both flaps, then sutured the sides back up using skewers. Finally, I was on the right track! Like a coffee cake with a nice swirl of streusel in the center, this turkey's meat boasted an attractive layer of herbs in every slice yet still had enough "unherbed" portions to provide welcome contrast. On the downside, the procedure was labor-intensive, and the bird was difficult to flip (the skewers got caught in the roasting rack). Was there a less invasive (and less tacky-looking) way to achieve similar results?

Racking my brain for ideas, I borrowed a technique the test kitchen had developed for stuffing a thick-cut pork chop. Using a paring knife, I made a 1½-inch vertical slit in the breast meat and created an expansive pocket by sweeping the blade back and forth, being careful not to increase the size of the original slit on the surface. This newly created void covered an interior surface area nearly as large as the butterflied breasts. In this space, I rubbed a small amount of herb paste (too much and the herbs began to taste raw and strangely medicinal). This method yielded flavor that was just as good as the butterflied version. Who would have thought that treating a turkey like a pork chop was the secret to true herb flavor?

Now that I'd upped the three-pronged method I'd started with to a four-pronged affair, I realized that rearranging the order of my herbal assaults made sense. I began by applying the paste underneath the skin (directly onto the flesh), then inside the newly created pockets (reversing these two steps caused the skin at the incision site to widen and tear), inside the cavity, and, finally, over the skin.

Go to www.cooksillustrated.com
- The drippings from this turkey can be used to make our **Best Turkey Gravy**. Key in code 11052 to get the recipe.
- Recipe available until December 31, 2005.

Steps to Serious Herb Flavor

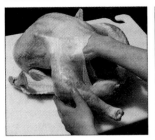

LOOSEN
1. Carefully separate skin from meat on breast, thigh, and drumstick areas.

RUB
2. Rub herb paste under skin and directly onto flesh, distributing it evenly.

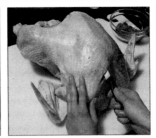

STAB AND SWEEP
3. Make 1½-inch slit in each breast. Swing knife tip through breast to create large pocket.

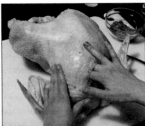

STUFF
4. Place thin layer of paste inside each pocket.

MASSAGE
5. Rub remaining paste inside turkey cavity and on skin.

Parsley, Sage, Rosemary, Thyme, and More

Until now, my herb paste had been a combination of parsley, sage, rosemary, and thyme. It was time to focus on its details. When used alone in large quantities, strong herbs such as piney rosemary and minty sage were overpowering and needed to be balanced with the softer flavors of lemony thyme and fresh, grassy parsley. As a general rule, the more pungent the herb, the less I used in the blend (less sage than thyme, and even less rosemary than sage). Alliums—minced shallot and garlic—boosted the savory, aromatic qualities of the mixture, while a minimal amount of lemon zest contributed a fresh, bright note. (Too much, however, left tasters complaining of artificial, "Pledge-like" off-notes.)

In terms of paste construction, some fat was necessary, but too much thwarted the crisping of the skin. Although melted butter tasted great, it also tended to congeal on the cold surface of the turkey. Olive oil and a small amount of Dijon mustard, on the other hand, smoothed the mixture out into a fairly emulsified, easily spreadable paste.

Once my herb-swathed turkey was roasted to perfection, allowed to rest, and carved up, I watched as tasters marveled over its fancy appearance and deep, fragrant aroma. Plain Jane

no more, this tasty bird would liven up any holiday table.

HERBED ROAST TURKEY
SERVES 10 TO 12

If roasting an 18- to 22-pound bird, double all of the ingredients for the herb paste except the black pepper; apply 2 tablespoons paste under the skin on each side of the turkey, 1½ tablespoons paste in each breast pocket, 2 tablespoons inside the cavity, and the remaining paste on the turkey skin. Roast breast side down at 425 degrees for 1 hour, then reduce the oven temperature to 325 degrees, rotate the turkey breast side up, and continue to roast for about 2 hours. Let rest 35 to 40 minutes before carving.

If roasting a 14- to 18-pound bird, increase all of the ingredients for the herb paste (except the black pepper) by 50 percent; follow the instructions below for applying the paste under the skin, in the breast pockets, and in the cavity; use the remaining paste on the skin. Increase the second half of the roasting time (breast side up) to 1 hour, 15 minutes.

If you have the time and the refrigerator space, air-drying produces extremely crisp skin and is worth the effort. After brining, rinsing, and pat-

ting the turkey dry, place the turkey breast side up on a flat wire rack set over a rimmed baking sheet and refrigerate, uncovered, 8 to 24 hours. Proceed with the recipe.

Turkey and Brine
- 2   cups table salt
- 1   turkey (12 to 14 pounds gross weight), rinsed thoroughly, giblets and neck reserved for gravy (if making), tailpiece removed

Herb Paste
- 1¼   cups roughly chopped fresh parsley leaves
- 4   teaspoons minced fresh thyme leaves
- 2   teaspoons roughly chopped fresh sage leaves
- 1½   teaspoons minced fresh rosemary leaves
- 1   medium shallot, minced (about 3 tablespoons)
- 2   medium garlic cloves, minced or pressed through garlic press (about 2 teaspoons)
- ¾   teaspoon grated zest from 1 lemon
- ¾   teaspoon table salt
- 1   teaspoon ground black pepper
- 1   teaspoon Dijon mustard
- ¼   cup olive oil

1. **FOR THE TURKEY AND BRINE:** Dissolve salt in 2 gallons cold water in large stockpot or clean bucket. Add turkey and refrigerate 4 to 6 hours.

2. Remove turkey from brine and rinse under cool running water. Pat dry inside and out with paper towels. Place turkey breast side up on flat wire rack set over rimmed baking sheet or roasting pan and refrigerate, uncovered, 30 minutes. Alternatively, air-dry turkey (see note above).

3. **FOR THE HERB PASTE:** Process parsley, thyme, sage, rosemary, shallot, garlic, lemon zest, salt, and pepper in food processor until consistency of coarse paste, ten 2-second pulses. Add mustard and olive oil; continue to process until mixture forms smooth paste, ten to twelve 2-second pulses; scrape sides of processor bowl with rubber spatula after 5 pulses. Transfer mixture to small bowl.

4. **TO PREPARE THE TURKEY:** Adjust oven rack to lowest position; heat oven to 400 degrees. Line large V-rack with heavy-duty foil and use paring knife or skewer to poke 20 to 30 holes

RECIPE TESTING: **Stabs in the Dark**

We stopped at (almost) nothing to pack our roast turkey with herb flavor. Here are two of our more unorthodox, and less successful, attempts.

MORE OOZE THAN AAHS
Multiple incisions stuffed with herb paste looked like puncture wounds oozing green stuff.

POST-OP COMPLICATIONS
Intricate surgery gave us the flavor we wanted, but certainly not the right look. And the procedure was truly unwieldy.

in foil; set V-rack in large roasting pan. Remove turkey from refrigerator and wipe away any water collected in baking sheet; set turkey breast side up on baking sheet.

5. Using hands, carefully loosen skin from meat of breasts, thighs, and drumsticks. Using fingers or spoon, slip 1½ tablespoons paste under breast skin on each side of turkey. Using fingers, distribute paste under skin over breast, thigh, and drumstick meat.

6. Using sharp paring knife, cut 1½-inch vertical slit into thickest part of each breast. Starting from top of incision, swing knife tip down to create 4- to 5-inch pocket within flesh. Place 1 tablespoon paste in pocket of each breast; using fingers, rub in thin, even layer.

7. Rub 1 tablespoon paste inside turkey cavity. Rotate turkey breast side down; apply half remaining herb paste to turkey skin; flip turkey breast side up and apply remaining herb paste to skin, pressing and patting to make paste adhere; reapply herb paste that falls onto baking sheet. Tuck wings behind back and tuck tips of drumsticks into skin at tail to secure.

8. **TO ROAST THE TURKEY:** Place turkey breast side down on prepared V-rack in roasting pan. Roast 45 minutes.

9. Remove roasting pan with turkey from oven (close oven door to retain oven heat). Using clean potholders (or wad of paper towels), rotate turkey breast side up. Continue to roast until thickest part of breast registers 165 degrees and thickest part of thigh registers 170 to 175 degrees on instant-read thermometer, 50 to 60 minutes longer. (Confirm temperature by inserting thermometer in both sides of bird.) Transfer turkey to carving board; let rest 30 minutes. Carve turkey and serve.

COOK'S extra

Go to www.cooksillustrated.com
- Key in code 11053 for the results of our **turkey tasting**.
- These results will be available until December 31, 2005.

EQUIPMENT TESTING: **Turkey Tools**

We wouldn't roast a turkey without five basic tools, all of which have multiple kitchen uses. (We've listed the winners of previous tests below.) But what about all those turkey-only gadgets that show up in stores every fall? We tested 20 items and found a few worth considering.—Garth Clingingsmith

THE BASICS

LARGE COOLER
If you lack refrigerator space for brining, add six to eight ice packs to a cooler.

ROOMY ROASTING PAN
Preferably Calphalon Contemporary Roasting Pan ($100).

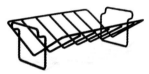

NONADJUSTABLE V-RACK
Preferably Norpro Nonstick Roasting Rack (model #270, $9.75).

INSTANT-READ THERMOMETER
Preferably Thermapen (model #211-006, $75).

FAT SEPARATOR
Trudeau Gravy Separator with Integrated Strainer (model #099-1105, $9.99).

WORTH CONSIDERING

STUFFING BAG
There's no easier way to get stuffing into and out of the bird. We like the Regency Turkey Stuffing Bag ($2.50 for two).

LACING KIT
Straight poultry lacers fasten the cavity shut. We like the No-Sew Turkey Lacer ($1.95 for 6 pins and 1 lacing cord).

HEAT CONDUCTOR
Odd as it may look, a hollow metal tube inserted in a stuffed bird conducts heat and speeds cooking. Try the Roasting Wand ($14.99).

TURNING FORKS
Most of our test cooks make do with big wads of paper towels, but a few prefer the leverage provided by Poultry Lifters ($9.95).

STEP-BY-STEP | CARVING THE BREAST

The wings and legs on our Herbed Roast Turkey can be carved just as they would be on any other turkey, but the breast, which is stuffed with herb paste, needs some special attention. Here's how to ensure that every slice has a nice swirl of herbs.

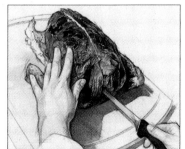

1. With wings facing toward you, cut along both sides of breastbone, slicing from tip of breastbone to cutting board.

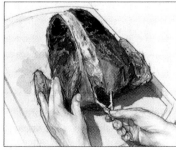

2. Gently pull each breast half away to expose wishbone. Pull and remove wishbone.

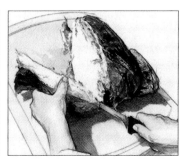

3. Using knife tip, cut along ribcage to remove breast completely.

4. Place entire breast half on cutting board and cut on bias into thin slices. Repeat step 3 along other side.

ILLUSTRATION: RANDY GLASS

Pasta with Hearty Greens and Beans

This classic recipe from the Italian countryside deserves a place on the American table.
Could we streamline it without forfeiting flavor?

⇒ BY REBECCA HAYS ⇐

Italians have a knack for transforming humble ingredients into remarkable meals, and the rustic trio of pasta, hearty greens, and beans is no exception: When carefully prepared, the combination is sublime. But making something out of almost nothing takes time. In this case, dried cannellini (white kidney) beans are gently simmered until tender, then garden-fresh greens are cleaned, cooked, and seasoned. Tossed together with al dente pasta and a sprinkling of Parmesan, the result is rich and satisfying. If I could find a few shortcuts yet retain the complex flavors of the Italian original, this dinner could become a regular in my midweek repertoire.

A Bitter Beginning

The hearty greens that Italians usually mix with pasta and beans include turnip, dandelion, chicory, mustard, broccoli rabe, collards, and kale. And there's a five-step approach for reducing the bitterness most of them possess: Blanch, shock (dunk in ice water), squeeze dry, chop, and sauté. The upside? When handled this way, the bitterness is tamed and the resulting greens are robust but not overpowering. The downside is that the whole process demands precious time and multiple pieces of kitchen equipment.

Two of the choices, kale and collard greens, were absolute standouts: Tasters noted their appealing vegetal and mineral qualities but made not one mention of bitterness, giving me new hope for a straightforward cooking method. Sure enough, a simple sauté tasted great, but the quantity of raw greens necessary for this recipe meant that I would have to cook them in three or four batches. The solution was a sauté/braise combination. I quickly wilted half of the greens in a hot pan with olive oil, aromatic onions and garlic, and spicy red pepper flakes and then squeezed in the

Kale (seen here) and collard greens have a mild, sweet flavor that works well with pasta. Bitter greens (mustard, dandelion, turnip, and chicory) are best saved for other recipes.

remainder of the raw greens. I poured in chicken broth to serve as the braising liquid, and, 15 minutes later, tender, flavorful greens were mine.

Finishing Touches

As for the pasta, I'd run across a few references to whole wheat spaghetti and decided to try it—despite some skepticism among a few health-food-fearing colleagues. I prepared a batch, served it up, and braced myself for the reactions. Surprise: Tasters unanimously preferred the nutty flavor of whole wheat pasta to traditional semolina pasta for this dish. In fact, the more potent dimension of flavor provided by the whole wheat pasta was the missing link, adding complexity that brought the beans and greens into a pleasing harmony.

To finish up, I worked in some heavy-hitting ingredients to compensate for the flavor deficiency of the canned beans (the obvious shortcut to cooking them myself): hearty pancetta, acidic tomatoes, briny olives, and earthy fontina and

Parmesan cheese. Still more garlic, in the form of bread crumbs or chips, contributed headiness and welcome crunch.

One last note: I knew from experience that draining the pasta and finishing it in the sauce helps to integrate the components of a dish, and this one was no exception. Just a few minutes of simmering went a long way toward joining the gutsy flavors. Now I can have classic Italian comfort food, even when time isn't on my side.

WHOLE WHEAT PASTA WITH GREENS, BEANS, PANCETTA, AND GARLIC BREAD CRUMBS
SERVES 4 TO 6

Prosciutto di Parma can be substituted for pancetta. If you can't find a 13.25-ounce package of Ronzoni, the winner of our tasting (page 15), use ¾ pound of a whole wheat spaghetti of your choice.

- 2 large slices white sandwich bread (about 6 ounces), torn into quarters
- 3 tablespoons olive oil
- 6 garlic cloves, minced or pressed through garlic press (2 tablespoons)
  Table salt
- 3 ounces pancetta, cut into ½-inch pieces (about ½ cup)
- 1 medium onion, diced small (about 1 cup)
- ¼ teaspoon hot red pepper flakes
- 14 cups loosely packed kale or collard greens (1 to 1½ pounds), thick stems trimmed, leaves chopped into 1-inch pieces and rinsed, water still clinging to leaves (see page 30)
- 1½ cups low-sodium chicken broth
- 1 can (15 ounces) cannellini beans, drained and rinsed
- 13¼ ounces whole wheat spaghetti
- 4 ounces fontina cheese, coarsely grated (about 1 cup)
  Ground black pepper

1. Pulse bread in food processor until coarsely ground. Heat 2 tablespoons oil in 12-inch straight-sided sauté pan over medium-high heat. Add bread crumbs and cook, stirring frequently, until beginning to brown, about 3 minutes. Stir in 1 tablespoon garlic; cook, stirring constantly, until garlic is fragrant and bread crumbs are dark golden brown, about 1 minute. Season bread crumbs with salt, transfer to small serving bowl,

The Secret to Full-Fledged Flavor

Drain the pasta before it reaches al dente texture, then cook until tender in the brothy sauce. This technique allows the pasta to absorb the flavors of the sauce and to release its residual starch, which helps to thicken the sauce slightly.

and set aside. Wipe out pan with paper towels.

2. Heat remaining tablespoon oil in now-empty pan over medium-high heat, add pancetta, and cook until crisp, about 8 minutes. Transfer with slotted spoon to small bowl.

3. Add onion to pan; cook until starting to brown, about 5 minutes. Add remaining table-spoon garlic and red pepper flakes; cook, stirring constantly, until garlic is fragrant, about 30 seconds.

4. Add half of greens to pan; using tongs, toss occasionally, until starting to wilt, about 2 minutes. Add remaining greens, broth, and ¾ teaspoon salt; cover (pan will be very full); increase heat to high and bring to strong simmer. Reduce heat to medium and cook, covered, tossing occasionally, until greens are tender, about 15 minutes (mixture will be somewhat soupy). Stir in beans and pancetta.

5. Meanwhile, bring 4 quarts water to boil in Dutch oven over high heat. Add spaghetti and 1 tablespoon salt; cook until pasta is just shy of al dente. Drain pasta and return to pot. Add greens mixture to pasta, set over medium-high heat, and toss to combine. Cook until pasta absorbs most of liquid, about 2 minutes. Add fontina; adjust seasoning with salt and pepper. Serve immediately, passing garlic bread crumbs separately.

Pasta with Not-So-Hearty Greens?

Because of their substantial texture and more asser-tive flavor profile, we prefer kale or collard greens in these recipes, but spinach makes a satisfactory substitute. Follow either recipe, replacing kale or collards with two 10-ounce bags crinkly-leaf spin-ach, trimmed, chopped into 1-inch pieces, and rinsed, water still clinging to leaves (about 16 cups), and reducing chicken broth to ¾ cup. After adding second half of spinach to pan, cook for 2 minutes, until spinach is completely wilted. Continue with recipe as directed.

WHOLE WHEAT PASTA WITH GREENS, BEANS, TOMATOES, AND GARLIC CHIPS

SERVES 4 TO 6

If you can't find a 13.25-ounce package of Ronzoni, the winner of our tasting (see photo at right), use ¾ pound of a whole wheat pasta of your choice. If you like, pass extra-virgin olive oil for drizzling over the finished pasta. For a vegetarian dish, substitute vegetable broth for chicken broth.

- 3 tablespoons olive oil
- 8 garlic cloves, 5 cloves sliced thin lengthwise, 3 cloves minced or pressed through garlic press (1 tablespoon)
  Table salt
- 1 medium onion, diced small (about 1 cup)
- ½ teaspoon hot red pepper flakes
- 14 cups loosely packed kale or collard greens (1 to 1½ pounds), thick stems trimmed, leaves chopped into 1-inch pieces and rinsed, water still clinging to leaves (see page 30)
- 1½ cups low-sodium chicken broth
- 1 can (14½ ounces) diced tomatoes, drained
- 1 can (15 ounces) cannellini beans, drained and rinsed
- ¾ cup pitted kalamata olives, roughly chopped
- 13¼ ounces whole wheat spaghetti
- 2 ounces Parmesan cheese, finely grated (about 1 cup), plus additional for serving
  Ground black pepper

1. Heat oil and sliced garlic in 12-inch straight-sided sauté pan over medium-high heat. Cook, stirring and turning frequently, until light golden brown, about 3 minutes. Using slotted spoon, transfer garlic to plate lined with paper towels. Sprinkle lightly with salt.

2. Add onion to pan; cook until starting to brown, about 5 minutes. Add minced garlic and red pepper flakes; cook, stirring constantly, until garlic is fragrant, about 30 seconds.

3. Add half of greens to pan; using tongs, toss occasionally, until starting to wilt, about 2 minutes. Add remaining greens, broth, tomatoes, and ¾ teaspoon salt; cover (pan will be very full); increase heat to high and bring to strong simmer. Reduce heat to medium and cook, covered, tossing occasionally, until greens are tender, about 15 minutes (mixture will be somewhat soupy). Stir in beans and olives.

4. Meanwhile, bring 4 quarts water to boil in Dutch oven over high heat. Add spaghetti and 1 tablespoon salt; cook until pasta is just shy of al dente. Drain pasta and return to pot. Add greens mixture to pasta, set over medium-high heat, and toss to combine. Cook until pasta absorbs most of liquid, about 2 minutes. Stir in 1 cup Parmesan; adjust seasoning with salt and pepper. Serve immediately, passing garlic chips, extra-virgin olive oil, and Parmesan separately.

Chocolate 101

From shopping to chopping, our no-nonsense guide puts an end to chocolate confusion. BY SEAN LAWLER

Chocolate Basics

Chocolate liquor, a dark, pasty liquid made by grinding the nibs extracted from dried, fermented, roasted cacao beans, is pure, unsweetened chocolate, the base ingredient for all other processed chocolates. About 55 percent of chocolate liquor is *cocoa butter*, a natural fat responsible for chocolate's unique texture. Its melting point is close to body temperature, which explains why chocolate melts so smoothly in your mouth but stays solid and shelf-stable at room temperature. Suspended in the cocoa butter are particles of ground *cocoa solids*, which carry the chocolate flavor.

Chocolate Buyer's Guide

Given the many types of chocolates available in stores today, people often want to know how they differ and whether one can be readily substituted for another. The first question is fairly straightforward (and answered in these pages), the second one is anything but. Different types of chocolate vary tremendously in flavor, and their behavior in recipes can be fussy and unpredictable. For this reason, *Cook's* recipes often employ more than one type of chocolate to achieve complex, multifaceted flavor. That said, we've provided some of the standard substitution formulas below.

UNSWEETENED CHOCOLATE

What It Is: Pure chocolate liquor that has been cooled and formed into bars.

Cooking Tip: Because most unsweetened chocolates are starchy and unrefined (see "Conching," below right), unsweetened chocolate is the traditional choice for recipes in which a bold hit of chocolate flavor is more important than a smooth or delicate texture (think brownies).

Substitution: Replace 1 ounce unsweetened chocolate with 3 tablespoons cocoa powder + 1 tablespoon butter or oil.

CAUTION: This substitution ignores the many important differences between butter, oil, and cocoa butter. A pan of fudgy brownies made with cocoa powder and butter will usually turn out cake-like and dry. (Best for small-quantity substitutions.)

TEST KITCHEN WINNER:
★ SCHARFFEN BERGER Unsweetened Chocolate, $11.00 for 9.7 ounces

COCOA POWDER

What It Is: Chocolate liquor fed through a press to remove all but 10 to 24 percent of the cocoa butter. To counter the harsh, acidic flavor of natural cocoa, the powder is sometimes treated with an alkaline solution, or "Dutched." Cookbooks often claim that Dutching "mellows" chocolate flavor, but our tasters disagreed. Without the distraction of natural cocoa's harsh acidity, the more subtle, complex chocolate flavors came to the fore. We think Dutched cocoa tastes best, although it is interchangeable with natural cocoa.

Cooking Tip: Cocoa powder contributes a lot of chocolate flavor with little additional fat, making it perfect for hot beverages or recipes that already contain plenty of butter, such as cakes and cookies. In the test kitchen, we often "bloom" cocoa powder in a hot liquid such as water or coffee. This dissolves the remaining cocoa butter and disperses water-soluble flavor compounds. The result? A deeper, stronger chocolate flavor.

Substitution: None. Chocolates have too much fat to take the place of cocoa.

TEST KITCHEN WINNER:
★ CALLEBAUT, $20 for 2.2 pounds (mail order)
Best Supermarket Brand: DROSTE Cocoa, $5.49 for 8.8 ounces

WHITE CHOCOLATE

What It Is: Technically not chocolate because it contains no cocoa solids. To meet government standards for "white chocolate," this product must contain at least 20 percent cocoa butter, which is usually de-odorized to remove any naturally occurring flavors that might overwhelm white chocolate's mild flavors of milk, sugar, and vanilla.

TEST KITCHEN WINNER:
★ CALLEBAUT, $8 for 1 pound

WHITE CHOCOLATE CHIPS

What It Is: Many "white chips" contain palm oil in addition to (or instead of) cocoa butter and do not qualify as "white chocolate." We prefer the brands with the most fat, be it cocoa butter or palm oil, for their softer texture, especially in cookies or brownies eaten straight from the oven.

TEST KITCHEN WINNER:
★ GUITTARD Choc-Au-Lait White Chips, $2.79 for 12 ounces

MILK CHOCOLATE

What It Is: Candy bar chocolate. Milk chocolate must contain at least 10 percent chocolate liquor and 12 percent milk solids.

Cooking Tip: Because of its relatively weak chocolate flavor (milk chocolate is usually more than 50 percent sugar), we don't use it in very many recipes. Good for nibbling.

TEST KITCHEN WINNER:
★ PERUGINA Milk Chocolate, $2.59 for 4 ounces

SWEET CHOCOLATE

What It Is: Think milk chocolate without the milk. Also called sweet dark chocolate, it is just that—extremely sweet. While it must contain at least 15 percent chocolate liquor, it is often more than 60 percent sugar. Sweet chocolate is sold by the Baker's company as German's Sweet Chocolate Bar.

Cooking Tip: We have little use for the stuff, even in our German Chocolate Cake recipe.

Conching The transformation of bitter, unsweetened chocolate liquor into the sweetened milk and dark chocolates on store shelves takes place through a refinement process called *conching*. Sugar, vanilla, soy lecithin (an emulsifier), and other ingredients (including a supplement of pure cocoa butter) are added to the chocolate liquor, and the mixture is rubbed and smeared against rollers until homogenous and smooth. The process also aerates and heats the chocolate, driving off some of the volatile compounds responsible for chocolate's natural bitterness. The result is a smooth-melting chocolate with a mellower, more palatable flavor. The U.S. Food and Drug Administration has divided sweetened chocolates into several broadly defined categories: milk chocolate, sweet chocolate, and bittersweet/semisweet chocolate.

BITTERSWEET/SEMISWEET CHOCOLATE

What It Is: A catch-all category. The government makes no distinction between "bittersweet" and "semisweet" chocolates. To be called by either name, the chocolate must contain at least 35 percent chocolate liquor, though most contain closer to 50 percent and many "high-percentage" chocolates have 70 percent chocolate liquor or more. If comparing chocolates made by the same company, it is fairly safe to assume that the bittersweet variety contains more chocolate liquor than the semisweet; otherwise, the terms are of little value.

Cooking Tips: With relatively strong chocolate flavor and a smooth texture when melted, these are the chocolates to use for sauces, frostings, custards, and icings. While many tasters enjoyed the complex flavors of the expensive, high-percentage chocolates eaten raw, for cooking we preferred the chocolates that were proportionally higher in sugar. Ghirardelli Bittersweet, our test kitchen favorite, is 44 percent sugar, while most of the high-percentage entrants in our tasting were 30 to 35 percent sugar.

Substitution: Replace 1 ounce bittersweet or semisweet chocolate with ⅔ ounce unsweetened chocolate + 2 teaspoons granulated sugar.

CAUTION: Because it has not been conched, unsweetened chocolate will not provide the same smooth, creamy texture as bittersweet or semisweet chocolate.

TEST KITCHEN WINNER:
★ GHIRARDELLI Bittersweet Chocolate, $2.29 for 4 ounces

CHOCOLATE CHIPS

What It Is: Real semisweet or bittersweet chocolate, only with a slightly lower fat content (about 27 percent), which improves the chips' stability. Some manufacturers replace a portion of the cocoa butter with palm or other vegetable oils at the expense of texture.

Cooking Tip: While we don't recommend using chips in chocolate sauces or puddings, they do produce acceptable results when substituted for bittersweet or semisweet chocolate in a simple brownie recipe.

Substitution: Chop up bar chocolate for cookies when chocolate chips are not on hand.

TEST KITCHEN WINNERS:
★ GUITTARD Semisweet Chocolate Chips, $2.79 for 12 ounces, and NESTLÉ Semisweet Chocolate Chunks, $2.50 for 11.5 ounces

Working with Chocolate

Chopping Chocolate

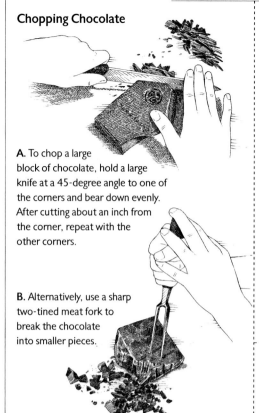

A. To chop a large block of chocolate, hold a large knife at a 45-degree angle to one of the corners and bear down evenly. After cutting about an inch from the corner, repeat with the other corners.

B. Alternatively, use a sharp two-tined meat fork to break the chocolate into smaller pieces.

Melting Chocolate

A. Double Boiler: The traditional method for melting chocolate is in a heatproof bowl set over a pot of barely simmering water. Stir occasionally.

B. Microwave: Microwave chopped chocolate at 50 percent power for 2 minutes. Stir chocolate and continue heating until melted, stirring once every additional minute. If melting butter with chocolate, add the butter at the 2-minute mark when stirring the chocolate.

Storing Chocolate

Never store chocolate in the refrigerator or freezer, as cocoa butter can easily pick up off flavors from other foods. If chocolate is exposed to rapid changes in humidity or temperature, sugar or fat may dissolve and migrate, discoloring the surface. This cosmetic condition, known as *bloom*, is not harmful—bloomed chocolate is safe to eat and cook with.

To extend the life of chocolate, wrap it tightly in plastic and store it in a cool, dry place. Milk and white chocolates should last for six months to a year; dark chocolates will last for several years.

Decorating with Chocolate

To create chocolate curls for cake decorating, scrape a block of chocolate with a sharp paring knife, anchoring the block carefully with your other hand. Pick up the shavings with a toothpick or tweezers.

To write with chocolate, put chopped semisweet or bittersweet chocolate in a zipper-lock bag and melt, either in a microwave or by submerging in hot water. Snip off a tiny piece from one corner. Holding the bag in one hand, gently squeeze out the chocolate as you write.

The Taming of Hunter-Style Chicken

The original chasseur was a preparation fit for even the sorriest spoils of the hunt.
Could we adapt this dish to the tamer, milder birds bagged at the local market?

⇒ BY SARAH WILSON AND JOLYON HELTERMAN ⇐

Like most "hunter-style" dishes, *chasseur* (French for "hunter") began as something of a culinary makeover—a dose of creative Renaissance cookery meant to assuage the downsides of dining on fresh-killed game bird. Smallish pieces disguised the intricate surgery necessary for extracting wayward bullets, while white wine, wild mushrooms, and aromatic herbs helped mask musky, gamy flavors. Hours of gentle stewing transformed the tough flesh into fall-off-the-bone morsels, just as the stewing liquid eventually thickened into a hearty, flavorful sauce.

Centuries later, farm-raised chicken has eclipsed partridge as typical dinner fare. But most "chicken chasseur" recipes remain trapped in the past, blithely hacking up the tamer (and more dependably bullet-free) birds into unappetizing chunks or dousing the milder meat with enough potent herbs to temper a cauldron's worth of gamy grouse. Even the versions that get the flavors right struggle with adapting the cooking method. Game birds (then and now) have fairly dark meat throughout, making cooking times roughly equivalent from section to section; by contrast, a chicken's white and dark meat cook at different speeds. Add to that the modern prejudice against flabby, uncrisped skin and we had a long way to go to update this classic dish.

Piece Talks

Most current chasseur recipes opt for breaking down a whole chicken, searing the pieces, then braising them in wine and stock. True to the original? Perhaps—but by forgoing such "authenticity" in favor of either white meat or dark meat only, we could eliminate one of our timing problems right off the bat.

Which path to choose? Thighs are the closest a farm-raised chicken gets to game-bird consistency, and that's the route we usually choose when braising chicken. The rich, fatty dark meat becomes meltingly tender when braised. But the reality is that most Americans (and many of our test cooks) prefer white meat. We decided to see if we could develop a chasseur recipe with lean breasts. Given the tendency of white meat

For chicken with crisp skin, hold the sauce until serving time.

chicken to dry out and become stringy when braised, we knew this would be a challenge.

Searing four breast halves in a 12-inch skillet crisped the skin, but just half an hour of simmering later, the skin returned to mushy flab and the meat was very dry. Reducing the braising

time was problematic—either the chicken wasn't cooked through or the sauce was watery and thin. For this recipe to work, it was clear that chicken and sauce would have to spend some time apart. Perhaps if we took the braised chicken breasts out of the pot before they were done and threw them under the broiler to finish cooking, we might get crisp skin and have the opportunity to thicken the sauce. Brilliant theory, so-so results.

The best way to ensure crisp skin *and* juicy meat was now obvious: Sear the pieces in the pan, then roast them in the oven. While the chicken roasted, we could finish the sauce in the skillet. In other words, we would cook the meat and sauce separately—from start to finish. Totally unconventional (this was supposed to be a braise), but we had run out of options.

So what did we sacrifice by forgoing the half-hour braise? Not much, it turned out. Presented with two versions of the recipe—one with braised chicken, the other cooked with our hybrid method—tasters unanimously preferred the latter. Not only was the skin crisp—and evenly browned—but the sauce had time to thicken. What about the transfer of flavors between chicken and sauce that braising would allow for? While the connective tissue in dark meat chicken melts during braising and fortifies the sauce, chicken breasts evidently have little to offer the sauce other than the *fond* (browned bits)

How We Did It: Great Pan Sauce and Perfectly Cooked Breasts

Braising, which is the traditional choice for this recipe, works well with dark meat chicken but not breasts, which turn out parched and stringy. Here's how we retooled this classic dish to make sure we got perfectly cooked chicken breasts.

SEAR
Sear chicken breasts in a hot skillet
until browned on both sides.

ROAST
Roast chicken breasts on a rimmed
baking sheet to cook them through.

BUILD A SAUCE
Meanwhile, build the sauce in the
skillet using leftover drippings.

PHOTOGRAPHY: CARL TREMBLAY

in the pan. As for the chicken, it was plenty tasty when served with the sauce.

Fiery Finish

With the timing and texture problems ironed out, all that was left to do was to marry the flavors of the sauce to our nicely roasted chicken breasts. The original chasseur would have used whatever wild mushrooms were growing nearby. But in a blind taste test, plain button mushrooms were surprisingly good.

Deglazing the pan with white wine and chicken stock was fine, but deglazing it with a touch of brandy and flambéing it first was better. Enough of an improvement to call for this daunting—yet actually easy—cooking technique? Yes. In a repeat test, even the test kitchen's most hardened skeptics had to concur that the flambéed brandy added a welcome hit of sweet complexity that the sauce was otherwise lacking.

Unlike cacciatore, where tomatoes define the sauce, the modern version of chasseur uses them as no more than an accent. A mere ⅓ cup of drained canned diced tomatoes was sufficient. In typical pan-sauce fashion, we finished the sauce by whisking in cold butter and fresh herbs—in this case, the victorious tarragon and parsley.

At last, we had a chasseur fit for the modern-day bird with its lean white meat—and ready for dinner in just an hour. Would 15th-century game-bird hunters have preferred this elegant, streamlined version? Hard to say. But for 21st-century grocery shoppers, it's a sure shot.

CHICKEN CHASSEUR
SERVES 4

If fresh tarragon is unavailable, double the amount of fresh parsley; do not use dried tarragon. Egg noodles or mashed potatoes make a good accompaniment to Chicken Chasseur.

- 4 bone-in, skin-on chicken breast halves (10 to 12 ounces each), trimmed of excess fat and skin
  Table salt and ground black pepper
- 2 tablespoons vegetable oil
- 8 ounces white button mushrooms, cleaned and sliced ⅛ inch thick (about 3½ cups)
- 1 medium shallot, minced (about 2 tablespoons)
- 3 tablespoons brandy or cognac
- ½ cup dry white wine
- 3½ cups low-sodium chicken broth
- ⅓ cup drained canned diced tomatoes
- 3 tablespoons cold unsalted butter, cut into 4 pieces
- 1 tablespoon minced fresh parsley leaves
- 1 tablespoon minced fresh tarragon leaves

1. Adjust oven rack to middle position; heat oven to 400 degrees. Sprinkle chicken evenly with salt and pepper. Heat oil in 12-inch skillet over medium-high heat until almost smoking. Add chicken breasts skin side down and cook without moving them until skin is crisp and well browned, 5 to 8 minutes. Using tongs, turn chicken pieces and brown on second side, about 5 minutes longer. Place browned chicken skin side up on rimmed baking sheet and set aside.

2. Pour off all but 2 tablespoons fat from pan. Add mushrooms and cook over medium-high heat until mushrooms start to brown, 6 to 8 minutes. Reduce heat to medium and add shallots; cook until softened, about 1 minute longer.

3. Remove pan from heat and add brandy; let stand until brandy warms slightly, about 10 seconds. Wave lit chimney match over skillet until brandy ignites. Return pan to medium-high heat and shake skillet until flames subside. Add wine; using wooden spoon, scrape browned bits from pan bottom. Simmer briskly until reduced to glaze, about 3 minutes.

4. Add broth and tomatoes and simmer over medium-high heat; simmer briskly until liquid, mushrooms, and tomatoes measure 1½ cups, about 25 minutes.

5. While sauce simmers, place chicken in oven; roast until internal temperature reaches 160 degrees on instant-read thermometer, 15 to 20 minutes. Transfer chicken pieces to serving platter and tent loosely with foil.

6. When sauce is properly reduced, whisk in butter, one piece at a time, until melted and incorporated. Add parsley and tarragon and adjust seasoning with salt and pepper. Spoon sauce over chicken and serve immediately.

TASTING: White Wines for Cooking

When a recipe calls for "dry white wine," it's tempting to grab whatever open bottle is in the fridge, regardless of grape varietal. Are we doing our dishes a disservice? Sure, Chardonnay and Pinot Grigio may taste different straight from the glass, but how much do those distinctive flavor profiles really come through once the wines get cooked down with other ingredients?

To find out, we tried four different varietals and a supermarket "cooking wine" in five recipes: braised fennel, risotto, a basic pan sauce, a beurre blanc, and chicken chasseur. In our tests, only Sauvignon Blanc consistently boiled down to a "clean" yet sufficiently acidic flavor—one that played nicely with the rest of the ingredients. Differences between the wines were most dramatic in gently flavored dishes, such as the risotto and beurre blanc. In contrast, all five wines produced similar (and fine) results when used in chicken chasseur, no doubt because of all the other strong flavors in this dish.

But what's a cook without leftover Sauvignon Blanc to do? Is there a more convenient option than opening a fresh bottle? To find out, we ran the same cooking tests with sherry and vermouth, wines fortified with alcohol to increase their shelf life. Sherry was too distinct and didn't fare well in these tests, but vermouth was surprisingly good. In fact, its clean, bright flavor bested all but one of the drinking wines. And at $5 a bottle (for Gallo, our top-rated brand of vermouth), you can't argue with the price. –Garth Clingingsmith

HIGHLY RECOMMENDED
OUR FAVORITE
➤ Sauvignon Blanc
Crisp, clean, and bright, this wine was strong enough to share the spotlight with other ingredients but refused to steal the show.

MORE THAN MARTINIS
➤ Dry Vermouth
A pleasing sweet/tart balance made this fortified wine a close second. And, after being opened, it can sit on the shelf for months.

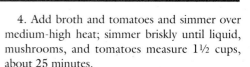

RECOMMENDED WITH RESERVATIONS
INTO THE WOODS
➤ Chardonnay
Most inexpensive Chardonnays are simply too oaky from barrel aging for most recipes. When cooked, "oaky" became bitter, not woody.

TOO SWEET
➤ Riesling
This wine's fruity sweetness paired well with a few recipes but was out of place in other dishes.

TOO SHY
➤ Pinot Grigio
While this slightly acidic, mild wine won't ruin a recipe, it won't improve it much either, adding only a "generic wine-iness" that fades quickly into the background.

NOT RECOMMENDED
SALTY DOG
➤ Cooking Wine
The salt used to preserve inexpensive cooking wine makes it unpotable.

NOT A TEAM PLAYER
➤ Sherry
Complex sherry worked well with the robust flavors in chasseur, but its "earthy" notes dominated the simple beurre blanc and risotto.

Go to www.cooksillustrated.com
- Key in code 11055 for the results of our **tasting of eight brands of vermouth.**
- This information will be available until December 31, 2005.

The Ultimate Linzertorte

What's the secret to making a perfect version of this Old World tart?

⇒ BY THE COOK'S ILLUSTRATED TEST KITCHEN ⇐

An unusual technique turns a rich nut crust and simple jam filling into an elegant tart.

The ingredients for linzertorte couldn't be easier to prepare. A food processor produces the buttery nut crust, and the raspberry jam filling is something you buy. It's the process of transforming these two components into a finished tart that can drive perfectionists (like us) over the edge. You can make a homely but still delicious linzertorte with only modest effort, but for the holidays, we think it should look its best.

Easy Going

A linzertorte is more crust than filling, so we started there. Walnuts made for a bitter, soft crust. Our tasters preferred a mix of about 2 parts hazelnuts and 1 part almonds. Toasting the nuts was worth the extra step, but skinning the hazelnuts—a messy and irksome process—was not.

As bizarre as it may sound, a hard-cooked egg yolk is standard in many classic recipes. Several sources credited this unlikely ingredient with creating a supremely tender dough—but tender to a fault was more like it. Dough made with a cooked yolk was frail and crumbly. Instead, a single raw egg moistened and

bound the dough nicely. Of the traditional spice choices, tasters endorsed cinnamon and allspice but rejected cloves. So far, this was smooth sailing.

Roped In

Rolling the dough (and getting it into the pan) is where this recipe hit rough waters. The standard method of rolling out the dough and gingerly fitting it into a tart pan was futile, as the delicate dough cracked and split. Patting the dough in place by hand yielded an uneven and unattractive crust.

After much consideration (and failure), we hit upon an unconventional but reliable method. We took a portion of the dough and rolled it out directly on the surface of the removable bottom disk of the tart pan, stopping just shy of the edges. We then dropped the tart pan bottom into the fluted ring and pressed the dough by hand just to the edges. To form the sidewalls, we took pieces of the remaining dough, rolled them into ropes, and gently pressed them partway up the walls of the tart pan. Success!

As for the lattice, our attempt to sidestep rolling out dough and cutting strips was a failure; we tried crosshatching ropes of dough, but they looked odd, and their wide girth made them unpleasant to eat. The best that could be done was to roll out the rather sticky dough between sheets of parchment or plastic wrap, cut the strips, and then chill them thoroughly. And forget about weaving the strips as you would if making a pie. Linzertorte dough lacks the fortitude necessary for that kind of manipulation. Instead, by placing the strips one by one in precise order over the jam-filled tart, we found we could mimic the effect of a basket-weave design.

Half-Baked Idea

Yet our linzertorte still fell short of perfection. Beneath the layer of jam, the bottom crust was soft and slightly floury, as if underbaked. Adjustments in oven temperature were of no avail. We were forced to take more drastic measures: First, we prebaked the unfilled pastry. Though this worked, it was yet another step, one that required pie weights and foil. (Without weights, the sidewalls slipped in the oven.)

We reconsidered for a moment. The bottom crust posed the problem, not the sides. So we threw together another dough, lined only the

bottom of the tart pan—stopping short of creating the walls—and prebaked sans pie weights. The crust was now fully baked and crisp. Once cooled, it was easy enough to use the remaining dough to form the sides of the tart shell. After a quick slick with jam and the arrangement of the lattice strips, we were ready to bake the tart.

To add some glitter and glow, we brushed the dough with cream and sprinkled it with coarse turbinado sugar before baking. Served with a final flourish of whipped cream, this tart finally delivered on the promise of its rich heritage.

LINZERTORTE
MAKES ONE 11-INCH TART, SERVING 10 TO 12

Study the instructions before laying down the first lattice strip; once the dough softens, it becomes difficult to work with. In addition, the strips cannot be repositioned once they have been put in place because of the stickiness of the raspberry filling. If, while you are trying to form the lattice, the strips become too soft to work with, rechill them until firm. If strips tear or crack, simply piece them together as you form the lattice—any breaks will become almost unnoticeable once the tart is baked. Lightly sweetened whipped cream flavored with kirsch or framboise instead of vanilla is the traditional accompaniment. The tart keeps well for a day or so.

Pastry
- 1 cup (about 5 ounces) unblanched hazelnuts
- ½ cup (about 2 ounces) blanched almonds
- ½ cup plus 2 tablespoons granulated sugar
- ½ teaspoon table salt
- 1 teaspoon grated zest from 1 lemon
- 1½ cups (7½ ounces) unbleached all-purpose flour
- ½ teaspoon ground cinnamon
- ⅛ teaspoon ground allspice
- 12 tablespoons (1½ sticks) unsalted butter, cut into ½-inch cubes and chilled
- 1 large egg
- 1 teaspoon vanilla extract

Filling
- 1¼ cups (13½ ounces) raspberry preserves
- 1 tablespoon juice from 1 lemon

Glaze
- 1 tablespoon heavy cream
- 1½ teaspoons turbinado or Demerara sugar (optional)

1. **FOR THE PASTRY:** Adjust oven rack to lower-middle position and heat oven to 350 degrees. Toast nuts on rimmed baking sheet, stirring once, until lightly browned and fragrant, about 8 minutes. Cool nuts to room temperature. Do not turn off oven.

2. In food processor, pulse nuts, sugar, and salt until very finely ground, about eighteen 1-second pulses. Add lemon zest; pulse to combine. Add flour, cinnamon, and allspice; pulse to combine. Scatter butter pieces over flour mixture and pulse until butter lumps are no larger than peppercorns and mixture resembles coarse meal, twelve to fifteen 1-second pulses. In small bowl, use fork to combine egg and vanilla. With machine running, pour in egg mixture through feed tube; process until dough forms large ball, about 10 seconds.

3. Turn dough out onto work surface; press together to form cohesive mound. Divide dough into 2 pieces, one piece slightly larger than other (larger piece should weigh about 15 ounces, smaller piece about 13 ounces). Flatten each piece into 5-inch disk; if not using immediately, wrap each piece tightly in plastic wrap and refrigerate up to 48 hours. (If refrigerated until firm, let dough stand at room temperature until soft and malleable, about 1 hour, before proceeding.)

4. Cut parchment round to fit 11-inch tart pan with removable bottom. Spray bottom and sides of tart pan with nonstick cooking spray. Separate bottom from sides of tart pan; line bottom with parchment round and spray parchment with cooking spray. Place smaller dough disk on center of parchment-lined tart pan bottom, place sheet of plastic wrap over disk, and roll out disk until just shy of pan edges. Drop pan bottom into fluted ring and remove plastic wrap. Using hands, press dough into even layer until flush with sides of tart pan. Using dinner fork, poke holes uniformly in dough; set tart pan on baking sheet and bake until beginning to brown around edges, 15 to 18 minutes. Set baking sheet on wire rack and let crust cool to room temperature.

5. Pinch piece of dough about size of Ping-Pong ball from larger dough disk; roll with hands against work surface to form ⅜-inch-diameter rope. Place rope against side of cool prebaked tart bottom. Repeat with additional dough (you will have some left over for lattice), connecting ends of ropes. When entire inside wall of tart pan has been lined, use finger to gently press rope into flutes of pan, creating walls about ⅝ inch high (walls should not be as high as rim of tart pan). Set tart pan aside on baking sheet.

6. Reshape remaining dough into disk and roll between two large sheets parchment sprayed lightly with cooking spray into 12-inch round about ⅛ inch thick (if dough becomes too sticky and soft, refrigerate or freeze until firm and workable). Peel off top layer of parchment. Using ruler sprayed lightly with nonstick cooking spray and pizza cutter or chef's knife, neaten edge of

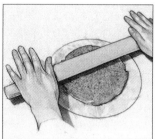

dough round, then cut round into ¾-inch-wide strips (you will need 10 strips). Slide parchment with dough onto baking sheet; cover loosely with parchment. Freeze 20 minutes or refrigerate 40 minutes until firm but not fully stiff.

7. **FOR THE FILLING:** Meanwhile, in small bowl, stir raspberry preserves and lemon juice together. Spread preserves evenly in tart shell.

8. **TO ASSEMBLE, GLAZE, AND BAKE:** Invert dough strips sandwiched between parchment; peel off top layer. Using icing spatula as needed, lift one of longest strips from center of round and lay across center of tart at 1 o'clock/7 o'clock position. Lift second long strip and lay across center of tart at 3 o'clock/9 o'clock position. Lift short strip and lay across tart parallel to first strip, near

edge of tart. Working clockwise, repeat positioning of outer strips parallel to central strips; you should now have 6 strips in place. Lift one of remaining strips and lay across tart parallel to and equidistant from central and edge strips. Working clockwise, repeat until lattice is complete with 10 strips. Press excess dough against rim of tart pan to trim.

9. Gently brush lattice strips with heavy cream and, if using, sprinkle with turbinado sugar. Bake tart (still on baking sheet) until deep golden brown, about 50 minutes. Cool on baking sheet on wire rack to room temperature, about 2 hours.

10. **TO SERVE:** Remove outer tart pan ring. Slide thin metal spatula between parchment paper and bottom crust to loosen. Slide tart onto serving platter. Cut into wedges and serve.

The Best Chocolate Butter Cookies

Chocolate butter cookies usually taste bland or surrender their crisp, delicate appeal to a chewy, brownie-like texture. How about great flavor and great texture?

⇒ BY ERIKA BRUCE ⇐

No holiday is complete without a heaping plateful of decorated butter cookies, a colorful display of shapes, sizes, and flavors. I'm always tempted to reach for the darkest and most alluring in the bunch—the chocolate butter cookie—only to discover a tasteless imposter. Sadly, a cookie that *looks* like it's made of chocolate is no guarantee that it will *taste* like it's made of chocolate.

Wanting to put an end to this cookie charade, I started by sampling eight chocolate butter cookie recipes. Most produced a bland and disappointing chocolate cookie—no surprise given the paltry amounts of chocolate they called for. These were no more than plain butter cookies shaded with a couple tablespoons of cocoa powder. The few recipes that did deliver on chocolate flavor, by adding heavy doses of melted bittersweet or unsweetened chocolate, were texturally deficient—either hard and wafer-thin or soft and chewy, like a brownie. Apparently, cramming big chocolate flavor into a tender, crisp cookie was going to be a serious challenge.

Taste versus Texture

I started out with the test kitchen's classic crispy butter cookie recipe, which calls for sugar, butter, flour, and salt (1 part butter to 1½ parts flour, by weight). For the chocolate, I added 4 tablespoons of cocoa powder. Not enough chocolate flavor. Next I tried adding melted unsweetened chocolate, but these cookies turned out hard and crunchy, and they also spread too much in the oven.

Back at the drawing board, I decided I needed a quick review of chocolate basics (see "Chocolate 101" on page 16). One notable difference between types of chocolate is the percentage of cocoa solids and fat. Even the darkest of the sweetened chocolates—bittersweet—has only 35 percent flavor-contributing cocoa solids, the balance taken up by sugar and cocoa butter. Cocoa powder, however, has a much higher percentage of cocoa solids (up to 90 percent). For chocolate flavor in its purest form, without the extra fat, cocoa powder was clearly the best candidate. (In addition, melted chocolate had adversely affected texture in all of my tests.)

I steadily increased the cocoa powder in my

Applying a bittersweet chocolate glaze to cocoa-packed cookies helps spotlight chocolate's starring role.

recipe until it reached ½ cup (double the original amount). But this was as far as I could go; while the chocolate flavor had noticeably improved, the texture was again compromised—this time because of starch—and the result was a dry, pasty cookie. I cut back on starchiness by reducing the flour, but this now butter-heavy dough produced a cookie that was too tender and crumbly. I tried

adding an egg as a binder, but the dough became wet, sticky, and difficult to roll out. What if I used just the yolk and dumped the white, the part of the egg that contributes the most moisture (and the most stickiness)? These cookies were winners. I settled on two yolks and had dough that could be rolled out and baked successfully.

Flavor Boost

I found that increasing the vanilla extract brought out the aromatics in the chocolate, and adding a teaspoon of instant espresso powder boosted the deep roasted notes. As I dissolved the espresso powder in a small amount of boiling water, I wondered if "blooming" the cocoa powder in the hot water might boost the chocolate flavor. (The theory is that hot water melts away the remaining cocoa butter, freeing up volatile flavor compounds.) Unfortunately, the 3 tablespoons of water needed to bloom the cocoa powder returned the dough to a soft and sticky mess. I turned to the large amount of butter at my disposal and melted 4 tablespoons of it, just enough to make a warm paste out of the cocoa and espresso powders. Blooming the powders in melted butter really helped to boost the underlying chocolate flavor of the cookie.

The rich aroma coming out of the oven proved that heat also aided in the release of chocolate flavor compounds. But, as we have discovered with other baked chocolate desserts, those compounds are better left in the cookie than lost to the atmosphere. To avoid losing too much flavor, I had to take the cookies out of the oven at just the right

Key Steps to Maximum Chocolate Flavor

ADD COCOA SOLIDS
Start with cocoa powder. It has more cocoa solids than other forms of chocolate and the most intense flavor.

UP THE COMPLEXITY
The bitter, roasted notes of espresso powder accentuate similar qualities in the cocoa powder.

"BLOOM" IN HOT BUTTER
Mixing both powders with hot, melted butter makes more flavor molecules available to taste buds.

moment—trickier than it sounds, as visual clues are hard to detect in this dark dough. The secret is to use a fork or finger to gently press the center of a cookie; slight resistance tells you the cookies are done. (If the cookies are baked until they darken around the edges, they will turn slightly bitter and lose much of their complexity.) When cooled properly, the cookies will have a strong chocolate flavor and a perfectly crisp texture.

Many home cooks avoid recipes that call for rolling out dough. Although this dough can be rolled out easily and then cut into decorative shapes, it can also be rolled into a cylinder, sliced into coins, and then baked. But, no matter how you slice it, these chocolate butter cookies will truly taste as good as they look.

CHOCOLATE BUTTER COOKIES
MAKES ABOUT 4 DOZEN 2½-INCH COOKIES

Natural cocoa powder will work in this recipe, but we found that Dutch-processed yields the best chocolate flavor. Espresso powder provides complexity, but instant coffee can be substituted in a pinch. The dough can be wrapped tightly in plastic wrap and stored in the refrigerator for up to three days or in the freezer for up to two weeks. Defrost frozen dough in the refrigerator overnight, then let stand at room temperature until firm yet malleable, about 30 minutes. The cookies are refined enough to serve plain, but a dusting of sifted confectioners' sugar or chocolate glaze is a nice touch. Baked cookies can be stored in an airtight container at room temperature for up to three days but should be dusted with sugar or glazed the day they are served.

20 tablespoons (2½ sticks) unsalted butter, softened to cool room temperature (about 65 degrees)

½ cup (about 2 ounces) cocoa powder
1 teaspoon espresso powder
1 cup (7 ounces) sugar
¼ teaspoon table salt
2 large egg yolks
1 tablespoon vanilla extract
2¼ cups (11¼ ounces) unbleached all-purpose flour

1. Adjust oven rack to middle position; heat oven to 375 degrees. Melt 4 tablespoons butter in medium saucepan over medium heat. Add cocoa powder and espresso powder; stir until mixture forms smooth paste. Set aside to cool, 15 to 20 minutes.

2. In standing mixer fitted with paddle attachment, mix remaining 16 tablespoons butter, sugar, salt, and cooled cocoa mixture on high speed until well combined and fluffy, about 1 minute, scraping sides of mixing bowl once or twice with rubber spatula. Add yolks and vanilla and mix on medium speed until thoroughly combined, about 30 seconds. Scrape sides of bowl. With mixer running on low, add flour in three additions, waiting until each addition is incorporated before adding next and scraping bowl after each addition. Continue to mix until dough forms cohesive ball, about 5 seconds. Turn dough onto counter; divide into three 4-inch disks. Wrap each disk in plastic wrap and refrigerate until dough is firm yet malleable, 45 to 60 minutes. (Alternatively, shape dough log, 2 inches in diameter and about 12 inches long; use parchment paper or plastic wrap to roll into neat cylinder. Chill until very firm and cold, at least 1 hour.)

3. Roll out 1 dough disk between 2 large sheets parchment paper to even thickness of ³⁄₁₆ inch. (If dough becomes soft and sticky, slide rolled dough on parchment onto baking sheet and rechill until firm, about 10 minutes.) Peel parchment from one side of dough and cut into desired shapes using cookie cutter(s); using thin metal spatula, place shapes on parchment-lined baking sheet, spacing them about 1 inch apart. Gather dough scraps and chill. (For cylinder-shaped dough, simply slice cookies ¼ inch thick and place on parchment-lined baking sheets.)

4. Bake until cookies show slight resistance to touch (see photo above), 10 to 12 minutes, rotating baking sheet halfway through baking time; if cookies begin to darken on edges, they have overbaked. Cool for 5

Determining Doneness

When the cookies are ready to come out of the oven, they will show slight resistance when gently pressed. If they yield easily, they are underdone and need more time to crisp; if they begin to darken at the edges, they have baked too long and will taste burnt and bitter.

minutes, then, using spatula, transfer cookies to wire rack; cool completely. Repeat steps 3 and 4 with remaining dough disks and scraps, rerolling scraps just once. Decorate as desired.

BITTERSWEET CHOCOLATE GLAZE

Melt 4 ounces bittersweet chocolate with 4 tablespoons unsalted butter and whisk until smooth. Add 2 tablespoons corn syrup and 1 teaspoon vanilla extract and mix until smooth and shiny. Use back of spoon to spread scant 1 teaspoon glaze almost to edge of each cookie. (If necessary, reheat to prolong fluidity of glaze.) Allow glazed cookies to dry at least 20 minutes.

GLAZED CHOCOLATE-MINT COOKIES

Follow recipe for Chocolate Butter Cookies, replacing vanilla extract with 2 teaspoons mint extract. Glaze cookies with Bittersweet Chocolate Glaze and dry as directed. Melt 1 cup white chocolate chips and drizzle over glazed cookies. Let dry at least 20 minutes before serving.

MEXICAN CHOCOLATE BUTTER COOKIES

In medium skillet set over medium heat, toast ½ cup sliced almonds, 1 teaspoon ground cinnamon, and ⅛ teaspoon cayenne until fragrant, about 3 minutes; set aside to cool. In food processor fitted with metal blade, process cooled mixture until very fine, about 15 seconds. Follow recipe for Chocolate Butter Cookies, whisking nut/spice mixture into flour before adding flour to dough in step 2. Proceed with recipe, rolling dough into log. Roll chilled log in ½ cup raw or sanding sugar before slicing.

Go to www.cooksillustrated.com
- Key in code 11056 for **Chocolate-Orange Butter Cookies with Chocolate Brandy Glaze**.
- Recipe available until December 31, 2005.

TECHNIQUE | SIMPLE TRIMMINGS

DRIZZLE WITH CHOCOLATE
Melt chocolate chips in the microwave on low power or in a bowl set over a saucepan of simmering water. Transfer to a plastic sandwich bag. Snip off one corner of the bag, then drizzle.

ROLL IN SUGAR OR NUTS
Roll the chilled cylinder of dough in ½ cup sanding (coarse) sugar or chopped nuts, such as pistachios, almonds, or pecans, just before slicing into rounds and baking.

Rescuing Buttermilk Mashed Potatoes

Replacing the butter and cream with buttermilk doesn't work. (Unless you like curdled, parched spuds.) So what's the secret to tangy, creamy mashed potatoes?

⇒ BY REBECCA HAYS ⇐

Recipe writers like to tout buttermilk as a miracle ingredient, claiming that this naturally lean product (made by adding bacteria to skim or low-fat milk) creates the illusion of butter and cream. But do any of these butterless recipes deliver?

In a word, no. The recipes I tried produced potatoes that were curdled, crumbly, chalky, and dry. In fact, other than a low calorie count, the grainy, thirsty potatoes had only one thing going for them: the distinctive tang of buttermilk. But this trademark tart flavor was in fact so alluring that I decided to continue my investigation.

I sketched out a plan: First and foremost, I was going to add some butter! Because of the flavorful, creamy buttermilk, I wouldn't need to add a truckload, but I decided that fat-free potatoes just aren't worth choking down. Second, I wanted an everyday recipe, streamlined enough for frequent dinner-table appearances. I also had to develop a curdle-proof technique. While most recipes instruct the cook to heat the buttermilk, what resulted was an unappealing mix of watery, coagulated liquid and grainy curds.

Curdle Hurdle

Tackling the curdling problem first, I tried to skip the heating step, but that wasn't the answer: Buttermilk curdles at 160 degrees, a temperature reached almost instantly when the cold liquid hits steaming-hot potatoes. I pulled out an instant-read thermometer and started adding buttermilk to the potatoes when they dropped below the 160-degree mark. This worked, but talk about fussy! I kept searching for a viable solution and came across sources suggesting pinches of baking soda (to neutralize acidity) or cornstarch (for stability). Neither trick worked. I knew that high-fat dairy products like half-and-half aren't prone to curdling. What if I fattened up the buttermilk with some melted butter? Bingo. When mixed with room-temperature buttermilk, the melted butter acted as an insulating agent, with the fat coating the proteins in the buttermilk and protecting them from heat shock.

No Jacket Required

The test kitchen has found that simmering whole russet potatoes in their jackets yields true potato flavor and a rich, silky texture; peeled and cut russets cook up with a thin taste and texture. Could I simplify the cooking method by switching my choice of potatoes? Peeled-and-cut red potatoes were dense and pasty when mashed, but peeled-and-cut Yukon Golds made creamy, smooth mashed potatoes. Why do Yukon Gold potatoes respond better to this technique than russets? Russet potatoes have more starch and therefore absorb a lot more water than lower-starch Yukon Golds. So while mashed russets become soggy if peeled and cut before cooking, the less absorbent Yukon Golds turn out just right.

Settling on amounts of butter and buttermilk was a delicate balancing act. Too much butter obscured the buttermilk flavor; too little tasted too lean. After many trials, I settled on 6 tablespoons butter and ⅔ cup buttermilk. These amounts allowed plenty of tartness to shine through—and while this wasn't diet food, I didn't have to think twice about going back for seconds. So when it comes to buttermilk mashed potatoes, all you need is the right potato and the right technique. And a little butter.

BUTTERMILK MASHED POTATOES
SERVES 4

To achieve the proper texture, it is important to cook the potatoes thoroughly; they are done if they break apart when a knife is inserted and gently wiggled (see photo). Buttermilk substitutes such as clabbered milk do not produce sufficiently tangy potatoes. To reduce the chance of curdling, the buttermilk must be at room temperature when mixed with cooled melted butter.

2   pounds Yukon Gold potatoes, peeled and cut into 1-inch chunks
    Table salt
6   tablespoons unsalted butter, melted and cooled
⅔   cup buttermilk, at room temperature
    Ground black pepper

1. Place potatoes in large saucepan; add cold water to cover by 1 inch and 1 tablespoon salt. Bring to boil over high heat, then reduce heat to medium and simmer until potatoes break apart when paring knife is inserted, about 18 minutes. Drain potatoes and return to saucepan set on still-hot burner.

2. Using potato masher, mash potatoes until a few small lumps remain. Gently mix melted butter and buttermilk in small bowl until combined. Add butter/buttermilk mixture to potatoes; using rubber spatula, fold gently until just incorporated. Adjust seasoning with salt and pepper; serve immediately.

BUTTERMILK RANCH MASHED POTATOES

Follow recipe for Buttermilk Mashed Potatoes, adding 1 medium garlic clove, minced; 3 scallions, white and green parts sliced very thin; 2 tablespoons minced fresh parsley leaves; and ⅓ cup sour cream along with butter/buttermilk mixture in step 2.

Go to www.cooksillustrated.com
- Key in code 11057 for **Buttermilk Mashed Potatoes with Leeks and Chives.**
- This recipe will be available until December 31, 2005.

The Secret to Buttermilk Mashed Potatoes

NOT QUITE DONE
Potatoes that remain intact when pierced with a paring knife need more cooking.

JUST RIGHT
Potatoes that break apart when pierced with a paring knife are ready to be mashed.

OVERDONE
Potatoes that have begun to disintegrate will result in soupy mashed potatoes.

When mashed potatoes turn out dry, it's partly because the starch granules haven't ruptured and broken down. Thorough cooking makes the granules dissolve, yielding mashed potatoes that are smooth rather than grainy.

Mix Masters

KitchenAid has dominated the standing-mixer market for decades, but can it cream a new batch of competitors with 1,000-watt motors, cavernous bowls, and lofty price tags?

⇒ BY JOLYON HELTERMAN ⇐

For dedicated home bakers, choosing a standing mixer used to be a piece of cake. You strolled down the KitchenAid aisle; you selected a size. The competition? Mostly glorified eggbeaters mounted on stands—fine for whipping cream and stirring cake batter but pretty much useless for heavier tasks involving cookie dough or bread.

Recently, though, numerous high-end models have whirred onto the scene to give KitchenAid a run for its money. Most have raised the stakes with huge bowl sizes and seriously ramped-up wattage. While KitchenAid's largest mixer is 6 quarts (most are 5), now 7 quarts and larger aren't uncommon. KitchenAid's basic model runs on a 250-watt motor; the new models tout ratings of 700, 800, even 1,000 watts! Naturally, prices have soared. Hobart—a maker of industrial-grade mixers—has rolled out a new 5-quart consumer model priced at a cool $1,500 and change.

How much mixer does a home cook need? To test the field thoroughly, we bought 18 different mixers of every shape, size, and price—from a budget $100 model up to the $1,500 Hobart. Our lineup included Bosch (two models), DeLonghi (two), Electrolux, Farberware, Hamilton Beach (two), Hobart, Jenn-Air, KitchenAid (four), Sunbeam (two), and Viking (two).

A Baker's Dozen

Standing mixers should be able to beat egg whites, whip cream, incorporate butter and sugar ("creaming"), mix stiff cookie dough, and knead basic bread dough. I started with a test that would quickly thin the ranks: 15 minutes of medium-duty kneading on a rustic bread dough. (If all you need a mixer to do is beat egg whites and stir cake mix, you're better off spending $70 on a good hand-held mixer instead.) Any mixer that couldn't finish the job was out of the running. Hacking, screeching, shuddering, even pausing—all fine, so long as the resulting dough was acceptable and the mixer survived.

First up was the Jenn-Air Attrezzi, a smart, stylish number that huffed and puffed its way through the first few minutes of kneading, then hacked flour out of its sleekly contoured etched-glass bowl. As smoke wafted from the motor, I reconfirmed the fire extinguisher's proximity but resisted pulling the plug. After 3:50, the motor stalled and never started again. Next, the diminutive KitchenAid Classic wheezed and trembled through the exer-

cise, but 15 minutes later both mixer and dough were fine. The $1,500 Hobart whirred calmly from start to finish. And so it went—for 18 rounds.

All in all, these mixers were truly a noisy, convulsive lot. But only six failed outright, either stalling out irreversibly or leaving portions of dough unincorporated: Bosch Solitaire ($899.99; the cheaper Universal model survived), Farberware ($99.99), Hamilton Beach 5-Quart ($349.95; the 7-quart survived), Jenn-Air ($349.00), and both Sunbeams ($98.95, $129.99). Just 12 mixers, then, would advance to the remaining rounds.

Design Matters

For the next several weeks, the triumphant dozen tried their luck in a variety of mixer challenges: kneading pizza dough, mixing cookie dough, whipping cream, and beating egg whites. In the end, we developed clear mixer-design criteria.

First, there's mixing motion. The two most common are stationary beaters (with rotating bowl) and "planetary action," when a single beater rotates on its axis while spinning around a stationary bowl (similar to the way a planet moves around the sun). Planetary action proved far superior—the agitator simply makes it to more areas of the bowl. Three stationary models (Farberware, both Sunbeams) choked on dough in the elimination round: Either the bowl stopped moving or the beaters got too clogged to rotate. Another stationary-style mixer, albeit a more unusual design, the Electrolux DLX-2000 ($469.95) has a rotating bowl and all its inherent problems (ingredients get clogged on the agitator while the bowl spins ineffectually). One mixer opted for another approach entirely. Shaped like a food processor, the Bosch Universal ($369.99) has an agitator that rotates on a spindle. The Bosch wasn't bad at kneading, but when creaming and whipping, its tendency to fling ingredients to the sides rather than integrate them in the middle proved detrimental to the final consistency.

Second, forget cavernous bowls. Unless you regularly make multiple loaves of bread, 5 to 6 quarts is plenty. To accommodate the extra volume, DeLonghi, Hamilton Beach, and Viking built the bowls of their 7-quart models up, not out: The resulting urns are nearly impossible to scrape down

without dirtying a shirt sleeve, and small amounts (think two egg whites) get lost in the depths.

We also prefer slightly squat bowls, which compensate for the lost height with a more spacious bottom surface and by flaring out to a wider mouth. By distributing ingredients lower and wider, these models had less opportunity to fling the contents up the sides beyond the beater's effective range of motion. The net result? Less need to scrape. The other advantage of shallower distribution—coupled with a wider paddle (more leverage)—is less work by the motor. The 5-quart mixers by DeLonghi and Viking have squatter, flared bowls, while the 6-quart KitchenAid Professional 600 made up for straight sides with the most spacious bottom surface of any planetary-action mixer in the lineup.

Most mixers come with three attachments: a dough hook (for kneading), a paddle-shaped flat beater (creaming dry and wet ingredients), and a wire whisk (whipping). The minor differences from model to model aren't worth reporting, with a few exceptions. First, most flat paddles are, in fact, flat. The exceptions were the DeLonghi and Viking paddles (5-quart models only), which feature slightly bent-out edges, a three-dimensional touch that proved remarkably effective for creaming. If only the Viking could keep its slick-shaped beaters locked securely in the socket: With both Viking models we tested, the dough-caked attachments constantly plunged into the bowl during scraping sessions, thanks to a poorly designed locking mechanism and the disproportionate weight of the attachments themselves.

Finally, the DeLonghi, Hamilton Beach, and Viking mixers earned extra credit for an ingenious method of adjusting beater clearance. Each attach-

Bowl Shape Speaks Volumes

Testers developed a knack for diagnosing some mixer tendencies just by noting the proportions of the bowl. Our favorite? Squat and flared.

STRAIGHT AND NARROW
Minimal flour spray, but stacked contents mean constant scraping and harder work for motor.

SQUAT AND FLARED
Some flour spray, but slightly wider bottom and flared sides mean easy access and minimal scraping.

ment can be lengthened or shortened by turning a washer near the top. With the KitchenAids, only the mixer arm can be adjusted, making it a pain for cooks who prefer closer bowl contact with one attachment than with the others.

Power Games

If I hadn't included the Hobart in the lineup, I might never have discovered the sneaky truth behind wattage ratings. Most mixers list their power in watts; Hobart is the only one to use horsepower. When I learned that ⅙ HP equals a mere 124 watts, I scratched my head in puzzlement. How could this quiet, powerful workhorse have the lowest wattage rating in such a hacking, shuddering group (from 250 watts to 1,000 watts)? Turns out Hobart is the only mixer to list output power rather than input power. What's the difference? Output wattage is the amount of power the motor actually produces—which flows out of the motor, moves through the mixer arm, and, ultimately, smacks the ingredients around. Every other mixer lists input wattage, which is simply the power that flows from the electrical outlet into the mixer's motor.

What does input wattage tell you about the power of a mixer? Absolutely nothing—it's purely a marketing gimmick. To wit, the six models that failed the bread dough test (our initial round) had power ratings ranging from low to high, mostly high (275, 350, 400, 450, 700, 700). In addition, every other test showed absolutely no correlation between mixer performance and wattage. (If manufacturers were willing to provide output wattage

figures, comparison would be easy, but this key bit of data is never offered.)

The Dye Is Cast

Beyond output power, it was clear that design was crucial to successful mixing. For a better measure of a mixer's efficiency, then, I devised a final test. Mixing 4 cups of pizza dough in each bowl, I added 10 drops of yellow food coloring to one side of the dough and 10 drops of blue to the other. How long would each mixer take to knead the dough completely to a uniform green color—with no individual specks of yellow or blue?

Incorporation times varied significantly. The slowest mixer had gone from speckled blue and yellow to a uniform green in just over 11 minutes. The quickest? A speedy 3:45. From fastest to slowest: KitchenAid Professional 600 (3:45), Bosch Universal (4:45), DeLonghi 7 (5:03), Hobart (5:30), Viking 5 (5:30), DeLonghi 5 (5:33), Hamilton Beach (5:39), Viking 7 (6:30), KitchenAid Artisan (7:20), KitchenAid Accolade (7:42), KitchenAid Classic (8:52), and Electrolux (11:15). And wattage? Clearly unrelated.

So is KitchenAid still the mixer to beat? Yes. Three mixers survived the gauntlet of tests without showing fatal flaws: the KitchenAid Professional 600 ($369.99), the 5-quart DeLonghi ($349.95), and the Hobart ($1,503.08). Given that $1,500 is far beyond most test cooks' budgets, the kitchen was split down the middle between the KitchenAid and the DeLonghi, but our test results give a slight edge to the KitchenAid.

The Standing Mixers We Tested

RECOMMENDED

KitchenAid Professional 600
Mixer to Beat

DeLonghi 5-Quart
Expert Creamer

Hobart
Quiet Workhorse

RECOMMENDED WITH RESERVATIONS

Viking 5-Quart
Attachment Disorder

DeLonghi 7-Quart
Gaping Bowl

KitchenAid Artisan
Weak Knead

RECOMMENDED WITH RESERVATIONS (continued)

KitchenAid Accolade
Awkward Pauses

Viking 7-Quart
Buggy Whip

Hamilton Beach 7-Quart
Bad Vibrations

Bosch Universal
Side Issues

NOT RECOMMENDED

KitchenAid Classic
Shaky Situation

Electrolux Assistent
Lost in Space

RATING STANDING MIXERS

RECOMMENDED	TEST CRITERIA		TESTERS' COMMENTS

KitchenAid Professional 600
CAPACITY: 6 quarts
PRICE: $369.99
WATTAGE: 575
DYE INCORPORATION: 3:45

KNEADING: ★★★
CREAMING: ★★★
WHIPPING: ★★★
DESIGN: ★★★

FEATURES: "Spiral" dough hook, flat beater, wire whip, pouring shield, bowl lift

With 18 models tested, a KitchenAid still came out on top—though just barely edging out the DeLonghi. With 575 watts (the median for the group), it plowed through 4 cups of dough almost two minutes faster than most "super-wattage" models. Ideal 6-quart capacity distributed wide (rather than tall) made for easy scraping and additions, if a bit more flour spray.

DeLonghi DSM5
CAPACITY: 5 quarts
PRICE: $349.95
WATTAGE: 780
DYE INCORPORATION: 5:33

KNEADING: ★★★
CREAMING: ★★★
WHIPPING: ★★★
DESIGN: ★★★

FEATURES: Nonstick dough hook, "crimped" nonstick flat beater, stainless whisk, splash guard, tilt head

Watching this compact mixer expertly cream butter and sugar into a uniform consistency was a thing of beauty. Flared bowl and well-sized attachments kept ingredients "low in the bowl" and minimized scraping. A bit more composure during heavy workloads might have broken the near-tie for first in its favor.

Hobart N50
CAPACITY: 5 quarts
PRICE: $1,503.08
WATTAGE: 320
DYE INCORPORATION: 5:30

KNEADING: ★★★
CREAMING: ★★★
WHIPPING: ★★★
DESIGN: ★★

FEATURES: Dough hook, flat beater, wire whip, bowl lift

"Purrs like a kitten," said testers about this industrial-strength lion, as it calmly processed rustic dough, oatmeal cookies, and anything else we threw its way. Narrow bowl mouth (the narrowest) made it awkward to add ingredients, and turning off power to change speeds was a pain—but not as much as transporting the 55-pound beast.

RECOMMENDED WITH RESERVATIONS

Viking VSM500
CAPACITY: 5 quarts
PRICE: $440.00
WATTAGE: 800
DYE INCORPORATION: 5:30

KNEADING: ★★★
CREAMING: ★★★
WHIPPING: ★★★
DESIGN: ★★

FEATURES: Dough hook, "crimped" flat beater, wire whip, transport wheels

If Viking ever figures out the "locking" concept, this 5-quart model might be the mixer to beat. Shaft-arm lock required ridiculous force to slam shut, but the real tragedy was how often attachments plummeted from the poorly designed socket during scraping breaks.

DeLonghi DSM7
CAPACITY: 7 quarts
PRICE: $449.95
WATTAGE: 980
DYE INCORPORATION: 5:03

KNEADING: ★★★
CREAMING: ★★★
WHIPPING: ★★
DESIGN: ★★

FEATURES: Nonstick dough hook, nonstick flat beater, stainless whisk, splash guard, tilt head

The DSM7 suffered the plight of tall, cavernous bowls—difficulty whipping small amounts and awkward scraping of sides. ("The hardest part is keeping yourself clean," noted one tester.) Despite huge-sounding wattage, more shaking and screeching with heavy loads than many other models.

KitchenAid Artisan
CAPACITY: 5 quarts
PRICE: $249.99
WATTAGE: 325
DYE INCORPORATION: 7:20

KNEADING: ★★
CREAMING: ★★★
WHIPPING: ★★★
DESIGN: ★★

FEATURES: Dough hook, flat beater, wire whip, splash guard, tilt head

Kneading caused audible strain on the motor, as did adding heavy dry ingredients (oats) to cookie dough. Creamed and whipped like a pro—an economical choice for infrequent breadmakers. Narrow bowl mouth hindered tidy addition of dry ingredients.

KitchenAid Accolade 400
CAPACITY: 5 quarts
PRICE: $299.99
WATTAGE: 400
DYE INCORPORATION: 7:42

KNEADING: ★★
CREAMING: ★★★
WHIPPING: ★★★
DESIGN: ★★

FEATURES: Dough hook, flat beater, wire whip, splash guard, tilt head, delayed start

More wattage (more money) than the Artisan, but consistently performed at a lower level. This "deluxe" motor sounded weaker, and attachments seemed ill designed for the slightly tweaked bowl shape. Some hated the "delayed start" feature, preferring the Artisan's immediate response.

Viking VSM700
CAPACITY: 7 quarts
PRICE: $499.95
WATTAGE: 1,000
DYE INCORPORATION: 6:30

KNEADING: ★★★
CREAMING: ★★★
WHIPPING: ★
DESIGN: ★

FEATURES: Dough hook, flat beater, stainless whip, tilt head, transport wheels

Same problems as the VSM500 (plummeting attachments, "slam lock" shaft design), and the two egg whites we'd hidden at the bottom of the cavernous bowl remained safe from agitation, no matter how far down we adjusted the whip attachment. This "1,000-watt" machine did seem powerful, but not more so than more modestly labeled motors.

Hamilton Beach CPM700
CAPACITY: 7 quarts
PRICE: $469.00
WATTAGE: 800
DYE INCORPORATION: 5:39

KNEADING: ★★
CREAMING: ★★
WHIPPING: ★★
DESIGN: ★★

FEATURES: Dough hook, flat beater, wire whisk

The CPM700's 5-quart sibling stalled permanently during the elimination round, and this one stalled twice before finishing the task. Separate on/off switch is awkward, and mixer arm lurched violently. Large bowl presented usual problems for small amounts.

Bosch Universal Kitchen Machine
CAPACITY: 6 quarts
PRICE: $369.99
WATTAGE: 700
DYE INCORPORATION: 4:45

KNEADING: ★★★
CREAMING: ★★
WHIPPING: ★
DESIGN: ★

FEATURES: Dough blade, egg whip, plastic lid, 6-cup blender

Shaped like a food processor with mixer attachments, the Bosch did a commendable job when kneading bread dough. But the decentralized mixing space (a "doughnut" around a central spindle) kept less cohesive contents from meeting in the middle. Condensation from the lid affected dough moisture.

NOT RECOMMENDED

KitchenAid Classic Series
CAPACITY: 4½ quarts
PRICE: $249.95
WATTAGE: 250
DYE INCORPORATION: 8:52

KNEADING: ★
CREAMING: ★★
WHIPPING: ★★
DESIGN: ★★

FEATURES: Dough hook, flat beater, wire whip, tilt head

Amid hefty contenders, KitchenAid's smallest model seemed more like a toy. The Classic did a fair job of creaming and whipping, but it wasn't cut out for kneading dough and had a chronic case of the shakes. You're better off opting for the more powerful Artisan, which costs the same.

Electrolux DLX-2000 Assistent
CAPACITY: 8 quarts
PRICE: $469.95
WATTAGE: 450
DYE INCORPORATION: 11:15

KNEADING: ★★
CREAMING: ★
WHIPPING: ★★
DESIGN: ★

FEATURES: Plastic whisking bowl, dough hook, beater, roller/scraper

Wide bowl allowed easy access and capacity for nine bread loaves, but cookies, cakes, and even single loaves got lost in the abyss. The roller tool's grooves are a haven for butter, and the least intuitive user interface in the lineup had us constantly re-deciphering the manual before every task.

These mixers, also "Not Recommended," were eliminated after failing to knead dough acceptably: Bosch Solitaire MUM7400 (700 watts, $899.99), Farberware (350 watts, $99.99), Hamilton Beach CPM500 Commercial (700 watts, $349.95), Jenn-Air Attrezzi JSM900 (400 watts, $349.00), Sunbeam Heritage (450 watts, $129.99), Sunbeam Mixmaster 2366 (275 watts, $98.95).

Is Coffeehouse Coffee Best?

We secretly replaced our tasters' favorite gourmet coffee with supermarket beans.
Could they tell the difference? Our taste tests yielded surprising results.

⇒ BY JOLYON HELTERMAN ⇐

My daily coffee ritual begins promptly at 6:30 a.m., when I plunk down $3 and change for a customized, 15-syllable concoction laced with enough caffeine to get me through half the morning. Hours later, I retrace the two-and-a-half-minute trek from the test kitchen to the local Starbucks coffeehouse, where my dealer (aka barista) starts portioning out my usual fix before I even make it up to the counter.

Trembling with product satisfaction, I stock Starbucks beans at home as well; given my daily routine, it's quite convenient. Ironically, it's when the company took the convenience factor up another notch—offering its whole beans at the grocery store—that my eyes began to wander. Amid the instant-coffee "crystals" and the tin cans of preground coffee sat several shelves' worth of whole-bean coffee brands. Some hailed from other coffeehouses, vying (like Starbucks) for a piece of the lucrative coffee-aisle action; others were straight-ahead supermarket brands, priced per pound at less than what I normally pay for a single iced-venti-no-foam-latte.

Could any of them compete in taste with my old standby? To find out, I bought eight whole-bean coffees at the supermarket. For each brand, I chose the "house blend," or whatever medium roast was widely available.

Tasters' Choice(s)

Test kitchen staffers first tried the coffees brewed regular strength. The differences were striking. Some coffees were strong and smoky, others tasted light and "chocolaty," still others boasted hints of caramel or molasses. For a few of the brands, the tasting sheets overflowed with invective decrying bitter, rancid, or harsh qualities. Most surprising, Starbucks came in not first but *fifth* out of the eight samples. "Burnt, with a bitter aftertaste," said one taster. "Like gnawing on charcoal," said another. Top honors went instead to Green Mountain Roasters and Eight O'Clock, which tasters found complex and well balanced.

By no stretch am I a trained coffee expert, but I also wasn't convinced that I've been blithely sucking down "burnt coffee" twice a day. So I devised one more test—a tasting of coffee with milk. Why? An informal poll revealed that more than two-thirds of the *Cook's* staff (including me) add milk to their coffee, and it seemed only fair to try the brands that way, too. So I brewed up eight

more pots, added ¾ cup warmed whole milk to each, and summoned 25 soon-to-be-jittery tasters into the test kitchen for another tour.

Sure enough, preferences changed. This time, Green Mountain and Eight O'Clock, the plain-coffee champs, ended up in the lower ranks—bland and insipid, according to tasters. In contrast, Starbucks landed near the top, along with Millstone and Seattle's Best, two other fairly assertive coffees. The bitter, burnt notes that had menaced tasters in the first round were suddenly "robust" and "complex" when tempered by the milk. Simply watered down? Not quite. Additional research revealed that the proteins in milk (and cream) bind some of the bitter-tasting phenolic compounds, reducing the bitterness and intensity of the coffee flavor.

Dark Matter

So far I had based my analysis on tasters' subjective descriptions. But there was a better way. In general, the longer a coffee bean roasts, the darker and more strongly flavored it becomes. Although it's possible to make a rough comparison of roast darkness by eyeballing alone, experts use an instrument called an Agtron to measure exactly how much light the beans reflect. The higher the Agtron reading (that is, the more light the beans reflect), the lighter the roast: An Agtron reading of 85 would indicate an ultra-light, almost tealike coffee; the darkest French roast out there would be closer to 15.

To find out how roast darkness lined up with taster preference, I sent the samples to a lab that specializes in coffee analysis. The Agtron readings differed markedly. From darkest to lightest: Starbucks (34.9), Millstone (36.5), Seattle's Best (40.0), Chock Full o' Nuts (40.3), Green Mountain (48.0), Folgers (48.9), Eight O'Clock (51.4), and Dunkin' Donuts (59.9).

From this data, I made two important discoveries. First, according to coffee-industry standards, the four darkest coffees in our lineup (Starbucks through Chock Full o' Nuts) are considered "dark" roasts, while

the remaining four (Green Mountain through Dunkin' Donuts) are "medium." Second, roast darkness correlated with our tasting-room experience: Green Mountain and Eight O'Clock, both lighter roasts, triumphed in the plain tasting yet proved too mild in the milk round. By contrast, the three darkest roasts (Starbucks, Millstone, and Seattle's Best) were the milk-round champs.

Still troubling was how to explain Chock Full o' Nuts, Folgers, and Dunkin' Donuts—three brands that stubbornly refused to play by the light-roast/dark-roast rules.

Grounds for Dismissal

Luckily, some of the best discoveries happen by accident. The lab I hired to measure roast darkness had included several other tests for the same fee. Most of the data seemed better suited for a coffee dissertation than a magazine article—"package integrity" scores, moisture levels, and so forth. When I reached the last line, however, I noticed an odd-sounding measurement: "6 quakers," read one report; "1 quaker," read another. I had no idea what a quaker was, but given that my three problem coffees—Chock Full o' Nuts (7), Folgers (8), and Dunkin' Donuts (9)—had the most, I was determined to find out. Turns out, a *quaker* is coffee-industry jargon for an underdeveloped coffee bean that fails to get sorted out before the roasting stage. Less dense than a regular, mature bean, quakers can wreak havoc on the coffee's flavor profile, imparting a spoiled taste to the brew. So desirable is quaker-free cof-

Watch Out for Quakers

GOOD BEANS   **QUAKERS**

The beans on the left may come from the dark side, but it's the pale ones on the right that visit evil upon a good brew. Quakers—light-colored, underdeveloped beans found in most commercial coffees—impart a rancid, "spoiled peanut" taste to the entire pot. In the tasting room, we had better luck with low-quaker-count brands.

Coffee Shelf Life: The Age-Old Question

While testing supermarket coffees, we were careful not to brew up beans that had passed the "Guaranteed Fresh Until" date printed on the package. As coffee beans age, they lose moisture and oils that are important for aroma and flavor, and older beans are more likely to have been contaminated with oxygen (even in "airtight" packaging).

When we noticed that some of our coffees had expiration dates that were months away, we called manufacturers to find out what these designations mean. To our surprise, there's no standard for coffee shelf life: Green Mountain and Dunkin' Donuts said they roast beans six months before the date on the package. Most of the rest roast beans one year before that date. But Chock Full o' Nuts, which lost points for stale taste, gets roasted a whopping two years before the package date—in our case, a year and a half before we tasted it. It all goes to show that coffee, unlike wine, doesn't improve with age. —J.H.

---

fee that beans are graded based on quaker count, and buyers are willing to pay a premium for beans that come up clean in spot tests.

The lab had found quaker counts in our coffees ranging from 0 to 9—based on a 100-gram sample (just over a cup). Do those numbers really matter to the casual coffee drinker? In a word, yes. In a 1-pound (455-gram) bag of Millstone coffee, you would expect to find just 4½ quakers total, while in a 1-pound bag of Dunkin' Donuts coffee there might be 40.

How much training would I need to identify quakers? None at all, said Mané Alves, the lab's director. "Open up any bag of [one of the high-quaker-count brands]. You will see them—beans that are lighter colored than the rest." So I dumped several bags of coffee onto the countertop and, sure enough, the coffee was crawling with them! I began sorting and an hour later had a cupful of quakers. How awful could these pale beans really be? I had my answer minutes later, when I brewed a fresh pot of coffee made entirely from quakers. The smell was putrid enough, but the first taste dispelled any suspicions that quaker count was merely some academic exercise. The experiment isolated a taste I've always associated with bad gas-station coffee but conflated (incorrectly) with the burnt taste that comes from leaving the pot on the burner too long. Suffice it to say a quaker is indeed something best avoided.

Beyond roast darkness and quaker count, the experts also acknowledged that the brands in our lineup draw from raw (or "green") beans of varying quality. But spending a mint on prime beans doesn't guarantee a tasty brew. For example, says Alves, Starbucks and Seattle's Best "consistently buy better green beans" than the other brands, but the dark roasting they undergo obscures many of the nuances.

TASTING SUPERMARKET WHOLE BEAN COFFEE

Twenty *Cook's Illustrated* staff members tasted eight whole-bean coffees from the supermarket (in all cases, the medium roast or "house" blend) at regular brew strength plain and with ¾ cup whole milk (per 12-cup pot). The coffees were analyzed by Coffee Lab International of Waterbury, Vt., for roast darkness and "quakers," underdeveloped beans that negatively affect the flavor profile of a batch. The Agtron index is a measure of roast darkness, as determined by a spectrophotometer of the same name; the lower the index, the darker the roast. **The coffees are listed below in two groups—lighter roast and darker roast—in order of test kitchen preference.**

LIGHTER-ROAST COFFEES

GREEN MOUNTAIN COFFEE ROASTERS Our Blend
- **$7.49 for 12 ounces**
- **Agtron: 48.0 Quakers: 6**
Soft, balanced, and pleasantly acidic, this was a lighter roast even the dark-roast camp could get on board with. Hints of caramel and fruit.

EIGHT O'CLOCK COFFEE Original
- **$4.99 for 13 ounces**
- **Agtron: 51.4 Quakers: 6**
We liked this inexpensive brand's smooth body, its nutty, almost chocolaty flavor, and its "toasty aroma," especially in the plain tasting.

FOLGERS Classic Supreme
- **$3.99 for 12 ounces**
- **Agtron: 48.9 Quakers: 8**
"Yuck—from my dad's old thermos," recalled one taster. "Reminds me of bad truckstop coffee," said another. The strong astringency was fine with milk but bothered tasters in the plain round.

DUNKIN' DONUTS Original Blend
- **$8.49 for 16 ounces**
- **Agtron: 59.9 Quakers: 9**
The lightest roast of the group failed to impress our tasters. ("Chocolaty but thin—is there coffee in here?") Unpleasant "molasses" off-notes, a bitter aftertaste, and the highest quaker count in our lineup.

DARKER-ROAST COFFEES

MILLSTONE Colombian Supremo
- **$7.99 for 11 ounces**
- **Agtron: 36.5 Quakers: 1**
This brand was neck-and-neck with Starbucks for winning over our dark-roast enthusiasts. The deep, smoky, "chocolaty" flavor profile with a bitter finish proved a good foil for milk, but some of our light-roast camp found it "harsh."

STARBUCKS COFFEE House Blend
- **$9.39 for 12 ounces**
- **Agtron: 34.9 Quakers: 1**
This self-proclaimed "light roast" from Starbucks was darker than any other coffee in our lineup. Fans praised the rich, "almost chocolaty" flavors and deep, smoky aroma, but others found it burnt.

SEATTLE'S BEST COFFEE Seattle's Best Blend
- **$7.69 for 12 ounces**
- **Agtron: 40.0 Quakers: 0**
Not a quaker to mar the flavor profile, but tasters still weren't that impressed. Dark and smoky, yet this brand lacked the complexity to round out such strong flavors. "Smells like tar."

CHOCK FULL O' NUTS SoHo Morning Roast
- **$5.79 for 12 ounces**
- **Agtron: 40.3 Quakers: 7**
The three bags we sent to the lab had three different roast darknesses. (The company says it was aiming for about 40.) Every version our panel tasted was plagued by metallic off-notes, "bracing acidity," and a "cardboard" aftertaste.

So where did we come out? Turns out it is possible to get good whole-bean coffee at the supermarket, but you may have to spend close to Starbucks prices. Millstone ($7.99 for 11 ounces) and Starbucks ($9.39 for 12 ounces) were our favorite darker roasts, while Green Mountain Roasters ($7.49 for 12 ounces) and Eight O'Clock (a cheap $4.99 for 13 ounces) were the best for light-roast fans and those that drink their coffee black.

COOK'S extra

Go to www.cooksillustrated.com
- Key in code 11058 for **our testing of coffee grinders**.
- This information will be available until December 31, 2005.

Well-Rounded Cookie Cutters

Shape isn't the only factor to consider when choosing a set of cookie cutters. Over many years (and many batches), we've developed fairly specific criteria, from sharp cutting edges and sturdiness to adequate height and ease of use. Keeping these traits in mind, we tested cookie cutters made from traditional stainless steel, enamel-coated metal, plastic, copper, and rubber-topped stainless steel on our Chocolate Butter Cookies (page 23).

It was no surprise that the metal cutters—with their thin, sharp edges—did the best job cutting out well-defined shapes, while the plastic cutters—with thicker, duller edges—tended to turn out slightly imperfect cookies. In terms of height, cookie cutters with less depth than the standard 1 inch were difficult to remove from the dough, requiring careful maneuvering to avoid marring the final shape (one ½-inch-tall model stuck at the edges). Cookie cutters with rounded tops—or, if you can find one, a rubber-grip top—were also preferred. One cookie cutter with sharp edges on both top and bottom cut into our hands as well as the cookies.

We recommend easy-to-find traditional stainless steel for most cookie-cutting tasks. Copper cookie cutters (equally good performers) require maintenance and cost more than twice as much.

SHARP ON ONE SIDE, SOFT ON THE OTHER

Tasting Heritage Turkeys

Heritage turkeys—rare breeds touted for their complex and distinctive flavor—get lots of hype around this time of year. Given the countless hours we've spent in the test kitchen coming up with tricks for giving woefully mild-tasting traditional turkeys any semblance of flavor, we were intrigued enough to investigate. Is one of these birds worth as much as $125 (even if that includes shipping)?

Turkeys used to have a lot more in common with wild game birds. They were relatively small, with a fairly even distribution of muscle (meat) between breast and legs, and they had a varied diet (mostly grass and insects), one of several factors that contribute to complex-tasting meat. After World War II, demand increased dramatically for inexpensive poultry and for mild-tasting white meat.

Turkey producers responded by selectively breeding more birds for larger breasts. The birds also matured more quickly, giving the meat less time to develop flavor, and they were fed bland-tasting but economical grain. Producers also confined the birds to smaller pens, reducing their opportunity for exercise (another contributor to meat flavor). Called Broad-Breasted Whites, these are the birds found in every supermarket today. In recent years, groups like the Society for the Preservation of Poultry Antiquities have begun a crusade to bring the old-style breeds (nearly extinct by the late 1960s) back to the dinner table.

But how do they taste? To find out, we conducted a blind tasting of three heritage-turkey breeds: a Narragansett, a Bourbon Red, and an American Bronze. Suspecting that the turkeys might vary from farm to farm, we included a second Bourbon Red and a second American Bronze from different sources. We also threw in our favorite supermarket turkey (Plainville Farms) for comparison.

Did the heritage turkeys live up to their reputation for complex, distinctive flavor? That's an understatement. Most tasters, raised on milder specimens, were rattled by the strong flavor of these turkeys, not to mention the surprising range of textures—from chewy, dry, and leathery to greasy and tender. The dark meat was the most controversial, with its assertively gamy flavor and dark mahogany hue.

The regular turkey from Plainville Farms finished second overall, bested by just one heirloom, the American Bronze ($38 for a 14-pound bird, plus $40 packing and shipping), which we ordered from a Tennessee farm called Peaceful Pastures. This bird boasted dark meat that was rich tasting but not livery (and not off-puttingly dark in color). The white meat was more fully flavored than conventional turkey yet without the strange sour or mineral off-flavors that plagued the other heirloom turkeys in the tasting. Our tasting also revealed that buying a particular breed by no means guarantees a particular flavor profile. Our other American Bronze, purchased from a farm in California, came in last, thanks to a much gamier flavor than its Tennessee counterpart.

HEARTY GREENS

Collard greens and kale have tough, thick stems that must be trimmed before they can be used in recipes, including the pasta dishes on pages 14–15. Here's how we accomplish this task in the test kitchen.

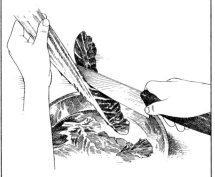

Hold each leaf at the base of the stem over a large bowl filled with water. With a chef's knife, slash the leafy portion from each side of the stem. Discard the stem.

SHOPPING WITH THE TEST KITCHEN: **Hot Sauces**

As often as we use hot pepper sauce in the test kitchen, we've never given much thought to brand. Considering that most are made from a basic combination of red peppers, vinegar, and salt, does brand even matter? We rounded up eight supermarket samples to find out.

First, we sprinkled each sample atop a portion of steamed white rice. Across the board, tasters deemed one sauce a knockout: Frank's won points for its "bright" and "tangy" notes and potent heat. Tasters also liked La Preferida Louisiana Hot Sauce, which was a tad hotter. Surprisingly, Tabasco, the brand most often found in restaurants and on pantry shelves (including our own), came in dead last. Why? The searing heat masked any other flavor in the sauce, and most found the thin, watery body to be unappealing. "Bitter, like pepper skin," said one taster.

To see how our winner and loser would fare in a cooked application—with other flavors in the mix—we pitted Frank's RedHot against Tabasco in a breakfast strata made with bread, cheese, eggs, onion, and hot sauce. The results were split. Some tasters enjoyed Tabasco's spicier edge, while others preferred the fuller, more tomatoey complexity of Frank's. For sprinkling on top of the cooked strata, however, nearly all tasters once again picked Frank's RedHot as their favorite for its fuller flavor and more "luxurious" body. One taster put it succinctly: "Tabasco is an ingredient, while Frank's is a condiment." Save Tabasco for adding heat to recipes.

THIS SAUCE SCORCHED THE COMPETITION

KITCHEN SCIENCE: Rescuing Rock-Hard Fruit

Can anything be done to ripen fruit at home? It depends on the fruit. In some fruits, known as climacteric, ripening continues after harvest. In others, known as nonclimacteric, ripening occurs only on the plant; it stops once the fruit is picked. Bland, rock-hard climacteric fruits (apples, apricots, avocados, bananas, blueberries, cantaloupes, figs, kiwis, mangoes, nectarines, papayas, peaches, pears, plums, and tomatoes, for instance) all have a shot at becoming sweet and juicy (that is, ripe) someday. In contrast, nonclimacteric fruits (including cherries, honeydew melons, pineapple, citrus, grapes, raspberries, and strawberries) may get softer over time, but they will not ripen further at home.

The ripening process in many fruits is controlled by ethylene, a colorless, odorless gas produced in minute quantities by the plant and its fruit. For climacteric types, once the amount of ethylene reaches a certain threshold, the fruit bursts into ripeness; naturally, this process takes some time. But what if we hastened the process by exposing unripe climacteric fruit to ripe fruit already producing copious amounts of ethylene? To test this idea, we purchased a basketful of hard, unripe supermarket pears along with a few ripe bananas. The experiment was simple: We would place three unripe pears and two very ripe bananas in a tightly rolled-up brown paper bag (to concentrate the ethylene) and a similar group in a tightly rolled-up paper bag without bananas. (Don't try to ripen fruit in plastic bags; it will spoil first. Moderately porous paper bags allow a small amount of oxygen to enter, helping the pears produce enzymes that prevent them from spoiling as they ripen.)

NOT READY   **RIPE AND READY**

A special stain applied to an unripe pear turns bluish-black in the presence of starch. After several days in a paper bag with bananas, another pear from the same batch has very little staining, indicating that most of the starch has been converted to sugar and the fruit is now ripe.

Three days later, we checked the progress. The pears stored by themselves (no bananas) were slightly softened but still tasted tart and astringent. The pears stored with the ripe bananas? Soft and deliciously sweet. When we gave the banana-less pears another full day, however, they reached full ripeness. So a simple paper bag works—including ethylene-bloated bananas merely speeds the process along. –Guy Crosby, Ph.D., Food Scientist

Dried Mushrooms

While developing our recipe for Daube Provençal (page 7), we noticed disturbing differences in quality from one package of dried cèpes to another. More commonly known by their Italian name, *porcini*, dried cèpes should be large and thick (left photo) and either tan or brown—not black. Avoid packages with lots of dust and crumbled bits (middle photo) and keep an eye out for small pinholes, telltale signs that worms got to the mushrooms (right photo). Eyeballing is good, but smelling the mushrooms (especially if sold loose) is also helpful to judge quality. Purchase dried cèpes with an earthy (not musty or stale) aroma; mushrooms with no aroma at all are likely to have little or no flavor.

Packages of "wild mushroom mix," found in some stores, should not be substituted for cèpes. Although these mixes sometimes include cèpes, they also often include lesser-quality mushrooms whose flavor profiles may not suit the dish.

LARGE AND THICK   **CRUMBLY**   **WORM HOLES**

Avoid cèpes with worm holes (right) or broken, crumbly bits (center). The best cèpes are large, thick, and tan or brown, with a fragrant, earthy aroma (left).

RECIPE UPDATE

All-Season Peach Cobbler

Several readers wondered if frozen peaches would make a passable substitute in our **Fresh Peach Cobbler** (July/August 2004). A straight substitution of frozen peaches for fresh proved a disaster. Even after the peaches were defrosted, then macerated in sugar and drained (the method we used in the original recipe to remove excess liquid), they still exuded too much moisture when baked. The resulting biscuit topping was deplorably soggy, and the peaches were swimming in runny liquid.

The solution involved making three alterations to our recipe. First, we reduced the peaches from 2½ pounds fresh fruit to 2 pounds frozen to compensate for the discarded pits and skin. To remove even more liquid, we also halved the amount of peach macerating juice added back to the dish before baking (⅛ cup instead of ¼ cup) and baked the peaches longer (15 to 20 minutes instead of 10 minutes) before applying the biscuit topping. As good as cobbler made with fresh-picked specimens from the peak of peach season? Maybe not. But it's a worthy approximation the other 11 months of the year.

Prefab Holiday Cookies

Readers who found themselves overwhelmed by holiday cookie-baking marathons asked if there was any way to ease the last-minute frenzy by making and freezing cookies ahead of time. To find out, we baked up our **Spritz Cookies** (November/December 2004) and tried freezing them in zipper-lock bags.

A week later, we placed the cookies on a baking sheet and "refreshed" them in the oven for 4 to 5 minutes (a method that works with other cookies). While the taste and texture were on par with a fresh-baked batch, appearance was another story (top photo).

We had more success when we formed the cookies, froze them right on the baking sheet (bottom photo), and transferred them to zipper-lock bags for storage until ready to bake. Then we

PREBAKED COOKIES LOOK SLOPPY

PRESHAPED COOKIES LOOK NEAT

When looks matter, frozen prebaked cookies just don't cut it. Preshaping and freezing, then baking, saves time without sacrificing appearance.

simply placed them back on the baking sheet and proceeded with the recipe. (The frozen cookies needed 2 to 4 minutes extra baking time.)

Grilled Steak Inside

Several readers asked if we could find a way to bring our **Grilled Marinated Flank Steak** (May/June 2005) indoors during the colder months. Broiling yielded spotty browning and pan-searing caused the exterior to burn, so we turned to a combination method used in restaurants: pan-roasting. This method involves developing the exterior crust on the stovetop and finishing the steak in the oven to get the interior up to temperature. –Compiled by Nina West

IF YOU HAVE A QUESTION about a recently published recipe, let us know. Send your inquiry, name, address, and daytime telephone number to Recipe Update, Cook's Illustrated, P.O. Box 470589, Brookline, MA 02447, or write to recipeupdate@bcpress.com.

Go to www.cooksillustrated.com
- Key in code 11059 for **Spritz Cookies**.
- Key in code 110510 for **Cobbler with Frozen Peaches**.
- Key in code 110511 for **Pan-Roasted Marinated Flank Steak**.
- Recipes available until December 31, 2005.

≥ BY GARTH CLINGINGSMITH ≤

EQUIPMENT TEST
Wine Keepers

MAKESHIFT WINE SAVER
Can this 99-cent water bottle outdo a $109 gadget?

Our March/April 2005 recommendation of the VacuVin Vacuum Wine Saver ($9.99) begat a slew of reader letters suggesting other methods of saving leftover wine. A few recommended we do without pricey "wine preservation systems" and use a much simpler (and cheaper) tool: an old water bottle. We went to the kitchen to test the water bottle, the VacuVin, and three additional gadgets.

We removed equal amounts of wine from bottles from the same case and "preserved" the leftovers for 10 days. The PEK Preservation System's Wine Steward Preservo ($109, plus argon cartridge refills) houses the bottle in a chamber of argon gas, while Winekeeper's The Keeper ($99.95, plus nitrogen canister refills) uses a keg-like tap system to dispense the wine and, as it is used, replace it with nitrogen. Wine for Later's small decanters ($49.95) accommodate a half- or quarter-bottle of wine; in our tests, though, the included glass stoppers leaked. In the end, not one of these contraptions kept the wine quaffable.

A small plastic water bottle with an airtight, screw-top lid proved much more effective. Tasters found wine kept in sealed plastic bottles to be just as drinkable as that preserved with the VacuVin Vacuum Wine Saver. One caveat: The VacuVin allows you to store any amount of wine in the original bottle. You must fill the plastic bottle completely to eliminate air.

EQUIPMENT UPDATE
Instant-Read Thermometer

Our test cooks use our top-rated instant-read thermometer, the ThermoWorks Thermapen, many times a day. So when we noticed new versions of it, we had to check them out. The probe tips containing the thermocouple sensors in the Super-Fast Thermapen (THS-211-076, $85) and the High Accuracy Fast Thermapen (THS-211-072, $98) have been reduced to almost half the diameter of the original. We found that the thinner probe tips shave about four seconds from the standard model's already-fast 10-second response time, but that speed comes at a cost. During testing, we accidentally bent, then broke, the thin tip. In addition, the High Accuracy Fast model sacrifices broad range for more precise readings (the maximum temperature reading dropped from 572 to 199.9 degrees, making it impossible to check the temperature of frying oil, for instance). We'll stick with the more durable, plenty-fast-enough standard Thermapen (model THS-211-006, $75).

EQUIPMENT TEST
No-Skid Mixing Bowls

Chasing a wobbly mixing bowl across the counter as you whisk, fold, or stir is no fun. That's why no-skid bowls struck us as a good idea. We gathered six and put them to the ultimate test: making mayonnaise.

Both Oxo models had narrow bases that made them wobble a bit. The KitchenAid, Rosti, and Amco bowls were steadier, but we preferred the Norpro Beating Bowl Set ($29.95), which had a separate "Grip Ring" that let us tilt the bowl (useful when whisking small amounts). Is the no-skid bowl a must-have item? No, the old kitchen trick of coiling a

BOWLED OVER
A no-skid base helps steady this bowl.

damp kitchen towel around the base of a regular bowl works almost as well. Still, if you make a lot of mayonnaise or whip cream by hand, the Norpro might come in handy.

DO YOU REALLY NEED THIS?
Finger Guards

Nicks and cuts are always a danger when working with knives. We wondered if finger guards—small metal or plastic plates that come between your fingers and the knife blade—might help. We bought three finger guards and enlisted several kitchen novices to try them alongside our seasoned test cooks.

FINGER PROTECTION?
We'd just as soon chop more carefully.

Neither group was impressed. The guards do prevent cuts, but they are very awkward. The plastic DigiGuard Finger Protector ($3.29) was the most comfortable of the three tested. If you're prone to knife wounds, you might consider trading speed and efficiency for safety, but none of our novice testers wanted to take the DigiGuard home.

EQUIPMENT UPDATE
Salad Spinners

In 1999, we spun gallons of greens dry in eight different spinners and found two that excelled. Six years later, both the Zyliss and the Oxo are still spinning along in the test kitchen, but our test cooks have come to favor the Oxo, with its one-handed pump action, over the Zyliss, with its pull cord, which has sometimes failed to retract. Zyliss has updated its pull cord with the Easy Spin Salad Spinner with "glide-wheel motion" ($24.99), so we gave it another spin.

The cord on the redesigned Zyliss does retract more reliably than its predecessor. And, as in the original tests, it dried greens just a little more effectively than the Oxo. But the Oxo is nearly as efficient and still easier to use. Both are recommended options.

Sources

The following are sources for items recommended in this issue. Prices were current at press time and do not include shipping. To confirm prices and availability, contact companies directly; check www.cooksillustrated.com for updates.

Page 3: EXOGLASS SPOON
• Matfer Bourgeat Exoglass Spoon (11 7/8"): $5.66, item #B00070M78Q, Amazon.com (www.amazon.com).

Page 3: WHAT IS IT?
• Poffertjes Fork: $2.99, item #11422, Fante's Kitchen Wares Shop (800-443-2683, www.fantes.com).

Page 13: TURKEY TOOLS
• Calphalon Contemporary Roasting Pan: $100.00 (www.calphalon.com).
• No-Sew Turkey Lacer: $1.95, item #3940, Sur La Table (800-243-0852, www.surlatable.com).
• Norpro Nonstick Roasting Rack (13" by 10"): $9.75, item #103249, Cooking.com (800-663-8810, www.cooking.com).
• Poultry Lifters: $9.95, item #217916, Cooking.com.
• Regency Turkey Stuffing Bag: $2.50 (for two), item #135061, Sur La Table.
• Roasting Wand: $14.99, item #120108, Fante's.
• Trudeau Gravy Separator: $9.99, item #8711, Fante's.

Page 27: STANDING MIXERS
• KitchenAid Professional 600 Series: $369.99, item #KP26M1XNP, Amazon.com.
• DeLonghi DSM5 5-Quart: $349.95, item #B0002XGSN8, Amazon.com.

Page 30: HEIRLOOM TURKEY
• American Bronze Turkey: $38 for 14-pound turkey, Peaceful Pastures (615-683-4291, www.peacefulpastures.com).

Page 32: INSTANT-READ THERMOMETER
• Standard Penetration Thermapen: $75.00, item #THS-211-006, ThermoWorks (800-393-6434, www.thermoworks.com).

Page 32: NO-SKID MIXING BOWLS
• Norpro Beating Bowl Set (model 10367): $29.95, item #B00023DIEU, Amazon.com.

Page 32: SALAD SPINNERS
• Oxo Salad Spinner: $24.99, item #628331, Target Stores (800-591-3869, www.target.com).
• Zyliss Easy Spin Salad Spinner: $24.99, item #559669, Target.

RECIPES
November & December 2005

COOK'S EXTRA: New Recipes Available on the Web This Month
To access the following free recipes, go to www.cooksillustrated.com and enter the code listed after each recipe.

www.cooksillustrated.com

Join the *Cook's* Web Site and Get Instant Access to 12 Years of Recipes, Equipment Tests, and Tastings!

Web site members can also join the *Cook's* bulletin board, ask our editors cooking questions, find quick tips and step-by-step illustrations, maintain a private list of personal favorites (recipes, quick tips, tastings, and more), and print out shopping lists for all recipes.
Yours Free: As a paid Web site member, you will also receive our **2005 Buying Guide for Supermarket Ingredients.** Simply type in the promotion code **CB56A** when signing up.

Here's Why More Than 80,000 Home Cooks Subscribe to Our Web Site

Quick Search for 'Best' Recipes: Access to every recipe published since 1993.
Cook's Extra Recipes: Continued access to the recipes that don't fit in each issue of the magazine, including many flavor variations.
Updated Cookware Ratings: Charts of all buying recommendations published in the magazine (you can download them), plus frequent updates on new models and price changes.
Tasting Results: You'll have access to every tasting published in the magazine, in addition to tastings conducted for Web members only.
Questions for the Editors: Paid members can ask our editors questions by e-mail and are guaranteed a response.
Magazine/Book Customer Service: Pay invoices, give gifts, handle returns, check your subscription status, and more.
Visit Our Bookstore: Order any of our books online and also qualify for special offers.

AMERICA'S TEST KITCHEN TV SHOW

Join the millions of home cooks who watch our show, *America's Test Kitchen*, on public television every week. For more information, including recipes and a schedule of program times in your area, visit www.americastestkitchen.com.

Daube Provençal, 7

Pasta with Greens, Beans, Pancetta, and Garlic Bread Crumbs, 14

Sweet Potato Casserole, 9

Herbed Roast Turkey, 12

Chocolate Butter Cookies, 23

Chicken Chasseur, 19

Buttermilk Mashed Potatoes, 24

Roasted Green Beans with Red Onion and Walnuts, 10

Linzertorte, 20

PHOTOGRAPHY: CARL TREMBLAY, STYLING: MARIE PIRANO

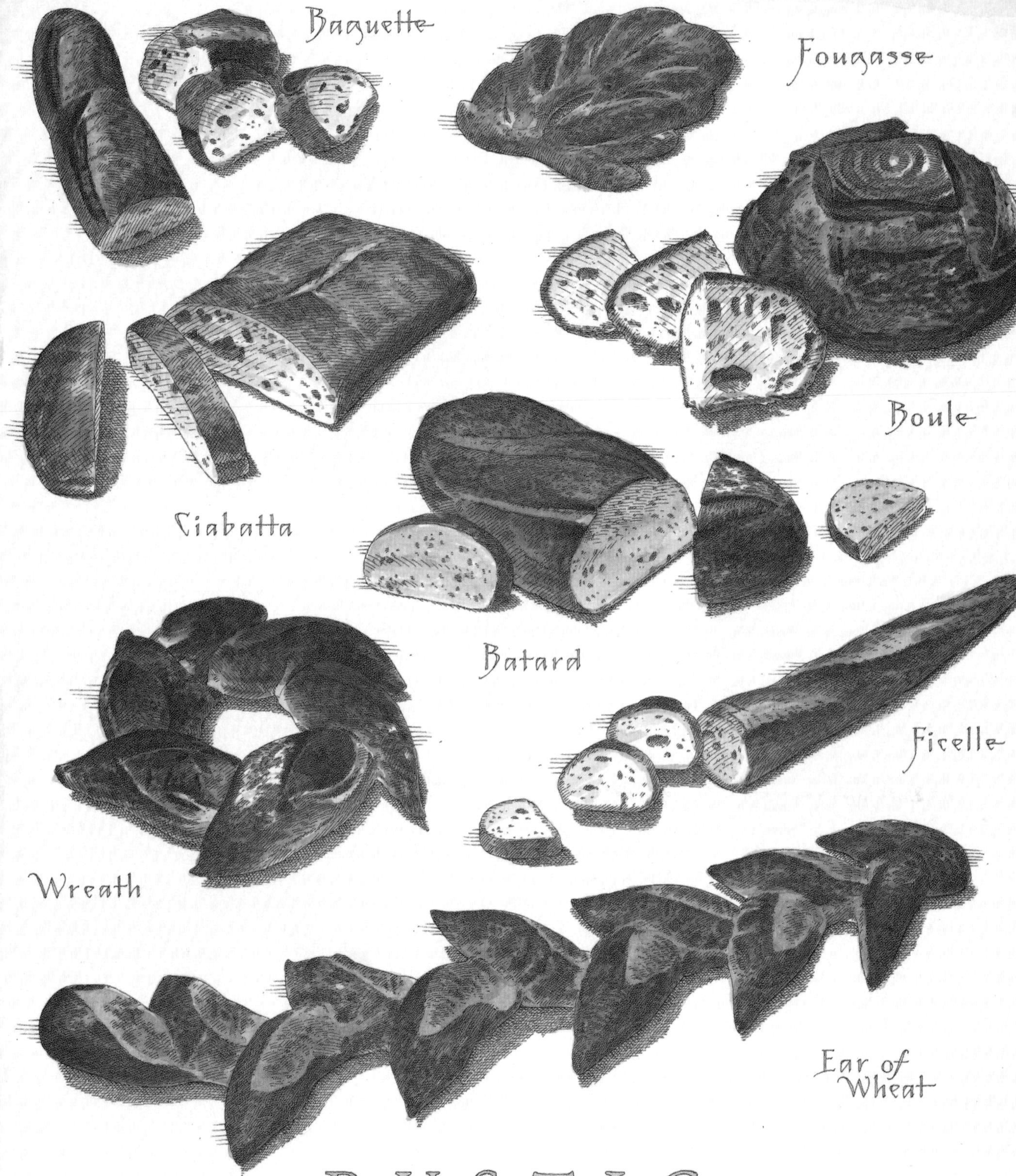

Baguette

Fougasse

Boule

Ciabatta

Batard

Ficelle

Wreath

Ear of
Wheat

RUSTIC
BREAD SHAPES